INSIDE

AMERICAN MOTORCYCLING

AND THE

AMERICAN MOTORCYCLE ASSOCIATION

1900 ~ 1990

HARRY V. SUCHER

FIRST EDITION

Inside American Motorcycling And The American Motorcycle Association. 1900 - 1990

First Printed July 1995

Manufactured in the United States of America

ISBN: 0-9627434-1-0

info**sport**™

Production and Distribution Services by Infosport Publications
30011 Ivy Glenn Drive, Suite 122
Laguna Niguel, Ca. 92677
714-249-2270

Layout & Design by Nancy Wegrowski

This book is dedicated to the memories of Thomas Callahan Butler, Vernon L. Guthrie, and Leslie D. Richards, pioneer motorcyclists, professional journalists, and veteran members of the industry who early on recorded the history of the domestic motorcycle industry and its constituent organizations concurrent with their eras. When through political intervention their efforts were rejected, they passed the torch to the author in the hope that at some future time their works could be a part of an updated overview of the subject to the end; that, as such, it could become a permanent part of the ongoing saga of American transportation history.

AUTHOR'S PREFACE

For over five decades I have been actively collecting and recording the history of our domestic motorcycle industry and the various makes of machines that were a part of it. What with the present popularity of motorcycling there has been a growing interest in the part of even casual motorcyclists in the historic backgrounds of both the sport and industry, as well as the constituent organizations that came along to support them.

Yet at times there was a certain discouragement along the way in knowing that there was a time when motorcycling and its attendant history suffered a declining interest to the point where there were few who considered such worth remembering.

In spite of this, my interest in the subject was sustained by a small but influential number of pioneers and veterans within the sport and industry who considered the history of domestic motorcycling as an important facet of the saga of our country's transportation, and offered support and encouragement for its preservation.

During the two decades following World War II when enthusiasm for motorcycling enjoyed a resurgence due to the importation of a broader range of machines, journalistic activity accompanying it quite naturally received enhanced public support, which included my own participation.

The fortuitous change in public attitude brought forth both the encouragement as well as the collaboration of certain veterans within the industry for the production of formally presented histories regarding motorcycling. This resulted in the production of my histories of two prominent makes of American machines: the Indian story "the Iron Redskin" and "Harley-Davidson: The Milwaukee Marvel," the first editions appearing in 1977 and 1981 respectively.

While certain aspects of the history of the constituent organizations that came along to support the growing motorcycle movement were by necessity included as an integral part of the story, it was clearly impossible to accord them the comprehensive treatment in one-make histories that they rightly deserved.

To this end, it was ultimately suggested that an historic overview of the entire domestic motorcycle movement was in order, including an in-depth coverage of the various accompanying organizations that ultimately led to the founding of the American Motorcycle Association, the background and history of such being an integral part of the sport and industry. As such a work had never before been undertaken, it has been intended to fill a past overlooked segment of the saga of American transportation.

This present work, like my previous efforts, entailed a vast amount of background research, yet also relied heavily on the contributions from and collaboration with a substantial number of past and present members of the domestic motorcycle industry, and thus must be considered as essentially a team effort.

The history of American motorcycling has been by necessity an uneven and often chaotic entity due to the various economic and social influences that have occurred along the way, so is that of the concurrent organizations that supported it. As the story unfolds, the reader will become aware of the many bizarre and sometimes incomprehensible aspects of the activities both within the industry as well as its accompanying associations. In this regard it must be remembered that there is ever public conflict and controversy involving any type of sporting competition. Then as motorcycling in the United States was but a marginal industry for many years, those engaging in it were often operating in a state of desperation in order to survive.

CONTENTS

INTRODUCTION

"It is more important to provide material for a true verdict than to gloss over disturbing facts so that individual reputations can be preserved."

Captain Sir Basil Liddell Hart
In his Preface to "The History of the First World War"

Successful books invariably receive substantial support before they are written. This is true with this one, which is an historic overview of motorcycling in the United States and the constituent organizations that came into being to accompany it. The current public interest in motorcycling has focused attention on the previous lack of a formally presented history of the industry from its beginnings to the present day. In recognition of the significance of such a work, prominent members of the industry along with its sporting figures have contributed both assistance and encouragement to this professionally researched and scholarly presentation.

The history of American motorcycling and its accompanying organizations is unique in the annals of the United States transportation saga in that, through the years, it has pursued an uneven, chaotic, and often controversial course. This may well be due to the fact that motorcycling in America never attained status as a means of personal transport as it did in other countries. As a discretionary purchase, it attracted only those who sought it for recreation or as an outlet for competition riding.

In the early years of the century, however, the motor bicycle gained public acceptance as it offered economical personal transport at a time when the contemporary automobile was too costly for the average man. With rapid technical progress stimulated by an active market, some 65 manufacturers came to supply 75,000 units annually. This era of optimism had early on created an awareness for the need of a constituent organization to regulate both the growing sporting activities as well as to protect the industry from certain public antipathy toward two-wheeled transportation from the previous introduction of the safety bicycle. This need was met by the formation of the Federation of American Motorcyclists (FAM). Founded in 1903 it fulfilled at least partially its needed role after 1909 as motorcycling was approaching its prewar zenith.

The onset of the European war had a devastating effect on the industry. The inevitable inflation brought on costing and production problems to many of the lightly financed manufacturers. Then the supply of cheap component parts from overseas was cut off, together with the market loss of young men now facing the uncertainties of military conscription. 85% of the manufacturers dropped out of the game, many entering unrelated fields of endeavor.

The FAM collapsed due to both the above conditions along with the effect of problems with management and the loss of a financial base. To save a necessary constituent organization, the manufacturers took over the remnants, forming what was now known as the Motorcycle Manufacturers and Allied Trades Association (MM&ATA). With financial control, the factories were now in charge of the industry's destiny, a move which was to have a lasting impact of future events.

The postwar boom in motorcycle sales failed to materialize due to the now accelerated production of cheap automobiles with only three of the strongest

INTRODUCTION

manufacturers left to compete for a greatly reduced market. Organizational problems within the MM&ATA saw a further reorganization in 1924 with the forming of what was now known as the American Motorcycle Association (AMA). Now firmly integrated with the manufacturers, the industry as well as the AMA was now controlled by the factories, including sales, marketing and the regulation of competition activities.

Viewing with alarm the now reduced and static market, as a gesture of self protection, the heads of the factories working through the AMA adopted a policy of news management. Controlled press releases now promulgated a sugar-coated image of excellence of product along with highly inaccurate optimistic production and sales figures. Also suppressed were the reports of growing rider dissatisfaction with the undemocratic and monopolistic factory control of AMA competition rules and general policy matters. While this served the immediate needs of the industry, the lack of independent editorial comment tended to isolate it from outside influence which could have prevented what was now becoming an incestuous situation. In casual observation of the scarcity of motorcycles seen on the road, the general public viewed the industry's position as confusing. The whole matter was now unconvincing to an increasingly skeptical group of professional journalists, thinking members of the trade, and not a few individual riders.

Further problems appeared with the onset of the depression. Ignatz Schwinn ceased production of Hendersons and Super X's, citing the depleted market, concentrating on his more lucrative bicycle manufacture. That left Harley-Davidson and Indian as the sold contenders facing further declining sales from private purchasers that was not materially aided by the small volume market from law enforcement bodies and a limited number of commercial buyers. An ill-fated attempt to forge reciprocity competition agreements with Canadian riders was but a thinly veiled attempt to take over their markets and resulted in bitter enmities that lasted for decades. An unfortunate bitter fratricidal warfare broke out between the enthusiasts of both makes, said to have been fostered by factory representatives which further eroded the industry's public image. This was a somewhat incongruous situation as the top management of both had been holding clandestine annual meetings in defiance of federal trade laws to fix retail prices and coordinate policy ever since 1921.

The AMA was further reorganized in 1928 with Earl C. Smith installed as Secretary-Manager soon also to act as Harley-Davidson's paid Publicity man-

ager. The AMA's next move to strengthen its policy of new management was to take financial control of the last ailing survivor of a once-viable trade publication, the Los Angeles based "The Motorcyclist," affording a now complete editorial and news domination of all aspects of the sport and industry.

Among the enquiring reporters who sought to unravel the complexities of this journalistic fairyland was Dr. Harry V. Sucher, a California motorcycling enthusiast with considerable communication skills, who inaugurated investigation into domestic motorcycle history in what was to become a lifetime of effort. It was fortunate that at that time most of the pioneers of the industry were available for interview providing the authentic background for material of historic accuracy. There was a limited amount of material in the AMA archives as much had been either removed or destroyed, especially when certain controversial matters were under consideration. In any case, most of the pioneers who were on hand at the birth of the industry were anxious to see true facts rather than fictionalized distortions recorded as history and cooperated willingly with the author.

The post-World War II era saw continuing problems within the industry. The sudden influx of imported foreign machines in the middleweight category opened a market that had been heretofore neglected by the domestic manufacturers creating a new group of riders. The AMA, through the Competition Committee, staffed by factory representatives, rigged the rules to at least keep domestic machines competitive. With Indian now moribund, Harley-Davidson was now the sole AMA protagonist. The AMA had severed its connection with the "The Motorcyclist" as its official new organ and its long suffering publisher, Arthur E. Welch, was now free to offer editorial support for a reorganization of the AMA to include rider participation. In addition, he opened the' pages of the magazine for comments on the matter which met with massive response. Staff member and editor, Paul Brokaw, offered a series of articles comparing various makes of machines a heretofore forbidden area of discussion. Also facing the industry was the matter of an emerging free thinking "outlaw" element in motorcycling, the "biker" mode with its suggested social protest advocacy and its impact on the motorcycling public image.

It was during this period that Dr. Sucher's source material had been organized to the point that he was able to present articles to trade publications, especially those devoted to antique interests. This ultimately led to the publication of a comprehensive history of the Indian motorcycle entitled "The Iron Redskin." This was in response to the evergreen

INTRODUCTION

public interest in this defunct but still highly revered make. With the depth of research and cooperation from competent authority this book was at once accepted worldwide as a definitive work which also included sidebar coverage of the Ace, Henderson and Crocker machines.

This work then suggested that a similar effort should be made in behalf of Harley-Davidson and with the cooperation and support of many enthusiasts and past and present dealers and factory employees this was accomplished with the publication "Harley-Davidson: The Milwaukee Marvel" with sidebar reference to Excelsior. The book represented the first time that a comprehensive and objective history of this famous make had been presented. Both works, taken together, were a refreshing alternative to the formerly published accounts of factory "histories" that were self-laudatory anthological accounts prepared by publicity managers as mainly promotion efforts.

These two books now stood as benchmarks by which the quality of future works were to be judged and, in fact, encouraged a number of journalists to venture into additional esoteric motorcycling subjects. Some produced photographic coffee table type volumes featuring special interest models. A discerning reader will note that many of these books utilize material based on Dr. Sucher's original research, although credit is not always given to the source.

The British essayist, Thomas Carlyle, stated that "history is the distillation of rumor," and is also made up of "innumerable biographies." In his works Dr. Sucher has effectively separated fact from fantasy and has added human interest and anecdotal touches that bring the stories to life.

After the two post-war decades of infighting between the two domestic makes, the conflict with foreign importers and the ongoing complaints of riders that they were excluded from participation in AMA management, the latter body had lost much of its effectiveness. This situation was further complicated by the massive invasion of the domestic market by the Japanese. As the Harley-Davidson - controlled AMA adamantly refused to allow the Japanese to be admitted to its membership, it followed that Milwaukee who then enjoyed by 4% of the market was refusing any participation in AMA affairs to firms that were now controlling 85% of the market.

With the AMA's now impotent position and the advocacy of the industry's prime interest at a standstill, a group of insurgent AMA members took over both AMA management and its treasure in a decisive move. The Milwaukee-controlled Competition Committee which had long dominated all AMA affairs was abolished, and a new body, now called the Competition Congress with democratic rider representation replaced it. While members of the industry had a place in the new organization, they no longer were in complete control.

To serve the needs of the trade and commercial aspects of motorcycling, the Motorcycling Industry Council (MIC) was formed as a separate body. Dedicated to these interests, the MIC today provides sales and marketing research and advisory projections together with legal counsel and other services. A notable activity has been the sponsorship of rider education seminars and the promotion of motorcycle safety.

With this separation of the AMA into two distinct organizations, and now freed of its long-standing internal battles over policy control, it has been able to provide a more effective agency for the promotion of motorcycle affairs and a more harmonious supervision of competition. It also provides protection from adverse government regulation, the freeing of recreational areas for motorcycle use, opposition to insurance restrictions, and exposing unconstitutional barring of motorcycles from certain public parks, recreation areas and public roads. With these activities it today warrants substantial support from motorcycling enthusiasts.

As a complex undertaking with multifaceted applications, many aspects of modern motorcycling are highly controversial. There are those today, often within the industry, involved in contention for political power, who believe that the industry's past should best be forgotten. On the other hand many enthusiasts, including past and present industry leaders, believe that it should be dignified by a formal presentation of both its evolvement and its various internal interactions down through the years. Among the latter are two past AMA Presidents, two former Executive Directors and the Founding and current President of the Motorcycle Industry Council who have given their wholehearted support to this project.

Dr. Sucher, with his lifetime contacts with the industry and his close association with and cooperation from most of the principals involved, has assembled and intensely interesting and authoritative account of the subject. His in depth research, factual analysis, and dispassionate objectivity assure the reader an accurate and highly evocative overview of American motorcycling history.

Joseph Hope
Co-founder and first President
Motorcycle Industry Council

ACKNOWLEDGEMENTS

The author's interest in motorcycling began well over a half century ago. The thought of some day recording the history of the American motorcycling industry is recalled as coming on gradually, although by the mid-1930's much data was already in hand. As personal interest in the project grew, continuing interviews and conversations with central figures in both the sport and the industry were carried on well through the early 1970's, when at long last, sufficient information was assembled to enable the undertaking of formal presentations suitable for publication.

An early interest in motorcycling history was indeed fortuitous, as in the beginning there were sufficient pioneers present within the industry whose recollections of their own participation, as well as the activities of others, could give firsthand accounts of important significance.

Happily, many of these pioneers still survived well into the 1960's when my formal presentations were being organized. This made it possible to again review with them much material that was a matter of controversy, or where certain recollections were in dispute with others who had lived through the same era. This helped insure the most reasonable historical accuracy.

A serious problem in the research of domestic motorcycle history is that during its period of near redundancy between the wars there existed a lack of both quality and accuracy in journalistic reporting.

There was also the significant fact that certain forces within the industry sought to deliberately suppress and often distort the facts of certain contemporary events. This ultimately had the effect of obscuring true facts, confusing the historian, and distorting public opinion, later giving rise to much needless speculation.

Indeed, it may be stated that within the country's general industrial community the course of events attendant to the history of the domestic motorcycle industry are perhaps the most controversial within the saga of American transportation.

It is obvious that the extent of the inquiry and research into the history of the domestic motorcycle industry has been monumental; encompassing exhaustive examination of available documentary evidence, as well as extensive interviews with survivors who were contemporaries of the historical period of the sport and the industry. This latter activity involved many hundreds of interviews and literally thousands of conversations, and happily resulted in obtaining substantial contributions of such priceless historical materials as personal diaries, journals, copies of correspondence with various factories, photographs heretofore unpublished, catalogs, and other materials pertinent to the subject. In all cases the material submitted was exhaustively cross-checked with other contemporary sources, with no information being accepted as authentic until it was subjected to the most searching examination.

The author has previously recognized the contributions of the many historic figures in domestic motorcycling in his published one-make histories. Rather than repeating these again, it has been thought appropriate in this instance to now mention those who were not only in accord with the necessity to at long last record a definitive history of the U.S. motorcycle industry and its organizations, but who took both an active and interested part in cooperating with the author in providing material and personal support in the project. This fact tends to guarantee the authenticity of their conclusions about the domestic motorcycle industry.

In addition to the principal authorities quoted, the author also acknowledges the contributions of the many dealers, sports figures, and factory personnel who contributed to the broad scope of the subject. Added to these are the observations and opinions of literally hundreds of veteran motorcyclists and also those who later added their contributions regarding the more recent developments within the industry. Many of these same people were interviewed independently by Jerry Hatfield incidental to the preparation of his book on the specialized subject of American motorcycle sport.

In the further interest of brevity, and to avoid repetitiousness, certain significant historical events already discussed in the author's previous works will be referred to only in the Annotations so that previously unpublished data may be more fully described.

ACKNOWLEDGMENTS

JOHN WORTH ALEXANDER
(1900-1975)

Youthful motorcyclist during the belt-drive era, later collecting an impressive number of pioneer machines. He was a noted authority on the technical details of the products of this era.

LORIS R. (HAP) ALZINA
(1893-1972)

Pioneer motorcyclist, mechanic, and early day competition rider. He was an Indian dealer in Oakland, California after 1921; and after 1949 was the West Coast distributor for BSA, Incorporated. He was very active in organized as well as sport motorcycling, and a long-time member of the AMA Competition Committee.

ERLE ARMSTRONG
(1891-1982)

Pioneer bicycle racer and motorcyclist, joining the Indian Company in 1909. For many years he was head of the production force and was a recognized authority on all aspects of domestic motorcycling history.

WILLIAM A. BAGNALL
(1926-)

Youthful motorcyclist and journalist who was employed by the Western Journal Publishing Company in 1949. He was later the Editor of "The Motorcyclist" in 1953, and subsequently purchased the magazine. He was elected President of the AMA in 1968, prior to which he campaigned for AMA affiliation with the FICM. He was subsequently given the Dudley Perkins Award for his services to the sport and industry.

ERWIN G. BAKER
(1882-1960)

Youthful bicycle racer, physical fitness exponent and professional acrobat in Vaudeville; later engaged in pioneer motorcycle competition with indifferent success. He gained fame in later years in long distance records runs, such as 1913-1916 Desert Races, and in a number of transcontinental solo runs with various makes of cars and motorcycles. He was given the nickname "Cannonball" by news reporters, an appellation he did not like.

C. GERALD BARKER
(1899-1982)

A Canadian motorcycle enthusiast who was active in the British Empire Motorcycle Club in Toronto for many years, organizing many social and competition events. A voluminous writer, he made many contributions to local club publications, and collected much data on past and contemporary Canadian motorcycling history, which was later made available to the author.

CHARLES D. BASKERVILLE
(1906-1992)

The son-in-law of Arthur E. Welch, owner of the Western Journal Publishing Company, he assisted with the production of "The Motorcyclists" after World War II. On Welch's retirement in 1949, he became both the Editor and Publisher of the magazine. He carried forward Welch's campaign for a more democratically oriented AMA.

NELSON A. BETTENCOURT
(1900-1981)

Harley-Davidson dealer in Vallejo, California, who made the acquaintance of the author in 1932, when the latter moved to the U.S. Army Arsenal at Benicia. He encouraged the author's research into domestic motorcycling history, and introduced him to many of the dealers and factory people of the 1930's era.

JOHN R. BOND
(1913-1990)

Graduate engineer and a post-World War II designer at the Harley-Davidson factory. He later founded "Road and Track" automotive magazine, which set new standards of excellence for domestic automotive publications. He possessed a broad knowledge of domestic transportation history.

DEWEY BONKRUD
(1905-1993)

Youthful motorcyclist and competition rider and club man, noted as a mechanic and tuner. He later gained recognition as an authority on pioneer and vintage motorcycle mechanics, restoring many such engines and machines in his later years.

PAUL BROKAW
(1909-1988)

Life-long motorcycle and aviation enthusiast who participated in many aspects of the sport and industry; being successfully both a Harley-Davidson and Indian dealer, as well as holding a brief tenure as the Editor of "The Motorcyclist" between 1947 and 1949. He campaigned for a more democratically oriented AMA, and as an outspoken critic, was the center of much controversy.

DON J. BROWN
(1929-)

Youthful motorcyclist and competition rider as well as a journalist, and edited Floyd Clymer's "Cycle" magazine between 1953 and 1956. For the next decade he was the Sales Manager for American Triumph in Los Angeles. He was also an executive for the American Suzuki Corporation, and in later years became a marketing consultant to the industry. He possesses a comprehensive knowledge of latter day domestic motorcycling history.

SPANGLER ARLINGTON BRUGH (1912-1969)

A mid-western medical student who studied drama and later gained fame in Hollywood motion pictures under the stage name of Robert Taylor. He was also an enthusiastic motorcyclist, and was a long-time member of the Hollywood Motorcycle Club, taking part in mild competition events, such as enduros and English type trials. He favored Harley-Davidson EL machines, later switching allegiance to Triumphs.

MAX BUBECK
(1917-)

Teen aged pre World War II motorcyclist who gained prominence in post war competition. He won the Greenhorn Enduro in 1947 on an Indian Four, later campaigning briefly on an Indian Warrior, and took part in a series of enduro type events. He set a solo record of 134 mph on a 101 Indian Scout fitted with a specially tuned Chief motor tuned by Pop Schunk and owned by Frank Chace in a dry lake course. In later years he sponsored an annual Death Valley run for antique machines. In 1993 he made a cross country run on a 1915 Indian to commemorate the exploits of Erwin G. "Cannonball" Baker. He was subsequently inducted into the Indian Hall of Fame.

THOMAS CALLAHAN BUTLER
(1889-1974)

A graduate of the famed Virginia Military

ACKNOWLEDGMENTS

Institute and a pioneer motorcyclist, he became a Southern distributor for Excelsior in 1910, and changed to a similar position with Indian in 1912. He was later a member of that factory's sales force and was active in the early affairs of the FAM, and M&ATA and the AMA. He collected a vast file of early historical motorcycling material, and once contemplated writing a history of domestic motorcycling. He later made this material available to the author.

ALLAN CARTER
(1904-)

Youthful mechanic and later a production expediter for the duPont Automobile Company in Wilmington, Delaware, between 1924 and 1931 when production ceased. He later bought the company to service the surviving duPont cars, closing down the operation in 1937 to serve as a production executive at the Indian Motorcycle Company, where he remained through the war years. He is an authority on the World War II affairs of that company.

JUDSON A. CARRIKER
(1889-1978)

Youthful motorcyclist and a Pope, Thor and Wagner dealer in Santa Ana, California in 1908. He became an Indian dealer in 1910, and in 1912 was appointed West Coast Competition Manager, tuning factory supplied racing equipment. He later sold Cushman products. He was active in organized motorcycling, FAM, M&ATA, and later AMA, and possessed a vast file of historically valuable factory publications and correspondence.

JOHN CAMERON
(1914-)

A hard-riding clubman who was a "two cam" Harley-Davidson enthusiast, and was an authority on the care and tuning of these models. He unsuccessfully tried to enter a supersports MotoGuzzi in the 1949 Daytona classic. In later years, he, along with Lance Tidwell, entered antique sidecar outfits in long distance enduro races for vintage vehicles.

ALFRED RICH CHILD
(1891-1985)

A British born salesman and promoter par excellence who joined the Harley-Davidson factory as its Southern Traveler in 1920, and in 1924 established an import branch in Japan. He later, in 1930, manufactured a Japanese version under license as the Rikuo, while still handling Milwaukee products. Banished from Japan in 1937 by a militaristic government, he left the industry for a time, later rejoining it in 1944 as the U.S. importer of English BSA products. A gadfly of the domestic industry, he campaigned for a free domestic market. Possessing a vast file of personal as well as factory material, and being long acquainted with the Harley-Davidson founders, he was an important source of historical background information.

RICHARD CHILD
(1914-)

The only son of Alfred Rich Child, he reactivated the Harley-Davidson import business in Japan in the 1950's, and continued his father's role in collecting historical data on both Harley-Davidson as well as the Japanese industry.

CHARLES CLAYTON
(1921-1993)

Youthful motorcyclist and later journalist who founded a publication, "Cycle Sport" in the early 1960's. He later established a more comprehensive journal, "Cycle News," which offered voluminous coverage of both competition events as well as general news related to the domestic industry. In maintaining an independent editorial viewpoint, he was frequently a severe critic of certain policies of the both the industry and its constituent organizations. "Cycle News" was, for a time, published in both Western and Eastern editions, before consolidating into one large national publication.

J. FLOYD CLYMER
(1895-1970)

Precocious boy automobile salesman, early day motorcyclist and competition rider who campaigned for both Harley-Davidson and Excelsior and won the 200 Mile National at Dodge City in 1915. He was later a dealer for Excelsior, Indian and later Harley-Davidson. He later entered the publishing field with his famous motor scrap books, and later purchased "Cycle" magazine. He was involved in numerous motorcycle marketing activities, but his operations were clouded somewhat by a larcenous nature, having served a term in a federal penitentiary for mail fraud. In later years he helped to reactivate the Trailblazers Club, an association of pioneer motorcyclists.

ALBERT BENTON COFFMAN
(1879-1951)

A pioneer who once was sales manager for Yale Motorcycles, he became a trade fair marketing promoter, and was later involved in executive positions in the management of the FAM, M&ATA, and later the AMA. He left the industry in 1928 to deal with a diversity of other products on the trade fair circuit, but kept in touch with it nevertheless. Possessed of an encyclopedic memory and a vast file of memorabilia, his material and recollections have been an authoritative source of domestic motorcycling history.

EUGENE W. "PETE" COLMAN
(1916-)

Teenage flat track star in the earlier days of that sport, and later variously connected with the industry both as an appointed AMA referee on the West Coast, and later, as an executive in the American Triumph Corporation.

ARTHUR A. CONSTANTINE
(1888-1972)

Graduate engineer and one-time designer for the Thor concern. A later employee of General Motors Buick Division, he joined Harley-Davidson in 1920 in the engineering department, creating an electrical system for the Sport Twin and later updating the "J" models. He designed a preliminary projection for a 45 cubic inch V-twin which was rejected by Harley-Davidson's management; later taking it to Excelsior where it ultimately became the Super-X. He updated the Henderson Four into the "K" models in 1928, leaving the industry with the close of Schwinn's motorcycle production in 1931. He was later consultant to the Indian Company in their attempts to resurrect the ill-fated Torque models. His photographic recall was of great value in the preservation of industry history.

FRANK COOPER
(1908-)

Industrial engineer who once operated an Indian agency in Los Angeles, taking over the Western states distributorship of AJS-

ACKNOWLEDGMENTS

MATCHLESS after World War II. He engineered improvements in their performance in competition, and was an active promoter of off-road and enduro events. After the collapse of Associated Motorcycles, he briefly had his own make of two stroke machine, based on the Italian Ilo, manufactured in Mexico.

GEORGE RANDOLPH CRAINE
(1898-1990)

A member of a wealthy and socially prominent Virginia family which owned Southern textile mills, he studied drama and appeared in stage productions in New York before gaining fame in Hollywood as Randolph Scott. He was a pioneer motorcyclist, owning belt-driven machines as a schoolboy, and later was active in the Hollywood Motorcycle Club, favoring Harley-Davidson EL models. The western roles that brought him popularity were at variance with his eastern sophistication, and he later retired from films to become a stock broker.

ALBERT G. CROCKER
(1882-1962)

An engineer who once worked for Thor and later Indian, he became a dealer and later distributor in Kansas City, taking over the same make in Los Angeles in 1929. He began the manufacture of flat track speedway machines in 1934, and brought out his high-performance custom-built big V-twin road machines in 1936, which were in limited production until 1941. He also built a few scooters, as well as contracting for general machine work and foundry production at his premises at 1346 Venice Blvd. in Los Angeles.

BASIL H. DAVIES
(1879-1967)

An English Anglican clergyman and pioneer motor-bicyclist who became an early industry historian, and for many years wrote a weekly column in the Illiffe press "Motor Cycle." The same firm published his history of the British industry in 1950, "Motorcycle Calvacade," which included much first-hand information from the surviving pioneers. Under the pen name of "Ixion" he was an undisputed authority. He supplied the author with valuable data on post-World War II British motorcycling.

JIM DAVIS
(1899-)

Early day competition rider from the age of fourteen, he gained fame on the board tracks, riding for both Indian and Harley-Davidson in various years. Retiring in 1937, he organized several motorcycle law enforcement bodies in Ohio and adjacent states. The only surviving veteran competition rider who gained awards from the FAM, M&ATA and AMA, he is a revered figure in the annals of domestic motorcycle sport.

DONALD J. DOODY
(1951-)

An Irish born Canadian citizen with an interest in both antique motorcycling as well as its history, this latter-day Canadian historian provided valuable assistance to the author in gathering the more important facts of industrial as well as organizational history of Canada.

FRANCIS I. duPONT
(1872-1943)

The son of Francis Gurney, he was an inheritor of financial interests in the vast duPont chemical-industrial empire in Delaware, and subsequently, founded a prestigious stock brokerage firm on Wall Street that bore his name. He was an investor in the reorganized Indian Motorcycle Company in 1923, and had a hand in saving that company from oblivion, in company with with his younger brother, E. Paul. The author's late father, Victor E. (1880-1966), was one of his many brokerage clients.

E. PAUL duPONT
(1887-1950)

An early investor in the reorganized Indian Motorcycle Company, and in company with Francis I., gained majority share holdings and the presidency of the Indian Company. A graduate engineer, he had manufactured small gasoline engines for Naval launches during World War II, and in 1919 had launched the duPont automobile, an assembled vehicle of better than average quality. He was also responsible for the design of the 841 Model shaft-drive motorcycle for military use in 1943. Possessed of an optimistic and light-hearted outlook, he exhibited a persuasive and attractive personality.

STEPHAN duPONT
(1915-)

The elder son of E. Paul, and also a graduate engineer, he joined the Indian Company in the late 1930's, and as a member of the AMA Competition Committee, he sided with the Davidsons in proposing a 6.5:1 compression ruling that was intended to eliminate competition from British machines. He also served on Indian's Board of Directors.

T. JACQUES duPONT
(1923-1989)

A son of E. Paul, he became a competition rider during the 1950's and was a perennial entrant in the Isle of Man TT contests, favoring Matchless machines. A professional photographer, he contributed many pictures to the AMA publications in the immediate post-World War II era.

ALEXIS I. duPONT
(1928-)

A son of E. Paul who, in later years, operated a 200 acre general aviation airport at New Garden, Pennsylvania. Here is housed a private family museum holding many mechanical artifacts of E. Paul's past as well as representative Indian machines. He has also preserved the financial records of the Indian Company, as well as the Indu Operations, in the family mansion adjacent to the Hagley Museum in the Brandywine Valley.

WILLIAM CRAPO DURANT
(1861-1947)

A one-time wagon manufacturer who entered the automobile industry during the early days and founded General Motors. Losing it to Pierre S. duPont after World War I, he organized Durant Motors featuring Star, Durant and Flint automobiles. More of a promoter than a business man, he made and lost several fortunes. With an encyclopedic recall, he enumerated the early history of the motor-buggy and motor-bicycle era.

JOHN M. EAGLES
(1931-)

Life-long motorcyclist, expert mechanic, and innovative engineer. By profession an industrial engineer, he also possesses an intense interest in antique motorcycles, and has restored many examples, including several for

ACKNOWLEDGMENTS

the author. He is an acknowledged authority on the technical details of the Indian and Harley-Davidson machines.

JAMES FORREST "BUD" EKINS
(1930-)

Youthful motorcycle rider and mechanic who early on began assembling a large collection of antique machines and also gained fame as a desert enduro and Catalina Island Grand Prix contestant, as well as representing the U.S. in Europe at the FICM sponsored International Six Days Trials. For many years he supplied stunt riders and machines for various Hollywood motion picture and television productions. He is noted as an authority on the technical details of early belt-drive machines, as well as those of later vintage. He later organized runs for pre-1916 antique machines.

FLOYD EMDE
(1919-1994)

Youthful motorcyclist and later Harley-Davidson and Indian dealer in San Diego, California, who won the 1948 Daytona contest on an Indian Sport Scout. He was later a dealer in Japanese imports for many years.

DON EMDE
(1951-)

The son of Floyd who grew up in the motorcycle business and, as a star competition rider, won the 1972 Daytona on a two stroke Yamaha. In later years he entered the publishing and sales promotion field. He has been active in the affairs of both the AMA and the Motorcycle Industry Council, and is an authority on the latter-day history of the domestic industry.

EARL FLANDERS
(1913-1985)

Life-long motorcyclist and competition buff who later established a BMW dealership along with a motorcycle accessories business. For many years he was a District 37 AMA referee, and also managed the AMA Speed Trials at Bonneville.

AUTHOR "SKIP" FORDYCE
(1910-)

A one-time carnival stunt rider and thrill show operator who later operated a very active Harley-Davidson dealership in Riverside,

California. He also sponsored the active Riverside Bombers Motorcycle Club, and helped to promote many enduro and race events in that area. For many years, his attractive wife, Ruth, was active in the Motor Maids of America. Fordyce is remembered in history as defying Harley-Davidson's restrictive one-make edict in assuming a concurrent Triumph franchise.

ROLAND "ROLLIE" FREE
(1902-1984)

Youthful motorcyclist, mechanic, Indian dealer and later, a mid-western distributor for Indian in Indianapolis, Indiana. He was active in AMA affairs, and sponsored a number of competition events and was later an authority on the history of the industry and organized motorcycling. He later established some solo speed records on the dry lake with Vincent HRD machines.

JOSEPH FRUGOLI
(1901-)

A Harley-Davidson dealer in the author's home town of Santa Rosa, California, after 1925. He sponsored several local competition riders, including Al Scoffone, and also endeavored to keep a couple of the author's early elderly machines in running condition. He possessed a large file of early day catalogs and historical factory correspondence.

RAY E. GARNER
(1893-1972)

A one-time member of Indian's factory sales force and later a dealer and distributor in Portland, Oregon. He was also a contributor to various motorcycle trade publications, actively supported the early AMA, as well as briefly supported the abortive Federation of Western Motorcyclists. He was an authority on early day motorcycle history, and ended his career as a dealer in Japanese machines.

VERNON GUTHRIE
(1882-1947)

A professional educator who entered the industry as a salesman and later sales manager for Perry Abbott's Pope and Wagner and later Harley-Davidson dealerships in Portland, Oregon. He became a factory traveler for Milwaukee in 1915, and was responsible for building that company's strong western repre-

sentation during the next decade, helping to establish most of their long-time dealerships. He left the company in a dispute over factory policy matters, and later became a free-lance automotive journalist in Southern California. He possessed a vast file of historical industry material and wrote voluminous preliminary manuscripts. He later encouraged the author's historic research and provided much valuable background material.

WALTER F. HADLEY
(1899-1976)

A mid-western agricultural equipment salesman who was formerly connected with the J.I. Case Company. He kept in close contact with Harley-Davidson's attempt to sell the company in the 1960's to such heavy manufacturing firms as De Laval, International Harvester, John Deere, etc.; and as a non-motorcyclist, collected a large file of historic material.

JERRY H. HATFIELD
(1938-)

A youthful motorcyclist and latter day historian with a special interest in the technical details of antique machines. With the author's encouragement he produced "American Racing Motorcycles" in 1982, and later, "The Indian Motorcycle Buyer's Guide" and "Inside Harley-Davidson, 1903-1945." All of these offer valuable information on the technical details helpful to restorers.

THEODORE H. HODGDON
(1905-1984)

A graduate of Northeastern University and a member of Indian's advertising staff from 1926 to 1932. An enthusiastic collector of trade history as well as a journalist, he continued to write for trade publications after leaving the industry. He helped to found the Antique Motorcycle Club of America in 1954; was its perennial Editor, and gave much useful advice to antique restorers. He later headed the Eastern Branch of BSA, Inc., between 1955 and 1965 . Also an amateur aviation enthusiast, in collaboration with Arthur Constantine he designed an adaptation of the Henderson K model fours for light airplane use. He also wrote "The Golden Age of the Fours," his special field of motorcycling interest. Later he provided the author with

Acknowledgments

much valuable material and encouragement in historical projects.

JOSEPH HOPE
(1929-)

Prominent in the sales and marketing fields, he was once the Retail Sales Manager for the Honda dealership in Long Beach, California. He was later Western Sales Manager for BSA Western, and later National Director of Public Relations for BSA and Triumph, as well as serving a term as President of the Motorcycle Safety Foundation. He was later a key figure in the reorganization of the American Motorcycle Association, and was the co-founder and first President of the Motorcycle Industry Council when the trade members of the AMA were integrated into that body. He was later Vice-President and General Manager of the Western branch of Norton-Villiers.

JULES HORKY
(1909-1988)

Youthful motorcyclist and one-time manager of Indian's retail factory sales outlet. He later became E.C. Smith's assistant in the management of the AMA headquarters, tabulating competition and membership records; ultimately possessing an intimate knowledge of on-going AMA affairs. A modest and self-effacing individual, he performed invaluable service to the AMA during a critical period in its history.

ALAN R. ISLEY
(1936-)

A graduate of the University of Indiana with a degree in general business and marketing. Was employed for several years by the Starcraft Corporation of Goshen, Indiana, manufacturer of pleasure boats and recreational products. Was later General Sales Manager for Kawasaki, and hence a Class B member of the American Motorcyclist Association. He was active in the reorganization of that body, and with the institution of the Motorcycle Industry Council, was elected its first President, a position he holds at this writing.

WILLIAM E. JOHNSON
(1905-1962)

An able corporate attorney well connected in Southern California business circles and a motorcycling enthusiast. He owned a control-

ling interest in an Indian agency, and in the late 1930's secured the import rights for Ariel and Triumph machines. He did much to promote a new interest in motorcycling, and encouraged many budding competition stars with his sponsorship.

LOREN C. "HAP" JONES
(1903-1990)

A pioneer motorcyclist and competition rider favoring "two cam" Harley-Davidsons. He later switched allegiance to Indian, and in the mid-1930's secured a franchise in San Francisco. A tireless promoter of the sport, he featured perennial field meets, social events, and his "birthday parties" which entertained thousands of enthusiasts through the years. He subsequently founded a prosperous accessory business. He possessed a vast file of historical material, and encouraged the author in his historical research. The author purchased his first British motorcycle, a 1936 Villiers powered lightweight, from Hap during his student days.

MALDWYN JONES
(1891-1989)

A pioneer motorcyclist who was associated with Merkel and Excelsior. A competition rider of note, he was a member of Harley-Davidson's championship "wrecking crew" after World War I. A gifted tuner and practical engineer, he was a noted builder of racing engines, and in later years was a development engineer with the Wheeler-Schebler Company. He had a wide acquaintanceship with pioneer members of the industry, and had an encyclopedic memory of practical trade events and industry personnel and had much influence on the preservation of its history.

EDWARD LAWRENCE KRETZ
(1911-)

A youthful motorcyclist who early on developed an individualistic riding style that vaulted him into prominence as a competition star. First, winning a big National race at Savannah in the mid-1930's, he next won the first Daytona 200 in 1937, and from then on was a formidable contender for nearly two decades. His aggressive charging style of riding, combined with his relentless courage and flair for showmanship, made him a universal favorite. Twice voted the most popular rider on the AMA circuit, he loyally supported

Indian until the end of its days, and then racked up notable records on Triumphs. He later operated Indian, BMW and Honda dealerships. He encouraged the author in his historical research and contributed much valuable material, and also is a valued personal friend.

EDWARD LAWRENCE KRETZ, JR.
(1932-)

A competition rider of note during the early 1950's under the tutelage of his famous father. While his career was brief, he racked up two National championships and a number of other victories. For many years he was in a business association with his father.

LINTON J. KUCHLER
(1916-)

Youthful production assistant in the Harley-Davidson factory just prior to World War II. After returning from the service he was a dealer for the same make in Ann Arbor, Michigan. In 1956 he was appointed as an assistant to E.C. Smith at the AMA headquarters, succeeding to his office in 1958 when E.C. retired. He resigned in 1966 to become the Competition Manager for the National Stock Car Racing Association (NASCAR), a post he held for many years.

ARTHUR OLIVER LEMON
(1893-1972)

An automotive engineer who worked with William and Thomas Henderson and went with them to Excelsior when Ignatz Schwinn bought Henderson. After the Hendersons left, he remained with Schwinn to create the Ace and stayed to redesign the Henderson to Schwinn's liking. On William Henderson's death, he joined the Ace organization, entering the wholesale bicycle business when Ace failed. When Indian acquired the Ace rights in 1972, he joined Indian to oversee Indian-Ace production and remained in Springfield until 1934, when falling four sales prompted him to again enter the bicycle field. Along with Arthur Constantine, he remained as the definitive authority on the history of four cylinder production in the domestic industry.

EARL L. LeMOYNE
(1869-1962)

An early day bicycle competition rider and

ACKNOWLEDGMENTS

physical fitness advocate who took up motorcycling before the turn of the century. He was said to have brought the first model, an Orient-Aster, to Los Angeles in 1899. He organized and participated in the initial motor-bicycle races in the Los Angeles and San Diego areas. Later a successful building contractor, he built many of the first large buildings in Los Angeles, including the Union Railway Station in 1928. He later engaged in philanthropic work and gave away millions of dollars to charity. He later enjoyed recounting the events of the pioneer motorcycle activities. A modest and unassuming individual, he always referred to himself as "just an old carpenter."

ELMO LOOPER
(1917-1971)

A noted tuner and competition rider who was also a gifted innovative engineer. He favored both Norton Internationals and the Los Angeles built Crockers. After World War II he bought out the remaining Crocker components. He was noted as an authority on Crockers, and restored the author's 1938 model.

FREDERICK A. LUDLOW
(1895-1984)

Early day competition rider, first with Indian and later as a member of Harley-Davidson's famed "wrecking crew." He had the distinction of winning five National Championships at Syracuse in 1921 during one race. He later racked up several solo speed records on specially tuned Hendersons and Indians at Bonneville. He made an unsuccessful attempt for the world's record at Bonneville in 1937 on an eight valve, 61 cu in. Indian. He spent the rest of his life as a motorcycle patrolman in Pasadena. An authority on early day competition, he was a favorite speaker at various club gatherings. He once toured the country lecturing and exhibiting racing films.

PERRY E. MACK
(1878-1951)

Pioneer motor-bicycle designer who was responsible for the P.E.M. (his initials), as well as the Jefferson and Waverly, and later designed the first commercially produced U.S. ohv design in V-twin form for the Pope concern. He also produced a limited number of similar engines during the brief cycle-car

boom for several manufacturers. For many years he was chief engineer for Briggs and Stratton. He was an authority on early day motorcycle history, and was acquainted with most of the pioneer figures.

RUSSELL E. MARCH
(1937-)

With a business and legal background in education, he was once Sales Manager for American Honda, and later filled the same office with Buco Helmet Company, a subsidiary of the American Safety Corporation, maker of safety equipment for automobiles. A Class B member of the American Motorcycle Association, he was subsequently elected to succeed William T. Berry's troubled administration as Executive Director. While his tenure of office was characterized by controversy, he inaugurated an affiliation with the FIM, the international control body of motorcycle sport, and promoted the expansion of AMA activities to broaden its appeal to motorcycle riders. He also secured larger quarters at Westerville, Ohio, that presently serves as AMA headquarters.

WILLIAM H. "BILLY" MATHEWS
(1912-1981)

Noted Canadian tuner and competition rider who favored Norton Internationals, and was often sponsored by J.M. McGill, the Canadian distributor. He also campaigned in the U.S. in the late 1930's with signal success, winning the Daytona 200 in 1940, and narrowly placing in the post-World War II events as well. He later joined the Fred Deeley organization as a shop foreman and was an authority on Canadian competition history.

ARMANDO MAGRI
(1914-)

A noted California competition rider and a protege of Sacramento Harley-Davidson dealer Frank J. Murray. He won Pacific Coast Championships, and was a frequent entrant at Daytona. He took over the dealership in 1952, and for many years sponsored other young competition riders.

EMMETT MOORE
(1912-1993)

For many years prominent in the motorcycle trade, and was an executive in the American

branch of BSA, Inc., under Ted Hodgdon. He became an authority on early motorcycle history, especially Indian, and was one of the founders of the Antique Motorcycle Club of America in 1954. He wrote frequently for trade journals, and possessed a vast file of historical data.

FRANK J. MURRAY
(1892-1956)

Early day Sacramento Harley-Davidson dealer and sponsor of numerous aspiring competition riders. He possessed a vast file of historic catalog and shop manual material. The author purchased an EL model from his agency in 1950.

JOHN NOWAK
(1909-)

A long-time Harley-Davidson factory employee and, for many years, the manager of its service department. He was in charge of the development of military motorcycles for World War II, and headed the experiments on the various prototypes, such as sidecar shaft drives, and variants of the WLA and WLC models. He possesses an intimate knowledge of Harley-Davidson history.

JOHN J. O'CONNOR
(1875-1962)

Early day professional bicycle racer and a compatriot of George M. Hendee. He was an advertising and publicity director for Indian, and later, Editor of "The Pacific Coast Motorcyclist and Bicyclist" (later called "The Motorcyclist"). A voluminous writer, his exaggerated Victorian prose set the style for others, but his fictionalization of people and events rendered much of his reporting questionable as to its accuracy. Of a larcenous nature, he was, through the years, involved in a number of both questionable as well as illegal financial dealings, such as: his abortive attempt to manage his Federation of Western Motorcyclists, which was short lived, and his theft of funds from the California Motor Officers Association's retirement account. Steadfastly promoting himself as the elder statesman of American motorcycling, he died penniless in a dingy Los Angeles rooming house.

Acknowledgments

FLOYD ODLUM
(1898-1978)

A successful financier who at one time owned General Dynamics Corporation, RKO Pictures, Atlas Corporation, the Titeflex branch of which built the last Indian models in the early 1950's. He claimed to have had a role in Ralph B. Roger's acquisition of Indian in 1945 . The husband of famed aviatrix Jacqueline Cochran, he enjoyed a spectacular career as a free-wheeling financial tycoon. In later years he claimed to still hold the manufacturing rights and trademarks of the Indian Company.

HERBERT OTTAWAY
(1912-)

Youthful competition rider and associated with his father in the operation of an amusement park in Wichita, Kansas. He later turned race promoter, and was frequently in contention with E.C. Smith over the validity of AMA sanctions. He operates a private motorcycle museum with a large collection of historic machines, together with much motorcycling memorabilia, and has an encyclopedic memory of early competition events.

JOSEPH C. PARKHURST
(1926-)

A rider with a special interest in off road and trail events. At one time he was on the staff of John R. Bond's prestigious "Road and Track" magazine. He subsequently founded "Cycle World," based on the latter's high standards of journalistic and technical excellence, which set a new standard in domestic motorcycling journalism. Adopting an independent editorial policy, he often ran counter to the ideas of the motorcycle establishment. He later sold the magazine to CBS Publications, and continued to advocate off road recreational riding. He has authoritative knowledge of the post-World War II era.

DUDLEY PERKINS
(1893-1978)

Pioneer enduro and hill climb competition rider, he became a Harley-Davidson dealer in San Francisco in 1915, founding a three generation firm that still exists. A tireless promoter of both the social as well as the competition side of motorcycling, he enjoyed acquaintanceships with nearly all of the early pioneers. He possessed an encyclopedic knowledge of domestic motorcycling history, as well as that of FAM, M&ATA and AMA affairs. He was an early supporter of the author's research into history.

SAMUEL WEST CECIL PIERCE
(1913-1982)

Youthful rider and one-time Harley-Davidson and Indian dealer, as well as a free-lance industrial designer and promoter of various business enterprises. He expressed a fanatical interest in Indian, and after its end of manufacture he criss-crossed the country buying up surplus parts and used machines. He operated an extensive Indian restoration and parts supply business for many years, and kept many old machines on the road. He later earned the well deserved title "Mr. Indian."

JOSEPH A. PETRALI
(1905-1974)

A natural born competition rider as well as innovative engineer. As a teenager he rode for both Harley-Davidson and Excelsior, and assisted Arthur A. Constantine with the development and testing of the Super-X. He became Harley-Davidson's sole professional rider in 1931, being a "Peashooter" exponent and competed on hill climbs as well. He also worked with William Ottaway and Hank Syvertsen in the development of the ohv 61 cubic inch EL models. He made a record run at Daytona on a specially built EL racing machine. Petrali resigned in 1938 to build race car engines with Joel Thorne in Los Angeles, and in 1940 became Howard Hughes' director of flight services. He was an engineer on the famous one-time flight of the legendary Spruce Goose. In later years he headed the AAA Contest Board, supervising the speed trials at Bonneville. A gregarious and friendly individual, he was much sought after as a speaker at automotive and motorcycle gatherings, and possessed a vast knowledge of technical and political transportation history. He offered the author inspiring support in his historical research.

CORA EVELYN REARDON
(1894-1957)

A clerical assistant and office manager in the AMA headquarters at Columbus, Ohio, after 1928, and had an intimate knowledge of the internal affairs of that body. Her acquaintanceship with E.C. Smith enabled her to chart the internal political interplay within the Competition Committee, the reports of which enabled a historical analysis on the actions of that body.

LESLIE D. "DICK" RICHARDS
(1895-1974)

A pioneer motorcyclist, active club member and journalist and historian. He was prominent in the affairs of the FAM, and had a hand in the organization of the M&ATA and then the AMA. He was formerly Assistant Editor of "Motorcycling and Bicycling Illustrated," in which he campaigned for a reorganization of the FAM; and after 1920 was the Publicity Manager for the Indian Company. In 1925 he became an Indian dealer in Denver, Colorado, and cooperated with Harley-Davidson dealer Walter W. Whiting in building up active motorcycling interest in that area; the two sponsoring active clubs. He possessed an encyclopedic knowledge of early domestic motorcycling history, and was widely acquainted with the principal figures in the sport and industry. He later collaborated with the author in outlining his one-make histories.

ROXY D. ROCKWOOD
(1929-1990)

Post-World War II motorcycling sports announcer, who was a perennial favorite on the West Coast scene; notably at the long-running competition venue at the Los Angeles Ascot Speedway. He possessed a complete understanding of the past and contemporary performance of every competing rider on the country's sporting circuits.

RALPH BURTON ROGERS
(1909-)

A mid-1930's industrial organizer and financier who merged his group of diverse companies with the Indian Company when he gained a controlling interest as well as the presidency of that organization in 1945. He merged the Torque Engineering Company's European-type designs with Indian's to produce a new line of machines in 1949, which, unfortunately, were not technically successful. He lost control of the company to the British Brockhouse group in 1950. While he attempted to bring modern merchandising and

ACKNOWLEDGMENTS

sales techniques to American motorcycling, he remains as a figure of controversy attendant to the failure of Indian.

ANGELO ROSSI
(1901-1993)

Long-time Indian dealer in the author's home town of Santa Rosa, California, which was combined with an active bicycle sales outlet. The author's first bicycle was purchased from him in 1924, and later a first Indian, a 1927 Chief, in the early 1930's. Rossi indulgently supplied the author with a collection of catalogs and other Indian literature, and encouraged his historical interest in motorcycling.

WILLIAM J. RUHLE
(1878-1952)

A pioneer motorcyclist and competition rider, also active in the affairs of the FAM, M&ATA and later the AMA. For several years he was in partnership with Roy Artley, both of whom were participants in the pre-1920 San Diego-Phoenix Desert Races. Both enjoyed a wide friendship with other West Coast pioneer riders and dealers.

EDWARD RYAN
(1884-1966)

Pioneer competition rider and early day dealer in Pope and Wagner machines. For many years he was a prominent Excelsior dealer, and was a perennial entrant in the San Juan Capistrano Hill Climbs, along with Floyd Clymer, Dudley Perkins and Hap Alzina. In later years he owned a Harley-Davidson dealership in San Pedro.

EUGENE RYHNE
(1904-1989)

Early day West Coast competition rider and hill climb exponent, winning the National Championship for Exelsior in 1930. He was also a noted mechanic and tuner, and was the shop foreman for Albert G. Crocker in the manufacture of the Crocker speedway and road models.

JOSEPH SARKEES
(1926-1986)

Post-World War II Ariel and Triumph dealer in Sacramento, California, and a charter member and active participant in the British Motorcycle Dealers Association. He later han-

dled other British makes such as Douglas, and lightweights such as Excelsior (British), Famous James, and others. He was an active participant in club sports, and sponsored competition riders as well. The author purchased several machines from him during this era.

CLAUDE SALMON
(1886-1963)

A pioneer motorcyclist and a long-time Harley-Davidson dealer in Oakland, California. He possessed a comprehensive knowledge of the history of the belt drive days, and encouraged the author's historical research with much helpful advice and source material.

CONRAD SCHLEMMER
(1912-)

Youthful motorcyclist and competition rider in the mid-west, with emphasis on hill climbing. He was briefly a Harley-Davidson dealer in the 1950's, and has a special interest in Milwaukee competition machines. He offered valuable technical advice to the author in the production of Harley-Davidson history.

REGINALD SHANKS
(1909-)

Canadian pioneer rider and Harley-Davidson dealer in Vancouver, British Columbia. His brother, Robert, operated an Indian agency on the same premises at 97 Fort Street. An authority on early day north-of-the-border motorcycling, he aided the author in summarizing the history of the sport and industry in Canada.

THOMAS SIFTON
(1903-1990)

Early day rider and tuner, as well as an innovative engineer. A long-time Harley-Davidson dealer in San Jose, California, working independently he re-engineered Milwaukee's 45 cubic inch V-twins into potent racing machinery. Often at odds with the factory due to his independent approach, at the same time he made possible an impressive number of victories; first with his shop foreman and star rider, Sam Arena, and later the equally-able Larry Hedrick. He later prepared the 500 cc BSA twins that garnered a one-two-three victory at Daytona in 1954, under Alfred Rich Child's sponsorship. In later years he supplied

special competition products and custom accessories to the trade. Milwaukee's racing records improved after he shared some of his advanced methods with factory engineers.

ERNEST SKELTON
(1923-)

Veteran motorcycle mechanic and specialist in metal fabrication. With a special interest in Crocker motorcycles, in company with Charles Vernon, he traced the ultimate fate of a number of these rare machines produced in Los Angeles between 1936 and 1941.

EARL C. "E.C." SMITH
(1889-1977)

Industrial salesman, trade show promoter, occasional sidecar driver, motorcycle competition organizer, and Secretary-Manager of the AMA from 1928 to 1958. His dedicated and tireless efforts on behalf of the sport and industry are credited with holding both together during the lean years of domestic motorcycling. His forthright and often dictatorial manner was an ongoing source of controversy, as was his sometimes capricious and arbitrary decisions; but no one disputed his dedication or his capacity for intensive effort. He was never known to reveal the critical internal workings of the AMA Competition Committee that governed the rider's affairs, but was always willing to discuss the matters of broad policy.

ELLWOOD STILLWELL
(1905-1967)

A veteran Canadian motorcyclist and competition rider who in the early 1930's was among the first to showcase British machines in competition events south of the border by entering such supersports machines as Rudges and Norton Internationals. He subsequently collaborated with Ivan J. Stretten and C. Gerald Barker in the preservation of early day Canadian motorcycle history, his observations later being made available to the author.

JOHN STOKVIS
(1916-)

Together with his now deceased brother, Edward (1912-1971) he participated in the founding of the Torque Engineering Company in Connecticut during WWII. They engaged a former engineer of the Indian Motorcycle

ACKNOWLEDGMENTS

Company to design lightweight motorcycles for an anticipated U.S. post war market. Two prototypes were purchased by Ralph B. Rogers for integration into the tradional Indian line.

IVAN J. STRETTEN
(1892-1956)

Canadian enthusiast who was active in early day competition affairs, he later moved to Michigan where he contributed both to club life and motorcycling journalism. With a broad interest in the history of the sport and industry, he had privately published a series of paperback books that featured photographs and brief captions of historical interest. In later years his reporting was featured in "The Motorcyclist" magazine.

LT. COL. JACOB GUNN SUCHER
(1893-1949)

A graduate of the U.S. Military Academy at West Point, New York, class of 1919, and a cousin of the author. As an ordinance and transport officer, he was familiar with military motor vehicles, and was also a sidecar driver. He offered the author much assistance in this field, and encouraged his historical research.

JOSEPH TERESI
(1941-)

Youthful motorcyclist and mechanic who settled in California and in the 1960's began altering both American and British motorcycles to the custom biker mode. He later concentrated on Harley-Davidson machines with an eye to both increasing their performance and lightening their weight. He subsequently established an outlet for aftermarket parts and accessories. He was also credited for inaugurating the extended fork configuration. In the 1970's, in company with Lou Kimsey, he established "Easyriders" magazine which exemplifies the biker mode and lifestyle. Expanded as Paisano Publications, other titles of the same theme were added. What with increased circulation and the addition of foreign language editions, Paisano commands the world's largest volume of motorcycle magazines in circulation.

FRANCIS N. "SHORTY" THOMPKINS
(1921-)

A teenage competition rider and a prominent West Coast racing star after World War II, specializing in Ariel machines. He was very active in the post-World War II decade, and entered a large number of events with signal successes.

ERWIN TRAGATSCH
(1920-1989)

Czechoslovakian born engineer who at various times was employed or associated with various motorcycle manufacturers on both the European continent as well as in England. As a journalist, he spent many years of his life researching the orgin and location of manufacturers of all the motorcycles produced in the world since the earliest days of the motor bicycle. In cataloging well over two thousand makes, he was careful to note which were prototypes and those which were bona fide commerical productions offered for public sale. He selected about sixty-five such makes for author's inclusion in the Appendix.

EDWARD TURNER
(1901-1975)

Prominent British motorcycle engineer and designer who helped to revitalize the ailing Ariel concern with his innovative square four cylinder machine in 1930. He later created the famous vertical twin "Speed Twin" Triumph, which set a new fashion in British design. He worked with William E. Johnson in setting up the latter's Los Angeles dealer-distributorship in 1937. After 1950, he spent much time in the States, where he enjoyed the Hollywood social scene. Sometimes described as temperamental and unapproachable, he extended the courtesy of several lengthy interviews to the author, in which he described his accomplishments and rendered an analysis of the current marketing and sales of British machines.

EVELYN GUNN VAN WORMER
(1853-1941)

The author's maternal grandmother and the widow of Clement Harry Van Wormer (1848-1915), a one-time prominent California agriculturalist and land speculator. She was a cousin of Wilbur Gunn (1859-1920), an Ohio resident who experimented with motor bug-

gies and motor bicycles in the latter years of the Nineteenth Century. He later moved to England and manufactured motorcycles and then founded the Lagonda Car Company in 1906. It was her interest in transportation subjects, unusual for a woman of her time, that prompted her to generously subsidize the author's initial research into domestic motorcycling history.

GRAHAM WALKER
(1894-1963)

Early day British motorcyclist, competition rider, journalist, and later a BBC motor sports announcer. He campaigned with Sunbeams in the 1920's, and later took part in a one-two-three victory at the Isle of Man TT races, on Rudge machines. He was later Editor of the Temple Press sponsored "Motorcycling," and gave strong editorial support to the promotion of the sport and industry. He favored the author with some extensive correspondence regarding both the past and current marketing status of the British industry.

JOSEPH A. WALKER
(1907-1979)

Youthful rider and mechanic who once traveled internationally with flat track star Loyd "Sprouts" Elder as his mechanic. He was later the shop foreman in William E. Johnson's Indian agency, and in 1946 became a partner with Jack Wager in a Harley-Davidson dealership in Santa Ana, California. Through the years he collected a vast file of industry memorabilia, much pertaining to Harley-Davidson affairs. His knowledge of that company's financial doings was of great help to the author in his research into that make's history.

ED YOUNGBLOOD
(1940-)

With college degree and teaching credentials as well as an advanced degree in English literature, he was at one time a staff reporter for Charles Clayton's "Cycle News" and later its Managing Editor. He was appointed by AMA Executive Director Russell March to revitalize the official AMA publication, "American Motorcycling." He was at one time a temporary Executive Director of the AMA, was later given permanent status, and ultimately was designated officially as AMA President.

CHAPTER ONE

THE EARLY YEARS 1900-1910

The development of the motorcycle was dependent on the evolution of the bicycle. The history of both runs a parallel course during the closing years of the 19th century and the opening years of the 20th.

The primitive bicycle, the hobby horse or "boneshaker" that appeared in Europe during Napoleon's reign, consisted of two light wagon wheels suspended below a wooden bar and was propelled by the rider's feet. A later type, which appeared in the United States, employed cranks and levers to engage the driving wheel, but was too clumsy and heavy to gain public acceptance. By the mid-19th century someone discovered that if a driving wheel of from 4-1/2 to 6 feet in diameter (depending on the stature of the rider) were activated by pedal cranks through the axle, such gearing could afford locomotion commensurate with his leg power.

The "high-wheeler" or "penny farthing" bicycle did not become popular until about 1860 when the manufacture of both light steel tubing and the tangentially spoked wire wheel could be utilized to reduce the overall weight. The Micheaux brothers in Paris and the Starley group in England were the first to produce these machines in quantity for commercial sale. The high wheeler, however, was an unsafe machine. A fall due to fouling the high wheel in a rut or striking some object, led to many injuries and even fatalities.

A. K. Starley invented the "Safety" bicycle in 1885 in the form much as it exists today. The economic and social possibilities of cheap personal transportation were such that by 1890 there was a world-wide boom in manufacture and sales.

In the meantime, numerous experimenters on both sides of the Atlantic were developing the internal combustion engine. In France Etienne Lenoir demonstrated the poppet valve principle, along with the use of intermittent electric current for ignition. Nicolas G. Otto, and his pupil, Gottlieb Daimler, coincidentally with Siegfried Markus, developed petrol engines during the 1870's and 1880's.

As the highwheeler, which was obviously unsuited for the application of an engine,[1] passed from the scene, it was now obvious that a lightweight gasoline engine might well be fitted to the frame structure of the Safety bicycle. Such did not become a reality, however, until two Frenchmen, Count Albert De Dion and Georges Bouton, perfected the small petrol engine that was at once powerful and light enough to be adapted to a motor bicycle.

While the two marketed their own version as a light motor tricycle in 1895, many contemporaries frankly copied their designs, as the patent situation was at that time quite vague.

World-wide attention was focused on the motor bicycle as a low-cost alternative to the expensive automobiles of the day, as by that time the bicycle itself was in use by untold millions of people all over the world.

In the United States, the bicycle craze was evidenced by more than 3 million units in use by 1895. Not only that, the social aspects were such that hundreds of bicycle clubs came into existence- some oriented toward family participation and touring, but also for those who were interested in sporting competitions such as speed trials, racing, and endurance runs. Early in the century small wooden ovals or velodromes of 1/6 to 1/4 mile circumference were built in many of the nation's larger cities by race promoters, and the names of many of the competition stars became household words. In such an atmosphere of public enthusiasm, the

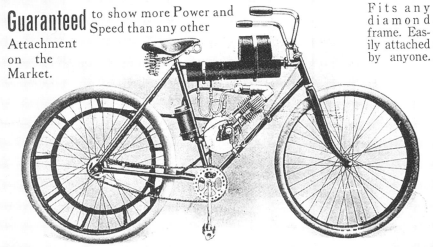
stage was now set for the motor bicycle. Public attention was further enhanced by the fact that several nationally circulated magazines dealing with the subject were already in place, the first being "The Bicycle World" founded in 1877. Each of these publications now featured a section on motorcycle technology.

A significant introduction of the

motorcycle to the public was now seen in the racing velodromes where they were used as pacing machines to precede a racing bicyclist in order to "cut the wind" and provide a pure example of the competitor's speed capabilities. One Kenneth Skinner imported some De Dion type engines for use in pacers at New York's Madison Square Garden in 1898. A bicy-

"The Horseless Age" was the first publication devoted to "Motor Cycles," the name that was coined for the two, three and four wheeled vehicles that were powered by something other than a horse.
Don Emde Collection.

"Cycle And Automotive Trade Journal" was introduced after the turn of the century. It featured a section in each issue devoted to motorcycles.
Don Emde Collection.

cle mechanic named Carl Oscar Hedstrom gained notoriety in building reliable pacing machines, some being built as tandems, and laid the foundation for his first road-type machines built in 1901.

The early motorcycles actually in production for commercial sale were largely built by existing bicycle factories who possessed the financial background for experimentation and prototype development. A prominent New England factory in Waltham, Mass. marketing the Orient cycles offered the first actual production machine in 1899 as the Orient-Aster, using a French-made copy of the De Dion-Bouton engine. In 1900, the Marsh Cycle Company in nearby Brockton offered a similar machine. In the same year, Colonel Albert A. Pope announced that motorcycle development was being undertaken at his large factory in Hartford, Connecticut. Pope was one of the first manufacturers, having established bicycle factories both at that location as well as in Waverly, Mass. and Toledo, Ohio for the manufacture of high wheelers as early as 1875 after studying the progress of the industry in Europe. The Indian motorcycle was launched in Springfield by George M. Hendee on the work of Hedstrom in 1901, with marketing being undertaken through the former's already established retail outlets for his Silver King bicycles that had been manufactured since 1895.

Other pioneers entering the field were the "Minneapolis from Minnesota" in 1901, the "Mitchell" in Racine, Wisconsin, the "Columbia" in Westfield, Mass., the "Wagner" in St. Paul, together with a number of unnamed prototypes, all in the same year.

Added between 1902 and 1905 were the "Auto-Bi" from Buffalo, New York, the "Dyke" from St. Louis, the "Curtis and Erie" from Hammondsport, New York, "Freyer-Miller" from Cleveland, Ohio, the "Holley" from Bradford, Pa., the "Geer" from St. Louis, the "Merkel" from Milwaukee, the "Rambler" from Racine, the "Reading Standard" from Reading, Pa., the "Steffy" from Philadelphia, and the "Thor" from Aurora, Illinois. The latter make utilized Hedstrom engines as they were under contract to make these for Indian and, as a part of the agreement, could use these in their own machines. William S. Harley and Arthur Davidson were making their first machines, but as a more or less backyard venture until they formally entered the industry in 1907.

To the above firms who formally placed machines in production must be added several dozen prototype machines assembled by individuals who perhaps intended to enter the industry, but for one reason or another, probably mostly finan-

cial, never actually produced machines for sale.

The motor bicycle of 1900 was actually just that, a heavyweight standard pedal cycle with pedaling gear intact for getting the machine under way and for braking via the standard coaster brake, but with an engine placed within the frame, driving the rear wheel through pulleys placed on the engine shaft carrying a leather belt of either flat or V-type to the large pulley on the rear wheel. To afford the proper gearing, the rear pulley was usually nearly the same diameter as the wheel rim itself. The fuel tank, tool carrier, ignition coil, battery box, and other items were then fastened, or "clipped" at various points on the frame.

The early machines were without any spring suspension, the bicycle type forks being of the solid type, the only resilience being from a standard bicycle saddle. The whole aspect was such that it was later categorized as the "clip on" era.

While the early machines were quite light, usually under 125 lbs. of unladen weight, they were also, as converted pedal cycles, flimsy. What with the vibration from the small engine and the hammering from the solid forks, and considering the generally bad roads of the period, motorcycling was not for the aged or infirm.

The actual ability of the rider to control the machines under way, as compared to today's offerings, could be nothing short of frightening. With but uncertain throttle control of the primitive carburetors, engine speed was actually regulated by manipulating the spark control, a poor compromise at best. Primitive clutch action was effected by means of a spring-loaded idler pulley set on the end of a movable lever that kept the belt in tension. The ultimate result was that locomotion was an all-or-nothing affair. While fairly easy to control in rural going, the problems of negotiating the heavy traffic of that day in cities were formidable. The streets were filled with pedestrians and skittish horse- or mule-drawn vehicles, with their attendant droppings, prone to panic when subjected to the unfamiliar staccato noise of the exhaust.

The pioneer motorcyclist also had to be something of a mechanic. Any journey required the carrying of a full set of tools. The uncertain metallurgy of the day produced valves prone to warp and burn, piston rings that seldom retained their tension, together with fragile ignition components and unreliable dry batteries, all necessitating a supply of critical spare parts. A roadside overhaul was ever imminent.

A notable feature of most of these creations was their potential speed. Compared with the three-mile-an-hour average of a pedestrian, the ten-

THE EARLY YEARS 1900-1910

The designated four founders of the Harley-Davidson Motor Company. (from left) William A. Davidson, Walter and Arthur Davidson, and William S. Harley. The last two named developed the original machine between 1901 - 1903, the first two joining the Company upon its incorporation in 1907. This photograph was taken about 1910. *Harley-Davidson Motor Company.*

Oscar Hedstrom, the designer of the original Indian "Moto Cycle," poses in 1901 with one of his earliest creations. *A.F. Van Order Collection.*

THE EARLY YEARS 1900-1910

The premier issue of "Motorcycling" featured a shot on the cover titled "The Hillclimb." The hill might look trivial today, but with less than five horsepower it would have been a challenge.
Don Emde Collection.

mile-an-hour average of the bicyclist, and the twelve-mile-an-hour canter of a good riding horse, the average wide open velocity of a 2-3 hp motor bicycle was anything from 40 to 50 mph, providing a smooth enough road was available. This capability, combined with a usually ineffectual exhaust silencer, could make the motor bicycle a terrifying spectacle when under way.

While the bicycle was coincidentally soaringly popular, some public condemnation had already been experienced from non-cyclists who thought large groups of cyclists proceeding down a street, such as in a club outing, or the twenty-mile-an-hour speeds in short bursts ("scorching") constituted a public hazard. Then, too, large groups of parked cycles in cities obstructed doorways, limited general sidewalk access, and otherwise brought public disapproval. As it was, the many bicycling clubs and associations formed for both social and sporting activities found themselves in concert to provide political strength to combat those who would restrict their activities.

Almost immediately many of the larger bicycle clubs, especially in the larger cities, found themselves with ancillary subdivisions made up of those members who now possessed motorcycles. Within a short time, large numbers of these riders branched out to form exclusive motorcycle clubs outside of the parent organizations.

While the motorcycle was originally conceived as an enhancement of the cheap bicycle as low-cost transport to complement the then high-priced automobile, the competitive aspects at once became apparent.

The world's first bona fide motorcycling organization was founded in Europe in 1901. A loose confederation of motorcycling bicyclists from France, Germany, Austria and Italy formed an organization to sponsor what was optimistically termed a racing association. The first international event was held in France in 1903 being termed the International Cup Race. This turned out to be a fiasco as the organizers had shortsightedly limited the dry weight of the entrants to a maximum of 100 lbs. At the weighing-in, competitors were seen to be hacksawing off extraneous parts of their machines in order to qualify. The resultant flimsy machines, many fitted with large engines, often disintegrated on the course or simply collapsed after a few miles, injuring a number of riders. Noting the need for mandating more wholesome machines, the International Cup Organization soon led to the formation of what is the present FICM, the international body that regulates world-class competitions.

At about this same period, the Auto-Cycle

Union was founded in Great Britain for the same purpose, and organized motor cycle sport was at last to become a reality.

In the United States, with the growing proliferation of sporting motorcycle clubs, a formal organization for both legislative protection and regulation of competition, along with an organized system of record keeping, was seen to be mandatory.

The story goes that the first attempt to form a national motorcycling organization came on September 7, 1903. Motorcycling members of the New York Bicycle Club, now enjoying their own organization, met with members of the newly-formed Alpha Motorcycle Club to form the nucleus of a national organization which was to be called the Federation of American Motorcyclists. It was reported that of the 92 motorcyclists present, 44 contributed $2 each for a year's membership dues. The officers of the two clubs then offered to meet together to work out the details of the new organization.

From the few sketchy articles that survive from this period it might well be inferred that this initial organizational meeting was a more-or-less spontaneous affair, but this was not the case.

The bicycle trade magazine "The Bicycle World," had, in common with a couple of similar but lesser publications, been devoting space to the growing sport of motor bicycling, along with news of ongoing technical advancement. In the Fall of 1902, motorcycling was rapidly assuming such popularity that the publishers decided to change the format to "The Bicycle World and Motorcycle Review."

Meanwhile, in the popular "Letters to the Editor" section there had been a growing number of correspondents advocating the formation of a national association of motorcyclists. This was advocated for both the purpose of regulating and governing the now-growing popularity of motorcycle sport, and for the protection of motorcyclists from the same hostile legislation that had already been experienced with bicycling activities.

One of the more prominent correspondents was one George H. Perry of New York City who had experienced what he described as police harassment in receiving a citation for not registering his motorcycle as a motor vehicle in that city. Being well acquainted among both bicyclists and motorcyclists in the New York area, he subsequently attended a number of informal meetings with several groups who also felt that at long last motorcyclists should become organized.

Plans were formulated during July and August for a formal organizational meeting, and the King's County Wheelmen's Club President offered the use

THE EARLY YEARS 1900-1910

(Above) Posed behind the big brick factory building of the Aurora Automatic Machinery Co. in Aurora, Ill. is the Thor team entered in the 1908 F.A.M. New York-Chicago endurance run. R.W. DuSell is the center figure in this print made from an old cracked glass negative. The other riders are, unfortunately, unidentified. The machines are 1908 Thor singles. All three finished the grind through more than 900 miles of the mud and gravel roads of the era, with DuSell making a perfect score. *Emmett Moore.*

(Below) Members of a motorcycle club affiliated with the Federation of American Motorcyclists in the endurance run from New York to Chicago in 1908 take a rest stop in Toledo, Ohio. Such events were popular with early sporting motorcyclists, and tested the mettle of their machines. Note the preponderance of detachable celluloid collars, fashionable men's wear in that era. *Emmett Moore.*

THE EARLY YEARS 1900-1910

"The Bicycling World and Motorcycle Review" became so named in 1902. It was originally "The Bicycling World." *Don Emde Collection.*

of their meeting hall in Brooklyn.

Perry and some associates sent out a number of printed flyers to other clubs in the vicinity, including a special invitation to George M. Hendee of Springfield, Mass. who had once been a prominent highwheel amateur bicycle racer before he retired to form his bicycle manufacturing concern that in 1901 came to include the manufacture of Indian motorbicycles in company with Carl Oscar Hedstrom.

The meeting, as conducted by Perry, included sufficient supporters of the formation of a national motorcycle organization that it resulted in what was described as a landslide victory for the proponents, the vote being reported as unanimous. It was further decided that the name of the new organization was to be The Federation of American Motorcyclists. The results were published in the September 12th issue of "The Bicycle World and Motorcycle Review," reporting that as of that date the organization was founded. However, as will be seen, the structure of the FAM and the writing of its constitution and bylaws had yet to be accomplished. In a subsequent series of meetings held that Fall in various locations in the New York area, Robert G. Betts of New York was elected President, and George H. Perry was elected Vice-President. Perry had been suggested for the Presidency, but he demurred, stating that business commitments mandated that he soon move his residence to New Haven, Connecticut. However, in the structuring of the FAM area representatives were also elected, and Perry subsequently agreed to serve in that capacity for the Eastern District. As there were already many letters in hand from clubmen motorcyclists in various areas of the country approving the formation of the FAM, certain of these were elected in absentia to fill area representative posts. Bernard B. Bird was elected to represent the Western District in St. Paul; William W. Austin the Southern District in Daytona, and Donald E. Campbell of San Francisco the Pacific District.

In staffing the various areas of the country into such districts, the plan was to have each of the representatives appoint "governors" in each state within their original jurisdiction. These in turn would administer local affairs - a rather ambitious projection that anticipated a vast growth of the FAM in the future.

Following the initial executive organization, a committee of the President, Vice President, and other officers began drafting a constitution and bylaws which were completed that December and printed in "The Bicycle World and Motorcycle Review."

CONSTITUTION

ARTICLE I

Section One. The title of this organization shall be the Federation of American Motorcyclists.

Section Two. Its objects shall be to encourage the use of motorcycles and to promote the general interests of motorcycling; to ascertain, defend and protect the rights of motorcyclists; to facilitate touring; to assist in the good roads movement; and to advise and assist in the regulation of motorcycle racing and other competition in which motorcycles engage.

ARTICLE II

Section One. For convenience of government this Federation shall be subdivided into four districts, which shall be styled Eastern, Southern, Western and Pacific Districts, respectively.

Section Two. The Eastern District shall comprise the New England States, New York, New Jersey, Delaware and Pennsylvania.

Section Three. The Southern District shall comprise the states of Maryland, Virginia, West Virginia, Kentucky, Tennessee, North Carolina, South Carolina, Georgia, Florida, Alabama, Mississippi, Louisiana, Texas and Arkansas.

Section Four. The Western District shall comprise the states of Ohio, Indiana, Michigan, Illinois, Wisconsin, Minnesota, Iowa, Nebraska, South Dakota, North Dakota, Kansas, Montana, Wyoming, Colorado, New Mexico, Oklahoma, and Indiana Territory.

THE EARLY YEARS 1900-1910

Section Five. The Pacific District shall comprise the states of Washington, Oregon, California, Nevada, Idaho, Utah and Arizona.

ARTICLE III

Section One. Any person of good character owning a motorcycle shall be eligible to membership.

Section Two. All applicants shall be endorsed by at least one member of the Federation, or by two reputable citizens of the town in which he may reside, and shall be addressed to the Secretary and be accompanied by the membership fee of $2 per annum, which the Secretary shall transmit to the Treasurer within six days after its receipt.

ARTICLE IV

Section One. The officers of the Federation shall be a President, a Vice President for each of the four districts, a Secretary and a Treasurer. These shall constitute an Executive Committee in which the management of the Federation shall be vested. They shall be elected at the annual meeting, which shall be held between July 1 and September 15, at such place as the Executive Committee may decide, and of which date and place not less than thirty days notice shall be given; twenty-five members personally present shall constitute a quorum.

Section Two. There shall be the following national committees, of five members each, named by the President: Membership; Legal Action; Competition; Roads, Touring and Hotels; and Transportation and Facilities.

Section Three. In addition to the National Committees enumerated in Section Two, the Executive Committee shall be empowered to appoint additional committees where needed to facilitate the implementation of Federation policy. *2

The Constitution was ratified by both the Executive Committee sitting as a quorum, as well as by delegates representing the previously designated FAM districts, at a special meeting held in New York City in March of 1904. In addition, President Betts was re-elected for another term. He served until August of 1905, at which time George H. Perry, one of the original FAM organizers, was elected to succeed him.

In the meantime, a Competition Committee was appointed to hammer out the regulations of motorcycle sport. The first decision was made to follow in the footsteps of the National Cycling Association in the governing of two-wheeled sport, but this was soon superceded by new regulations which dealt with motorcycles only.

During 1905, the matter of racial participation in FAM affairs was discussed. A Southerner, William R. Pittman, went on record as opposing blacks being admitted to membership. After some discussion, President Betts moved that racial matters be set aside until such time as they became an issue affecting the membership as a whole.

Perry was re-elected President during the 1906 national meeting held that year at Rochester, New York. Further clarification of the competition rules was made with Speed and Racing events being separated from Economy and Reliability runs.

Arthur Douglas, newly appointed Competition Chairman, suggested that in order to promote safety in motorcycle sport, the horsepower of the machines be limited to five, and that engine displacement should be limited to 50 cubic inches.

A study of the published reports of FAM proceedings appearing in the contemporary trade magazines between 1906 and 1912 reveals some pertinent facts regarding the actual structuring and scope of FAM influence.

In the first instance, the Executive branch had little power, as its base of support from the general membership was, in most cases, strictly limited. As an all-volunteer organization, delegates from clubs or acting as individuals from various parts of the country had perforce to travel to the national meetings at their own expense. As a result, few of the same people attended more than one meeting if this involved lengthy travel. With such a turnover, normal continuity of participation was limited. An examination of the lists of names of those appointed to various committee positions shows dozens of names of people who appear only once, with no other records of any activities or contributions made to FAM goals.

While many worthwhile activities were either planned or mandated, such as the sponsoring of legislation at local levels to enforce effective silencing of exhaust systems, or the authorization of competent repair facilities with FAM sanction, there is no record that any such activities were ever carried out.

Another vexing problem was the on-going financial weakness of the FAM. As originally mandated, each member was assessed $2 per year dues; one-third of which was to remain with the district, the other two-thirds being forwarded to the National Executive Committee. The outlying districts and club organizations protested that their share was insufficient for their own operation, and, in the majority of cases, funds to the National FAM were never sent.

The lack of local financing from dues was generally augmented by the charging of small entry fees to contestants in the Economy and Reliability runs to defray the expenses of the referees and contest officials.

The central authority of the FAM, referring again to the matter of travel expense, therefore, tended to be concentrated among officers who resided in areas adjacent to New York City where the FAM was founded. This quite naturally led to resentment from members and clubs in more dis-

tant areas who rightly claimed that they enjoyed little or no representation.

Another problem was the staffing of competition events with competent referees and contest officials. While local members may well have participated with enthusiasm, their lack of experience in such matters, and their resultant errors in either judgment or in the proper supervision of the event, led to many protests and not a little ill feeling among the contestants. While the FAM Competition Committee established sets of rules for various types of events, their rather loose interpretation on the part of a horde of inexperienced officials resulted in a most chaotic situation.

The marketing of motorcycles in the early years followed the lead of the bicycle trade in advertising in the trade magazines of the day. In the days before radio and television there were vastly more publications dealing with subjects of broad interest than there are today. Some of these reaching national stature, and circulating in the millions were "The Saturday Evening Post," "The Woman's Home Companion," "The Ladies Home Journal," and several others. In addition, rurally circulated farm journals enjoyed a wide following, as in those days the country's population was centered on agri-

Ralph DePalma was an early convert from bicycle racing to motorcycles and was possibly the world's first motorcycle "factory rider." He later switched to auto racing and became one of the biggest stars of that sport.
A.F. Van Order Collection.

THE EARLY YEARS 1900-1910

Ray Seymour in 1908 on a Thor twin cylinder racer. He went on to become a big star on the board tracks for the Indian factory.
A.F. Van Order Collection.

Earl LeMoine was one of the first motorcyclist enthusiasts in the Los Angeles area. He is seen here in 1901 on an Orient with a French-made Aster motor.
A.F. Van Order Collection.

culture. Successful bicycle and later motorcycle manufacturers quite naturally advertised in these publications.

Another popular advertising alternative of the day was that of product exhibits at the hundreds of agricultural fairs that were promoted all over the country. These historically took place in the autumn of the year after the crops had been gathered and before winter set in. The largest of these were usually sponsored by state governments, but there were often many regional or country fairs quite impressive in scope.

Added to this, national expositions to celebrate some patriotic event were in vogue, such as the National Centennial of 1876 held in Philadelphia; the Columbian Exposition held in Chicago in 1892, and the St. Louis Exposition of 1914 held to celebrate the anniversary of the Louisiana Purchase. Such large-scale events usually continued over a year's time.

The actual staging of individual exhibitions soon came into the hands of promoters who specialized in such work, and who acted as manufacturers' agents in contracting for space and in helping to design the format of the exhibit. In addition, associations of dealers or wholesalers would form a group to contract for an exhibit, often of differing makes within the same scope of activity. One of these who concerns us in the bicycling and motorcycling sphere was one Elias Klaus Brinkerhoff. Born in Russia to Jewish parents in 1858, the family moved to Holland ten years later to escape one of the many waves of persecution meted out by the Czars. The elder Brinkerhoff, who had assumed a Dutch-sounding name, was said to have gone for a time to Paris to learn the intricacies of bicycle manufacture, returning later to Amsterdam to open his own repair shop. Bicycling had been popular in Holland since its earliest days due to the flat terrain. Young Brinkerhoff learned his trade from his father and emigrated to the United States in 1880. He was first employed in the giant Pope factory in Hartford. Possessed of a gregarious personality, he soon joined the Sales Department. He later struck out on his own and became an exhibition promoter throughout the midwestern States, contracting with such leading makers of bicycles and motorcycles as Yale, Thor, Dayton, Minneapolis and others.

After 1906 he always donated desk space at his various exhibits for a local FAM club meet to solicit new riders not yet affiliated. For this goodwill gesture he was cited by several National FAM Presidents, as well as receiving testimonials from numerous dealer associations and manufacturers.

Another well-known promoter of FAM recruitment was Richard J. Warnock, long-time Secretary of the Alpha Motorcycle Club in New York City. Acting on his own he assisted the National Secretary in mailing out printed flyers to the secretaries of the various bicycle and motorcycle clubs listed in the appropriate columns of the trade magazines, pointing out the advantages of FAM affiliation.

In 1905 L. E. Fowler, a graduate engineer as well as a journalist became the editor of "The Bicycling World and Motorcycle Review." Inaugurating a strong editorial policy, he was later joined by Carl A. Neracher as an assistant, the two later collaborating in the launching of the well-known Cleveland motorcycle in 1915.

Another equally strong publication which also vigorously supported the growth of the FAM was "Motorcycle and Bicycle Illustrated," edited by Henry W. Parsons, who had expanded its scope from the original "Bicycle Illustrated." He was also a tireless advocate of the necessity for the industry's technical progress.

These publications were soon joined by another widely circulated paper that included the automotive field, "The Automobile and Cycle Trade Journal." Being of a more technical orientation, its emphasis was more on vehicular mechanics than club and organizational news.

In many ways these journals resembled the already established Iliffe and Temple Press sponsored magazines in Great Britain, "Motorcycling" and "The Motor Cycle," in taking independent positions regarding the strengthening of the industry, as well as advocating the strong organization of the sport.

Motorcycle sport of this period consisted mostly of Endurance or Reliability runs of varying lengths held on public roads. Sometimes billed as Economy Runs, they were designed to test the usefulness of various makes. They were less oriented to out-and-out speed contests in deference to the public opinion of non-riders, many of whom had already condemned bicycle racing in the same context.

Indian gained much of its early reputation by competing in such events, shrewdly promoted by ex-bicycle competitor George M. Hendee. Harley-Davidson, after its formal entrance into the industry in 1907 with an enlarged factory and augmented financing, followed the same format. Walter Davidson gained national recognition when he won a FAM-sponsored National Endurance Race around Long Island in the summer of 1907.

These contests also served the purpose, with

THE EARLY YEARS 1900-1910

C. Will Risden was one of the first motorcycle dealers on the west coast. He is seen here in 1905 on one of the Indian racers he sold.
A.F. Van Order Collection.

Ralph Hamlin posing on an Orient motorcycle at Agriculture Park in Los Angeles in 1902. This site would later become the Los Angeles Coliseum.
A.F. Van Order Collection.

strong encouragement from the more substantial manufacturers, of discouraging the activities of the numerous marginal and cheap-jack manufacturers who were turning out inferior machines simply to capitalize on a new market. Some of these fly-by-nights were actually selling inferior copies of now well-established makes. Many of these machines would simply disintegrate after a few miles on the road.

The general production of motorcycles during this period was facilitated by the availability of component parts from a number of manufacturers who had also supplied, or were still supplying, the bicycle trade. Some of these were made in the United States, but many were imported from Europe where both bicycling and motorcycling were in full swing. Two of the largest of these in the United States were the Harry R. Geer Company of St. Louis (sometimes advertised as a "Harry 0.") or the Rochester Cycle Company. It was thus entirely possible for a handy mechanic to order sufficient components to build his own machine much as is done today with modern aftermarket products. Even in the early days it was possible to purchase on the open market either completed engines or in rough castings for individual machining.

There is sufficient evidence to suggest that numbers of individuals wishing to enter the motorcycle trade purchased such components, affixing their own or some fabricated make name on the tanksides, as well as handymen who fancied the challenge of building up a machine to their own specifications. Most of the projected commercial manufacturing attempts expired before they got off the ground, but more often than not they were able to procure some publicity in a trade magazine announcing the launching of a new make. This may well explain. the many reports that anywhere from 150 to 250 makes of motorcycles once appeared in the United States. The accidental finding of one of these expired dreams in later years has muddied the waters still further.

While the idea was not a bad thing in itself, the fact that many of the components were cheap productions, built down to a price, made for a troublesome and short-lived machine. Some of the early makes actually in production for a time suffered from the fitting of such parts.

In the spring of 1905 the still confused picture of organized domestic motorcycling was complicated further with the announcement that a new national motorcycle association was being formed. Tentatively named the National Association of Motorcyclists, this fledgling organization was the brain child of Guy T. Green of Camden, New Jersey.

Assisting him was Charles A. Bright who was also an Orient enthusiast. This make had attained some sporting successes in the New Jersey area after the manufacturers had replaced their roadster-type pedal cycle frames with a heavier type. Another improvement was a more powerful version of the Aster engines made in France that were original copies of the earlier De Dion-Boutons.

In addition to the Orient exponents, there were also a number of Indian fans in the group who hoped that George M. Hendee might add his support to a new association.

The first National Association of Motorcyclists-sponsored race was held at Providence, Rhode Island in September,1906. A few more events catering to both Orient and Indian riders were held that autumn and on into the 1907 spring session. In the end, Hendee, who was an original supporter of the FAM refused to offer any support, stating that more than one national body would simply dilute the effort of both.

The only supporter of note of the NAM was ex-bicycle racer turned motorcyclist, Ralph de Palma, who was an Orient rider. He later told the author in 1952 that an Orient won the first recorded road race in the U.S. between Irvington and Milburn, New Jersey in 1901. De Palma went on to gain world fame in the automobile racing world, together with his nephew and protege, Peter de Paoli.

The American motorcycle industry was encouraged by the winning of the first British 1,000 mile Reliability Trial by T. K. "Teddy" Hastings on an Indian. A member of the Crescent Motorcycle Club of the Bronx, New York, Hastings made the journey at his own expense. He repeated the performance the following year, this time sponsored by George M. Hendee. The all-chain drive fitted to his machine was declared a deciding factor on a difficult course.

By 1905-1906 it had become apparent to motorcyclists in general that the roadster-type pedal cycle with "clipped on" propulsion components was but a short-lived and uncomfortable compromise at best. The more forward-looking manufacturers were now at once investigating updated design with strengthened loop-type frames to extend the wheelbase for better handling and to place the engine nearer the ground for a lowered center of gravity. Some type of sprung fork was now thought mandatory, as both the discomfort to the rider and the danger of fractured blades, not to mention the early disintegration of the machine had now become a critical issue.

The now standard copies of the original De Dion-Bouton engines were already being subject to

THE EARLY YEARS 1900-1910

The rarest of all Indians, the original 1901 model. It was known as the "Camel Back" due to the shape and position of the fuel tank. Shown is an early model with the small gas tank. *A.F. Van Order Collection.*

A 1903 Model Indian with the larger gas tank. *Indian Motocycle Company.*

The single cylinder model four years later. The same basic look, but certain modifications are apparent. *A.F. Van Order Collection.*

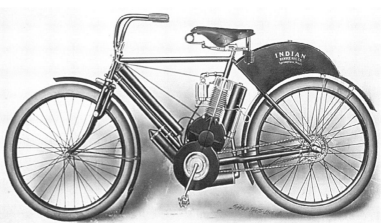

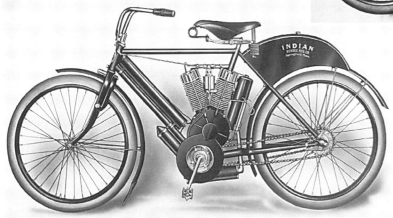

In 1907 Indian also featured a V-twin model. *A.F. Van Order Collection.*

The sale of motorcycle clothing during the salad days of American motorcycling was as extensive then as it has become today. Leggings were a very popular item in those days due to the fact that engines were not very oil tight and a rider's clothing could be virtually ruined in one day due to the oil spray.
Motorcycling and Bicycling.

critical evaluation, and there were numerous experiments with various types of mechanical inlet valves to replace the old atmospheric types that became quickly choked with carbon after low mileages. Magneto ignition was the coming vogue to replace the earlier fragile and undependable dry cell batteries.

But the most critical and perhaps controversial problem was that of improving the drive train. The simplicity of the initial belt drive had the advantage of low cost and provided a "soft" application of power, especially when the alignment of the light frame and the necessity of smoothing out the impulses of a vibrating engine were to be considered. But the large diameter rear wheel pulley was prone to fouling with mud, and the attempt to use the standard belt tensioning idler pulley to act as a primitive clutch for control in urban traffic left much to be desired.

While the chain offered a more positive drive with the possibilities of more compact drive

sprockets that could keep the rear wheel from being choked with mud, it proved to be more harsh than the flexible belts. Early supporters of the chain-drive principle such as Indian, Reading-Standard and Thor were themselves not wholly satisfied with it until they had devised a species of cushioned drive sprockets to offer a modicum of flexibility. The obvious answer was some form of mechanical clutch combined with a change speed gear box.

In the meantime, those manufacturers retaining belt drives were given a slight respite in 1909 when Victor Bendix, proprietor of the then small tool and gear concern that bore his name, invented a free engine clutch that could be placed in the way of the engine pulley and which now took the place of the formerly rather crude belt tensioning control. Designated as the "Eclipse" it was at once fitted to many makes of machines as an optional accessory. The device worked fairly well, albeit being somewhat fragile and requiring judicious application.

Faced with these and other technical problems, most of the early bicycle or bicycle component manufacturers who entered were now faced with the necessity of enhancing their design staffs and otherwise expending reserve or borrowed capital on prototype development if they wished to stay in the game.

The inevitable role of motorcycle competition began early on, as witness the turn of the century contests featuring such competitors as Earl Le Moyne, C. Will Risden and Ralph Hamlin. Orient-mounted Hamlin won the first track race at the old Los Angeles Fairgrounds (then known as Agricultural Park) in 1902, defeating Risden. Hamlin was a pioneer bicycle dealer and later an Orient exponent gave early prominence on the West Coast to this make.

The hundreds of country fair horse tracks gave ample opportunity for elaborating on this theme, although the all-weather riding conditions of the west and southwest focused the greatest interest in those regions.

These speed contests at once showed the weakness of the belt drive. A tuned engine's extra power demands caused much belt slip, and if the tension was increased unduly, the inertia forces caused wringing or distortion of the frame. Indian, Reading-Standard and Thor machines featuring chain drives showed their superiority in the beginning, and inspired some enthusiasts running other makes to adapt or convert their belt drives to this mode.

An early West Coast Indian competitor was Ray Seymour, a protege of Jake de Rosier, Indian's first professional rider. Thor was represented by

THE EARLY YEARS 1900-1910

The start of a race in Santa Ana, Calif. circa-1910. *A.F. Van Order Collection.*

(Above) A 1904 Merkel
with its proud owner.
A.F. Van Order Collection.

Paul Derkum, who later became a race promoter, along with Albert Earhart who was later joined by Howard Schaeffer. Flying Merkel machines were initially developed for racing by a youthful employee, Maldwyn Jones, who gained fame as a tuner and builder of racing specials. After C. Will Risden acquired an Indian franchise, he provided factory racers for newcomers such as Ben Bresee and Will Samuelson.

As track racing spread to the East, the FAM Competition Committee established regulations which designated the number of contestants allowed on tracks of varying width. Standing starts were mandated, and time trials were suggested to weed out the slower riders. Amateur and professional categories were established, and trailing feet or "footing" on the turns was prohibited.

All in all, the end of the first decade of the twentieth century marked a turning point in the history of domestic motorcycling. The need for updated and more specialized machines was now apparent, with technical improvements to the early De Dion-Bouton-based designs and the urgency for reliable drive trains with substantial clutches and change speed gears.

The former Endurance and Reliability runs were losing their appeal in the face of the more spectacular out-and-out speed contests. This fact was to see the dawning of a new age of motorcycling activity.

For Those Who Know

"To a man who has never raced and cut the corner close, perhaps the above conveys no sense of humor, but to the racing man who has "been there" once or more times, and has seen or felt what happened when something slipped a cog, there is more than humor in the picture. The rider who can cut close and does it right, often wins. The fence seems to draw the rider toward it. Sometimes luck enters into the situation. Artist Merrick has told the story with wonderful vividness, because he knows."   *Motorcycling... August 11, 1910*

CHAPTER TWO

AMERICA'S GOLDEN AGE OF MOTORCYCLING 1910-1915

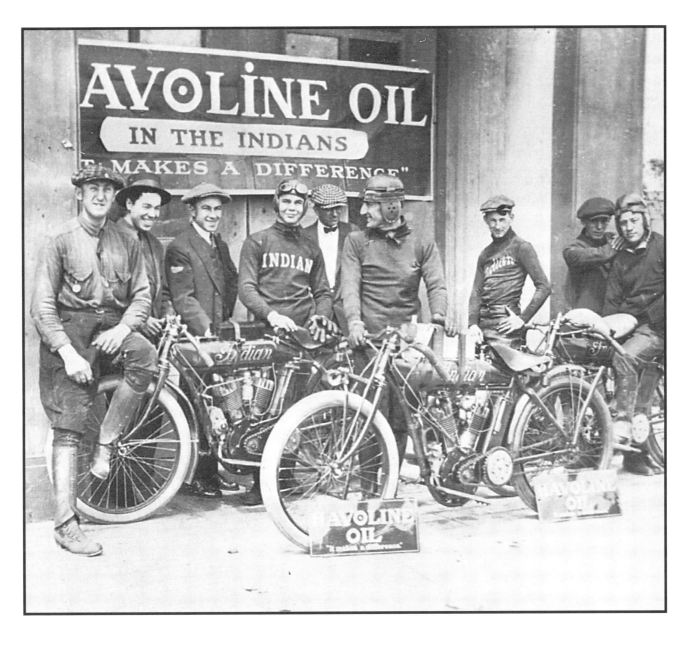

AMERICA'S GOLDEN AGE OF MOTORCYCLING 1910-1915

By 1910, motorcycling interest had increased to the point where it is estimated that over 125,000 machines were registered throughout the United States. Their main employment, in spite of the burgeoning interest in competition, was in utility ride-to-work models as the cheap mass-produced automobile had yet to make its appearance. The initial curved dash Oldsmobiles cost about $650, a substantial sum in those days, and Henry Ford's immortal Model T had just been introduced the year before with a price of $859. These compared unfavorably with the $175 to $200 asked for a good motorcycle.

Motorcycles were now coming into widespread commercial use. Law enforcement bodies were utilizing them for traffic control, and were apprehending "speeding" motorists, runaway horses and "scorching" bicyclists. Certain commercial firms, such as telephone, telegraph and delivery services were also utilizing them. The rapidly expanding rural Free Delivery Postal Service saw many contract carriers using the larger capacity single- and twin-cylinder types to make their rounds.

The "clip on" days were happily over, and the many pioneer manufacturers who did not prefer to update their products into more substantial models simply ceased production or went into other fields of endeavor. The more prominent of these were Auto-Bi, Columbia, Duck, Dyke, Geer, Holley, Mitchell, and Orient, along with a couple of dozen lesser makes. An exception to these was the Curtiss, whose advanced engines gained early recognition within the industry. Their innovator, Glenn Curtiss, favored going on into aircraft production, and his motorcycle patents were taken over by the Marvel concern.

The more prominent makes now moving forward with more advanced designs were Indian, still the sales leader; Excelsior, which enjoyed an expanding market with the built-in advantage of Ignatz Schwinn's in-place bicycle retailing outlets; and Harley-Davidson, who had just acquired an enlarged factory and additional capital for expansion. Other progressive manufacturers included Merkel, Thor, Reading Standard and Pope, a part of the established bicycle and automobile empire, together with lesser known makes of small production.

It must be emphasized that motorcycle production among the various manufacturers was controlled by the degree of financing available, or, perhaps, the lack of it. Indian, Excelsior, and Harley-Davidson inaugurated a program of aggressive market expansion, along with the capital to accompany it. Most of the early pioneers had neither the means or managerial talent to implement such, and were of necessity limited by minimal manufacturing facilities and production potential to command other than a localized market. The second string manufacturers such as Merkel, Thor, and Pope were already subsidized by their suppliers of unrelated products. In addition, some of the smaller firms, due to financial and physical limitations, were forced to rely on bought-out engines and other components for their assembly.

While all of these companies carried on general advertising programs in the several popular trade magazines, their solicitations were aimed at the market for additional sales agents. While some national representation was acquired in this manner, it was far less effective than placing traveling representatives in the field, which could entail substantial costs.

A notable technical advance during this period was the development of the four-cylinder motorcycle. Designers since the earliest days of the industry had projected the multi-cylinder engine to afford smoother running power plants and reduced vibration. Alexander Binks in England had actually built a few such machines which were in-line fours set either across or longitudinally in the frame. But it was not until 1905 that the first practical four was offered by a subsidiary of the great Belgian National Arms factory, known as "FN", standing for "Fabrique Nationale d'Armes aux Guerre." This

AMERICA'S GOLDEN AGE OF MOTORCYCLING 1910-1915

Thomas Callahan Butler.
Horton Studios.

Leslie D. Richards.
Houston Photographers.

machine, designed by Bert Kelecom, was to set the fashion for this type of motorcycle for several decades. Kelecom's belt-driven prototype models, featuring a small side-valve engine, were soon superceded by a two-speed model with a clutch and chain-drive. A couple of seasons later, shaft drive was offered as an option. In the United Stated two engineers, working independently, were each to bring out their own FN-inspired versions. One was William Henderson, who, with the help of his brother, Tom, exhibited his first prototype in 1909. The other was built by Percy Pierce, the son of George N. Pierce, who was already in production with the Great Arrow (later, Pierce Arrow) automobile.

Henderson's model was more advanced, having overhead-inlet and side-exhaust valves (F-head). The single-speed, belt-driven prototypes fitted with a heavy-duty Eclipse clutch were superceded by two-speed sliding gearboxes and chain-drive in the production versions, which were announced for the 1910 season after Henderson was able to secure financing to set up a small factory in Detroit.

The Pierce machine, which was actually engineered by L. E. Fowler, was intricately built and superbly finished, its design further enhanced with an integral two-speed transmission and shaft drive. A smooth running model, as was the Henderson, its performance was handicapped by being fitted with a T-head engine whose broad combustion chamber profile and consequent reduced compression ratio limited its performance.

In spite of its obvious advantages and fine finish, the Pierce did not sell well, as its $400 retail price then represented a lot of money for the average motorcycle buyer. Pierce also marketed a similarly designed single cylinder model for $250, again well over the competition in price. After manufacturing about 3,500 machines, the Pierce went out of production in 1913, leaving the field to the more competitively priced Henderson.

As a footnote to early Four history, the FN was briefly imported into the United States after 1905 by a New York City dealer through the Dutch import-export firm of Stokvis and Sonen of Amsterdam. Originally priced at $385.30, it attracted much journalistic but less buyer attention, and was withdrawn three years later after sales were disappointing.

After 1910, most of the leading factories concentrated their prototype efforts on the development of the V-twin engine. This was mandated by the now booming interest in the motorcycle as both a utilitarian and commercially oriented machine in relation to the vehicular operating conditions then existing throughout the United States.

Those persons whose memories encompass only the post World War II transportation scene, where the country was crisscrossed by multi-lane cement surfaced freeways, would have difficulty in visualizing the primitive conditions of the nation's roads during the first two decades of this century. Outside of the principal cities and larger towns whose roads were paved with either cement, bricks, or cobblestones, the outlying roads and highways were sometimes graded for drainage and overlaid with a layer of gravel. But most of them, and even portions of the transcontinental routes, were merely unsurfaced wagon tracks that became bottomless quagmires after every rain. Such conditions not only called for substantial engine power, but at once demonstrated the limitations of the belt drive, as the rear wheel pulley as well as the belt became immobilized with mud and would usually slip even when simply wet.

The utilization of an extra cylinder in the form of a V-type engine was the obvious answer for more power, as was the need for an improved gear change mechanism.

As far as the engine enhancement went many vehicular historians have in some cases carelessly dismissed the V-twin design as an expedient to fit the diamond-shaped motorcycle frame. However, in the technical sense, the type has much to recommend it. With the addition of just thirty-to thirty-five pounds of weight (the size of the average early-day cylinder and piston assembly) the displacement of the engine could be doubled with the output of more than twice the power of the single. In addition, carburetion problems were not increased by any lengthening of the induction manifold and the engine was commendably narrow and compact, even when compared to the single.

After 1912, the V-twin model accounted for the majority of sales, although most of the manufacturers still fitted single gear chain drives. These commonly consisted of a primary and secondary chain drive, with a heavy-duty Eclipse-type clutch being carried on the countershaft. A pedalling gear was still fitted, a relic of the earlier days when it was needed to set the machine in motion and provide a coaster brake for braking. The newer models similarly employed the pedalling gear for starting up, although by this time Corbin and New Departure, the leading suppliers of these proprietary items, had earlier offered more substantial units to suit the requirement of the now heavier machines. In the absence of kick start mechanisms, motorcycles were still started up by initially pedalling the machine with the exhaust valves raised,

(Below) A 1912 9-35 Model Harley-Davidson. Note the idler pulley that could be adjusted to act as a primitive clutch. *George Hays.*

(Below bottom) An Indian board track racing machine of 1915 vintage. This example was reputed to be the identical model ridden by Johnny Seymour, fitted with interchangable single cylinder 30.50 and 61 cubic inch twin engines for his 1926 record-breaking runs at Daytona Beach. *Russell Harmon.*

the former still offering the classic "light pedal" assistance on the more formidable hills. Another optional method of starting was to place the machine on the rear stand, and apply the pedals. After the engine fired, the clutch was released, the machine taken off the stand, the rider next mounting and feeding in the clutch with appropriate manipulation of the throttle.

The earliest "change-speed gears" followed later bicycle practice in utilizing a planetary two-speed gear mechanism located in the rear hub. These were fitted in such leading makes as Harley-Davidson, Theim and Thor. The former incorporated the clutch as well, the latter two fitting the clutches on the countershaft. Due to the limitations of the planetary system within the space involved, only two speeds were possible. These change-speed gears also made practical the fitting of sidecars which were superior to the earlier forecars or passenger trailers in both weather protection and keeping road dirt and dust off the passenger. A solo, single geared machine, with the gear ratios

suitably reduced for this work then provided performance that is best described as melancholy.

The hub gears had the disadvantage of adding weight where it was intensified by the rear wheel hammering on the poor roads of the period, together with the difficulty in keeping the long rod control mechanism (that extended upward and forward to a lever on the tankside) in proper adjustment.

Perhaps the most effective demonstration of both change-speed gears, as well as their fitting in conjunction with the countershaft, was the fitting of a specially designed mechanism of this type to the Indian V-twins that were prepared by the factory for the Isle of Man TT races held in 1911. Such were suggested by William H. (Billy) Wells, the British Indian importer since 1909, who urged George M. Hendee to enter the island contest as an advertisement for American machines which, even in those days, were more substantially built than either British or Continental types. The Indians easily managed a 1-2-3 win over the 37-mile mountain course where the two speeds provided a flexible negotiation of a rather demanding course.

What with the limitations of the two speed hub gears, most of the more progressive manufacturers at once inaugurated prototype work on countershaft gear boxes, and by 1915 three-speed gears, mostly of the sliding type, were offered, although most still offered single geared models as economy options at lower prices.

By 1912, most manufacturers now offered mechanical inlet valves as standard, although a few still offered engines with the older atmospheric valves as an option as economy models.

Through ongoing technical articles in the trade magazines, the more prominent designers became well known to those interested. These included Walther Heckscher, originator of the Excelsior; William S. Harley of Harley-Davidson; L.E. Fowler of Pierce, Carl Oscar Hedstrom of Indian; William Ottaway of Thor; Charles Gustafson of Reading Standard; Perry E. Mack of Jefferson; E. E. Metz of MarschMetz; and, later, M & M; R. W. Spacke, maker of proprietary singles and V-twins; Andrew Stand of Joerns Motor Company, who made the Theim and later the Cyclone; Joseph Merkel of both Miami and Flying Merkel, and William C. Schrack of Emblem. As time went on, many of these men were associated with various other makes within the industry.

With the now rapidly growing popularity of motorcycling and the reported increase in national registration of machines to 175,000, the numerical strength of the FAM quite naturally increased. This was not only due to the increase in public owner-

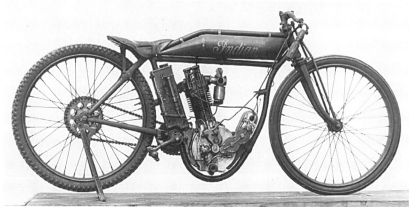

ship, but from the ongoing journalistic support, the publicity through membership solicitations at the trade fairs and exhibitions, and to the growing public interest in motor sports and competitions involving both automobiles and motorcycles.

At the end of 1911, National FAM Secretary Le Roy Cook announced that there was now a paid up membership of 6,780 riders. While this number appears small in relation to the number of registered machines, it must be remembered that the vast majority of converts to motorcycling, noted since 1905, were utility riders whose main objective was low cost transportation, Then, too, with the population of the country then centered in rural areas, most of these were outside the parameters of club life.

It was possible after 1905 and on through 1912 to purchase a good quality single-cylinder machine, with either belt or chain, for about $200. This was considered bargain transportation.

At the National FAM Convention held in Albany, New York in 1911, the newly elected President, Alvin L. Barker, chaired a gathering of members of the Competition Committee which further elaborated on expanded rulings covering various competition events, machine classifications, and stressed the need for local referees and officials to apply these uniform mandates. In spite of increased membership and strong editorial support from the trade press, the efficiency and influence of the FAM was still handicapped by several weaknesses in its organization.

The National officers were still unable to muster the authority to collect a sufficient percentage of the membership dues; local chapters complaining that these were needed to finance their own activities. Due to the fact that these officers were forced to expend personal funds for attendance and participation in national and regional committee meetings, the administration remained centered in the New York area, its national headquarters being centered adjacent in such cities as New York, Rochester or Albany. As this led to what was considered a more or less inbred situation, FAM officials and general members in areas such as the Midwest, South, West and Southwest complained that they lacked sufficient representation. This state of dissatisfaction ultimately caused a formal intention on the part of a Southern enthusiast, Gustave Aubuchon of Atlanta, who, in 1912, proposed the formation of a Confederation of Southern Motorcyclists to serve the needs of motorcyclists in that part of the country. The Aubuchon family had long been prominent in that region, being in possession of a considerable for-

tune from the operation of a large plantation in Georgia, as well as several sugar processing mills in Cuba. The elder Aubuchon, who had been a captain in the Confederate Army, was presently an automobile dealer in Miami, holding a franchise for Pope-Hartford, a prominent luxury car.

While the number of motorcyclists as well as motorists was proportionately more limited throughout the South than in other parts of the country, the younger Aubuchon was of the opinion that an Association catering to the interests of the riders of the old Confederacy could have merit. Aubuchon's influence was not inconsiderable, as he was a new, but active distributor of Excelsior machines for the Southern region.

This proposal, aired in a letter to L. E. Fowler, attracted no little attention. The South was still a distinct entity, somewhat isolated from the rest of the country due to its own background and the upheavals engendered by the Civil War were still at issue with many wounds still unhealed.

It was during this period that the names of a number of prominent men who had served their time in the earlier years of the industry came into widespread attention among the motorcycling community. Thomas Callahan Butler was born in Palatka, Florida, in 1889 to well-to-do parents. He graduated from the famed Virginia Military Institute with a degree in Engineering, and was also a pioneer motorcyclist. Envisioning the need throughout the South for economical transportation, he became an early advocate, and in 1910 became an Excelsior dealer in Atlanta, being thereafter anointed a distributor for the Southern States. After noting Indian's prominence in sales and national and international sporting successes, he decided to drop Excelsior. He then sent a telegram to George M. Hendee offering to take on the Indian line. The latter accepted his offer and Butler at once was given a franchise and the Southern distributorship in the spring of 1912.

Butler first came into national prominence by at once opposing Aubuchon's advocacy of a separate regional motorcycle association, citing the already ineffectual position of the FAM and the weakening and divisive effect that the formation of such a body could have on both the sport and the industry. Aubuchon had persisted in contacting various dealers throughout the South, and actually promoted two Endurance runs and a couple of races in both Georgia and Florida during the 1912 and 1913 seasons. He failed to gain sufficient popular support, however, and in 1913 he dropped motorcycles in favor of assuming Pope-Hartford car dealerships.

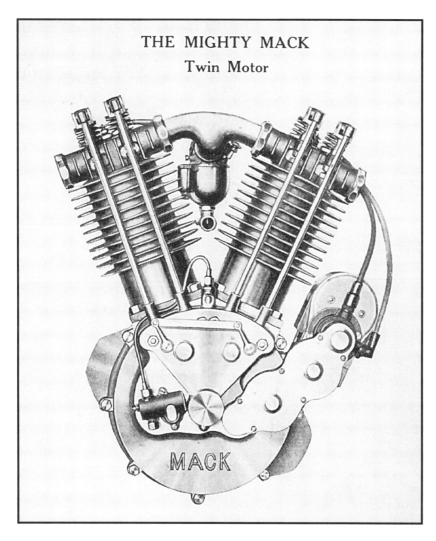

THE MIGHTY MACK
Twin Motor

MACK

Perry E. Mack designed a 61 cubic inch ohv V-twin engine in 1911 and offered it to the trade. The last Pope motorcycles were fitted with it, representing the first of it's type to appear on the American marke. It was also fitted to a few prototype cyclecars, including the Steco designed by Perry himself.

Butler later became a member of Indian's factory sales force in Springfield and is today remembered for his initial efforts at collecting and preserving the early history of the motorcycle industry.

Leslie D. Richards was born in Long Island, New York in 1895, and by 1910 had become a pioneer motorcyclist. He took an immediate interest in both motorcycle sport as well as FAM affairs, and, with a talent for journalism, played an important role in the industry and in the preservation of its history as well as that of organized motorcycling.

Vernon Guthrie was born in 1879 near Portland, Oregon, and was educated as a teacher in Oregon State Teachers College. He left the classroom in 1909 to become Sales Manager for Perry Abbott's Reading-Standard agency in Portland, to which was added a Harley-Davidson franchise in 1912. In 1915 he accepted the position of Western District Manager, coordinating his activities with those of Dudley Perkins in San Francisco, the Western distributor for Harley-Davidson. He was ultimately responsible for building Harley-

Davidson's strong network of Western dealers. He installed such later prominent dealers as William J. Ruhle in San Diego; Rich Rudelier in Los Angeles; Claude Salmon in Oakland; Nelson Bettencourt in Vallejo; Joe Frugoli in Santa Rosa, and several others in California and the Pacific Northwest. Known for his dedication to the cause and his pleasing and persuasive personality, he also collected and preserved much important history of both regional and national importance. In later years he was an automotive journalist.

The outstanding leaders in the motorcycle industry who reached early prominence included Arthur Davidson, who followed George M. Hendee's lead in personally crisscrossing the country soliciting dealers. His opposite number at Indian was Frank J. Weschler, a non-motorcycling enthusiast who was noted for his managerial abilities and who became the actual chief of Indian's operations after Carl Oscar Hedstrom left the Company in 1913. Ignatz Schwinn, majority owner of the vast bicycle manufacturing and merchandising empire, Arnold-Schwinn & Company, rapidly built the Excelsior operation into a world-wide enterprise.

As the motorcycle industry came of age after 1910, it was soon noted that the fastest growing sales area was the West and Southwest. This area was attracting the greatest population growth due to its economic opportunity and its favorable climate. This meant that an enthusiast could enjoy all-year riding, a condition not found in other parts of the country. By 1912 it was noted that 40% of new machine sales occurred in that area.

To cater to this growing interest, a new trade magazine "The Western Motorcyclist and Bicyclist" was founded in Los Angeles in 1910. In its early masthead it proclaimed "to serve and promote the special interests of Western riders."

The more aggressive motorcycle manufacturers had been quick to take notice of the importance of the Western markets. Indian set up C. Will Risden as its first California dealer in 1907 and as its far-west distributor in 1909. Arthur Davidson came west to explore the territory during 1911 and 1912 and through their pioneer dealer, Dudley Perkins, a strong dealer network was in place before World War I. The dealer network was subsequently strengthened by the work of Vernon Guthrie after 1915.

A notable Western campaign was launched at the time by Reading Standard. A relatively small company never assembling more than 2,000 units per year, it marketed some of its products locally in Pennsylvania, the rest being allocated to a surprisingly large network of dealers on the West Coast, extending to Honolulu as early as 1911. Other concerns with similar outputs such as Pope, Thor and Merkel and Yale also had a few agencies in place during this period.

The growing popularity of the motorcycle as a utility vehicle, whose scope was soon enhanced in the big twin field, spawned a four-wheeled version known as the "cyclecar." The popularity of the motorcycle in France had, in 1910, inspired one M. Bourbeau to devise and market the first of such vehicles. The idea was to expand the simplicity and economy of the motorcycle into an area of enhanced appeal that included lateral stability and better weather protection for two or more passengers. Bourbeau's simplified car which he named the "Bedelia" quite naturally included such motorcycle components as wheels, engines and drive trains built into a lightweight chassis which was to set an international if short-lived vogue.

The frame, which turned out to be somewhat flexible, was a narrow ladder-like structure made of hardwood longerons which carried a light, coffin-like metal body. The engine was placed in front with a torpedo-shaped fuel and oil tank above it. The primary chain drive extended rearward to a countershaft that carried a pair of pulleys that ran outside the frame rails and drove both rear wheels via large diameter pulleys. A primitive clutch was provided by hanging the rear axles within a slotted carrier that could be moved back and forth and was operated by a lever beside the driver who was seated behind the passenger. Brakes were provided by a drum on the countershaft that carried a contracting band. The steering was also ultra simple consisting of a straight axle articulated in the center to accommodate undulations in the road. It was hung on a pivot, its action being controlled by a wire-and-bobbin device much as in a boy's soap box racer. An English observer, in contemplating this somewhat frightening vehicle, noted that the passenger would arrive at the scene of the accident before the driver!

In spite of its crudities, the cyclecar became somewhat in vogue in both the continent and Great Britain and the idea was not slow in coming to the United States where American artisans developed their own version.

It was at this point that A. B. Coffman became a prominent figure on the domestic motorcycling scene, who for the ensuing two decades would have a significant influence on both the industry and the sport. Albert Benton Coffman was born in 1878 in Rahway, New Jersey where he attended local schools. He was a member of the Benton family which produced a number of scholars and

The general public was provided with a full overview of the motorcycle sport in the September, 1915 edition of "St. Nicholas" magazine.
Don Emde Collection

educators. His mother, Julia Benton, was a grand niece of the famous Thomas Hart Benton, a distinguished United States Senator from Missouri who was responsible for drafting the historic compromise dealing with the issue of slavery.

Young Coffman was an early day bicyclist and motorcyclist and in 1905 joined the Consolidated Manufacturing Company of Toledo, Ohio, manufacturers of bicycles, accessories and, later, the Yale-California motorcycles.

As a gregarious and aggressive individual, Coffman gravitated to salesmanship and he was soon Consolidated's travelling representative for the midwestern states. He was soon placed in charge of designing and setting up display and exhibit booths. Noting the opportunities for broadening his scope in this field, he resigned from Consolidated in 1909 to become a freelance operator contracting with bicycle and motorcycle firms for space at such functions and having displays designed and built to their order.

With his business contacts, he was soon aware of the weaknesses inherent in the FAM and noted that the various motorcycle manufacturers did not have their own trade association as did the bicycle makers, the latter having organized the Cycle Trades Industries in 1897. Up to this time the leading motorcycle manufacturers wishing to display machines in national trade fairs were integrated into that body. It was Coffman's contention that the motorcycle industry had grown to the point that it needed its own manufacturers' association.

During 1910 he contacted the owners of each of the factories actively manufacturing machines, pointing out the advantages of such an organization and suggesting their attendance at an organizational meeting to be held the following year. This meeting was held in June of 1911, at Columbus, Ohio with representatives of 27 manufacturers present. Plans were outlined for the drafting of a constitution and bylaws and Coffman was elected interim President. In the meantime, Coffman, in his role as a trade fair promoter, continued to advocate the organization and solicit members.

After 1910, the country was swept with a wave of enthusiasm for all forms of motor sport. The novelty of motor vehicles had now passed and public interest centered on competition. As soon as machines used in competition were fitted with chain drives, or where they could be converted from belts, motorcycle racing became a standard fixture on large numbers of horse tracks and the county fair circuit. There was also growing interest in motorcycle racing on velodromes, a most sophisticated venue built for bicycle racing dating from the turn

Flying Merkel Racer
7 H. P. (60.86) BOSCH MAGNETO

Our two *Special Models* are essentially *speed* machines in every particular. The greatest care and skill is exercised in the designing and construction. They are built and assembled under the direct supervision of our Mr. Merkel. They are of the latest and lightest possible rigid loop frame construction. Every ounce of superfluous weight is removed and their entire construction in every minute detail is designed to develop the greatest possible speed.

Our 1909 Specials made an enviable record in track and special road events the past season. Judging by the past, we have every confidence that our 1910 specials will prove the fastest motorcycles in the world.

The Flying Merkels were a force to be reckoned with during the heydey of competition. A number of these machines were built for public sale between 1910 and 1915 when motorcycle production ceased. Maldwyn Jones and Cleo Pineau were the most prominent Merkel exponents, and campaigned with them until the early 1920's.

of the century. These steeply banked board ovals were rather small in circumference, usually one-quarter to one-third of a mile around. Due to the narrow courses contests were limited to four contestants and match races between two riders were preferred. Most of the velodromes and motordromes were built adjacent to nearly every large population center in the country. This made team racing popular, and match races were often held between local champions who had beaten all local comers and extended their scope to regional contests.

The majority of these board ovals were built on a promotional basis by John Shillington Prince. A one-time high wheel bicycle racer in England, Prince came to the United States in the late 1880's after representing Humber cycles in Australia. After his retirement in the mid-1890's he turned promoter, and, with a background in engineering, he conceived the idea of the velodrome. He subsequently crisscrossed the United States contracting for these and, in some cases, held a financial interest in them.

Early day contestants included Paul Derkum, representing Thor; Jake de Rosier and Fred Huyck

riding for Indian, and Cleo Pineau and Maldwyn Jones on Flying Merkels. Most of them frequently rode for several makes, as did other riders, depending on what type of financial arrangements could be made with either distributors or the factories.

It was during this period that Indian, whose founders were both competition enthusiasts, took the lead in both participation and manufacture of limited numbers of competition machines. In 1911 Carl Oscar Hedstrom devised both single and V-twin versions of his original designs as four and eight-valve models, all being of the valve-in-head type. Indian gained an early lead in both velodrome and later motordrome and board track racing with such models.

Not to be outdone, Excelsior, Merkel and Thor built a few such machines, but as their resources were far less than Indian, they did not have the funds to field other than a handful of individual riders.

A frequent competitor, usually riding an Indian, was one Erwin G. Baker, a physical culture exponent, health food advocate, and a one-time vaudeville acrobat and professional bicycle racer. Baker was noted as entering horse track races as early as 1909, but with only occasional success. He was later to gain much notoriety in long distance events, such as endurance runs in the East and Midwest, and the noted desert races held between San Diego and Phoenix. He subsequently became a professional endurance rider and featured many makes of both motorcycles and automobiles in both Three Flag and transcontinental rides. He made his last ride on an Indian Sport Scout in 1941 at the age of 60.

In 1912, A. B. Coffman gave notice that another annual meeting of the American Motorcycle Manufacturers Association was to be held in Chicago in July. In spite of publicity in the trade press, only a handful of manufacturers' representatives expressed their intention to attend, so for the time being Coffman cancelled the event.

With the ever-increasing public interest in motorcycling, a brisk trade in accessories came into being. Such items included tools, improved electrical fittings, luggage carriers, clothing of all types, as well as lighting sets for night riding. Up to this time few of the factories supplied such, the buyer having the option of either carbide or acetylene types, as technical progress in adapting electric lighting to a vibrating machine had yet to overcome its limitations.

By 1913, motorcycling competition was in full swing, and the FAM, with its lack of coordinated control, was hard pressed to keep abreast of the latest developments. With the proliferation of

The Aurora Manufacturing Company was a pioneer producer of a comprehensive line of household appliances, and entered the motorcycle field with Thor machines, their trade name, right after the turn of the century. Thor enjoyed some competition successes after 1909 when the talented William Ottaway became the head of engineering. Motorcycles were dropped when WWI began in 1914, and the firm concentrated on their lucrative home appliance business.

the motordromes, the promoters made their own rules and they were in financial control and could mandate rules to their liking. In many cases they gave lip service to the FAM, designating their meets as FAM-sanctioned, no doubt to seem to legitimatize their offerings.

The situation was somewhat more formalized where individual FAM-affiliated clubs sponsored

either track races or long distance endurance runs, as the organizers considered themselves more obligated to comply. The big problem was in organizing and training referees and timers to do a proper job. In a 300-mile road race held at Savannah in 1913, inaccurate lap counting caused a dispute as to whether Maldwyn Jones or Bob Perry was the winner. The painful frequency of such poor supervision turned both riders and organizers against the FAM, and probably as many "outlaw" events were run as those which were "officially sanctioned."

In general, it may be stated that the FAM then consisted of a membership contained within a number of motorcycle clubs which gave lip service to the national body. They labelled their contests as FAM-sanctioned, but contributed little money to the national headquarters, as it had no positive authority over internal club affairs. In the absence of any authorized personnel to travel about the country to oversee FAM affairs, national business appeared to be transacted by correspondence only.

The constitutionally mandated system whereby FAM affairs in each state were to be administered by a "Governor" was ineffective. As some states, such as those in the old West, had little if any organized motorcycling activity, it was not heeded. In more populous states with much activity, there were simply too many events for one official to oversee.

In the Fall of 1912, a group of Chicago motorcyclists, under the leadership of Dr. W. S. Paterson gained control of the National FAM. A member of a group of motorcycling enthusiasts, Paterson's campaign stressed the fact that the New York clubs had monopolized the national FAM for too long. While this was true, at the same time the Northeastern clubs had together contributed sufficient funds to the National governing body to keep it afloat.

Paterson, a physician and a member of a wealthy Chicago family, was born in 1868 and was at once a physical culture exponent, pioneer competition bicyclist, and an early day motor bicycle enthusiast. He was the perennial President of the prestigious Chicago Motorcycle Club, which, in conjunction with other clubs in Northern Illinois, was responsible for the promotion of an active program of competition as well as social activities. He had attended a number of the FAM's national conventions, and early on had advocated strengthening competition activities by selecting an active National Competition Secretary.[1] In 1910 he had suggested that Elias K. Brinkerhoff be appointed to fill that office in the thought that as a travelling trade show promoter he would be in a strong position to

AMERICA'S GOLDEN AGE OF MOTORCYCLING 1910-1915

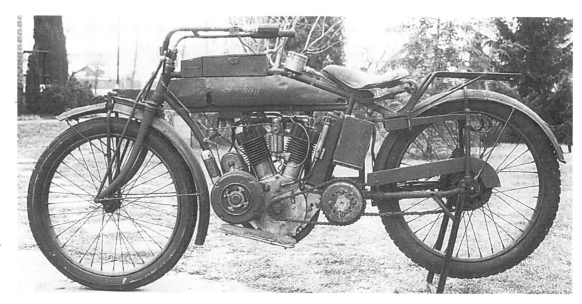

A very rare 1914 Indian 61 cubic inch Hendee Special. This was the first attempt to fit electric starting to a motorcycle. The model was discontinued due to the lack of effective storage batteries, after about three hundred examples were assembled, and conventional kick-start mechanism was supplied.
Sucher Collection.

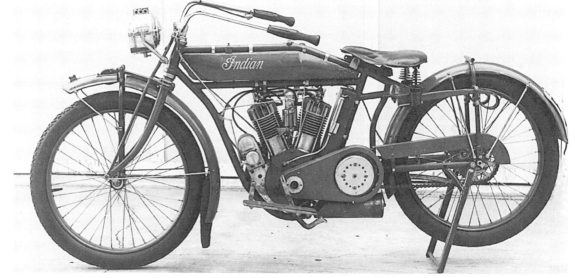

A single-geared 61 cubic inch 1914 Indian V-twin. Both Harley-Davidson and Indian featured such models during this era as low cost economy models for utility riders where high speeds were not required.
George Hayes.

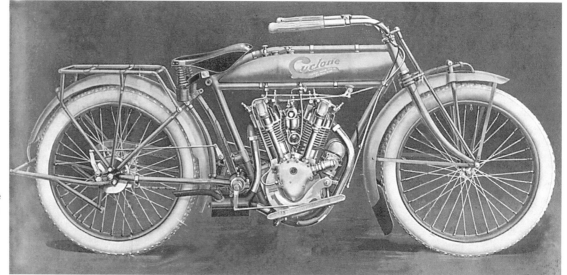

A 1915 Cyclone, a motorcycle with many innovative features at the time. It was built by the Joerns Motor Company of St.Paul, Minnesota.
A.F. Van Order Collection.

28

The Wagner was a soundly built motorcycle from a firm that concentrated on the product of single cylinder motorcycles. Many of its components were brought out from the Harry R. Geer Company of St. Lewis. It was Harley-Davidson's chief competetor for sales to Rural Free Delivery carriers of the U.S. Mail. Production ceased in 1915. *Motorcycling Illustrated.*

oversee this important aspect of FAM affairs.

Paterson was overruled, however, as with the widespread prevalence of anti-Semitism, others of the national officers reasoned that it might be impolitic to appoint the Jewish Brinkerhoff. While such sentiments are unpopular today, in those days ethnic prejudice was prevalent. Between 1880 and 1911, about twenty million immigrants were admitted to the U.S. at the behest of the then-powerful industrialists who foresaw the need for an exploitable labor force to man the rapidly growing number of manufacturing facilities that had multiplied with the growth of the country following the Civil War. Many of the native born citizens feared the loss of their jobs and various groups of these, such as the Irish, faced much resentment. At any rate, the national officers had already appointed one J. P. Thornley, a New York City physician, to act as national Competition Chairman. As shall be

seen, Thornley was soon to become a figure of much controversy.

Paterson at once advocated an active FAM national competition program, not only to strengthen interest in sports, but to bring more public attention to motorcycling affairs. In this vein, Paterson, who was an active tourist, suggested that a series of big National Championship races be inaugurated. In 1913, while travelling with a group of friends on a tour of the Midwest, he noted the general popularity of motorcycling in that area. He suggested that Dodge City, Kansas be the site of such contests as a big three-mile oval was already in place on the prairie on the outskirts of that city. It was through his efforts that a series of such races were held at Dodge City from 1914 to 1916, this location then being billed as the "Indianapolis of Motorcycle Racing." It was also largely due to Paterson's efforts that the annual road races at Savannah were also a FAM fixture during the same period.

It was during the years of 1913 through 1916 that the country saw an unprecedented public interest in motor sports, including both automobile and motorcycling events. Dirt track racing was a feature of most state, county and regional agricultural fairs. In addition, motorcycle club activities were flourishing with numerous social activities, field meets, endurance runs, and other events in cities and towns all across the country. In addition to the Dodge City and Savannah fixtures, a series of desert races were inaugurated over the then-primitive route between San Diego and Phoenix.

As successors to the ill-fated and overly-dangerous motordromes, Jack Prince was busy in these years crossing the country building large mile-and-over wooden speedways in such cities as Atlanta, Chicago, Kansas City, Springfield, Denver, Beverly Hills, Fresno, Rockingham (New Hampshire), Altoona, (Pennsylvania) and other locations. These were built between 1914 and 1917 and also catered to the auto racing boom.

The year of 1913 was significant both from the standpoint of domestic and national motorcycle history. The newly elected President Woodrow Wilson and the Congress, controlled by the Democratic Party, enacted a progressively applied individual income tax which was to be a matter of controversy in the ensuing decades.

At the behest of certain banking and political interests, the Federal Reserve Act of the same year laid the foundation for the gradual devaluation of the dollar to place more money in circulation. Previously the law mandated that all paper currency be backed by an equivalent amount of gold. This had insured the constant value of the dollar

AMERICA'S GOLDEN AGE OF MOTORCYCLING 1910-1915

(Right) Showing the steep angle of a board track.

(Below) The Yale from the Consolidated Manufacturing Company was a popular pre-World War I seller who concentrated on V-twins after 1912. A distinguishing feature was the casting of the cooling fins of the cylinders to stand parallel to the ground. Production ceased in 1915.
Western Motorcyclist and Bicyclist.

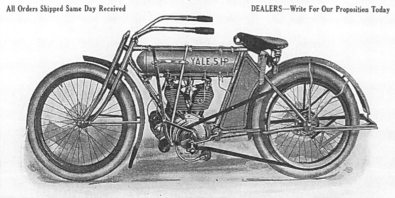

"PIGS IS PIGS"

BUT THERE IS A DIFFERENCE IN DROP FORGINGS

Most any old steel may be forged, but efficient service requires special steel, scientifically prepared for the particular purpose.

YALE drop forgings are made from "Arrow Tip" steel which we have selected after careful tests of everything in the market.

There is also a vast difference in the handling and treatment of the forgings after they leave the hammer.

Our drop forging plant is one of the largest and best equipped in the country, and we make thousands of special forgings of the highest grade for many of the biggest and best automobile builders in the business.

The YALE MOTORCYCLE naturally gets the best we can produce, which means the height of mechanical perfection in every detail, and YALE FORGINGS are largely responsible for the absolute dependability for which the YALE is famous.

REAL QUALITY—YALE QUALITY

begins in the forge shop and foundry and can be attained only when every detail of production is carried out in a single plant under unit management and inspection.

Write today for catalogue that tells the whole story of YALE PERFECTION. Four models—4, 5 and 7 horsepower.   Prices, $210 to $285.

All Orders Shipped Same Day Received   DEALERS—Write For Our Proposition Today

which was worth the same amount in 1813 as it was in 1913. The new law allowed far less gold backing for paper currency, and, as a result, an ongoing inflation occurred which has continued ever since.

1913 also saw the high water mark of domestic motorcycle production, with 71,000 units being sold. Indian was still the sales leader with over 31,000 machines (41% of the market), with 13,000 Harley-Davidsons; 11,000 Excelsiors; 10,000 Flying Merkels; 6,500 Thors and 5,000 Popes. The balance of the market was shared by the manufacturers of smaller production capacity.

This was also the year in which Harley-Davidson's management decided to enter the field of competition. This facet of motorcycling had been totally ignored by them in earlier years, the emphasis being on utility transport and commercial uses. Harley-Davidson was one of the leaders in this field that it shared with similar makes such as Wagner, Jefferson and Iver Johnson. While Walter Davidson had won some endurance contests during earlier years, and numbers of private owners made credible showings in similar contests, the company made it a practice to disclaim any pretense of competition, although stressing the fact that such contests proved the durability and dependability of its products. With the growing public interest in motorcycle sport, and the publicity attendant to the sporting prowess of Indian, along with Excelsior, Merkel and Thor, it was now apparent that successful competition by

AMERICA'S GOLDEN AGE OF MOTORCYCLING 1910-1915

Charles "Fearless" Balke at the Playa del Rey board track near Los Angeles in 1912. As the nickname suggests, he was an agressive rider. *A.F. Van Order Collection.*

Dr. J. P. Thornley
F. A. M. national competition chairman

Harley-Davidson was now necessary for survival.

To this end, William Ottaway, who since 1909 had been the chief designer for Thor and responsible for their earlier competition program, was hired in December of 1912 to develop a competition program for Harley-Davidson. Ottaway had no doubt seen the handwriting on the wall as far as Thor's continuing interest in competition was concerned as that company was showing more interest in their lucrative tool and household appliance business.

With strict orders to develop only Harley-Davidson's present models of engines without incurring the added expense of new designs, Ottaway set to work upgrading the current line of dependable but somewhat stodgy power plants. The result was to open a new chapter in domestic motorcycle history.

1913 was also the year in which Carl Oscar Hedstrom surprised the industry when he severed his connection with the Hendee Manufacturing Company and retired to private life. While Indian's success to date had been phenomenal, its growth had been aided by the public sale of large blocks of both common and preferred stock enabling the expansion of its factory space as well as production.

During this same year Excelsior's competition fortunes improved with the hiring of A. J. "Jock" McNeil as Chief Designer and Competition Manager. McNeil, a Scottish immigrant, had already gained considerable success with V-twin machines powered with J.A. Prestwich engines. McNeil's subsequent "big valve" twins were to make Excelsior a formidable machine in competition.

The increased growth of the motorcycle industry, with national registration approaching 250,000 units in 1913, quite naturally stimulated much journalistic attention. The two leading trade magazines had, by this time, increased their output to twice a month publication and their leadership in circulation was now challenged by another Chicago-based magazine, "Motorcycling," that was now a weekly. For the growing Western market, a new publication, "Pacific Motorcyclist" had been founded in Los Angeles the year before.

The trade publications of this era mostly followed a rather florid and bravura style of writing. This trend was inaugurated by John J. O'Conner, a one-time bicycle racer and a contemporary of George M. Hendee in the high wheel days. O'Conner already enjoyed a somewhat checkered career in the bicycle trade, having been discharged as Sales Manager for a prominent manufacturer in 1909. He was subsequently hired by Hendee to fill the position of Publicity Manager for Indian, and edited it's in-house publication, "Honest Injun" as well as writing most of their sales literature. In 1915 he came out West and obtained the position of Editor of the "Pacific Motorcyclist" where he expanded on his flamboyant and often inaccurate style of reporting.

With all this accelerated activity, FAM membership quite naturally increased, it being reported that 8,567 members were on the rolls in the Fall of 1913. This increase was effected by the simple expedient of requiring that any participants in the large numbers of rallies, picnics, organized runs, and other activities be paid up members of the FAM. While this had an encouraging effect upon the organization's prestige, its practical effect was minimal as only small amounts of the funds were

31

AMERICA'S GOLDEN AGE OF MOTORCYCLING 1910-1915

A 1915 photograph of the Breeze brothers on their 1915 J model Harley-Davidsons. Apparently one Solar headlamp sufficed to conduct both riders at night on the rural roads of Illinois farming country!
John Breeze.

A well-dressed Harley rider. Circa-1915.

relayed to the National headquarters.

Another problem in the FAM's administration was its inability to exert effective control over the selection and appointment of referees, stewards and other contest officials throughout the country where clubs and other nominally FAM-affiliated bodies were giving lip service to the National organization. but were actually paying very little attention to its mandates. Once the various officials in the far-flung localized areas of the country were appointed,their tenure of office was prolonged by popular local consent and often the appointment of individuals by the National headquarters to replace them was ignored.

In this regard a crisis erupted in when Lee Humiston, riding an Excelsior, made his record-breaking run on the board track at Playa del Rey, California, at just over 100 mph on December 30, 1912. In this case FAM President Paterson had just appointed a new West Coast referee, one Elmer Collins, who submitted a sanction request for Humiston's record run attempt. The incumbent referee, Howard Gates, refused to resign, however, and Humiston found himself in the middle of a jurisdictional dispute. While the record was allowed to stand, the National officers deemed it unfair to negate Humiston's record and the resultant ill-feeling brought about by the warring factions caused a serious impediment to the amicable conduct of Western FAM activities.

Later that Fall, a similar episode occurred at a race meet in Syracuse, New York. E. P. Donaldson, the incumbent referee, had been deposed by FAM Competition Chairman, Dr. Thornley, just before the meet and all prior collected sanction fees were impounded. The position was then filled by Frederick Temple, who refused to honor his predecessor's rulings. A near riot ensued when the race meet failed to be started on the designated date.

The whole problem was coincidentally complicated by the fact that Dr. Thornley had been exhibiting erratic and inconsistent attitudes toward his responsibilities together with the problem of inexperienced local officials handling competition affairs. A positive note despite the FAM's inconsistencies was the participation of many motorcycle dealers in both the social and competition aspects of the sport. In some areas several dealers would band together to sponsor a mass ride to some central location for picnics and field meets. Many of these gatherings were sponsored by one or more clubs, often with local dealer cooperation, all of which promoted fellowship and camaraderie among riders. Many of the more thoughtful people within the industry hoped that such gatherings, fostering family participation, might somehow counterbalance the heavy emphasis on racing and speed competition. This was true particularly in regard to board track racing which was, at best, a gladitorial contest with often bloody consequences. While

AMERICA'S GOLDEN AGE OF MOTORCYCLING 1910-1915

A group of riders getting ready for action at Omaha, Nebraska in 1914.
A.F. Van Order Collection.

A pacing machine, used primarily in bicycle racing is getting some attention.
A.F. Van Order Collection.

there was much public support for this type of racing, the thundering and fire-belching 61's represented a type of machine that few spectators could identify with in a personal sense. An effective FAM public relations gesture was the 1913 issuing of a 32-page instruction manual covering the operation and maintenance of motorcycles. Ostensibly written by FAM Secretary W. B. Gibson, it was in reality freely based on a similar work issued by the Iliffe Press in England.

It was during America's Golden Age of motor-

cycling that its products found sufficient markets overseas to inaugurate an extensive export program. The earliest sales leader, Indian, established its first export contact in 1909 in Great Britain, after T. K. Hastings effectively demonstrated an early Indian twin's prowess in that country's 1,000 mile Reliability Trial in 1907 and 1908. William H. (Billy) Wells, a pioneer motorcyclist and one-time importer of the German Vindec machines, undertook to arrange an export agreement with George M. Hendee. Wells subsequently entered Indian

33

machines in the Isle of Man races, with factory backing, culminating in the spectacular 1-2-3 win in 1911. Wells continued to support competition with the aid of his protege, a young rider named Charles B. Franklin. Wells was subsequently elected to Indian's Board of Directors after his purchase of a large block of Indian stock, and attended at least one Board meeting a year except for the war years.

Indian later expanded its exports to Europe, through the Dutch firm of Stokvis and Sonen, as well as to South America, Africa and Australia.

Excelsior first expanded its activities to Canada, establishing a branch in Toronto in 1912 after Indian had preceded them in 1910. Schwinn engaged the firm of Vandergroot and Haas to handle its exports to Europe in 1913, and, at the same time, opened a branch in London. Limited numbers of Excelsiors also were exported to Australia before the war.

Harley-Davidson executed an agreement with Duncan Watson in England just before the war, and extended its activities to Canada during the same period, but did not develop its later extensive export program until after 1920.

The smaller manufacturers such as Merkel, Pope and Thor all opened Canadian branches in Toronto between 1911 and 1913, and a few Merkels and Popes were exported to Australia as well.

While motorcycle manufacture in both Great Britain and Europe exceeded that of the United States during the pioneer years, their types of machines were less suited to colonial use than those of American origin. Due to the relatively shorter distances required, and the presence of better roads, foreign machines were generally of lighter construction and were fitted with engines of usually not over 500 cc's. This latter emphasis was subsequently emphasized in competition where all classes were of a half liter or less which tended to discourage the development of larger engines. Then, too, the economic conditions overseas mandated lower cost machines with smaller fuel demands due to the high cost of fuel. The American V-twins and fours of full liter or more of cylinder displacement and their more rugged construction were well suited to colonial conditions and could operate with heavy-duty sidecars or commercial side vans as well. Export programs were an important item in domestic motorcycle economics after 1920, as will be seen.

Technical progress in American motorcycle design advanced rapidly in the immediate prewar years. The average 61 cubic inch twin now developed at least 15 to 18 hp through improvements in valve timing and combustion chamber profiles.

Spring frames also appeared, with Indian, Merkel, Pope and later Cyclone all offering various types of rear springing.

In spite of the accelerated manufacture and strong market (with its accompanying active competition program and widespread club activities) two events occurred in 1914 that were slowly to exert a strangulating effect upon the domestic motorcycle market.

In the Spring of 1914, Henry Ford, whose production of the Model T was rapidly assuming extensive proportions, announced that he was doubling the $2.50 per day wages, then common throughout all domestic industries for production workers, to $5 per day. He stated publicly that the now substantial enthusiastic public response to his products made this possible. Of course there was the obvious reason that if ordinary wage earners were paid on this scale they could well afford to purchase Ford products.

The immediate response from other industrialists was one of alarm. It was stated that Ford's proposal would undermine the nation's economic system, cause runaway inflation, and tended to be socialistic. At the same time, other heavy industries saw the necessity of falling into line, and within a couple of years, all major producers had raised production wages to Ford's figure.

The effect upon the motorcycle industry was profound. The inevitable effect of the doubling of production wages presaged the problem of survival in a highly competitive industry.

Almost immediately on the heels of the wage problem came the declaration of war in Europe. While political observers had been watching the growing tension between Germany and the other major powers, the general public was not unduly concerned. The effect of this upon the domestic motorcycle industry was the almost immediate rise in the cost of critical materials due to the inflationary effects of wartime demands. Another critical factor was the loss of the source of a variety of component bicycle and motorcycle parts imported from Europe at lesser cost than those available domestically. These included such vital items as ball and roller bearings, ignition parts, Bosch and Harz magnetos, component wheel assemblies and many other small parts. Not only were the European sources diverted to war material, but there was also the dislocation of shipping facilities due to the threat of submarine warfare.

Faced with such problems, many of the smaller manufacturers suspended production at the close of the 1914 production season. This situation did not at once involve the larger manufacturers such

AMERICA'S GOLDEN AGE OF MOTORCYCLING 1910-1915

Indian factory racer Jake DeRosier won over 900 races in his career. Sadly, he died of complications from a board track racing accident a year after it happened.
A.F. Van Order Collection.

SPROCKETS

Hydraulic Pressed Steel Co.
Cleveland, Ohio

as Excelsior, Harley-Davidson and Indian who had already undertaken to become largely independent of foreign suppliers, and who had captured sufficient share of the market to give them the advantage of high volume production.

While the whole industry was approaching perilous times this was not immediately apparent to the public at large. The so-called Big Three could now look forward to lucrative government contracts for the U.S. defense effort, and still controlled a large share of the bicycle market.

In some areas the larger firms were actually in a state of expansion. Many of the retail dealers in the larger cities had moved into large and often opulent quarters that rivalled those of the automobile dealers in scope. The retail trade was still growing, as witness the expansion of the important Western markets that were enhanced by all-weather riding conditions. The motorcycle market was further enhanced by the sudden increase in sales of sidecar outfits.

It was during this period that the four-cylinder Henderson became a popular seller. It was favored by law enforcement officers as being more com-

fortable to ride in their 10-12 hour shifts due to its lack of vibration. It was also popular as a deluxe sidecar machine. William Henderson's modest factory had, since 1913, been running behind on orders. With but modest financing, Henderson's current facilities could produce only about 2,500 units per year.

In line with the growing Western market, Tennant Lee, in association with Charles J. Haddock, secured Henderson's California distributorship. With a well-financed operation, extensive premises were secured on San Francisco's Van Ness Street, then, as now, known as "Automobile Row."

With the general preoccupation with the news of the war in Europe, there was little public notice of the problems of the domestic motorcycle industry. In fact, many of the firms suspending production made no public notice of the fact, and took advantage of the time left to hastily assemble and ship to their dealers the final run of their models from the usual backlog of component parts. The trade press, ever mindful of advertising revenue, made no mention of the now perilous condition of the industry.

(Above) In March of 1915, a 300-mile road race was held in Venice, California. Seen here are a group of Indian riders who participated in the event. From left to right are: Erwin "Cannonball" Baker, Charlie Balke, Fred Jakobe, Dutch Myers, Freddie Ludlow and K.H. Verrill.
A.F. Van Order Collection.

Some more thoughtful members of the industry, however, cognizant of the danger signals, sought ways to improve their own position. In a move to consolidate the survivors, and to seek means of strengthening their position, William C. Schrack, the owner/manager of the Emblem Company suggested that the presently dormant Motorcycle Manufacturers' Association, as initially organized by A.B. Coffman, be reactivated. The hope was that as a united body the remaining motorcycle and accessory firms might arrive at some helpful solutions.

Schrack mailed formal invitations to all prospective members in October, calling for a general meeting to be held in Chicago the following month. This time the response was promising and, among those attending were Arthur Davidson, Frank J. Weschler, Ignatz Schwinn, Thomas Henderson, Joseph I. Merkel and A. B. Coffman. Also attending were representatives of such ancillary suppliers as Firestone Tire and Rubber, B. F. Goodrich, Persons and Mesinger Saddles, Delco-Remy, Edison Electric, Budd, Kelsey-Hayes and Rochester Wheel Manufacturers, and about a dozen other suppliers of related motorcycle components.

During the three day meeting, the formal organization of the Association was affirmed, along with a pledging of mutual cooperation in the promotion of the good image of motorcycling. A committee was appointed to investigate the availability of firms with facilities to mass produce standard bearing sets and multiple hardware items univer-

sally utilized by all makes of machines.

Also discussed was the current ineffectual condition of the FAM but, in the light of more immediate problems, no formal action was taken.

Competition activities were carried forward through 1914 and 1915, with emphasis on such big national features as Dodge City, Savannah, and the yearly San Diego to Phoenix Desert Classic, together with a heavy schedule of board track racing. There were also many continuing localized sporting events at country fair venues, as well as social activities and milder competition events among the hundreds of motorcycle clubs.

While there was lip service given to the FAM in regard to the advertising and announcing of sanctioned events, due to the haphazard manner of sanctioning and rules control from Dr. Thornley's New York office, its influence on these affairs was practically nonexistent.

Matt Brinker (Brinkerhoff) continued to act as the principal trade fair impresario, but with more commitments than he could handle he often referred events to A. B. Coffman, who, since his recent resignation from the Consolidated Manufacturing Company, was devoting all his time to trade promotion.

The regional and local trade fair concept was expanded in 1908 by the Cycle Traders Association. In that year they had inaugurated a National event which was usually held in alternate years in either New York's Madison Square Garden or at the Coliseum in Chicago. Billed as the

(Top) Freddie Huyck is shown on an Indian twin cylinder racer at Agriculture Park.
A.F. Van Order Collection.

(Above) California rider Lincoln Holland is seen here in 1910 with a single cylinder Monark.
A.F. Van Order Collection.

With Merkel and Thor phasing out both their manufacturing and competition support, the sporting scene was now dominated by Excelsior, Harley-Davidson and Indian, although a few loyal privateers continued to field the discontinued makes. By the 1914 competition season, Harley-Davidson, under the skilled hands of William Ottaway, now had well-organized racing team, titled the "Wrecking Crew" by some newsman, and was strongly challenging the long time leader, Indian. By 1915, Harley-Davidson was strong enough to sweep the board by winning all of the big Nationals. Much of its success was due to the superior team organization perfected by Ottaway, with his insistence on good health habits for team members and his use of blackboard signals displayed along the track to direct team strategy in slipstreaming and boxing in competitors. He was ably assisted by C. C. Welborn.

While the retail motorcycle market was still holding firm with emphasis on sidecar sales, total production for the industry dropped to 62,000 units for the 1914 sales season.

In 1915, the "Big Three" (Excelsior, Harley-Davidson and Indian) all brought out improved models. These featured three speed sliding gear transmissions, together with optional "all electric" models at a premium price. These featured generators and batteries to activate head lights, tail lights, and sidecar lights. Many experienced riders still preferred proprietary acetylene lighting sets, however, as neither the generators or batteries of the time were wholly reliable, the latter having an especially short life.

Henderson now offered a three-speed transmission as standard on their four, with full electric equipment as well. The popularity of this model prompted several other small manufacturers to experiment with four cylinder prototypes, the most prominent being the Gerhardt. None of these ever reached production, however.

The Pope, whose sales leader by 1912 was an advanced overhead valve 61 cubic inch V-twin with rear springing now offered a two speed transmission. The make was now lagging behind its usual 5,000 to 6,000 yearly production due to the death of Colonel Pope in 1910 and subsequent problems within the management that succeeded him. Car production ceased in 1912 and motorcycle production dwindled after that, with only a limited number of units available during 1916 and 1917.

An especially critical loss to the industry was that of the Flying Merkel. It was originally built in Milwaukee by a small company founded by its designer, Joseph I. Merkel. A single cylinder belt

National Cycle Show, it came to include participation by the growing number of motorcycle manufacturers, most of which were then offshoots of the bicycle manufacturers themselves.

After 1912, the shows were held in the same venues, but were billed as the National Motorcycle and Bicycle Shows.

As a portent of things to come, the name of Earl C. Smith was being mentioned at intervals as promoting race meets in the Ohio and Indiana areas.

AMERICA'S GOLDEN AGE OF MOTORCYCLING 1910-1915

(Above) One of the biggest events of the year prior to World War I was the 300-mile race at Dodge City, Kansas. Seen here is the flying start in 1915.
A.F. Van Order Collection.

Dave Kinnie was a Cyclone factory racer during that company's heyday.
A.F. Van Order Collection.

AMERICA'S GOLDEN AGE OF MOTORCYCLING 1910-1915

The noted "Red" Parkhurst at the famous Dodge City, Kansas track on one of William Ottaway's Model II racing machines with an improved pocket valve engine. Under the latter's tutelege, Milwaukee's famous "Wrecking Crew" dominated U.S. competition between 1915 and 1921.
Harley-Davidson Motor Company.

drive machine, it was of better than average quality, with such advanced features as light weight (only 90 pounds) together with a single lever control that adjusted both the throttle and spark, and a silencer integral with the frame. Merkel's product attracted the attention of a small bicycle manufacturing plant in Pottstown, Pennsylvania, The Light Manufacturing Company, who made an offer to effect a merger between the two concerns. Merkel accepted their proposition, and moved his operation to Pennsylvania, the motorcycles now being named the "Light Merkel." This new model, launched in 1909, featured a swinging arm rear frame, activated by a coil spring enclosed in a fore-and-aft tube under the saddle. Also included was a telescopic fork, being externally a conventionally constructed curved tube with a bracing strut hut concealing a spring loaded sliding tube inside it. This fork provided such effective handling that several subsequent makes such an Indian, Excelsior and, later, Harley-Davidson and British JAP racing models adapted copies to their racing models.

After a couple of seasons, Merkel was given the opportunity to join the Miami Cycle and Manufacturing Company of Middletown, Ohio, a large scale bicycle manufacturer who wished to incorporate Merkel's motorcycles. Merkel took the offer and at once added a 61 cubic inch V-twin to

his line, with the option of either belt or chain drive and solid or spring rear suspension. Later in the 1914 sales season, a two speed transmission and an impulse starter were added.

Now named "The Flying Merkel" both twin and single cylinder racing models were offered, and Merkel's official factory sponsored racing team of Maldwyn Jones, Cleo Pineau (who later joined Indian), Frank Laird, and A. G. Chapell (a former Indian competitor) gained numerous victories in the big sports events during the 1913 and 1914 seasons.

Merkel's success was due mostly to the advanced design of the engines, being liberally supplied with ball bearings (advertised as "the ball bearing engine"). The variable oil feed was interconnected with the throttle and overcame the usual lubrication failures common to the engines of those days.

While Merkel enjoyed substantial national distributorship through a large number of dealers and gained much fame in competition, the engine was expensive to make. With the supply difficulties and inflation problems due to the war, the larger Merkel models were phased out in the spring of 1915, leaving only a lightweight moped-like machine in limited production. Bicycle manufacturing was carried on for some years, however.

39

The triumphant Harley-Davidson team celebrate after the 1915 Dodge City race. Winner Otto Walker, seen on the left, averaged 76.20 miles per hour.
A.F. Van Order Collection.

In its heyday the Miami firm produced 100,000 bicycles and nearly 10,000 motorcycles per year (1912-1914) and enjoyed a sterling reputation for superior products.

As matters stood by 1915, with so many motorcycle firms suspending production, it was noted by experts within the industry that fully 85% of the manufacturers were now out of the game, along with dozens of makers of accessories and ancillary manufacturers. However, as will be seen, total domestic motorcycle production did not at once decline unduly as the Big Three were increasing production to hopefully take over the entire market.

As it was, the roster of manufacturers who momentarily survived, aside from the Big Three, were a rather curious group. Reading-Standard, though never producing over 2,000 units per year in the best of times, was still viable due to their far-sighted participation in the Western market, most of their production being relegated to a network of dealers in that area. Iver-Johnson, whose principal product was firearms, had entered the bicycle field during the initial boom and produced a limited number of motorcycles of both single and V-twin types, beginning in 1907. Their machines were hand built and of superlative quality with many advanced features, but were aimed at the utility rather than the roadster or sporting market, and

were most often preferred by commercial users, such as rural mail carriers. After 1915, they concentrated production on their two speed 61 cubic inch V-twin. These were actually available, on special order, until 1924 or 1925, but after 1915 only about a thousand models were sold.

The Schickel, perhaps one of the most individualistic machines ever produced in the United States, was also a survivor. Its designer, Norbert Schickel, was somehow connected with a foundry in Stamford, Connecticut, which, while conducting general fabrications in metallurgy, specialized in aluminum products. The Schickel was distinctive in that it was one of the few serious domestic designs that was based on the two-stroke engine principle. It was created by its designer as an ultra simple and economical machine whose principal employment would be in the commercial sphere. The high torque characteristics of large capacity two-strokes were already well known, and Schickel carried the idea a step further in concentrating on two single cylinder models, one of 500 cc and the other of 650 cc capacity, both intended for heavy duty passenger or commercial sidecar work.

Another unique feature was the extensive use of aluminum, the frame and fuel tank being cast integrally, together with the standing legs of the leading link fork. These and the iron engine cast-

AMERICA'S GOLDEN AGE OF MOTORCYCLING 1910-1915

Battle on the boards.
Circa 1910.
A.F. Van Order Collection.

ings were made by the manufacturer, the balance of the cycle parts, wheels, mudguards, saddle, handlebars, etc. being standard bought out components. The initial 1912 machines were fitted with belt drives and a heavy duty Eclipse clutch. Later models featured chain drive and a two speed gear box.

In very limited production and enjoying mainly a local market, most of the machines sold were fitted with proprietary sidecars, this market at the time being served by at least a dozen manufacturers who provided universal type fittings to suit a wide variety of customers' machines. The Schickels were actually available until 1924 or 1925 mostly to special order. An innovative surprise in 1915 was the Cyclone motorcycle, made by the Joerns Motor Company of St. Paul. This company had built the Theim motorcycle, a sound if undistinguished single cylinder and V-twin machine that in 1912 fitted a two speed hub to its larger models. This model was discontinued in 1914 to make way for an advanced design by Andrew Strand, which featured a 61 cubic inch V-twin machine with rear spring and a three speed transmission that had a bevel gear and shaft driven overhead cam shaft and magneto drive.

The new engine proved to be a potent performer, and a racing machine ridden by Don Johns made a spectacular showing in a number of cham-

pionship races, although minor faults caused several early retirements that indicated more prototype developments were in order. In the meantime, financial and managerial problems intervened in the company, and after about 150 roadster machines and half a dozen racers had been assembled, production was suspended early in 1916.

A newcomer in the lightweight utility market was the two stroke Cleveland. It was designed by engineers L. E. Fowler and Carl A. Neracher for the Cleveland Motor Company of Cleveland, Ohio, which was already marketing the Cleveland and Chandler automobiles. The machine was more or less conventional, but the vertically positioned single cylinder engine was set across the frame. It featured an overhung crank, the prototype engines being clutchless and connected via a bevel gear to a belt drive pulley, control being partly effected by a compression release. Production models, however, were fitted with a flywheel clutch that carried both a magneto and a two speed gear, the final drive then being by chain.

A simple and rugged design, being a basic machine offered without electric lighting, it was initially marketed through general merchandise channels. The emphasis was on utility and with no pretense as a sporting vehicle, as its top speed was about 35 mph. With a national advertising cam-

41

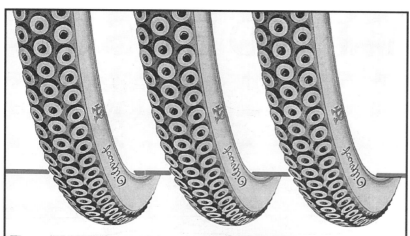

paign, conducted largely in non-trade media, the Cleveland soon became mildly popular with ride-to-work buyers and newsboy types, and was subsequently handled by many regular motorcycle dealers. In 1920, C. Will Risden became its West Coast distributor. In production until 1925, about 5,000 units were assembled annually, about one half going to the export market.

In the meantime, the central management of the FAM became more and more centralized within the New York area, its activities minimally supported by a number of active originally chartered clubs within that vicinity. Direct contact with clubs, as well as members in the South, Midwest and far West was, by this time, almost nonexistent.

While some of the organized competition was billed as being conducted under official FAM sanction, the latter practice became almost comical, as the eccentric Dr. Thornley as National Competition Chairman was appointing referees

that were now deemed unacceptable to the established clubs, many of whom simply ignored his mandates and proceeded with locally appointed officials. As Thornley also ignored the directives of the National FAM President Paterson, as well as the legally constituted Board of FAM directors, the whole operation was by this time almost totally ineffectual.

At this juncture, Dr. Paterson, in a last ditch attempt to save the FAM, called for a special meeting of all available National FAM officers, Committee members, and as many of the FAM affiliated club representatives that could be mustered. This meeting convened in February of 1915, at the Algonquin Hotel in New York City. In opening the meeting, Dr. Paterson noted that most of the members assembled were from the New York and Northeastern areas, and that, aside from the small contingent of Chicago members that had accompanied him, the Southern and Western areas of the country were without representation.

Speaking from a prepared text, Paterson proposed that a Competition Chairman should be hired who would be free to travel about the country to oversee motorcycle sporting affairs and form a personal liaison with former FAM affiliated clubs that had strayed from the fold. He also proposed that the financial structure of the FAM be strengthened, and that Dr. Thornley be at once removed from office, citing his flagrant flouting of official mandates to desist in his activities. To this end, he proposed the nomination of A. B. Coffman as a new FAM President, pointing out that in his capacity as a trade fair promoter and his past and present association with the trade, he could be in a strong position to administrate the affairs of an office that could benefit from his ability to travel widely.

During the subsequent discussion, the question was raised as to the propriety of selecting Coffman, who, as a commercial trade fair promoter, would then be in a conflict of interest situation in the handling of FAM affairs. Paterson countered with the thought that in light of the fact that none of the members could suggest anyone else as an alternative, the FAM would continue to decline.

In later years, Coffman related to the author that Dr. Paterson had contacted him in regard to his assuming the National FAM Presidency and had made a special trip to Toledo to visit him at his home to confer with him concerning his proposed FAM reorganization. (In regard to the New York meeting, Paterson was so confident that the gathering of FAM representatives would accept his proposal and elect Coffman that he suggested that the latter come to New York for the meeting, but stay

AMERICA'S GOLDEN AGE OF MOTORCYCLING 1910-1915

Indian rider Harry Glenn at the Atlanta board track in 1914.
A.F. Van Order Collection.

in an adjacent hotel out of sight of the members until Paterson could convince the FAM officials to accept both his proposals and Coffman's election.)

After continued discussion, the FAM members accepted Paterson's recommendation, and to the surprise of some of the assemblage Coffman made his rather dramatic appearance before the meeting. In accepting the FAM Presidency, Coffman made it clear that the FAM would be expected to advance the funds for his initial travelling expenses. The representatives of several clubs present agreed to about $250, whereupon Dr. Paterson contributed the same amount from his personal funds.

The next order of business was to both select a new Competition Chairman and the forcible elimination of Dr. Thornley. Paterson suggested one John L. Donovan, an active motorcyclist and long time member of the Chicago Motorcycle Club, for the position, stating that the election of a midwesterner would allay the feeling among the membership that the FAM was mostly a New York and Northeastern organization. Donovan was elected on a unanimous ballot, and G. B. Gibson, the long time National Secretary from Massachusetts was re-elected to that post for another term.

At the conclusion of the meeting, Coffman recalled that both he, Dr. Paterson, and a number of FAM-affiliated club members from the New York area met to plan the strategic removal of Dr. Thornley from his office.

As a result, John Weyler, of the Bronx

Motorcycle Club, and C. D. Scherson, of the Crotona Motorcycle Club based on Long Island, engaged a prominent New York trial lawyer, Thomas J. Meighan, to attempt the legal removal of Dr. Thornley. On March 23 the latter was legally served with an order to show cause why he should not be removed from office.

In a rather surprising move to fight the FAM, Dr. Thornley retained a noted Baltimore jurist and former prominent political figure, one Charles J. Bonaparte (1851-1921),[*2] who was the grand nephew of the late Emperor Napoleon. Bonaparte filed a demurrer, requesting a bill of particulars from the FAM litigants. This was provided by Meighan, outlining Dr. Thornley's eccentric behavior and his refusal to abide by the rulings of the FAM Executive Committee.

After Bonaparte reviewed the presented bill he concluded that his client legally had no vested rights in an office that was essentially an appointive one, and on April 10 he submitted to Meighan a confession of judgment. While this legally terminated Dr. Thornley's term of office, he did not quit the post until a group of New York FAM club members entered his premises and physically removed him from the building.

Coffman related that his first official act as the FAM's new travelling President was to journey to New England and, starting in Boston, he visited a number of past and present FAM clubs, offering encouragement to the membership. At the same time, he stirred up various controversies in his travels by removing from office some of the uncooperative contest officials who were Thornley appointees. Coffman was accompanied for a part of the way by Secretary Gibson.

Coffman continued his journey to his home base in Toledo where he went on to visit a number of clubs and dealers in the Ohio and Indiana area. At this juncture, another event occurred which was to have an important bearing on both his and the FAM's future.

The Panama Canal, the hundred-year-old dream of politicians and shipping interests, was completed in 1914. Visualizing its impact on international trade in the Western Hemisphere, certain commercial interests throughout California, and San Francisco in particular, decided to stage what was billed as the International Pan Pacific Exposition in that city. With the planned construction of extensive facilities on a prominent site near the Golden Gate bridge, trade fair promoters were at once invited to negotiate contracts for exhibit space.

While the ranks of the motorcycle manufactur-

ers were already thinning, the management of the Big Three all expressed interest in participating, as did several Bay area dealers and the still-surviving retailers of Reading-Standard, Thor, and Flying Merkel. C. Will Risden, with some assistance from the factory, was placed in charge of the Indian exhibit. Excelsior's California distributor, Tennant Lee was to fulfill a like office. Harley-Davidson's management decided to offer their representation to Matt Brinker, still the country's leading trade fair impresario. However, Harley-Davidson decided to withdraw the offer and retained A. B. Coffman who later stated that his handling of Harley-Davidson's extensive exhibit brought his trade promotional career into enhanced focus.

Brinker, who by this time had amassed a tidy fortune, decided to visit his relatives in Holland. While shipping and especially passenger travel had been severely dislocated by the U-boat menace, he managed to secure passage on a British freighter sailing from New York to Le Havre. Departing on September 24, the ship was torpedoed about 50 miles south of the Scilly Island on England's south coast. While some of the crew managed to launch a lifeboat and reach shore, Brinker was not among the survivors.

Another signal event of 1915 was the sinking of the Lusitania by a German U-boat in May, with the loss of over 1,200 lives, many of them women and children. This warlike attack on what was then thought to be an unarmed passenger vessel aroused world wide revulsion. It was learned some 50 years later, however, that the ship actually carried munitions in her forward hold, the fact being concealed by the collusion of the shipping company and the Collector of the Port of New York. At any rate, anti-German sentiment reached a fever pitch in the United States. While President Woodrow Wilson, an ostensible peace candidate, counseled forbearance, many people were favoring a declaration of war on Germany. The net effect on the American economy was that industrialists projected the manufacture of war material in the preparedness climate, and many strategic materials came into short supply.

As far as the motorcycle industry was concerned, the market had softened markedly due to the phasing out of a number of the locally manufactured makes. The surviving marques were now faced with growing inflationary costs, together with the inevitable demands for higher wages on the part of employees.

A. B. Coffman returned to Toledo in July, following the installation of his Pan Pacific Harley-Davidson exhibit, and found to his dismay that his reputation among the FAM membership had suffered. There were comments that he had neglected FAM business to operate his own affairs, together with the fact that there was still ill feeling extant over the controversies in the Thornley affair. He also found that in his attempts to initiate a more positive leadership in the FAM, there were comments that he was an arrogant and domineering individual who tended to ride roughshod over the feelings of others.

In an effort to solicit and enhance rider support, Coffman induced several of the surviving manufacturers to include a prepared advertising statement urging riders to join the FAM. In the hope of strengthening his appeal, he had written to the appropriate officers in the American Athletic Association, the American Automobile Association, the Auto-Cycle Union of Great Britain, the FICM

AMERICA'S GOLDEN AGE OF MOTORCYCLING 1910-1915

Harry Lewis and Charlie Suddeth show off their Excelsiors prior to a race in Omaha, Nebraska in 1913.
A.F. Van Order Collection.

President, as well as the fledgling Canadian Motorcycle Association, suggesting that the FAM be considered as an affiliate. In due time he received replies acknowledging the FAM and his solicitation. Coffman then included the names of these organization in his appeal, obliquely inferring FAM affiliation which did not actually exist.

In commenting on his phase of FAM history, Coffman stated that he had attempted to convey the impression of a strong central FAM leadership, a factor that had too long been lacking. He also noted that he felt constrained to neutralize the discouraging effect the European war was having upon the domestic motorcycle market, with the growing threat that if the U.S. embarked on a preparedness program there could well be a selective service draft of the young men who made up a goodly portion of motorcycle buyers.

A helpful publication that appeared in 1915 was a book entitled "Motorcycles" by Victor Page, a French-born mechanical engineer who had previously published similar works on automobiles and aircraft engines. It was a voluminous work and covered both theory and practical application of mechanics, covering the mechanical details of most of the leading domestic makes of machines together with a few British and French types. As a popular seller, the book went through several editions, but unfortunately was not updated due to the author's untimely death in 1918. After being out of print for many years, it was reproduced as a paperback in its original text by Post Motor Books in 1971, and is still a useful handbook for those interested in restoring antique machines. It is notable that since its initial publication, there were no other similar hard cover books published domestically until nearly three decades later.

During the years between 1912 and 1915 when domestic motorcycling was most popular, the more prominent trade magazines already mentioned had expanded their offerings to twice-monthly publication. One, "Motorcycling," became a weekly. Well supported by the advertising revenue from nearly fifty manufacturers and a large number of accessory suppliers, these publications normally had a content of from 80 to 150 pages. To sustain reader interest, many news items were carried dealing with the activities of the hundreds of motorcycle clubs. Also

Don Johns, one of the best racers of the pre-World War I era.
A.F. Van Order Collection.

included were numerous small articles concerning activities of members of the trade and on-going competition activities, both local and national.

The sporting activities of this era have been covered only in a general aspect, as the more important competition events have already been treated to an in-depth discussion in the author's previous works.

There was one series of such events that deserve special mention, however, as being significant not only for their efficient organization but for their influence on technical progress in contemporary motorcycle design. These were the desert races over the 450 mile distance between San Diego and Phoenix, that were featured under FAM auspices starting in 1913, and held annually until 1916, when they were terminated in deference to the nation's defense effort.

A formidable course extending over the wilderness of the Southwestern desert area, it followed the sometimes indistinguishable unimproved wagon tracks first followed by the early day pioneer migrants to California. Participation entailed great personal risk, from the heat or the possibility of becoming lost if the trail was inadvertently strayed from, with death from both hunger and thirst a real possibility. Then there was the hazard of encountering roving bands of renegade Apache Indians or Mexican bandits who often crossed the border to steal cattle.

In spite of this, the races always attracted a substantial group of contestants, and their participation and exploits form an interesting saga in the history of American motorcycle sport.

As the Isle of Man race in 1911 pointed out the necessity for change-speed gears, so did the Desert Races in the States after 1913. The substantial numbers of single geared machines entered initially did not fare well, as the usual 11-1 ratio provided insufficient power over steep hills or through deep sand, and insufficient speed on the flat to keep them in contention with competitors who had variable gears. After 1913, all the leading makes were fitted with variable gears.

CHAPTER THREE

CHAOS AND REORGANIZATION
1916-1919

CHAOS AND REORGANIZATION 1916-1919

At the 1916 National Motorcycle and Bicycle Show held in New York's Madison Square Garden, machines from Dayton, Merkel, Pope and a few other makes were entered, in addition to models from Harley-Davidson, Indian and Excelsior. However, only the latter Big Three were still in production.

1915 had been a satisfactory sales year with about 9,000 units from Excelsior, 16,500 from Harley-Davidson, 26,000 from Indian and about 1,900 from Reading-Standard, along with a handful from the others. But with the economic and supply conditions caused by the war, increased retail prices somewhat restricted trade. The Emblem concern, with modest production, announced that it was soon to abandon the domestic market in favor of the export field. William G. Schrack halted production of his 76 cubic inch V-twin and concentrated on a lightweight V-twin intended for the European market.

Motorcycle competition was actively carried on, with Harley-Davidson's famous Wrecking Crew winning most of the big nationals. Indian, still undaunted, saw Charles Gustafson (assisted by his son, Charles Jr. and Charles B. Franklin, the former Irish racing star and now a designer) experimenting with updated competition engines.

With the war in Europe now becoming intensified, President Woodrow Wilson was reelected on the promise of "Keeping Us Out of the War." Motorcycling in general received favorable publicity, along with other types of motor transport during the U.S. Army's Punitive Expedition into Mexico in the spring of 1916. Mexico's 1910 revolution was still unresolved, as the the newly elected President, Francisco I. Madera, had been deposed and assassinated by Victoriano Huerta, only to shortly suffer a similar fate himself at the hands of Venustiana Carranza. In the meantime, a bandit-turned-general, Pancho Villa, was not only disputing Carranza's authority in the north, but was crossing the border to raid towns in New Mexico and Arizona. Carranza then authorized the U.S. government, quite naturally outraged at the killing of its citizens, to send their own troops into his country to hopefully capture Villa. A force of 5,000 regulars under the command of General John J. Pershing crossed the border, utilizing motor transport in the form of trucks, automobiles, four Curtis JN-D training airplanes, and motorcycles.

Equal numbers of Excelsiors, Harley-Davidsons, and Indians were used in both solo and sidecar versions for scouting and liaison work, giving generally reliable service, attesting to the soundness and adaptability of the now universal U.S heavyweight V-twin concept.

While the wily Villa easily evaded capture in the remote vastness of his own familiar area, the campaign was significant in that it provided an initial experiment in mechanized warfare, a modern departure from the long traditional horse cavalry and the use of horse-drawn vehicles.

A.B. Coffman's activities on behalf of the FAM came to a halt when he announced that he had exhausted the rather meager travelling funds allotted to him the previous summer by the National Executive Committee. After some delay, that Committee called a meeting in Philadelphia in July, where Coffman stated his case and suggested executive action to enable him to carry on his work. With the Committee divided in opinion as to what course to next pursue, Coffman offered his resignation as President, stating that being kept in limbo impeded personal business affairs which now required his attention.

The Committee then selected Shelby Falor, Sales Manager of the Motorcycle Tire Division of the Goodyear Tire and Rubber Company of Akron, Ohio, to succeed him. Noting the now critical decline of general FAM membership to fewer than 4,000, with only limited amounts of dues being remitted to the National officers, Falor launched a direct mail appeal to the remaining members and surviving affiliated clubs to reactivate the "governor" concept of state organized FAM groups. As

CHAOS AND REORGANIZATION 1916-1919

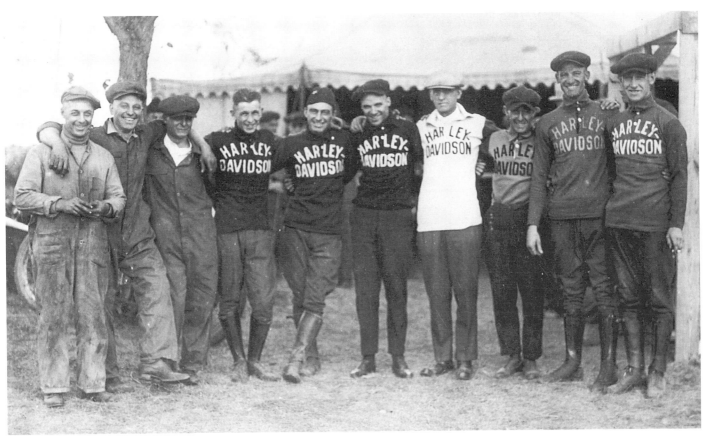

The Harley-Davidson factory team at the 1919 Marion, Indiana 200-mile race. Shown are (from left to right) mechanics John Morey, Frank Trespeci and Hank Syvertsen, along with Ralph Hepburn, Ray Weishar, Albert "Shrimp" Burns, Team Manager Bill Ottoway, Maldwyn Jones, Red Parkhurst and Otto Walker.
A.F. Van Order Collection.

this move further weakened the already ineffectual FAM administration, the already sketchy overseeing of regional and local referees and contest officials was now non-existent.

At an emergency meeting in Akron held in August, it was noted that former local FAM clubs and regional cadres were no longer bothering to seek official sanctions for ongoing competition events, the suggested local organizing of state FAM authorities being almost totally ignored.

With the national membership roster now standing at just over 2,000, and with but $340 remitted to the National Treasurer, President Falor, with the concurrence of the officers present who did not even constitute a quorum, ordered that due to the now-imminent possibility of being drawn into the war, all official FAM activities and competition programs be suspended until the cessation of hostilities.

This was actually a rather oblique face-saving gesture on the part of the National officers, and was in effect an unofficial disbanding of the FAM as originally organized.

In retrospect, the FAM enjoyed a brief span of but six years of activity, starting in 1909 when sufficient motorcycles were registered to give a certain scope to both club and competition activities. In truth, the FAM had accomplished some purpose

in highlighting the fact that both the trade, private owners, club members and competition events required a national organization aimed at promoting motorcycling affairs. The FAM supervision of at least a portion of the country's motorcycle competition activities accentuated the fact that without some pretense of a central authority the sport could well regress into total chaos.

In the late fall of 1916, and following the mandate of the U.S. Congress that the nation was to proceed on a war preparedness footing, the War Department called for bids from private firms for a myriad of products. From the lessons learned in the Mexican campaign, large numbers of trucks were called for, in addition to a certain number of passenger cars and motorcycles.

There was a brief discussion in official circles that perhaps the motorcycle industry should be required to design special machines for use by the armed forces. But the time factor involved could be a critical issue, and the standard roadster types had already proved themselves in the Mexican campaign.

The reaction of the Indian company was now significant, as it was to have a direct bearing on the future of this leading domestic manufacturer.

George M. Hendee as Indian's sole surviving original partner and the actual founder, announced

A.F. Van Order was a life-long motorcyclist and founder of the Trailblazers, a motorcycle fraternal organization based in Southern California.
A.F. Van Order Collection.

been largely overlooked since 1910 and the rise of the big twin popularity. Then, too, some of the more thoughtful people within the trade may well have considered that the attention to the development of racing machines may well have focused undue attention on the more hazardous aspects of motorcycling. While some of the machines now offered were more or less conventional types, others were not.

In the fall of 1914 Excelsior announced the introduction of a simple two-stroke lightweight with single geared belt drive with an Eclipse clutch, offered at $135. It appeared in 1915 with a two speed gear box at a slightly higher price.[1]

For the 1916 season, Indian offered a similar machine, but with a two-speed gear box and all chain drive, powered by a two stroke for $150.[2]

In 1916 the Miami company, after phasing out their heavyweight V-twin and single cylinder Flying Merkels, re-entered the market with a heavy-weight pedal cycle with a spring fork powered by a small four stroke engine. Featuring a standard pedalling gear, it was much like a modern moped.

None of these machines attracted much public notice as they were notably underpowered and were dropped for the 1917 season, although the Miami manufacturing rights were sold to another firm, and, under the name of Evans, appeared for a few more years.

Indian re-entered the market with the Model 0, another lightweight with a horizontally opposed 15 cubic inch twin that owed much to the contemporary popular English Douglas. It was a comfortable and smooth running machine, but with only 15 cubic inches of engine displacement its mild performance elicited little interest and it was dropped after 15 months of limited production.

The Shaw Motor Company of Galesburg, Kansas, turned back the clock to the pioneer days by offering an engine kit to motorize standard pedal cycles which could also be purchased as complete units. They also offered a toy racing car that could be bought disassembled featuring a small single cylinder engine of their own manufacture.

Another rather novel power application for standard pedal cycles was the motor wheel. This device was originally patented and produced in limited numbers in England by E. C. Wall as the Wall Motor Wheel after 1910. It consisted of an engine with a 20" wheel that could be attached to the near side of the rear wheel of a bicycle, the whole being able to accommodate itself to the bicycle's lateral movement by means of an articulated frame. Manufacturing rights for the U.S. were secured by the A. 0. Smith Motor Company who marketed it

his intention to retire in October. What with the continual issuing of shares after 1910 to finance the Company's activity, majority control passed out of the hands of Hendee and Hedstrom by 1913. The latter, put off by the new intrusion of non-motorcycling shareholders into the affairs of management, elected to dispose of his shares and resign. Hendee, lately facing intensified pressure from the majority shareholders, felt that he no longer relished the continuing struggle.

At this point, a new Board of Directors, headed by John F. Alvord as Company President, decided to maximize profits by going all out for War Department orders by allocating nearly all of the output of big twins to this market. Frank Weschler, who had assumed more and more of the company's managerial duties since 1913, was ordered to prepare bids for submission to the authorities.

After the United States declared war upon the Central Powers in April of 1917, Thomas Callahan Butler, through his political connections in Washington, was appointed as the civilian head of a War Department cadre to recruit a force of technicians and mechanics to serve in special units overseas to maintain army machines. He was given a leave of absence from his job by Frank Weschler, but the war ended before Butler had more than a few units organized.

In the meantime, certain surviving manufacturers had decided to concentrate some of their emphasis on the utility market, an area that had

CHAOS AND REORGANIZATION 1916-1919

Ray Weishar (#2) leads Ralph Hepburn (#4), Shrimp Burns (#5) and Red Parkhurst (#6) in a 200-mile race in 1919 at the original Ascot racetrack in Los Angeles. Hepburn was the eventual winner.
A.F. Van Order Collection.

under their own name. The Wall attachments had the engine connected to drive the wheel via a short chain, but the Smith version was made more compact by attaching the wheel directly to the camshaft which afforded the proper gear ratio. The production rights were later secured by the fledgling Briggs and Stratton concern who made further modifications. They also offered the device with a small, very lightweight four wheeled buckboard, the unit being attached to the rear of the vehicle. A few units were also adapted to powering ultralight railways speeders, the unit being fixed to position the wheel on top of one rail.

While speeds up to about 20 miles per hour were attainable as a bicycle attachment, they suffered early failures from the vibration and road shock to the head bearings as well as damage to the

wheels. The power units did not work well on rough roads which upset both the carburetion and magneto timers. Considered largely as a novelty, the units were in production until about 1924.

Another and still less orthodox power unit was the motor wheel offered by the Dayton Sewing Machine Company, formerly manufacturers of the well-built Dayton big twins. This unit comprised a small engine carried within a disc type wheel which was intended to replace the standard front bicycle wheel, the forks being slightly spread apart to accommodate it. As an unsprung unit subject to road shocks, the device never worked well and was soon withdrawn from production.

The general public apathy to both ultralight motorcycles, as well as the less orthodox devices illustrated the innate conservatism in the public mind concerning their desires, and the need for the manufacturers to supply machines that offered both sound construction and adequate road performance.

The eagerly awaited War Department bids were at long last advertised early in 1917. Indian's money hungry Board of Directors at once decided to go all out and relegate nearly all of their sizable production capabilities to the preparedness effort, stating privately that high profits could accrue from a cessation of the usual sales efforts and attendant advertising. Their first bid was for twenty thousand 61 cubic inch Powerplus models, standard except for slightly lowered gearing, at $187.50 each, with $49.50 for required sidecars. As this model, with its rear springing and general design was a fairly expensive machine, the bid price per unit would offer only a small profit.

The short sightedness of Indian's Board in offering nearly all of their production to the War effort was immediately apparent, as it would mean withholding machines from the civilian market, then served within the United States by over 1,100 dealers.

Harley-Davidson, while wishing to participate

Pope machines were prominent since the earliest days of the motorcycle industry, and were a part of the bicycle and automobile manufacturing empire founded by Albert A. Pope. After 1912, heavyweight V-twins were emphasized, with ohv engines designed by Perry E. Mack. The company floundered from poor management after Pope's death in1910. The last motorcycles were assembled by the Westfield Manufacturing Company from components left over from 1914 manufacture.
Western Motorcyclist and Bicyclist.

Look at These Lines!

COMPARE this illustration with that of any other motorcycle on the market. See if you can find one that appears cleaner-cut, more trim or more business-like than the Pope.

Notice how the lines of the Pope express its strength and solidity; how its slightly rakish construction suggests the speed of which it is capable.

Notice how every line harmonizes with every other; how every detail blends into the whole artistic triumph.

You will find no better example of

the law that the more nearly perfect a thing is mechanically, the more it tends toward harmony in design.

Notice the free space all about the Pope motor that makes it easy to get at; the clearance between motor and gas tank that permits the removal of cylinder heads, cylinders and pistons without taking motor out of frame.

Combined with all the Pope advantages and exclusive features, the Champion of the Hills, finished in the well-known red-striped gray, is one of the most attractive outfits seen on the road.

Westfield Manufacturing Company

5 Lozier Ave.   Westfield, Mass.

Makers of *Columbia* Bicycles

Two more shots of action at the Ascot track. The one mile oval had a very hard surface which allowed for close high speed racing.
A.F. Van Order Collection.

The New York-based "Motorcycle Illustrated" was a leading publication of the early motorcycle days.
Don Emde Collection

in the preparedness drive, took a more rational view of the matter and somewhat cautiously offered a bid similar to Indian's on 7,500 three-speed magneto- equipped J models, again their standard offering, but with lowered gearing.

The result was that Harley-Davidson was at once able to supply machines to its civilian customers with the potential to break into Indian's leading position as Indian's customers were not only shortchanged on their orders for new machines, but faced a shortage of spare parts as well. In some cases, Indian dealers dropped their franchises in favor of Harley-Davidson.

Ignatz Schwinn, with smaller motorcycle production, was also cautious, allocating but 3,500 machines for the 1917 War Department bidding. In addition, a few Clevelands were accepted for messenger service on domestic army installations.

As matters turned out, Indian supplied a total of 41,000 machines to the Government during 1917-18, the latter half of which were at a slightly higher price, the Company having been able to renegotiate its original contract in the face of wartime inflation. In addition, about 6,000 machines were allocated for export or were of the limited production K models in 1916 and the O models in 1917 which were sold on the home market.

Harley-Davidson delivered a total of 15,000 military machines in the same period. Its total production for 1917-18 amounted to 17,356 and 19,328 respectively, allowing them a substantial number of machines for the domestic market which enabled them to take advantage of Indian's preoccupation with war production.

Current FAM affairs went, A. B. Coffman and William Schrack had held an emergency confer-

CHAOS AND REORGANIZATION 1916-1919

The start of the 1919 200-mile race at Ascot. Winner Hepburn is #4.
A.F. Van Order Collection.

A 1920 vintage motorcycle competition rider's safety helmet. Before the days of fiberglass, the protection afforded by thick leather must have been minimal.
Dude Hartman.

ence with Shelby Falor in September, 1916, following his announcement of the suspension of FAM activities. Falor defended his action on the grounds that the general membership had fallen to the point that there were no longer any funds forthcoming for even minimal operation. He also noted that most of the earlier competition records had been lost during the furor over the Thornley affair, that numerous complaints had been received concerning contested competition results, and that he himself was totally discouraged.

At this juncture, Coffman and Schrack sent out a form letter to all of the surviving manufacturers, together with copies to some of the principal trade suppliers, briefly outlining the crisis in FAM affairs and calling for a meeting of the American Motorcycle Manufacturers Association, and inviting other interested parties within the industry. While this Association had been but loosely organized after its finalizing in 1914, it was obviously the only choice for a possible resolution to the problems of the FAM.

After receiving sufficient response, Coffman arranged for the group to meet early in November with representatives of all of the surviving manufacturers together with other interested parties such as those from Firestone and Goodyear, Delco—Remy, etc.

The meeting, which was chaired by William Schrack, consisted mostly of discussions of ways and means of strengthening the FAM. For this purpose, he suggested that a reorganization be effected to include principal suppliers of components to the

trade, such as tires, electrical parts, wheels, and all others who supplied bought-out items. He stated that it was obvious that with the now decimated ranks of prime manufacturers, such an organization could not function without the support of everyone who was connected with domestic motorcycling.

A committee consisting of Coffman, Shelby Falor, Arthur Davidson and William Henderson was appointed to study possible pre-organizational structuring, and render a report of their findings for a subsequent meeting scheduled for the following February. It was their conclusion that resulted in the founding of what was to be called the Motorcycle and Allied Trades Association. Thomas Henderson was elected President; Arthur Davidson, Treasurer, and E. F. Hallock, representing the suppliers, as Secretary.

No formal documentation of a constitution was offered, but rather a simple preamble such as was adopted for the original American Association of Motorcycle Manufacturers. This was included in the initial Minutes as:"The organization is open to all manufacturers of motorcycles and components of high ethical purpose whose aim is to further the best interests of those engaged in the industry and allied trades, and to protect its members from unjust restrictions and exactions."

The initial formation of the M & ATA had as its purpose the revitalization of the FAM, the current problems of the industry itself being put aside for the moment.

New FAM officers were then elected, including Robert G. Betts, President; Shelby Falor, Vice

CHAOS AND REORGANIZATION 1916-1919

Roy Artley competed in many different types of events in the teens and early twenties including flat track racing, hill climbs and cross country record runs.
A.F. Van Order Collection.

Red Parkhurst won the 1919 Marion race. He completed the 200 miles in three hours and six minutes.
A.F. Van Order Collection.

President, and Theodore R. Thomas, Secretary. Henry Parsons was installed as interim Competition Chairman, and this group, in a series of separate meetings, conducted an analysis of the FAM's past failed policies and endeavored to suggest corrective measures.

An important item of discussion was the suggested advocacy of making motorcycle competition safer by restricting the engine sizes to 30.50 cubic inches and under, as the speeds of the 61's commonly seen since 1912 had risen progressively up to 115 mph.

In the meantime, Henry Parsons, in a series of articles and editorials in "Motorcycle and Bicycle Illustrated," suggested that the FAM was being strengthened and sought reader opinion on what additional corrective measures might be applied. Subsequently numerous letters were received from readers highlighting the general dissatisfaction of motorcyclists with the FAM.

During this period the scope of the surviving trade magazines had narrowed markedly. This was due, partly, to the drop in advertising revenue, and a general decline in motorcycle sport due to the absence of numbers of able bodied young men who were now involved in the war effort. Outside of Parsons' publication, there was little note taken of general industry decline and very limited discussion of the problems of revitalizing the FAM.

In the meantime, Parsons' publication staff had been augmented by the appointment of Leslie D. "Dick" Richards as Associate Editor. Richards had become an active member of the Long Island-based Crotona Motorcycle Club in 1913, and was subsequently elected its Road Captain, organizing a number of long distance and endurance runs on Long Island in conjunction with other clubs in the New York vicinity. He had enlisted in the U.S. Navy in 1915, serving aboard the destroyer "Paulding" as a radio operator. Upon his discharge in 1917 he joined Parsons' staff in the Fall. The "Paulding" was later to enjoy much notoriety when assigned to the Coast Guard to assist in suppressing the liquor traffic by apprehending many of the motley fleet of vessels that were supplying thirsty Americans with illicit spirits during the Prohibition era.

Richards, who had long been a critic of the FAM's ineffectual status, was now assigned to give editorial voice to the cause of strengthening organized motorcycling.

Contemporary changes in the industry included the purchase by Ignatz Schwinn of the Henderson operation. Schwinn had noted the popularity of that machine, despite the limitation of production due to inadequate facilities and financial

base, as well as his own third place position as a big twin producer behind Indian and Harley-Davidson. He reasoned that by adding Henderson with its more extensive facilities and financial base, production could be greatly expanded.

William Henderson and his brother, Thomas, were at first hesitant to sell, noting their strong luxury tourist and law enforcement market that was absorbing all the machines they could produce. But, in the end, Schwinn's reported median six figure offer was too much to refuse and the deal was consummated in November, 1917. The sales agreement mandated that both the Hendersons join Excelsior as production managers, along with young Arthur O. Lemon who was hired in 1915 as an engineering assistant.

Lemon in later years stated that from the beginning he had doubts about the new situation, as the Hendersons were free-thinking and independent in their attitudes, with Schwinn being somewhat of an obtuse personality with a reputation for recalcitrance.

In the spring of 1918, Harley-Davidson decided to attempt to penetrate the middleweight utility market, but with a model more substantial than Indian's now ill-fated K and Model O machines. Accordingly, William Harley and William Ottaway set to work and in due time were testing the prototype of what was to become the Sport Twin. The model was quite similar to Indian's Model O in being an opposed twin, again based on the English Douglas, but a somewhat larger and heavier machine with the engine being enlarged to 37 cubic inches. With good pulling power and a top speed of about 45 mph, the result was a very smooth-running and easy-to-start machine with "go anywhere" capabilities.

Just prior to the final prototype testing of the new Sport Twin, Harley-Davidson hired a new publicity manager, a young motorcycling enthusiast named Julian C. (Hap) Scherer, a former sales manager for the Firestone Tire Company. Scherer was an advocate of the expansion of motorcycle interest into the middleweight category. The fall of 1919 saw Scherer at once inaugurated into an ambitious publicity campaign, riding one of the first Sport Twins on a transcontinental run, as well as setting a record in the Three Flag Run from Canada to Mexico.

Another industry news item was that Carl A. Neracher had resigned from the Cleveland Motor Company, manufacturers of the mildly popular two stroke Cleveland, in order to attend to the sales promotion and marketing of a new type of utility motorcycle.

Pioneer Indian motorcycle dealer Bernard E. Andre's establishment at 913 Quarrier Street in Charleston, West Virginia. He also held franchises for Excelsior, Henderson, and Smith Motor Wheels. A belt drive Flying Merkel is seen on the sidewalk. Andre is at the right in the doorway. The photograph was taken in 1916. *Richard A. Andre.*

In the fall of 1918, the news leaked out that Indian's Charles B. Franklin was overseeing the prototype testing of a new model. This was destined to become the famous Scout, which was to mark a turning point in the company's fortunes. According to Franklin's biographer, Thomas Callahan Butler, the basic design was originally worked out in 1912, before he joined the Indian organization. Franklin was employed at the time as an electrical engineer by the city of Dublin, Ireland. He was an experienced motorcyclist and competition rider, and had become familiar with several makes before joining with William H. Wells' Indian group.

In reviewing the development of the Scout in later years, Butler told the author that he had suggested that Franklin lower the machine's silhouette by specifying 20" rather than 22" wheels, and shortening the frame to make a more compact

machine. As it was, the project was rather a gamble, as the Scout's 37 cubic inch engine was less powerful than the then-fashionable 61 cubic inch that had become the standard offering of the industry leaders. On the other hand, both Butler and Franklin had agreed that a middleweight machine could well be the best of both worlds in providing an economical utility machine that also offered good performance, which had been the Waterloo of both the K and O models. A further advantage was that the Scout had a simple but sturdy cradle-type frame, plus unit construction of the engine and gear box so the production costs were less than that of the Powerplus. The Powerplus, like Excelsior's C model and Harley-Davidson's J model, carried an excessive number of component parts from their bits and pieces design involvement. It was on this point alone that Butler, as sales manager, was able to convince Indian's Board of Directors to proceed

CHAOS AND REORGANIZATION 1916-1919

The author's adventurous cousin, Joseph Martin, rode this 1914 single geared J model Harley-Davidson from Indiana to California in the summer of 1919. What with bad roads, or the lack of them and rainy weather and heavy mud, the trip took twenty-eight days. This was the first machine that the author was familiar with. *Sucher Collection.*

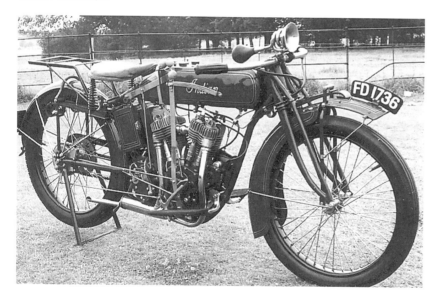

A 1920 Indian Powerplus owned by Vintage Motor Cycle Club member Golin Spong. Note the flat English style handlebars. *Jeff Clew.*

with its introduction.

In the late fall of 1918, the Hendersons resigned from Excelsior. There was an ongoing friction between them and Schwinn over the overall design characteristics of the Henderson Machine. Its basic concept was as a rather compact machine with a low silhouette which did not suit Schwinn, who thought that it should be made more impressive in size as a luxury touring and law enforcement machine, together with the fact its F-head engine was rather expensive to produce and

should be of side valve configuration.

The Hendersons argued that with an already well-proven design with a large following, the machine should be continued as such. Added to this, there were ongoing personality conflicts between the often irascible Schwinn and the free-thinking Hendersons.

The Hendersons' departure was highlighted by more unpleasantness when Schwinn threatened to sue them for a breach of their purchase contract, especially when the Hendersons signified their intention to enter the market with their own version of an updated Four.

Schwinn then offered Arthur Lemon the position of Chief Engineer, with carte blanche approval to design a new but simplified version of a four cylinder design. Lemon recalled that he viewed the matter with mixed emotions, but with a very generous salary offer, he accepted. A significant addition to Excelsior's engineering staff was one Everett M. De Long, a four cylinder enthusiast who had once been the protege of the Hendersons.

In the meantime, a committee consisting of A.B. Coffman, William Schrack, and Arthur Davidson, suggested that in order to successfully implement any reorganization of motorcycling, the manufacturers' association should be more formally organized. This had been suggested in 1916, but the exigencies of the war had apparently intervened. At any rate, at a meeting held in Chicago in January, 1918, the American Motorcycle Manufacturers Association was reorganized to form what was now called the Motorcycle and Allied Trades Association. While now made up entirely of trade representatives, its expressed purpose was to replace the still-ineffectual FAM and to serve the causes of both the trade and private owners, and to govern and regulate competition activities.

The first step was to draw up a set of rules to govern competition. There were now two general classes of competitors; amateurs and professionals who might be in the employ of the factories. The amateur class (those who had never competed for cash purses) was subdivided into two further classes - novices and experts - the former being riders who had never won or placed in any formally organized competition.

Guidelines were also set up to govern the granting of sanctions for competition events, whether by clubs or professional promoters. In the matter of Board tracks, no event would be sanctioned on courses less than a mile in circumference or less than one hundred feet in width. No more than four riders could be started in any one heat. On dirt tracks, no more than six riders could be on

The Excelsior motorcycles were a part of Ignatz Schwinn's bicycle empire, and after 1912 concentrated on heavyweight 61 cubic inch V-twins. One of the last of the industry's later survivors, the manufacture of motorcycles ended with the depression in 1931.
Western Motorcyclist and Bicyclist.

the front row for the start, more than that number being accommodated in ranks of no more than six riders behind the leaders. In all cases, pole and rank positions were governed by places attained in a previous time trial.

It was also made clear that the M&ATA would not sanction any events that did not guarantee to operate under M&ATA rules, and that all officials and referees must be cleared by the M&ATA who would then mandate enforcement of any and all M&ATA rules.

To give further effect to this intent, it was also announced that a Competition Committee would be formed which would have full authority to act in the name of the M&ATA and make and enforce whatever rules deemed necessary for the proper control of all sporting events having to do with motorcycle competition in the United States.

Shortly after, another directive was issued stating that all riders wishing to compete in M&ATA sanctioned events must be registered beforehand in order to strengthen that body's central control and to ensure that all previously mandated rules would be observed.

While all motorcycle competition was now under the industry's control, it was hoped that a strict adherence to M&ATA rules would lead to a strong riders' and owners' organization that could be both democratic and self-sustaining.

The first Competition Committee Chairman elected was Henry Parsons who had long been a leader in the FAM reorganization advocacy, and who, in his position of power as the editor of the then-leading trade publication, could at once inaugurate a vigorous campaign to encourage well organized competition.

Parsons at once published a series of editorials outlining the goals of the reorganized body and urged all riders to register to allow for their affiliation within the program; that clubs could be chartered catering to such groups of riders, and that for a nominal fee of 50 cents, a central registry of all such riders could be established.

To provide the all-important financial strength that had long been the weakness of the FAM, the M&ATA membership decided upon a schedule of contributions from its members to support the new program. Each motorcycle manufacturer would be assessed $100 per year. Individual allied trade suppliers, who sold at least $20,000 worth of equipment to the trade would be assessed $50 per year. As all dues were to be paid in quarterly installments, an ongoing cash flow could be assured. Under this system, prime manufacturers were designated as Class A members; trade suppliers as Class B, and individual private members as Class C, with an annual assessment of $1. In addition, competition riders would pay an additional 50¢ fee per year for their registration.

At this juncture, Robert G. Betts resigned as President, and Irwin D. Allen, an Excelsior-Henderson dealer of Akron, Ohio, was elected in his place. As the FAM was still technically, if not actually, in existence, Allen can be described as the FAM's last chief executive. Upon assuming office, he at once mailed a form letter to all present or former FAM clubs, soliciting their support for a reorganized FAM. Upon receiving little response, he reported to the M&ATA Executive Committee that, in his opinion, an entirely new national motorcycling organization should be formed, and offered either to aid in this, or step aside as President in favor of another who might offer a fresh approach.

W.B. Gibson. It was unanimously agreed that a new organization under a new name should be launched, if only to erase the tarnished image of the FAM and give the whole movement a fresh start. In order to present a strengthened image of motorcycle sponsorship, it was decided to amend the originally selected Motorcycle and Allied Trades Association to Motorcycle Manufacturers and Allied Trades Association, underscoring the backing of the concerns who were wholeheartedly involved in all aspects of the motorcycle trade.

One important manifestation of this strength had been to bail out the expiring FAM from an accrued indebtedness of $4,200 that had been building up since 1916. It had been at this critical juncture that the FAM management had embarked on a program to establish a group of dealers as well as independently owned repair shops that were officially approved by the FAM. The thinking behind this was the well known fact that many of the repair shops, and even some of the dealers, were guilty of unethical conduct. The idea had been conceived by Secretary W.B. Gibson, who had dispatched one Stanley Gallagher, a former Harley-Davidson factory employee, to inspect a selected group of motorcycle establishments in New York and New Jersey to evaluate their operations and recruit them into what was to be called an "FAM Approved" category. Gibson terminated the program when it was soon noted that the expenses of the project had exceeded the money available. This added to other mounting FAM deficits for office rent and supplies, postage, and the overseeing of competition affairs, such as they were.

With the general dissatisfaction from motorcyclists at large with FAM activities, coupled with the growing demands from creditors, the top management of Harley-Davidson, Indian, Excelsior, and Emblem, had, in a hurriedly called meeting in Chicago, somewhat reluctantly put up the funds on a pro-rata basis to pay off the deficit. The overriding thought had been that continuing troubles from within the FAM would further prejudice efforts to regain public confidence through a more effective organization.

With the new national organization now designated the MM & ATA, the organizers set about to correct the long-time weakness of the FAM in establishing a firm financial base, as well as providing the necessary executive control. It was suggested that a new executive be chosen from within the ranks of one of the manufacturers, with an official headquarters to be located at one of the establishments, with the advantage of permanent office facilities and secretarial help. Both the Davidsons

In the meantime, Henry Parsons and Leslie D. Richards offered on-going editorial advocacy in their magazine for the formation of a reorganized national motorcycle association under a new name, with most of the other trade publications following suit. In a review of some of these contemporary offerings, some of the editors went overboard in predicting a new era of success for the industry and satisfaction for owners, usually couched in the flamboyant prose popular in that day.

In the fall of 1919, a representative group of motorcycle manufacturers and allied trade members met in Chicago under the banner of the M&ATA. Included in the group were Arthur and Walter Davidson, Frank Weschler, Ignatz Schwinn, William Schrack, the Henderson brothers, Henry Parsons, L.D. Richards, Shelby Falor, and several former FAM officers, including veteran Secretary

Chaos And Reorganization 1916-1919

A formidible competition mount was the "big valve" Excelsior originally developed by Irish racing star Jock O'Neil. The X's established many records in the early days, with active factory riders such as Carl Goudy and Bob Perry.

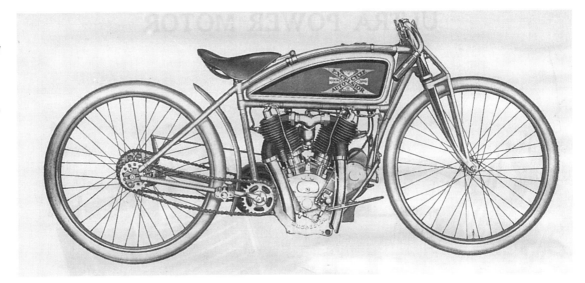

The Indian Scout designed by Charles B. Franklin and introduced in 1919 set new standards for middleweight motorcycle design. Well received domestically, it was also popular on the export market, and was Indian's sales leader between 1920 through 1927 when it formed the basis for the immortal 101 model.

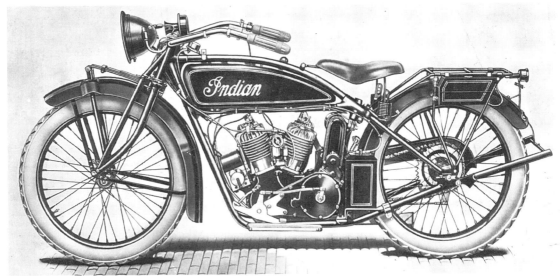

Don Emde Collection

and Schwinn at once vetoed the idea of offering the MM & ATA any ancillary services.

At this juncture, Frank Weschler suggested that Douglas Hobart, a graduate engineer and a full-time draftsman in Indian's Engineering Department, be installed as the first President of the MM & ATA. He described Hobart as a long time motorcycling enthusiast who had entered the game as a protege of Bernard "The Terrible Swede" Swenson, a former high wheel bicycle racer and compatriot of George M. Hendee, who was a early-day Indian dealer in Providence, Rhode Island, and presently a distributor.

Hobart, in partnership with one Claude Coulter, had recently, under Swenson' sponsorship, established an Indian dealership in Hartford, Connecticut. He was still a part-time employee at the factory, however, driving to Springfield two days a week to assist Charles B. Franklin.

Weschler stated that Hobart, who had agreed to a previous proposal in the matter, could oversee MM & ATA affairs while in Springfield and that the Company would provide both office facilities and secretarial help.

The assemblage, after some consideration, accepted Weschler's rather generous proposal, noting mainly its financial advantages, and the Executive Committee made arrangements for what FAM records still existed to be transferred from Irwin Allen's premises in Akron to Springfield. To allow ample time for this and the setting up of Hobart's office, it was stipulated that he would be officially recognized as President of the MM & ATA in January, 1920.

While the foregoing account of the long-delayed official demise of the FAM and the official launching of the MM & ATA has been somewhat concise by the author in the interest of brevi-

CHAOS AND REORGANIZATION 1916-1919

William Ottaway was the innovative mechanic and practical engineer who, at the turn of the century, became interested in the internal combustion engine. He was for a time the chief designer for Thor, updating their engines for a brief foray in competition. In 1913 he was hired by Harley-Davidson to update their utility type engines, and was responsible for Milwaukee's preeminence in racing between 1915 and 1921. He finalized all of their designs until his retirement in 1942. *Harley-Davidson Motor Company.*

In the early days, motorcycling was considered a "mainstream" sport. Shown is a motorcycle accessory catalog produced by New York's Gotham Sporting Goods Company. *Don Emde Collection*

ty, the whole affair was actually very drawn out and filled with complexities, and the summation of events had to be somewhat truncated in the interest of space considerations. With the virtual collapse of the FAM in the Spring of 1916, followed by the problems of liquidating its indebtedness during 1917 and 1918, there were some three years of organizational effort before the interested parties were able to formulate a set of rules so that both organized motorcycling and its attendant sporting activities could at least function. Then there were several more months of effort before the MM & ATA could be formally launched. As a self-protective endeavor on the part of both the surviving manufacturers and their suppliers to save the industry, the new organization represented the cooperative efforts of a relatively large number of

people. As a historical aside, during the many meetings held during 1918 and 1919, it had been suggested that the new organization be designed as the American Motorcycle Association. While this was briefly considered, it was ultimately considered by a majority that the name was too similar to that of the FAM, and further, it did not emphasize that the whole motorcycle industry itself was now in support of the new organization; both managerially as well as financially, in an effort to regain the confidence of motorcyclists at large.

The volume of correspondence involved during this period was awesome. The veteran FAM Secretary, W.B. Gibson, volunteered to oversee it, and was so appointed by the Executive Committee to serve on a quasi-official basis.

The actual details of the launching of the MM & ATA and the events attendant to it were lost to history for many years. This was due to rather uneven coverage by the contemporary trade press, as well as through later deliberate destruction of most of the MM & ATA records, which will be subsequently described.

After several years of intense searching, the author was able to assemble a skeleton group of the more accurate reports. I was most fortunate to be able to interview many of whom had preserved some of the official records through their own interest in the matter, all of which contributed to the preservation of what is today considered an acceptably accurate history.

As an aside to the demise of the FAM, surviving pioneers who were active motorcyclists and active participants in FAM affairs before World War I have offered some interesting comments in the matter from their own observations and experiences. These included such well known figures as Hap Alzina, Dudley Perkins, L.D. Richards (who was especially active in FAM affairs), Thomas Callahan Butler, August and Anton Freirmuth, Jim Davis, Fred Ludlow, Claude Salmon, Arthur Le Moyne, and others who generously accorded the author extensive interviews.

The cumulative opinions gathered from these contacts indicated that the original organization of the FAM was faulty. It was originally conceived as a rider's organization to unite them through local club participation as a democratic body, but soon passed to the control of a succeeding group of wealthy men. As motorcycling enthusiasts, they attempted to create a competition aura with a special emphasis on an elite societal ambiance, which already existed in horse racing. The concept of an elitist emphasis on the sporting side of motorcycling was at once at variance with the position of

CHAOS AND REORGANIZATION 1916-1919

A well designed motorcycle of the pre-WWI era was the Pope. The company was founded by Colonel Albert A. Pope, a boy officer who was awarded a brevet rank at the battle of Gettysburg, founded a bicycle manufacturing empire in 1872, and later included both automobiles and motorcycles. The example shown was of advanced design, with a Mack designed ohv engine, three-speed gearbox, and rear springing. With Pope's death in 1910, the vast conglomerate floundered through insufficient management. The last motorcycles were assembled in 1915.

The last ever big twin Iver-Johnson assembled in the late 1960's by an enthusiast who located the last of the component parts for these machines in a storage area of the Iver-Johnson arms factory. Designed as work horse utility models, these machines had a top speed of about 40 mph, but were favored for commercial sidecar use and by contract rural free delivery U.S. mail carriers for their ability to negotiate the bad roads of the first two decades of the Twentieth-century.
Richard Renstrom(from the Bud Ekins Collection)

the average motorcycle owner. He was, more often than not, a blue collar artisan or clerical type who was basically interested in low cost utility transportation in an age and time when the newly invented automobile was far too costly to own and operate for other than the well-to-do.

With such a concept, the opulent FAM hierarchy quickly abolished any semblance of democracy within the rank and file membership. The decisions were made from on high; first from the New York group with its domination, and later moved to Chicago. With the consequent minimal financial contributions from the members at large, much of this was provided from the private contributions of the national officers, who ran the FAM as an autocratic fiefdom. With such a background, in retrospect, it is indeed remarkable that the FAM held together as long as it did.

At any rate, by the summer of 1919, motorcycling competition activities were again officially under way, stimulated by the return of thousands of discharged young men from the military service who were anxious to return to both civilian employment and sporting activities. Many of the dormant clubs were reactivated, and many new ones established.

The trade press, eager to support the industry, printed in glowing terms the promise of a revitalized national organization. Former active FAM referees and officials (those who had enjoyed the approval of riders and clubmen in their respective districts) were urged to sign up for participation in the MM & ATA, which was now declared the sole governing body of the U.S. motorcycle sport. To this end, A.B. Coffman, with the assistance of L.D. Richards, set forth a new set of rules which covered board track

Leslie "Red" Parkhurst was a factory sponsored Harley-Davidson rider. He won many events in his career in addition to setting world speed records at Daytona Beach, Fl; in 1924. Here he is sitting on one of the trick Harley factory racers.
A.F. Van Order Collection

racing, dirt track competition, road racing, hill climbing, club rules, etc. In doing so, the attempt was made to iron out elements that had engendered rider's complaints with the former FAM.

The so-called "Big Three" among the surviving manufacturers, Excelsior, Harley-Davidson, and Indian, at once set about reorganizing their previous competition activities. Harley-Davidson revived their famous "Wrecking Crew" that had held prominence since 1916, and Indian, led by Charles Franklin as designer and Charles Gustafson, Jr. as Competition Manager, were already trying out new prototype racers to challenge them. By 1920, motorcycle sport was in full flower, supported by a war-weary population eager and willing to resume civilian diversions in motor sport.

As to affairs within the industry, William Henderson announced that a new four-cylinder machine of original design, named the ACE, was going into production at a new factory organized in Philadelphia.

Harley-Davidson was hurrying the completion of an enlarged factory complex on the site of their original factory on Juneau Avenue. This project had been launched with newly acquired financing in 1918, following the hopes of increased sales records enjoyed during the neglect of the civilian market during the war.

A reorganized company to manufacture the once bankrupt Militaire Motorcycle Company, formerly located in Buffalo, obtained a factory in Springfield, across the street from Indian on Wilbraham Avenue, and announced a sales campaign for 1920. The Militaire was a curious car-like vehicle with wooden-spoked artillery wheels and retractable stabilizing wheels and propelled by a four cylinder air-cooled engine with a sliding

gear transmission. A highly original design by R.F. Sinclair, produced briefly before the war in both single and four-cylinder models, it was intended to appeal to both automobile and motorcycling interests. Due to technical difficulties, only a few machines were produced. The company closed down only a few months later.

The two-stroke lightweight Cleveland, which had been popular before the war with utility riders and was enjoying a healthy export trade, resumed production with a slightly warmed-over model.

The A.O. Smith Company, which had acquired the original E.C. Wall patents in England before the war and had been in limited production, sold the rights to the newly organized Briggs and Stratton Company (who mainly marketed small industrial engines) who put it into limited production.

Joseph Merkel's lightweight power cycle design was sold by the Miami concern, which decided to concentrate on the bicycle market, to another manufacturer who marketed it briefly as the Evans. Merkel attempted to re-enter the market with another motor wheel of his own design, but ran into financial problems after a short time. What was left of his efforts was taken over by Indian, who marketed the device along with one of their heavy duty bicycles, but quit the market after disappointing sales.

Norbert Schickel's foundry in Hartford, Connecticut, continued to manufacture the large capacity two-stroke singles he had devised just before the war. Preoccupied with other products, the machines were assembled and sold by special order only; the slightly updated 1915 model being available until 1924.

The Iver Johnson concern, mainly involved with their long-established lucrative arms firms manufacturing, continued a very limited production of their massively constructed two-speed V-twin, also on a special order basis. This rugged machine, a favorite with rural contract mail carriers for its mud-slugging power, was continued in its 1915 guise until 1924. Less than a thousand machines were turned out during the ten year period.

In the face of the market dominance by the Big Three, as well as the problems of financing, numbers of aspiring designers were obviously discouraged from entering the field. Those who had hoped for a post-war resurgence of well-liked products from Pope, Thor, Flying Merkel, Dayton, and other lower production manufacturers were disappointed when their mentors elected to specialize in other fields of endeavor.

An ominous portent for the domestic motorcycle industry was an announcement in the automo-

Chaos And Reorganization 1916-1919

Port-Au-Prince, Haiti, 1916. Three United States Marines attached to the U.S. Naval Occupation Forces with their 1913 single-geared Indian single cylinder motorcycles.
U.S. Naval Historical Center

bile trade publication, "Motor Age," editorializing on the now accelerated public demand for automobiles and the registered number of no fewer than 387 manufacturers. The Ford Motor Company and the reorganized General Motors Corporation under Pierre S. duPont were the leaders of the industry; Chrysler was not yet in existence. The balance of the smaller manufacturers offered what was known in the trade as "assembled" cars, these being made from bought out components supplied by the myriad of ancillary firms that now offered a wide range of automotive products.

As a paradox to the sudden drop in motorcycle sales in the face of the massive production of cheap cars that offered great carrying capacity, comfort, and effective weather protection, was a renewed boom in bicycle popularity. With the significant increase in population from the baby-boom of the first two decades of the century, there was now a growing market of youthful riders. In addition, many adults were buying increasing numbers of bicycles as ride-to-work machines. While public transport in the form of trolleys and buses were expanding, their slowness and overcrowding in many cases made personal transport attractive, weather permitting.

In spite of the apparent uncertainties of the post-war motorcycle market, the manufacturers brought out no less than four rather unconventional models in 1919.

Harley-Davidson's top management, undaunt-

ed by the failure of Indian's lightweight opposed-twin Model O, brought out a similar but middleweight machine, also based on the contemporary popular British Douglas, called the Sport Twin. A more rugged offering, it had a top speed of 45 mph and possessed sufficient power with its 37 cu. in. engine to be a go-anywhere machine. It was almost wholly designed by William Ottaway, in consultation with Sir Harry Ricardo (the British flow-metrics expert) regarding its combustion chamber profiles.

Ireland-born Charles B. Franklin was a youthful motorcyclist in the pioneer era. His father, a prosperous metal salvage dealer, was able to send him to the Dublin Technical College, where he received a degree in electrical engineering in 1901. He became a competition rider, and became attracted to Indian after T.K. Hasting's victory in the U.K. He became associated with W.H. Wells, and rode an Indian to 2nd place in the famous 1911 Isle of Man 1-2-3 triumph. While employed by the City of Dublin in their electrical power plant, he was a part-time Indian dealer sponsored by Wells. He was offered a position in Indian's engineering department in 1916, and in the Fall sailed for New Orleans from Lisbon, taking the southern Atlantic route to avoid the German U-boat menace.

His personal ideas concerning motorcycle design were first formulated about 1912. When Indian was considering its post-war program, his idea of what he considered to be a progressive

A group of military side-car drivers with Harley-Davidson outfits on the flight line at the U.S. Army Corps training field at Love Field, Texas in 1917.
U.S. Army Signal Corps

design was the soon-to-be immortal 37 cu. in. Model G Scout. With some modifications to better suit the American market, as suggested by sales force member Thomas Callahan Butler, the model was announced in the late spring of 1919. As a middleweight easily started machine with a top speed of 55 mph, it had a broad appeal even in the heyday of the heavyweight 61 cu. in. V twin, which was faster but weighed 100 lbs more and required some athletic ability to kick start.

At the other end of the scale was the rather unorthodox Neracar, the brain child of one Carl A. Neracher, with a two-stroke engine patterned on the contemporary Cleveland from the board of the same designer, L.E. Fowler. This machine had a low step-through platform type body, center pivot steering, and extra-wide mudguards for all-weather protection. Its drive train was through a friction disc fitted to the crosswise mounted engine. Its speed was regulated by a counterwheel which could be shifted across it.

Neracher launched the project from a factory in Syracuse, New York. Funds were provided by a group of wealthy investors, headed by King Gillette, who had become a multi-millionaire from his innovative razor blades. The Neracar was promoted as less of a motorcycle than a new era in personal transport. Its lightweight, modest speed and low riding position gave it an appeal as an every-person machine. It was advertised in the general magazine media, such as the "National Geographic," and farm and family oriented magazines. Of a rather sound design and rugged construction, it was a transportation bargain at $185.

While sales were encouraging, with numerous

motorcycle dealers adding it to their other lines, the mass sales envisioned by the hopeful investors did not materialize, and they withdrew their support in 1924. The design had been coincidentally produced in England, with fair results, the Neracar being in limited production until 1928, but fitted with a 250 cc British made sidevalve engine.

A less practical design was the Auto-Ped, a small two-wheeler on the pattern of a child's sidewalk scooter with 12" wheels fitted to a low platform body. The small two-stroke engine was carried over the front wheel, its control effected by moving the stem-type handlebar back and forth to activate the spark and throttle adjustments. Designed to carry the sole rider in a standing position, it was suited only to short journeys. Its small size in heavy traffic could be daunting to the non-motorcycling owner it was intended for. Its New York based manufacturer turned out several hundred of these curious machines, hawking them through the larger department stores in New York City and Boston. The idea was simultaneously offered in England, where it met with the same lukewarm response, and was withdrawn from production after a few months and heavy financial losses.

While as noted many members of the domestic motorcycle industry went to great lengths to strengthen the position of both the post war market as well as the attendant organization for public participation, the subsequent results in the end were not overly encouraging. Certain economic forces affecting the general transportation picture were to shortly relegate the motorcycle to a basically marginal status within it.

CHAPTER FOUR

THE GREAT DECLINE
1920-1930

THE GREAT DECLINE 1920-1930

A fter World War I the United States emerged as a world leader with enhanced political and economic power. Virtually unscathed by the Great War, its might was now enhanced by the industrial expertise resulting from the acceleration of mass production for the war effort. This experience helped to fulfill the pent-up demand for civilian goods and services now that the uncertainties of war were over.

With a soaring prosperity, Americans were now eager for labor-saving household appliances, the extended communication from telephones and the newly developing radio, sophisticated labor-saving machinery for both agriculture and industry, and above all, enhanced personal transportation.

The position of the motorcycle industry was noted in relation to the accelerated production of automobiles that had started in 1919. Harley-Davidson and Indian, whose cavernous factories were capable of turning out 35,000 units per year had, in 1920, found a market for one-half that number. The decrease in sales saw Harley-Davidson with a $3 million debt service on its new factory, and Indian found itself in critical need of replacement tooling facilities.

Ignatz Schwinn was in far better condition due to the cushion of his soaring bicycle manufacture, and turned out nearly 4,000 four-cylinder Hendersons. Mindful of the falling market for the V-twins of his two chief rivals, production of the formerly popular 61 cubic inch V-twin that had been the backbone of his motorcycle production since 1915, was cut back to special orders only, and he shipped less than 100 units in 1920.

While the U.S. was leading the world in automobile production, other parts of the world had yet to see much progress in that field, and motorcycles overseas were now the best compromise. As the heavyweight American models with their rugged construction were the best alternative, especially in colonial conditions, the American factories sought to exploit this market as a cushion against falling domestic sales.

Harley-Davidson, through Sir Duncan Watson's operation in England, sought to expand its European market, with additional efforts toward South Africa and Australia. Indian renewed its ties with Stokuis and Sonen in Holland, competed in the other areas with Harley-Davidson, and paid special attention to the Japanese and Asian markets.

In the face of the popularity overseas of American machines, William Schrack of Emblem announced that he was closing down his domestic sales organization in favor of an export only program, featuring his newly designed lightweight 32 cubic inch V-twin aimed at European markets.

Aurthur A. Constantine did not like to have his picture taken. This rare photograph was taken by Ted Hodgdon with the designer aboard a 1931 Henderson four.

THE GREAT DECLINE 1920-1930

Reading-Standard, whose small production was hampered by its wide range of models, bravely attempted to expand the European market along with its small penetration of the Western U.S., Hawaii, and even franchised dealers in the South Seas, Fiji and Tonga.

While export was to become a critical factor in supporting the American motorcycle industry in the face of the diminishing market, the top management of the Big Three saw the danger in admitting this as an admission of defeat at home. The general public was never allowed to know that in the ensuing decade from 45% to 55% of all production was sold overseas.

Neracar and Cleveland were enjoying sufficient sales to keep their small factories in operation as the utility market still was attracting customers, and Iver-Johnson and Schickel could scarcely be counted, as neither assembled more than 1,000 units to special order between 1915 and 1924.

Motor sports were now attracting accelerated public attention as an outlet after its curtailment during the war years. The infamous Black Sox baseball scandal in Chicago in 1919, where players were found to be rigging games at the behest of gambling interests, had momentarily caused public disapproval of that sport. There was also much interest in prize fighting, but its often brutal aspects elicited some public disapproval.

A built-in venue for both automobile and motorcycle racing was now available at the hundreds of horse tracks that existed throughout the country in both state and county-sponsored fairground sites. They had long been a fixture in American life where harvest festivals were held each fall, this in an age when the majority of the population lived in rural areas. In addition to races being held during the fair periods, the tracks were further available to promoters who could schedule

meets during the spring and summer.

The great board tracks that flourished between 1919 and 1924 were also a big attraction for spectator interest, both for cars and motorcycles. Their principal mentor, Jack Prince, promoted both the building as well as the upkeep of these vast ovals after the war, there being one or more in operation adjacent to many of the country's larger population centers. While the boards were a prominent showcase for motorcycling, many thoughtful heads of the industry often doubted the extent of their role. While it was a crowd-thrilling spectacle to watch the thin-tired, thundering and fire-belching 61's circling the course at speeds now approaching two miles a minute, the races frequently produced bloody accidents. It was thus difficult to assume that the average spectator could equate himself riding such a dangerous machine.

In 1919, Henry Parsons, as MM & ATA Competition Chairman, with the assistance of former FAM President R.G. Betts had planned a large number of National and Regional motorcycling contests. Two-hundred mile races were planned for Elgin, Illinois and Marion, Indiana, along with a revival of the pre-war Dodge City; Sheepshead Bay, New York; and Le Grande, Oregon Classics.

In addition, hill climbing was now coming to the forefront as an alternative to horse track and speedway racing. Before the war, most hill climb contests were rather tame affairs, where stock machines contended on infrequently traveled rural sites, or on private road areas. After 1920, more spectacular venues in the form of steep courses on off-road hills were utilized. The slopes, invariably in rural areas, were anything from 45 degree to 60 degree angles, many of the latter actually being non-negotiable.

In place of street roadsters, specials intended only for the purpose were developed, with elon-

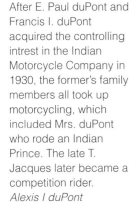

After E. Paul duPont and Francis I. duPont acquired the controlling intrest in the Indian Motorcycle Company in 1930, the former's family members all took up motorcycling, which included Mrs. duPont who rode an Indian Prince. The late T. Jacques later became a competition rider.
Alexis I duPont

THE GREAT DECLINE 1920-1930

(Top) The middleweight, opposed twin-cylinder Harley-Davidson "Sport" was based on an earlier British-made Douglas motorcycle. It was on the market from 1919 to 1923.
A.F. Van Order Collection

(Above) The Immortal Harley-Davidson JDH "two-cam" model produced in limited numbers during 1928 and 1929. A high-performance machine, it established a cult following that exists until this day.
George Hays

gated wheelbases and especially tuned engines. These were often overhead valve specials, sometimes tuned for blended fuels or alcohol, and with very small fuel tanks and lightweight forks to cut down weight.

Both the factories as well as the MM & ATA Competition Committee encouraged hill climbing activities, as the sites could be utilized with little prior preparation, and minimal expenses were incurred to promote an event. This made it an ideal source of interest for club activity, where other promotions such as dirt track meets or road races entailed much more organization.

Competition rules subsequently formulated saw the establishment of both 45 and 80 cubic inch unlimited classes. An "A" class covered factory machines with special engines and blended fuels, more often than not entered by professional riders. The "B" class covered the same engine displacements, but were restricted to modified stock engines burning commercial gasoline.

Hill climbing was not only a crowd pleaser, but was ordinarily not overly hazardous to the rider, provided the technique of getting clear of the machine once it attained its stalling points or began

to wind itself over backward was perfected.

Early day "slant artists," as they were called, included Orrie Steele, Augustus "TNT" Terpenning, Dudley Perkins, Hap Alzina, Eddie Ryan, and the perennial Howard Mitzel. In later years there were Gene Rhyne, Joe Petrali, Joe Herb, Sam Arena, and Conrad Schlemmer, to name a few.

During the 1920's and 1930's the short subject newsreels that were shown in motion picture theaters usually featured a 30 to 60 second shot of hill climb action.

The emphasis on racing saw much activity in the competition departments of the Big Three. All were conducting experiments with specially designed engines. Harley-Davidson and Indian built limited numbers of four and eight-valve specials of the overhead variety. Excelsior's Jock McNeil designed an overhead camshaft model, of which six or seven were built for both their sole professional, Bob Perry, and selected privateers. The lightly financed Reading-Standard concern had also recently purchased the rights to the Cyclone overhead cam V-twin from the Joerns Manufacturing Company of St. Paul. Joerns had discontinued the make after assembling only about 150 Roadster machines and half a dozen racers in 1916, after a year's production. But without the funding required to overcome its initial teething troubles, this once very promising design faded from the picture.

Harley-Davidson and Indian, after fielding a few examples of their eight-valve specials, reverted to engines based on their bread and butter models. This was partly to reduce expenses, and because their appearance was like the production models. The support of factory racing teams was highly expensive with star riders drawing up to $20,000 per season in salary and bonuses. Added to this were the expenses of transporting managing personnel and mechanics and providing their accommodations during the competition season. The factory managers often questioned the support of racing, with the post-war public decline in sales, but with its popularity as a spectator sport, it appeared as the most effective media to showcase the industry.

Excelsior dropped official competition participation after its star rider, Bob Perry, was killed in practice at the Ascot Speedway in Los Angeles on one of the super fast "cammers." In his grief, Ignatz Schwinn ordered a halt to all race bike production. Excelsior's participation was now limited to two privateers, Waldo Korn and J.M. McNeil, who between them still owned 2 or 3 engines.

THE GREAT DECLINE 1920-1930

A rider's eye view of the 101's instrumentation, with ammeter at left, electrical switches on the right, and auxiliary hand-operated oil pump below the fuel filler caps. The Stewart Warner Speedometer was an optional extra.
George Hays

The classic Indian V-twin engine design pioneered by Charles B. Franklin in his 1919 Scout. The example shown is a 1929 101 Scout.
George Hays

As it was, immediate post-war competition was dominated by Harley-Davidson's now famous Wrecking Crew, who won nearly all of the big nationals between 1919 and 1921. Much credit for their victories was given to William Ottaway's superb organization and team tactics, together with the competent assistance of R.W. Enos and C.C. Wilborn.

Indian bravely stayed with the game, however, with Charles Franklin's special two-carburetor side valvers, which were ultimately triumphant on the board tracks.

Side-car racing after the war was featured in dirt track events after 1920, utilizing the Flexible made side-cars with hinged axles that enabled the outfit to be banked on the turns. Bill Minnick and William P. Governor were the star drivers for Harley-Davidson, with Floyd Dreyer flying the flag for the Wigwam. Due to a number of accidents sustained by a handful of private aspirants, (mostly resulting in fatalities for their passengers) side-car racing was banned after 1925.

Harley-Davidson's finest hour to date took place on the fast track at Syracuse, New York on August 21, 1921. Star rider Fred Ludlow, a veteran pre-war Wrecking Crew member, was noted as having an exceptionally good running motor at the start of the 20-mile National and William Ottaway signaled his teammate to give him the lead. Ludlow then forged to first place and won the feature race easily. He won no less than five National Championship races that day for Harley-Davidson.

The following month the team was sent to Phoenix for a 100-mile National. Following another solid win, President Walter Davidson abruptly announced that the team was being disbanded and ordered its members to return to their homes rather than to Milwaukee. With no funds forthcoming for salaries and expenses and no train tickets provided, the team members were forced to pawn their watches and solicit quick loans from dealers and attendant enthusiasts to get home. The decision was based on Harley-Davidson's poor sales showing for the year, being at a low mark of 11,000 units.

Ludlow had previously been given a provisional promise for a position with the factory's engineering department, but with the cutback in personnel, such was not to be. Ludlow made up a collection of racing action motion pictures from newsreel excerpts, and toured the country with a side-car outfit exhibiting them to motorcycle clubs. He incurred the wrath of President Davidson, who claimed there were too many scenes of competing makes! Ludlow subsequently changed his allegiance to Indian and became the shop foreman for C. Will Risden in Los Angeles.

As Indian was still in contention, many of Harley-Davidson's star riders changed to the Wigwam, such as Curly Fredericks, Jim Davis, Charles Balke, and Ray and Johnny Seymour (no relation). Indian now dominated the boards, easily overcoming the challenge of a few privateers who were handicapped by not having official factory support.

A little-known vignette of American motorcycle sport was the brief advocacy of cyclecar racing during this period. One Charles Garrison, a former Indian factory mechanic now employed by Bernard Swenson, built such a vehicle that resembled a standard sprint car in miniature, a spidery machine with a narrow streamlined body with motorcycle wheels. Powered with a 74 cubic inch Powerplus engine which was mounted on the right rear side of the body to catch the airflow, the gearbox was inside the body driving a solid rear axle via a chain. With components donated by Frank Weschler, Garrison built two such models, and these were displayed in exhibition heats during race meets on the boards at Sheepshead Bay, New York, and Rockingham, New Hampshire. Noting Weschler's cautious sponsorship, Jack Prince approached Walter Davidson about Harley-Davidson building a similar set of machines for an added feature of racing competition. Davidson at once vetoed the suggestion on the grounds of both expense and the fact that the cyclecar, on the domestic market at least, was now a redundant proposition. It was also noted that the very fast examples were deathtraps without any braking system. At a later meeting with Davidson, Weschler agreed that cyclecar racing was an ill-advised proposition. Garrison's car was later unearthed in the storage area of the vast State Street factory.

A rather obscure episode in the history of the Motorcycle Manufacturers and Allied Trades Association was the dropping of the word "Manufacturers" from the title. The Executive Committee thought it best to downplay the role of the manufacturers, seeing that the recovery of organized motorcycling was now well underway. Then there was also the fact that the Committee was attempting to overcome the former autocratic stigma of the FAM by emphasizing the democratic makeup of the club structuring. A few of the surviving letterheads bear the former title from 1919 through mid-1920, before the new masthead was in place. The organization was then publicly referred to as the "Motorcycle and Allied Trade Association," or more simply, the "M&ATA" in

A 1929 Indian Chief, showing details of classic Indian fork mechanism.
George Hays

In the early 1920's the United States Tire Company put up billboards describing local histories as an advertising campaign. Carl Holton oversaw these projects, traveling with a Harley-Davidson sidecar outfit.
Alfred Rich Child

journalistic reference.

Post-war personnel changes included the resignation of L.D. Richards as Associate Editor of "Motorcycling and Bicycling Illustrated," and his acceptance of the position of Publicity Manager for Indian. One of his advocacies was the promotion of the idea of the production of more lightweight models by the leading factories to extend the scope of motorcycling. He continued to write articles for his former employer, Parsons, as well as for other trade journals, and was a staunch supporter of the M&ATA.

Arthur A. Constantine, a graduate engineer and, since 1909, employed by the Buick Automobile Company, joined Harley-Davidson's engineering staff in 1920 as an assistant to William S. Harley. His first assignment was to design an electrical system for the Sport Twin, which heretofore had been offered with magneto ignition and acetylene lighting as an optional extra.

Arthur Lemon, now Excelsior's chief designer, had produced an entirely new Henderson machine. At Ignatz Schwinn's suggestion it was a larger edition than the original and had a side valve engine that was cheaper to manufacture than the original F head.

In the meantime, William Henderson had launched his newly designed Ace. It immediately attracted favorable attention, as it followed his original format that had proved successful, although it differed in both detail and component dimensions in order to avoid legal difficulties with Schwinn.

A milestone in Harley-Davidson history was the hiring in January 1920 of Alfred Rich Child, whose activities had a significant role in future events. Child had arrived in the States as an immigrant from England well before World War I, as a penniless young man who found such successive employment as a janitor, handy-man, butler, government tax collector at the Port of New York and haberdashery salesman. He ultimately became a traveling representative for a wholesale bicycle and hardware concern that was opening up markets in the southern United States, as well as in Cuba, Haiti, and certain other islands in the Caribbean. He saw the value of commercial side-car outfits, and finally applied for a sales position with Harley-Davidson in the fall of 1919.

President Walter Davidson was convinced of his abilities as a salesman and Child was hired and immediately sent on the road; first in the New York area, and then to the southern states to oversee dealer activities there. [1]

In the meantime, "Hap" Scherer, as Harley-Davidson Publicity Director, was already traveling

THE GREAT DECLINE 1920-1930

(Above) The decades-old trailing link front suspension as fitted to all V-twin Indian models from 1910 through 1941.
George Hays

(Above right) An Indian hill climber of the late 1920's. Note the fitting of a small fuel tank and the single cylinder lightweight Prince forks to save weight.
George Hays

the country demonstrating the capabilities of the Sport Twin as a versatile vehicle that combined both economy and adequate all-around performance. He conducted a number of long distance journeys, reporting his experiences in a series of articles in the trade journals. His most spectacular trip was one through the notorious Death Valley, then a little traveled wasteland with scarcely distinguishable wagon tracks and no tourist facilities. As a middleweight enthusiast, Scherer aimed to promote an alternative to the dominant heavyweight V-twin. He was also providing a competitive look at Indian's 37 cubic inch V-twin Scout, which was enjoying a good response within the parameters of the reduced motorcycle market, both at home as well as overseas export markets.

At the same time, the motorcycle was being overwhelmed by the burgeoning automobile market, with 402 makes listed in the trade press. Most of these consisted of the so-called assembled car, which were being built by relatively small firms utilizing bought out components but with modest production and thus catering to a more or less local market.

Henry Ford, however, was dominating the market, with his vast River Rouge plant turning out an ever increasing flood of Model T's. General Motors, now controlled by Pierre S. duPont and shrewdly managed by Alfred P. Sloan, was in high gear with their compact 490 Model Chevrolet. The irrepressible William C. Durant, with newly acquired financing, was making a comeback with his Durant Motor Company. He concentrated on his Star car, similar in concept to the Model T but with a somewhat better styling, and also offered the mid-range Flint, a sound

if undistinguished vehicle.

With these three and other more obscure low priced makes, and selling prices of under $500 for the simpler versions, just a little above the cost of a heavyweight V-twin side-car, the latter was seen to disappear literally overnight.

It was at this juncture that the motorcycle industry found itself participating in a new era of a more sophisticated approach to sales and marketing, which heretofore had proceeded on a more or less haphazard basis.

This came about through the automotive world, when one Norman Shidle, a young engineer with a flair for journalism, founded an automotive trade magazine in the fall of 1918, called "Automotive Industries." Filled with well-written and timely articles on technical subjects, such as sales and marketing, it at once found acceptance.

In spite of the boom in automotive sales, Shidle noted that there were numerous failures among the smaller manufacturers. These, as he noted, were not through a lack of public demand, but rather because the manufacturers did not produce the type of models that the public demanded. The reasons cited were inefficient internal management of material and component procurement, lack of inventory control, and ineffectual cost control procedures.

Shidle published his findings in a series of articles which were well received by the industry. To enhance his coverage, Shidle paid the tuition for his young assistant, Raymond Prescott, to attend a graduate course in advanced economics at Columbia University. With this very scholarly and in-depth approach, Shidle was subsequently recog-

THE GREAT DECLINE 1920-1930

The Noel McIntyre
Special
Harry V. Sucher

nized as the instigator of the critical science of sales and marketing.

L.D. Richards, who was closing out his journalistic career in favor of taking an active part in the sales field of motorcycling, had been informally conferring with Henry Parsons as well as with other thoughtful people within the motorcycle industry. Their ultimate conclusion was that a more scientific approach was needed to attempt to solve the numerous problems now besetting it.

Early in 1920, Richards approached Shidle with the proposal that similar studies be made of the motorcycle industry, since his automotive analysis was well received. Shidle, who was not aware of the motorcycle industry's problems, stated that he could undertake such a study only if he could have access to sales and production figures from past years from the more prominent manufacturers.

In recounting the events to the author in later years, Richards stated that he realized he was treading on dangerous ground. With the distressed condition of the market and the growing intensity of intra-industry competition, production and sales figures, as well as the details of individual factory practices were a closely guarded secret, and any employee who divulged such matters would no doubt face instant dismissal.

But spurred by the seriousness of the situation, and well acquainted with Hap Schere:, Harley-Davidson's Publicity Manager; Charles Clelland, Reading-Standard's like number; as well as the like number of Excelsior (whose name today is forgotten, unfortunately); Richards made it a point to privately discuss his proposal with each one. Surprisingly enough, all his conferees agreed with the logic of his proposal.

Contingent with his January, 1920 appointment as Publicity Manager at Indian, he called a more formal meeting with the others on his list and it was decided to meet privately with Shidle inci-

dental to the National Motorcycle Show held that year at New York's Madison Square Garden.

Following this, the conspirators met in secret for an intense two-day session at the Waldorf Astoria Hotel, with Shidle promising to make an in-depth, but confidential survey of the motorcycle situation following the receipt of each firm's representation of their sales, production, and manufacturing procedures.

Richards was also encouraged by the coincidental appointment of Charles B. Franklin as Indian's Chief Engineer. This followed the resignation of Charles Gustafson, who was somewhat miffed at the success of Franklin's Scout after he had gone on record as opposing the Board of Director's decision to put it into production. Gustafson went on to form his own engineering company to design racing equipment. His son, Charles Jr., elected to remain with Indian as its Competition Manager, a position he held for the next decade. Richards noted that Franklin, as a graduate engineer, was more committed to the fine points of plant management than his predecessor was.

At this point, Excelsior's Engineering Department was augmented by the hiring of Everett M. De Long as Arthur Lemon's assistant. A graduate engineer, he was also a motorcyclist with a special interest in four-cylinder power plants. He had worked briefly with Lemon previously in the Henderson organization, and following Lemon's break with Schwinn, had engaged in free-lance automotive design assignments.

With the generally indeterminate state of the motorcycle market, the manufacturers now turned their attention to the Western states, which even in the pioneer days enjoyed the greatest proportionate volume of sales. With all-weather riding climate and a sparsely populated area, it promised boundless economic opportunity and enhanced motorcycle sales.

The pioneer Los Angeles Indian dealer since 1907, C. Will Risden, with factory cooperation, sponsored the establishment of C.C. "Hop" Hopkins in San Francisco in 1910 who then aided Hap Alzina in obtaining a franchise in Oakland in 1921.

Dudley Perkins enjoyed an active Harley-Davidson dealership in San Francisco after 1915. He, in turn, sponsored an Oakland dealership headed by Claude Salmon just after the close of the war. Factory traveler Vern Guthrie subsequently helped to establish other dealerships in Vallejo, Stockton, and small towns up and down the Central California valley.

The Great Decline 1920-1930

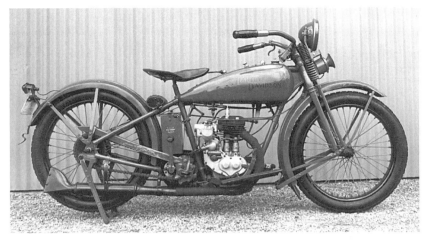

(Top) A near original 1926 21 cubic inch Model A "Peashooter" once owned by the late De Duchene. An economical and dependable machine, it was more popular on the export market than it was domestically.
Harry V. Sucher

(Above) An all original 1930 VLD Harley-Davidson from the Bud Ekins collection.
Harry V. Sucher

Perry Abbott secured franchises in Portland, Oregon, after 1909, which included Reading-Standard, Pope, Wagner, and after 1912, Harley-Davidson. He was also the West Coast distributor for Reading-Standard, which included Hawaii and the Pacific Island area. A later satellite Harley-Davidson dealer in the Portland area was Dawes Rice.

After the war Harley-Davidson had unsatisfactory relationships with its dealerships in both Los Angeles and San Diego. In San Diego the Appeal Manufacturing Company held the initial franchise and directed most of its energies to the wholesale and retail bicycle business. Vern Guthrie ultimately recruited Rich Budelier, an economics instructor at the University of Colorado and a Harley-Davidson enthusiast, to take the San Diego franchise. As a supersalesman with an ebullient personality, he successfully reestablished the facility. Two years later Guthrie persuaded him to take over the Los Angeles dealership, which he held successfully for many years. Budelier's San Diego operation was then awarded to William J. Ruhle who, with enduro-star Roy Artley, held the dealership for many years.

Excelsior was well represented in San Francisco

with Henderson by the partnership of Tennant Lee and Charles J. Haddock, who opened an impressive operation on Van Ness Avenue's famous "automobile row," where many makes of luxury cars were featured. As a young schoolboy the author recalls their large showroom with an impressive array of potted palms and luxurious furnishings.

The distribution of motorcycles by the factories differed somewhat between the Big Three. Harley-Davidson utilized the Milwaukee factory travelers in various parts of the country to keep in contact with the dealers. The only exception to this was their establishment of a warehouse facility in San Diego when they were having problems with the Appeal Group. Eric von Gumpert, their long-time Export Manager, also acted as Traffic Manager to oversee the shipments of both machines and accessories.

Early in the game Indian set up dealer-distributorships in some of the larger cities such as, Providence, Rhode Island; Wilmington, South Carolina; Kansas City, Missouri; Oakland, California and Portland, Oregon. Their operators were charged with both serving the dealers in their areas as well as encouraging the participation of new franchises.

With small early production, newly established Ace managed to persuade a number of disaffected Henderson dealers to handle their machines, although the manufacture of this surprisingly popular machine was short lived.

In the early 1920's Big Three franchises did not always limit themselves to their primary suppliers. While the factories involved tried to discourage this, it was some years before they mandated sole representation. Many dealers added another make, such as the Excelsior twin and Ace and Henderson fours. Large numbers of dealers added lightweight Cleveland and Neracar, which provided entry-level motorcycling.

Reading-Standard, with a V-twin competitive to both Harley-Davidson and Indian, was mostly isolated, hampered by its small annual production. A few pioneers who had offered them before the war stayed with the make, but after the war they were scarcely in the running.

Reverting to the M&ATA activities at this point, the Competition Committee, headed by Henry Parsons and including the Davidsons, Frank Weschler, Ignatz Schwinn, and representatives of Firestone Tires, Goodyear Tires, and other minority suppliers, inaugurated a rider participation program that was to add substantial interest in motorcycling from the general riding public as well as club members. This was the Gypsy Tour

THE GREAT DECLINE 1920-1930

Motor Officer Edward Peters of the Adanac, British Colombia police Department with his 1930 Indian 101 Scout.
Donald Doody

The helical geared primary drive designed by Charles B. Franklin and fitted to the early model G Indian Scout from 1919 on and later incorporated into the Chief models in 1923. The units were fitted to all V-twins until 1934.
George Hays

program, which was to be an on-going feature for three decades.

This consisted of organized rides, advertised as an officially sponsored M&ATA activity, implemented throughout the country by the dealers of all makes as well as through cooperation of the clubs. These usually took place three or four times a year, and were mainly scheduled to coincide with such national holidays as Memorial Day, Fourth of July, Labor Day and were especially emphasized if they fell on a three-day weekend. Another mode of scheduling was to announce a Gypsy Tour in conjunction with some big National Competition meet, such as a major hill climb, road race, or dirt track contest.

More often than not, various dealers would advertise the tours in their area to attract their customers who were not club affiliated. Emphasis was on orderly behavior, unaltered silencing systems on participant's machines and proper attire. The clubs generally took this as an encouragement to turn out in their respective distinctive outfits. Almost without exception, one of the feature events at the gathering rendezvous was a contest for the best turned out club, with prizes for either the cleanest or the best equipped machines.

The sight of well turned out riders proceeding in an orderly fashion over the roads was an excellent showcase of motorcycling to the spectating public, who might well be encouraged to join in the sport.

Participation was, of course, dependent on holding M&ATA membership and while by this time most clubs enjoyed 100% membership as the criteria for a M&ATA chartered club, unaffiliated riders had to pay the mandated $1.00 dues to obtain a membership card to participate, thus swelling the membership rolls statistically for the M&ATA.

THE GREAT DECLINE 1920-1930

In referring to the Shidle marketing survey, the four Publicity Chairmen had met in secret with him for two or three additional conferences, their absences from their factories being explained on the pretext of taking care of other commitments. Shidle was finally able to render his confidential report to each of the participants individually in November of 1920. For the time being and by prior agreement, it was decided not to reveal the findings to either the management of the factories involved or to the trade media and thence to the general motorcycling public.

A tragic event for Indian in the fall of 1922, was the death in a road accident of Bernard A. "The Terrible Swede" Swenson, a distributor and prominent dealer in Providence, Rhode Island. Swenson had represented Indian ever since 1905, and as a tireless promoter for motorcycling and active in establishing Indian franchises along the Eastern seaboard, both his active sponsorship of motorcycling activities and his promotional role were sorely missed. His widow carried on the business for a time in partnership with the shop foreman.

Another loss was sustained in December, when William Henderson was struck down by a car that was driving out of a filling station in Philadelphia. With massive skill fractures, he died without regaining consciousness. Arthur Lemon, still employed by Schwinn, was offered the position of Chief Engineer, which he accepted. He was subsequently joined by Everett M. De Long, who now transferred his loyalty to Ace. De Long, long noted for his dedication to air-cooled, four-cylinder designs, had lately gained additional recognition for his collaboration with Erwin G. "Cannonball" Baker, the noted long distance record breaker, in working on an experimental prototype of another type of four. This had been based on an Indian Powerplus chassis with two sleeved down Powerplus V-twin type engines placed side-by-side and sharing a common crankshaft. Lack of available financing ended the venture before production could be instituted.

The promotion of club activities and the emphasis on average rider participation in the Gypsy Tours, which, incidentally, also encouraged individual touring, was a fortuitous substitute for the spectator sport of board and dirt track racing, which was in decline at this point. Harley-Davidson and Excelsior were no longer officially sponsoring either, and Harley-Davidson had already sold off their fleet of about twenty-five racing models to favored riders. Indian, through their long tradition of competition, carried the flag alone, but their consistent winning in the face of diminished competition created a rather colorless situation when the results of factory sponsorship put aspiring privateers at a serious disadvantage.

Board track racing continued with some loss of public interest until 1924. At this point both wind and weather had caused the deterioration of these vast timbered edifices, along with the encroachment of suburban growth and rising real estate values, which brought a penalizing tax burden. Then, too, as an often bloody spectacle and as a hazardous gladiatorial contest, editorial condemnation was ever present. Thoughtful members within the factories' top management were also of the opinion that, in many ways, racing had been a detriment to the industry in fostering a sport that emphasized the dangers of two wheel transportation.

It was also at this point that the top management of the surviving factories came to the conclusion that close cooperation between them was now advantageous in the face of what was fast becoming a marginal place in the transportation field.

At the last big 200-mile National held in Syracuse in August, 1921, the Davidsons and Frank Weschler agreed on private meetings between them to be held at stated intervals for the purpose of discussing mutual problems and policies. Accordingly, a meeting was held in the Waldorf Astoria Hotel the following month with Arthur Davidson, Frank Weschler, L.D. Richards and Alfred Rich Child in attendance. Over a private dinner of Lobster Thermador, the discussion of generalities resulted in a price fixing agreement involving similar models of machines mutually produced. It was agreed that with the current state of the market, a price war between the domestic factories would be disastrous for all concerned. In recounting the events of the meeting to the author, Childs and Richards both stated that Ignatz Schwinn, while invited, did not attend, citing the reason that with the Excelsior Twin phased out of production his sole four-cylinder model was not sold in a competitive price range of the others' V-twins.

These meetings, which were to be annual events for the next eighteen years, were quite naturally held in secret. Price fixing was illegal under the terms of both the Sherman and Clayton Acts passed by Congress earlier in the Century at the urging of President Theodore Roosevelt. But, at the same time, such mutual agreements in U.S. industry between nominally competing manufacturers were quite common. There was actually little fear of any serious prosecution if apprehended due to the political climate prevailing at the time. The corrupt Harding Administration, struggling in a welter of their own corruption, had the Attorney General

THE GREAT DECLINE 1920-1930

The late William Hoecher with his 1929 DLD 45 cubic inch Harley-Davidson. The initial model of Milwaukee's "45" series, it shared the frame of the 30.50 single, and in place of cranking the down tube, the generator was driven by a shew gear and was fitted parallel to the front cylinder, giving it the nickname of "the three cylinder Harley."
George Hays

Harry L. Daughtery, hard-pressed to soft pedal the news of both the government's as well as his own illegal activities.

The revealing of the clandestine meetings between the concerned Publicity Managers and the results of the Shidle survey at last came to pass during the spring of 1921.

Harley-Davidson was currently producing a two model range: the 61 and 74 cubic inch variants of the long running J-series and the Sport Twin. At this juncture, Vice President William C. Davidson, in charge of production and noted for both his practical knowledge of metallurgy and his ability to run a tight ship, informed the Board of Directors that with the slump in production, costing factors were becoming critical. He advocated the dropping of the Sport Twin, and rationalizing production by concentrating on the "J's" only. President Walter Davidson informed Hap Scherer of this proposal, as the latter had managed an aggressive sales campaign on its behalf during the past two years. Scherer at once protested, pointing to the need for middleweight machines to provide a broader spectrum of the market and the urgency in offering a model that could better attract entry level riders, together with the mild success the Sport Twin was enjoying on the export market. He then revealed the context of Shidle's findings, which stated that the heavyweight V-twins were difficult to start and were best suited to athletic riders, and that instead of emphasizing speed and power the focus on utility type models would expand the market. In the subsequent discussion, Scherer was forced to reveal his participation with the representatives of other manufacturers.

This enraged Davidson, who for many years had developed an almost paranoiac fixation with maintaining secrecy regarding the Company's internal affairs, and he fired Scherer on the spot.

When the news of this circulated throughout the industry, there was much sympathy for Scherer, as he was generally very well respected within the trade and many riders as well as dealers were of the opinion that the promotion of the Sport Twin was sound policy, noting the popularity of the Indian Scout. At any rate, the Sport Twin was phased out in the fall of 1922, after over 6,000 units had been assembled. Limited numbers were produced from component parts still on hand in 1923 and 1924, which went to the export market, where the model had enjoyed its best acceptance. Its mild reception on the home market was credited to both the dominance of the Indian Scout and the fact that the V-twin had the weight of tradition behind it, although the Sport Twin was a soundly designed machine and gave good service.

Scherer was hired by Rich Budelier in Los Angeles as Sales Manager in his now successful dealership, much to Walter Davidson's chagrin, and continued to promote the Sport Twin as long as it was available.

In the meantime, affairs at Indian had taken a critical turn. While Indian had enjoyed capable management from Frank Weschler ever since 1916, the problem was the non-motorcycling shareholders who had acquired voting control of the Company, and an absent President Henry H. Skinner, who took little part in company affairs. Being more interested in stock speculation and funding their own estates, the shareholders were loathe to vote funds for company operation and Weschler was hard pressed to obtain funding for the needed tooling for the ill-advised all-out war contract fiasco that crippled civilian production, or for the tooling up for the Scout, which proved to be Indian's salvation.

The present problem was the Indian Sales Department, under its Manager J.B. McNaughton, who appeared unable to accurately project ongoing sales. This resulted in an oversupply of bought-out components and raw materials that saw Indian stagger under excessive overhead. Added to this, there were labor problems with the Machinist Union, and widespread pilfering of both materials and components, which were being sold in clandestine marketing.

At this juncture, Richards informed Weschler of the Shidle involvement and his participation in it. He presented a digest of Shidle's conclusions concerning the need for both marketing surveys as

THE GREAT DECLINE 1920-1930

well as more efficient methods of quality and cost controls of the entire operation.

Richards later told the author that Weschler was at first taken aback concerning his participation with representatives of the other companies, but quickly saw the logic of Shidle's recommendations. He put Richards in charge of setting matters aright, much to McNaughton's chagrin, whose tenure of office had been long based on his cronyism with the original founders. After a thorough housecleaning and overhauling of company operations, Indian gradually recovered from its near disaster of the winter of 1921-1922, and managed to assemble no less than 7,500 Scouts, which was the vital factor in providing the much needed cash flow. The popularity of the Scout caused Weschler to order Charles B. Franklin to design an enlarged version of it, which was to be called the Chief. He also ordered the phase-out of the long-running Powerplus model which had been the backbone of Indian's line since 1916, after well over 100,000 units had been produced.

Henry Clelland was less fortunate at Reading-Standard in pointing out that too small production that involved too many models caused irrational production, coupled with inefficient cost controls had long been responsible for the firm's ongoing difficulties. Top management refused to consider Shidle's recommendations, and with finances almost exhausted, the staff was greatly reduced, including the discharge of Clelland. The company began entering competition events after purchasing the manufacturing rights to the overhead cam V-

twin Cyclone engine from the Joerns Company. It was too late, however, and operations were suspended in the fall of 1922. An attempt at a revival was made in 1924, but when promised financing did not materialize, the Reading-Standard became history. Clelland joined the sales force of Goodyear, and ultimately obtained a franchise for Huppmobile cars in Newark, New Jersey.

With the knowledge that the contents of his survey were now a matter of public record, Shidle sent copies of his recommendations to various trade publications, but only Henry Parsons aired the article entitled, "Where is the Motorcycle Going?"

During his initial investigation into the production and marketing problems of the automobile industry and later that of the motorcycle, Shidle sent his young associate, Raymond Prescott, to Columbia University to study advanced economics. In later years the two collaborated in what was probably the origins of modern sales and marketing techniques.

The trade press generally ignored the post-war changes within the motorcycle industry, and one cannot find any critical suggestions in the editorial pages of that day. Most probably their editors did not want to jeopardize their advertising contracts, although such were drastically reduced as succeeding manufacturers of both machines and accessories dropped out of the market. The only editor and publication that offered any real constructive critiques was Henry Parsons in "Motorcycling and Bicycling Illustrated," and also featured a number of articles by L.D. Richards who was not reticent about sug-

Racing was almost an every-weekend attraction during the Spring and Summer season. The photograph shows a typical scene at the old Ascot Speedway in Los Angeles in 1920.
Hughes Photos, L.A.

THE GREAT DECLINE 1920-1930

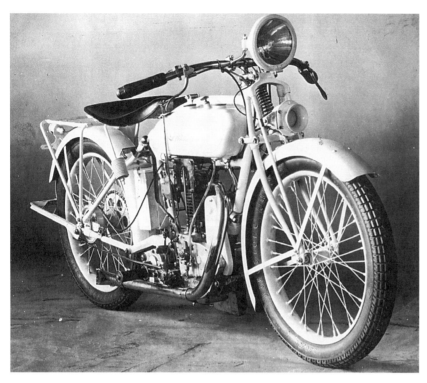

The ohv 21 cubic inch Indian Prince model of 1926. Originally intended to compete with Harley-Davidson's "Peashooters" in this newly inaugurated competition class, Indian decided to concentrate on their successful 61 cubic inch board trackers, leaving the smaller class to Milwaukee. A few private owners entered 21 cubic inch competition, but without factory sponsorship, had but little success. In the end, only about two-hundred ohv Princes were ever assembled.
T.A. Hodgdon

gesting changes in current factory policies.

With declining scope and content, the quality and style of most of the trade magazines suffered. The general public did not know that these publications were owned by firms that produced a group of offerings that included a diverse range of subjects such as gardening, agriculture, building trade subjects, or mechanical matters; the motorcycling magazines were only one facet of their operations. As the content declined, most of the surviving journals were produced by one editor with limited clerical help. Much of the reporting was performed by amateur journalists for a negligible fee (or even gratis for the honor of seeing their names on a byline) who would submit reports of competition events and industry affairs. The accuracy of much of this reporting is suspect, and later researchers and historians often puzzle over the diversity of content from separate authors or reporters dealing with the same event, with often inconsistent spelling of names and even varying tabulations of the results.

Motorcycling journalism in the 1920's was largely taken over by the factories themselves with their house journals. Harley-Davidson published their long-running "Enthusiast" since 1916. Indian, after 1910, featured similar offerings in "Honest Injun," later called "The Wigwam News," and ultimately "The Indian News." These publications were sent out to individual customers and supplied in bulk to dealers for distribution. They appeared quarterly and sometimes on an every-other-month

basis. Of course, these were of a sales oriented nature, together with human interest stories about individual riders, tour reports, service and maintenance hints, and reports of recent competition results. These latter generally emphasized contests where the make in question was the victor.

Late in 1920, certain of the members of the Competition Committee considered the matter of an affiliation of the M&ATA with the international governing body of motorcycle sport, the Federation Internationale of Competition Motorcyclists (FICM) [*2] whose headquarters were in Geneva, Switzerland. Such a move had been briefly advocated by A.B. Coffman in pre-war FAM days, but then the organizational problems had made such a move impossible. Henry Parsons, however, reasoned that with the withdrawal of Excelsior from active competition, such a move might stimulate a renewed interest within both the industry and the membership of the M&ATA.

Such an affiliation had also been suggested by W.H. "Billy" Wells, British importer of Indians and a member of that company's Board of Directors since 1914. He noted that with the popularity of American V-twins and their often spectacular performances at Brooklands, FICM membership would be a factor in boosting sales.

The M&ATA Board voted that Parsons should look into the matter by opening up correspondence with Geneva. While agreeing, Parsons had his hands full in managing his magazine, overseeing competition affairs, and the fact that he was unable to travel extensively to keep in personal contact with the growing number of clubs. In the meantime, he had relegated much of the excess correspondence to Douglas Hobart, titular President of the M&ATA, who had been overshadowed by Parsons with more direct contact with the membership. This latter situation had been encouraged by the Davidsons, Schwinn and Weschler, who saw control of sporting activities as the most effective way for the industry to control the affairs of domestic motorcycling. At this juncture, Parsons informed Hobart that he was now in charge of negotiations with the governing committee of the FICM.

Hobart enlisted the aid of Billy Wells to act as an intermediary, noting his closer proximity to Geneva. Wells enthusiastically accepted the assignment, and enlisted the cooperation of C.T. Loughborough, who had headed the British Auto-Cycle Union as Secretary-Manager since its founding in 1909, and which had long been affiliated with the FICM.

Loughborough agreed to act as intermediary, but warned Wells at the outset that the proposed

THE GREAT DECLINE 1920-1930

Bernard E. Andre, pioneer Indian motorcycle dealer of Charleston, West Virginia, poses with a 1902 Indian that was subsequently restored by the Indian Company and presented to the Smithsonian Institution. The 1930 photograph also shows John G. Thompkins on an Indian four sidecar outfit and a classic Packard automobile in the background.
Richard B. Andre

international M&ATA affiliation could encounter difficulties. The main stumbling block could be the disparity of engine sizes between American and British competition machines. The popularity of the 61 cubic inch Yank machines were outside the FICM mandated 30.50 cu.in. (500 cc) "half-liter" piston displacement. The relative shorter travel distances and the better roads had fostered the British and European development of lighter machines with smaller engines, and thus, the half-liter measurement now limited their competition machinery to this formula.

However, Loughborough stated that he saw no valid reason why a new racing class could not be created to accommodate the Americans; the question being whether the Americans would be willing to scale their orientation toward a place in the FICM formula.

The top management of both Harley-Davidson and Indian were receptive at that point to the idea. Harley-Davidson flushed with victory over the impressive performance of the Wrecking Crew; and Indian, well behind in the dirt track Nationals, could take pride in their spectacular domination of the board tracks, also pointing to their signal successes in record breaking at Brooklands.

While Excelsior was not officially sponsoring competition, enthusiasts such as Irish racing star Jock McNeil, Waldo Korn, Ray Creviston, as well as Wrecking Crew member Maldwyn Jones, now experimenting with smaller capacity machines, were still carrying the flag as privateers.

Hobart prepared a formal proposal to be relayed by Wells to Geneva, and the latter made an appointment to visit the FICM headquarters in the fall of 1920. The mission was aborted, however, when Wells, preparing to embark for France on the Folkstone Ferry found that he had neglected to bring his passport.

During the winter of 1921 and 1922, Wells made no less than three trips to Geneva. The FICM Competition Committee asked Wells searching questions concerning the general state of the American industry, noting the large number of firms that ceased production after 1915. Wells countered that motorcycling in the States was now attracting a healthy following, citing that support of the Gypsy Tours had enjoyed a turnout of 25,000 riders during 1920, and that over 40,000 had participated during 1921 and 1922, each contributing $1.00 dues to the M&ATA treasury, making organized U.S. motorcycling now a viable proposition.

The Committee also queried Wells about whether the M&ATA would actually put in place half liter competition classes, which had been much discussed but never implemented. Wells' answer was that before Arthur Lemon had left

THE GREAT DECLINE 1920-1930

This Harley-Davidson 21 cubic inch ohv "Peashooter" was built as a factory special by the late Joe Petrali. It's engine was a frank copy of the contemporary J.A. Prestwich model that was highly successful in international competition. Designated as the CAC model, for some reason it's final development was never undertaken. Note the Merkel-type fork.
Joe Petrali

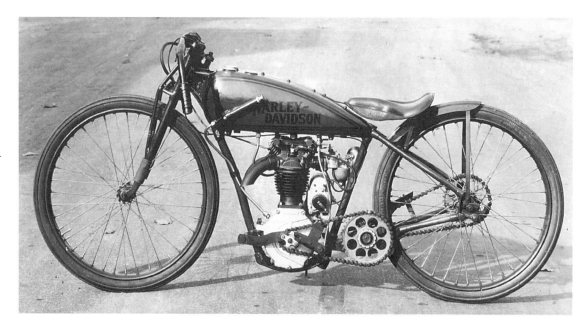

Excelsior to join Ace, he had persuaded Schwinn to allow some prototype experiments with a single-cylinder 30.50 cubic inch engine. This was in essence one half of the "big valve" V-twin that had been previously developed by Jock McNeil, and was currently under test by Maldwyn Jones and ex-Indian star Paul Anderson, who had briefly campaigned with an example in New Zealand and Australia. The Committee noted these facts, but reiterated that they had yet to see substantial encouragement on the part of the M&ATA for this class of machine. They further noted that while Harley-Davidson and Excelsior had both terminated official support of racing, the sale of 61 cubic inch racing machines to favored riders was still emphasizing large displacement competition. Also mentioned was Indian's continuing support of board track racing, again a class not favored in Europe and only sanctioned in a limited way at Brooklands' concrete oval as a full liter class.

In his next visit to Geneva in 1922, Wells announced that Charles B. Franklin had been directed by Frank Weschler to inaugurate experiments with 350 cc and 500 cc prototypes, and that Franklin had procured several makes of British single-cylinder machines for testing and evaluation in connection with anticipated emphasis on the International formulas.

During these negotiations, Hobart and Wells exchanged a heavy volume of correspondence, Hobart forwarded copies of this to Henry Parsons, who in turn kept the M&ATA Competition Committee apprised of the state of the FICM negotiations.

The conferences with the FICM hit a snag, however, regarding the speed records allegedly established by Harley-Davidson's Racing Department at Daytona Beach in the winter of 1921. Milwaukee had heard that Indian was planning an all-out assault on the world's straightway speed records, and accordingly, had sent William Ottaway, R.W. Enos, Wrecking Crew riders Fred Ludlow, "Red" Parkhurst, and several factory mechanics to the famed Florida beach venue. Ludlow ran a specially tuned pocket valve 61 cubic inch standard roadster-engined machine through the trap at 103 mph. Parkhurst racked up a phenomenal 114 mile per hour run with a similar engine that had been bored out to 68 cubic inch, which was said to be a prototype of a 74 cubic inch version that was slated to be competitive to a 74 cubic inch Powerplus engine that had just been introduced by Indian. In their press releases describing the events, Harley-Davidson stated that they had officially terminated any further development of eight valve specials, and henceforth would concentrate on perfecting production type pocket valve designs.

The FICM took exception to the accuracy of these well-publicized records that had received much attention in the American trade press. While the runs had been made on an up-and-back basis, the factory had tabulated the fastest time before the wind only, which was contrary to the long standing rules of both the parent FICM and the Auto-Cycle Union as well. Loughborough told Wells that under no circumstances would the FICM accept such results.

The Great Decline 1920-1930

Following a voluminous report of the negotiations between Wells, Loughborough and the FICM which was rendered to Henry W. Parsons by Hobart, a meeting of the M&ATA Competition Committee was held in Chicago. Present were the Davidsons, Weschler, Schwinn; members Dudley Perkins, Hap Alzina, Eugene Shillingford, and a few more prominent dealers. In a lengthy two day meeting, nothing concrete was settled concerning the advisability of prolonging the FICM negotiations. While it was admitted that international affiliation might well help the domestic export trade, it was also noted that the possibility of foreign machines being imported to the U.S. might well offer unwanted competition on an already depressed American market. *3

At the same time, it was also agreed that the institution of smaller capacity classes in the U.S. might well be in order. Both factories had already sold most of the factory racers to private owners, but with the limited numbers and the nearly exhausted supply of spare parts to keep them running, they were coming to the end of their days. It was also apparent that the inherent dangers in the use of the very potent 61's that could attain speeds of well over 100 mph was a hazard to the riders as well as courting adverse public opinion in the face of a number of fatalities on both track and speedway.

President Walter Davidson suggested that the industry should promote increased encouragement to hill climbing, which was a growing popular sport, was far less dangerous, and entailed less expense to promote. At any rate, the meeting ended with the agreement that the development of both 21 and 30.50 cubic inch machines should be encouraged.

In the meantime, the FICM Secretary, Alonzo Biaggi wrote a letter to Wells in which he stated that the FICM Board of Governors would sanction the M&ATA affiliation only if the 61 cubic inch class be confined to the U.S., and that such would not be allowed to compete in either the Auto-Cycle Union's venue at the Isle of Man or in any European events. He also stated that the Governors felt that Wells was out of line in attempting to obtain sanctioning for American machines, which was interpreted as being mostly a showcase for their export activities. To counter Wells' oft-repeated reference to Brooklands, it was also stated again to both Wells and Sir Duncan Watson that American big twin records were segregated as a local entity at that venue.

Again, Hobart rendered a digest of the extensive correspondence to Parsons and, in the end, the Committee decided to table the matter pending further developments. This action, in the historical sense, marked the adoption of a policy of American isolation from International motorcycle sport that was to continue for the next forty years.

In the meantime, the ranks of the American motorcycle industry were depleted still further when the Evans Power Cycle production was terminated by the Rochester manufacturing firm that had assembled about 3,000 units since 1920; substantial numbers had been exported to Holland, Belgium and Germany. A German firm subsequently bought the patent rights and continued to manufacture this moped type machine with its 112 cc two stroke engine in limited numbers until the early 1930's.

In the spring of 1923, the Henderson brothers' Ace concern in Philadelphia was in financial trouble, mainly because their selling price of $325,000 was insufficient to cover their costs of manufacture. In a reorganization attempt, the operation was moved to an unused leather tanning factory in nearby Blossburg, where about 200 more units were assembled. With the failure to obtain additional financing, Ace finally expired in the fall, after about 5,000 units had been built since its founding in 1920. The Ace had enjoyed instant popularity with many former Henderson enthusiasts. It also enjoyed some popularity as a law enforcement machine, especially where the officers worked under contract, and supplied their own machines.

The following year, the remnants of the company were purchased by Michigan Motors of Detroit, but financial problems again intervened and only a few machines were assembled, mostly from components left over from the Blossburg operation.

During this same period, Indian was undergoing a corporate reorganization. In the early spring of 1923, Frank Weschler met with the Board of Directors and stated that he could continue as Vice President and General Manager only if he were given more authority over Indian's operations. It was noted that it was his heroic single-handed efforts during the critical years of 1921 and 1922 that had saved the Company from oblivion. It was emphasized that Weschler required full authority to make decisions without having to continually consult with a mostly absent Board of Directors, and that his autonomous control would be needed now that the Company was on a firm footing.

The Board saw the wisdom of Weschler's request, also recognizing his role in saving the Company. President Henry H. Skinner resigned in his favor, but retained his seat on the Board.

THE GREAT DECLINE 1920-1930

The Excelsior factory team at Ascot Park in 1920. From left to right are Wells Bennett, Bob Perry, team manager and engine designer J.A. McNeil, and Joe Walters. McNeil, who had previously raced Cyclones himself, designed this overhead cam engine that closely resembled a Cyclone engine. Sadly, Perry was killed on the bike just a few minutes after this photo was taken. As the story goes, Ignatz Scwinn ordered Excelsior's racing program halted immediately due to the accident, so the new engine was never developed fully.
A.F. Van Order Collection

Harley-Davidson factory racers Red Parkhurst and Freddie Ludlow (seated in sidecar) set a number of individual and team speed records on the beach at Daytona Beach, Florida in 1924.
A.F. Van Order Collection

THE GREAT DECLINE 1920-1930

Weschler was also awarded $100,000 in preferred Indian shares in recognition of his long years of dedicated service.

The Company was now reorganized; the name being changed from the Hendee Manufacturing Company to the Indian Moto Cycle Company. The "r" was dropped to avoid patent litigation from any other motorcycle manufacturer. In addition, a new block of common stock in the amount of $500,000 was placed on the market with the approval of the U.S. Securities and Exchange Commission.

It must be noted in passing that large blocks of stocks were purchased by Francis I. and E. Paul duPont, brothers and members of the famed duPont family.

Under Weschler's efficient management, Indian entered into a period of prosperity (within the limitations of the contemporary market) which has often been described as its Golden age. The limited advocacy of the affiliation of the M&ATA with the FICM was terminated when, in the reorganization of Indian's Board of Directors, Billy Wells was no longer included. It was later considered an oblique method of terminating further advocacy of international affiliation.

In the late spring of 1923, Henry Parsons reviewed both his position as Chairman of the Competition Committee of the M&ATA, as well as the relations of that body to the sport and industry. He had long considered that he had been handicapped to some degree by his inability to travel extensively to more closely monitor both club and competition affairs, and contemplated resignation. While the M&ATA was on a more or less firm financial footing with the healthy income from club registrations, membership rolls which were enhanced by the Gypsy Tour program, and sanctions from the promoters of both dirt and board track racing, there was the matter of rule enforcement in competition and the growing number of "outlaw" or unsanctioned competition events.

Parsons also noted that his growing responsibilities with "Motorcycle and Bicycle Illustrated" required more effort, as the publishers were pressuring him to expand the scope of the magazine for more attention to the bicycle trade, which was accelerating in the face of the static motorcycle market.

At a special meeting of the M&ATA held in Chicago in July, where members of the Competition Committee as well as other trade representatives and organized club members were present, Parsons brought up the matter of a reorganization as well as the institution of a firmer full-time management of competition affairs. He cited the well-remembered problems of the FAM,

where an aggressive control of activities had never been achieved, and noted that with the generally satisfactory position of the M&ATA its present advantage should be maintained. He also stated that the matter of deciding the type of motorcycle competition in regard to machine type and design should be seriously considered. He also mentioned the results of the Shidle survey, and hoped that the factories would now consider the development of dependable and economical smaller machines to offer a low cost alternative to the ever-growing production of automobiles.

The Board was rather taken aback with Parsons' expressed intention to resign and, after some general discussion, suggested that he retain his office until the fall which would allow for other arrangements to be made.

Parsons' remarks relative to the ever growing production of automobiles was well taken. Some 250 makes of cars still survived, most of them small local productions and assembled types. Ford and General Motors had been rapidly expanding and, with increased production, expanded dealer network and limitless financial resources, now dominated the market. In addition, Walter P. Chrysler, a former railroad mechanic, was now entering the field with a sophisticated version of the well known Maxwell.

The market was presently dominated by Ford, whose activities had expanded to operating his own steel mills, coal mines, and even rubber plantations in South America and Malaysia, not to mention his own shipping line and expanded assembly plants in Canada and Great Britain. Even with the proliferation of domestic makes, Ford's approaching attainment of 15 million units now saw every other car on the country's roads representing one of his products.

Ford production was of such magnitude that in 1923 he was able to offer a roadster model at $265, with the touring model at $285. These were, of course, the starker versions: the options of an electric starter and balloon tires were a $20 option for each.

In addition, General Motors' 490 model Chevrolet and Star from Durant Motors had increased production of somewhat less ungainly vehicles in plain form at $395.

Ford's production at his expanded Manchester plant in England was such that Parliament levied a horsepower tax, based on the cylinder bore of the engine, that offered an effective handicap to their sales in an effort to save the struggling domestic industry from foreign competition.

In the meantime, board track and horse track

PREPAREDNESS
Where It Counts the Most—

MOST MILES PER DOLLAR

Firestone
Gum-Dipped Tires

racing on the country fair circuits were winding down. This was due partly to the shortage of racing machines, the diminished interest in the boards, and the often ragged and poorly organized fairground contests that were challenging M&ATA rules by being the unsanctioned "outlaw" variety.

Most of the board speedways were now dismantled or inoperative, the only survivors on the Eastern seaboard being Altoona, Newark, and Rockingham, New Hampshire. Tracks still operating on the West Coast were Beverly Hills, Playa del Rey, Fresno, Cotati, and Tacoma. The Cotati oval was Jack Prince's last project, operating from 1921 to 1925, when it was dismantled. The author, as a young schoolboy, was privileged to attend a couple of the later meets here; one of which featured an unofficial solo run record by Johnny Seymour on an Indian clocked at 117.5 mph!

At the same time, both Harley-Davidson's and Indian's Engineering Departments were engaged in prototype work on small capacity single-cylinder machines. Charles B. Franklin was working on side valve, overhead valve and overhead camshaft models. William Ottaway, assisted by Arthur A. Constantine and Hank Syvertson, was evolving a two model range of both side valve and overhead valve 21 cubic inch singles.

Both factories were considering the export field, and the growing popularity of motorcycles overseas, particularly in England, with the hope that small capacity models had become the standard fare. The more highly developed American heavyweight V-twins were still popular in far flung colonial areas of the world, but in limited production in England and Europe, and it was hoped that lighter weight American made models could compliment the former.

As it was, penetration of the surviving makes on the domestic scene was more or less closely drawn. Indian was the best seller in its home area of the Northeast, as well as the Eastern seaboard and within the states of the old Confederacy.

Harley-Davidson dominated the mid-western heartland, with both makes in strong contention for the larger markets in the West, where 65% of the sales of the whole industry existed.

Excelsior's sales outlets were mostly confined to the larger cities (much of their market being to law enforcement) even at the penalty of higher prices than the V-twins. Cleveland and Neracar, in the very minor utility and non-sporting market, were also centered in the larger cities. They were offered by either Harley-Davidson or Indian dealerships, and sometimes in hardware and sporting

good stores. By the mid-1920's, there were approximately 2,500 dealer outlets for all makes, with Harley-Davidson having the edge in representation. Domestic sales of both makes were about equal, but Harley-Davidson now had more overseas representation, which accounted for their larger production.

Henry Parsons scheduled a meeting of both the Competition Committee and the general membership of the M&ATA at his editorial offices in Chicago in October of 1923. In reviewing his position within the organization, he had already made up his mind to resign, with the suggestion that A.B. Coffman be appointed as his successor. He had considered Coffman's long service to the sport and industry, dating from his participation in former FAM activities. He also considered Coffman's commercial representation of both the cycle and motorcycle industries as a trade show promoter, together with his freedom to travel when required, as his operations up to this point were not of a fixed base variety. Coffman told the author in later years that Parsons had conducted a series of private meetings with him to discuss his appointment before the formal M&ATA meeting. Coffman freely admitted that he had not been overly popular with some of the M&ATA, due to his alleged dictatorial manner on occasions. Parsons countered that a firm hand was needed in a critical managerial position, and that the lack of such was at the heart of former problems within organized motorcycling. At any rate, Coffman agreed to take over Parsons' post as Manager of the Competition Committee if he were accepted by a majority of the M&ATA membership. Parsons and Coffman worked out a series of proposals for both an organizational and competition program for the forthcoming meeting.

While Coffman's name was mentioned by Parsons at the October meeting, no definite action was taken on his appointment, and it was noted that a majority of those present who were familiar with Coffman's past record appeared to favor his appointment.

Noting that the M&ATA membership was well alerted to substantial changes to be instituted within the M&ATA structure, Parsons scheduled a general meeting to be held, again in Chicago, in January, 1924. Parsons called the meeting to order, introduced Coffman, whom he stated was attending in a provisional capacity but who had been invited to present both his own as well as Coffman's proposals for a reorganization of the M&ATA and a revitalization of general motorcycling activities. He then opened the meeting and called upon

THE GREAT DECLINE 1920-1930

One of the most popular events at a 1920's dirt track race was the sidecar race. Here in Greeley, Colorado on Sept. 17 1920, the Indian Flexi sidecars of Floyd Dreyer (and his curious passenger) and Floyd Clymer (on the outside) lead the Harley sidecars piloted by Frank Kuntz and a rider by the name of Foote. Foote was the winner.
A.F. Van Order Collection

Coffman to summarize the position of the sport and industry to date.

Coffman opened the discussion by calling for increased recognition of both the 21 and 30.50 cubic inch classes, noting that most of the industry was now agreed that the promotion of smaller capacity machines to enhance market penetration as well as safer competition factors was in order.

He suggested that for ongoing competition a series of five, ten and twenty-five mile races for 30.50 machines be scheduled for all areas, with sectional winners being invited to compete for National titles. Added to this was the provision that the 21 cubic inch class of machines, if sufficient interest was forthcoming, could be accorded the same schedule. Noting that interest in the 61 cubic inch class had diminished, he suggested that continuing provision for competition be maintained, stating that traditional interest in this class of machine had existed since well before the war. A broad spectrum of events would include five, ten, twenty-five and three hundred milers. Identical sidecar events were to be allowed, although sentiments against such events due to the previous number of fatalities might cause their future elimination.

In answer to comments from the floor that the large number of projected events was a bit ambitious, considering the current lack of public interest in motorcycling, Coffman countered that offering a broad range of possible events permitted the clubs as well as outside promoters a wide choice from which to select whatever type of meetings were best suited to various regional appeal. In any case, sanctions would have to be obtained well ahead of

time to avoid conflicts.

For the benefit of the average rider, Coffman suggested that a vigorous promotion of the Gypsy Tours be continued for their value in promoting the social and touring aspects of the game. It also fulfilled the need for watchfulness to combat the ever-growing problem of adverse motorcycle legislation, and could encourage club members to qualify as well-informed competition officials and referees. He cited the fact that the lack of qualified officials and referees had always been a serious problem in organizing well run competition events, and that poorly run M&ATA sanctioned affairs had caused the increase in outlaw events that provided a poor public image. He also stated that steps should be taken to enhance the public image of motorcycling, by discouraging the open exhaust syndrome and encouraging both riders and clubs to dignify their dress and deportment.

Coffman then called upon Parsons to report on the M&ATA's past and present financial status. Parsons stated that while the income from both club and individual rider participation in the Gypsy Tours had brought in an encouraging increase in membership, administrative difficulties within the clubs had resulted in shortfalls when funds were not remitted to headquarters. The declining number of sanctioning fees from the waning popularity of racing was also a factor. This was especially true in board track racing as the promoters, who made their own rules outside of M&ATA mandates, still contributed at least $25 for each event for the privilege of advertising official sanction in years past.

He further stated that the hoped-for 1919 aim

THE GREAT DECLINE 1920-1930

Ray Weishar poses after winning the 1920 Marion 200-mile race.
A.F. Van Order Collection

of a democratically controlled national organization without factory support was still far in the future. Without factory support, riders themselves would be unable to cope with the inconsistent funding problems.

At this point, Coffman resumed the chair and advocated a restructuring of the M&ATA to avoid the pitfalls of the former FAM and to strengthen the authority of central management. To promote individual rider support, so necessary to form a broad base of activity, he suggested adopting the name "The American Motorcycle Association" in place of the M&ATA designation. This change would play down the dominant role of the manufacturers and trade suppliers, and give the general membership a more positive feeling of participation. To give effect to this intent, Parsons suggested that a steering committee be formed to perfect the organizational details and to elect a president.

This suggestion was acted upon with the appointment of the Davidsons, Henry Alexander of Cleveland, Frank J. Weschler, and Frank Schwinn as committee members, with Coffman as an ex-officio member. It must be mentioned that neither Iver-Johnson nor Schickel representatives were members of the manufacturers group, as they had declined to participate due to their marginal involvement in the industry. While both were selling machines on a special order basis, neither had manufactured any component parts since 1920, and their minimal output was based on assembly of their 1915 designs. In fact, both firms had sold substantially less than a thousand units each since their initial manufacture and introduction in 1915. Neracar, who was not represented either, had declined motorcycle designation.

Trade suppliers included representatives from Goodyear, Firestone, Messenger, Kelsey-Hays, Michigan Wheel, Genet (a duPont-owned supplier of electrical components), New York Mica, Wheeler Scheduler, B.F. Roger Sidecars, Pennzoil, and a few others not recorded.

In its ultimate organization as finally approved, the association was in reality a two-tiered affair. The M&ATA was to remain as the manufacturers body, together with supplier members. The AMA, as it was to be popularly designated, consisted of individual rider members, club members and their auxiliaries, and was governed by the Competition Committee under the executive control of its chairman, also known as the secretary-manager. He was to oversee all competition affairs with authority to enforce the rules as well as to oversee the by-laws of the affiliated clubs. The President of the AMA was to be the titular head of

both the M&ATA as well as the AMA, and in practice was to act as a go-between for the manufacturers and trade suppliers and the Competition Committee. This rather unorthodox arrangement was to stimulate the appearance of a rider's organization that governed the activities of both individual riders and club affairs, while also regulating competition affairs. The theory was that the riders' group was to be financially self supporting, but at the same time, the M&ATA stood ready as a last resort to fund any shortfall in the income from rider and club dues, Gypsy Tours, competition sanctions, or possible outside gratuities. [*4]

The financial structuring of the supporting M&ATA was as follows: Class A members were manufacturers fabricating complete machines including Indian, Harley-Davidson and Excelsior, which were assessed $100 per year dues, payable quarterly. Class B accessory manufacturers, doing at least $20,000 worth of business each year with the trade, were assessed a $10 initiation fee and yearly dues of $50, payable quarterly. Class A and Class B members had equal voting power.

Individual riders and club members were charged $1 per year dues, with a $5 per year assessment for each chartered club, which, under the rules, was mandated to include only bona fide individual members. In addition, those dealers wishing to advertise as AMA supporters were assessed $3 per year for the privilege. This group cumulatively was designated Class C, but had no voting power.

While in principle this proposed financial structuring was intended to support AMA activities, practical experience had already indicated that the actual collections from Class C memberships might fall short, and the M&ATA members agreed that in the future their membership might be required to submit to additional assessments if shortfalls should occur.

Following the adoption of the AMA organization, the M&ATA elected as president one George T. Briggs, president of Wheeler Shebler Company. For many years his company had supplied most of the carburetors to the trade, and he had been an active supporter through the years of both the FAM and the M&ATA. His name had first been suggested by Walter Davidson, who also made the point that it might be best for all concerned that the M&ATA executive should not be connected with any of the principal manufacturers. At any rate, Briggs was elected on an uncontested ballot, along with Arthur Davidson as Vice President.

The American Motorcycle Association subsequently designated January, 1924, as the official

THE GREAT DECLINE 1920-1930

Ray Weishar was a top star of the late-teens and early twenties. His luck ran out at a race at the Legion Ascot track in Los Angeles in 1924. He was killed when he hit a bump on the track and swerved into the outside railing.
A.F. Van Order Collection

Paul Anderson on a Harley-Davidson 30.50 cubic inch single. This model actually has a 61 cubic inch V-twin motor with the front cylinder blanked off. In 1925, Harley-Davidson went into production of a conventional single cylinder design to become known as the "Peashooter."
A.F. Van Order Collection

date of its founding. Its finalization did not really occur until late in March, due to the large amount of organization work that still had to be accomplished. President Briggs, Secretary/Manager Coffman and Vice President Davidson were also stated as having been installed in office in January, but were not formally installed until March as well. *5

At a meeting of a partial group of M&ATA members that was held in June, both President Briggs and Chairman Coffman emphasized that in the future it was hoped that public announcements and publicity connected with motorcycling affairs would emphasize the AMA designation. In playing down the role of the M&ATA to the media as well as the general public, it was hoped that rider approval, long a problem in organized motorcycling to date, would be enhanced by the emphasis on a rider-oriented organization. At any rate, as a concession to the sequence of events that were to govern the future of American organized motorcycling, it was to be the Chairman of the Competition Committee who would to be in executive control. In a minor way, the waters were somewhat clouded by the fact that in 1919 there was a brief consideration of naming the FAM's successor the American Motorcycle Association, and somehow a batch of membership cards with this designation were printed; a few of which still survive. With the official action of reorganization effected in 1924, it is logical to assume that, with official adoption of the new name, it should be considered correct in the historical sense.

Much was made of the reorganization in the trade press, but unfortunately, most of the amateur journalists of the day offered ambiguous and garbled accounts of the proceedings. The only accurate reporting of the proceedings in their correct chronological order was quite naturally to be found in Henry Parsons' "Motorcycle and Bicycle Illustrated." The author was fortunate in being able to unearth a copy of this article, as well as Coffman's outline of the agenda of the various meetings, along with his personal recollections in an interview conducted in 1947. Also of value were the recollections later recorded by L.D. Richards, who was present at all of the proceedings, as well as those of Thomas Callahan Butler.

In passing, mention must be made of the somewhat indeterminate role of Douglas Hobart as the officially elected M&ATA President from 1920 through 1923. While he acted as Chairman on occasion for M&ATA meetings and carried on much of the routine correspondence and record keeping, the real authority during this period was in the hands of Henry Parsons. Parsons, as

Competition Chairman, oversaw competition rules and dealt directly with rider and the affiliated club affairs. On the other hand, Hobart performed yeoman service in the lengthy negotiations between the M&ATA and the FICM governing board through Billy Wells and C.T. Loughborogh of the British Auto-Cycle Union. While the negotiations ultimately failed to arrive at a satisfactory conclusion, the final result of the isolation of American motorcycle sport from international competition was, in itself, a historic milestone in the history of American motorcycling.

In the end, Hobart became somewhat sensitive regarding his actual role, which ultimately saw him acting as a secretary rather than a president. In later years, he often privately confided to others that he was the first President of the M&ATA, which, in reality, was his official designation. In addition, he sometimes referred to himself as the first AMA Chief Executive, all of which had a tendency to blur the dividing line between the role of the M&ATA and the AMA in the historical sense.

Hobart's role in organized motorcycling affairs did not end with the election of A.B. Coffman to the Presidency of the M&ATA and the AMA, however. In the interim, he had somehow learned of the sub-rosa meetings conducted annually between Frank Weschler and the Davidsons, beginning in 1921. The heads of both companies managed to keep the meetings secret, the only other outsiders being aware of it and present at the meetings were Indian's L.D. Richards and Harley-Davidson's Alfred Rich Child. Indian's President Skinner was also aware of the meetings, and gave his tacit approval, but never attended any of the meetings during his tenure of office that ended in 1923.

In passing, Hobart had hoped that he could continue on as President. But at the AMA-M&ATA's additional organizational meeting held in March, George T. Briggs of Wheeler-Schebler was elected president, much to the relief of Coffman, who already considered that he had a formidable task confronting him.

At any rate, Hobart's reaction to the knowledge of the clandestine meetings was immediate. Being a somewhat idealistic person, and perhaps with some latent hostility at being passed over for office, he confronted Weschler personally concerning the matter. He remonstrated with him concerning the illegality of such collusion, and the consequent risk of prosecution under existing laws governing corporate conduct. Weschler responded in his usual diplomatic manner, emphasizing the present critical state of the motorcycle industry. He cited the loss of sales caused by competition from cheap cars, and the

If You Want the Utmost in Motorcycle Enjoyment and Satisfaction—

Ride a Henderson

EXCELSIOR MOTOR MFG. & SUPPLY CO.

THE GREAT DECLINE 1920-1930

Both the Indian and Harley-Davidson companies introduced their own "in-house" publications as a means to show riders enjoying their products on the open roads and winning races.
Don Emde Collection

realistic necessity for the manufacturers, as sole survivors of a new weakened industry, to seek extreme measures to remain in the picture.

While the matter might have ended at that point, Hobart fired off letters to both President Davidson and Ignatz Schwinn, expressing his strong disapproval of their conspiratorial meetings. In response to this outburst, the three top management executives engaged in a series of long distance telephone conferences concerning how to deal with Hobart, as well as how to prevent him from spreading his findings to the other members of the industry as well as the general public. Walter Davidson was particularly adamant about the possible damage Hobart might have caused, and Weschler assured him that immediate steps to quiet the matter would be undertaken in Springfield.

L.D. Richards, who was aware of the matter, later told the author that Weschler, no doubt wisely, did not at once remove Hobart from his position with Indian for fear of subsequent declarations. Instead, he offered to strengthen the Indian dealership in Hartford, where he had lately participated on a part time basis. At the same time Hobart's employment at Springfield ended on the premise that it would be to his advantage to devote full time to the Hartford operation. Hobart ultimately agreed, but more or less withdrew from active participation in AMA-M&ATA affairs, and was a low profile dealer until his sudden death from a heart attack in 1937.

The Hobart affair and its repercussions did not end at that point, however. During the fall of 1923, while Hobart was still in office, Charles B. Franklin had completed prototype work on a 21 cubic inch overhead camshaft single intended for competition. Hobart accepted it officially as an entrant in M&ATA sanctioned events. When the news came out, it at once enraged Walter Davidson, whose Milwaukee engineers had not yet readied their own singles for the same application. He accused Hobart of using his office to give his company an unfair advantage. In the end, the rather premature action on Hobart's part came to nothing, as Jim Davis left Indian's professional racing team to join Harley-Davidson. Before leaving, he entered just one event with the new engine, but failed to place due to mechanical trouble. *6

In the meantime, A.B. Coffman kicked off the 1924 season by sending out form letters to all AMA members. He outlined the details of the new organization with an explanation of the new competition classes and their rule schedules, with the approval of the Committee, but without mention of the M&ATA, although under George T. Briggs'

signature. Not mentioning the M&ATA was intended to emphasize the rider's dominant role in the proceedings.

The majority of competition victories in 1924 went to Indian, however, as they still retained their professional team. But Jim Davis was able to gain a National win for Milwaukee in the 30.50 cubic inch class. In the absence of a machine of this type, Davis rode a "61" with the front cylinder deleted, the engine being re-timed to run in this configuration.

With no 61 cubic inch events scheduled that year in deference to 30.50 emphasis, Paul Anderson, who had done well the previous year on a Maldwyn Jones-designed Excelsior, switched to Harley-Davidson and won a 200 mile National on another "half-sixty one".

A number of personnel changes within the industry occurred in 1924. Thomas Callahan Butler resigned from Indian to become the Sales Manager for C.W. Risden's active Indian agency in San Francisco. Here he was able to renew his friendship with his old acquaintance, Hap Scherer, who was still with Harley-Davidson's Rich Budelier. Before leaving Springfield, Butler had suggested that the production of fan cooled versions of the Indian engines would be a sales factor in the growing interest in small industrial engines. Weschler vetoed the idea as complicating his efforts to restore Indian's lost footing. Butler's point was well taken, however, noting the growing success of Briggs and Stratton and Kohler and Kohler in this new field.

As an aside to motorcycling history, a pioneer designer, Perry E. Mack, had recently joined Briggs and Stratton. Born in 1878, as a boy cyclist he had lived through the transition from the high wheeler to the safety type bicycle, and after some engineer training he entered the field of motorcycle design with his own make, called the "P.E.M." The rights of both his single and twin-cylinder designs were later purchased by the Waverly concern, who marketed them before World War I as both the Jefferson and the Waverly. Mack later designed a 61 cubic inch V-twin with overhead valve configuration for cycle car use in 1913, and later designed a similar motor for the last Pope machine built until 1915. For many years he was the chief engineer for Briggs and Stratton, and was with them almost until the time of his death in 1951. His recollections, transcribed by the author just before World War II, form an interesting chapter in domestic history.

A former Wrecking Crew member, Fred Ludlow joined C. Will Risden as a mechanic after failing to obtain a position with Harley-Davidson in Milwaukee. He was promoted to the position of

THE GREAT DECLINE 1920-1930

Ralph Hepburn won many motorcycle races including the prestigious Dodge City 300 in 1921. He later switched to cars and was killed in the Indianapolis 500.
A.F. Van Order Collection

Shop Foreman, and subsequently became a motorcycle officer for the city of South Pasadena and later, Pasadena, a position he retained until his retirement in 1955.

Leslie D. Richards resigned as Indian's Publicity Manager and moved to Denver, Colorado, in December, 1924, in deference to his wife's health. He founded a parcel delivery business using Indian commercial sidecar outfits. A year or two later he was offered and accepted the Indian franchise in Denver.

Floyd Clymer, the precocious boy car salesman and later motorcycle racing star (winner of the Dodge City 200 Miler in 1915 for Harley-Davidson) had represented Indian for a time, along with Excelsior. He had won a number of hill climb events for Excelsior, along with Pikes Peak enduros. He let the agency lapse, however, for the promotion of his once famous "hole-in-the-windshield" auto spotlight. Of a somewhat larcenous nature, Clymer was involved in various enterprises, one of which got him a federal conviction for mail fraud and he was sentenced to a term in Leavenworth Penitentiary in 1930.

In the increasingly important western motorcycle market, Ray E. Garner's Indian franchise in Portland was made a factory branch. Garner was a tireless promoter of the sport and wrote many articles for the trade press advocating clean dealerships and more attention to sales techniques.

Vern Guthrie, Harley-Davidson's western factory traveler, had established two additional dealerships in California: Frank J. Murray in Sacramento and Joseph Frugoli in Santa Rosa, the author's boyhood home. He reactivated Harley-Davidson's strength in Portland by settling a long standing dispute between two feuding dealers in the area, George Blanton and Dawes Rice.

Albert G. Crocker, a former engineer with Arthur Constantine at Thor and later with Indian's operation in Springfield, had his Kansas City dealership expanded into a distributorship. A new Indian outlet in Atlanta was established with George T. Bullard as manager.

In 1924, Arthur Constantine was ordered to restyle Harley-Davidson's long running J series, which appeared for the 1925 season with a streamlined fuel tank, lowered seat position, and wider mudguards to conform to the updated styling trends recently introduced by Indian and Excelsior. He was also working with William Ottaway and Hank Syvertson on the finalization of the side-valve and overhead-valve versions of a new 21 cubic inch single-cylinder model. This design team also introduced a new 61 and 74 cubic inch pocket valve design of "two cam" configuration, which was intended to power an updated hillclimb machine. Hillclimbing was now coming into new prominence as a professional as well as a club activity.

In 1924, in order to enhance its Japanese market, Harley-Davidson entered into an agreement with Alfred Rich Child, to open a factory branch in Tokyo. Indian had dominated this market since 1919, with 500 to 800 units being shipped each year. Indian had become a cult with well-to-do Nipponese enthusiasts, reinforced by Crown Prince Hirohito's purchase of a Chief sidecar outfit.

The energetic Child soon expanded Harley-Davidson's former small activity there, and worked both sides of the street in selling military sidecar outfits to both the Japanese army as well as the Chinese warlords on the mainland. He later manufactured a Japanese version of later Harley-Davidson models under license as the "Rikuo" (King of the Road), along with Milwaukee-made machines imported to compete with his own product.

Harley-Davidson soon became the dominant import in Japan, even with competition from imported, cheaper British machines. The author, who made a tour of Japan in 1984, noted many examples of both Milwaukee made as well as Rikuo models. The former dated before World War II, and the latter had been terminated in 1960. A further excursion into inner Mongolia also saw fair numbers of old machines still in use, and even a donkey cart fabricated from the chassis of a long obsolete J model sidecar!

In the meantime, the three surviving manufacturers, working through the M&ATA and the AMA, sought to strengthen the domestic market. Rider and club participation was encouraged through continuing promotion of the Gypsy Tours and National Rider's Rallies. The growing weakness of the trade press was somewhat overcome by the emphasis in the in-house factory publications, each now promoting "brand name" loyalty. The importance of non-standard exhaust systems in arousing public anti-motorcycling sentiment was stressed, as was correct rider deportment, along with a continuing watch for anti-motorcycling legislation.

A.B. Coffman was active in traveling about as much as possible on AMA business, but his activities were complicated by the demands of his growing trade fair promotions that often featured unrelated products such as household appliances, farm equipment, and furniture. While he encountered some criticism for engaging in these opposing activities, Coffman argued that his $200 per month, plus expenses, from the AMA did not cover his family demands.

While board track racing was now all but dead, the dirt track county fair circuits were also declining due to the lack of 21 and 30.50 cubic inch development. Public tastes were also changing with the growth of interest in sprint car racing, which was readily adaptable to the horse track venues. The aftermarket activities of the many independent manufacturers, who were offering a myriad of products to enhance the starkly functional Model T Ford cars, were now a factor in racing.

Many large cities, as well as smaller towns, now had their local car racing aspirants, which saw hundreds of events staged throughout the spring, summer and fall seasons. While Ford was the most popular for these conversions, other larger makes

were often subjects for conversion for participation in advanced classes.

In the face of growing competition from the automobile, both as a transportation entity and a sporting spectacle, and in the face of lackluster public interest, the Competition Committee met in the summer of 1923 to consider another problem. National Motorcycle Shows had been held after 1909, usually in conjunction with bicycle shows staged by the Cycle Traders Union up until the war years, and had been revived in 1919 with a disappointing participation from the motorcycle industry because of the decline in the number of manufacturers. These events had been staged each alternate year at New York's Madison Square Garden and Chicago's Coliseum, except for the 1921 show that was held in Atlanta.

In 1923, however, the Cycle Traders Union decided that public interest in such shows was declining due to the current standardization of models, and were becoming an unnecessary expense.

A.B. Coffman, however, urged that the M&ATA go it alone in 1924 to show the determination of the industry, and developed plans to present an exhibit at the Chicago venue. In order to offer something new in the way of stimulating public interest, he tentatively offered the proposition that a selected group of foreign exhibitors be invited to attend. He was urged along in this idea by Henry A. Parsons, who was campaigning for the American development of middle and lightweight machines based on the current overseas types now offered in Great Britain and Europe. When Coffman mentioned this possibility to the M&ATA it elicited a storm of protest. The assembled representatives of the big three were adamant in their opposition, calling attention to the current static condition of the domestic market. Furthermore, none of them were in a position to offer models competitive with foreign lightweight machines, not to mention the real danger of foreign competition from imports which might spell the early death knell of the domestic manufacturers. In the subsequent heated discussion, Henry Parsons' past critiques of the industry in their failure to develop non-traditional designs were vigorously condemned, and Coffman himself was severely censured for even contemplating such a proposition.

During a subsequent stormy session, Frank Schwinn brought up the matter of the forthcoming suspension of production by both Iver-Johnson and Schickel, who were running out of long-past manufactured parts. It was also noted that Neracar and Cleveland were planning to leave the industry, along with Briggs and Stratton abandoning the Motor Wheel, and Shaw dropping its bicycle

THE GREAT DECLINE 1920-1930

(Above) Gene Walker was one of the very best riders of his day, riding both Harleys and Indians. He won numerous events until he was killed in 1924 at Stroudsbury, Pa. when he hit a tractor on a warm-up lap.
A.F. Van Order Collection

(Below) His jersey covered with dirt and oil, Bill Brier takes a breather after a long distance race in Sioux City, Ia.
A.F. Van Order Collection

motors in favor of garden tractor production. It was emphasized that these last defectors represented lightweight motorcycling, a further indication that American buyers, by tradition, had already rejected the very type of machines that Parsons and Coffman were suggesting to promote.

In later years, Coffman told the author that he regretted his poor judgment in bringing up the matter, and that in so doing he had stirred up sufficient resentment among the manufacturers that it prejudiced his standing from then on with the M&ATA membership.

At any rate, Coffman went ahead with plans for the 1924 show. As he privately surmised, public support was minimal, the show ending up as more of a social gathering for the staff and management of the manufacturers and allied trades. In spite of this, one final national motorcycle show was held in Chicago in 1927.

Subsequent to the 1924 National Motorcycle Show debacle, President Walter Davidson called a special meeting at the factory and ordered the Harley-Davidson sales force and all factory traveling representatives to attend. In an impassioned address he reviewed the present static condition of the industry, the redundant condition of the domestic market, and what he termed the critical situation where the domestic factory's survival was dependent on exports to generate the cash flow necessary for their survival.

Davidson also noted that to broaden Harley-Davidson's penetration of the market, the factory was to embark on a program of establishing part-time dealerships in the smaller towns and rural areas where the operators could engage in employment in non-related industry while representing the company after-hours or on weekends.

In referred to the details of the exclusive handling of Harley-Davidson products, dealer compliance with this mandate would be a strong factor in the yearly review of their franchise renewals.

California's Vern Guthrie, who attended the meeting, later told the author that it was his opinion that Davidson was referring especially to Cleveland, which many dealers had handled since their introduction in 1915. While Cleveland was rumored to be phasing out their long running lightweight, it was also suspected (from inside information) that they were planning to introduce another model of larger sized cylinder capacity.

Guthrie also noted that Harley-Davidson had been in a rather critical financial situation since going into debt for the new factory building in 1920, anticipating a post-war motorcycle boom that failed to occur. The serving of this indebted-

THE GREAT DECLINE 1920-1930

ness, for the building as well as for the extensive new tooling purchased, plus the halving of the anticipated post-war sales, had caused the company to seek financing outside the original family groups of the founders. A good portion of these funds were obtained from the sale of shares to the Wood family, a well-to-do group of Milwaukee capitalists. At any rate, the Davidsons held only a slight voting majority with their residual of 51% of the company stock. This was a bitter blow to the founders, who continually mentioned in company literature that they remained as a family-owned enterprise, and subsequently, took great pains to keep the details of company financing a closely guarded secret.

At this point Indian was in somewhat better financial condition due to the flotation of an additional stock issue incidental to the 1923 reorganization. But with the fall of their market after 1920, Indian, like Harley-Davidson, was carrying the overhead of a large plant facility where it utilized only a small area of the available space. Then too, it was in need of new tooling to either replace or augment the installations brought in during Indian's salad days between 1910 and 1914. Following the near failure of the company during 1921 and 1922, Frank Weschler, now in sole charge, was treading a very careful course in controlling costs and in avoiding any over-expansion. Also, there was the ever present spectre of surprise actions on the part of the non-motorcycling shareholders, who had ultimate control of the company fortunes through the use of their votes.

The annual price-and-policy fixing meeting between Frank Weschler and the Davidsons was held in the Blackstone Hotel in Chicago at the end of August 1924. Alfred Rich Child, who had made a return trip to Milwaukee from Japan to address some export problems, was able to attend. After the usual amenities, Arthur Davidson brought up the matter of the current public image of motorcycling and the importance of projecting the news of the industry so as to put the sport and industry in a good light. He suggested that henceforth all news of industry affairs should be controlled by the factories themselves through the issuing of press releases to the trade magazines. He further suggested all articles and feature stories regarding each make in question should be subject to prior review by the factory in question, along with the privilege of censorship of any content considered detrimental or prejudicial to the best interests of the industry.

Davidson alluded to the amateurish and often inconsistent articles frequently encountered that were being written by casual correspondents. He was particularly irked by the writings of Henry A. Parsons, who was often critical of the directions of the industry and often at odds with established policies, although he admitted that Parsons' publication was generally better than most.

He also touched on the subject just aired within his own organization, namely that of restricting the sale of products by franchisees to those of the one factory.

Weschler responded that he agreed that the public image of the industry was, as always, an evergreen subject. But he warned that any attempt to muzzle the trade press could well result in much editorial resentment, as professional journalists ever cherished the principle of editorial integrity. Weschler suggested that before the factories embarked on a program of total censorship, the Publicity Managers from each factory should routinely submit more press releases that outlined in-house policies that could, in an oblique manner, slant the writer's thinking in the desired direction.

In the matter of restricting dealer's handling of products of other suppliers, Weschler stated that Indian dealers had long handled both Clevelands and Neracars, and he thought that in the absence of the availability of similar in-house products, the offering of these machines not only increased dollar volume for the dealers, but were valuable as entry level machines for prospective motorcyclists.

After some discussion, it was decided to observe the outcome of the coming year before making a final decision on the matters of trade publication control and the restriction of dealer's product management.

However, during the following spring Walter Davidson implemented both restrictions of dealer products and trade press control in respect to Harley-Davidson's policies, and issued his mandates at a factory dealer and factory traveler's meeting held in Milwaukee in April. *7

At a closed meeting between top management and the factory travelers, some of the latter, including Vern Guthrie, reported that in many cases the dealers in their respective territories had not taken kindly to the news of a forthcoming prohibition concerning the sale of outside products. While the Motor Wheel market was indeterminate, the handling of Clevelands and Neracars was cited as being a distinct sales advantage as an offering of lower cost entry-level utility machines.

President Davidson countered that he had definite knowledge that Cleveland was soon to announce a large capacity machine, and as such, the factory would not countenance the introduc-

THE GREAT DECLINE 1920-1930

One of the all-time racing greats, Jim Davis on an Indian board tracker. He won numerous championship events for both the Indian and Harley-Davidson factories during his long and illustrious career.
A.F. Van Order Collection

tion of outside competition.

In a discussion of news control of trade press content, he emphasized that with the current state of the market only material tending to enhance the image of the sport and industry should be relayed to the public. He further announced a fact that was no longer a secret; that the company was soon to offer a lightweight machine that would at long last provide Harley-Davidson buyers a utility type machine.

President Davidson's statements regarding Cleveland were well taken, as in the fall of 1925, the Ohio factory announced that their long running lightweight two stroke was being discontinued in favor of a similar model to be powered with a small four-cylinder air cooled engine. This was a rather surprising move in light of the fact that Cleveland had enjoyed an exclusive niche in the domestic motorcycle market for a utility type machine that appealed to newsboys and ride-to-work owners not interested in sporting activities.

The engine design for the new model was a 45 cubic inch in-line air cooled four, but was of the long outmoded T head configuration, the intake and exhaust valves with separate camshafts on opposite sides of the cylinders. This made for an unusually wide combustion chamber which result-

ed in an exceedingly low compression ratio that greatly reduced its potential power output. While an easily started and smooth running machine, a $100 price increase over its original two stroke with only a ten mph increase in speed, made it hardly an attractive proposition.

Cleveland's designer, L. E. Fowler, was formerly an automotive engineer, and was said to have been much impressed with an early Pierce-Arrow engine of the same type, although by the mid-1920's, the T head was considered obsolete.

Indian's single-cylinder, side valve 21 cubic inch Prince was announced in the fall of 1924, for the 1925 sales season. The experimental overhead camshaft prototypes were not placed in production, due to high manufacturing costs, nor was the overhead valve variant. A well made machine of simple design, it was priced at $185, and was received with mild enthusiasm at home, although it was to be given a good reception on the export market.

Harley-Davidson showcased their new 21 cubic inch single-cylinder models in 1925, with Joe Petrali entering some exhibition race events with the overhead valve version. The side valve version with many identical cycle parts, intended as a utility model, was announced with both models in production for the 1926 sales season. The overhead valve edition was soon to be known as the "Peashooter," due to its somewhat unfamiliar small size when appearing on the tracks, although it was a good performer and tuned examples were capable of 80 mph.

The mid-1920's saw the emergence of Petrali as a star who was to exhibit his extraordinary riding skills in both track racing and hill climbing. He was born in 1905, and at an early age showed a marked aptitude for mechanics. He dropped out of school to repair motorcycles and, as a teenager, became the protege of Charles "Fearless" Balke, a veteran competition rider. He subsequently rode Harley-Davidsons and Excelsiors, after Maldwyn Jones left to join Wheeler-Schebler. He was next hired as a professional by Harley-Davidson to campaign with Peashooters.

It was also during this period that Erwin G. Baker continued to garner much personal publicity for his spectacular transcontinental record runs, as well as his "Three Flag" rides from Mexico to Canada. He rode various makes of motorcycles such as Ace, Henderson, Indian, Excelsior, Cleveland and Neracar, as well as repeating these performances for various makes of automobiles. An early day track competitor with mediocre success, he found his forte in endurance rides, and gained the name "Cannonball," coined by news

THE GREAT DECLINE 1920-1930

writers, which he disliked, but which followed him to the end of his days. He made his last run in 1941 at sixty years of age on an experimental Indian Sport Scout with a rotary valve engine which he had designed.

In 1925, C. Will Risden expressed his intention to retire, and entered into negotiations with Thomas Callahan Butler to take over the franchise. During their discussions, one A.F. Van Order, a protege of Rich Budelier, entered the picture with more substantial financing, and almost overnight acquired Risden's interests. Within a few weeks, however, a sudden conflagration destroyed the building along with several dozen machines and the extensive parts inventory. Van Order and Budelier were subsequently suspected of arson, but insufficient evidence spared them from prosecution. The episode was long a topic of conversation and speculation among veteran dealers of both makes. Central Los Angeles was without a central Indian agency until 1928, when Albert G. Crocker transferred from Kansas City to re-establish it.

Butler moved to Idaho where he engaged in engineering consulting work for mining and lumber interests, but with his wide acquaintanceship in the motorcycle industry, he kept in close touch with it until his death in 1976. His diaries, journals, and collection of factory correspondence was a very important factor in the preservation of domestic motorcycle history.

Vern Guthrie resigned from Harley-Davidson in 1925, as a result of his disagreement with Walter Davidson over his growingly restrictive policies toward his dealerships, particularly in the West. Guthrie considered this a retrograde step in public relations and a minus factor with his on-going contacts with the western dealership that he had been the prime mover in establishing. A sincere individual with a persuasive personality and a charismatic manner, he was well respected throughout the industry with both conferees and competitors.

Guthrie subsequently took a franchise for Hudson and Essex cars in Monterey Park, California, and when that venture failed in 1930, he became a free lance journalist dealing with automotive and transportation subjects with the news media in the Los Angeles area. His vast collection of source material regarding his long experience in the motorcycle trade (which he made available to the author) was an important adjunct to the preservation of its history.

In the spring of 1925, an important export outlet for the American motorcycle industry was terminated when Great Britain's Chancellor of the Exchequer announced that henceforth a 33% import tax would be levied against all foreign automobiles and motorcycles.

The English economy had yet to recover from the effects of the war. While their motorcycle industry was prospering as an alternative to low cost transportation, their auto industry was still in the doldrums. Coupled with this, additional income was needed to aid in retiring their war indebtedness.

Sir Duncan Watson and Billy Wells both closed down their import concerns; Excelsior also terminated operations at their small independent outlet. These firms maintained spare parts depots in London until 1929 or 1930. Harley-Davidson continued to be represented by Frederick Warr, who sold a few machines from his modest premises in Fulham between the wars. His son reopened the business after World War II.

Arthur Constantine was discharged by Walter Davidson in the summer of 1925, over a dispute concerning the former's independent designing of a new 45 cubic inch V-twin. Rumor had it that Indian was planning a 45 cubic inch version of its still-popular 37 cubic inch Scout, which made it logical to offer a slightly higher powered version. In noting the trend toward middleweight machines, Constantine was of the opinion that they could now penetrate a new segment of the market.

Davidson took exception to Constantine's spending a part of company time on an unauthorized project, but also to the design of the machine. It was a permutation of what Constantine considered the best features of both Harley-Davidson and Indian. The cycle parts were in essence a slightly elongated 21 single, but with a pocket valve 45 in. V-twin engine that had an Indian type in-unit helical gear drive to the transmission.

Constantine was hired at once by Schwinn, bringing his proposed design with him. He once told the author that Schwinn had been thinking of inaugurating a new middleweight design to broaden Excelsior's penetration of the market, and fortunately, his new idea had appeared when the often irascible Schwinn was in a receptive mood. The profile of the new twin was slightly altered to conform to the former Excelsior outline, and prototype work was started immediately. It was announced to the public in February 1926, being designated the "Super-X." With thick cylinder walls, it was capable of being bored out to 61 cubic inch to offer a somewhat more powerful variant.

Walter Davidson, who was put out with the Schwinns for their immediate association with Constantine, called for a meeting with them in Chicago for the ostensible purpose of inquiring into the recently noted discount selling of their

THE GREAT DECLINE 1920-1930

Eddie Brink is shown here in 1925 aboard one of the new single exhaust port Harley-Davidson Peashooters. *A.F. Van Order Collection*

Henderson fours to the law enforcement market. Schwinn had long known of the price-and-policy agreements between Harley-Davidson and Indian, but had had no reason to participate as his recent sole production had been the fours, which retailed at much higher prices than either of their twins.

At any rate, Davidson queried Schwinn as to just why he had discounted his fours from $455 to $365, which represented a direct factory sale to buyers, less the usual dealer markup. Schwinn told Davidson that, with the sudden loss of the British market and with cancellations from New Zealand and Australia from dealers (who were in fear of like tariff barriers from those countries) he had ended up with 250 units in storage.

Davidson warned Schwinn of the dangers of price cutting within the industry in the face of current market conditions, and the cash flow problems attendant to low volume productions.

The subject of retail pricing for the new 45 and 61 cubic inch Super-X's was now brought up, and Schwinn rather haughtily informed Davidson that as premium quality supersports machines, he expected to move them at least $25 to $35 more than comparable Indian Chiefs, Scouts, or Harley-Davidson's J model V-twin, and that he would fix his own prices.

Frank Schwinn in later years told the author that, in his opinion, the Davidsons actually called the meeting to ascertain the ultimate retail pricing of the Super-X's, as the matter of the four discounting was not of immediate concern as a non-competitive model.

The financing of the motorcycle operation was

never a critical problem for the Schwinns, as their operation was based on the high volume and very profitable bicycle operation that had long offset their low volume motorcycle market.[8] Ignatz Schwinn was also intensely proud of his long production of America's luxury machine. While its yearly numbers were small, averaging 1,600 to 2,200 units, nearly half went to export on firm overseas markets, and half of the domestic sales went to law enforcement. The balance of the domestic sales went to the few well-healed riders who could afford to pay a non-competitive price for a luxury machine.

At the subsequent price-and-policy fixing meeting between the Davidsons and Frank Weschler later that fall, the prices of the Prince and the side valve Peashooters were fixed at $210. The Prince's pricing had been raised to compensate for the redesigning of the original wedge shaped fuel tank which was a rather unattractive feature. Weschler was undecided as to whether or not he planned to go into full production on an overhead valve Prince model, but if he later did so, he agreed to match the $265 price set by the Davidsons for their overhead valve Peashooter.

During this period, the Davidsons were seriously considering entering the four-cylinder market, and in the spring of 1925 had awarded Everett M. De Long, the Henderson's and Arthur Lemon's former protege, a contract to produce a prototype model.

The Davidsons at once rejected De Long's initial proposal for an in-line four as not capable of being rationalized into their current J Model production. De Long's next proposal was a V-type four that was, in essence, two sleeved down 61 cubic inch J engines set side-by-side, geared to a common crankshaft, mated to an outrigger shaft on the present J gear box. This design closely followed a similar prototype De Long had built in conjunction with Erwin G. Baker for a proposed manufacturing product in 1920.

Walter and Arthur Davidson were impressed with the result, as was Alfred Rich Child, who examined the machine that fall during his annual visit to the factory to coordinate his activities with the company in Japan. Child later told the author that the project was vetoed by Production Supervisor William C. "Big Bill" Davidson as still being too much at variance with current models to be economically produced. As this Davidson made the principal decisions in such matters, and was respected for his long and successful record in rational factory production, the project was abandoned.

At the annual meeting of the M&ATA and the AMA Competition Committee in January, 1926 in

THE GREAT DECLINE 1920-1930

Cincinnati, Ohio, the still critical state of affairs within organized motorcycling was discussed. A.B. Coffman, who chaired the meeting, opened the discussion with the statement that financial income had declined, even with the growing strength of the clubs and the popularity of the Gypsy Tours. He laid this to both a lack of proper communication with the Chicago headquarters and the failure of club officers and Tour promoters to forward the proper funds. He further stated that his inability to make frequent visits to the clubs, as well as to attend important previously sanctioned competition events, had resulted in laxities in these event processes so that an excessive number of "outlaw" events were being conducted throughout the country, with consequent further loss of revenue.

Coffman also mentioned that support of the AMA from the dealers was lacking in many areas, again partly due to a lack of communication with headquarters and his inability to cover that area in personal visits.

Coffman mentioned that both his salary and expense money were inadequate to cover the proper performance of his duties, and that during the past several months he had been forced to contribute funds from his personal business involving trade promotions. Even at that, he reported that there was now only $600 in the treasury. In the matter of cutting expenses, he mentioned that eliminating the annual motorcycle show had been a wise decision, in agreement with the Cycle Trades Union which had come to a similar decision regarding the show's necessity.

There were some comments from the floor taking Coffman to task for not keeping in closer contact with the clubs as well as attending more of the important competition events. Coffman somewhat heatedly retorted that he had already explained his difficulties in covering such a broad spectrum of endeavor, together with the growing personal as well as organizational financial problems.

Frank Weschler suggested that an alternative practice of reinforcing factory loyalty as well as AMA support on the part of competition riders, which he inaugurated in 1923, was to financially reward Indian riders who either placed or won competition events. Those winning or placing in National events were sent checks of from $25 to $50 to augment their prize money. Winners or placers in less important contests were given $10 to $20 gift certificates redeemable for either parts or accessories at their local dealers.

The Schwinns countered this with the statement that they were not willing to follow suit, as they were no longer offering factory support to competition riders. The Davidsons were noncommittal, as it was known that they were averse to dispensing any gratuitous funds to riders. Nevertheless, Weschler continued his monetary recognition of Indian contestants until the end of his tenure with Indian in the fall of 1927.

The Board meeting in question ended with the members voting to continue with their original AMA subsidization, with Coffman promising to redouble his efforts at enhancing club, rider and dealer support.

Early in 1925, an unsubstantiated rumor circulating throughout the industry had it that a firm in New Jersey was planning to import foreign motorcycles, a possibility that had disturbed the domestic manufacturers ever since the discussion concerning possible FICM affiliation.

President Walter Davidson was acquainted with Wisconsin's senior U.S. Senator, Robert M. La Follette (a progressive Republican and unsuccessful presidential candidate in 1924) who had national stature as a prominent political figure. Davidson at once contacted him to investigate the possibility of an increased protective tariff which might be instituted for enhanced protection for the domestic motorcycle industry. It was noted that a tariff of 10% of the landed value of automobiles had been enacted in 1920, which was one of the reasons that Rolls Royce had organized an assembly plant in Springfield, Massachusetts. In the midst of the discussion, Senator La Follette died suddenly and was succeeded by his son Robert, who was appointed by the Governor of Wisconsin to fill out his term and with whom Davidson subsequently conferred.

The author, who is remotely related to the La Follette family, was later informed that Davidson was told it would require a substantial sum of money to hire a lobbyist to promote such a proposal to the Senate's Committee on Tariffs. Davidson informed Frank Weschler and the Schwinns regarding the matter, as well as members of the AMA Competition Committee. As the rumored importation of foreign machines did not materialize, the matter of raising such funds was tabled for the time being.

The Davidsons, however, continued to review the situation regarding the Cleveland Motor Company, together with their previous warning to their dealers against handling Cleveland machines. The issue was still very much alive, as many Harley-Davidson dealers favored the make as an entry level sales stimulant. They were still in sympathy with the popular factory traveler Vern Guthrie, who had quit Harley-Davidson over his advocacy of the dealers continuing the sales of this make.

A. B. Coffman

THE GREAT DECLINE 1920-1930

Earl Armstrong (middle) was a development rider for the Indian factory. He looks quite "race-worn" in this photo having just finished a long distance event. On the right is another famous Indian rider, Cannonball Baker. *A.F. Van Order Collection*

President Davidson pointed out that the western states distributor of Cleveland was the prominent San Francisco Indian dealer C. Will Risden, and he issued a factory directive that "he didn't want Harley-Davidson people doing business with Risden."

Meanwhile, William G. Schrack terminated his limited production of export-only Emblem light V-twins at Angola, New York, having purchased the assets of the bankrupt Pierce Bicycle Company. Other pioneers who deserted motorcycles for bicycles included Thomas Henderson, who entered this field shortly after the death of his brother William, and Arthur Lemon who, after the end of Ace's Blossburg production, entered the bicycle export business.

The AMA Competition Committee again had a brief contact with the FICM headquarters in Geneva regarding some new speed records racked up by Johnny Seymour for Indian at Daytona Beach. Representing both the 30.50 and 61 cubic inch classes, Charles Gustafson, Jr., Indian's Competition Manager, utilized the same stripped down frame for both, the engines being exchanged. Runs of 116 mph for the four-valve single and 132 mph for the eight-valve twin were recorded. The results were forwarded to Geneva along with a certification from the electric timing device supplied by the American Automobile Association. But again, as one-way down-wind runs, the FICM refused to accept them in the international sense, and merely logged the results as "...the American records." As such, they remained unchallenged for the next decade.

During the summer and fall of 1926, Frank Weschler became involved in negotiations with the owners of Michigan Motor Company over the possible purchase by Indian of the manufacturing rights of the defunct Ace. While this group had been issuing press releases concerning the pending revival of the make, efforts at obtaining sufficient financing had been futile up to this point.

Indian, through Weschler's heroic efforts, was now in a very sound financial situation. Production since the 1921 crisis had been stabilized at between 7,500 and 8,500 annual units, a strong export market as well in place, and loyal Indian enthusiasts supported a modest but stable purchasing rate on the home market. With manufacturing efficiencies established, the company had a sizable balance of well over $800,000 in the treasury. At any rate, Weschler was at last able to purchase the Ace rights for $125,000, and shortly after a freight train load of tooling, dies, and finished and semi-finished parts arrived at the State Street factory.

THE GREAT DECLINE 1920-1930

Box bodied sidecar out-
fits enjoyed some popu-
larity in the late 1920's for
commercial delivery use.
The machine is a 37
cubic inch Indian Scout.
Leslie D. Richards

Theodore A. "Ted" Hodgdon, a young 1926 graduate of Northeastern University who had just joined Indian's Advertising Department, has left us a graphic picture of the integration of the Ace into the company's model range. The initial Aces were as assembled in 1924, but to rationalize production the engine was fitted to a modified Scout frame a year later. Introduced at the high retail price of $450, production was limited, the bulk of the small output being sold to law enforcement, as a four was ever the choice of officers having to spend long hours in the saddle.

In the fall of 1925, Leslie D. Richards was per-suaded by factory representatives to take over the franchise in Denver. Up to this point it had been held by Floyd Clymer, who had incorporated it with an Excelsior franchise in 1919. But Clymer had been neglecting his motorcycle business and sales in favor of promoting his famous hole-in-the-windshield automotive spotlight, and his Indian franchise was now being revoked. With Clymer's refusal to relinquish his premises or parts stock, Richards, with some financial help from Weschler, established what was soon to be one of Indian's most active far west dealerships, which he formally

opened in the spring of 1926.

At this point Indian was developing its 45 cubic inch version of the well established 37 cubic inch Scout to offer competition to the newly intro-duced 45 cubic inch Super-X. It was announced in the fall of 1926, for the 1927 sales season.

In 1927, one James A. Wright was instrumental in affiliating his company with the M&ATA. He was both the sales manager and a minority stockholder in the Mica Company of Albany, New York. This firm had been founded in 1920, and was in direct competition with the Geneto Company in supplying sparkplugs and carbon brush components for mag-netos and generators for automotive and industrial engines, and motorcycle components.

Wright joined Mica in 1925, and at once sought to expand the sale of products to both the manufacturers as well as the general trade. During the following year, when the company joined the M&ATA, he took an active role in its affairs. As an energetic and personable individual, he sought to expand both Mica's business as well as the promo-tion of the motorcycle trade. Traveling much of the eastern seaboard in sales promotion, he quickly built up a wide acquaintanceship within the motor-

THE GREAT DECLINE 1920-1930

Noted dealer, promoter and racer Floyd Clymer created his own publication in the 1920's to promote his line of motorcycles and accessory products. He later published "Cycle" magazine and a line of motorcycle repair manuals that still carry his name today.
Don Emde Collection

cycle industry.

The general condition of the AMA at this point had remained more or less static. A.B. Coffman, well aware of its problems, along with his own in attempting to carry on with inadequate financing, took his problems to a general meeting of the M&ATA Board of Directors held in Chicago in May of 1927. It was noted that there had been numerous complaints from various clubs and individuals promoting competition affairs, saying there had been too many delays in implementing requests for sanction. Often the meets were held before sanctions were even formally received. There were also numerous complaints from contestants that the receipt of awards and trophies was often months late. Coffman cited the lack of sufficient clerical help in his Chicago headquarters to properly handle the volume of mail.

In a prolonged three day meeting, it was decided to forgo for the present any more national motorcycle trade shows. The last one held the previous January in New York's Madison Square Garden had been sparsely attended. The only outstanding feature had been Indian's exhibit of a red painted Ace with Indian's transfers on the tanksides, and Arthur Lemon in attendance to greet Ace fans with the news of Springfield's acquisition of the manufacturing rights. Coffman, who had managed most of these shows since 1920, freely admitted that the lack of public interest in motorcycling had come to the point that the expenses to the industry involved were no longer worth the effort.

In the end, Coffman promised to make further attempts to communicate to both riders and dealers the need for enhanced AMA support, with a special effort being directed toward the clubs.

Meanwhile, Indian introduced a 45 cubic inch version of their long-running 37 cubic inch Scout for 1927. The Prince single was carried on, together with the new Indian Ace and Chief models, giving a five model range.

The 45 cubic inch four-cylinder Cleveland that replaced their two stroke model proved to be a failure. The T head configuration developed insufficient power to provide a speed of over 40 mph, which was only 16 mph faster than the two stroke which had been sold at over $100 less than the new model.

It has long been a historical mystery why L. E. Fowler, an experienced automotive designer and one time journalist, ever settled on such an archaic design. At any rate, Cleveland's management decided to try another design, and hired Everett M. De Long to develop a replacement.

Harley-Davidson's William Ottaway, with the

help of a newly hired speed tuner, Henry "Hank" Syvertsen, worked out a high performance variant of its veteran pocket value J type engine. It was based on the alcohol burning hill climb engine that had been developed in conjunction with Arthur Constantine in 1924, utilizing the crankcase design of the 1920-1921 overhead valve eight-valve racing engines. This modification provided a set of cams for each of the valves and enabled more latitude for speed tuning. This gave Harley-Davidson a range of six models for 1928, 61 and 74 cubic inch standard big twins; the two cam variants of the same; together with the side and overhead valve 21 cubic inch singles. The overhead valve model was in more limited production, however, as it was less suited for utility work and required much tinkering to keep its somewhat sketchily lubricated valve gear in adjustment.

Excelsior's top management ordered Arthur Constantine to update their two model range of the four-cylinder DeLuxe and the V-twin Super-X. The Deluxe especially needed attention, as it had been carried forward in Arthur Lemon's side valve form since its introduction in 1920. In the search for more power, the compression ratio had been progressively raised until the engine had lost some of its original reliability.

In the middle and late 1920's the country was enjoying unprecedented economic prosperity. With the war debt retired, the expansion of industry and a myriad of business concerns catering to an ever growing consumer demand, there were also extensive export demands for U.S. products all over the world. The only dark cloud on the horizon was the plight of the nation's farmers, whose income was curtailed by the competition from more cheaply produced foodstuffs from abroad.

The surviving motorcycle factories kept in close contact with their dealer outlets by means of traveling representatives whose job it was to keep their retailers informed of the latest technical developments at the factory, supply sales aids and advertising matter, as well as to keep management informed as to their overall status.

The commercial traveler had become a fixture on the American business scene following the industrial and business expansion after the Civil War. Before the days of sophisticated advertising and general communication, the personal contact between manufacturers and their retail outlets was logically served by direct communication. Possessing personality traits of both the Gypsy and the adventurer, an ongoing optimistic outlook needed to instill continuing confidence in his contacts, the commercial traveler needed the stamina

THE GREAT DECLINE 1920-1930

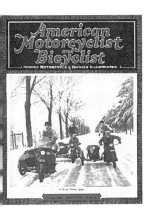

Don Emde Collection

to endure the interminable train rides as well as the loneliness of the often dingy commercial hotels that adjoined the far flung railroad stations of rural America. As a seemingly permanent character in the fabric of society's fanciful stories of the legendary erotic adventures of these worthies with casually encountered farmers' daughters, they became woven into American folklore.

Through the years, both the Davidsons and Frank Weschler were known to comment upon their relationships with their traveling representatives and the numerous problems encountered in their management. The Sales Departments usually projected an itinerary to be followed by the factory men with set dates of arrival at various locations. As a check on their activities, the Sales Manager or his assistant might often make a surprise visit to any given destination along the route to ascertain if the traveler was, in fact, covering his territory properly. In some cases, the representative was supposed to travel in a factory owned sidecar outfit, which afforded a means of carrying samples of accessories and personal baggage. Spot checks were often made to be sure such vehicles were not left at home in favor of a more comfortable car.

Another problem was the fact that in some instances the travelers brought along female companions, which were sometimes not their wives, in open defiance of factory policy. In most cases, however, the representatives were honest and upright and performed a valuable service in forming a close liaison between the dealers and the factory and did much to enhance their sales methods.

In the spring of 1927, a spearhead in the long feared invasion of foreign motorcycles occurred when Reginald "Reggie" Pink, an English immigrant and one time mechanic at Brown Brothers New York City Harley-Davidson agency, executed an import agreement for a number of prominent British makes and opened a showroom in the Bronx. Pink had, for a couple of seasons past, entered an opposed twin Douglas super sports machine in numerous local hill climbs and speed trials with creditable results. Other makes offered at one time or another included Norton, Velocette, Rudge, Triumph and Ariel. Pink no doubt concluded that, as the largest center of the nation's population, there would be sufficient iconoclastic motorcyclists who might be disposed to try a new approach to the sport.

At any rate, Pink's operation prospered until he closed the doors in 1945. There were no other foreign motorcycle importers known to be in operation during the 1920's, although a handful of them were reported to have been brought in by private

individuals directly from the factories.

In June of 1927, a change in the Indian Motorcycle Company's ownership occurred when the majority of the voting shares of preferred stock was acquired by Louis J. Bauer and his brother Charles. For some years the two had operated a successful machine tool manufacturing concern in Dayton, Ohio. Their acquisition of Indian was with the expressed intention to carry on with motorcycle production, together with the utilization of the unused space in the vast State Street factory for the manufacture of other products.

Frank J. Weschler was at once offered the position of general manager, although he was obviously to be replaced as president by Louis J. Bauer. In considering this offer, Weschler was reported as having been less than pleased with such a prospect. In retrospect, Indian's survival after the 1921 debacle had been due wholly to Weschler's heroic efforts. Following the 1923 reorganization, Indian production had been both stabilized and rationalized, the dealer organization had been strengthened, and an effective competition campaign had been maintained. In addition, profits had increased to the point that there was well over $800,000 in the treasury, which made possible the purchase of the manufacturing rights to the Ace which materially strengthened Indian's marketing position.

Before the Bauer incursion, Weschler had hoped to use at least a part of the accrued profits to purchase much needed new machine tooling as well as projected prototype work on updated models. Bauer differed from Weschler's projections by suggesting that Indian's surplus be utilized for diverse products, as well as for speculation in the stocks of outside companies, a common practice during the frantic economic expansion of the middle and late 1920's. It was at this point that Weschler decided to resign from the company and, according to associates, he simply "took a walk" on August 27th. His last official act occurred a few days previously when he met with Arthur Davidson, William Ottaway, and Ray E. Garner for the annual Harley-Davidson/Indian price and policy fixing meeting.

It is certain that those present learned of Weschler's decision before either the Bauers or anyone else at Springfield! During the next month Weschler was offered and accepted the presidency of the Baldwin Chain Company at nearby Pittsfield, which, along with Duckworth, supplied the driving chains for the domestic motorcycle industry.

While paradoxically a non-motorcyclist, Weschler nevertheless had been dedicated to the well being of the industry for nearly all of his adult

THE GREAT DECLINE 1920-1930

life. A person of unswerving honesty and resolute of purpose, he was also congenial with associates and competitors alike, and his kindness and consideration to all brought him universal respect and affection from others within the industry. As an ongoing member of both the AMA and the M&ATA, his influence was substantial within the industry until his untimely death in 1935.

Other events within the industry during 1927 saw the Schwinns order Arthur Constantine and his engineering staff at Excelsior to update the Henderson Four and Super-X models for the coming sales season. Harley-Davidson's top management began prototype testing of a new range of machines to replace the now dated, long running J series, Harley-Davidson's offering since 1914. It was planned to drop the overhead-inlet, side-exhaust "pocket valve" configuration in favor of side valve types. According to later statements by William Ottaway, the J cylinder configuration had become increasingly expensive to produce. While both the standard as well as the limited production of "two cam" models had been subjected to minor face lifting along the way and had been well received by Harley-Davidson enthusiasts, it was now thought best to inaugurate a new series of models.

At Indian, the Indian-Ace was being facelifted in consultation with Arthur Lemon, with improvements to the original 1919 Ace engine and an integration of its cycle parts with the current Scout as a rationalization of production. The 37 and 45 cubic inch Scout models were also scheduled for an updating by Charles B. Franklin.

L. E. Fowler's archaic four was being replaced at Cleveland with an entirely new machine of streamlined appearance and compact design that featured a four-cylinder 45 cubic inch motor based on William Henderson's original F head concept. As conceived by Everett O. De Long, it was essentially a machine of medium weight with an 80 mph top speed.

As a reflection of the now static condition of the domestic motorcycle industry, its attendant trade press had markedly declined, "The Motorcyclist and Bicyclist Illustrated," formerly "The Motorcycle and Bicycle Illustrated," as well as "Motorcycling" were greatly reduced in content and were now appearing quarterly. They were soon to disappear from the market, followed a couple of years later by "The New American Motorcyclist and Bicyclist," a one-time revival of "Motorcycling Illustrated," which ended up virtually in pamphlet form and folded in 1931.

The only really healthy trade press survivor in the late 1920's was the "Pacific Motorcyclist," for-

merly "Pacific Motorcyclist and Bicyclist," published in Los Angeles, as the principle center of motorcycle activities existed in the West. The magazine's position as an effective trade organ was somewhat diminished by the attitude of its Editor, John J. O'Connor. As an egocentric, self-styled elder statesman of domestic motorcycling, his flair for exaggeration and the dramatic seriously compromised normal journalistic integrity.

The net effect of the lack of effective journalism generally and the regional bias promoted by O'Connor tended to obscure the true position of the industry at home, and also kept the motorcycling public in ignorance of the international situation. Due to (rather than in spite of) the economic upheavals in both Great Britain and on the continent of Europe following the war, the motorcycle overseas had come into its own. In England motorcycling had become soaringly popular due to the need for basic transportation and the high cost of fuel. A secondary condition was its competition role that offered a healthy public diversion.

By 1929 there were nearly 750,000 motorcycles of all types registered in the United Kingdom, topping automobile registrations by a substantial margin. Many of these were sidecar outfits for both commercial and family use; the latter fulfilling the transportation requirements of a young family. Motorcycles had also come into widespread use on the Continent, although there was more of an emphasis on smaller capacity utility ride-to-work types.

The healthy state of the overseas industry, especially in Great Britain, had led to the development of an effective trade press. Two weekly journals, "Motorcycling" from Illiffe, and "The Motor Cycle" by the Temple Press, enjoyed a wide circulation from both reader interest as well as advertising support from the trade, and were able to adopt a strong independent position that in its objectivity enhanced the industry. Searching road tests of new models appeared in nearly every issue, as well as evaluations of accessories, clothing, etc., which enabled a reader or potential buyer to assess his own requirements, a condition that was almost never observed in the U.S. where the declining state of the industry was such that publishers were afraid of losing advertising revenue if any but lavish praise were bestowed on any new model or related product.

In late 1927 it became painfully apparent that all was not well within the AMA. A.B. Coffman, handicapped by lack of funding, the necessity to conduct his own business affairs, and the shortage of clerical help in his Chicago headquarters, found

UNITED STATES
ROYAL CORD
MOTORCYCLE BALLOON

THE GREAT DECLINE 1920-1930

Freddie Ludlow had a fascinating career on motorcycles. He raced dirt and board track events for both the Indian and Harley factories. He later focused on speed records, setting them at Daytona (seen here), Bonneville, and at various locations in Southern California. When his racing days were over, his love of motorcycling remained and he spent many years as a motorcycle policeman in the Pasadena, Ca. area.
A.F. Van Order Collection

himself unable to keep abreast of requests for sanctions and the prompt awarding of trophies. In January of 1928 he wrote to M&ATA President George Briggs, the Davidsons and James Wright about the present situation within the AMA along with his intention to resign his office.

In the meantime, John J. O'Connor launched a series of editorials in the "Pacific Motorcyclist" commenting on the deteriorating AMA situation. He suggested that in view of the difficulties in communication between the AMA clubs and appointed AMA referees and competition officials with the Chicago headquarters, that it might be advantageous for western motorcyclists to form their own association.

AMA President Briggs, who was suffering from ill health at the time, at once requested that James Wright ascertain O'Conner's intentions in the matter. Wright responded by taking O'Connor to task for taking a public stand against the AMA at a critical period in its existence, and suggested that he should at least have sought prior discussions with AMA and M&ATA officers before opening up the subject of forming a new association. He further commented that with the present AMA organization in a weakened state, splitting the country into two organized groups would undoubtedly result in a further deterioration of organized domestic motorcycling.

O'Connor, according to both Coffman and Wright, ignored Wright's communication, and proceeded to editorialize on the need for a western

organization, tentatively named the Federation of Western Motorcyclists.

While some AMA and M&ATA members were attracted to this proposal, many veteran motorcyclists who were acquainted with O'Conner personally were skeptical. O'Conner, in spite of his long career as a motorcycle journalist, was generally not well thought of by many of his contemporaries due to his long history of questionable financial undertakings. Their antipathy was further aroused when, in a subsequent editorial, he suggested that he himself act as the Competition Chairman for the proposed FWM. He further proposed that all appointments for a new set of contest officials for the western states, California, Oregon, Washington, Nevada and Idaho, which were to be included in the FWM, be undertaken.

O'Conner further augmented support for his proposal by printing letters from readers in the "Pacific Motorcyclist" who were favorable to FWM formation. Early trade supporters were Indian's western representative, Ray E. Garner and Paul A. Bigsby, a pioneer motorcyclist, skilled mechanic and tuner who had just joined Albert G. Crocker's newly acquired Indian franchise in Los Angeles, the latter having just given up the Indian factory branch in Kansas City. Bigsby was also a promoter of sorts having recently organized some races in the San Joaquin Valley.

To give further effect to his intent, O'Conner traveled through both California and Arizona, visiting as many motorcycle clubs as could be induced to convene for his benefit so that he might explain the details of his proposed FWM. In elaborating on its organization, he stated that his magazine would be designated as the official FWM publication, and that a $1 per year dues to be assessed each rider member would also include a year's subscription to the magazine. Sanctions for FWM competition events would be issued at fees varying from $5 to $25, according to the scope of the event, which would be collected by O'Conner.

R.B. Fairmarsh, "Pacific Motorcyclist" publisher, went along with the idea in its initial stages, but soon began to have doubts about giving it his unqualified support. Contemporaries have suggested that Fairmarsh always viewed O'Conner's various activities somewhat warily, noting his past reputation regarding financial matters. While the FWM would, if successful, undoubtedly increase the magazine's still modest subscription rate, it was noted that O'Conner himself was to have sole jurisdiction over the collection and dispersal of the funds.

While the proposed FWM aroused some interest among club members and others interested in

THE GREAT DECLINE 1920-1930

Theodore A. Hodgdon

Don Emde Collection

promoting competition events who had experienced difficulties in contacting the AMA headquarters, a number of prominent members of the trade voiced their disapproval. Both Hap Alzina and Dudley Perkins were among these, stating that the domestic industry was simply not strong enough to support two organizations. In defense of the FWM, O'Conner assured his critics that competition and/or AMA membership cards would be honored for any and all FWM events, and that he proposed friendly cooperation in all policy matters involving both groups.

Still unconvinced of the merits of the FWM, Alzina and Perkins contacted all of the dealers by means of personal mailings outlining their opinion that further attention should be given to strengthening the AMA rather than supporting a new splinter organization that was projected to be under the control of just one individual; namely, O'Conner.

In spite of substantial opposition from a number of influential Harley-Davidson and Indian dealers, joined now by Excelsior-Henderson distributor Tennant Lee, O'Conner managed to gain some interest in the FWM, and by the summer of 1928 he had sold about 200 memberships and issued sanctions for races in Los Angeles, Fresno, Lodi and Idora Park in Oakland.

It was at this juncture that Coffman submitted his resignation as AMA Competition Chairman to M&ATA President George Briggs, citing past administrative and financial problems together with his discouragement over the new threat to AMA unity from the FWM. Briggs induced him to carry on until he could call a meeting of the M&ATA Board of Directors to further discuss the future of the AMA. This conference was held in Chicago on August 3, 1928, and in addition to Wright representing the New York Mica Company, there were in attendance Frank Schwinn of Excelsior, Henry G. Alexander of Cleveland, Louis J. Bauer of Indian, and Arthur and Walter Davidson.

The agenda of the meeting included: a discussion of the future of the M&ATA, the administrative problems of the AMA, the selection of a new Competition Chairman, the matter of funding ongoing AMA activities, the possibility of the manufacturers sponsoring a trade magazine in the face of presently declining trade journalism, the need for enhanced trade advertising rather than excessive emphasis on competition, discount retail pricing to law enforcement buyers, and the stimulation of enhanced rider interest in AMA affairs.

In the matter of the M&ATA, it was suggested that the motorcycle industry might consider amalgamating with the automobile industry, now that

the trade suppliers no longer had a public showcase in the discontinued national motorcycle shows. The matter of selecting a new Competition Chairman was tabled pending more study by James Wright. The decline of both quality and content of trade journalism was noted, but Walter Davidson was firmly opposed to the manufacturers getting into the publishing business. He was also against any joint participation of the manufacturers in trade advertising, as suggested by Louis Bauer. Retail price cutting in favor of law enforcement buyers, as admitted by Frank Schwinn, was frowned upon by both Bauer and Walter Davidson.

In addition to an already crowded agenda, the group voted to accept Coffman's resignation as Competition Manager and AMA Secretary. Noted were both his refusal to continue in the office, as well as his ongoing inability to maintain a firm control over AMA affairs. In addition, George T. Briggs offered his resignation as AMA President, citing his ongoing health problems.

In noting James Wright's enthusiasm for promoting the organization's affairs, together with his efficient handling of numerous assignments given him by the ailing Briggs, he was nominated for the office of AMA President by Walter Davidson, who in the recent past had experienced an ongoing rapport with him. With his good relationships with the balance of the supplier-members, Wright was elected to the office by a unanimous ballot. At the same time, Arthur Davidson was similarly re-elected as Vice-President, although a sudden illness had prevented his attending this meeting.

It was ultimately decided, in concluding the session, that the financing of the AMA should be worked out among the manufacturers on a pro rata basis, and that the upgrading of both the administration and the scope of AMA activities was of the utmost importance.

Upon returning to Milwaukee, Walter Davidson wrote a memorandum of the meeting for the benefit of William A. and Arthur Davidson, William B. Harley, and T.A. Miller, then a principal shareholder. In later years, William Ottaway secured a copy of this memo that is still in existence.

In the meantime, Harley-Davidson's Engineering Department was testing prototypes of the previously mentioned side valve engines in view of replacing their long running pocket valve J series, together with a new 45 cubic inch side valve model that was to share its cycle parts with a new side valve 30.50 single. While the pocket valve 61 and 74 cubic inch J models had undergone continuous minor refinements during the past decade, the rather complex cylinder castings with integral

THE GREAT DECLINE 1920-1930

One of the "mega-stars" of the period was Otto Walker. He won numerous events on the big board tracks, dirt tracks, and even set speed records at Daytona Beach, Fl. riding this 61 cubic inch pocket-valve Harley.
A.F. Van Order Collection

heads was becoming increasingly more expensive to produce.

Arthur Constantine at Excelsior was putting the finishing touches on an updated Super-X 45, which was to have an optional 61 cubic inch model, as well as his newly designed "K" Model fours that were now featuring the original F head configuration of William Henderson.

Everett M. De Long had already completed his new Cleveland 61 cubic inch four, a very compact design that also was based on the original Henderson formula.

Indian's Charles B. Franklin had just restyled the 1927 45 inch Scout that was now designated as the 101. As an attractive dual purpose utility and sporting mount, it was to attract some public attention within the somewhat lethargic motorcycle market.

In spite of the almost instant acceptance of the 101, all was not well at Indian. The Bauer's program to diversify Indian's offerings had not fared well. The program was to include a shock absorber to be fitted to the leaf type springs of contemporary automobiles; a light car designed by Louis' son Jack, powered with an Indian Chief engine-gear unit; and an outboard marine engine.

With endless unforeseen delays and numerous production problems, these new projects were rapidly sapping Indian's cash reserves. Worse still, motorcycle production was being impeded, right when the popular 101 Scout was attracting numer-

ous new buyers. Perhaps a more serious blow was the continuing desertion of a number of Indian dealers, who for the past year had seen the decline of motorcycle production and saw a substantial number of orders for the Scouts not being filled.

In the meantime, James Wright, in seeking a replacement for A.B. Coffman, was seriously considering appointing one Earl C. (E.C.) Smith as AMA Competition Chairman and AMA Secretary. A native of Ohio, Smith had received a common school education and was later a salesman for a petroleum company and also had an interest in an automobile accessory business. While not known as an active motorcyclist, he had shown an early interest in former FAM activities in the Ohio area, and had been an official FAM referee beginning in 1914. During the early 1920's he had given further support to the M&ATA-AMA reorganization, and had acted as both a competition referee and a race promoter in both Ohio and Indiana. He possessed a wide acquaintanceship within the industry, including prior contacts with Wright and, in fact, had already broached the subject of being a candidate for Coffman's position. Wright had been impressed with Smith as a possible candidate, not only for his long interest in motorcycling activities, but also for his reputation for honesty and for being a somewhat aggressive and forthright individual.

Wright subsequently had several conferences with Smith that fall in the matter. Also, Smith conferred with Coffman concerning details of the position and heard Coffman's description of the many problems he had encountered during both his tenure of office with the FAM as well as the AMA. Wright also conferred with the Davidsons, Schwinn, and Henry Alexander concerning Smith's proposed appointment. This was accepted and, on October 15, 1928, Smith was formerly appointed as Secretary of the AMA and Chairman of its competition committee.

The salary arrangement with Smith included $400 per month with flexible per diem payments for travel and a $50 monthly allowance for office expenses. To cover this, and to retire a $1,500 deficit from the past year, the representatives of the four manufacturers agreed to subsidize the AMA's financial obligations. This was to be a temporary expedient to the hoped-for resurgence of the AMA's rider support. Harley-Davidson now enjoyed the largest dealer representation, due in part to Indian's past and current financial difficulties, coupled with the fact that both Excelsior and Cleveland had always occupied a minority status in such representation. Because of this, it was decided to pro-rate the subsidization of each accordingly on

The Great Decline 1920-1930

a varying scale. Harley-Davidson would contribute $3,500; Indian $2,500; Excelsior $1,500; and Cleveland $500.

In addition, Harley-Davidson executed a parallel agreement with Smith to serve as their part time publicity representative, taking the place of the veteran Crolius S. Lacey who was retiring, at a salary of $200 per month. While this action could be construed as a conflict of interest, it was entered into with the full knowledge of James Wright as well as the rest of the manufacturer's representatives, who, according to Wright's later statements, were in agreement that the strengthening of Smith's financial position could also enhance his effectiveness within the AMA.

Critics of both the AMA and Harley-Davidson in later years took exception to the latter's majority position within the AMA hierarchy. Some took the position that the Davidsons took advantage of Indian's then-weakened financial and marketing situation. This was not the case, however, as the whole matter was undertaken with the agreement of all of the principals.

Following the October meeting, Smith met with Coffman in order to effect an orderly transfer of authority, and all of the current AMA and FAM records were shipped from Chicago to Smith's office in Columbus. Included were two standard four-drawer filing cabinets containing Coffman's extensive collection of catalogs and sales literature relating to dozens of now defunct motorcycle manufacturers, along with originals and copies of Coffman's voluminous correspondence having to do with past FAM and AMA matters.

Shortly afterwards Smith mailed copies of a lengthy statement to the remnants of the trade press, as well as to current paid up AMA members and clubs. In this he outlined goals for a strengthened and reorganized AMA. He also extended his compliments to Coffman in recognition of his past two decades of service to domestic motorcycling. Included was a brief statement from Coffman, extending his compliments to Smith along with a plea of augmented membership support of Smith's efforts, which were now to be handled as a full time proposition.

The current reduced circumstances of the AMA were reflected in the fact that the paid up membership had dwindled to 4,200, with only 64 AMA chartered clubs remaining on the roles. At once Smith opened an office in a residence at 252 North High Street in Columbus, that had been converted for this purpose. With a staff of one, Alice G. Brimmer, Smith inaugurated his revitalization campaign on January 1, 1929.

In noting that racing and, most particularly, hill climbing were currently well established, Smith gave first priority to building club activities to strengthen organized motorcycling, along with a public relations campaign to gain acceptance of motorcycling activities among the general public. In order to implement this, Smith took to the road that spring in a sidecar outfit supplied by Harley-Davidson, along with a motion picture projector and a collection of motorcycling films loaned by the Firestone and Goodyear Tire Companies. His strategy was to visit the established clubs in various areas and solicit their help in contacting individual motorcyclists in adjacent areas for the purpose of organizing additional clubs. In expanding his contacts, Smith sent out quarterly newsletters from Columbus to a hopefully growing list of established clubs and presently unaffiliated members soliciting their support.

At a meeting of the M&ATA manufacturers held that summer in Chicago, Smith was able to report some progress, along with the suggestion that the manufacturers increase their advertising coverage in the general media. The Davidsons were particularly supportive in this suggestion, and were openly critical of the other manufacturers who, up to this point, had not emulated Milwaukee in promoting their products in nationally circulated magazines.

A new dimension in motorcycle sport was introduced in the spring of 1929, in the form of short track racing, which had been inaugurated in New Zealand a couple of seasons before. One of its principal exponents, an Australian named Lloyd B. "Sprouts" Elder, had taken an exhibition team to South America the preceding fall in the hope of introducing it there. Elder brought his team to California and established a circuit that included Los Angeles, Fresno, Emeryville and Oakland. The author attended several races at Oakland's Idora Park during that summer, where Elder had a track laid out around the perimeter of the baseball stadium.

This form of racing was conducted on a track that could be either flat in its surface or slightly banked, and required the use of very lightweight machines. As contrasted with straight line operation, the theory of broadsliding the machine against centrifugal forces was employed, the rider "crossing over" the steering and supporting his weight largely on a steel plated boot on the turns. Specially prepared ultralight British Douglas and Rudge machines were raced initially, a number of which were imported by Elder, the class being based on overhead valve 30.50 engines.

Motorcycle Equipment Company of New York was a leading accessory supplier in the early days.
Don Emde Collection

THE GREAT DECLINE 1920-1930

The AMA Competition Committee approved the sport, but specified that 45 cubic inch side valve American machines were also eligible for competition. This was rather a futile gesture, however, as the Yankee 45's, even with their high torque characteristics, were no match for the ultralight single-cylinder Rudges or light twin Douglases. A later Class A designation allowing alcohol fuel eliminated American machines entirely.

After 1930, when the earlier Rudges and Douglases came to the end of their days, the newly developed J.A. Prestwich 500 cc overhead valve motors in specially built frames dominated the sport.

While the flat track or speedway competition was nominally governed by a skeleton set of AMA rules, promoters later formed a Speedway Association which worked out their own formula.

E.C. Smith's early contact with John O'Conner's FWM, following his initial membership and club organizational journey through the Midwest, took the form of a conciliatory letter to O'Conner, wishing the new group well and offering reciprocal competition between AMA and FWM cardholders. While most of the M&ATA members had at once taken a dim view of O'Conner's move in forming a rival organization, they could appreciate Smith's political expediency in taking a wait-and-see attitude, as the FWM was already showing organizational problems.

While O'Conner still enjoyed substantial support from Paul A. Bigsby in the Los Angeles area, Ray E. Garner in San Francisco, and Perry Abbott in Portland, there were now certain apparent deficiencies in his administration. It was noted that his approval in sanctions was often late and that he frequently allowed competition events to be scheduled on concurrent dates in adjacent areas. Aside from the usual $10 fee, he frequently acted as the Chief Judge and Referee himself, enlisting unpaid volunteer help in running the events. These volunteers were inexperienced and inaccurate in recording lap times and winning and placing sequences. While O'Conner was ultimately able to sell about 300 memberships, the news content of the "Pacific Motorcyclist" deteriorated in favor of constant editorial emphasis in support of FWM organizational affairs, along with lavish praises of the implied growing scope of its activities.

In the meantime, the fortunes of the Indian Company went from bad to worse. The Bauer's campaign to popularize their patent shock absorber failed to penetrate the automobile accessory market, in spite of an expensive sales effort that involved hiring a staff of salesmen to promote it. The light car

project was terminated due to technical problems with the fitting of a Chief power unit, and the outboard motor introduction received a negative response from the dealers, the majority of whom were not located adjacent to navigable waterways.

Indian motorcycle production had been reduced to only three models: the Chief, Four, and 101 Scout; the former now as a 74 cubic inch. The 61 model had been dropped in 1927, along with the Prince Single. The output of these models had been cut back due to the firm's ongoing financial difficulties, in spite of the fact that there was a substantial demand for the 101.

With cash reserves all but exhausted, Indian's motorcycle production nearly ground to a halt. The day was saved in several ways by Hap Alzina, who raised cash from San Francisco Bay area bankers to fund company payrolls (after long-suffering Springfield bankers refused to advance further short term credit) and made hurried train trips to the factory with the needed funds.

In the summer of 1929, the Bauers surveyed the wreckage they had wrought and called it a day, surrendering their majority holdings of preferred stock at thirty cents on the dollar. A new group entered the picture that included one Charles A. Levine. This group selected Russell J. Waite, a current minority stockholder, as President. He was a member of a wealthy and socially prominent family in Charleston, South Carolina. With Waite and his family's long standing political connection in that state, the Levine group may well have thought that he could bring some prestige to the company. For some reason, the Bauers retained their seats on the Board of Directors, although they were now in the minority.

Waite took office on July 10, 1929, and at once issued a statement that the company was in a state of reorganization. Faced with a greatly reduced output of motorcycles, along with a badly decimated dealer organization, Waite saw the need for drastic measures for recovery. He offered James Wright the position of General Sales Manager, with carte blanche authority and a generous expense account to implement whatever steps he considered necessary to revitalize the company. Waite had been impressed with Wright's organizational abilities during his initial efforts with the M&ATA and AMA and, as an incentive, offered him certain options in the future purchase of Indian stock. Wright at once accepted and, upon resigning from the New York Mica Company, took office on September 1, 1929.

The annual sub-rosa price-and-policy fixing meeting between Indian officials and the

THE GREAT DECLINE 1920-1930

Davidsons took place on September 20 in New York City, Waite leading the delegation from Springfield in company with James Wright. Walter Davidson was accompanied by Alfred Rich Child, who was currently on his annual visit to Milwaukee from Japan.

While the customary agreements were hammered out, both Child and Wright later told the author that the meeting was somewhat strained, as the rough-hewn Davidson and the aristocratic Waite were of conflicting personalities. Davidson later referred to Waite as "...a stuffed shirt," with Waite characterizing Davidson as "...defensibly boorish."

Later that month, Henry G. Alexander announced that Cleveland was suspending production of their latest 61 cubic inch four-cylinder model until further notice. The reason cited was that the company was undergoing a financial reorganization pending a projected merger with the Huppmobile Motor Company. The Cleveland Motor Company had been organized in that industrial Ohio city in 1913, to manufacture the Chandler automobile which was developed as an assembled model but featuring their own engines and a number of advanced design concepts that put it a cut above many of its contemporaries.

The Cleveland two stroke utility motorcycle had been launched in 1915 from the same factory, and produced about 5,000 machines per year until 1925, half of which were exported.

The two four-cylinder models had been less successful, but Alexander noted privately that their lack of sales of the improved 45 and 61 cubic inch models had been due to the lack of dealer representation; caused in part by the 1923 gentlemen's agreement between Milwaukee and Springfield limiting the offering of outside makes of machines. Alexander further stated that a hoped-for reintroduction of motorcycles would occur later the following year.

On October 24, 1929, the notorious Black Friday that had been predicted by some economists occurred when the country's speculative bubble burst and the New York Stock Exchange suspended trading. The post war expansion that had gone into high gear after 1922, and reached fantastic proportions after 1925, had touched off unbridled speculation in the stock market. This was fueled by the late growing practice of buying on margin; i.e., the purchase of stock issues with a small down payment, the balance to be forthcoming on demand. But with nearly 60 million dollars outstanding in war debts due to the failure of the war-ravaged Allied powers to keep up their repayment, a shortage of hard currency in the U.S. resulted. This,

coupled with an almost frantic rush to purchase stock issues that were artificially spiraling in value on margin, ultimately led to disaster when there were no more funds available to shore them up. Hundreds of millionaires (on paper) were wiped out overnight, taking a number of banking institutions along with them.

The initial effect of the crash was not immediately felt, except for a gradual deflation of the dollar. Most business firms adopted a cautious attitude regarding any future expansion, prodded by the majority of the banking institutions, which at once began a critical assessment of their loan portfolios.

On January 25, 1930, E.C. Smith called a special meeting of the principal M&ATA members. This included the following manufacturers' representatives: the Davidsons, James Wright, Frank Schwinn and the now dejected Henry G. Alexander, together with representatives from Firestone, Goodyear, Delco, Budd and Kelsey-Hayes, Genetco, and a few others at the AMA headquarters in Columbus.

Overlooking for the moment the stock market debacle, he expressed cautious optimism concerning the future of the industry, as well as encouragement from his recent AMA membership drive which had brought the membership roster up to 5,800 with 93 chartered clubs now on the roles. He expressed the hope that the other manufacturers would follow the Davidsons' suggestion that the industry should increase their advertising schedules to include more of the general media. He further extended his condolences to Wright and Alexander concerning their current financial difficulties, as did other members present.

Harley-Davidson had already launched their updated 1930 sales program with a five model range, their largest offering to date. This included the side-valve and overhead valve 21 singles, a new 30.50 model that shared its cycle chassis with the newly designed side valve 45 twin, together with the new top-of-the-line "V" series of Big Twin model side valvers in commercial, standard, and sporting versions, along with optional modifications for their use with both passenger and commercial sidecar bodies.

The largest group of Harley-Davidson customers who favored big V-twins were generally less than happy with the new V series, as these were handicapped in their performance by being substantially heavier than the former well proven, long running J series, but actually developed slightly less power. These had been subject to minor improvements through the past decade, the 1929 models having beefed up frames, improved

108

THE GREAT DECLINE 1920-1930

Shrimp Burns of Oakland, Ca. was one of the most aggressive riders of his day. A popular rider, he rode very hard and recorded many victories during a career which unfortunately ended with Burns' death in a race at Toledo, Ohio.
A.F. Van Order Collection

cylinder finning, and a new throttle controlled lubrication system. Then too, the small production two cam high performance 61 and 74 in. models had already gained a place of honor among many Milwaukee enthusiasts, and there were many requests from both riders and dealers that this model be continued.

William Ottaway perhaps inadvertently added fuel to the flames in his close contacts with many "two cam" enthusiasts. A man of methodical mind and a cautious engineering innovator, he kept a meticulous journal attendant to his engine modifications, and worked out a set of recorded graphs of performance tables and horsepower readings. One set of these showed both power and torque readings for the two cammers, showing that both exceeded the readings for the V series engines. He had sent out a number of copies of these to two cam speed tuners upon their requests. When Walter Davidson heard of the matter, he was understandably furious, and castigated Ottaway for giving out what he considered company secrets, not to mention the downgrading of a succeeding model. A few copies of these are still in existence, highly treasured by veteran two cam devotees.

The new V series introduction also received a further setback when it was found that its light pattern flywheels, installed to enhance the machine's acceleration, were of insufficient weight to dampen its excessive vibration. While acceleration was improved, the machine shook so badly that it was distinctly uncomfortable at speeds over 50 mph. In

response to a storm of protests from buyers, the engineering department instituted a crash program of redesign, and heavier flywheels together with enlarged engine cases were soon dispatched to the dealers. In the end, a total of 1,326 machines required rebuilding, a fact not appreciated by the dealers who received no compensation for the shop time involved.

The new 45 fared only a little better with its light pattern frame and gear box being somewhat overstressed for the twin-cylinder engine. In order to fit the engine within the single's frame, the generator was positioned along the axis of the front cylinder and driven by a skew gear. This unorthodox fitting led to the popular designation for the model as "...the three-cylinder Harley." This did not work well in practice, as the mechanism was subject to failure due to inadequate bearing surfaces. The long stroke engine also did not develop as much power as was anticipated, and proved to be no match in its performance when compared to the already popular Indian 101 Scout. Harley-Davidson enthusiasts generally considered that both models had been launched without adequate prototype testing.

The company's only solace at this time was the selling of the rights to manufacture the V series Big Twins in Japan to Alfred Rich Child for $75,000, which partially made up for the losses incurred in its initial failure.

During this same period Indian was scarcely more fortunate. Plagued by cash shortages and a problems in motorcycle production which hampered the sales of the popular 101 Scout, its dealership network was universally disenchanted with the prospect of having to market automobile shock absorbers, a failed light car, and an odd-sized outboard marine engine. In the interval, newly hired Sales Manager James Wright was hurriedly crisscrossing the country in an effort to shore up the company's now defecting dealerships.

Indian's market for its four-cylinder model, its engine a slightly updated 1919 design which was sold mostly to law enforcement bodies for suburban police patrol, was also being seriously challenged by Excelsior's updated K model, which was a vastly superior machine. In point of fact, Arthur Constantine's updated V-twin and four models proved to have few, if any, teething problems when compared to its larger rivals.

On the competition side, the picture had changed considerably in the late 1930's. With the deterioration of the board tracks and the decline of public interest in horse track racing, the emphasis had come to center on hill climbing. After Harley-

THE GREAT DECLINE 1920-1930

Frank J. Weschler (1879-1935) was the general manager of Indian after 1916, until he served as President from 1923 through 1927.
Indian Motorcycle Company

Davidson's withdrawal from its former extensive racing program, its principal stars, such as Jim Davis, Ralph Hepburn, Fred Ludlow, M.K. Fredericks, and others, saw their former venues disappearing. The last ever board track event took place in the spring of 1928, at New Hampshire's Rockingham Board oval when M.K. Fredericks made a solo run against time on a 61 cubic inch factory machine for a last ever record of 120.2 mph. With the track already in disrepair, a group of local club members had refurbished its surface for a final event. A few days later, the track was dismantled in favor of a new real estate development.

To cater to the new interest, which now had its major support from various clubs catering to sporting riders, all three factories built a limited number of special hill climb machines. Most were, by this time, 45 cubic inch V-twin models modified for burning alcohol fuels, which could be employed for both 45 and 80 cubic inch Class A events. Indian supplied about two dozen machines based on their 45's first assembled in 1925. Excelsior fielded a new 45 overhead valve designed jointly by Arthur Constantine and Joe Petrali, who had lately been employing his self-taught design theories. Harley-Davidson also fielded a like number of 45's, augmented by a few 21 cubic inch overhead valve specials which formed a new class, with Fred Reiber from the Midwest being their principal exponent.

The seesaw domination of various aspects of sport by the three surviving makes during the 1920-1930 decade was due more to the amount of money that the factories were willing to devote to competition rather than to the marked superiority of any one make. Harley-Davidson's major victories from 1920 through 1921 were largely due to vast expenditures lavished on their Wrecking Crew. Indian's resurgence of prosperity after 1922 saw the Redskins dominant in all but the 21 Class, which they ignored. Harley-Davidson's eventual interest in this class made them dominant within it, to the exclusion of participation in the larger categories. Excelsior did little during this period after their early withdrawal from the small displacement class in 1923, although it allowed Joe Petrali to win a few records with their newly introduced 45 Class in 1925 and 1926. Harley-Davidson practically withdrew from competition during 1928 and 1929 in favor of developing new bread-and-butter models, allowing Indian to take all of the big nationals during those years.

Eugene "Gene" Rhyne came forward to take all the national hill climbs for Excelsior in 1930. Aside from the factory specials allotted to expert riders,

there were many hill climb machines built up by handy owners and dealer's mechanics for less important events promoted by local clubs. E.C. Smith was hard pressed to enforce his self-centered campaign to police these events and enforce his edict against "outlaw" or non-sanctioned meets. A particular problem was that many AMA cardholders competed in both by entering under assumed names.

The emerging popularity of short or flat track racing during this period was largely due to the fact that a course could be easily and cheaply laid out on any level field with only a few hours work with a road grader. This obviated the complications and expense of hiring the use of a fairgrounds track, where promotional costs could be considerable when balanced against an uncertain gate receipt.

In the meantime, support for John J. O'Conner's FWM was waning. His grandiloquent promises of large scale promotions and efficient management of races and hill climbs were not fulfilled. In addition, he attempted to oversee each event with a minimum of referees and officials, and it was noted that these were less effective than the former AMA appointees had been. In addition, promised prizes and trophies were seldom awarded, if at all. It soon was generally considered that O'Conner was managing the FWM as a one man show for his own financial gain.

In the meantime, R.A. Fairmarsh was becoming disenchanted with the whole affair, most particularly as the support for the "Pacific Motorcyclist and Bicyclist" was waning. Most serious was the diminishing advertising revenue. This was due not only to the falling away of trade support, but for the past two or three seasons support from the bicycle trade had also fallen. Adult bicycling activity had steadily declined, due both to the ever-increasing automotive sales as well as constant improvement in suburban and urban public transport. The cycle manufacturers were now concentrating on the youthful market, which had been growing in recent years, and now advertising in youth oriented magazines such as "St. Nicholas," "The Youth's Companion," and "Boy's Life." Wishing now to concentrate his efforts on other unrelated trade publications included in his roster, the magazine was put up for sale. In October 1930, it was purchased by the Western Journal Publishing Company of Los Angeles for the negotiated price of $4,500. It had been noted within the trade that its circulation was "...below 15,000 copies per year," but was actually far lower than this figure.

Arthur E. Welch, a newspaper reporter since the turn of the century on various Southern California publications, had also been retained as

THE GREAT DECLINE 1920-1930

an advertising salesman since 1908 for "Westways," the official publication of the California State Automobile Association, an affiliate of the American Automobile Association. In 1918, he entered the general publishing field with his own company, the Western Journal Publishing Company, with some financial backing from his wife's mother. In addition to his sales activities for "Westways," he was soon publishing a magazine for the building trade, "The Building Contractor of California," along with another called, "Architectural Products." In addition, he composed catalogs, advertising material, and brochures for other business concerns. With a long standing interest in automotive affairs, he reasoned that a motorcycling magazine could be a welcome addition for added revenue. While he also included motorcycling as an additional project, he was actually a non-rider; his sole contact with the sport being as an occasional sidecar passenger.

O'Conner had originally sought to purchase the magazine but had lacked the necessary capital. He had previously sought privately to discourage some other potential buyers, and when Welch and Fairmarsh appeared to be in their final negotiations, he filed legal action against Fairmarsh, claiming that the latter through a verbal agreement had tendered him a half interest in the magazine, and demanded one half of the proceeds of the sale. O'Conner had no actual grounds for this action, but Fairmarsh ultimately bought him off for $350 so that he could conclude the matter with Welch.

Welch planned to strengthen the magazine by expanding its neglected Eastern coverage. He engaged in new freelance reporters to supply news from that area, expanded the advertising content, and distanced himself from any association with the new defunct FWM, whose numerous problems had actually turned many trade people as well as riders against it.

Paul A. Bigsby, once a staunch FWM supporter, inadvertently helped to turn the tide. He now advocated a general return to the AMA fold, used his still valid AMA Competition card to promote some short track races in Fresno and Lodi, as well as organizing the Los Angeles Forty-five Inch Club. This Club was made up of sporting riders who were mainly 101 Scout enthusiasts.

With O'Conner now safely out of the picture, Welch took personal charge of the magazine, although the name of a young assistant named Howard B. Rose was placed on the masthead as Editor.

Meanwhile, the situation at Indian had gotten worse. The group in control, headed by Charles A.

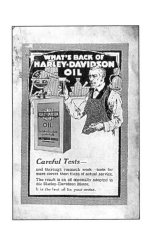

Levine, had been attempting to raise money through Indian's assets to gain control of an aviation company on Long Island to build airplanes based on the successful designs of Guiseppi Bellanca, several of which had completed long distance flights. With the redundant position of Indian's cash flow, Levine had actually ordered some of the machine tooling sold, portions of which were actually being removed from the production area. News of this at once came to the attention of one of Indian's prominent minority shareholders, Francis I. duPont, who, in company with two of his younger brothers, Eleuthere' Paul and Archibald, had invested in Indian stock following the 1923 reorganization. Francis I., who was also the owner of a then-prestigious Wall Street stockbrokerage firm, at once considered the possible damage to the company, and immediately dispatched E. Paul to Springfield. E. Paul was able to put a stop to the removal of Indian's tooling on legal grounds. In the meantime, Francis I. had become aware of Indian's now precarious condition through its recent mismanagement, and at once conferred with E. Paul to consider what steps could be taken to save the company.

Succeeding duPonts, such as Lammot and T. Coleman, who headed the company during the Civil War, utilized their now enormous profits to diversify the firm's efforts into other areas, such as chemicals and petroleum products. After the turn of the century and the accelerated demand for munitions of war, the company, under Pierra S. III, diversified into one of the world's largest multinational organizations whose holdings included General Motors.

E. Paul and his sons were all interested in mechanics, the former having obtained his degree in engineering from the University of Pennsylvania. As a boyhood tinkerer, he built his own version of a motor bicycle in 1900, using a Steffy designed version of a De Dion-Bouton engine.

As an offshoot of the family petrochemical and explosives empire, E. Paul also owned the Ball Grain Powder Company, along with other properties acquired through inheritance, together with a blue chip stock portfolio managed through his brother's brokerage firm. In 1915, he organized an engineering firm in Wilmington, Delaware that manufactured small gasoline engines for launches used by the U.S. Navy in World War I. In 1919, he organized the duPont Motor Company which manufactured automobiles. As products assembled largely from bought-out components, they were nevertheless of outstandingly high quality and were built in small numbers for the carriage trade.

THE GREAT DECLINE 1920-1930

In his analysis of the Indian situation, E. Paul considered the company's vast unused facilities that could be utilized for other products, although he did not, as others had done, visualize the sacrificing of the motorcycle business or its subordination in favor of other products.

While duPont was considering the acquisition of Indian, in consultation with Francis I., the control of Indian passed from the Levine group to another which was controlled by one Norman T. Bolles, who was elected President as a replacement for Russell Waite. Bolles described himself as an engineer but, in reality, he was better known as a stock and securities manipulator with an extremely shady reputation from his previous dealings on Wall Street.

At that time, Indian's financial structuring consisted of 100,000 shares of preferred stock that was nominally in the hands of the Board of Directors, which paid 6% per annum, with 1,000,000 shares of no par common stock that was owned by the public at large. Bolles issued an additional 10,000 shares of common stock, and proceeded to inflate its value through a "bull pool" promotion.

During a number of shareholders' lawsuits against Indian's management, the duPonts went about buying up as many shares as was necessary to gain majority control. This was effected in June 1930, when E. Paul was elected company President, with a new Board of Directors that included his brother Francis I. A holding company was then organized by E. Paul, called the "Indu" Corporation (a contraction of Indian and duPont) into which the Ball Grain Powder Company and other duPont industrial holdings were integrated, which was then, of course, registered under the very liberal laws of Delaware, a state which was politically controlled in those days by various branches of the duPont family.

The new owners were now faced with the monumental task of reorganizing the company, strengthening its production methods, and rebuilding its shattered dealer force that was seriously demoralized by the depredations of the past three administrations.

Norman T. Bolles' activities regarding the watering of Indian's stock, along with his subsequent relationships with other companies, came under the scrutiny of a Congressional investigation in 1932, chaired by Fiorella H. La Guardia. Bolles subsequently served a term in the federal prison at Atlanta as the result of his illegal stock manipulations with Indian and other companies.

F. Gardiner Coffelt, Vice President and General Manager of the Highland National Bank of Springfield made the comment that he had "never, in twenty-five years of experience, ever encountered a worse gang of crooks than had taken over Indian." As it was, public confidence in Indian was all but destroyed.

During the initial period of the duPont reorganization of Indian, the Hupp Motor Company of Detroit had taken over the Cleveland Motor Company the year before. They announced that both the Chandler and Cleveland cars were to be discontinued, that the four-cylinder motorcycle would not be revived, and only the smaller Huppmobile models would be assembled in the Cleveland plant. This was due to the sudden drop in automobile sales following the stock market crash, which naturally was most severe on the smaller manufacturers. Hupp attempted to sell the manufacturing rights and tooling of the motorcycles, but there were no takers, and the small motorcycle production force was disbanded. In all, less than 500 of each of the 45 and 61 cubic inch Clevelands were ever made.

Everett M. De Long undertook freelance engineering projects when he appeared to be succumbing to the effects of alcoholism. It was later discovered that he was actually suffering mental derangement from the effects of an inoperable brain tumor, and he died hopelessly insane in 1934. A very tragic ending for a highly respected and talented automotive engineer.

During 1929 and 1930, E.C. Smith's energetic promotion of the AMA in both membership and organized club recruitment brought substantial results, due in the main (according to Smith's own statements to the M&ATA Board of Directors) to his extensive travels across the country to personally visit both private riders as well as dealers and trade members. The cause was aided by the help of many prominent dealers of the day who realistically supported the premise that without a formal organization of motorcyclists generally, both the industry and sport were doomed. Prominent among these were Brown Brothers (Harley-Davidson) in the Bronx, Eugene Shillingford (Indian) in Philadelphia, P.T. Bullard (Indian) in Atlanta, George Gonzales (Indian) in New Orleans, Knuths (Harley-Davidson) in Milwaukee, to name a few.

On the West Coast W.J. Rhule (Harley-Davidson) in San Diego, Rich Budelier (Harley-Davidson) and Albert G. Crocker (Indian) in Los Angeles, Hap Alzina (Indian), Dudley Perkins (Harley-Davidson) and Claude Salmon (Harley-Davidson) in the San Francisco Bay area, and Nelson Bettencourt (Harley-Davidson) in Vallejo.

THE GREAT DECLINE 1920-1930

The biggest race to win in the teens and early twenties was the Dodge City 300-mile event. Held in the hot July sun, the race was the annual showdown between Indian and Harley-Davidson. This shot taken in 1920 shows the Harley team that was on hand that year. From left to right are team manager Bill Ottoway, Maldwin Jones, Ralph Hepburn, Freddie Ludlow, Otto Walker, Ray Weishar, Jim Davis, and Harley engineer Hank Syvertsen. Weishar, previously shown with his pig, is holding what looks like a coyote in this photo!
A.F. Van Order Collection

These latter dealers were particularly supportive, especially after the divisive efforts of the new discredited John J. O'Conner and his ill-fated FWM.

These, and many other dealers, aided the cause by promoting AMA affiliation to their customers, participating in or even sponsoring local clubs, and in inaugurating or participating in the promotion of competition events. Smith was able to report a nearly 15% rise in AMA support to the M&ATA Directors in the summer of 1930. While the sobering news of the recent stock market crash was still fresh, the country generally had yet to feel the full weight of an economic recession.

A sour note in AMA progress was noted that summer, however, involving Leslie D. Richards, Walter W. Whiting, Floyd Clymer and H.D. Cooper in the Rocky Mountain area adjacent to Denver. Clymer, a former Excelsior exponent, after winning a National Championship at Dodge City in 1915 for Harley-Davidson, accepted their franchise in Denver in 1916. The agreement was cancelled in 1918, following a policy dispute between Walter Davidson and Clymer. Another pioneer motorcyclist, Walter W. Whiting, was awarded the dealer-

ship. Clymer than took on an Indian dealership, but his inactivity in motorcycling attendant to his marketing of his once famous hole-in-the-windshield automobile spotlight caused Indian to revoke his agreement in 1925, and awarded it to Richards, who was then utilizing Indian sidecar outfits in a local parcel delivery operation.

Richards and Whiting shared a mutual interest in promoting lightweight motorcycles for both utility and entry level riders, and each sold substantial numbers of Harley-Davidson and Indian singles. Although business rivals, Richards and Whiting became warm personal friends, and acted together to sponsor two local motorcycle clubs as well as to be indirectly responsible for the formation of three more clubs in areas outside of Denver.

In this favorable climate, motorcycling interest in the Denver area was high, stimulated in part by growing numbers of entry level riders buying singles, with active club participation that ultimately resulted in 100% AMA membership. At this juncture, Walter Davidson informed Whiting that the factory could not countenance his friendly cooperation with Richards, as he considered it bad policy

113

THE GREAT DECLINE 1920-1930

The riders are being bump-started for the 1921 Dodge City 300-mile race. Once the engines were running, the riders did one lap to get into a formation, thus starting like a car race with a "flying start."
A.F. Van Order Collection

Hap Alzina
Don Emde Collection

for Harley-Davidson dealers to be friendly with their opposite numbers handling competing makes, to quote "...especially Indian!" Whiting took strong exception to this, stating that his past cooperation with Richards had promoted a pleasant atmosphere in the Denver area, that general sales had been rewarding, and that their mutual sponsorship of the clubs had done much to stimulate interest in both competition activities as well as much sociability. Davidson was adamant, however, and during the resultant recriminations between the two he revoked Whiting's franchise.

In the meantime, Clymer, who apparently had been made aware of what had transpired, was obviously waiting in the wings and took over Whiting's franchise with financial backing from one D.P. Cooper, under whose name the dealership was resumed. Clymer had retained a large stock of Indian parts from his past franchise, and immediately purchased an additional stock of late model parts from other sources, along with a number of late model used Indian machines. He advertised both these and his parts stock at giveaway prices with the result being that Richards was driven into bankruptcy.

The result of this affair caused great consternation among motorcyclists in the Denver area, most of whom sympathized with both Richards' and Whiting's plight. A number of them wrote letters of protest to E.C. Smith, James Wright, as well as to Ted Hodgdon, Dudley Perkins, Hap Alzina, and other known members of both the M&ATA and the AMA Competition Committee. Smith at once advised the latter that the Denver episode was a

factory affair that was outside AMA and M&ATA jurisdiction, and that it would be impolitic for people not directly involved to interfere.

Richards moved to Texas shortly afterwards and established an airplane repair business in Houston. Whiting subsequently entered the retail automotive accessory trade. First hand accounts of the affair were later related to the author by both Richards and Whiting's nephew, Robert L. Braithwaite. As an aftermath, E.C. Smith ceased to make public the membership rosters of both the M&ATA or the AMA Competition Committee in order to make them less accessible to inter-industry controversy.

In any case, the affair seriously weakened the position of the AMA in the Rocky Mountain area for a time, as without effective sponsorship club interest waned. Sufficient numbers of riders dropped their memberships to effect the loss of about 250 riders from the AMA roles.

M&ATA President James Wright called a general meeting of the group in Columbus. In attendance with Wright and Smith were the Davidsons, Frank Schwinn, representatives from Goodrich and Firestone, Delco-Remy, Person's Saddles, Pennzoil Company, and as a special guest and new member, E. Paul duPont, newly elected President of Indian.

Smith opened the meeting and stated that in spite of a few setbacks, the AMA's position had lately gained strength with a modest increase in individual memberships and club registrations. He further stated that the industry must police itself in the evergreen problem of poorly kept dealer's premises, and that individual motorcyclists should

THE GREAT DECLINE 1920-1930

The Excelsior factory team at the 1920 Marion event. From left to right are Paul Anderson, Warren Cropp, Hugh Murray, J.A. McNeil and Joe Wolters. Note the screens on Anderson's and Wolter's bikes. They were used to keep the rocks out of the rider's faces.
A.F. Van Order Collection

be encouraged to both deportment and personal appearance to hold up an improved public image.

In the matter of the AMA-M&ATA structuring, he emphasized that the long standing hope that the AMA might someday become a democratically controlled rider organization, as envisioned back in the former FAM era, could not be attained in the foreseeable future. With the redundant state of the industry and the small numbers of motorcyclists, as compared with the overall population, on-going trade financial support and centralized management could only keep the AMA together.

Noting the weakened position of the trade press, Smith emphasized the importance of the current in-house publications, the "Enthusiast" and the "Indian News," in maintaining a contact with individual riders and in keeping them informed of ongoing AMA competition and social activities. He also stressed the need for continued dealer support for both competition activities as well as the Gypsy Tours, which were still receiving good rider support.

He also urged that Excelsior and Indian follow Harley-Davidson's policy of advertising in the general public media. To this, E. Paul duPont responded by pointing out the recent $1,000 full page advertisement he had recently placed in the "Saturday Evening Post," then the country's most widely read weekly magazine with a circulation of over 8 million copies.

Due to the upturn in the AMA's financial picture, which had resulted in a modest surplus in its treasury, Smith requested and received a reduced

subsidy from the manufacturers of $1,000 from Harley-Davidson, $750 from Indian, and $500 from Excelsior. This was in addition to the usual $100 per annum dues from the latter, together with the usual $50 per year contribution from each of the ancillary trade suppliers.

The meeting was concluded amid a general air of good feelings, with strong support for Smith for his past efforts. While there was in fact some general public apprehension concerning the country's economic future following the recent collapse of the stock market, its repercussions had yet to be seriously felt, and the motorcycle industry had yet to suffer any serious consequences.

The appointment of Smith to manage AMA affairs was without a doubt a turning point in its previously uneven history. He had shown courage in taking an aggressive posture in the enforcement of competition rules, running the risk of being branded as overly dictatorial, as had been Coffman's fate in pursuing a similar course. Smith had long been an admirer of Kenesaw Mountain Landis, the one-time appellate court judge who had been appointed National Commissioner of professional baseball. Landis' job was to police the conduct of both the clubs and the players following the loss of public confidence after criminal elements had infiltrated the sport. Smith envisioned himself in a similar role in keeping all aspects of motorcycle competition above board.

Much of the controversy surrounding Smith and his activities in the AMA could be attributed to

THE GREAT DECLINE 1920-1930

A rolling start on a board track.
A.F. Van Order Collection

his multifaceted personality. With a chameleon-like character, Smith could at once be charming, diplomatic, and persuasive. On the other hand, he could at times be unreasonable, petty, and vindictive. Many of his decisions could be capricious, illogical, and arbitrary. Yet, no one could fault his dedication to the best interests of both the sport and the industry. Possessed of a photographic memory, he never appeared to forget the name or appearance of anyone casually encountered. This quality was employed effectively in spotting competitors at various events who sometimes competed in outlaw events under assumed names.

The motorcycle sporting scene at this point was still centered on hill climbing. In addition to the factory stars that were supplied with special machines, many mechanically inclined clubmen were building up their own versions from miscellaneous parts. A growing diversion in Southern California was the holding of speed trials on Lake Muroc, a hundred square mile prehistoric lake bed near Lancaster. Jim Davis, now attached to the Wigwam, made a number of unofficial records here on specially tuned Indian Scouts and converted former board trackers between 1927 and 1930.

The 101 Scout, by this time the machine of choice for sporting owners, was much in vogue. Its performance could be enhanced by "stroking," i.e., fitting cut down Chief flywheels which, by using short skirted pistons, could increase the displacement to 57 cubic inch With the fitting of racing

valve cams and extra strong valve springs, a 100 mile plus per hour speed was possible. Paul A. Bigsby, working out of Albert G. Crocker's establishment, designed an accessory overhead valve sequence for the Scout that was based on the 1925 factory devised racing specials that was an attraction to handy owners seeking the ultimate in 45 cubic inch performance.

In summarizing domestic motorcycling progress during the 1920-1930 decade, it may well be said that some technical advances in design were offset by a steadily declining public interest. Registrations nationally fell from 175,000 in 1920 to 135,000 by 1929. While the industry produced around 25,000 units per year, half or more of these were exported to foreign markets, which, in effect, kept the manufacturers marginally viable.

As a further indication of the decline in motorcycling popularity, the population of the country within the decade grew from 105 to 128 million. Automobile registrations in 1920 were 8 million, increasing to 28 million by 1930. During this interval, six makes of machines: Ace, Emblem, Evans, Iver-Johnson, Neracar and Schickel, ceased production. In addition, several talented motorcycle designers such as Perry E. Mack, Joseph Merkel, Everett M. De Long, all soon to be joined by Arthur Constantine, turned to other pursuits. The picture was truly discouraging to an ever-shrinking number of motorcycling enthusiasts, especially as the country was rapidly proceeding to economic disaster.

CHAPTER FIVE

THE WORST YEARS OF THE GREAT DEPRESSION 1931-1934

The Worst Years Of The Great Depression 1931-1934

During the winter of 1930-1931, the effect of the stock market crash was becoming apparent. With the steady deflation of hard currency consumer buying diminished, household appliances, various luxury goods, and automobile sales were the first to be affected. The latter suffered particularly, as car production had accelerated greatly since 1927. The industry had produced over 11 million cars during the past three years. The first to be hurt were the dozens of makes of assembled cars from small factories, usually serving their own regional markets, and by the end of 1930, most of these had closed their doors.

As largely a discretionary purchase, the sale of motorcycles fell off alarmingly, although there was still some market for commercial and law enforcement uses. The export market held fairly firm until the 1931 sales season, when the effect of the economic decline came to be felt worldwide. The resulting unemployment from the decline of these diverse markets added to the problem with an abrupt drop in general purchasing power.

Early in 1931, a substantial number of motorcycle dealers, particularly in the smaller towns and rural areas which were the first to feel the economic pinch, dropped out. All three factories at once sought to open a sales campaign to law enforcement agencies in a growing desperation to find cash buyers. Excelsior was particularly active in this field, as four-cylinder machines had been the choice for such use since before 1920, and had been preferred by officers who rode eight to ten-hour shifts and appreciated their smooth running qualities. The new K and KJ Hendersons had been particularly popular for their now advanced design. In municipalities where the officers purchased their own machines and were compensated on a per diem basis, the Hendersons were often the favorites, as their initial high selling price could be readily recovered.

In order to meet this competition with the now somewhat obsolete four with its slightly updated 1920 engine, Indian's Municipal Sales Manager, W. Stanley Bouton, was authorized by President duPont to offer special fleet deals to several large cities that had long used them, such as New York, Oakland, New Orleans, and Atlanta. Such deals were worked out with an agreement with the local dealers in each case. In fleet transactions, both the factory and the dealers reduced their mark-ups, the latter hoping to recoup the loss by having the subsequent repair and service work.

Arthur Constantine later reported that Schwinn, who had but 200 domestic franchised dealers, mostly in the larger cities, inaugurated a practice of selling the K police model at a 25% discount, the usual dealer's commission, to law enforcement agencies in areas where there was no regular dealer. The K models were particularly popular for extended highway as well as suburban patrol work, as their updated engines could stand up to high speed pursuit. The Indian fours were not suited to the latter employment, as their now-obsolete engines would more often than not succumb to lubrication failures under such use. The Indian Chief and Harley-Davidson's big twins held up much better under severe conditions, although the redesigned VL's were sometimes prone to blown head gaskets during high speed running.[*1] The initial V models, with their light pattern flywheels, were later mentioned as having been built to the Davidson's demand for hoped-for enhanced acceleration to compete with their competitor's four-cylinder machines.

While law enforcement sales had long been looked upon as helpful for both prestige and advertising value, many factory people as well as dealers came to look upon such sales as a necessary evil. The complications of the human predicaments involved could be endless. Purchasing agents could be unreasonable in their demands for price concessions in fleet sales, which then demanded considerations from the dealers, if involved, if the latter were not to be antagonized. In some cases, various government agencies would demand a rotation

The Worst Years Of The Great Depression 1931-1934

A 1930 Harley-Davidson Model C 30.50 cubic inch single. Note the twin bullet headlights. The chromed wheel rims and exhaust system are non-standard. Owned and restored by Colin Light of the Vintage Motor Cycle Club of Great Britain. *Jeff Clew*

arrangement between makes, presenting the problem of one factory having to take its opposite number's machines as trade-ins. In some cases, avaricious civil servants and politicians demanded under-the-table kickbacks as a part of the transactions. At the local level, some police departments demanded special rates for service and repairs. Some officers might demand personal service in the way of clothing, goggles, or even service and repair work on their own personal machines, all to be then charged to the municipal account.

In some areas, the manufacturers would seek help from state or local politicians in setting up specification requirements in their contracts that could favor their own products for future sales. The practice had been inaugurated by Harley-Davidson in the late 1920's, and was subsequently taken up by Excelsior and Indian. At any rate, with the onset of the depression, together with the very real threat that a world wide depression could well reduce the export market, general law enforcement sales at home became an important issue.

On March 31, 1931, Ignatz Schwinn announced to his staff that all motorcycle production was to be immediately terminated. This came as a distinct shock to both the industry as well as

the many loyal enthusiasts who had long favored the Henderson and Super-X models. The reasons for Schwinn's move soon became apparent. Motorcycle production at the great Courtland Street plant had never been carried on in sufficient volume to return other than a modest profit. The operation was being largely subsidized by the bicycle production that in 1929 had topped 600,000 units. Schwinn himself was variously described by contemporaries as a rather complex personality, being highly opinionated, stubborn, often irascible, and frequently abusive toward subordinates. Not the least of his emotions was his intense pride in his personal accomplishments, fueled, it was stated, by his humble beginnings as a mechanic in a German bicycle factory in Stuttgart.

According to Arthur Constantine, Schwinn had increased the production of the Henderson following his purchase of the marque from the Hendersons in the fall of 1917, expanding from 2,500 yearly units to 4,500 in 1919 and 1920. When the 1921 slump in the industry occurred, production of the 61 and 74 cubic inch V-twins had been reduced to negligible proportions, in the theory that the Henderson had a better sales potential as a leading domestic four cylinder model. Following

THE WORST YEARS OF THE GREAT DEPRESSION 1931-1934

National Cash Register Company of Tokyo used this car in their Service Department. Its carrying capacity is eight of the largest size registers made, also ample supplies of paper tape, lubricant, etc.
Alfred R. Child

brief competition from the ill-fated Ace, Schwinn held a monopoly until Indian resurrected the latter in the fall of 1927.

Motorcycle production at Excelsior dwindled after 1925, even with the introduction of the newly-designed Super-X. From that time until 1929, there were but 900 to 1,200 fours and 400 to 600 twins produced annually, scarcely sufficient volume to insure a substantial cash flow. Another problem involved the building of sidecars. As a heavyweight machine, about half of the sale of fours involved sidecars, especially on the export market. Up until 1925, Excelsior, in common with Harley-Davidson, obtained its sidecar bodies from the B.F. Rogers Company in Chicago.*2 When the company suspended its sidecar production that fall, Excelsior was forced to set up a small production line, again with insufficient output to make the operation profitable.

Excelsior, with its small output, was never well represented with dealers, most of whom were centered in the larger cities. Many of these, faced with strong competition from Harley-Davidson and Indian, stocked few, if any, Super-X twins which were not competitively priced. Most of the latter were carried by dealers in the Midwest adjacent to Chicago. As it was, about half of all Excelsior products were exported, the Super-X being especially popular in Australia and New Zealand.

The updated 1929 fours saw some increase in production, with about 3,800 K models coming off

the line between the late fall of 1928 and March of 1931. About 1,900 Super-X's were made during the same period. With the whole operation running at little more than a break-even point financially, it is little wonder that Schwinn faced the prospects of both a domestic and world wide depression with some trepidation. Other factors included in the picture were that Schwinn was 75 years old, not in the best of health, and his only son, Frank, was partially crippled from a boyhood attack of infantile paralysis, and had but a passing interest in motorcycling.

Perhaps the most telling blow, according to Constantine, were some mechanical problems afflicting the last K models. In order to cut costs, Schwinn had ordered some low cost electrical components from some obscure manufacturer. About 250 fours intended mostly for law enforcement were so fitted between October 1929, and January of 1930. In November, the California State Highway Patrol ordered 150 of these, which showed early failures of the electrical systems. These were unable to stand up to high speed running when the pursuit lights and siren were in operation. Similar problems were encountered in police units sold in Indiana and Ohio. The consequent loss of Henderson prestige was considerable.

A group of senior employees approached Schwinn with the proposition of leasing the facilities to continue production. Schwinn vehemently refused to consider it, stating that if he couldn't

THE WORST YEARS OF THE GREAT DEPRESSION 1931-1934

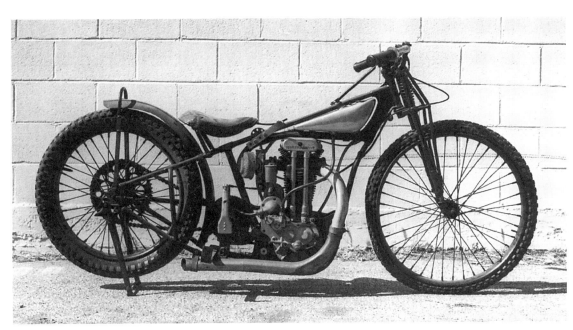

The Harley-Davidson 30.50 CAC Model designed by Joe Petrali in the early 1930's. Its engine was based on the current J.A. Prestwich models used in Class A competition. It was never fully developed.
George Hays

conduct motorcycle manufacture, no one else would be allowed to take over the make. Constantine later offered the opinion that both the lack of financial backing and managerial experience on the part of the proposers influenced Schwinn's decision.[*3]

A few more models were assembled from on-hand components that spring, mostly to fulfill prior law enforcement contracts. The remaining parts stock was sold to the Ballak Cycle Supply Company, also located in Chicago, and for many years helped to keep Excelsiors and Hendersons on the road. Constantine resigned to join the engineering department of the Bendix Corporation, where he remained for several years.

In the meantime, E. Paul duPont and his new Board of Directors were attempting to straighten out Indian's tangled affairs. The most pressing problem was to increase the production of the now famous 101 Scout. As a medium-sized compact machine, its advanced engine design (which was both simple yet powerful, through its efficient combustion chamber design and good breathing characteristics) developed surprising power for its cylinder displacement. With Indian's race-bred heritage, it was renowned for its good balance and superior handling characteristics. Light enough to attract entry level buyers, yet powerful enough to fulfill the demands of law enforcement, it was perhaps the closest model to an all-purpose machine yet produced by the domestic industry, and has been revered by historians as possibly the best all-around domestic machine ever made up until that time. According to veteran factory employees, about 16,750 units were produced between the

spring of 1928, through the fall of 1931, and there were still unfilled orders from dealers.

The Indian operation was reorganized with Loren F. Hosley, the former plant manager for the duPont car production, being installed as Vice-President and General Manager. Production Foreman George Mason transferred some automobile parts from the Wilmington plant to Springfield, and the last few duPont cars were assembled in the factory's basement.

Many veteran Indian employees were retained, such as Production Foreman Erle Armstrong, who oversaw all actual machine production and quality control.

In later years duPont commented that the operation was staffed by a number of employees who constituted what may best be termed dead wood, cronyism being rampant from past days. Many of these were left over from Indian's salad days under Frank Weschler, who hated to fire anyone.

A technical advance in product finish was inaugurated with the substitution of duPont paints, which were now sprayed instead of the former dip tank method.

James Wright and three assistants of the sales force were now crisscrossing the country attempting to mend fences with the dealers, and assuring them that factory activity was now centered on motorcycle production only and that the Company's position was now materially strengthened by duPont ownership. This was being effected by the structuring of the Indian Corporation, which integrated duPont's more profitable holdings with the Springfield operation. It had at one point been planned to inaugurate the limited production of air-

THE WORST YEARS OF THE GREAT DEPRESSION 1931-1934

The 45 cubic inch Super X. This 1930-1931 model was restored by the late Dewey Bonkrud. An optional engine bored out to 61 cu. in. was also available.
George Hays

craft engines, utilizing a part of the State Street plant's vast unused spaces, but Indian's now precarious position together with the uncertainties of the economic situation, caused this project to be shelved. The immediate problem was the deteriorated condition of Indian's tooling facilities, much of which were not only nearly worn out, but had been seriously depleted through the selling off of a part of it during the Levine ownership. Partial replacements were made, some of which were purchased as used equipment from other now idle Springfield factories.

The initial announcement of E. Paul duPont's involvement with Indian came as a surprise to most members of the country's financial community. He was a member of one of America's most prominent industrial and financially powerful families. His substantial inheritance together with his association in the automobile industry and his activities with the Ball Grain Powder Company, not to mention his connections with his brother's important stock-brokerage business, had gained him much public recognition. When the news of both E. Paul's and Francis I.'s involvement with Indian was made public, both in the New York Times and the Wall Street Journal, not a few eyebrows were raised along Wall Street, considering the unsavory reputation that the Indian Company now had because of the publicity attendant to the depredations of its recent owners.

What had been overlooked by contemporaries and even later acquaintances was the fact that E. Paul had pursued a lifelong interest in things mechanical ever since his boyhood days. It was also not generally known that he had graduated from the University of Pennsylvania with a degree

in mechanical engineering. With a background of good fortune from the obvious advantages of inherited wealth and aristocratic social position, duPont at once personified the polish and sophistication that inevitably accompanied it. Yet at the same moment he exhibited both a warm and pleasant personality, approaching life with a cheerful and sometimes bantering attitude. In a later personal interview, the author was pleased to note that he was altogether a kindly and sensitive individual.

In contrast to most of the past leaders in the domestic motorcycle industry, his background and position made him unique in that he had not risen from the working class ranks, a fact well recognized by his new contemporary competitors, the Davidson brothers and Ignatz Schwinn.

In the meantime, Arthur Welch was now attempting to rejuvenate the ailing "Pacific Motorcyclist", which had been reduced to near pamphlet form through the recent FWM debacle together with John J. O'Conner's self-serving policies. With a depicted advertising content and a subscription list of less than 6,000, its future appeared far from promising.

Welch at once published editorials emphasizing that the new management was dedicated to the best interest of both the sport and industry and that both helpful and objective reporting of these activities was to be the order of the day. He also touched on his long career in journalism, as both an experienced reporter and his expertise in the publishing business.

Welch also wrote a long letter to E.C. Smith outlining the past difficulties that the magazine had experienced, explaining his aims to correct past troubles, and pledged his support of the AMA, along with his intention to report the ongoing activ-

122

THE WORST YEARS OF THE GREAT DEPRESSION 1931-1934

ities within the sport and industry in a fair and objective manner. Smith favored him with a cordial reply, and within a few weeks made a special trip to the West Coast to confer with Welch concerning cooperation in AMA policy matters. Smith also stressed the fact that with the growing critical state of the industry, only manufacturers and others advertising in the magazine as selling their products through dealers should be given contracts, with direct mail vendors being excluded. Welch later told the author that he saw the wisdom of this policy, as with dealer support he could expand the advertising so necessary for the magazine's survival. As an initial gesture of encouragement, Smith also contracted for space in which to list the names and addresses of individual motorcycle dealers in various areas of the country, giving prominence to those who have been long-time AMA supporters.

With the now increasing economic pinch, AMA clubs as well as sporting activities were seen to be declining in scope. Some dealers in the Northeastern states, however, led by the veteran Indian dealer N.H. Coulter of Providence, sponsored a regional Gypsy Tour on Labor Day in 1931 that was well supported. Another well established fixture that still enjoyed good rider and club support was the Jack Pine Run. This famous event had been originally sponsored by the Muskegon Motorcycle Club in Northern Michigan, founded by veteran Harley-Davidson dealer Oscar Lenz. It featured an enduro-type run through cut over logging country, including colonial type abandoned logging roads as well as cross country segments, and was considered as most demanding on both rider and machine.

Incidental to conferring with Welch in Los Angeles, Smith called on a number of clubs in that area, as well as one in Reno and two in Salt Lake City in order to offer them encouragement. A visit to the Denver area was less than successful, as there were still mixed feelings toward the absence of AMA-M&ATA intervention in the recent Clymer-Richards-Whiting affair. The two surviving clubs refused to reinstate their former 100% rider membership or to renew their charters. As a footnote, Clymer had only a short time to profit from his new Harley-Davidson dealership. He had just been convicted in the District Federal Court on charges brought by the Postal Service for mail fraud. It transpired that Clymer had established a marketing service that offered to find, for an advance fee, commercial outlets for various new inventions and other products, in association with a young woman, Vera Martin. When no action was

forthcoming from Clymer, and in the face of numerous complaints, postal investigators gathered sufficient evidence to sustain a conviction. Clymer was sentenced to two and one-half years in the Federal Prison at Leavenworth, Kansas. With good behavior, and later becoming a trustee, Clymer served but fifteen months. Miss Martin was acquitted for lack of evidence.

In May 1931, an unfortunate series of events occurred which were to end the "entente cordiale" that had existed for the past decade among the management of the principal motorcycle manufacturers. President Walter Davidson, in an announcement released through his area factory representatives, offered direct factory sales of VLG Police models to any bona fide state or municipal law enforcement body. The terms were $195 cash for each unit, but with the provision that the machines they were replacing be taken in as a trade-in. The privately expressed intention was to junk the trade-ins, ostensibly to remove them from the marketplace to clear the way for the sale of new machines. It had been noted along the way that large numbers of used machines in the hands of private riders, in the more expensive category of big twins and fours, had been acquired at police auctions. Many dealers had long expressed the opinion that such machines, while usually showing high mileages of 40,000 to 50,000 miles, were generally sound mechanically, as they had in most cases been well maintained while in service. At any rate, cash buyers were usually able to acquire such units for about half the cost of the same new models. It appeared that Harley-Davidson's strategy in the matter was to clear the market of such machines.

The looming area of controversy, however, was the fact that the dealers themselves were not to participate nor would they receive their usual 25% commissions. Their immediate disapproval at once appeared to be justified. As we have seen, the discounting of retail prices for law enforcement sales, particularly in regard to fleet sales, was an already established practice within the industry. But in the past, both the dealers and the factory shared the discounting.

The sentiments of the Indian forces were no less negative. Not only did they feel that Harley-Davidson was engaging in unfair cutthroat competition, but the intention to junk several hundred still serviceable machines, many of them Indians, could cause a further serious depletion within the ranks of private motorcyclists that would be detrimental to both the sport and industry.

During the ensuing years, the author sought the opinions of a number of prominent dealers of

In the 1930's Los Angeles Indian dealer Al Crocker went into production of his own line of motorcycles. His first machine was a Speedway racer. He later dropped it in favor of a high performance V-twin which he produced in small numbers until the start of World War II.
Don Emde Collection

THE WORST YEARS OF THE GREAT DEPRESSION 1931-1934

The November 1932 issue of "The Motorcyclist" was its first as the official AMA publication.
Don Emde Collection

both makes. These included such Harley-Davidson stalwarts as Dudley Perkins, Claude Salmon, Rich Budelier, W.J. Rhule, and the Brown brothers, together with Indian dealers Hap Alzina, Hap Jones, Guy Urquhart, W.J. Montgomery, and others. These and other Indian dealers were opposed as much on the grounds of the ill will it created within the motorcycle community as they were on the competition field. The Harley-Davidson dealers were of the opinion that the matter did more harm than good between the company management and its dealers, as members of the latter, already discouraged by the drop in sales due to worsening economic times, simply cancelled their franchises. Both groups agreed that the consequent fratricidal war waged between some of the enthusiasts of each make did much to further denigrate motorcycling's already poor image.

According to later statements by William Ottaway and Alfred Rich Child, the company made a $30 profit on each unit, and also had to assume the administrative burden of taking in and junking the trade-in machines. Following the general storm of protest within the industry, the offer was terminated that summer, after 300 machines had been delivered under the scheme.

During this period, Harley-Davidson offered Joe Petrali a position in the company, ostensibly as their now sole professional rider but also for his engineering and tuning expertise. He was already an acknowledged expert in that field, aside from his natural and very diverse riding skills. In recounting the events of the matter to the author in later years, Petrali stated that the salary of $40 a week was an attraction, together with the opportunity to work with William Ottaway, following his severance with Excelsior and the termination of his relationship with Arthur Constantine.

In noting the now virtual disappearance of all the trade magazines, and in consideration of Welch's solicitation of AMA news and announcements, E.C. Smith conceived the idea of combining their forces. This would not only be of mutual economic advantage, but would possibly assure the continuation of the surviving trade magazine which was highly essential in providing a much needed public forum for the sport and industry.

Smith wrote a letter to Welch outlining his proposal, and the two met that fall in Los Angeles. Welch later told the author that Smith's initial proposal was attractive. The AMA would pay the production fees, together with payment of a somewhat less than standard space rate for certain announcements. The AMA and the magazine would each receive 50 cents of the dollar-per-year subscription rate which would also include a year's AMA membership. In addition, all proceeds from advertising space would remain with the magazine. Smith also offered to solicit the services of a number of freelance journalists across the country who had previously reported on sports events for both "Pacific Motorcyclist" as well as published trade journals, in order to provide proper national coverage.

After some thought, Welch decided to accept Smith's offer, which was made contingent upon its acceptance by James Wright and the M&ATA Board of Directors. A formal legal agreement was never drawn up; the matter was to be effected by a letter of proposal and a letter of acceptance exchanged by both parties. Wright and the Board readily passed favorably on the matter. Welch later commented that the agreement gave the magazine a much-needed financial boost, although he never anticipated the controversies that would later arise between himself and Smith.

Late that summer, James Wright, as Indian's Sales Manager, sent copies of a letter to their dealerships. It stated that due to the company's ongoing financial problems, together with the economic state of both the motorcycle business and the country, the 101 Scout production would be terminated in September in order to further streamline production. This announcement at once aroused a storm of protest from most of the dealerships. Many of them pointed out that Indian's main appeal throughout the past decade had been the various Scout models, which had gained worldwide acceptance, and that many dealers' present survival had been dependent upon the 101's popularity even though motorcycle sales were in the doldrums. Hap Alzina was especially bitter, as he was currently selling relatively large numbers of the model, and had in fact saved the day for its continued production when he had supplied its financing during the company's 1929 crisis. The situation was further complicated by the fact that Indian's management at that point declined to reveal their future plans for a replacement model.

James Wright reported that he did not expect the usual annual price-and-policy fixing meeting between himself and the Davidsons to be called that year, due to their recent factory direct sales campaign and the breaking of the gentlemen's agreement on price fixing with Indian. But at the end of August, Arthur Davidson telephoned James Wright that the two would have some very important business to discuss, so a meeting was arranged for September 15th at the Blackstone Hotel in Chicago. Wright was accompanied by Municipal Sales Manager W. Stanley Bouton. Alfred Rich

Child, who was in the States for his annual conference in Milwaukee, was also present.

According to a later report of the meeting by both Wright and Child, Davidson opened the proceedings by stating that he had knowledge that the War Department was considering calling bids for a limited number of big twin sidecar outfits to replace some of the 1917 and 1918 JD and Powerplus models from World War I that were still in service on many stateside as well as overseas Army posts. He suggested that noncompetitive bids would insure that each factory could then supply an equal number of units. He suggested a bid price of $295 per unit. While Bouton retired briefly to calculate Indian's cost figures, Wright suggested that the Davidsons would have the edge as their VL models were fitted with a reverse gear and the Chiefs were not. Davidson replied that in any case Indian could have an edge because the net out-the-door cost on the Chief was less than the VL's because of the latter's greater number of component parts. He suggested that Indian was in a position to make a price concession if the matter became an issue.

Wright at once brought up the matter of the Davidson's recent cut-rate municipal sales campaign, which had caused the meeting to open on a somewhat strained note. Davidson responded by stating that his company was in somewhat desperate financial straits due to the drop in both domestic and export sales, and that they had on hand a surplus of VL machines due to a cutback in Child's orders for Japan. This fact was at once corroborated by Child.

Davidson continued that he wished to lay on the table the matter of the problems with their 45 cubic inch twins, stating they were currently planning a replacement model, as the original had been found to be technically inferior with its unorthodox generator fitting and its light pattern frame and forks which were insufficiently strong for the demands of export. He noted that if Indian was dropping their current 101 model that sold for $295 FOB during the past year, in the interest of rationalizing production, that Indian's management might concede that their new 45 could be offered at a lower price, noting the condition of the market. Wright replied that the Davidsons could offer any price they wished, as long as the 101 was now off the market. Concerning the pricing on the proposed War Department contract, Bouton stated he would need more time to confer with production people before rendering a decision.

As it was, Indian's management decided what they hoped would solve the problem by merely fit-

ting the engine-gearbox unit into the Chief's chassis. Anchored to a frame that was 100 pounds heavier, the new model, catalogued as the Standard Scout, brought forth a scream of protest from the dealers, as its resulting performance could best be described as melancholy. A few of them actually cancelled their franchises over the matter, especially in cases where Scout sales and service work had been their prime source of income.

The discussion of the War Department matter came to naught, as the procurement officers noted the drop in Congressional appropriations for the armed forces, which were then at minimal strength. The various branches were ordered to retire any defunct surplus equipment and to repair and maintain as much of the old material on hand as was possible.

The late fall and winter of 1931 and 1932 saw the country's economic situation deteriorating even further. The shortage of hard currency caused thousands of businesses and manufacturing concerns to fail. Consumer buying, due to widening unemployment, dropped alarmingly. Many of the nation's railroads were in serious financial trouble; and many banks, especially in rural areas, were approaching insolvency. The Republican administration, led by President Herbert Hoover, attempted to promote some recovery by making low cost loans available to industry through the government-backed Reconstruction Finance Corporation.

The position of the now nearly dormant motorcycle industry was no less acute. As a largely discretionary purchase, held up mostly by a few commercial and law enforcement sales, production had fallen to a total of less than 8,000 units between the two factories, Indian's share being under 3,000. A part of the loss was due to the falling export sales, of which Harley-Davidson had the lion's share, with Alfred Rich Child formerly absorbing from 1,800 to 2,000 units per year in Japan. His sales were still holding fairly steady, as large numbers of VL sidecar units were still being purchased by Chiang Kai-Shek and other war lords in China.

Both firms were saddled with 19th Century-type multi-story facilities with centrally-powered machinery via the old leather belt and jackshaft principle that left no provision for an assembly line system. The units were moved about the plant on dollies for the adding on of various component parts.

Both factories terminated substantial numbers of more recently hired management and production personnel. According to Indian's Ted Hodgdon, numbers of people recently hired to fill middle management jobs were discharged, and most of the

Indian's one time Advertising Manager Ted Hodgdon with a 1929 KSS Velocette brought from England by Charles B. Franklin for examination and evaluation during his experiments with overhead camshaft engines.
Theodore Hodgdon

department heads were placed on a three day work week with a corresponding reduction in salary.

Indian's production force was largely on piece work, being paid on a per-unit fabrication scale. By tradition, Indian employed two classes of artisans. The more skilled machinists fabricated parts and finished castings during the winter months, those on an hourly rate drawing from 45¢ to 75¢ per hour. Often being farmers, fisherman, or skilled in other trades, they pursued these avocations in the spring and summer, with less skilled workers assembling and crating the finished machines as orders were received, working at a much reduced rate of 25¢ per hour and up.

Harley-Davidson laid off low seniority employees and spread what work there was among those remaining by having each individual employed for two or three days per week; this allowed a greater number to at least buy food for their families. Hourly wages at the Juneau Avenue plant were then scaled from 25¢ to 75¢ per hour.

The only proposal within the industry for a new model during 1931 was Charles Franklin's prototype of the Dispatch-Tow. This was a three-wheeled rickshaw-like vehicle based on the 101 Scout designed to allow a single driver to collect or retrieve a disabled automobile by means of a folding tow bar attached to the fork. With the discontinuance of the 101, the project was shelved. The following year Harley-Davidson picked up the idea, basing it on their 45 twin, which was then carried on as the long running Servi-Car, widely used commercially and as a traffic and parking control vehicle by law enforcement.

It was during this time that Indian's management began to farm out a number of its smaller machining and fabrication operations, finding that it was more economical to have the work completed by small specialist firms. A number of these were located adjacent to the main factory in Springfield, but some were in other parts of the country. For several years Albert G. Crocker of Los Angeles had a contract to machine main bearing crankpins. Harley-Davidson was less inclined to follow this practice, claiming that possible production problems occurring in outside suppliers could hold up production.

Early in 1932, an unfortunate episode occurred that complicated the already strained relationships brought on by Harley-Davidson's factory-direct law enforcement sales program. Dealers for both makes reported that Harley-Davidson factory representatives had been, in some cases, referring to the newly installed Indian President, E. Paul duPont, as "that New Jersey Jew". This appellation was clearly a misnomer, as the duPonts were Aryan French and had always been located in and adjacent to Wilmington, Delaware. There was never any evidence that the Founders themselves had any connections with the spreading of this rumor. A number of veteran dealers for both makes subsequently told the author that in their opinion some of the traveling sales supervisors were at fault, apparently enlarging on the Founder's well-known anti-semitic sentiments.

At any rate, duPont felt sufficiently incensed by the matter to become a surprise visitor at the annual price-and-policy fixing meeting held that year in Chicago. Milwaukee representatives were Arthur Davidson, Alfred Rich Child, and James Wright and W. Stanley Bouton from Springfield. In a highly strained atmosphere, duPont took Davidson to task for his company's broadcasted ethnic slurs against his family. Davidson at once disclaimed all managerial responsibilities in the matter, but stated that steps would be taken to investigate the source and offered duPont his apologies for any anguish caused for himself and his family. DuPont accepted his statements and apology, and the two shook hands. DuPont then extended his friendship to the Davidson family and left the meeting.

But further damage to the formerly cordial relationships between the two factories had already taken place. Many of the larger clubs with owners of both makes within their memberships split into separate groups. The subsequent fratricidal warfare damaged the image of both the sport and industry still further. It led to some incidents of physical combat at both on-the-road encounters as well as at competition events, and furthered a serious blot on American motorcycle history.

In the late spring, Indian announced a new lightweight model in the form of the Pony Scout, a 30.50 cubic inch V-twin; its engine a sleeved-down version of the long running 37 cubic inch Standard Scout. As a Depression-inspired model, prototype testing and retooling were avoided, as the model was a resurrection of the chassis parts of the Prince single, the jigs and dies of which were already on hand. As a further measure of economy, the helical gear drive to the transmission was dispensed with in favor of a single row primary chain contained within a sheet metal case. This new model, said to have been the brain child of Vice President and General Manager Loren F. Hosley, illustrated Indian's disenchantment with single cylinder machines. The Prince terminated in 1928, never having caught on well in the domestic market. The Pony was to have better acceptance due to its enhanced performance, having a top speed in standard form of close to 65 mph.

The retail pricing of Harley-Davidson's and Indian's various models during 1932 and 1933 were somewhat at variance, as by mutual agreement. The top-of-the-line Chief and Big Twin were identically priced at $325. In the absence of the 101 Scout, Harley's 45 was set at a rock bottom $235, with the 30.50 single that shared the same chassis at $225, and the 21 single being dropped to $195. The new Pony model was set at $250, with an economy model sold without the usual steering friction dampers, euphemistically called "ride controls", fixed at $225. The Four was continued in very limited production at $445, this being dropped the following year to $395.

As the year of 1932 progressed, the economic depression had reached catastrophic proportions. From thirteen to fifteen million people were out of work; over 5,000 of the nation's banks were failing; half of the railroads were in bankruptcy; businesses and manufacturing plants were failing everywhere; and one-fourth of the country's farmers were under foreclosure. Various branches of state and local governments had already trimmed their labor forces, cut back on expenditures, and curtailed both non-essential and some essential services as their tax bases eroded. In many cases local governments were stretching their meager budgets to provide soup kitchens to feed the hungry and homeless.

It was later shown that a part of the problem facing the United States was its recently-erected tariff barriers that had at once stifled world trade. The farmers, particularly in the Midwest, had not shared in the general 1920's prosperity, largely due to the importation of cheap foodstuffs as well as overproduction at home. The McNary Haugen bill passed by Congress for the relief of agriculture, as well as a general trade bill in the form of the Smoot Hawley Act, were not enacted in time to alleviate the import problem.

As makers of a largely discretionary purchase, the motorcycle industry was particularly hard hit, both plants having instituted drastic cutbacks in production the year before. About one-third of the franchised dealerships of both companies, mostly in the smaller towns and villages, simply disappeared. Many long established dealerships in the larger centers drastically cut back their operations and moved to less favored lower cost locations. Many took on unrelated pursuits, such as saw filing, appliance repair, welding and general machine shop services. A relatively large percentage of the dealers later reported that for several sales seasons not a single new machine was sold. A few of the Indian dealers took franchises for the American Bantam car, a recent Yankee version of the British Austin Seven, which even at a retail price of $445 found few takers.

It could be considered that the motorcycle might well have become a depression vehicle, but such was not the case. Due to the recent high production of automobiles after 1927, there was now a glut of millions of used and many discontinued

Racing legend Joe Petrali was featured on the cover of the October, 1931 issue of "The Harley-Davidson Enthusiast." He is shown winning a hillclimb event at Muskegon, Mich. *Don Emde Collection*

makes of new cars available, all at rock bottom prices. Due to their small production and specialized nature, late model used motorcycles held their value proportionately better than cars, but many older models changed hands in private sales for very little.

With an oversupply of cheap gasoline at 15 to 18 cents a gallon and lubricating oil at 10 cents a quart, automobile operation, at least in the United States, had never been the economic problem it was overseas.

The situation was reversed in Europe and particularly in Great Britain, then the world leaders of the industry. Of the 100 odd firms active before 1930, only half survived by drastic cutbacks in production. Most of them now resorted to making stark, small capacity models, usually with sweated labor. Large numbers of lightweight machines powered by two stroke units, usually from Villiers, formed the backbone of the new depressed market.

Motorcycling competition had by this time all but disappeared, except for the odd event that was more often than not of non-sanctioned outlaw nature. Joe Petrali, as the sole surviving factory rider, won the 1931 and 1932 National Hill Climbs for Harley-Davidson over weak competition.

Noting the crisis state of the country and motorcycling in particular, E.C. Smith called a special meeting of the AMA-M&ATA at Columbus in September. With the inability of the factories to sponsor any professional riders, and the lack of available funds for former promoters to stage such events, it was noted that only a few short track events were being staged; These events were mostly in California and were put on more as entertainment than as out-and-out competition, and had mainly local appeal. Small tracks operated sporadically during the spring and summer at Idora Park, San Mateo, Lodi, Sacramento, Fresno, Merced and Los Angeles. Eugene W. "Pete" Colman, an early competitor as a teenager, recalled that an attempt was made to introduce the sport into Florida by a group of western riders, but without success. The teams nearly ran out of food money before they could return home. Sparse crowds buying 50 cent tickets produced scant income. Interest in this sport was further limited by the fact that specialized machines were required, as cut down 45 cubic inch domestic roadsters were too heavy and lacked the necessary power to perform well. After the original supply of Rudge and Douglas machines wore out, specially built 190 lb. speedway models fitted with the newly developed 500 cc overhead valve alcohol burning J.A.P.'s by the British J.A. Prestwich firm had become standard.

In view of the severe cutback in motorcycle sport, the drop in machine registrations due to rider unemployment, and the consequent disbanding of many of the organized clubs, Smith proposed a new AMA program of motorcycling activity that might attract universal participation by the surviving private owners in order to stave off a total collapse of interest. In this, Classes A and B, which would include speedway, would remain intact for hopeful later resurgence. The emphasis would now be on Class C, which was to foster the riding of standard machines in competition events tailored to their technical limitations, with strict rules against modifications to the engines from stock. To further enforce these rules, machines would have to be ridden on the road and not transported to meets, and have only a minimum of equipment, such as headlights, front mudguards, saddlebags and rear mudguard tail pieces to be removed after arrival.

In the interest of safe competition speeds, only 45 cubic inch side valve engines with disconnected brakes could be used for dirt track events. But 45 cubic inch and 74 cubic inch machines with intact brakes could be entered in cross-country or field meet types of events. Class B hill climb events for amateurs could be fitted with tuned engines, but fuels were restricted to standard octane gasoline, and steel lug tractor type rear wheels were not permitted, although automotive type tire chains could be used.

After some discussion, the group adopted the Class C concept. Young Theodore A. (Ted) Hodgdon, present as an Indian representative, suggested that English-style Trials events be also included, as well as Tourist Trophy type events. This so-called TT designation, if compared to the classic Isle of Man road races, was actually a misnomer. Road racing as such had long been outlawed by the AMA. The American TT course was laid out as a closed circuit, which mandated a couple of right and left turns and a jump, and was in practice usually effected by bringing in additional dirt material to a racetrack. This TT class was opened to both 45 and 74 inch classes with standard brakes permitted.

Smith particularly called attention to the fact that stroker type Indian Scouts with 57 inches of displacement were to be barred from all Class C events. Similar Harley-Davidsons appear not to have been so modified by practical mechanics, as 74 inch Big Twin lower ends could not readily be made to fit in the 45's engine cases.

With general approval of his proposal, Smith announced that the Competition Committee would hold further meetings during the winter to finalize

THE WORST YEARS OF THE GREAT DEPRESSION 1931-1934

An ohv Harley-Davidson "Peashooter" hill climber owned by former slant artist Conrad Schlemmer. *Conrad Schlemmer*

the new rules, and that a public announcement would be made regarding their adoption early in 1933. As it was, the institution of Class C in AMA competition was to have a far reaching effect upon domestic motorcycle sport for the next four decades.

It was also during the winter of 1932 and 1933 that Smith conferred with Arthur Welch concerning the general policies of the "Pacific Motorcyclist", which Welch, taking cognizance of its now sole position in the country's trade magazine field, had changed to simply "The Motorcyclist".

Welch later recalled that with the AMA footing the $200 per month printing costs, the publication could carry itself with the advertising revenue, which came to about the same figure.

Contrary to some popular opinions, most companies publishing small magazines required some volume activity to insure adequate cash flow, and the Western Journal Publishing Company was no exception. In this case, there were three magazines being produced at this time, together with a number of catalog and brochure printings for unrelated business firms. Welch's staff therefore actually spent only a limited portion of their time producing "The Motorcyclist", and although somewhat knowledgeable on the subject, they were in no way specialists in the field.

Following the initial issues carrying the announcement of The Motorcyclist's official representation of the AMA, Smith terminated his newsletter that had been issued sporadically to the registered clubs and general membership, now utilizing the magazine for current AMA news and announcements. At the same moment, he assumed a natural proprietary interest in its general editorial policies, which ultimately led to certain journalistic weaknesses in the publication as well as a gradually growing series of disagreements with Welch.

In the first instance, both were in agreement that with the current critical state of the industry, the policy of advertising only products that were sold through dealers and excluding direct mail sales was a necessary procedure, as had been discussed.

Smith's next suggestion was that any controversial discussions relating to any present or future AMA or industry policies should be excluded. This, in short, mandated that the magazine would henceforth be both a total advocate as well as a propaganda medium, with its content slanted toward self laudatory reporting. This meant that anything objective or critical in the way of reported road tests of new models or any searching analysis of accessory offerings was taboo. Welch protested, stating that in his opinion such a policy would miti-

門倉商店運輸部

A 1930 VL Harley-Davidson big twin fitted with a Japanese designed rear car for commercial use in that country. Alfred Rich Child sold many of these unites for commercial use.
Alfred Rich Child

gate against technical progress and would negate any protective action for the benefit of consumers. He pointed out that the Temple Press and Illiffe publications in Great Britain, through their independent editorial policies, had done much to strengthen the British industry. Smith was in agreement on this point, but stated that the strength of the industry was such in Great Britain, in contrast to its weakness in the States, that any such domestic policy was impossible.*4

Smith further stated that reports of competition activities should be slanted toward glorifying the sport, omitting reports of accidents or injuries to contestants or spectators and the incidence of protests against referees and officials, thus painting an idyllic picture.

In subsequent statements made to the author in various interviews in later years, Welch stated that he could sympathize with Smith in his efforts to support the ailing industry. But at the same time, his basic reporter's instinct regarding the ethics of

accurate and objective reporting that he had developed through the years, gradually tended to rebel against what was to become an almost ironclad censorship by Smith. A growing conflict between the two did, as will be seen, ultimately occur.

In spite of the Depression, there had been a growing interest in amateur aviation in the country since the mid-1920's. This had been sparked initially by the Lympne flying contests in England between 1923 and 1926. With the lack of small aircraft engines caused by the slump in aviation progress since the Armistice, amateur designers had turned to motorcycle engines as the sole alternative. The disadvantages of the use of V-twins has already been mentioned, and in consequence, the four-cylinder Henderson became the model of choice. Developing 27 hp and weighing a little over 100 lbs. as converted, it afforded adequate if somewhat marginal power for a light airframe. It was later found to have deficiencies in lubrication. Theodore Hodgdon, as a budding aviation enthusiast, devised an improved oiling system with an enlarged lower crankcase housing with some technical advice from its designed Arthur Constantine. A pioneer light plane designer, Edward Heath, developed an ultralight high wing monoplane, which he called the Parasol, and subsequently offered kits for home construction, as well as finished airplanes from a small factory in Niles, Michigan, with the Henderson specified as the power plant. Heath made further modifications to the engine, and purchased about a hundred sets of castings from the Ballak Company in Chicago from the leftover parts stock. These engines, with the enlarged oil sump and modified manifold porting, were marketed as the B-4 model.

A horizontally opposed twin cylinder engine was devised by Lester Long, a pioneer Oregon light plane designer, utilizing 1923-1927 Harley-Davidson J cylinder and piston assemblies which he called the 'Harleyquin' but with his own crankcase and crankshaft castings and other modified automotive parts. He sold about 50 of these crankcases, along with building directions. Weighing about 90 pounds and turning out 30 hp at usable propeller speeds with little vibration, it was a successful conversion. He contacted Walter Davidson concerning its manufacture, but the latter considered the market too limited to make it a paying proposition.

1932 became a year of critical decision for the author in the pursuit of the facts of motorcycle history. Due to family problems at home, he was sent to live with a cousin, Lt. Jacob G. Sucher, a 1919 West Point graduate. He was stationed at the United States Army Arsenal at Benecia, located near the city of Vallejo, California. Then a rather somnolent post manned by a handful of personnel, it was a veritable museum of military artifacts of the past, with extensive warehouses filled with a variety of World War I equipment, along with many horse drawn vehicles left over from the Spanish American War as well as frontier days. Among the vehicles were about 450 unused 1917 Indian war department models still in their original shipping crates. Lt. Sucher, an ordinance officer, had been a military sidecar driver at his previous station at the Rock Island arsenal in Illinois.

It was here that the author met Nelson Bettencourt, a Harley-Davidson dealer in nearby Vallejo. Being adjacent to the active U.S. Naval Repair facility on Mare Island, he enjoyed a business selling motorcycles to the shore-bound sailors stationed on the various naval vessels and submarines that were undergoing refitting and repairing. These men lived in barracks and were subject only to light duties for months at a time, and substantial numbers of them took up motorcycling as a recreational outlet. Bettencourt, who was a cheerful and gregarious individual, had been a pioneer motorcyclist and a dispatch rider in France during his service in the A.E.F., and was recruited for his dealership in 1922 by the well-known Vernon Guthrie, popular Harley-Davidson West Coast factory representative.

Bettencourt confided to the author that his usual strategy was to sell a sailor a motorcycle, which after a few months, would be turned back to him for resale when the latter's ship was scheduled to leave Mare Island for sea duty. In some cases, he was able to sell and resell the machine to as many as seven or eight consecutive buyers! His attraction to the author was probably partly due to the access it gave him to the arsenal and the possibilities of machine sales to the soldiers, when several did in fact purchase both new and used machines.

The author's interest in motorcycle history had heretofore been confined to studying trade magazines, talking to various pioneer motorcyclists and perusing past and current catalogs and sales literature, generously provided by Santa Rosa Harley-Davidson and Indian dealers Joe Frugoli and Angelo Rossi. It was through Bettencourt that the author was able to meet other dealers, such as Claude Salmon in Oakland, Dudley Perkins and Tennant Lee, a former Henderson dealer, in San Francisco, and others. Vallejo was also one of the more important centers of motorcycling activity, with an active club co-sponsored by Bettencourt, that prompted various field meets and hill climbs that attracted participants from all over central California. The author was encouraged in his investigations, as Bettencourt pointed out that up to that point there had been little or nothing done in the way of formally preserving historic motorcycling material in the United States.

During that winter, E.C. Smith traveled through various parts of the country in an attempt to revive interest in club participation, which had been lagging, as well as promoting interest in the announced introduction of the Class C rules aimed at bringing private riders into sporting participation.

There was also the still pressing problem of the often bitter hostility between Harley-Davidson and Indian enthusiasts, which was giving motorcycling a poor image and disrupting club activities. In the spring of 1933, Smith reactivated his J sidecar outfit, and often in the company of Milwaukee factory traveler Fred Blixt, made visitations with clubs throughout the midwest in an effort to spread oil on the troubled waters.

It must be emphasized that while some of the dealers of both makes sometimes gave lip service to the brand name controversy, more often than not they did not become emotionally involved, and in most cases were on friendly terms. After all, they were all mostly dedicated motorcycling enthusiasts facing the same economic problems of marketing and servicing a discretionary product during the most difficult of times, and public knowledge of the existence of fratricidal warfare made for public condemnation of an already marginal commodity. Then, too, it was of advantage to be able to trade off with their opposite numbers for their own brand of machine on occasion when the product of another was taken in on new or upgraded machines.

While some of the dealers might have been somewhat rough-hewn characters, most of them were above the average in native shrewdness and business acumen, coping as they were with a product difficult to sell. In deference to their hobbyist involvement, many of them would go out of their way to make a viable sales prospect happy. Most were also willing to expend their own funds to support local club activities, as well as sponsoring annual picnics and promoting competition events to advertise the sport.

In spite of the difficult economic times, Arthur Welch noted an increase in rider and club support for "The Motorcyclist", now that it was officially affiliated with the AMA. Much of this support was aided by the editorial policies of "The Enthusiast" and "Indian News", which now appeared quarterly for the benefit of respective adherents and gave strong support to AMA participation and E.C. Smith's efforts. This was an encouraging trend, even though nationwide registration of motorcycles had fallen to less than 100,000.

At this time Welch noted that there was no material currently in print in the U.S. to disseminate technical motorcycling knowledge. This was in great contrast to the situation in Great Britain, where both Illiffe and Temple Press published yearly updates of their hard cover manuals on motorcycle mechanics and general knowledge for the benefit of new riders. For this reason, he engaged one Frank Johnson to write a rather condensed manual on motorcycle mechanics, covering past and current Harley-Davidson and Indian machines. Jameson was well qualified to offer this work. A graduate engineer, he had been briefly employed at the Milwaukee factory, had been a shop foreman at the once-prominent Excelsior dealership in Philadelphia, and was presently an Indian dealer in New England. Published by Welch in paperback form as a measure of economy, the book was euphemistically titled Questions and Answers, the author's anonymity preserved by the name Uncle Frank. Launched through the advertising section of the magazine at the bargain price of $1.50, it was an ongoing seller for many years, especially as it was periodically updated to cover subsequent models. Following Jameson's death after World War II, it was updated by "Motorcyclist" Editor Paul Brokaw who carried on the Uncle Frank authorship as its ghost writer. Back issues are sought after today by antique enthusiasts to aid in their restoration projects.

Another of E.C. Smith's AMA expansion projects during the spring of 1933 was to extend its scope to include Canadian riders and Canada's growing number of organized clubs.

Smith's reasoning was that with the ever-growing popularity of American made machines in Canada since before World War I, riders there would be receptive to both conduct competition events under AMA rules, and the possibilities of reciprocal activities across the border.

At this point, Smith might have been unaware that motorcycle marketing in Canada had undergone a recent change with the extension of a 'Buy British' program launched in England in order to stimulate trade and commerce with the Dominion countries, whose loyalty to the Mother Country was then more prevalent than it is today. The practical application of this drive was to induce the Commonwealth Nations to lower their tariff barriers against British goods, and England to lower her restrictions against the entry of Commonwealth products. The abolition of tariff rates on British motorcycles now made them more attractive to Canadian buyers, especially in the case of single cylinder medium weight models, as their first cost was substantially lower than heavyweight American machines.

Smith's visits were concentrated in the British Columbia area of the West Coast, as well as Ontario, Canada's more populous region. He found about twenty-five active clubs of various sizes, but many of these already had a somewhat loose affiliation with the Auto-Cycle Union of Great Britain. A couple of clubs of predominantly Irish members owed allegiance to the Irish Motorcycle Union. Reg Shanks, veteran Harley-Davidson dealer in Vancouver, later reported that Smith's main advocacy of Canadian-AMA affiliation was that it could bring enhanced authority in helping to suppress outlaw competition events on both sides of the border.

It was during these years that Smith assumed more authoritarian control over AMA and M&ATA

THE WORST YEARS OF THE GREAT DEPRESSION 1931-1934

This 1934 VL Harley-Davidson was built for the author by Johnny Eagles in 1985 from mostly new old stock parts supplied by veteran dealers. As a new machine, it represented authentic period performance and handling.
Steve Iorio

activities. James Wright recalled that both the Competition Committee and M&ATA Board members seemed not adverse to this, as Smith's total dedication to motorcycling's cause was evident, and that his aggressive action was showing results in an increase in both rider and club membership in spite of the hard times.

It was also noted that Smith continued in his dual role as a publicity agent for Harley-Davidson. The author recalls that he managed a trade exhibit for Milwaukee at the California State Fair held each fall in Sacramento during 1929 through 1933, borrowing machines from the local dealer, Frank J. Murray, to avoid shipping costs from Wisconsin. It is also recalled that he managed similar exhibits in Illinois, Indiana and Ohio during the same period.

Arthur Welch later recalled that Smith also solidified his editorial control over "The Motorcyclist" insofar as the imposition of his recently mandated AMA policies were concerned. While the reporting on and production of articles relating to competition events in the Southern California and adjacent areas was managed by Welch, Howard Rose, or freelance correspondents, the reporting of Eastern and Midwestern events was totally managed by Smith. He engaged his own correspondents, and all material was submitted to his Columbus office for review before being forwarded to Los Angeles for publication. With this censorship, Smith was able to present an idyllic picture of domestic competition. It also provided a means of denying coverage of foreign machine participation, which will be subsequently discussed.

Smith's censorship also extended to the isola-

tion of American riders from the international motorcycling scene, as he forbade the publication of a section on overseas reports of both the industry and competition events. Welch himself kept in touch with such events, however, by subscribing to both the leading British publications.*5

Welch later stated that he had at the time an ongoing sympathy for Smith's attitude, noting the current depressed state of the domestic market and the loss of a substantial part of the nation's dealerships. A large percentage of the survivors were still in dire straits, being housed in dingy and ill-kept quarters and scratching out a bare existence.

Welch was less in agreement concerning the proffered contributions of a number of former prominent members of the industry with reporting and literary abilities which Smith declared should not be given an airing. Thomas Callahan Butler offered a series of articles on his early day adventures selling Excelsiors in the Southern states. Leslie B. Richards offered to relate the history of the FAM, as did A.B. Coffman and several other veterans of that era. Young Ted Hodgdon, while a relative newcomer to the industry, had already gathered background material on several once popular but now defunct makes of machines, and there were a number of other qualified people who could have made worthwhile literary and historical contributions. Smith at once vetoed the airing of this type of material. His reasoning was (perhaps not totally illogically) that the industry was currently in such a condition that the review of its once promising past could only serve to amplify its present sorry state. He was particularly adamant about lay-

The Worst Years Of The Great Depression 1931-1934

In the 1930's, Speedway racing became popular on the west coast and in the northeast.
Don Emde Collection

Pasadena, California's Jack Milne became one of the big stars of the west coast Speedway scene. In 1937 he became America's first ever motorcycle World Champion when he won the World Speedway Final at Wembley Stadium in England.
Don Emde Collection

ing the history of the ill-fated FAM to rest in the face of his attempts to resurrect present organized motorcycling. Welch's position in the matter was, of course, weakened by the fact that the actual survival of the magazine was dependent on AMA financial support, and the fact that its demise might well be the coup de grace to the industry's future. At the same time, "The Motorcyclist" at once became a lamentably inaccurate and vapid news reporting medium, and consequently of limited value to later historians.*6

As a crowning affirmation of his oft repeated statement that "...we're not interested in past history, we're interested in selling new motorcycles," Smith discarded the contents of the files donated to the AMA when Coffman left his office in 1928. A.B. Coffman later told the author that the news of this brought him much personal anguish, as it represented a valuable history of both the sport and industry, as well as his own decades-long participation in organized motorcycling. While contemporary participants were ultimately able to piece the story together with much effort, much information was irretrievably lost.

During the earlier years of the Depression, both Harley-Davidson and Indian factories were being encouraged by dealers and owners to resurrect two popular models of the past; the two cam J's and the 101 Scout. Both models had been terminated due to difficulties at the time with production costs. Indian's management decided to produce an interim sports model specifically to accommodate the coming Class C competition class.

The new model, called the Motoplane, was fitted with the 45 cubic inch engine already in production and was based on the 1928 Prince chassis. To effect rock bottom economy, the helical gear primary with its expensive-to-make gears was eliminated in favor of a single chain primary within a sheetmetal case. The only innovative feature was a newly-designed dry sump oiling system, with a two-way pump and an oil chamber feeding it from the left tank half. Conceived from an idea mutually concocted by James Wright, Ted Hodgdon, and plant manager Loren Hosley, as a model whose prototype development was all but eliminated, the machine turned out to be perhaps the worst that Indian ever turned out. While the 30.50 engine appeared to work well in the Pony, the 45 cubic inch engine had too much power for the light frame, and under brisk acceleration would shed either the primary or secondary chain with dismal regularity due to frame whip. In addition, the oil pump was of insufficient capacity, and the oil habitually leaked into the crank case when the

machine was at rest. The light pattern clutch and gear box could not handle the increased power, and early failures here were the rule rather than the exception. After less than five hundred units were assembled, production was halted. The only saving feature was the fitting of cylinder barrels with larger inlet manifolds and a larger carburetor, which happily could be fitted to existing 101 Scouts for enhanced power. These were carried forward as spare parts for the long-lasting former models.

In the fall of 1932, Indian dealers and enthusiasts everywhere were saddened by the death of Charles B. Franklin at the early age of fifty-two. A life-long sufferer from breathing afflictions, he succumbed to emphysema. A graduate engineer, his early interest in motorcycling in his native Ireland had led him to experiment extensively in engine design, and he had advanced knowledge on what is known today as flowmetrics (having to do with gas exchanges, combustion chamber profiles, and valve efficiencies). He was responsible for most of Indian's competition, as well as its commercial success after 1920, and his advanced theories were still applicable until the last Indians were assembled in 1953. While Franklin had taken a leave of absence a few months before his death, his last effort was to lay out the preliminary designs of a new Scout model, which, as will be seen, was to have a very significant effect on both Indian's future and domestic motorcycle history.

Due to the incredibly hard times, motorcycle sport had been almost non-existent, except for a few hill climbs. Names frequently mentioned were Woodsie and Frenchie Castonguay in New England, along with Howard Mitzel, who campaigned for Indian. Fred Reiber and Joe Petrali were seen in the midwest, the latter sometimes joining with Windy Lindstrom in the west, all riding Harley-Davidson factory owned 45 cubic inch overhead valve machines built by the factory in 1930. A later rider was Joe Herb.

Short track speedway racing was attracting mild public support, mostly in the west where promoters had given it its greatest impetus. The names of its stars, who were later to gain recognition in other types of events, included Eugene W. "Pete" Colman, Jimmy Gibb, Pee Wee Cullum, Sam Pariott, Bo Lisman, Jack Parker, Wilbur Lamoreaux, Cordy and Jack Milne, Miny Waln, and Lloyd "Sprouts" Elder.

All speedway machines were now British type J.A.P. specials, domestic 45 cubic inch converted roadsters having long been outclassed. Together with Paul A. Bigsby, Albert G. Crocker, Los Angeles Indian dealer, was beginning experiments with his own version of the 30.50 cubic inch overhead valve fuel burning engine specified by the rules. While the speedway promoters gave lip service to the AMA, they operated under their own rules. E.C. Smith never exerted much authority over this phase of the sport, being content that the operators advertised AMA sanctioning in their programming and contributed a small fee for the privilege.

During this period, professional or factory-sponsored Class A competition was all but non-existent. As Indian had stopped hiring professional riders, Harley's Joe Petrali was now the sole professional, and he was expected to spend most of his time assisting William Ottaway and Hank Syvertsen in the Engineering Department. What Class A races there were centered in the very fast dirt oval at the State Fairgrounds in Syracuse, New York. Petrali would put in an occasional appearance there, together with privateer Lou Balinsky. The pair campaigned with three 21 cubic inch overhead valve Peashooters built in 1927, and in the absence of competition, simply toured around the track just fast enough to break the previous year's record. An Indian privateer, Al Toscani, sometimes put in an appearance on a converted 1928 overhead valve Prince, but was hopelessly outclassed without factory support. Petrali later stated that the whole affair was a waste of time, other than keeping Class A racing alive on paper. Veteran Jim Davis agreed, who at times had been alternately representing both factories.

In the meantime, the new Class C rules had been finally established by their official acceptance by the AMA Competition Committee. Smith at once launched a campaign to acquaint the clubs with the news, together with the publication of the rules in The Motorcyclist, as well as flyers mailed out to the various club officers. Heralded as extending competition to all private owners, Smith optimistically predicted a new era in general rider participation. A single line addition to the rules, almost unnoticed at the time, included 30.50 overhead valve engines within the 45 cubic inch side valve category, provided their cylinder compression ratios did not exceed 7.5 to 1. This ruling was to shortly bring on a controversy that was to plague American motorcycle sport for decades.

While the new 1933 rules specified the competition of strictly stock machines, as a paradox, the engineering departments of both factories were put to work devising rule beating innovations to their stock models. They were hoping that the provision that at least 100 examples of any new machines had to be advertised and sold before they were eligible for competition would be reduced.

While Milwaukee was concentrating on improved engine design, Indian embarked on the development of an entirely new model, which was later to gain immortality as the Sport Scout. Based on some preliminary work by the late Charles B. Franklin, the new model included ideas contributed by G. Briggs Weaver, former duPont automobile designer, plant manager Loren Hosley, production foreman Erle Armstrong, and James Hill, a newly hired technician with an already established reputation as a tuner.

Noting the still-present enthusiasm for the late-lamented 101, together with the dismal failure of the Motoplane, it was decided that the best course was to design an entirely new model. Based on the Prince, as were both the Pony and the Motoplane, the Sport Scout featured the open bottom Keystone style built-up frame, the engine and gearbox unit being carried in heavy plates. The engine had the same cylinder dimensions as the 101, but with enlarged cooling fin area and improved breathing capabilities. In order to rationalize production, the mudguards, fuel tank halves, chain guards, tool boxes, and other detail parts were built with the Chief dies and tooling. In addition, the new drive train, in common with the Chief, was now a four-row chain with a Weller tensioning device; both sharing the same clutch and gear set. In addition, both models now featured a two-way oil pump with dry sump return lubrication, the oil being carried in a chamber in the left tank half. In order to lighten the new machine, English-type girder forks were fitted, with suitable adjustable friction dampers. Prototype testing was concluded in the late fall of 1933, and the introduction of the Sport Scout appeared in the March 1934 edition of the "Indian News". Due to the current state of the market and small production, the machine did not appear in substantial numbers until the following fall.

In the meantime, Joe Petrali was testing prototypes of a 30.50 cubic inch speedway machine in Milwaukee. Provisionally designated as the Model CAC, its engine was based on the current J.A.P. design, but with Petrali's own modifications. While the machine showed promise, it was never fully developed as Walter Davidson ordered the project ended as a measure of economy.

In the spring of 1933, Smith's clerical assistant, Alice Brimmer, resigned in favor of marriage and eventual motherhood and was succeeded by two successive replacements whose tenure of office was short. Next hired was Cora Evelyn Reardon, the widow of a serviceman killed in the war, who served through the balance of the decade. Her recollections

Bo Lisman, the Long Beach Flash
Don Emde Collection

Don Emde Collection

of the AMA and E.C. Smith's activities formed an important source of the history of the organization through its particularly difficult period.

In addition to his recent efforts at recruiting and integrating Canadian riders into the AMA, Smith continued his efforts to build membership and encourage club activities. The Gypsy Tours, which had dwindled during the past three seasons, enjoyed a somewhat limited revival and aided in a small growth in AMA memberships. Club activities, such as picnics, scenic road runs, poker and turkey runs, were encouraged, and Smith mailed out one-page flyers with suggestions as to their organization and management.

To combat the often seedy personal appearance of many of the depression-weary riders evidenced at club functions, Smith suggested that members might adopt uniforms for wearing at club meetings and outings in order to present an enhanced public image of the sport. These usually took the form of high boots, peg top English style riding breeches, shirts and visored Persian style military caps. At prevailing prices, such outfits could be purchased for less than $25. Both factories offered to supply these through their own wholesale sources, which provided additional revenue.

Smith also diplomatically attempted to persuade dealers in the run-down premises, all too prevalent at the time, to spruce up their quarters. All of these constructive suggestions were given editorial support by Arthur Welch in the magazine, along with the publicity for individual club activities. Smith continued to monitor competition reports, most of which passed through his office, although many of the West Coast reports were handled by Welch's staff or from freelance correspondents. These journalistic efforts were reinforced by the quarterly in-house publications of the factories who elaborated on the various rider activities that supported their brand name.

The stimulation of individual participation in motorcycle sport now led, in the western states at least, to the more sporting concept of altering roadster machines as 'Bobbers', with elimination of front mudguards, removing the lower portion of the rear, and eliminating excess equipment.

At this point, E.C. Smith sent out a number of directives to club officials, stressing the need to enforce the AMA competition rules. As had been predicted, the inevitable cheating on the mechanical specifications of machines was a constant problem. Scrutineers were warned to be ever on the watch for Stroker Scouts, either built up as 57 inchers with Chief flywheels, or as 52 inchers with Harley 45 lower end assemblies. In order to

enhance acceleration, particularly in the long stroke Harleys, some home mechanics blanked out second gear, allowing for faster starts by eliminating the lag phase between first and top, all of which was in defiance of the rules.

Class C did not achieve any real prominence until the 1934 season. A 200 Mile National Championship and a 6-Hour Championship race held in Keene, New Hampshire was won by Arthur "Babe" Tancrede on a 1932 74 cubic inch Harley-Davidson VL. A 6-Hour TT at Macon, Georgia was a 1-2-3 win for Harley-Davidson, with Howard Almon on a 1931 DL, coming in first.

With the slow return of better times, in 1934 E.C. Smith suggested that an innovative event in the form of a 200 Mile Road Race be staged, with attendant national publicity. The site selected was an unused U.S. Army base at Jacksonville, Florida; a tarred section of streets winding through the area simulating actual road conditions. A large field of both competitors and spectators turned out that September for the event, which turned out to be a disaster in more ways than one.

As E.C. Smith was making tentative arrangements for the event, after receiving permission from the War Department through the Southern Corps Area to use the course, he was approached with an offer from a previously unknown promoter to stage the race. The man in question, a swarthy individual who introduced himself as Gil Lester, spoke of his previous association with automobile racing, dropping the names of several past and present Indianapolis contenders. His offer to finance the race, to provide $500 in prize money, a 10% commission to Smith, all for a 30% retention of the gross receipts, was attractive enough for Smith to accept.

On the day of the race, Lester and two associates occupied a converted fruit stand as a ticket booth, and processed about 5,500 paying entrants at $1.50 each. Half way through the race, Smith was given $500 for the purses; first place paying $300, second, $100, with consolation prizes of $50 for third and fourth places. At the end of the award ceremonies and the dispersal of the crowd, Lester and his associates were nowhere to be found, having quietly departed with the balance of the proceeds.

The much chagrined Smith, along with Arthur Davidson and James Wright, at once launched inquiries among Southern law enforcement agencies in an effort to identify Lester or to ascertain his possible whereabouts, but without success. An ultimate resolution of the mystery was forthcoming some six months later through the efforts of Hap Alzina. Alzina, who was politically well connected in the San Francisco Bay area through his substantial sales of Indian fours to law enforcement bodies, was also acquainted with William F. Knowland, publisher of the Oakland Tribune and himself influential in both local and national politics. Alzina requested Knowland to use his influence to secure cooperation in the matter from J. Edgar Hoover and the Federal Bureau of Investigation. Results from this source were not at once forthcoming, but through a tipster Knowland was put in contact with one Franklin P. Golliard, a former investigator with the Federal District Attorney's Office in Chicago, and who had once been liaison contact with the famous Elliot Ness who had waged a destructive war against Al Capone's illegal breweries in that city. Golliard reported that Gil Lester was none other than Guiseppi "Jo Jo" d'Allessio, a one time

Mafia street soldier for Johnny Torrio in New York, and afterward a contact man for Meyer Lansky with certain gambling casinos in Havana.

As the chances of running down d'Allessio were slim, and with the possibility of reprisals from organized crime against figures in the motorcycle industry, it was decided to drop the matter. While it was obvious that Smith had acted innocently in the matter, he received strong letters of advice from both James Wright and Walter Davidson concerning the future selection of race promoters.

Knowland later became a U.S. senator, and in an interview some years later, he told the author that J. Edgar Hoover for many years refused to publicly acknowledge the existence of organized crime. His thesis was that if his agents had contact with its members, their corruption might well be inevitable. He preferred the more spectacular efforts of gunning down individual bank robbers such as John Dillinger and Baby Face Nelson.

The Jacksonville contest itself turned out to be something of a fiasco. While the declared winner was Bremen Sykes on a Harley, with Rody Rodenberg and Roland (Rollie) Free second and third on Indian Scouts, in the opinion of the contestants and many of the spectators, a newcomer, Ellwood Stillwell of Toronto, Canada, on a 500 cc overhead cam Norton was actually first. Stillwell at once lodged a protest claiming that he had passed Sykes and kept his lead after the 163rd mile. Rollie Free later told the author that he had seen the incident, and that due to inept lap scoring, Stillwell had lost credit for an entire lap!

This incident, while almost unnoticed at the time, was most significant in domestic motorcycle history. It marked the beginning of the introduction of British machines into AMA competition events, as well as the ongoing participation of Canadian riders south of their border, together with the far reaching controversies that accompanied both.

The author's project of assembling domestic motorcycling history received practical encouragement when his maternal grandmother, with whom he had been sent to live following his parents' divorce in 1916, now offered to subsidize his efforts. Evelyn Gunn Van Wormer, the widow of Clement Harry Van Wormer (1848-1915), a one-time prominent central California agriculturist and land speculator, was also a cousin of Wilbur Gunn (1859-1920). A one-time engineer with the Singer Sewing Machine Company, he moved to England in the last 1890's and after engaging in both bicycle and motor bicycle manufacture, founded the Lagonda Car Company in 1906. It was no doubt her interest in his activities that made her aware of the fascination in transportation subjects, somewhat unusual for a woman in her era. Following the death of her husband, she continued to manage the family farms as well as continuing to engage in real estate activities. An educated woman, imbued with Christian principles and possessed of a high moral purpose, her kindness to the author during a difficult period in his life was always greatly appreciated. With her financial help it was now possible to greatly expand the scope of investigation and research.

The Indian Sport Scout did not appear on the market in sufficient numbers to become an important factor in Class C competition during 1934, for reasons previously mentioned. It contained a number of technical features that made it superior in some details to the contemporary Harley-Davidson WLDR that was a sports model based on the updated 45's introduced in the fall of 1931 for the 1932 sales season. Its cylinder dimensions were more square, which gave it an acceleration advantage when converted for racing. It was also available with optional magneto ignition, while the Harley-Davidson was not, which was a definite advantage in both weight saving and tuning possibilities, together with the fact that it was a somewhat lighter machine when stripped for competition.

On the other hand, the Harley had a strong clutch and transmission, compared with the Indian's now-archaic sliding gear type.

Whatever the difference, the early WLDR Harley-Davidsons were often able to win over the older 101 Scouts, even when the latter were fitted with Motoplane cylinders. The momentary technical advantages of the Sport Scout were soon to be challenged, as will be seen, by San Jose, California Harley-Davidson dealer Tom Sifton, a talented mechanic and practical engineer who rebuilt and re-engineered the long stroke 45's. Then, too, the abilities of the rider in any case were an important factor in machine performance.

In summarizing the effects of the Depression, both surviving factories continued to operate under much reduced circumstances. The main problem encountered in the depleted market was, of course, the reduced cash intake. Harley-Davidson suffered from an overall lack of operating capital, and suspended dividend payments on their stock, much to the consternation of the non-motorcycling shareholders. In an effort to bolster their still somewhat viable export business, they continued to offer a rather wide range of models: the 21 cubic inch side and overhead valve singles; a 30.50 cubic inch side-valve single; the WL 45 cubic inch twin; and the top-of-the-line 74 cubic inch V-models. With minor options in compression ratios and detail fittings, there were actually over thirty variant models within the basic three-model program.

For 1932, Indian offered what was basically a two-model range: the 74 cubic inch Chief (being optionally fitted with the former 101 engine gear unit as the Standard Scout) and the long running Four. In 1933 the Pony Scout and Motoplane were added, but in actuality were resurrections of the Prince chassis fitted with a formerly-offered engine.

Indian sustained heavy financial losses after 1930, not making reported profits until after 1935, according to financial reports rendered to the shareholders and the mandated public announcements as required by the Security and Exchange Commission in the Wall Street Journal and the New York Times. The Indian operation was incorporated into duPont's Indu Corporation, a holding company for duPont's other operations that also included the Ball Grain Powder Company. These later enjoyed substantial profits even during the depression years, which neutralized the losses from motorcycle manufacture. In addition, profits from the Ball Grain Powder Company soared briefly early in 1936 from the sale of armament materials to the Protagonists of the Spanish Civil War, before the U.S. Congress passed laws forbidding U.S. firms trafficking in war material.

In reference to the termination of Excelsior-Henderson production, Ignatz Schwinn shrewdly foresaw the coming severity of the Depression, and in doing so quit the game before sustaining any losses. Following the March 31st cutoff date, a small crew of assemblers finished sufficient models to fulfill outstanding orders, with most of the Hendersons going to law enforcement contracts.

By the mid 1930's American's commitment to the heavyweight big twin, as personified by the now re-engineered Harley-Davidson V-models and the Indian Chief, saw their ultimate development as rugged and generally trouble-free machines that were possessed of automotive type dependability. From the standpoint of quality, there was little variation. Either model was fully capable of a trouble-free transcontinental journey, needing only perhaps the addition of some lubricating oil and a possible adjustment of the rear drive chain. While their weight and bulk limited their use to mostly physically fit and possibly athletically inclined riders, their development catered to the now-established segment of the domestic market.

Two Depression casualties in the Indian organization's executive ranks were Ted Hodgdon and Arthur Lemon. Hodgdon was unable to meet the demands of his young family with his half-time employment in the Advertising Department and resigned to take full-time employment in a similar capacity with a local paper products company. He remained close to the industry, however, and subsequently performed freelance assignments at times for his former employer, writing advertising copy as well as contributing an occasional article to "The Motorcyclist".

Arthur Lemon, noting the severe cutback in the planned production of the four-cylinder models for 1933, resigned to enter the wholesale bicycle trade, and subsequently acted as export agent for several leading manufacturers. With only two hundred units planned for 1934, Lemon was afraid that both the model and his job were soon to be phased out.

A little known vignette of domestic motorcycle history was the tentative offering by both Harley-Davidson and Indian of fan-cooled adaptations of both single and twin-cylinder versions of their 45 cubic inch models as industrial engines.

The necessarily higher prices of these converted motorcycle engines mitigated their wide acceptance over the makes already on the market, however, and both companies withdrew from their manufacture after only a very few units were sold.

CHAPTER SIX

THE CANADIAN CONNECTION

THE CANADIAN CONNECTION

Since the turn of the century motorcycling affairs in Canada have had a significant impact on events in the United States. In the early years both public and private transportation developed more slowly in Canada than it did in the United States. The former, a vast area with comparatively few inhabitants, had but a small taxation base for either rail or road building. Rail connection between both coasts was not completed until 1886, the private contractors requiring a government subsidy to complete it.

While proper roads were in place early on in the central province of Ontario, and in the western province of British Columbia in the less-settled areas in the eastern sections and in the Great Plains region had to make do with primitive wagon tracks that were often impassable during inclement weather. As these regions were made more accessible after World War I by extensions of rail lines, some additional private and public transport was available in the form of gasoline-powered rail cars, track speeders, and even a few automobiles and motorcycle sidecar outfits fitted with flanged wheels. As a coincidence, the first private vehicle to make the initial transcontinental crossing was a 500 cc Ariel sidecar outfit piloted by one James Graham Oates, a transplanted Manxman, who made the difficult journey in the summer of 1928. The lack of roads forced him to convert his outfit to railroad use for much of the trip, having obtained prior permission from the proper authorities. It was not until after World War II that a motorist could make the crossing without passing over the border into the U.S. for much of the journey.[*1] This is not to infer that Canadians were not aware of the general world-wide progress in personal transportation. The world-wide boom in bicycling with the advent of the safety bicycle after 1890 was noted in the more populous areas, even though climatic conditions in the eastern and mid-western sections of the country precluded their all-season use. By 1900 numbers of early examples of motorcycles and cars were not uncommon.

Several experimenters constructed motor bicycles in both Ontario and British Columbia, fitting copies of the then almost standard De Dion- type engines. A Toronto firm, Queen City Cycle and Motor Company, marketed such a motor bicycle under the name of "Queen City" in 1903.

Climatic conditions in British Columbia and Vancouver area were more favorable for all-weather motoring, due to the warming effect of the Japanese current. With rarely any snowfall and but moderate rain, motor vehicles at once gained in popularity. Thomas Plimley imported several makes of British cars after 1900, along with such pioneer motorcycles as the Humber and Hobart. A few of these latter makes still survive in the hands of collectors. William H. Morrison, a local bicycle dealer in Vancouver, imported Indian motorcycles as early as 1904. The story goes that he visited the St. Louis Exposition in 1903, where he saw the Indian exhibit and met with George M. Hendee. Impressed with Indian's design, he immediately took a franchise. He was active for some years, Kenneth McFee later taking over the business. Another early Indian dealer was John S. Hall in Nanaimo after 1914, who also handled Excelsiors. The Shank brothers, Reginald and Robert, were early Harley-Davidson and Indian dealers respectively in the Vancouver area. Their father had emigrated to that city some years earlier, having been both a motor trader and aircraft engine dealer at the famous Brookland race course in England. He built a retail building at 97 Fort Street, his sons sharing the premises with their respective dealerships.

The Vancouver area had enjoyed a rather unique prosperity after 1900 as the principal trading port for the newly developing Alaska area following the Gold Rush of 1898. The exploitation of its vast forest products, mining, and fisheries was an economic stimulus that was of importance to a growing motoring trade.

Coincidental motorcycling activity noted in the Toronto area included pioneer Indian dealer

THE CANADIAN CONNECTION

In 1948, the Canadian Motorcycle Association issue with the AMA was a hot topic

Herbert Kipp, soon followed by Walter Andrews with Harley-Davidson, and William J. Porter with Reading Standard, who also imported small numbers of British machines.

As in the United States and other parts of the world, most of the early motorcycle dealers were already established bicycle retailers. A number of these Canadian concerns were soon bringing in such popular American makes as Pope, Thor, Merkel, Reading Standard, Wagner, Minneapolis, and others, as well as various British machines.

The Canadian government followed the lead of the mother country from the earliest days of the motor industry in considering the motorist fair game for heavy taxation. The result was a 10% import tariff, even though the Provinces had little in the way of a domestic industry. A later concession was a lowering of the tax to 5% on unassembled vehicles, envisioning this as a job enhancement for domestic labor. Indian took advantage of this by opening a small factory branch in Toronto in 1911, where components shipped from Springfield were assembled. After its incorporation in 1907, Harley-Davidson followed suit in 1912.

During the pioneer belt-drive era, motorcycling activity was limited mostly to the urban and suburban areas having paved (or at least gravel-surfaced) roads, due to the problem of mud or dust clogging the pulleys. But after 1910 and the advent of the chain drive, the scope of activity was greatly extended. The heavyweight V-twin American machines were favored during this time, especially in the rural regions, due to their high power development and rugged construction. Sidecar outfits, both as passenger or commercial, were popular especially as the third wheel facilitated extension of the more usual seasonal riding. Some solo enthusiasts fitted a light sidecar for off season use, often without benefit of changing the gearing. In some cases, a bare chassis was fitted for stability purposes only, often ballasted with a short section of railroad rail. During this time some domestic sidecars were being manufactured, with at least three firms active in the Toronto area, and one in Vancouver. American machines were also favored for law enforcement uses.

Perhaps the most extensive marketing effort in Canada was launched by the Fred Deeley organization in 1914, with headquarters in Toronto and soon afterward in Vancouver. The Deeley family pioneered motor trade in Great Britain after the turn of the century, and extended their activities to Canada, their initial effort being supported from the mother country. Several popular British makes including

BSA, Norton, AJS, Matchless, and others were featured, along with Riley and Humber cars.

In 1917, Harley-Davidson executed a distributing agreement with Deeley, with the opening of an assembly branch in Toronto, but the few franchises already in place had the option of maintaining their direct contacts with Milwaukee. Following the end of the war, Deeley extended their market by forming other satellite dealerships throughout the provinces.

Percy McBride, a pioneer Ontario bicycle dealer, acquired the distributorship for Excelsior and later Cleveland two-stroke machines. After the war he specialized in Hendersons, and opened a number of branches in the Toronto, Ottawa, Montreal, and Quebec areas.

In general, the marketing and distribution of motorcycles in Canada differed from that already established in the U.S., in that the enforcement of one-make sales was not mandated. This followed the marketing practices laid down by the Motorcycle Traders Association in England, which allowed a dealer to optionally handle a combination of offerings of various competing manufacturers. American machines were offered on the same basis, their makers not be able to mandate domestic restrictions as a condition of franchise. In most cases, the larger operations often offered two or more American makes from the same premises. It was also true that retail dealers exercised the option of dealing with the Canadian distributor, directly with the factory, or through private agreements with U.S. dealers to obtain their stocks from them. Even after Indian opened their factory branch in Toronto, Frank P. Broward preferred for reasons of his own to deal directly with Springfield. While Deeley was designated as the official Harley-Davidson distributor, William Ablitt, in northern British Columbia, continued to have his machines shipped from Milwaukee. On the other side of the coin, several of Deeley's outlets sold Indian spare parts and also repaired and serviced Indian machines; a source of ongoing conflict with the Davidsons!

A prime example of these complex marketing practices was recalled in the case of Palmer Rutledge, who operated Indian franchises in British Columbia. His stocks were usually shipped from Springfield via Spokane and trans-shipped across the border. But if a customer's order for a machine involved a model not presently in stock, he often obtained it from Indian dealer Ira Ordway in Seattle or from Ray E. Garner in Portland. He also had an ongoing agreement with Harley-Davidson's Dawes Rice in Portland to supply

THE CANADIAN CONNECTION

William H. "Billy" Mathews (1912-1982) was a preeminent Canadian Competition star equally known in the United States due to his spectacular win at the Daytona 200 in 1940 and his post WWII participation in the same contest. A Norton International exponent, he usually enjoyed the sponsorship of J.H. McGill, Canadian Norton distributor for North America. For a change of pace, he campaigned in England in the summer of 1948 on the speedway circuit, the photograph here shown having been taken at the West Ham venue on a J.A.P. Speedway Special.
Donald Doody

Canadian customers who preferred them, and maintained a large stock of spare parts for them as well. As a footnote to this rather bizarre situation, he also operated a franchise for Hudson and Essex cars that were shipped from Detroit, as well as for Austin cars from England that were supplied to him by Fred Deeley.

In later years Rutledge related details of another incident that occurred in the mid-1920's during this rather chaotic situation. Incidental to his yearly visit to the Indian factory, he stopped off at Milwaukee to visit the Davidsons. There he was not only royally entertained, but allowed to visit their Experimental Department where Joe Petrali and Hank Syvertsen were working on prototype models. The upshot of his visit was that he was offered a franchise for the Vancouver area, it being one of the periods where the Davidsons were at odds with Deeley over policy matters. Rutledge refused, privately stating that as long as he could obtain as many machines as he needed from Wisconsin, there was no point in tying himself up in any franchise agreement with the factory.

At that time, Indian was particularly strong in British Columbia, with active dealerships in neighboring Alberta, where both Calgary and Edmonton had strong representation. Yet dealers in both these areas also handled Milwaukee products, obtaining both new and used machines and spare parts through George Blanton, the franchised dealer in East Portland. While both the Deeleys and Herbert Kipp had parallel dealerships in the Ontario area, one George Freitas privately imported used and some new machines from the stocks of Knuth's Milwaukee dealership, one of the principals of which was related to the Davidson family by marriage.

Frank Weschler ultimately closed the Toronto factory branch in the 1923 reorganization of Indian, for reasons of economy as well as with the realistic recognition that the unauthorized trading conditions could not be controlled. Harley-Davidson continued through the years with their uneven and often stormy relationship with Deeley. In a recent action however, F. Trevor Deeley, representing the third generation, bought into the reorganized company and was awarded a seat on the Board of Directors.

The Canadian motorcycle market was strengthened in the mid-1930's with the establishment of a large wholesale and retail outlet by the Nicholson Brothers, A.L. (Lawrence) and J.B., Junior (Bernard), in Saskatoon. Both had become enthusiasts at a young age and had sent to England for a 148 cc Dot-Villiers in 1931 to enhance the scope of their newspaper delivery route. They next

obtained a 350 cc Douglas, and subsequently opened a dealership which was later to include BSA, Triumph, Ariel, Royal Enfield, and Panther. This establishment enjoyed a wide market in the growing prairie provinces of Saskatchewan and Manitoba, Canada's heartland, largely devoted to wheat growing and cattle grazing.

They also carried Indian and Harley-Davidson parts and accessories, and offered repair and maintenance services. In 1941 they authored their soon-to-be-famous book, "Motorcycle Mechanics and Speed Tuning", which went through several revised editions. Unable to find a publisher, a common problem with motorcycling journalists in those days, they had it produced privately. Their work was, incidentally, the first hard cover book of its kind published on the North American continent since the appearance of Victor Page's "Motorcycling" in 1915.

In general it may be stated that Canada was a proportionately better market for motorcycles than the United States in the between-the-wars era. The wage and salary scale being somewhat lower, motorcycles were attractive transportation from the economic standpoint. With a free market situation, in contrast to the factory-controlled monopoly in the States, Canadians had a broad choice of machines: from 98 cc upwards through middleweight 250, 350, and 500 cc models and on to heavyweight American V-twins. The availability of all these models at once brought both the younger and older enthusiasts into the game, a market not supplied south of the border where machine choice was restricted.

In addition, Canadian enthusiasts were not kept in a state of journalistic isolation. They had free access to the leading British trade journals which not only kept their readers informed, but through their advertisements exploited the free market concept. The exposure to the ongoing state of international sport was also a healthy stimulus to a broad interest in not only racing, but hill climbing, endurance and economy runs, trials events, field meets, and the attractions of organized club activities in general.

With both British and international influence on the sporting side, Canadian competition developed along the FICM class rulings. With restrictions only as to piston displacement without reference to compression ratios or detail engine modifications, both design progress and individual innovation were encouraged. The original Class C concept of the AMA (ostensibly to encourage amateur competition participation as promulgated in 1933) was not generally popular with Canadian

THE CANADIAN CONNECTION

sporting riders. This was augmented by the fact that the ruling was a factory rather than a rider's edict.

The Canadians, therefore, tended to base their competition rules on those of the British Auto-Cycle Union, which was also subjected to the International FICM. Motorcycle sport in Canada became popular after 1910 when the more numerous American makes sponsored racing and sold limited numbers of competition models. But after the restrictions of the war were lifted and the British motorcycle industry entered its Golden Age, both the Canadians' natural loyalty to their mother country and the logic of their competition rules for class racing led them to follow the International system.

A further stimulus to the sale of British machines was the "Buy British" campaign on the part of the mother country and the tariff concessions instituted between the Commonwealth countries that lowered their landed prices after 1930. As the English makes were already somewhat cheaper than the Yankee big twins, the tariff concession caused a sharp upturn in sales.

After 1935 there was an accelerated interest in competition, and during the spring and summer seasons there were major events scheduled nearly every weekend.

This activity quite naturally saw the formation of many new clubs, which oversaw the promotion of most of the various meets. A pioneer group, the British Empire Motorcycle Club, located in the Toronto area was one of the largest and most active in sports promotion. Leading member C. Gerald Barker, a long-time member of the trade with international connections, in later years did much to collect and record the more important aspects of Canadian motorcycle history. Another historian was Ivan J. Stretton, a competition rider of note in the early days who later reported on Canadian sports in various U.S. trade journals.

Club organization differed from that in the States in that the clubs in each province formed an autonomous group that was governed by the riders and in no way dominated by the trade. While journalists of the day often referred to the Canadian Motorcycle Association, such in fact did not formally exist until organized after World War II. There was a strong association of Western Canadian clubs since 1932 in British Columbia and Alberta which were informally administrated by Frank Carr, who also acted as a liaison with the clubs in the other provinces.

E.C. Smith, secretary-manager of the AMA, with the concurrence of the Board of Directors of the M&ATA, based their decision to attempt to organize AMA clubs in Canada because there was, at that time, no formally organized CMA as mentioned. With a projected AMA expansion across the border, increased membership along with club and dealer registrations and competition sanction fees, the needed cash flow to strengthen the AMA would be enhanced. Not the least of the considerations was that if Canadian competition and club participation was strengthened, the market for American machines already in place could be improved.

Smith, already mentioned, made his first excursion into Canada during 1933, with subsequent visits in 1934 and 1935, meeting with both dealers and various clubs. His sales pitch was that an enhanced AMA could strengthen both the sport and industry in both countries, and that a more rigid control of competition could help to counteract the ever present problem of unsupervised "outlaw" events. Another advantage cited was that in the offering of reciprocity in the matter of competition licenses, Canadian riders could expand their scope of participation by attending certain events in the U.S. when weather conditions were unfavorable in Canada.

The results of this campaign were that while Smith was able to both persuade some of the Canadian clubs to affiliate with the AMA, as well as inaugurating some new clubs, the resulting conflicts between those riders who did not agree with the AMA's established policies and Smith and the M&ATA ultimately brought on bitter feuding that was, in the end, detrimental to the best interests of both countries.

In the first instance, AMA affiliation brought with it the mandate of Class C rules, which both favored American-made machines and penalized Canadian owners of highly tuned British machines whose compression ratios were greater than the long mandated 7.5-1 dimensions.

Also, the lack of AMA recognition of the importance to the Canadians of the smaller displacement ACU-FICM classes tended to ignore what was already an integral part of their competition scene.

In addition, the Canadian club organizations already in place were happy with their autonomous status and democratic rider control, and did not take kindly to the fact that the AMA was governed by the trade without reference to any rider or private owner participation in its decision making.

It was also noted that the AMA did not countenance the type of competition events that were already popular in Canada. These included road racing and long distance endurance or economy

THE CANADIAN CONNECTION

The Norton Supersports machines fitted with both 350 and 500 cc overhead camshaft engines began as the CS-1 in 1928 as first designed by Walter Moore. As updated after 1931 by Arthur Carroll, they were known as "International" models. What with much prototype testing and participation in both international FIM events as well as the Isle of Man TT races, they developed as both superior handling as well as fantastically reliable performers. The example shown is a 1935 factory owned machine that was used to test carburetor adjustments on the famous Brooklands concrete speed course. The large muffler known as a "Brooklands Can" was fitted in deference to noise control in deference to requests from nearby residents. The author has in his collection a similar model but in road going form as restored by John Eagles.
Jeff Clew

type runs. These could be more readily organized in Canada, due to its vast sparsely populated regions together with the friendly cooperation of provincial government bodies that allowed the closing of both public country roads and even city streets for such events.

These latter were an anathema to the AMA, as the typical American Class C-oriented machines with their rigid suspension systems were more suited to broadsliding around horse tracks or hill climbing than the demands of road holding and the niceties of accurate steering.

Then, too, Canadian contestants crossing the border soon encountered what they came to describe as the politics of American regional competition, which had already been well noted in some cases by the American riders themselves, and which were already a matter of domestic controversy. This rather unique situation had to do with the spheres of influence long present in U.S. motorcycle marketing. Indian sales were greater in the northeastern, eastern and southern sections of the country. Harley-Davidson's greatest strength was the great mid-western heartland. This left both in contention for the more active west coast market. The result of this regional preference was that the appointed AMA referees and judges tended to favor the more popular make in their particular area when it came to enforcing rules and deciding close contests.

The issue of brand name favoritism among the appointed AMA officials has long been a central topic of conversation among veteran motorcyclists who entered various competition events

in the mid-1930's after the AMA's classic program came into being. While E.C. Smith was often reported as being philosophically in Harley-Davidson's camp, being politically oriented he was also known to favor Indian contestants in areas where the Redskins were more favored in the marketplace. While these occasional disparities came to be accepted by American contestants, Canadian riders who were used to a more tolerant atmosphere where an unfettered motorcycle market existed, often found this atmosphere difficult to accept.

The diversity of motorcycle makes available and the international type competition rules favoring more classes of machines created a larger percentage of owners who participated in various sporting events than was the case in the States. An attraction for Canadians in joining the AMA was the opportunity of entering additional meets south of the border through the reciprocity agreement offered. There were dozens of outstanding Canadian riders, a few of which became well known in American competition. Among these were Don McHugh (Harley-Davidson) and Jimmy Fergeson (Norton) of Brantford, Norman Teleford (Indian), Trevor Deeley (BSA and Harley-Davidson), and Jim Taylor (Norton) of Vancouver.

The rider who became the best known in American circles after 1934 was Elwood Stillwell, who actually won the first AMA sponsored road races at Jacksonville, Florida, and later entered several of the pre-World War II Daytona classics. A Norton exponent, his machine was a 1930 CSI 500 cc overhead cam International model that had been originally run at Brooklands by factory riders to test cam profiles. Another prominent Norton rider and early American entrant was George Pepper, who narrowly missed winning the 1935 Jacksonville, Florida classic.

The most famous of all, however, from the standpoint of his prowess on both sides of the border was William (Billy) Mathews. Born in 1912 in Saskatchewan, he became a boy rider and later a mechanic at Sturges Motors in Hamilton. Beginning his competition career in 1929, he rode various makes but ultimately chose the Norton. His later participation at Daytona will be subsequently discussed.

THE CANADIAN CONNECTION

In considering the careers of Stillwell, Pepper and Mathews, their generally outstanding successes were inseparably intertwined with the fortunes of the England-based Norton concern, and the 500 cc supersports International model which featured a single overhead camshaft.

The placing of the valves in internal combustion engines was found to be most critical to power development, and the earliest experimenters soon found that a valve-in-head engine made possible hemispherically-shaped combustion chambers that were the most power efficient. The fitting of such, however, necessitated the use of push rods mated to the crankshaft for proper timing of the induction and exhaust sequences, which activated a lever or rocker arrangement above the cylinder heads to activate the valves. While this arrangement, as refined through the years, worked well, there were inefficiencies in the system as there was some lost motion at both the lower end and the rockers due to the necessity for clearance to allow for heat expansion and prevent binding.

In an attempt to improve efficiency early experimenters soon devised an alternative system where the camshaft was fitted above the cylinder head, the drive being effected by either a vertical shaft with bevel gears at both top and bottom, or else by a system of sprockets and chains. The advantage here was that the clearances in the push rod mechanism were eliminated, together with the disadvantage of the consequent acceleration and deceleration of the push rods when activated by the cam gear.

The universal adoption of this system in the automotive and motorcycle industry was inhibited by the higher costs of its fabrication, the use of bevel gearing and shafts involving the most expense. In relation to motorcycle engines, the British J.A. Prestwich concern, a manufacturer of a variety of proprietary engines for the trade, experimented with a small number of overhead cam engines in the early 1920's. Other small firms, such as Chater-Lea and Velocette, engaged in limited production of "cammers", the latter adding a 350 cc sports model to their range in 1925.

The Norton concern's designer, Walter Moore, built a number of prototype engines on his own time, resulting in a 500 cc model which attained a victory in the 1928 Tourist Trophy races. Moore possessed a wide background in automotive engineering. His father had owned an early De Dion tricycle, and as a young man he was employed successfully in both the automotive and motorcycle industry, and before joining Norton worked for several years with the Douglas organization.

Moore's initial model, called the CS1 (Camshaft one) had a single overhead cam driven by bevel gears and featured a three speed Sturmey-Archer gear box. Norton's management encouraged his efforts, as they had supported racing since before Rembrandt Fowler had won the first 1907 TT race with a Peugeot engined machine. Moore resigned from Norton in 1929 to join the NSU firm in Germany, taking his designs with him, as the original patents had been taken out in his name. He was succeeded at Norton by a young engineer, Arthur Carroll, aided by a young Irish rider-mechanic named Joe Craig. Carroll refined the design further, adding a 350 cc model which was identical, except for cylinder dimensions.

Moore's prototype CS1 was subjected to the usual comprehensive testing by Brooklands, with detail modifications following its yearly appearances at the Isle of Man TT. After being additionally modified by Arthur Carroll it was renamed the "International", with the factory designation as the Model 30 for the 500 cc and Model 40 for the 350 cc versions. Its overall appearance remained virtually unchanged after 1932, except that a positive stop footchange close ratio four speed gear box was now fitted.

The resultant design was a machine that possessed a rugged engine that was capable of flat out running for at least 200 miles with remarkable reliability, coupled with a highly developed steering geometry that gave outstanding road holding and accurate steering, even with an unsparing rear frame.

As part of the author's research into the International's role in competition on both sides of the Atlantic, a well-worn but intact example built in 1936 was acquired by the author from Arthur Bennett in England in the mid-1960's. Its original registration documents indicated that it was used only for racing for two seasons, and was reputedly an entrant on the Isle of Man during its first year. In 1938 it was converted to road operation with the fitting of standard mudguards, silencer, tool box, speedometer, and lighting. As restored by Johnny Eagles, it typifies its own legendary attributes of impeccable handling and road holding. With its engine set up with a moderate compression ratio, it cruises happily at 70 mph, its tall gearing causing it to "fire off at every other telegraph pole" in the best Norton tradition.

A most spectacular early appearance of an International was at the second 200 Mile National Championship race held at Jacksonville in 1935, when George Pepper, of Belleville, Ontario, followed Elwood Stillwell's CS1 entry and disputed win the preceding year. Described as a naturally

THE CANADIAN CONNECTION

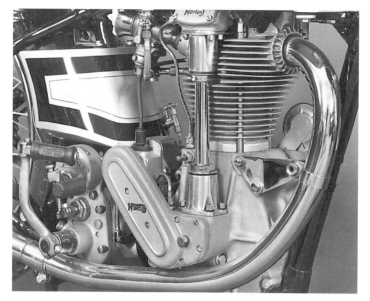

The Arthur Carroll version of Walter Moore's original design proved to be perhaps the most outstanding performer in motorcycle competition by the middle of the twentieth century, dominating international competition between 1932 and 1952. The Norton engines could be counted on to run flat out for at least 200 miles, and given a skilled rider who could make the most of the Norton's close ratio gear box, combined with the machine's legendary handling characteristics, a sure win was often possible. Due to its superior performance, AMA referees in certain districts barred Norton entries as being supersports specials, although a production machine cataloged for public sale and commercially produced in the required numbers made the Internationals legal entrants according to the AMA rule books.
Jeff Clew

skilled rider, Pepper kept well within sight of the leaders of the pack throughout the race, just behind front runners, Bill Carpenter on a Harley and Rody Rodenberg on an Indian Sport Scout. These two ran nearly side-by-side in a wheel-to-wheel duel for the latter part of the contest, with Carpenter running out of fuel in sight of the finish and coasting in just behind Rodenberg for a second place. Pepper was credited with third place four minutes behind the leaders, but both Rollie Free and Joe Petrali, who were spectators, later told the author that in their opinion his placing was actually less than a minute behind Carpenter. Pepper's machine was at once checked by the officials for its compression ratio, which was found to be spot-on 7.5 to 1. Pepper later stated that as usually set up at an 8.5 ratio and burning petrol benzole, as allowed in Canada, his machine was good for at least 112 mph. With a base plate fitted to reduce the ratio to the now standard AMA Class C ruling, and burning the required high octane gasoline, his top speed was now just over 100 mph. As the two contestants' machines were also capable of these top speeds, Pepper theorized that in spite of its lesser piston displacement, the Norton was able to stay with the leaders because of its close ratio four speed gear box that enabled him to keep it "on the cam", coupled with its now legendary steering and road holding, aided by its hand controlled clutch and foot type gear shift that make for quick changing.

In spite of Smith's extension of AMA hospitality and competition reciprocity in his sales pitch to the Canadians in his ambassadorial visits north of the border, Pepper's performance was given short shrift in the report of the race in "The Motorcyclist".

Prepared by one of Smith's southern ghost writers, much space was given to the details of the Rodenberg-Carpenter duel, with Pepper's name and make of machine being relegated to mention only in the box score listing at the end of the article. In spite of this, many of the 10,000 spectators present at the race were treated to their first exposure to the prowess of a foreign make.

Smith's ambivalence in the matter of the extension of AMA membership and reciprocity in sporting competition to the Canadians was at once a matter of concern to both the members of the AMA Competition Committee and certain leaders in the U.S. industry. In discussing the matter with the author in later years, Hap Alzina, Dudley Perkins, and James Wright ventured independent but similar opinions.

Smith at first thought that with the popularity of American machines, together with their somewhat broad and, to the Americans, somewhat unorthodox distribution and marketing, caused him to underrate the growth of the British machine market. He may have been unaware of the effects of the "Buy British" program that had its impact on the Canadian market after 1932, just about the period of his initial overtures across the border. On the other hand, members of the American industry could never be considered cordial to an invasion of foreign machines into the U.S., noting the already redundant state of the domestic market. James Wright was of the opinion that Smith had overrated his own capabilities of authority in the matter. Since 1930, he had been assuming an ever-increasing dictatorial manner in the administration of AMA affairs. The now industry-controlled Competition Committee had gone along with his assumption of this authority as he had within a short period greatly strengthened the AMA and provided strong decisive leadership, the lack of which had caused the ultimate failure of the late and unlamented FAM.

Veteran Canadian motorcyclists have informed the author that in Smith's initial proposals of AMA affiliation he had deliberately played down the presence of the now rigidly conceived Class C rulings for competition, and that not a few Canadian competition riders had somehow conceived the idea that the ACU-FICM rules would remain in place, for small displacement machines at least.

It must be noted that the premier competition events in Canada from the outset of the 1930's were based on the International FICM rules. In 1932, the British Empire Motorcycle Club inaugurated a road race in the Bayview Heights area of

THE CANADIAN CONNECTION

Ontario, a Junior 350 cc and a Senior 500 cc class event that was run in September. The noted multi-millionaire industrialist and racing driver, Kaye Don, donated a handsome trophy especially made for the event.

Edward Hughes of Toronto, on a 350 cc TT type four-valve Rudge, won the Junior event. The following year he represented Canada at the Isle of Man on a Sunbeam. In 1933, Herbert Blair, also mounted on a Junior Rudge, swept the boards to win in both classes.

With the Bayview course no longer available in 1934, the BEMC opted for another type of event, sand racing on the extensive beach at Wasaga, a vacation venue and summer resort on the south shore of Georgian Bay to the northeast of Toronto. The beach location was suggested by Victor Fox, an aviator who had assisted the Mollisons in using the sand for taking off on their West to East trans-Atlantic flight, and who considered the hard packed sand capable of providing a high speed course. A petition for use of the beach for competition was granted by the Provincial Government, and the meet was scheduled for the Canadian Thanksgiving Day, October 24th. Events offered included a 100 mile distance race, up and back along the beach on either side of the wire center line, a 20 mile Beginners race (these to include Junior and Senior classes) along with handicap races for all classes of machines up to 74 cubic inch, as well as sprint or drag race events.

Noted Canadian riders on hand included George Pepper (Norton); Tony Miller (Ariel Red Hunter); Len Duckworth and Jim Roston (BSA's); Morris Goldhart and Les North (Harley-Davidsons); and Jack Fergeson (AJS).

The meeting was somewhat marred by bad weather, so the committee changed the date to Queen Victoria's Day, May 24th, for the following year's races.

As the Wasaga contests became well established as Canada's premier motorcycling speed contests, Smith did not at once attempt to introduce any AMA-Class C type restrictions at this time. His affiliation efforts were confined to inviting established clubs to join with the AMA for the purpose of fraternizing with those south of the border, to join the ongoing Gypsy Tour rallies, as well as the opportunity to compete in stateside competition (under Class C rules). By 1935, about eight well-established clubs in the Ontario area had voted AMA affiliation, along with five in the British Columbia-Alberta Provinces to the west.

The Wasaga meetings were continued through the immediate pre-World War II years with increased popularity. The BEMC improved the course with the use of telephone communication along its length and the building of portable electric timing gear for the sprint and handicap races.

In 1936, the first American riders appeared, and as an anachronistic comparison to the Class C restrictions in place in the States, the two American factories utilized Wasaga as a testing venue for experimental racing engines. Romeo Masse on an Indian Scout, with an overhead valve conversion, was on the scene for the Unlimited Race. During the following year, Earl Robinson, the Detroit Harley-Davidson dealer, entered an experimental 61 cubic inch overhead valve EL model that had been reworked by Joe Petrali. Robinson was accompanied by his father-in-law, Jim Goulding, a former Australian resident who had recently undertaken the manufacture of sidecars and commercial-type rearcars. With his special equipment, Robinson was able to set up a new unlimited class record of 109.67 mph. Later unlimited records were also set by Dick Duchene on a Petrali-prepared EL, Harley-Davidson then gaining the honor of setting up the fastest speeds yet attained in Canadian competition.

Formidable Canadian riders enhancing their former performances included George Pepper, Jim Ferguson, and Bob Sparks on Norton Internationals, Bryan Sparks on a Vincent HRD, and several aspiring amateurs on the newly-introduced Triumph Speed Twins. After Harley-Davidson introduced its newly designed overhead valve EL 61, Phil Allchin, Dick Duchene, and Al Wilson entered them in the Unlimited Class.

After 1934, a number of the new Indian Sport Scouts appeared in various competitions. The one-time Indian distributor and dealer in Indianapolis, Rollie Free, recalled that he sold several machines to Canadian riders who evaded the Canadian import tax by purchasing Indiana registrations and a number plate for the nominal $2.00 fee. They then rode them across the border, posing as American tourists, then re-registered them in their home provinces as used machines.

Several Canadian riders subsequently went to England to compete in the Isle of Man TT as well as appearing on the now-popular Speedway circuit. Eric Chitty, from Hamilton, became the most prominent Canadian in the latter venue.

According to the recollections of a number of Canadian riders such as Billy Mathews, Ellwood Stillwell, and Jim Ferguson, as well as clubmen C. Gerald Barker and Frank Carr, E.C. Smith's ultimate strategy was to isolate the owners of American machines from Canadian affairs. As a

THE CANADIAN CONNECTION

factory controlled organization, Smith apparently was of the opinion that the AMA's prime function was the sales promotion of American machines, and that competition activities should reinforce this policy. In noting the current free marketing concept where dealers and distributors usually offered several makes of machines and often both Harley-Davidsons and Indians, Smith now approached the matter from the club angle.

Meeting initially with Harley-Davidson owners, mostly in the larger cities in southern Ontario, he suggested that clubs consisting of the exclusive Milwaukee enthusiasts be formed. His sales pitch was that with such organization, Harley-Davidson owners could conduct sporting events under AMA Class C rules, and that embarrassing competition from high compression British singles could be eliminated by the simple expedient of barring them from Harley-Davidson-AMA activities.

Smith had previously brought up the matter of the establishment of exclusive American machine clubs in Canada during a meeting of the Competition Committee in the fall of 1935, according to Hap Alzina. He noted that President Walter Davidson had been enthusiastic concerning the idea, and suggested that he had broached the matter with Smith beforehand, noting the Harley-Davidson's top management for many years past had encouraged the distancing of Harley-Davidson owners and dealers from the owners and activities of other makes.

The Indian contingent, however, was less than cordial to the idea. President duPont had relayed his negative sentiments to the Committee through Sales Manager James Wright. The feeling at Indian was that with the sales and marketing practices presently existing in Canada already well in place, the intrusion of the Americans in an attempt to introduce a separatist philosophy would be not only divisive but could very well antagonize Canadian motorcyclists in general. Wright further stated that Indian's management was enjoying the market they had established north of the border, and as long as Indian machines were being actively sold, they had no quarrel with the overall policies of the Canadian dealers and distributors.

The Competition Committee, with a majority of its members now Harley-Davidson factory personnel and dealers, voted to support Smith in the matter after Arthur Davidson had made an impassioned plea for the Committee to augment their support for the cause of American motorcycling. Minority Indian members on the Committee, Hap Alzina and Eugene Shillingford, later commented that Smith's proposal was well in line with the fact

that he was also on Harley-Davidson's payroll as a publicity agent.

While Harley-Davidson had, since 1928, enjoyed majority control of the Competition Committee, James Wright later told the author that Indian's top management at least was not unduly disturbed by this, and sometimes actually relished their minority status. As AMA affairs were generally known to be under Harley-Davidson control, the latter was, of course, faced with the responsibility of enforcing decisions that were sometimes unpopular with the general membership. Then, too, the preponderance of Harley-Davidson oriented referees and officials in many AMA-sanctioned competition events often created sympathy for the Indian marque within both the ranks of the membership as well as with usually less-than-interested spectators. Indian enthusiasts always claimed that Springfield machines had sufficient superiority in speed and power to frequently negate much official gamesmanship.

In spite of some internal opposition in the Competition Committee, Smith proceeded with his tacit organization of exclusive Harley-Davidson AMA sponsored clubs in Canada during 1935. By 1940, he claimed that no fewer than 21 such clubs were in place north of the border. Pioneer Canadian motorcyclists and historians have disputed this, however, including Billy Mathews, Ellwood Stillwell, Ivan Stretten, and C. Gerald Barker, who independently stated in later years that only eleven actually existed. These included one in Vancouver, one in Calgary, seven in various locations in Ontario, and two in Quebec.

Neither Indian's top management nor any Indian enthusiasts within the AMA Competition Committee ever officially encouraged the organization of one-make Indian clubs in Canada, although there were a number of such that had a preponderance of Indian owners within their membership. Many Indian owners also owned British machines, and at various times would enter them alternately in club-sponsored competition.

It is generally conceded that the Harley-Davidson-backed campaign by Smith to form a cadre of exclusive Milwaukee brand clubs in Canada, as well as the attempted importuning of certain north-of-the-border dealers into handling the make exclusively, in the end created much ill will among the Provincial riders.

The Canadians, used to the traditional British system of multiple brand dealerships, pointed out that this policy provided a broad spectrum of choice that increased motorcycling popularity by the offering of entry level machines.

THE CANADIAN CONNECTION

They also resented the fact that as minority makes on the Canadian market, the Americans had no business suggesting that AMA rules applied to British machines in the Class C concept inhibited technical development, not to mention the suppression of the innovative aspect on the part of individual riders and tuners.

The Canadians were somewhat hampered in presenting an official policy on behalf of their own club members and competition riders due to the fact that there was at that time no formerly organized Canadian Motorcycle Association. There was, however, an unofficial liaison between the clubs in the matter of the organization of various competition events. Most of the clubs in any given area were in the habit of sending out invitations to the competition riders of other clubs to participate, or else a blanket welcome in the case of some social events.

Another point of contention was that frequently the Harley-Davidson clubs, mostly in the Toronto area, were subsequently in the habit of scheduling club and competition events on the same date that had been previously announced by the mixed-make Canadian clubs, thus somewhat diluting the attendance of both, from the standpoint of spectator interest. This was a decisive factor prejudicial to the best interests of both factions.

While Smith and Harley-Davidson initially considered that they had in effect set in motion policies that might well promote the best interests of both the AMA and American motorcycles in Canada, the matter of the initially promised reciprocity in across-the-border competition soon arose to haunt them. The previously unrealized competition prowess of certain British models, such as the Norton Internationals, Ariel Red Hunters, and four valve Rudges had now become a factor to reckon with.

In the meantime, and to relish the effect of Smith's intent, C. Gerald Barker and Frank Carr had printed five hundred sequentially numbered cards with the words "Canadian Motorcycle Association" and "Competition License" underneath, together with a space for the bearer to fill in his name and local club affiliation, if any.

During the 1936 competition season, a number of Canadian riders crossed the border to enter AMA-sanctioned events in the midwest and northeast, including Billy Mathews, George Pepper, Edward Hughes, Tony Miller and others. In most cases they did well in both placing as well as winning; the preponderance of victories by Norton International machines giving rise to the privately expressed apprehension on the part of some of the Competition Committee officials regarding the "Norton Menace".[*2]

While these events were ostensibly conceived to promote good will between the sporting motorcyclists of both countries, in most cases the atmosphere was somewhat strained. The Canadian riders were quite naturally aware that the factory-controlled AMA was already attempting to dictate marketing conditions under which American machines were distributed in Canada. Then there was the overriding matter of the Class C ruling on a compression ratio that penalized British machines, together with the prohibition of blended fuels. As a further dampening effect, there was the recollection of the recent gamesmanship on the part of certain AMA officials and referees in the treatment that had been meted out to Ellwood Stillwell and George Pepper during their participation in the 1934 and 1935 Nationals.

A further cause for concern was the great lengths the AMA officials employed to check both the compression ratios and fuel tank content of the visiting competitors, inferring that they were intentionally intending to circumvent the rules.

At any rate, and in spite of some outstanding performances on the part of Canadian riders competing in AMA sanctioned events, reports of the results of these contests did not reach the national readership of the official AMA publication, "The Motorcyclist". Ivan Stretten, a Canadian-born resident of Michigan and now a naturalized U.S. citizen and contemporary motorcycle historian and journalist, told the author in later years that he had executed a prior agreement with Arthur E. Welch to write a column dealing with the results of these international contests for the magazine.

During his initial efforts in the matter in the fall of 1937, Smith got wind of the matter and in a long distance telephone call to Welch ordered him not to print the material. Welch at once protested, expressing confidence in Stretten's journalistic integrity, and noted that as long as Canadian participation in AMA competition was not an accomplished fact, it deserved journalistic coverage in the present sole outlet of U.S. motorcycling news.

Smith reiterated his opposition to any specific reports on the matter, giving as his reason that American and Canadian participation was presently undergoing organizational problems. He also emphasized his previous mandate that as long as the AMA was paying a part of the costs of "The Motorcyclist" production, it was still in control of the magazine's editorial policies.

Still wishing to retain Stretten's contributions, however, Welch engaged him to continue his recently offered column of midwestern motorcycling affairs under the heading of "Michigan Doings", but without reference to any coverage of Canadian participation.

In the meantime, Canadian and American relations were strained further when the chief AMA referee Carroll of Southern California's District 37 arbitrarily barred the entrants of Norton-powered "cammers" in TT and dirt track events in that area. The late Elmo Looper, a long time acquaintance of the author, and his brother, Maurice, were local mechanics and tuners of note. Being recent Norton enthusiasts, they fitted International engines in Model 18 frames, principally to utilize the lighter fuel tanks of the latter. Referee Carroll, in answer to the Looper's protests, stated that he based his ruling on the fact that the machines were non-standard, a purported violation of AMA rules. Looper then pointed out that Indian Sport Scouts were already being entered with 30.50-model fuel tanks and forks to reduce their top weight, and that Harley-Davidson 45 models were also to be noted with reworked tanks of smaller capacity, some of which were being offered to favored riders as factory built items.

Carroll was adamant, however, and Looper made a formal protest to the Competition Committee that went unanswered. Looper at once concluded that recent 1-2 finishes in race meets at the Los Angeles Ascot Speedway and their consistent headings in the preliminary time trials had been the Norton's undoing![*3] What with the current state of affairs, the enthusiasm for Canadian participation in American AMA-sanctioned events cooled markedly, although, as will be seen, some riders still focused on Daytona. By 1938, few competition riders crossed the border. In the meantime, gathering war clouds in Europe were already having a dampening effect on motor sport. The Canadian government began to institute preparedness measures in 1939, and with Great Britain's emphasis on building up its Air Force, Canada followed suit. Several large airfields were hastily established, and the government purchased one hundred Gypsy Moth bi-planes imported from Stag Lane and instituted a pilot training program. Many Canadian competition stars, as well as ordinary riders, enrolled in flight training, emulating their counterparts already enlisted in the Royal Air Force in the home country.

A number of Canadians distinguished themselves in the service of the mother country during the war in all branches of the service. One was notable competition star George Pepper, who flew a substantial number of missions as a fighter pilot in the Battle of Britain, and who lost his life in a sortie over the Channel.

So it was that by the opening of the 1939 competition season, most Canadian events, such as they were by that time, were confined to local motorcycle activities.

As a footnote to the aforementioned proceedings, Stephen duPont, E. Paul's oldest son and a recent addition to Indian's engineering staff, suggested to the AMA Competition Committee early in 1939 that the now-traditional Class C ruling of 7.5-1 compression ratio be lowered to 6.5-1: a move that would effectively bar all foreign overhead valve machines. It was noted that a recent succession of Canadian victories in the northeast, Indian's traditional sphere of influence, had not set well in Springfield.

In retrospect, and in view of the fundamental differences in the basic marketing and sporting orientation of the two countries, in the end it proved unfortunate that any official association between them was ever attempted. Although Smith never revealed any of his private opinions in the matter, it was later thought that his prime purpose in extending the AMA to Canada was hopefully to promote increased sales of American machines. Others were of the opinion that he over-optimistically estimated his executive abilities in attempting to de-emphasize the popularity of the FICM competition rules.

Veteran dealers, such as Hap Alzina, Dudley Perkins, Rollie Free, Marion Dedricks, George Blanton, and Ira Ordway, later expressed the opinion that if a somewhat stronger motorcycle industry that had the resources to develop a broader range of models had survived World War II, the Canadian free marketing concept applied domestically could have done much to expand the American market.

As it was, the scheme backfired as far as Smith and AMA Competition Committee were concerned, as an initial showcasing of British machines resulted in the United States, and Canadian riders were challenged to subsequently invade the American stronghold.

Much of the history of Canadian motorcycling was collected by the late C. Gerald Barker and was published through the Classic period in the newsletters of the British Empire Motorcycle Club. Much of this was made available to the author. Other valuable contributions were made by the late Ivan J. Stretten. His later recollections as well as some additional materials were organized by a young Irish-born Canadian motorcycling enthusiast, Donald J. Doody. A rather broad summary of this material was included in this chapter, along with the recollections of the many American motorcyclists whose experience paralleled this time in history.

Chapter Seven

The Competition Era 1935-1941

THE COMPETITION ERA 1935-1941

The year 1935 was notable for its somewhat improved economic conditions, and for a new era in the annals of domestic motorcycling. The newly adopted AMA Class C racing rules stimulated an increased interest on the part of private riders in motorcycle sport due to the broadened participation it offered. This was also enhanced by the increased interest in club activity, most of whom promoted various competition activities, both for their own members as well as in cooperation with adjacent clubs.

E.C. Smith continued his tireless promotion of club activity. The status of club membership was expanded to honor continuing membership with each renewal pin being numbered as to the years of service in club participation. Another innovation was the awarding of special recognition to clubs for the extent of their activities. The first to receive this honor was Fritzie's Roamers, a Springfield, Massachusetts group founded and sponsored by Frank L. "Fritzie" Baer, an Indian enthusiast and local dealer who operated his own sales outlet from the basement of the Indian factory. In presenting the award, Smith noted that the Roamers had received 2,000 column inches of favorable coverage in local newspapers, had sponsored two dirt track races with proceeds being donated to charities, and had gained local approval through their dignified dress and deportment.

The following year, Smith established a point system for the charting and recognition of club activities, with award categories for promoting field meets, club outings, attendance at Gypsy Tours, publicly advertised competition events, as well as general public service activities. Later that year he established an official AMA affiliation with the National Safety Council, with awards to both clubs and individual riders for miles of accident free riding accomplished.

A rather curious deficiency in ongoing AMA policy, however, was the lack of coordinated promotion of national newspaper publicity for major

competition events. What media publicity there was consisted of news items provided to local newspapers by the individual clubs who promoted the events. In answer to his critics, Smith stated that the current status of the AMA's finances precluded expenditures for extensive advertising, and that local clubs reporting to their own area newspapers was effective in itself.

The concept of long distance touring was fostered by the popularity of the ongoing AMA sponsored Gypsy Tours, which also were important social outlets for enthusiasts. This had much to do with the development of the accessory trade which came to accompany it. Through the middle and late 1920's the surviving factories supplied optional equipment in the form of both touring and law enforcement accessories. These included luggage carriers, saddle bags, wind and leg shields, handlebar muffs, spotlights intended for tourists, with sirens, pursuit lights, and later, radio equipment for police use. A notable accessory was the dual seat for double riding, developed by Harley-Davidson as the "Buddy Seat," and known as the "chumme-seat" from Indian.

This was considered an improvement over the traditional tandem saddle positioned over the back wheel, which could and did give the passenger a rough ride. It was not only safer, but could provide exhilarating contact with a female passenger. Another safety innovation was crash guards: the fitting of the fore and aft tubular type protecting the machine from damage if it happened to roll off the side stand.

The addition of such accessories categorized the machine as a "full dress" or "dresser", the mode suggesting the further addition of such extra fittings as exhaust pipe covers, extra clearance lights, chrome fender tips and bars. These allowed the enthusiast to customize his machine, and was an important source of profit for both the factory supplying them as well as the dealer, with the factory enjoying a 100% markup, and the dealer at least 50%. At field meets and club outings, prizes were

THE COMPETITION ERA 1935-1941

usually awarded for the "best equipped" machines, meaning the owner who spent the most money on additional items of doubtful utility.

The growing accessory market prompted dealers to engage in what became known as "stripping." A full dresser taken in trade would be stripped of its accessories, the new buyer then being encouraged to spend extra money on a new group of equipment. The items removed were held to sell to those who purchase older model machines, all such transactions adding to the dealer's cash flow.

For the 1935 sales season, Harley-Davidson withdrew its single cylinder models from the domestic catalogs, although the 30.50 single was assembled through 1937 for the export market;

mostly for the benefit of Alfred Rich Child who still had a market for it as a utility vehicle in Japan. With the almost universal popularity of the V-twin, American riders appeared to feel that the single was unsuited for real motorcycling. The point may have been well taken, as both the Harley-Davidson side valve Peashooter and the Indian Prince of like configuration were mild performers. The overhead valve versions of both, while offering substantially more power and capability of being tuned for racing, were not well suited to the average utility rider as their exposed valve gear was subject to constant adjustment, wore rapidly, and collected dust and dirt. As mentioned, the utility motorcycle in the U.S. lost out to the competition of the cheap used car, as the latter's Depression-era prices had fallen

A mid-1930's Classic. Charles Vernon's 1935 Indian Chief.
Harry V. Sucher

Michael Steckley with a newly restored 1938 Indian four.
Harry V. Sucher

THE COMPETITION ERA 1935-1941

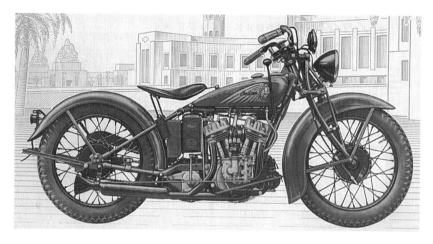

(Top) The 1940 Indian 30.50 Scout that formed the basis of the Wigwam's War Department models. *Indian Motorcycle Company*

(Above) The Author's 1938 Indian Sport Scout. *Harry V. Sucher*

to ridiculously low figures.

Indian had already phased out its updated Prince model in 1928, having paid little attention to the promotion of the overhead valve version, of which few were assembled. The Pony Scout, which was merely a Prince with a sleeved down standard Scout engine, proved to be a better seller; no doubt from its more acceptable performance and the fact that it followed the current following for a V-twin.

The newly introduced Sport Scout proved to be something of an embarrassment to both Harley-Davidson and Indian as well. With its high power-to-weight ratio (thanks to Charles Franklin's flow metrics) it could, if called upon, outrun the top-of-the-line Chief. It was especially potent if "stroked" with Chief flywheels and connecting rods, a common practice with sporting riders.

Skilled riders, such as Fred Ludlow and Rollie Free, engaged by the factory to undertake speed trials on dry lake desert courses, told the author if both models were tested concurrently, the throttles of the Sport Scout were ordered "rolled back" to give the Chief a 2-3 mph edge.

The Sport Scout also had a decided edge over the 74 cubic inch Harley-Davidson models, not only in top speed but also in acceleration. due to its enhanced breathing and over 100 pounds of less weight. Harley-Davidson enthusiasts continued to mourn the absence of the JDH "two cammers", citing their superior performance over the V models, although the latter was a much more dependable machine and was free from the petty adjustments that were part and parcel of cammer operation.

Harley-Davidson, in fact, had its engineering staff working on an overhead valve big twin ever since 1931. It was then considered that their side valve designs had been developed as far as was practical, according to Joe Petrali. William Harley, as titular head of the engineering department, relied heavily on William Ottaway, who had originally been retained in 1913 to improve the basic Harley-Davidson configuration. Ottaway was later assisted by another practical engineer, Hank Syvertsen, with the added contributions of the gifted Petrali after 1930. While Harley was well versed in engineering theory, his abilities appeared to have begun and ended with his refinements of the original work of De Dion and Bouton. His efforts being described by contemporaries as plodding rather than brilliant. At any rate, the staff came to the agreement that the best compromise in design would be to have the push rods work off a single nosed cam, as already proven in certain of the British J.A. Prestwich engines, with coil and battery ignition activated by a gear driven generator.

Petrali later told the author that a two cam mechanism was briefly considered, but that the noise of the added cams, together with the five pinion drive to the generator, had been a problem in some of the prototypes. A chain drive to the generator was considered for its simplicity, but was shelved because of being too similar to Indian's Sport Scout.

Coincidental to the overhead valve development, an 80 inch version of the V models was introduced in the fall of 1935, for the 1936 sales season, even though the series was to be phased out at the end of it. Known as the "U" models, they featured 1/4" more stroke which provided better torque for sidecar use but without enhancing the top speed. Both this and the continued 74 cubic inch model were now fitted with nine instead of seven stud heads, to correct their tendency to blow head gaskets during high speed running.

In retrospect, the V models as refined, were rugged, dependable machines, giving a comfortable ride with soft fork action and spring seat post. They were well accepted, mostly for heavy duty sidecar work as military models in the Orient, and were often the machine of choice for law enforce-

THE COMPETITION ERA 1935-1941

ment employment at home. Due to their relatively short production life, and under the handicap of a depressed market, only about 20,000 of the model were built, half of which were exported.

In 1984, the author was fortunate to obtain sufficient new old stock VL parts, supplied to him by veteran midwestern dealers who cumulatively had enough on hand to construct a complete machine of 1934 vintage; the first year that featured the contoured mudguards. With paint finish and careful assembly by Johnny Eagles, the mid-1930's ambiance of a new machine could be experienced!

In the summer of 1935, enthusiasts and members of the industry were saddened by the sudden death of Frank J. Weschler, then the President of the Baldwin Chain Company of Pittsfield, Massachusetts. A member of Indian's management staff since 1909, he had been appointed General Manager in 1913, following Hedstrom's resignation, and had been in virtual command of all company affairs following Hendee's resignation in 1916. His almost single-handed salvation of Indian in 1921-1922, and its subsequent recovery has been described, as has his presidency of the company during its salad days until his resignation in 1927. His dedication to both the cause of Indian and the well being of the industry were the hallmarks of his life. Weschler's kindness and congeniality had won him the friendship and respect of compatriots and competitors alike. His on-going connections with the Davidsons involving the conduct and policies of the industry had made longlasting and productive impressions. As a paradox, he had never been a motorcycle rider: his excursions were limited to being chauffeured as a sidecar passenger by some company associate.

The author left Benicia and returned to his home in Santa Rosa in 1934, at this time well into serious research regarding domestic motorcycle history. While enrolling in a science course in the local community college that would include premedical studies, a course in journalism was included as an elective. The mechanics and techniques of professional historic research were also explored under the tutelage of two helpful local librarians, Ruth Hall and Dagney Juell. Additional help was provided by the college librarian, Grace Jordan.

A significant breakthrough in the author's research occurred with a most fortuitous meeting in January 1935, with Vernon Guthrie at the West Coast Automobile Show held in San Francisco's Municipal Auditorium. Guthrie was attending in connection with his activities as a free lance journalist covering automotive affairs for his series of articles that were concurrently appearing in a num-

ber of Southern California newspapers. This introduction, which had been arranged by Nelson Bettencourt, led not only to access to Guthrie's broad knowledge of past and present motorcycling affairs, but also to his encouragement to the author to continue his pursuit of the subject. Guthrie noted that he had concentrated his journalistic attention on automotive subjects after finding that the general media, as well as publishing concerns, took a dim view of accepting offerings dealing with the almost redundant motorcycle industry. It was their opinion that there was insufficient public interest to warrant their attention.

Also noted was the indeterminate position of the motorcycle trade press being slanted toward promotional rather than objective reporting. Noted also was the amateurish quality of the reporting. At the same time, Guthrie went out of his way to provide to the author introductions to prominent members of the industry over the ensuing years, and also put at his disposal access to his vast files of motorcycling memorabilia, as well as some unorganized manuscript material dealing with early day historical events. Prophetically, he was firmly convinced that some time in the future formal attention to domestic motorcycling's past would attract public attention.

During the middle and late 1930's, both E.C. Smith and the Competition Committee, as the overseers of domestic motorcycling affairs, tended toward an increasingly projectionist attitude toward the industry. This was heightened by the experiences with the now aborted Canadian affiliation which many members of the industry considered to have been a mistake.

With a still-marginal market for domestic machines, the possible showcasing of foreign makes was, in some quarters, considered to be a real threat. Up to this point in time, Reggie Pink in New York City appeared to be the leading protagonist of British machines. He believed that an area of heavy population riders with esoteric tastes could exist in sufficient numbers to make his operation profitable. By 1937 he was offering such well known British makes as Ariel, Rudge, Douglas, Velocette, Triumph, along with a few Villiers engined lightweights. Of these, the newly introduced Triumph vertical twin was attracting the most attention. At the same time, Pink did not enter into any large scale import agreements with British manufacturers, nor did he ever, as far as is known, attempt to open any branch operations.

In the spring of 1936, Rudge enthusiast Paul Hanniford, a Pink customer, conceived the idea of forming an AMA club made up of owners of

155

THE COMPETITION ERA 1935-1941

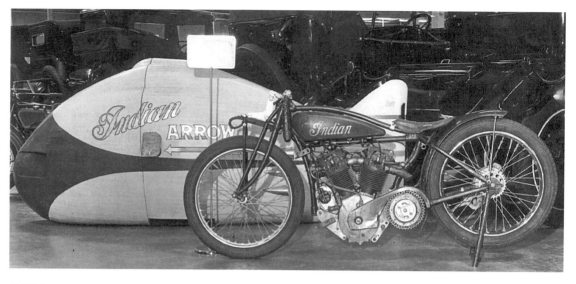

The Indian "Arrow" project which was used in Indian's ill-fated attempt to break the world's solo speed record with Fred Ludlow aboard at Bonneville in 1937. The machine was built up under Hap Alzina's direction by Marvin "Red" Fenwicke, and was fitted with a specially tuned 61 cu. in. ohv engine that was originally used in a factory board track machine in 1924. While fitted with the streamlined shell shown in the background, the aerodynamics were such that the machine became unmanageable around 125 mph and Ludlow narrowly escaped injury.
Harrah's Automobile Museum

Alfred Rich Child delivering the first 1936 EL Model to a buyer in Japan.
Alfred Rich Child

British makes. He contacted E.C. Smith concerning the chartering of such a club. Pink, who tacitly approved of the idea, refrained from publicly backing Hanniford, as he was an AMA member and held a competition license, and apparently did not wish to jeopardize his current AMA standing. Predictably, Smith refused to consider the proposal, stating in a letter to Hanniford that such a move would be divisive, and suggested that he and his associates should integrate themselves into one of the already established AMA clubs in the New York area. Hanniford, in reply, stated that there already existed divisive elements within the AMA as there were AMA chartered clubs throughout the country that consisted of exclusive groups of either Harley-Davidson or Indian owners. To this, Smith refused to answer.

Coincidentally, Jack Frodsham, a one time Velocette factory employee and a recent immigrant, established a dealership for Velocette in modest premises on West Pico Blvd. in Los Angeles. In noting the limited but potentially growing interest in Southern California for foreign machines, Frodsham also offered a line of accessories, tires, and other British components, including Lucas and Miller electrics. While Veloce Limited offered to supply the complete Velocette line, Frodsham concentrated on their two high performance models: the 500 cc MSS and the 350 cc overhead cam KSS. The latter model ultimately attracted substantial attention from sporting riders for its high performance capabilities as a 21 cubic inch machine: a size heretofore domestically considered as a mere utility mount.

The KSS, as a race bred machine with impeccable handling characteristics, was capable of being set up in three ranges of tune; the compression ratios being altered by the adjustment of the three shims fitted under the cylinder barrel, along with the Oldham coupling within the cam shaft drive. In good tune and using high octane fuel, the KSS was capable of top speeds of 70, 80 and 90 mph.

A Frodsham protege, Curly Harker, was able to set a 21 cubic inch record of 100 mph at Lake Muroc with a stripped and specially tuned KSS burning blended fuels—a new American record.

The author subsequently obtained a KSS from England that was rebuilt by Velo enthusiast Eddie Arnold of Glendale. With the engine set at Stage One, Arnold declared that the machine could be run continuously at full throttle, the stresses at this point would not be critical!

Frodsham later told the author that between

THE COMPETITION ERA 1935-1941

1935 and 1940 he was able to sell an average of twenty-five machines a year of both KSS and MSS models.

Another British invasion during the late 1930's in Southern California was announced by William E. "Bill" Johnson, a wealthy corporate attorney and motorcycle enthusiast, who was also the financial backer of an Indian agency in Pasadena. The story goes that Johnson noted a 1931 600 cc Ariel Square Four in Honolulu while on a visit to Hawaii and, being impressed with its performance, entered into a tentative agreement with the reorganized Ariel and Triumph concern in England for the importation of both makes.

Indian announced a revised version of its four cylinder model in the fall of 1935. The machine had undergone several face lifts since 1932, such as a heavier frame and restyled mudguards, all of which added weight, but without substantial improvements to the engine, which was essentially the same as offered by William Henderson in the 1919 Ace. Indian's Chief Designer, G. Briggs Weaver, who had been associated with E. Paul duPont in his wartime marine engine manufacture and the later duPont car, in an attempt to provide more power from this obsolete design, altered the valve gear into an unconventional overhead exhaust and side valve intake arrangement. While somewhat more power was

realized, the setup proved unreliable. As most of these models were sold to law enforcement, the subsequent complaints saw him attempting to improve the situation by fitting it with two carburetors in 1937, cataloging the model as the "Sport Four." Continuing problems led to the designing of an entirely new engine for 1938, but not until after 1,600 of the "upside-down" fours had been assembled during the previous two seasons to recover the tooling costs.

The annual price-and-policy fixing meeting between Indian's and Harley-Davidson's top management was held early in the spring of 1936, incidental to the special discussion of the Canadian situation as noted. Present were Walter and Arthur Davidson, Hank Syvertsen, E. Paul duPont, James Wright and W. Stanley Bouton. It was noted that with the growing divergence of the two company's range of models, the former close adherence in retail pricing could not be retained. Indian's Four, at $445, had no Milwaukee counterpart. The same was true with Harley-Davidson's forthcoming overhead valve 61 cubic inch E, whose manufacturing costs were stated as mandating a $395 price tag. Indian's 30.50 cubic inch Junior Scout had no Milwaukee counterpart, and there was no objection to lowering its price to $195. It was then agreed that Indian's 74 cubic inch Chief and the forthcoming updated Harley-Davidson 74 cubic inch side valve UL would both be offered at $340, but with a $10 premium for the 80 cubic inch ULH model. The Harley-Davidson 45 cubic inch WL and Indian's Sport Scout would remain at their former $300 parity.

The management of both factories noted the erosion of the foreign markets due to the worldwide Depression, as well as the effect of the political uncertainty in Europe due to the onset of the civil war in Spain. Also noted was the competition in the V-twin market from AJS and Matchless in England, although their machines were not as trouble free or rugged as the traditional Yankees.

While both Harley-Davidson and Indian had established marketing outlets in Spain's larger cities, such as Madrid and Barcelona, both factories had lately received direct orders for big twin military sidecar units from both of the warring factions. It was at once agreed that, due to the controversial nature of the conflict with the interjection of the opposing philosophies of Fascism and Communism, along with the world-wide condemnation of the war, the American factories should soft pedal any references to the use of their products in the war in company advertising.

James Wright later recalled, for the benefit of

THE COMPETITION ERA 1935-1941

Sam Pariott at Muroc Dry Lake for speed trials with his 30.50 cu. in. Crocker Speedway racer, foreground, and his 61 cu. in. Crocker V-twin. About 40 examples of the former were built between 1935 and 1940, and 65 of the latter were built between 1936 and 1941. The latter was reputed to be the fastest V-twin made in the U.S. during its short time of production, and could be ordered in any displacement between 61 and 90 cu. in.
Sam Pariott

the author, in reporting on the meeting, that a Spanish enthusiast and photographer, Ramon Hayes, had sent a number of photographs to Springfield showing Indian machines in combat situations, which Wright immediately destroyed.

E. Paul duPont enlarged on this theme, warning the top members of the industry that many of the world's manufacturers were currently under fire for supplying material to the combatants, including duPont's Ball Grain Powder Company. He noted that while the traditional duPont explosive production was a perennial target for pacifists, it had come under additional fire when its arrangement with the German I.G. Farbin, had been revealed. He saw no reason why the marginal domestic motorcycle business should not now be sheltered from public condemnation.

The duPont family was also much in the news during 1936 with the announcement of the forthcoming marriage of President Franklin D. Roosevelt's son, Franklin, Jr., to Ethyl duPont, a niece of Pierre S. and a cousin of E. Paul. The elder Roosevelt would only give his blessing to the marriage if the principals would agree to the withholding of their public announcement until he was safely re-elected on the first Tuesday in November. With his cultivated public appeal to the voters as a populist type of Chief Executive, he considered that a marital union between a member of his family and that of one of America's richest might somehow tarnish his image as a champion of the common man. At any rate, the scheduled Thanksgiving ceremony was the most glittering affair of the New York social season. In common with all the other second generation Roosevelt's matrimonial excursions, the marriage only lasted a short time.

Harley-Davidson's new overhead valve 61 cubic inch model was launched by the factory with some trepidation and little fanfare in the spring of 1936. With no special advertising other than the usual self-serving plaudits in the current issue of "The Enthusiast," 1,926 units were fed into the market.

The model was entirely new, with an updated heavy cradle frame, and a restyled fuel and oil tank; the mudguards of the previous V models being retained. Much of the prototype testing was conducted by William Harley's son, who suggested extensive adjustments to the steering geometry. A rather massive 650 lb. machine, it was of compact form in an attractively streamlined motif; typifying the ongoing commitment of the American industry's preoccupation with heavyweight machinery.

A point in question was the valve gear, with exposed rockers and oil lines feeding lubricant under pressure as a self-circulating system that replaced the former total loss type as seen in the former V production. The initial examples performed well, but the lubricant was forced out of the orifices over the rockers, with the return lines to the crankcase seemingly too small to accept the surplus. This fault aside, a design plus was the fitting of a massive four speed gear box of the constant mesh type with a drum controlled rotary shifter along with a massive multi-plate clutch.

The author was offered a test ride by Joe Frugoli on his initially received model. While the new EL showed a marked advantage in speed and power over the former V type, the author's legs were saturated with oil after a short run.

Both the dealers and a few initial buyers were predictably disappointed, and harking back to similar teething troubles with the initial V models in 1930, they questioned the factory's strategy in putting the E's into production without more thorough prototype testing. In commenting on the affair to the author, Petrali stated that the engineering staff was well aware of the problem but that President Davidson had signaled a go-ahead on assembly because a shortage of funds in the company treasury, in his opinion, mandated putting the machines on the market as soon as possible.

Alfred Rich Child later revealed that the company had hoped to sell him the Japanese production rights for a suggested $100,000 to add to his in-place line of Rikuo models. But on a 400 mile test ride through Japan on the initial sample, Child's son, Richard, noted both excessive oil leakage from the cylinder heads as well as rapid wear in the rockers themselves that put the machine out of tune to the extent that he barely was able to make the trip home. Child then declined to consider the purchase of the EL production rights, noting that the side valve models were best suited to the Oriental market.

The factory then instituted a round-the-clock program to correct the fault and, in the end, offered replacement kits of both covers and rockers with improved metallurgy for the initial production of 1,926 units.

The 74 and 80 cubic inch V models were phased out that fall, with newly designed side valve models of the same displacement, designated as the "UL" and "ULH" types that shared the same cycle parts as the "E" series.

The 45 cubic inch WL type was restyled utilizing the E and U cycle parts, such as the tank halves, mudguards, and other fittings to rationalize production. A rugged and dependable machine, it was somewhat heavy as updated, and was considered as a utility rather than a sporting machine with an actual top speed of less than 60 mph. It found favor with ride-to-work riders, and was popular on the export market, being favored by military and constabulary users in Central and South America where the generally poor roads precluded high speed running.

The 1936 models were carried until the opening days of World War II with very minor detail changes, together with the subsequently improved EL model after 1937.

A surprise announcement in the spring of 1936 was that former Indian dealer Albert G. Crocker was launching his own make of heavyweight V-twin. Crocker had dropped his Indian franchise in Los Angeles to manufacture his own make of speedway machine: a 500 cc alcohol burning design based on the current formula. For several years he had contemplated the building of his own design of a high performance V-twin, and had previously designed an overhead valve kit for attachment to Indian Chiefs and Scouts, in collaboration with Paul A. Bigsby, who, for three years, had acted as shop foreman at Crocker's extensive premises at 1346 Venice Blvd. in Los Angeles. In addition to performing general machine work, Crocker had, for some time, been turning out lower bearing assemblies for Indian, as well as performing various types of commercial aluminum casting work in his foundry facilities.

The Crocker motorcycle was a compact machine, based somewhat on the Indian lines with girder forks and a massive three speed gear box whose case was cast as an integral part of the frame. The engine was a nearly "square" bore and stroke overhead valve design, capable of being bored to accommodate cylinder displacements of anywhere from 61 to 90 cubic inch; each machine being more or less custom made to the buyer's specifications.

The machine was made almost entirely in Crocker's plant, except for electrical components, handlebars, saddles and the like. The fuel tank halves, footboard platforms, engine cases, tail lamp receptacles, and magneto drive covers were all of aluminum alloy, all made on the premises.

A noisy, somewhat intractable and difficult starting machine in unskilled hands and with a tendency to leak oil, it was, nevertheless, a potent performer that was 10 to 15 miles faster in stock form than the contemporary big twins of like displacement.

Fulfilling a long standing dream of its designer to create a really high performance motorcycle, it

THE COMPETITION ERA 1935-1941

Floyd Emde at Oakland in 1941.

Veteran Harley rider Jimmie Braithwaite with a factory supplied WR at the Ascot Speedway, 1940.
Joe Walker

at once found favor with those few hard riding enthusiasts who could afford to pay $75 to $100 premium over the less expensive competitors.

On the sporting side, there was now continuing interest in Class C competition, due to the possibilities of an aspiring amateur to enter the game at a modest cost.

At the same time, interest in speedway racing declined somewhat after the mid-1930's. The costs of acquiring a machine and maintaining a pit crew and a mechanic were substantial, and the competition limited the field to a few top riders. Then midget car racing became a preoccupation on the sporting scene after 1935, and was an attraction to those who could no longer afford to maintain full sized sprint cars.

A surprise announcement that fall was the launching of a new make of lightweight motorcycle, called the Servi-Cycle, by a small New Orleans engineering firm. The Simplex Company had been conducting mild experiments with moped-like machines ever since the onset of the Depression in the search for really low cost transportation vehicles. The Servi-Cycle was just that: a bicycle-like machine with an ultra simple two stroke 118 cc engine that featured an overhung crankshaft and a flywheel magneto that fired two sparkplugs to overcome the inertia of its low tension current. The drive was effected by two commercial type rubber V belts, the primary activating a centrifugal clutch under the saddle, the secondary to the rear wheel driving a pulley whose diameter was nearly that of the rim in order to provide the proper gearing, the whole having the aspect of a 1905 clip-on.

As a further concession to simplicity, no kick-start mechanism was fitted, the rider started off by paddling the machine with his feet, getting under way with the use of a compression release in the cylinder head.

Aside from a brief article in "The Motorcyclist" announcing its introduction, the manufacturers provided no further national advertising. The machine remained a purely local offering in the New Orleans area until after World War II.

As an adjunct to the increasing interest in motorcycling activities, a number of enthusiasts undertook some solo long distance runs. While these were not included in official AMA rules, and in fact were specifically forbidden, they attracted much general attention and enthusiasts' approval. Earl Robinson, the active Detroit Harley-Davidson dealer and competition rider, set a new transcontinental sidecar record of 89 hours, 50 minutes. His passenger was his attractive wife, Dorothy, an active rider, who was also a member of the Goulding family of sidecar manufacturers.[*1] Another Harley-Davidson enthusiast, Fred Ham, an athletic Pasadena motorcycle officer, revived the once-popular Three Flag run on a 1935 VLD for a record of 28 hours, 7 minutes from Tijuana, Mexico to Blaine, Washington, the Canadian Port of Entry. Shortly afterwards, Bill Connelly and Frank Dauria lowered Robinson's record to 69 hours, 46 minutes, with an 80 cubic inch VLU sidecar outfit. The record was not broken until 1959.

Indian competition star Rody Rodenburg claimed a new transcontinental solo record on a Sport Scout with a time of 71 hours, 20 minutes. This claim was later disputed with the allegation that Rodenberg was accompanied by a friend in an automobile who towed his machine at night while he slept!

At any rate, while these records were never officially recognized by the AMA (being outside the current Class C rulings) both factory advertising as well as the trade press gave much coverage to the intrepid travelers.

The accelerated AMA activities now put added responsibilities on the office staff at Columbus, headed by Cora Reardon, who by this time had one full-time stenographer and two part-time assistants. While she was able to take charge of much of the routine administration and correspondence, much of the detail decisions were within the province of E.C. Smith, who was more often than not traveling in the field. As a result, there was often delay in answering requests for sanctions, as well as in the awarding of trophies or commendations for winners of competition events. In consequence, there were numerous complaints from individual members as well as from club officials. In addition, there were difficulties in meeting the publication deadlines of "The Motorcyclist" for the inclusion of the reports of recent competition events. Upon their receipt at headquarters from the various correspondents, they were at once forwarded to Smith at various predesignated locations, where they were either accepted, rejected, or rewritten to suit Smith's policies before being forwarded to Welch's Los Angeles office.

In addition, Mrs. Reardon recalled that certain office files were kept locked by Smith and were in his private domain and off limits to office personnel. Items of correspondence marked "personal" and the minutes of both the meetings of the M&ATA Board of Directors and the Competition Committee were always carried by Smith in his briefcase. Much of this material was subsequently transferred to the Harley-Davidson headquarters in Milwaukee, either by Smith or by others. Mrs. Reardon also recalled that on more than one occasion certain of Smith's files were collected in Columbus by Walter Davidson, Jr., and loaded into Arthur Davidson's Franklin Airman sedan.

It was thought by some that these practices were carried out to conceal the details of Smith's private arrangement with Milwaukee in regard to his public relations work on their behalf. Although the M&ATA Board had long been aware of this arrangement, Smith later claimed that he kept much of the AMA's records from public view "to avoid having the Competition Committee subjected to public criticism."

As far as the personal makeup of the Competition Committee went, the names of its members at any given time were not often published in connection with reports of their meetings in "The Motorcyclist." The membership of the group was constantly changing, as attendance at the meetings required in most cases long distance travel. Thus, an appointed member might be willing to serve for a year or so, but with the economic conditions of the time, the continued expenditures for travel could well be a hardship. Then too, with the controversial nature of some of the Committee's decisions in the control of sporting events and rulings, many did not want to be identified with the Committee for too long a period.

In noting the prominence of the far west and southwest in motorcycling affairs, Smith sought to strike a balance with the east and northeast sections of the country in the matter of scheduling national sporting events.

The first big national event following the institution of the Class C rules was a 200 miler held at the fairground course at Keene, New Hampshire. Smith induced several of the newly reactivated clubs in the area to pool their resources to promote the event, which, following much advance publicity, drew a large crowd of both motorcyclists as well as spectators. Organized as a six hour TT event, it was won by Rhode Island police officer Arthur "Babe" Tancrede on a VLD Harley-Davidson, a 1932 vintage machine that was in generally stock form.

Later, in the summer of 1934, another six hour National was held at Macon, Georgia, this time a 45 cubic inch dirt track event. It was won by Howard Almond on a 1931 DLD Harley-Davidson in a close finish with a large field of contestants.

That fall a national road race was held at Camp Foster, Florida (an unused U.S. Army base) and was won by Bremen Sykes on another DLD. His win was disputed by a Canadian entrant, Elwood Stillwell, who was entered under the newly instituted reciprocal agreement by the AMA with north-of-the-border riders. Stillwell claimed that lap scorers overlooked one of his initial circuits on his 500 cc International Norton.

Following the second 200 Mile National road race held at Camp Foster in 1935, a dispute arose over the Rody Rodenberg-Bill Carpenter 1-2 placing over Canadian George Pepper. The Competition Committee decided to schedule future events such as TT contests in order to allow large displacement American machines to compete. It was thought that this move would make it more difficult for any future Canadian entrants on British machines to have an edge over 45 cubic inch Yankee contestants.

Class A short track racing was, by this time, failing in popularity in the west. A few eastern tracks, such as those at Coney Island, Newark, New Jersey, and Hershey, Pennsylvania, were still drawing sizable crowds.

At the same time, some of the older western tracks, such as those in Los Angeles, San Diego, Fresno, Modesto, Lodi, Redwood City, Sacramento and Chico, were revitalized as Class C venues, and were drawing fair public support for the racing season.

The now revitalized Gypsy Tours were being well supported when held concurrently with the big nationals in the northeast and east, as well as in such western venues as tours to Borrego Springs, Yosemite National Park, Lake Tahoe, Mt. Lassen Park and Mt. Hood. A well supported Northwestern Tour was held yearly for several seasons at the beach resort at Long Beach, Washington. It was estimated that well over 10,000 riders from Northern California, Oregon and AMA affiliated clubs in British Columbia attended this meeting through the 1930's, although there was some adverse publicity following fatal accidents sustained by some enthusiasts who participated in unauthorized drag racing during the 1936 and 1937 seasons.

AMA support was such during this period that E.C. Smith, in a report issued to the membership in 1936, noted that there were now 615 chartered clubs on the roster with 100% paid membership, together with 13,658 total membership, which included a few Canadian cardholders. The total income from registered dealers and clubs, general members, and the yearly dues from the manufacturers and trade suppliers was now sufficient to maintain the AMA, along with the added income from sanctioning fees, without any additional trade subsidies. Smith emphasized that the added income from the more casual Gypsy Tour participants, who bought cards in order to participate, was a most helpful adjunct.

The 1936 200 Mile National was scheduled at the state fairgrounds at Savannah, Georgia, again in deference to both southern and eastern motorcycle interests, and as indicated, was a TT event in deference to the hoped for dominance of American machines.

Held on the last weekend in January, this event saw the debut of Lawrence Edward "Ed" Kretz as a competition rider. A one time Imperial Valley hay truck driver and presently a mechanic with Floyd Clymer's Los Angeles Indian agency, Kretz made a remarkable showing as the winner at 70 mph over a very difficult course. As a courageous rider with a dramatic charging style and a hell-for-leather approach, he was soon to make a name for himself on the American racing circuit.

This event probably showcased the last time that strictly stock machines appeared in national competition in accordance with the formally instituted Class C rules. By the following season, both factory as well as dealer and private tuners began experimenting with altered valve timing, cam profiles, and port alteration. While this universal digression from the established rules, along with the tacit approval of the Competition Committee, has long been a subject of note and discussion on the part of motorcycle journalists ever since, none of these worthies have ever appeared to offer the real reason for it.

The author, who for many years has been preoccupied with the antecedents of the matter has, after extensive interviews with veteran factory people, competition riders and tuners, come up with what may well be the definitive answer. Such authorities as Hap Alzina, Dudley Perkins, Rollie Free, William Ruhle, Claude Salmon, Tom Sifton, Johnny Speigelhoff, Art Hafer and several others contemporary to the time, expressed the theory that it was the introduction of Indian's Sport Scout that was the principle reason.

Coming into prominence as a competition mount during the 1935 season, the Scout's nearly "square" bore and stroke, combined with its sophisticated flowmetrics, made it not only marginally faster than Harley-Davidson's DLD and WL models, but accelerated faster when coming out of the turns. The wider bore appeared to be the reason for the latter, as its piston speeds were capable of revving higher than those of the narrower-bored longer-stroked Harley-Davidsons.

In noting the initial spate of Scout victories, the Harley-Davidson dominated Competition Committee decided to approach the problem directly, and underground rumors immediately

THE COMPETITION ERA 1935-1941

Jack Cottrell, winner of the Oakland 200 in 1940.
Joe Walker

Cottrell poses with sponsor Dudley Perkins.
Dudley Perkins

began to circulate regarding permissible alterations to Harley-Davidson's 45 cubic inch engines. By the fall of 1936, AMA referees and scrutineers were only checking contestants' engines for still-illegal "strokers" and the still mandated 7.5:1 compression ratio.

The Sport Scout's initial advantage was only temporary, however. From San Jose, California, Harley-Davidson's Tom Sifton, a gifted practical engineer and noted local tuner was already re-engineering W type engines. He used an altered lubricating system, altered cam action and porting, which soon appeared in competition as a formidable rival to Springfield. As will be seen, Sifton engines were shortly to make a name for themselves, albeit without Milwaukee's blessing!

An important sporting venue established in the late 1930's was the dirt oval at Langhorne, Pennsylvania; a recreational area about 20 miles north of Philadelphia. Described as the world's fastest dirt track, it had been built in the mid-1920's for auto racing. In 1935, the Middle Atlantic Motorcycle Dealer's Association, under the leadership of Philadelphia Indian dealer Eugene Shillingford, with the assistance of Herman Voichick, managed the promotion of the initial AMA sponsored motorcycle race.

The course was particularly difficult, as there were no straights, but a circular run with a 5% grade in the rear portion that made it a broadsliding traverse all the way. The track was particularly suited to the riding style of Ed Kretz, who won the event no less than four times. Kretz's riding abilities had been honed when he taught himself trick riding on a dry lake bed near Baker, California, in 1931, when he managed a relative's service station in that desert village.

Other noted contestants at Langhorne included Ben Campanale, Frenchie Castinguay, Paul Albrecht, Chet Dygraaf, Red Wolverton, Joe Weatherly, Bobby Hill and Julian Woolyhad. In later years, Dick Klamfoth was also a prominent entrant.

Another noted course established in the 1930's was Laconia, an irregularly shaped oval that was mostly used to feature TT type contests. The initial 1938 event was inaugurated through the efforts of Fritzie Baer and his Springfield based Indian club. It was located in a park-like setting in the Belknap Recreation Area in New Hampshire, with adequate facilities for camping. The first running was noted as being the first time an amplifying public address system was used to keep the spectators in contact with the proceedings, and was manned by no less than Fritzie himself, who subsequently acted as the Master of Ceremonies in later prominent eastern

THE COMPETITION ERA 1935-1941

(l. to r.) Dick Milligan, H. Chronister, Glenn Rathbun and Ed Kretz at a Field Meet in San Pedro, 1936.
Glen Rathbun

Langhorne, 1938. (l. to r.) Lester Hillbish, Crocky Rodding, Frenchy Castonguay and Ed Kretz.
Ed Kretz

and northeastern events.

The initial 200 Miler was won handily by Ed Kretz, the course being well suited to his unique style of riding. As with Langhorne, Laconia always featured a Gypsy Tour in connection with its motorcycle events, and drew large crowds of enthusiasts from all over New England.

Following the initial Southern 200 Miler at Savannah, it was decided by the Competition Committee to move the event to Daytona Beach, Florida, which was already well known for its unlimited automobile speed trials on the hard packed sand. The Committee cooperated with the Southeastern Motorcycle Dealer's Association and several active clubs in the Florida area in planning the first event for 1937.

In 1936, the Competition Committee acceded to Harley-Davidson's request to change the Class C rules to bar pocket valve engines of any cylinder displacement that were also fitted with outside contracting rear brake assemblies. This removed the presence of the much cherished two cam Harley-Davidson JDH models from AMA competition. This 1928 high performance model had been a consistent winner over the former VL machines in various TT and hill climbing events, and the factory did not relish the thought of the two cammers now challenging the newly introduced EL models which carried a severe weight penalty as an initial handicap. This rule change was a source of regret to many two cam enthusiasts, including Al Toscani and Loren C. "Hap" Jones, who had been consistent campaigners and had several machines and a large supply of spare parts. Jones subsequently deserted Milwaukee and took an Indian franchise in San Francisco in 1937.

The new ruling also effectively removed the sometimes formidable competition of a group of Super-X's, highly tuned examples of which had been prominent winners in various parts of the country. While the Super-X's were suspected by some of having a less than rugged lower main bearing assembly, many were improved with the fitting of Harley-Davidson 45 flywheel assemblies.

E.C. Smith continued to promote club activities in the public relations sphere, presenting yearly awards to those clubs which garnered substantial news media exposure. He also continued his cooperation with the National Safety Council, with citations for clubs with accident free records.

Several clubs during this period were able to actually build and maintain their own club houses. With the ongoing income from locally sponsored competition events, coupled with the modest prices of available building sites, it was possible to con-

THE COMPETITION ERA 1935-1941

struct a suitable meeting place for around $2,000 if the individual members were able to do the actual construction themselves.

One of the problems of promoting competition events, especially the larger meets, was the lack of competent supervision in the matter of both the timing of the contestants and the tabulation of lap scores. Working mostly with inexperienced volunteers, few of whom actually possessed stop watches, there was the universal tendency for them to become absorbed in watching the race and lose track of the scoring. This led to many disputes instituted by the contestants over both winning and placing, as well as an accounting of the laps completed. In many of these cases, the actual winner or placer was selected by the flip of a coin; the loser being placated by being awarded identical prize money. The picture was further complicated by the often ambiguous reporting of sporting events by the usual group of amateur reporters, who rendered free thinking conclusions concerning the results. The results as printed in local newspapers frequently varied from the "official" results sanctioned for publication in "The Motorcyclist" by Smith, which often resulted in much local ill feeling.

In addition, crowd control at sporting contests was a problem, especially at hill climbs and TT races held in spread out venues encompassing large areas. Excited spectators tended to ignore unofficial patrol personnel, and few clubs or other promoters had the funds to hire professional law enforcement officers in an off duty capacity who could command more visible authority. In consequence, substantial numbers of spectators were injured and not a few met death as a result of encroaching on or crossing the courses, most of which were never reported in "The Motorcyclist" or noted in the official AMA records.

A continuing problem for E.C. Smith was the policing of "outlaw" events and keeping watch for AMA members holding competition licenses who were often in the habit of participating in them. A favorite deception was for the riders to compete in such events under assumed names. In 1936, Smith subscribed to a newspaper clipping service that kept him in contact with contests which were frequently outlaw in nature. He was particularly on the watch for photographs taken at such contests which might reveal the riders' identities. With his keen recall and photographic memory, not a few AMA cardholders were noted and received the summary year's suspension from officially sanctioned participation.

The coming 200 Mile National at Daytona Beach was the first major AMA sanctioned event to gain substantial national newspaper publicity. The beach course had long been in the public eye as a motor contest event, as it had been the location of these events ever since the earliest days of motor sport. Fred Marriot had first drawn public attention in 1906, when he piloted a specially built Stanley steam streamliner back and forth over a measured mile at the then-fantastic speed of 127.65 mph. Further attention was attracted between 1928 and 1935 when Englishmen Sir Henry Seagrave, Sir Malcolm Campbell and George Eyston had racked up unlimited solo automobile records there, followed by the Americans Ray Keech, Frank Lockhart and Lee Bible.

Glenn Curtis had electrified the motorcycle world in 1907 with his 137 mph world's record on his specially built V-8 aero engined two wheeler. Both Harley-Davidson and Indian had established motorcycle records at Daytona during the 1920's; the last being a record 132 mph run by Johnny Seymour on a 61 cubic inch Indian.

The beach course, as laid out for the initial race, was 3.2 miles in circumference, with one-half comprising the beach, the other a back stretch road behind it. The two were connected at either end by a semicircular banked surface that had a sand base covered with a mixture of clay and crushed rock. While the hard packed sand on the beach was smooth, the sand based back stretch was paved with a mixture of clay and coquino rock that was covered with tar and its many ruts posed a problem. Additional hazards were sudden high winds that could stir up ripples on the beach, and there was a sharp gradient on the north turn from the beach to the roadway. Another hazard at the south end was the proximity of a swamp filled with palmetto growth that could trap the unfortunate rider whose brakes failed or who overshot the turn. As a combination of road, track and a rough TT course, it presented a most severe challenge, and to complete the 200 mile distance it required 63 very tiring laps.

With a field of over 100 starters, the riders were lined up in ranks of 10, positions being awarded on the basis of times taken the day before in solo runs. The riders were flagged off at one minute intervals, posing problems of lap scoring.

The indefatigable Ed Kretz, with his usual charging style, blasted his way into an early lead. With his Indian Sport Scout never missing a beat, he was never headed and crossed the finish line for an elapsed average speed of 74.10 mph.

While the local press and "The Motorcyclist" carried glowing accounts of the success of the event, there were several complaints from both

THE COMPETITION ERA 1935-1941

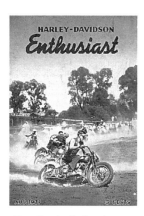

Don Emde Collection

The April, 1937 edition of "The Motorcyclist" featured Joe Petrali's record runs at Daytona Beach, Florida.
Don Emde Collection

contestants and spectators. Crowd control was woefully ineffectual, with two minor injuries and numerous near fatalities when spectators either crossed the course between riders or ventured too close to the infield.

Many riders were critical of the large group of volunteer judges and time keepers, who either misjudged or failed completely to tabulate the laps, or forgot to keep any records at all in their excitement of watching the race.

Another point in question was the primitive nature of the sanitary facilities that were inadequate to serve the needs of the large crowd. Many also thought that the purses were woefully small: $300 for the winner, $200 for second place, and $50 for the next two places. E.C. Smith evaded responsibility for this, saying that Walter Davidson and the Competition Committee were on record as stating that "...we don't want a bunch of rich kids racing motorcycles!"

Many riders expressed the opinion that the courses were unduly dangerous due to poor preparation, especially in the turns, where the clay and rock were quickly chewed up by the broadsliding contestants.

The spectacular win by Ed Kretz established his reputation as a star rider overnight, and he was signed as an Indian factory rider at a salary of $200 per month. This was quite a boost to a typical Depression style motorcycle mechanic who was presently working for Floyd Clymer's Los Angeles Indian agency for $18.50 per week!

While the Daytona races and other big national fixtures were to attract riders from all parts of the country, such entries were limited by both the expense of travel during hard times and the difficulties of transportation which limited most of the contestants to events in their local areas. The network of well made roads throughout the country was just starting to come into being, freeways still being decades away. As the original concept of riding a contestant's machine to AMA events was abandoned, they now had to be transported. Pickup trucks with beds large enough to accommodate motorcycles had not yet appeared, and high speed trucks capable of fast transport were far too expensive. The obvious alternative was to haul machines in a light trailer behind a touring car. As trailers were not yet commercially available, they were homemade using the front axle assembly of some junked automobile. Roadside tourist accommodations had yet to be extensively developed, and many contestants camped along the way to save money. The meager purses offered to winners and placers had to be considered in calculating the

financing of the trip. As matters stood, it took real motorcycling enthusiasm in the 1930's to support sporting participation!

During this period most of the competition events were of regional character. The scene of most of the competition activity at this time was in the western states, leading to the establishment of the Pacific Coast Championship circuit.

The mid-1930's saw two more attempts to break the existing solo speed record set by Johnny Seymour on a 61 cubic inch eight valve Indian special; the engine having been built by Franklin in 1924. Due to deficiencies in the timing mechanism, Seymour's speed of 132 mph was accepted as official only by the M&ATA, being noted in Europe but not accepted by the FICM.

On learning that Indian was contemplating another attempt with a new engine, Joe Petrali was ordered to build up a machine in Milwaukee. Accordingly, he and noted tuner Hank Syvertsen constructed a machine with a specially built version of the 61 cubic inch EL overhead valve engine fitted with special cams, porting, and magneto ignition. Conceived as a streamliner, it featured a disc-covered front wheel and a shroud over the rear. Hoping for a 150 mph record, President Davidson offered Petrali a $1,000 bonus if he could reach it.

The resulting attempt was nearly fatal for Petrali, who experienced a serious speed wobble when he reached 125 mph, which he explained was because of the noted aviation of the machine caused by the wind pressure on the fairings. He subsequently removed these, and ultimately managed a 137 mph run on prolonged full throttle over the measured mile. The factory attempted to conceal the fact of the machine's alterations by Petrali, but some local independent press coverage and the accompanying photographs gave the secret away.

Petrali later told the author that the machine was too heavy for its power, being some 200 lbs. heavier than Seymour's Indian, which was essentially a spidery board tracker. Davidson refused to award Petrali any bonus payment, although Petrali asked for a $500 payment, noting his near brush with death in the attempt. As far as the record went, factory travelers were reported as spreading the rumor that Petrali held the machine back in order to tempt Indian to top it; with a planned future assault by Milwaukee to be topped by another Petrali run. Whatever the result, the use of the revamped standard EL engine negated the adverse publicity concerning the teething problems of the original road going models.

Indian took up the challenge, however, and the

THE COMPETITION ERA 1935-1941

Jimmy Kelly, (#9) and Ed Kretz and Vaughn Dickerson tangle up on the south turn of the old Ascot Speedway.
Ed Kretz

racing mechanics built up another special, still using the basic 1924 eight valver but with improved breathing and special cams provided by Marvin "Red" Fenwicke, a noted tuner.

Instead of utilizing Daytona as Harley-Davidson had done, Hap Alzina, who offered to sponsor the project, elected to go to Bonneville, which, due to its hard salt surface, was considered safer than the beach course. Fred Ludlow, now a Pasadena motorcycle patrolman, was importuned to reactivate his record breaking, and a streamlined fairing was built by the aircraft mechanic that closely covered the entire machine.

The machine was trucked to the lake course in the spring of 1937, but the attempt ended in failure when, again at about 124 mph, a speed wobble with near aviation of the machine was experienced. Ludlow offered to make a run with the fairing removed, a la Petrali, but Alzina refused to permit it on the grounds of the excessive risks to the rider.

These 1936 and 1937 attempts at all-out solo records proved that a more or less standard frame and wheelbase configuration with streamlined shell coverage would become unmanageable at high speeds. This theory was vindicated again after World War II when the British star Noel Pope experienced the same problem with a similarly faired Brough Superior, also on the Bonneville course. Sponsored by Teddy Commerford, a London motorcycle dealer, Pope lost control at a similar speed, wrecking his machine in the crash, narrowly escaping fatal injuries.

Motorcycles had been widely featured in Hollywood motion pictures since the earliest days, initially in spectacular stunt sequences in Mack Sennett's "Keystone Kops" series, and later in stunt scenes worked into various action plots for variety. In 1934, after taking over Crocker's Indian franchise in Los Angeles, the indomitable promoter Floyd Clymer offered various studios Indian machines on loan for pictures. Several well known Indian riders, including Ed Kretz, donned grease paint to participate in the action. Regular actors often became riders, such as Cary Grant chauffeuring a somewhat apprehensive Irene Dunne on the back of an Indian Dispatch Tow in a chase sequence in "The Awful Truth."

Noting the predominance of Indians, Harley-Davidson enthusiasts complained that the Redskins were getting all the film footage, but the factory refused to donate any machines. Rich Budelier later offered some of his demonstrators as well as some used machines for picture appearances, and some of his shop mechanics also offered their personal machines to even Milwaukee's exposure.

By the mid-1930's, the author was well under way with his historical research into motorcycling history, with a substantial number of important figures within the sport and industry enlisted as supporters. A further viewpoint was augmented by exploration into the international scene by subscriptions to the British trade magazines. While there was gratifying response from nearly all of the people initially interviewed, the author was inevitably subjected to some good natured hazing on the part of some, no doubt because of his youth, obvious intensity, and his then all-too-apparent lack of sophistication. There was the occasional reference to "...that skinny kid who asked all those questions!" Yet, when these individuals were later presented with transcripts of previously granted interviews for the purpose of confirming their opinions and inviting corrections or further amplification, it was to their credit for their kindness and sensitivity that they were, almost with exception, cooperative.

The mid-1930's saw a resurrection of impetus for the trade union movement. There was much agitation on the part of champions of the working classes for organization of unions to allow for collective bargaining and to otherwise give the workers a voice in their own destinies. This movement had been gaining in influence since the end of the Civil War.

However, a conservatively oriented federal government, along with most state governments, was generally not supportive of the labor movement, favoring the capitalistic sentiments of the employers. It was a generally accepted theory that the iron law of wages decreed that employers should be able to set wages at the lowest possible figure that the workers would accept, along with hours and working conditions that met with minimum acceptability. Repressive treatment toward labor's agitation was such that elements of state's militia and even federal troops were called out occasionally to support employers in their efforts to import strike breakers to man their factories and otherwise suppress the militancy of revolting workers. The long, and often bloody, struggle continued for well over half a century. It was not until the election of the liberal thinking Franklin D. Roosevelt that labor, at long last, had a substantial champion when he recognized the rights of the working class to enjoy adequate wages and working hours and the privileges of collective bargaining.

The motorcycle industry, in its salad days, mostly enjoyed freedom from labor disputes, as the standard wage in industry was $2.50 for a ten-hour day before World War I. Henry Ford's doubling the wages of his workers had occurred just at the time when the dislocations of the war in Europe had the most serious effect on the industry as a whole.

The situation at Indian was unique in that the individualistic New England artisans often had interests in farming or fishing or other pursuits, and preferred seasonal employment. While there were labor troubles in Springfield after World War I, Frank Weschler foresightedly reached an agree-

ment with the local machinists union on wage scales, more often than not on a piece work basis. He also inaugurated a two tiered system where the more skilled workers fabricated and machined components in the late fall and winter and then less skilled and lower paid workers assembled machines as to dealer's orders in the spring and summer.

William Davidson, a one time foreman in a railroad shop, preferred steady employment of production workers, however, which was more in line with the general practice in the midwest industrial region. He was an exacting task-master, but exerted a paternalistic policy toward his workers, and was in the habit of presenting them with extra funds in the form of loans for unforeseen family emergencies, which could be paid back on their own terms, if ever.

It might be mentioned that none of the surviving big three factories, from the beginning, ever ran their production on assembly lines as was the later practice. The units were individually assembled with the frames wheeled about the factory to accommodate the work stations of individual assemblers.

At any rate, after the Wagner Act became law in 1935, the majority of the workers in industry sought to organize, especially in the Midwest and Great Lakes region where the bulk of such activity was carried on.

The biggest changes occurred throughout the automobile industry, where union organizers obtained concessions through collective bargaining with General Motors, Chrysler, Packard, Hudson-Essex, Nash, Willys, and other lesser survivors of the Depression. Henry Ford, however, always a foe of unionism, declined to arbitrate, and a number of bloody riots occurred at River Rouge when company police battled with striking workers over the admission of strike breakers into the plants. Under the tireless leadership of young Walter Reuther, a prominent leader in the formation of the United Auto Workers Union, Ford at eventually capitulated, and Reuther next turned his attention to other related midwestern industries.

During the summer and fall of 1936, union agents manned the gates of the Juneau Avenue factory, passing out leaflets urging union affiliation. William Davidson, secure in his faith in the loyalty of his workers, initially did not appear unduly alarmed by this, and was noted as stoically remarking "Let them come." While most of the older employees remained loyal to "Big Bill," a number of the younger workers, among them Johnny Speigelhoff, a budding competition star, did not,

THE COMPETITION ERA 1935-1941

Short track stars Jimmy Gibb (r) and Mutt Kelly show off the standard method of travel for competition riders in the mid 1930's. Jimmie is justly proud of his new Ford V8 sedan.
Ed Kretz

and there developed strong support for unionization among this group.

During this period William Davidson's health began to fail. A lifelong diabetic, his weight grew alarmingly, and the advice of his doctors regarding his excessive consumption of "good" food and drink went unheeded. During the winter he was stricken by severe phlebitis in his legs, and when the condition worsened, the doctors suggested amputation in an attempt to save his life. He never survived the surgery, however, and passed away on April 21, 1937, at the age of sixty-seven.

The passing of "Big Bill" was a severe blow to company operations. With his broad experience in shop and foundry practices, his working knowledge of metallurgy, and his ability to rationalize production procedures for economics, he had made valuable contributions toward the general high quality of the factory's products. He was also capable of inspiring loyalty in his work force, and many veteran employees would rather retain their jobs with the company at modest wages than seek higher pay in other types of industry.

His position in charge of production was filled by William Ottaway, with the assistance of Hank Syvertsen and Joe Petrali, who also contributed to engineering and design as well.

During the mid-1930's, certain events occurred which narrowed the domestic motorcycle's overseas markets. In the summer of 1937, a newly instituted militaristic government in Japan sought to exclude the presence of foreigners in their country who might well alert the world as to their program of re-armament. As a result, noncitizens and business operations owned by foreigners were asked to leave the country. Alfred Rich Child was given 60 days to close out his affairs, as were the managers of the Indian import agency. This meant a loss of an average of 1,000 yearly sales of Harley-Davidsons, and 400 to 600 Indians. The Japanese army was relying on the presently pro-

duced Rikuos for its heavyweight motorcycles.

The prolonged civil war in Spain also terminated the sale of American machines to that market, after a limited number of initial orders from the combatants when the conflict first got underway.

The British market was all but terminated due to the 33% import tariff, which had been imposed in 1925. The resurgence of motorcycle manufacturing on the European continent, which included Scandinavia, also introduced a competitive factor, but limited numbers of American machines were still being sold to those more affluent enthusiasts who preferred the big twin types. There was still a moderate demand for Harley-Davidson's 21 cubic inch singles, as well as for the 30.50 Indian Scout. Due to colonial conditions, there were still fair markets left in South Africa and Australia.

While the overall sales of machines had increased markedly since the worst years of the Depression, with both factories now realizing modest profits, the overall market demand had leveled off to the point where both factories were producing a total of about 20,000 units per year. The only encouraging factor in the export field was the purchase of fair numbers of American machines as military and constabulary units in Mexico, and Central and South America. This was counterbalanced in 1937 by Adolf Hitler's decree that henceforth the import of all foreign motor vehicles into Germany was to be banned in favor of promoting the home industries.

Late in the summer of 1937, Harley-Davidson's top management capitulated to the demands of the United Auto Workers Union and signed an agreement authorizing them to represent the company's production workers. In addition to installing shop stewards, a floor on the wage schedule was set at 45 cents per hour, that mainly covered women production workers and a few apprentices. As soon as the formalities were concluded, President Davidson summarily fired all those who had advocated union affiliation, contrary to the terms of the contract. Included was Johnny Speigelhoff, who at once changed his allegiance to Indian. Veteran production workers later stated that while their wage scale was somewhat improved, the traditional friendly atmosphere and spirit of camaraderie that had existed in the days of "Big Bill" was now gone.

Alfred Rich Child was unable to meet the 60 day deadline to quit Japan due to the length of time it required to liquidate his assets, but he was given an extension and left the following September. The Japanese allowed him to depart with his now considerable capital, except that the Rikuo operation was expropriated, its production now being diverted to military machines. Child went to Milwaukee, hoping to find a position in top management as a member of the sales force, but President Davidson informed him that there was no place for him. He was aware of the low salary scale that even the shareholding founders set for themselves, ostensibly to discourage middle management supervisors from asking for raises. President Davidson also reminded him that he had already acquired a substantial fortune from his various business activities in Japan and that the company had no situations that could offer comparable benefits. Child then accepted a position with the Lockheed Aviation Company as a Far Eastern sales representative, in deference to his long established contacts in that area.

The financial structuring of the two companies during this period was similar in that their ownership was in the hands of shareholders. Indian, as a public company whose stock was traded on the open market by laws of the Securities and Exchange Commission, published quarterly reports of company affairs, which involved the sales of stock, profits and losses and reports of personnel changes.

Indian's financial structuring was a two tiered system with 1,700,000 shares extant whose owners did not have voting privileges, and whose par value during Depression years varied from $3 to $6 per share. The preferred stock, the majority of which was owned by Francis I. and E. Paul duPont, carried voting privileges and was variously valued at $10 to $12 per share and paid 6% yearly dividends, payable quarterly in 1-1/4% increments.

On the other hand, Harley-Davidson was a closed corporation whose internal financial affairs were not made public, and in fact, were subjected to the utmost secrecy. After struggling with the servicing of the $3,000,000 debt incurred in 1918 for the construction and equipping of the Juneau Avenue factory, the founders opted to secure pri-

vate financing for the generation of operating capital rather than paying bank interest rates, the former being negotiable at more favorable conditions. Of the 40,000-odd shares extant, the founders of course retained at least 21,000 to maintain majority control. Of the balance, a portion was reserved for offering to individuals who would agree to purchase on a buy-back agreement at a stipulated later date at a slight profit.

The matter of President Davidson's almost paranoiac efforts to conceal the internal affairs of the company has long been a subject of much speculation. Former employees and one time shareholders have stated that company advertising had traditionally been oriented toward the emphasis that it was a family owned entity. This illusion would, of course, be shattered if the news got out that a substantial number of outsiders had a financial interest, which would tend to dispel the former declaration with a consequent downgrading of the importance of the four founders in the public mind. To reinforce the matter of secrecy, it was also reported that Board of Directors and public meetings were closed affairs that included the majority shareholders only, the "Star Chambers" aspect insuring that fewer individuals would be privy to company decisions.

Early on the founders also considered middle and lower echelon employees, including factory travelers, as readily expendable and the names, activities and contributions of such were never publicly recognized in company literature. This policy was said to have originated after the widespread publicity accorded to Hap Scherer and his activities attendant to the promotion of the Sport Twin. When Scherer was fired in 1922, the widespread sympathy he received from dealers and enthusiasts alike over his enthusiasm for middleweight models created great controversy.

While Harley-Davidson often appeared to go to extremes in concealing the inner workings of the company, it must be emphasized that reticence on the part of other manufacturers regarding similar matters was very much a part of the domestic motorcycle industry.

Arthur Constantine reported in later years that Ignatz Schwinn was highly sensitive regarding the small production of Excelsior products. This situation was influenced by the restrictive marketing practices of the between-the-wars period. While Harley-Davidson and Indian nominally serviced about a thousand dealerships, Excelsior only enjoyed, at best, a little over two hundred. A few dealers ordered Hendersons only, relying on law enforcement sales and the patronage of a limited

Don Emde Collection

THE COMPETITION ERA 1935-1941

John Cameron with his much modified 1917 JD Harley-Davidson in a Box Spring TT in 1936. This was the last event JD's could be entered in an AMA sanctioned event before they were outlawed by the Competition Committee. *Cycle Action*

number of enthusiasts who were able to afford a higher priced luxury model. With a limited market for the 45 and 61 cubic inch Super-X's, Schwinn preferred to promote these also in the luxury category, and they were always priced somewhat higher than their Springfield and Milwaukee counterparts to emphasize this appeal. Although invited on several occasions to join the Harley-Davidson and Indian price fixing cartel, Schwinn consistently refused.[*2] It was also true that he was forced on occasion to award price concessions incidental to law enforcement sales due to an overstocking of product. Further, he did not relish the idea of being called to account for discounting, which was always a bone of contention between the other two.

The duPonts were less concerned with secrecy, as they were used to managing public companies whose affairs were reported on Wall Street. In any case, the long standing critical situation at Indian was mitigated by the ownership of other diverse companies that were highly profitable. However, in later years, James Wright told the author that E. Paul duPont was somewhat sensitive to some Indian enthusiasts' criticism of the lack of design progress at Springfield, citing the continued fitting of the archaic sliding gear transmission, or the lack of production type overhead valve machines when their hand-built racing specials so

equipped were such outstanding performers. At times Indian's top management would admonish their critics that with modest sales in a depressed market representing a marginal industry, the vast expenditures required to alter ongoing production schedules were simply outside the realm of sound judgment.

Most of the professional journalists of that era; Henry Parsons, Leslie D. Richards, Lawrence E. Fowler, Arthur E. Welch, and others, were much in sympathy with the industry's position in the matter. More or less they agreed that a continuing theme in the trade publications of pessimism would be self-defeating by discouraging motorcycling's enthusiasts. On the other hand, most agreed that the current trend of unrealistic reporting of motorcycling events in general was somewhat self-defeating. To knowledgeable enthusiasts, especially in the case of competition riders after participating in any given event and experiencing the vagaries of the proceedings, it was a source of derision to then read a sugar-coated and inaccurate report of the activities in "The Motorcyclist."

Most of the more experienced motorcycling journalists were of the opinion that some mildly couched and constructive criticism of the current handling of motorcycling affairs and AMA policies could have had a constructive effect.

Enthusiasts of both makes continued to be offered entertainment in the in-house publications: "Indian News" and "The Enthusiast." Each quite naturally promoted name brand loyalty and offered comprehensive news items regarding club life and human interest articles concerning individual enthusiasts. Additional interest was provided by emphasis on Indian's prominence in motion pictures, together with Floyd Clymer's inducing the noted show business ventriloquist, Edgar Bergen, to purchase a Junior Scout. A number of photographs taken of Bergen posing on the machine, with Charley McCarthy suitably outfitted with helmet and goggles, were used in advertising.

Harley-Davidson gave considerable space to the Hollywood Motorcycle Club and its activities. Founded by Milwaukee enthusiast and prominent director Victor Flemming, it was co-sponsored by Rich Budelier. Primarily oriented toward Harley-Davidson owners, although some favored Indians, much emphasis was placed on the participation of such prominent stars as Clark Gable, Randolph Scott, Ward Bond, John Payne, Keenan Wynn, Robert Taylor and others; as well as well-known technical figures in the film industry.

These in-house papers were also a source of descriptions of ongoing technical details of various

THE COMPETITION ERA 1935-1941

E. Paul duPont's son Stephen and his wife Carol acted as the official host and hostess for the Indian Motorcycle Company in Springfield, Massachusetts. This mid-1930's photo taken by Stephen includes (l. to r.) Mrs. Ted Edwards, Jim Wright, Company Sales Manager, Carol duPont, Ted Edwards, Mrs. Hollowell, Bob Hollowell, George and Laura Greene.
Stephen duPont

new models, and surviving copies are much sought after by restorers.

In the spring of 1937, William E. Johnson finalized his arrangement with Edward Turner over the establishment of a branch dealership for Ariel and Triumph in Pasadena, which was housed in modest quarters on Avocado Street. Johnson phased out his Indian franchise, but continued to service Indian machines and to carry a supply of parts, an operation presided over by Shop Foreman Joe Walker.

With adequate financing, Johnson's operation became impressive in scope, especially at a time when many motorcycle dealerships were more often than not a marginal undertaking. Problems were encountered, however, when Johnson sought to purchase advertising space in "The Motorcyclist."

This episode was further complicated by the recent hiring by the American Journal Publishing Company of an additional advertising representative, one Chester T. Billings, during the preceding summer. With the return of somewhat better times, Welch's business increased through the heightened demand for general print material, such as catalogs and brochures, together with expanded content of his architectural and builders journals. It was his intention to have Billings assist "The Motorcyclist" editor, Howard Rose, in advertising solicitation.

But Billings, an enthusiastic motorcyclist, took such an interest in that aspect of the business that Welch, with Rose's acquiescence, installed Billings as editor. With the main emphasis on advertising solicitation, Billings traveled extensively in the Southern California area, also attending various motorcycling events and reporting on these as well as general AMA activities. E.C. Smith had spent much time in the area that winter, overseeing AMA business and overseeing the content of the magazine. In striking up an acquaintance with Billings, he was able to indoctrinate him with the ongoing policy of "managing" motorcycle news, as previously explained.

While Welch was still not wholly in agreement with his enforced arrangement with the AMA in the matter, Billings was, and for his cooperation Smith made him an AMA "Commissioner." At the same time, the Michigan resident and former Canadian competition rider, Ivan J. Stretten, was also awarded the same title for his agreement to follow the AMA journalistic line and to soft pedal his advocacy for the Canadian point of view in regard to the Class C AMA mandate on competition rules. Stretten later told the author he was willing to make some compromises in order to receive the small fees involved due to the small salary he received in his regular employment.

While some AMA members looked upon the

"Commissioner" designation as a comic opera counterpart of the politically appointed "Colonel" in the militias of the Southern states, or the numerous "Generals" extant in the armed forces of the dictatorships of Central American banana republics, nevertheless, Smith often found his commissioners valuable allies, especially in the administration of the affairs of the 38 regional AMA districts.

At any rate, William E. Johnson, on the opening of his new agency, at once planned an extensive general advertising campaign for his line of Ariel and Triumph. This included a proposed contract with Welch for a full page layout in "The Motorcyclist." On learning of this, Billings contacted Smith, then back in Columbus, questioning the advisability of granting such extensive coverage to an interloper on the American motorcycling turf. Smith replied that there was little that could be done to actually keep Johnson out of the magazine, but suggested that the coverage be limited to three column inches.

Billings, without consulting Welch, immediately contacted Johnson and stated that his overly extensive display be restricted in deference to the magazine's policy of catering to the interests of the American manufacturers.

An incensed Johnson cited his constitutional rights to free access to a public media, and threatened legal action under the protection of the federal antitrust laws. As Billings remained adamant, Johnson consulted the Beverly Hills law firm of Lantz, Leibowitz, and McConnell to ascertain the extent of his legal rights in the matter.

The author, in attempting to research the details of the matter, contacted Johnson in 1959 to ascertain the outcome of this action. Unfortunately, at this point Johnson was in a somewhat incoherent state due to the ravages of alcoholism, but he gave the author permission to contact his attorneys for the details. At that point in time, the law firm was no longer active, but one of the former partners, Arthur F. Lantz, Jr., was ultimately located in retirement in Palm Springs. He informed the author that the Journal Publishing Company had never been formally served with Johnson's complaint, but that a copy had been delivered to Welch that outlined Johnson's legal rights to public media exposure.

Welch telephoned Smith in Columbus and stated that he was not about to enter into litigation with Johnson in a case that he was certain to lose, and that on the advice of his own legal counsel he was going to offer Johnson a contract whether Smith agreed with him or not. Faced with these

facts, Smith backed down. Welch later recalled that he admonished Billings never to enter into any quasi-legal agreements with Smith without first obtaining his approval. Following this episode, relations between Welch and Billings remained somewhat strained until the latter resigned in 1941 to work in a defense plant.

Hard on the heels of the Johnson matter, J.M. McGill, Norton's North American distributor in Toronto, ordered a two column inch display in "The Motorcyclist" announcing his appointment and soliciting dealer inquiries. Jack Frodsham, the Los Angeles Velocette importer since 1935, also ordered display space. Both later stated they had not previously approached the magazine's top management due to the deteriorating relationship between the AMA and the Canadians.

It was at about this time that Emil August Recke opened modest premises in New York City with a franchise as the sole U.S. distributor for German BMW machines. He had been a mechanic in the German Air Force during the war, and later had been a production supervisor to the States.

His offerings included the side-valve horizontally opposed twin, the R75, that was to later be adapted as a German military model, and the Rennsport, a super sports model that had been developed for the European racing circuits and was capable of being fitted with a supercharger.

The venture did not fare well, even though Recke sponsored Joe Tomas, who had previously been a successful Norton International exponent, as his competition rider. It appeared that public sentiment against Hitler's activities had already reached the point that it mitigated against the purchase of German made products. It was reported that Recke sold only about two dozen machines before 1939, when the outbreak of the European war ended the project.

On the competition scene, Indian was now running ahead of Harley-Davidson for the 1937 season. After his spectacular win at Daytona, Ed Kretz went on to two consecutive National victories at Langhorne and Laconia. The Langhorne circuit had seen a spectacular performance by Indian the year before, when Lester Hillbish had won first place, with Indian garnering six of the first ten places.

Joe Petrali racked up a new American solo speed record at Daytona, as previously mentioned, breaking Johnny Seymour's ten-year old record on an Indian. Two similarly engined specials, also built up by Petrali and Hank Syvertsen, gained new records at the Wasago Beach course in Ontario, Canada.

Fred Ham, the athletic Pasadena motorcycle

Don Emde Collection

policeman, made a phenomenal 24-hour run on a specially tuned EL Harley-Davidson on the course at Lake Muroc. His 1,825 mile distance on the high desert course established no less than 43 new distance records between 50 and 1,800 miles. While the records were taken as non-stop, Ham quite naturally had to make pit stops for refueling and a couple of hour long delays occurred to adjust an overheated clutch. Nevertheless, Ham's powers of endurance were nothing less than remarkable, and much was made of his records in Milwaukee advertising.

Joe Petrali repeated his 1936 Class A win on a Peashooter in 1937 at Syracuse, a showcase win with the faithful Lou Balinsky following behind, there being no other competitors.

The Wigwam intensified its competition campaign with its racing Scouts, with Lester Hillbish campaigning in the East, and Ed Kretz in the West. The Castonguay brothers, Woodsie and Frenchie, were also much on the scene, and during the 1938 season Indian riders won all the Class C events in the half-mile category.

New solo speed records for ostensibly stock machines were set by Indian on the courses at Lake Muroc and Rosamond. Hap Alzina sponsored Fred Ludlow, who rode both Chief and Scout specials at speeds of 115.13 and 120.7 mph, respectively. These broke the previous records of 109.6 and 111.5 mph made in 1937 by Rollie Free at Daytona Beach. The machines used in both venues had been fitted with newly engineered V type manifolds and high lift cams, modifications worked out by Alzina's Shop Foreman, Marvin "Red" Fenwicke. The improvements were then incorporated into sports type production models, being cataloged as having "Bonneville" type engines.

A leading Crocker exponent, Sam Parriott, who specialized in dry lake speed trials, with the help of two other enthusiasts who acted as tuners, Bo Lissman and Elmo Looper, racked up a new Class C 74 cubic inch record for fuel burners at 129.49 mph. He also garnered a 500 cc (30.50 cubic inch) record for fuel burners with a converted speedway machine at 120 mph; these records being recorded in March 1938.

The first National Speedway Championship Class A races in the United States, featuring alcohol burning 500 cc overhead valve engines, were held at the Olympic Stadium in Los Angeles. In a three day meet in July 1934, such flat track stars as Pete Colman, Cordy Milne, Wilbur Lamereaux, Miny Wain, Gordon Johnson, Jimmy Gibb, Marcus "Mutt" Kelly, Bo Lissman, Earl Ferrand, Lloyd "Sprouts" Elder, Charles "Pee Wee" Callum, Byrd McKinney, and Cliff Self were on hand. Cordy

Milne was the ultimate winner, with Lammy Lamereaux second, and Byrd McKinney third.

The 1935 Championship races were held at the Fresno State College track, with most of the above-mentioned stars present, along with some newcomers. Sam Arena, a protege of Tom Sifton, added to his abilities of Class C track, TT and hill climbing with a foray on the cinders. Other new entrants were Ed Hinkle, Glenn "Shorty" Campbell and Manual Trujillo. Cordy Milne again topped the field, with his brother Jack tying with Miny Waln for second place. Pete Colman and Byrd McKinney tied for third.

The Speedway Nationals moved to the East Coast for 1936, the venue being the Tri-City Stadium at Union City, New Jersey. The standout performer was the East Coast star Benny Kaufman, but he was hard pressed by the Los Angeles rider Ed Hinkle. Some of the race results were contested due to faulty lap scoring, and some sportswriters reported that Kaufman and Hinkle ended up in a tied situation.

The 1937 Nationals, still held at Union City, saw Kaufman beating all comers, including a strong visiting Los Angeles contingent.

A noted contender on the eastern circuit was Bill Normyle, whose flamboyant style made him a crowd pleaser for two seasons. But his somewhat reckless approach caused him a near fatal accident in 1938, and he retired with crippling injuries.

The American speedway contests were scored on a point basis, with four riders competing in each heat. These were tabulated on a 4-3-2-1 basis, with the winners moving up by point accumulation. In Great Britain and Australia team racing was the rule, with two sets of contestants in each team, upward scores being tabulated by elimination. In this fashion, winning teams from the various stadiums met at season's end for the final eliminations that decided the National Championships.

In the States, the races were billed as being under AMA sanctioning. While a modest fee was forwarded to Columbus, the tracks actually operated under their own rules with their own judges and officials in charge. The sport paid only lip service to AMA supervision.

Class A speedway racing waned in popularity after 1938, the public interest then centering on midget car races. These attracted enhanced participation, as the cost of acquiring and maintaining a midget car was far less than that of Indianapolis sized spring cars. Speedway racing remained popular in Great Britain and Australia, however, and attracted huge crowds and a number of American riders, such as Jack Parker and the Milne brothers,

THE COMPETITION ERA 1935-1941

Wigwam's star riders at Ascot Speedway in 1937. (l. to r.) Sam Pariott and bo Lissman on 101 Scouts, Jack Milne, Ed Kretz, and Cordy Milne on Sport Scouts.
Craig Photos

as well as some from Canada, the most noted being Eric Chitty. It was Jack Milne's good fortune to become the first American World Speedway Champion in 1937. His teammate, Wilbur Lamereaux, was second, and brother Cordy was third. Many Australian riders competed in Great Britain, including Lloyd "Sprouts" Elder and Art Pechar, who entered with an Indian special.

Speedway activities were encouraged in Great Britain by the government, who, in noting the intense spectator interest and the huge crowds it attracted, gave special income tax concessions to the builders of these huge edifices, but also levied a heavy tax against the gate receipts. Between 1936 and 1939, huge tracks at Wembley, Harringay, and Crystal Palace operated in London; while Aldenshaw, Belleview and White City opened in Manchester. Others also opened in Glasgow, Blackpool, Wolverhampton, and Southhampton, with several small tracks in lesser cities that were training grounds for local aspirants.

In the final days, two other tracks, Lea Bridge and West Ham, were added to London. Speedway racing was an adjunct to what was later described as the Golden Age of motorcycling in the British Isles.

The original Class C concept of slightly altered standard machines had been abandoned by 1936, and factory specials in the hands of favored riders now dominated the winner's circle. Many Indian riders now fitted Junior Scout forks and fuel tanks to the Sport Scouts as a weight saving measure. Redskin tuners such as "Pop" Shunk, "Red" Fenwicke, Arthur Hafer, Bill Tuman, and factory

specialist James Hill, offered their talents in experimenting with altered port configurations, valve timing, and cam profiles. Howard Mitzel, the perennial hill climber, pioneered the cutting away of the heart shaped area between the valves to enhance gas flow.

Indian's initial theoretical technical advantages of the Sport Scout design were soon balanced off by the special W type engines from the Milwaukee factory. Milwaukee also built up some special lightweight cradle frames and small capacity fuel tanks, these machines being offered only to sponsored competitors.

Tom Sifton, as noted, had intensified his experiments with Harley-Davidson engines, especially since he took over the San Jose dealership from Fred Merlow in 1932, with the help of his star rider and shop foreman, Sam Arena.

In both cases, the 7.5:1 compression ratio mandated by the AMA for Class C competition was not a factor in side valve engineering, as their optimum rations seldom exceeded 6.5:1. The top limit was significant only to the engineering of the 500 cc overhead valve foreign made singles, as they were at their best when assembled over the 7.5:1 limit.

In 1938, E.C. Smith announced that there were presently 19,356 paid AMA memberships, with an increase of 687 registered clubs. He also noted an increase in sanctioned competition events to 674, which included track events, endurance runs, hill climbs, and TT races in 1937. This was topped in 1938 to 788. To further increase Class A memberships, Smith importuned the factories to require all

THE COMPETITION ERA 1935-1941

Fritzie Roamer Motorcycle Club receives an award fro the National Highway Safety Council for several years of accident free activities. Indian Sales Manager James Wright seated third from left, Club founder and Sponsor Fritzie Baer, as well as Springfield Indian dealer standing at right. *Indian Motorcycle Sales Company*

dealers attending regional dealer's meetings to secure them.

From this growth, the AMA was at long last financially self-supporting by 1937, with total receipts of $48,790. Smith's salary was increased to $4,800 per annum, which did not include the additional income he received from his private agreement with Milwaukee to perform certain public relations projects on Harley-Davidson's behalf.

Cora Reardon was promoted to the post of AMA office manager, with three full time clerk typists added to form the staff. She was also empowered to issue competition sanctions when requested, as well as to oversee trophy procurement. This was to counteract the complaints involving excessive delay in processing these matters in past years.

About 40 big twin Crocker motorcycles had been produced by 1938, their assembly being facilitated by Crocker dropping production of his 500 cc speedway specials due to the decline in interest in this competition. Sam Parriott, Bo Lissman and Elmo Looper continued to gain publicity for the fledgling make with their solo speed records attained on the dry lakes, although some of the bored-out large displacement specials were outside the accepted designations for official records. In addition, the redoubtable Bo Lissman racked up some notable wins in local TT races with a 74

cubic inch model in the Los Angeles area.

In the meantime, Walter Davidson, who had kept abreast of Crocker's activities from the beginning, and who was ever eager to stifle any sort of competition from others in a tenuous motorcycle market, sought ways to either terminate or at least hamper Crocker's production. Accordingly, and under Davidson's specific orders, Joe Petrali borrowed the 31st Crocker recently purchased by a Chicago enthusiast. With the owner's permission, the engine and transmission were dismantled in the shop of a local Harley-Davidson dealer under Petrali's supervision, and a series of detailed photographs were made by a professional industrial photographer, Austin Barnes. These were forwarded to Milwaukee for examination by the engineering staff to ascertain if any mechanical features infringed on Harley-Davidson patents. William Ottaway and Hank Syversten were of the opinion that the details of Crocker engineering were all well within the public domain, and that there were no grounds for legal action involving patent infringement.

By strange coincidence, the author acquired a well worn but complete Crocker from a midwestern collector in the mid-1960's, which was later identified by Petrali as the same machine that was examined by himself in the proposed patent infringement action against the Crocker organiza-

176

tion. Petrali still had in his possession copies of the photographs taken at the time of the dismantling, which bore the photographer's identification. This historic model was later restored by Elmo Looper and Ernest Skelton.

The outstanding performance of the rugged and well engineered Crockers attracted the attention of highway patrol officers in both Colorado and Arizona. One aspect of their consideration as the extra power required for the high altitudes encountered in parts of those states. The Colorado officials borrowed a 74 cubic inch model from motion picture actor John Payne for testing and evaluation. While in the end they placed no orders, Arizona officials did, and in 1940 purchased ten 74 cubic inch units which were fitted with enlarged fuel tanks to increase their cruising range. These gave good service through the war years until they were retired in 1946.

Petrali's association with Harley-Davidson ended with his resignation in the fall of 1938. As a full time employee since 1931, he had not only acted as their competition rider but also performed a credible amount of engineering and design work; first on the overhead valve Peashooter, next on the projected 30.50 speedway machine, together with having a hand in the development of the "E" series. In addition, he had competed as a hill climber, as well as keeping Milwaukee's flag flying as the leader of the now defunct Class A racing team.

In the spring of 1938, Walter Davidson suggested that the engineering department intensify their efforts in developing the Class C racing engines to counter the work of Tom Sifton on the West Coast. At this point, Petrali told the author that he considered himself frozen in a very limited salary situation, noting that some promises for cash bonuses for extra efforts were never fulfilled. He informed Walter Davidson that he would only consider participation in the Class C project if he were granted a substantial raise in pay.

Davidson demurred, pointing to the current hard times and the factory's cash flow problems due to minimal sales, but suggested that perhaps some adjustments could be made at a later date. Petrali noted that both Ottaway and Syvertsen had been paid certain cash bonuses behind his back, and with the consequent recriminations, he resigned.

In discussion the matter in later years with the author, Petrali stated that while times were indeed hard, the factory had lately been enjoying profits with careful attention to purchasing and rationalization of production, and he felt that his past con-

tributions had been such that he deserved better consideration. A remarkable individual in many ways, he had, since boyhood been immersed in both competition activities as well as engineering development, possessing outstanding native abilities in both fields. His competition career began with Harley-Davidson in 1921, subsequently with Excelsior, and received valuable engineering experience under the tutelage of Arthur A. Constantine in aiding in the development of the Super-X. His training was extended under William Ottaway, and he was able to demonstrate his own technical innovating capabilities as time went on.

Petrali's next activity was working with Joel Thorne in Los Angeles in the development of auto racing engines, and after learning to fly, was employed by Howard Hughes as the head of his flight services. He was aboard the famous Spruce Goose during its only flight over Long Beach Harbor. In later years, he headed the Contest Board of the American Automobile Association, managing the time trials at Bonneville as well as other venues.

Having left school to work with motorcycles, Petrali's formal education was at best limited. As his public recognition grew, he sought personal improvement by engaging a drama coach to polish his speech and public speaking abilities, and consulted a celebrity tailor to enhance his personal appearance. A friendly and gregarious individual, he enjoyed a wide circle of friends, and was always happy to share his experiences and knowledge in automotive and motorcycling engineering, as well as the sporting aspects of both. He had the misfortune to suffer heat exhaustion during the annual automotive Speed Trials at Bonneville in the late spring of 1974, and subsequently sustained a series of paralytic strokes which resulted in his death a few weeks later.

An incident in 1937 that was virtually unnoticed by the motorcycle industry, but which was to inaugurate a subsequent trend in two-wheeled transportation, was a small advertisement in a fall issue of "Popular Mechanics" magazine describing a small motor scooter being offered by the Cushman Motor Company of Lincoln, Nebraska. The company had been founded in 1902 by two cousins, Clinton and Everitt Cushman, who initially engaged in the manufacture of small gasoline engines for use in agriculture. Following an encouraging beginning, the company encountered financial difficulties during the Depression and it was ultimately taken over in 1934 by a local industrialist, John Ammon, and his son Charles, but they retained the Cushman name.[*3]

The scooter was offered with a choice of air cooled engines of Cushman design of either one or one and one-half rated horsepower. The cycle parts were simple: an unsprung fork attached to a platform body with the seat over the engine. Primitive springing was provided by balloon type 6" industrial tires. The early models had no kickstart, being push started by means of a compression release. In the spring of 1938, an extensive advertising campaign was launched, copy appearing in hobby and mechanical magazines, as well as in the official Boy Scout publication, "Boy's Life." Retailing for $92 and $109, the models offered a Depression bargain in low speed, economical transportation.

From the mid-1930's until the end of the decade both Harley-Davidson and Indian prudently rationalized production in their respective model lines. Milwaukee offered its top-of-the-line EL, accompanied by the identical 74 and 80 cubic inch UL's and ULH's, together with the 45 cubic inch WL and its accompanying three-wheeled Servicar. Indian offered the 74 cubic inch Chief and 45 cubic inch Sport Scout, both sharing many identical transmission and chassis components. In addition, the 30.50 cubic inch Junior Scout was carried forward as the "30.50," the name "Junior" was dropped as being thought somewhat derogatory. Also in limited production was the three-wheeled Dispatch Tow.

For 1938, a redesigned four-cylinder model appeared with a more rugged and updated engine to replace the long obsolete Ace type, which attracted increased sales for law enforcement use.

In addition, both factories were now producing a limited number of racing engines for the Class C category. Milwaukee's offerings were augmented by Tom Sifton's independently designed variants. For the sporting rider, Indian offered the specially tuned Bonneville models featuring high compression pistons, high lift cam gears and polished manifolding, which were known as "Y" motors, in either Chief or Scout models.

Both factories were also offering an ever increasing line of accessories for the encouragement of the "dresser" mode, for the increased cash flow of both factories and dealers.

A significant event in the spring of 1937 was the founding of the "Trailblazers" organization by A.F. Van Order. The Trailblazers featured an annual meeting of pioneer motorcyclists, many of whom were survivors of the earliest days of motorcycling and were still active. Van Order had absented himself from California for a time following a suspected arson induced fire that had con-

sumed C. Will Risden's Indian agency in 1925; allegedly to allow the statute of limitations to run out against possible prosecution. He later returned to act as sales manager for Albert G. Crocker's Indian agency. When Crocker sold the dealership to Floyd Clymer in 1934, Van Order opened an automotive insurance agency.

The initial meeting of the Trailblazers was held in an auditorium in Los Angeles in April 1937, attended mostly by pioneers in the Southern California area. Subsequent annual pre-war gatherings saw an encouraging increase in attendance from other areas of the country.

John J. O'Conner's next venture, following the collapse of his Federation of Western Motorcyclists, was to tour the western states in an effort to organize the various motorcycle officers into organizations within their respective areas to obtain better salary and working conditions as well as fringe and retirement benefits. The small numbers of motorcycle officers in such states as Nevada, Utah, Wyoming, New Mexico and Idaho declined to form separate organizations, but the idea was accepted in the more populous state of California. In 1936 O'Conner was able to put together a formal organization that included both state highway patrol officers as well as municipal units. O'Conner, as could be expected, promoted the formation of a benevolent fund, intended for both retirement as well as health and accident protection. In 1938, when the fund had accumulated about $30,000 from member contributions overseen by O'Conner in his capacity as secretary-manager of the association, he promptly disappeared with the money.

In reviewing the incident in later years, both Fred Ludlow, still a motor officer in Pasadena, and Captain Jack Shriver, of the State Highway Patrol, told the author that the group decided not to apprehend O'Conner. They were of the opinion that the legal expenses and the adverse publicity attesting to the laxity of the Board of Directors in not more cautiously overseeing O'Conner's management, would do more harm than good.

During the period in which he was overseeing the California Motor Officers' affairs, O'Conner attempted to purchase a residence at 944 Blaine Street in Los Angeles from the property's owner, Wilson C. Cravens, by trading him $4,000 worth of negotiable bonds. Cravens, whose suspicions were somehow aroused, suggested that O'Conner cash the bonds himself in closing the deal, but O'Conner demurred, stated that he was pressed for time to effect an early closure of the transaction. Cravens was able to take down the serial numbers

THE COMPETITION ERA 1935-1941

Harley-Davidson star rider Babe Tancrede, a Rhode Island motorcycle patrolman, at the 1938 Daytona races. The machine is a RLDR, motor number 36.
Ed Kretz

(l. to r.) Mechanic Lem Martinson, Ed Kretz, and Sam Pariott on the beach at Daytona for the 1938 race meet.
Ed Kretz

of the bonds, and checking with the Los Angeles Police Department, learned that they had been a part of the loot from a burglary in a Beverly Hills banker's home. O'Conner apparently got wind of Cravens' investigation and promptly disappeared before he could be questioned by the police.

As the self-styled elder statesman of American motorcycling, O'Conner was somewhat prominent in the early history of the sport and industry through his extensive journalistic efforts. He was a perennial contributor to the many trade magazines of the pioneer era, and for many years was the Editor of the "Pacific Motorcyclist," as mentioned. While he was acquainted with the majority of the early day figures within the sport and industry, he reported on their activities in a rather florid and bravura style that was embellished with fictionalized hyperbole that rendered the historical accuracy of his writings a doubtful entity.

The author was able to locate O'Conner in 1957, living in a rundown rooming house in the "Tenderloin" area of Los Angeles where he subsisted on meals secured from a rescue mission on skid row. O'Conner recounted an impressive sounding resume of his career within the domestic motorcycle industry, blaming the reports of questionable financial dealings on the machinations of disloyal former acquaintances. He demanded and received a substantial contribution from the author for each of three rather lengthy interviews, together with bottles of whiskey. Long ago abandoned by his wife and family, O'Conner subsisted partially on handouts from a few of his old acquaintances during his last days, passing away in the summer of 1962.

Attendant to the accelerated attention to dirt track and TT competition in the mid-1930's, hill climbing was also receiving increased popularity. Many of the established 45 degrees and 50 degree courses were being superseded by slopes of 60 degrees to 70 degrees which rendered them virtually unclimbable, but offered spectators enhanced gymnastics on the part of the contestants. An especially tough course was at Mt. Garfield, adjacent to Muskegon, Michigan, which defeated all comers for nine or ten years. It was ultimately topped by the great Joe Petrali who crested the 340 foot slope for an all time record of 12 seconds. During the same meet, Petrali beat out the veteran slant artist Orrie Steele, the perennial Indian exponent, who stalled out a mere 50 feet from the top. Local stars with high hopes were also defeated, including Claude Smith, Art Earlenbaugh and Adolph Lemaigre, who lost traction in lower levels.

While Petrali had entered the game at a later date than most of the perennials, he enjoyed con-

The Competition Era 1935-1941

Don Emde Collection

sistent experience in entering most of the larger meets between 1927 and 1937. Before 1930 he had entered his factory supplied, fuel burning Super-X's in such popular venues as Niles, Lansing and Battle Creek, Michigan; Green Bay, Wisconsin; Chicago, Illinois; Gary, Indiana; and Huntington, New York.

In the spring of 1938, the Competition Committee redefined the hill climbing rules for the 45 and 80 cubic inch categories, dividing them into "A and "C" classes. The "C" Class was subdivided into Novice, Amateur and Expert categories, with standard octane gasoline mandated as fuel. Class "A" categories included 74 and 45 cubic inch engines with either alcohol or blended fuels allowed at the discretion of the judges.

Class C riders wishing to move up to Class A were required to proceed through the Novice, Amateur, and Expert ranks via a point system based on their ongoing performances. The top Experts moved to Professional Class through elimination.

The National Championships for the A Class were held annually at either Mt. Garfield, Michigan, or Huntington, New York, and were limited to the fifteen top scorers.

According to established rules, each rider was allowed three trials, the fastest time or the best distance being accepted. In the event of ties, elimination heats followed. The scoring distance was the furthest point reached by the contestant's rear wheel. In cases where the rider came off but was able to hold the machine upright, it could be "walked" by supporting it in an upended position, with the rider standing behind it to manipulate the throttle. Such was an athletic endeavor that could add a bit of distance.

Large section rear tires with automotive chains fitted were permitted, but steel rimmed wheels with tractor type lugs attached were barred. All machines were required to be fitted with a spring loaded kill button device held open by a wooden peg attached to a cord secured to the rider's wrist. This was to prevent a riderless machine from either charging the slope or veering off into the crowd. The use of extremely steep courses was pioneered following World War I, with the establishment of the San Juan Capistrano venue 65 miles south of Los Angeles. Initial competitors were Floyd Clymer (Indian), Dudley Perkins (Harley-Davidson), and Eddie Ryan (Excelsior). Later competitors were Swede Matson and Harold Mathewson on Indians, and Mal Ord, Joe Herb and Lloyd "Sprouts" Elder on Harley-Davidsons.

Early day eastern devotees, in addition to

Orrie Steel, were "T.N.T." Terpennig, who ride both Indians and Excelsiors, and the perennial Howard Mitzel who campaigned with his Class A Indian Specials even after World War II when he had reached the age of 60!

Midwestern Milwaukee entrants were Conrad Schlemmer and Fred Reiber, sometimes joined by West Coast star Windy Linstrom. Another veteran Harley-Davidson rider was C.W. Hemmis, whose sons, Tom and Joe, carried on after World War II. Tom Sifton was also an early day competitor before he went on to specialize in engine development.

The Capistrano site was lost in the mid-1920's due to the sale of the property: the main West Coast venue next being a steep bluff north of Vallejo. Contests were sponsored there by joint action of the Vallejo and Oakland Motorcycle Clubs, usually managed promotion being in the hands of Nelson Bettencourt.

In order to encourage amateur participation, a 21 cubic inch class was established by the Competition Committee. This was almost wholly limited to Harley-Davidson Peashooters, due to the lack of overhead valve Prince Specials. Public interest was limited due to their performance being overshadowed by the 45 and 80 cubic inch classes.

Milwaukee subsequently importuned the Competition Committee to disqualify their two cam "J" motors of 1928 and 1929 vintage for hill climbing, as they tended to outperform the later EL motors introduced in 1936. This also eliminated the few remaining Super-X 45 and 61 cubic inch specials, which were especially formidable in the Class A fuel burning class.

A whole volume could be written describing the many spectacular hill climb events of this brief pre-World War II period, together with the lives and times of the many colorful riders who participated. The sport was revived for a brief time after the war, but never again rendered its one-time prominence.

With the emergence of a growing number of recognized star competitors during the late 1930's, E.C. Smith inaugurated the selection of what was billed as "The Most Popular Rider of the Year" contest with an announcement in "The Motorcyclist" in the spring of 1938. AMA members were urged to write the name of their favorite on a penny postcard. The result was that Ed Kretz was nominated with an overwhelming majority, and was awarded a trophy at the subsequent Daytona 200.

A noted west coast rider who carried the flag for Milwaukee but who, in reality, showcased the engineering work of Tom Sifton, was Sam Arena.

THE COMPETITION ERA 1935-1941

(l. to r.) Ben Capanella, Jack Horn, Babe Tancrede, Ed Kretz, and Johnny Speigelhoff at the 1939 Daytona races. *On-The-Spot Photos*

A motorcycling enthusiast from boyhood when he started riding a bicycle with a Smith Motorwheel, he later became an apprentice mechanic in the same San Jose Harley-Davidson dealership as Tom Sifton. When Sifton took over the business, Arena became the shop foreman and worked with Sifton in his engine development. At the outset of his competition career, Arena was a versatile rider, entering both track and TT events with much success, as well as making his mark in Class A speedway. In 1935 he joined Putt Mossman's speedway team that competed internationally in Australia, New Zealand and later in England. In 1936, he returned to the States where he garnered several second and third places in the big Nationals. He was also a successful entrant in the weekly Neptune Beach flat track events, and in 1938, won the Oakland 200 miler, making an all time record at 83 mph: 9 mph over the existing record.

The 1938 Daytona 200 was held on the same course as the previous year, but with little improvements made to the surface or spectator accommodations. Flushed with a successful competition season, Ed Kretz was a heavy favorite to win. He took an early lead and blasted his way around the course in his usual charging style. He had nearly lapped the field in the 29th mile when he was sidelined with a blown engine in his Sport Scout.

A dark horse rider, Ben Campanale, who had recently come forward in Southern California competition, had been entered as a factory rider on a WLDR Harley-Davidson; an out-and-out racing machine with a new engine that had enlarged cylinder finning, aluminum heads, and a revamped lubrication system that had been built by Hank Syvertsen and Joe Petrali. It was Petrali's last design effort for Milwaukee.

As advised by William Ottaway, Campanale ran a conservative race and slowly forged ahead to join the leaders of the pack. Sam Arena, riding a Sifton modified Harley-Davidson, was just ahead of Campanale in the 183rd mile when he went down in the north turn and filled his carburetor with sand. Campanale then turned up the wick and came in the winner.

While hailed as a milestone in AMA competition in an article written by Editor Billings in "The Motorcyclist," reporters for the general news media again noted the lack of adequate crowd control and sanitary facilities. Many of the entrants were again critical of the method of lap scoring, and several protests were filed regarding both this and the later reported positions, all of which were disallowed by E.C. Smith. Foreign observers were critical of the large number of riders, 115 in all, that were allowed to enter on the basis of the prior time trials, citing the congestion often noted at the turns, and the confusion resulting from the leaders lapping the field and being impeded by the slower riders.

It was during this period that the author ran afoul of the news managing policies of the AMA when he somewhat innocently submitted his first formal article to "The Motorcyclist." Early in the preceding year, he had entered into correspondence with Charles Markham, a staff writer for the British "Motorcycling" magazine, published by the Temple Press and edited by Graham Walker, one time racing star, TT winner, and later a commentator for motor racing events for the British Broadcasting Company. Markham, a professional mechanic who conducted most of the searching road tests on new models that appeared serially in the magazine, sent the author some technical material covering the Harley-Davidson and Indian 45 cubic inch engines. This included photographs of the offsides of the engines with the timing covers removed, together with some rough notes describing the timing systems and cam gear, with a comparison of the layout and the advantages and disadvantages of each.

The author, considering the subject a timely one, wrote an article based on Markham's observations, citing his interest as an overseas observer of the American motorcycling scene, and sent it to the editorial offices of "The Motorcyclist" in Los Angeles.

After some months had elapsed with no acknowledgement of the matter, a telephone call to

The Competition Era 1935-1941

Ed Kretz (#38) and a group of friends ride vintage Indian Chiefs at a country field meet and TT race.
Ed Kretz

Welch elicited the comment that he had not seen the article, and that it was no doubt in the hands of Editor Billings. Further questioning brought forth the somewhat guarded statement that while he was the publisher of the magazine, he did not have full executive control of the magazine's editorial or technical content.

Later that summer at a hill climb in Vallejo, the author encountered Smith, with whom, by this time he had a passing acquaintanceship. When queried about the fate of the article, Smith rather haughtily replied that only regular staff members of the magazine were considered sufficiently qualified to have their contributions published![*4]

In commenting on the episode in later years, Welch told the author that Chet Billings intercepted all material submitted by outside staff sources and forwarded it to Smith for his approval before considering publication. In this case, the article had been filed awaiting an early visit from Smith to the west coast. In any case, it was a standing AMA policy that nothing dealing with comparisons of a technical nature regarding either Harley-Davidson or Indian, or comparative road tests of an objective nature were to be aired in the magazine. To avoid any appearance of editorial censorship, any technical descriptions of mechanical details or descriptions of new models were written by the publicity writers for the respective factories and were printed intact as submitted.

It was subsequently brought to the author's attention later in the fall of 1938, that Walter Davidson had somehow gotten wind of his activities in the researching of domestic motorcycle history, and he had issued an inter-departmental memoranda that no middle management personnel were to grant the author interviews and that he was henceforth forbidden access to the premises at Juneau Avenue!

This official edict was well in line with the avowed company view that reporters, journalists, and historians were "...troublemakers who printed lies about the company," as reported by the late William Huddlestone, a one time staff writer for the Business Section of the Milwaukee Journal.

As one of Milwaukee's larger industries, Harley-Davidson activities quite naturally attracted substantial local media attention. The company frequently issued press releases regarding the announcements of new models, but reporters were more interested in news items involving the internal affairs of the company, which did not endear them to the management. Huddlestone later stated that President Davidson was particularly irked at the appearance of an article announcing a forthcoming Board of Directors meeting and the mention of Frank L. Wood, a prominent shareholder. This somewhat dispelled the carefully cultivated illusion that the company was a family affair, owned wholly by the original founders. Many of the human interest articles had as their source confidential reports to reporters from employees, who, more often than not, were paid a small fee for their information and whose identities were a carefully guarded secret.

The author was informed of the company's displeasure with his activities by Vernon Guthrie, who, as an automotive journalist, had kept in close touch with both Harley-Davidson's as well as Indian's activities even though he was no longer personally involved in the industry. He also stated that a report of the matter had been privately expressed to much of the dealership through the factory travelers, although they never appeared to take the matter seriously.

The author, whose enthusiasm at that time was tempered with an admixture of naivete, was somewhat taken aback by the episode, which subsequently prompted a letter from Guthrie. In it he stressed the fact that as a budding investigative reporter, rebuffs and denials were a part of the game and never should be taken personally. He further stated that along the way certain members of the industry, other than the Davidsons, were reticent about revealing some of the internal affairs of the industry.

"The researching and preservation of history is at once both an intellectual and scholastic undertaking. The Davidsons, with their working class background and limited formal education, have but little concept of either. Being pragmatic thinkers, they are quite naturally preoccupied with selling motorcycles, and shun public disclosures that might cast doubts on either the soundness of Company management or the direction of the industry. Then too, being involved in an undertaking that is both marginal in scope and not generally in public favor, they are quite naturally sensitive relative to their position within it. Both James Wright and Arthur Constantine have independently stated to me in confidence their concerns regarding the future of the industry. As realistic thinkers, they have no illusions regarding the generally negative public image of motorcycling. While as educated men they both feel a certain philosophical responsibility for the in-depth preservation of the industry's history. But they are also of the opinion that all of the salient facts had best not be aired contemporary, such being reserved for some future time when an overall view might be better presented in a dispassionate and objective manner."

Guthrie's summation proved true. While the author was in contact with both Wright and Constantine during the late 1930's, they did not offer a full disclosure of their experiences or refer to their own private material or journals until after World War II when they had severed all personal connections with the industry.

Arthur Welch later told the author that while he had been at variance with E.C. Smith's and the AMA Competition Committee's views on the necessity to manage industry news, he could appreciate their feelings in regard to the critical state of it. However, he was of the opinion that the continuing array of sugar-coated journalism as concocted by Billings as Editor and Smith as "Resident Censor" was often excessively transparent to even the most dedicated of motorcycling enthusiasts. He felt at times that even the still marginal industry could benefit from some constructive critiques.

The management of the Indian company during these years appeared little concerned with either their own image or the strict management of media content. This was no doubt due to the more relaxed atmosphere in Springfield, due to the improved financial situation of the company as well as the profitable position of the diverse industrial holdings of the duPonts that had carried Indian through the worst years of the Depression. Favorable too were Indian's labor relations, which were non-critical due to their generally good standing with the local unions and their acquiescence to the two-tiered system of production of component parts that was separate from their assembly.

Indian also benefitted from good relationship with their dealerships, fostered by their lack of restrictive policies regarding the conduct of their businesses or diverse product marketing.

Indian benefitted from a stable work force with small turnover of employees, the production supervisors being a convivial group of enthusiasts who were given wide latitude in the development of both detail improvements in the product as well as production efficiencies. The top management was sensitive to adverse comments regarding the lack of the development of overhead valve production models or the replacement of the long archaic sliding gear transmission systems, citing as always the profitability problems engendered by the Depression that mandated an overall status quo.

Domestic motorcycle production had leveled off in the late 1930's due to the loss of much of the export markets; production at both factories now running a close parallel. Much of the extreme bitterness that had grown between the enthusiasts of the two competing makes in the early 1930's had dissipated to some extent, although their in-house publications continued an attempt to foster brand name loyalty. The sporting competition was grow-

THE COMPETITION ERA 1935-1941

Ed Kretz at speed during a qualifying lap at Ascot.
Ed Kretz

ing intense now that the original Class C concept was all but forgotten, as each factory went all out to develop improved racing machinery.

In recognition of the general attitude of either indifference or hostility, a few of the more prominent dealers reasoned that combining forces of the two competing makes into dealer's associations of a regional nature might well combat this trend. Ted Hodgdon reported that steps were taken in the Northeast to form such an association in 1936. Similar efforts in the Carolinas and Northern Florida resulted in tentative steps to form a mid-Atlantic Motorcycle Dealers Association. Some of the prominent Western dealers, such as Hap Alzina, Dudley Perkins and William Ruhle, advocated such an organization in that area, with the idea of inaugurating a public relations campaign to improve motorcycling's image. But before any of these plans resulted in formal organizations, Walter Davidson sought to block the movement by instituting a network of Harley-Davidson Dealers Associations.

Davidson launched his proposal through a series of communications sent to the dealers as well as through personal contacts from the factory travelers to advocate the organization. Davidson based his promotion on the theory that this would help strengthen Milwaukee's market, but would also constitute a force to combat the anticipated competition from foreign imports. While imports at that time enjoyed a minimal market, the intrusion of Canadian competition riders showcasing

British machines and the aggressive sales campaign of British importers in the western market, which traditionally enjoyed 65 percent of the total national sales, was a cause for concern. In addition, it was Davidson's expressed desire that "...he didn't want Harley-Davidson dealers fraternizing with Indian people."

Regional dealers' meetings conducted by the two surviving makes after 1930 constituted an important role in national sales campaigns. These were annual affairs usually held in the late summer in connection with the announcements of new models for the ensuing sales season. In some instances, regional meetings were also held in the spring, incidental to the inauguration of the competition season.

These meetings were traditionally closed to the trade press, in an effort to keep projected sales strategies on a confidential basis. But they were not highly restricted as to individual participants, as factory representatives often invited prospective dealers to attend in the hope of encouraging their enthusiasm.

Specialty salesmen representing the factory component suppliers were also frequently invited to attend. They could then elaborate on projected technical improvements planned for the ensuing season.

With this somewhat lenient policy regarding attendance, the author was able to attend some of the dealers' meetings as an anonymous visitor through the connivance of representatives of both makes who were sympathetic to historical research of the industry. The convenient cover was the name badges issued to each participant; in the author's case indicating "Parts Department."

Dealer attendance at such meetings, in any case, was made mandatory to maintain a franchise, and in actuality was viewed by the participants both wearily as well as warily. With the static state of the contemporary motorcycle market, there was nothing really new or innovative in the way of new models for the forthcoming year. In any case, advance information on what few innovations there were had already been made available to the dealers through previously issued factory service material. There was generally nothing new in the way of sales campaigns, as sales brochures or newspaper advertising layouts, the latter usually requiring the financial participation of the dealers, were also a traditional practice and did not vary markedly from year to year.

The principle inducement for attending the meetings was the convivial sessions in an adjacent bar for the purpose of relaxing tensions and swapping trade and personal gossip with old acquaintances in the business. These social sessions were a welcome alternative to the familiar canned speeches of welcome and the reiterations of company policies with which all were long familiar.

Motorcycle dealers as a group, while sometimes rough hewn individuals, were generally men possessed of more than average business acumen, intelligence and native sophistication. Operating as they did in a industry that offered a rather narrow range of product that catered to a limited discretionary market traditionally outside general public favor, nimble wits and extreme sagacity were a necessity for survival. Then too, a basic enthusiasm and a dedication to the cause of motorcycling was a prime requisite.

The regional Harley-Davidson dealers' meetings were conducted either by President Walter Davidson or his brother Arthur, the perennial Company Sales Manager; both usually attending. With Walter in charge, he appeared in his familiar ill-fitting suit with mismatched accessories. His opening remarks, often delivered in a somewhat bombastic tone, included the pioneer and innovative aspects of the company's entrance into the industry, along with an account of its survival in difficult times. He also included self-congratulatory statements that, through conservative policies and careful management, its ownership remained in the hands of the founders and their families, and that, so far, the operation had been kept from falling into the hands of Jewish bankers!

He would then proceed to stress the necessity for brand name loyalty on the part of the dealers that should be instilled in enthusiasts, together with supporting the factory policy regarding the selling of merchandise that could be obtained only through factory sources. The growing selection of accessories was mentioned in connection with a generous display of such items that was placed on exhibit as part of the meeting. the substantial markups being an important adjunct to dealer profits.

Vice President Arthur, on the occasions he chaired the meetings, was usually less bombastic with emphasis on sales techniques and the importance of sponsoring social as well as competition affairs of a mild nature for the benefit of the average rider as a means of promoting brand name loyalty. He also stressed the ongoing factory policy that individual dealers make all out attempts to improve their sales volume each year, and that the granting of a franchise in any given area did not include a monopolistic control that excluded the awarding of another franchise within the same geographic boundaries, should the performance of the incumbent dealer not live up to the factory's expectations.

The regional Indian dealers' meetings were generally conducted by Sales Manager James Wright. As a genial and personable individual, he was generally well liked by the dealership for both his dedication to the Wigwam and his heroic efforts to rebuild the company following the Levine-Bolles debacle of 1929. With a rather informal approach, he usually touched on the glories of Indian during the pioneer period, its position of leadership in the sporting sphere and the present development of the Sport Scout that was enhancing club activities as well as formal competition. He also emphasized the accessory business, calling attention to the display of these items that was also a feature of the meetings.

Wright also had the rather curious habit of over-dramatizing whatever minor changes in detail finish were being incorporated in forthcoming models. This was in an era when the specifications of both makes were almost unchanged from year to year. He could rhapsodize at length over the inclusion of a metal plate, or a "dust shield" over the fork spring of a Sport Scout, or the repositioning of a tool box, or a deeper valance on a chain guard!

During one of these dissertations, the author recalls that a bored dealer was heard to remark, "...Oh hell, Jim, just paint it green and we'll sell it next year!"

E. Paul duPont sometimes attended these meetings, usually those located in the Northeast or along the East Coast, but he deferred to Wright's chairmanship and usually limited his remarks to the group and spent most of his time circulating among the dealers during the social parts of the gathering. A person of much personal charm, his lighthearted bantering and his friendly manner did much to further cordial relationships between management and dealers.

The matter of anti-Semitism, as publicly mentioned at times by the Davidsons, was in an oblique manner also expressed in Springfield. The Davidsons' sentiments were described by contemporary employees as having been fostered in the mid-1920's when the management in Milwaukee sought a bank loan to enhance their working capital. The story goes that the loan officer, who happened to be Jewish, suggested that a favorable decision by the bank would hinge on the tendering of a block of company shares as a part of the service fee, which was at once rejected by the Davidsons, who seemingly never forgot the incident.

A member of the duPont family once told the author, anonymously, that Indian's management did not go out of its way to recruit either Jewish employees or dealer representation. On the other

THE COMPETITION ERA 1935-1941

A late 1930's classic, this 1938 Indian Chief was favored by numbers of highway patrol bodies for law enforcement use, as well as tourists. The machine shown was found in derelict condition in an automobile graveyard in Needles, California, in the 1960's, and later restored by Johnny Eagles.
George Hays

A 1937 45 cu. in. WLA Harley-Davidson, fitted with non-standard sports type handlebars. The WR competition machines were based on this model, but the WLA's were themselves mild performing utility machines noted for easy starting and were sometimes favored by feminine riders.

hand, the multifaceted diversity of their holding corporations' interest at times necessitated dealings with Jewish members of the financial community in both New York and on Wall Street, which fact caused the duPonts to assume a neutral attitude for both their own interests as well as a public posture.

This attitude, both in the public as well as the private sense, on the matter of anti-Semitism is in

no way denigrating to the image of the domestic motorcycle industry in the historical sense, as such might be viewed in the light of public sentiments of that time.

During the earliest days of the colonial settlement of America, immigration to the New World was stimulated by the opportunity to escape the social, economic, and religious oppression that had long existed in Europe. It was not surprising that these people brought their prejudices with them. The Puritans and Separatists who gravitated to New England had already rejected the formalism and dogma of the Church of England, which was basically that of Roman Catholicism. The adherents of the latter who chose to immigrate found it expedient to form their own groups in Maryland, largely as a matter of self protection.

During the rapid industrialization of the United States following the Civil War, many working class people viewed with alarm the flood of European immigrants who were being freely admitted to the country at the behest of the powerful industrialists who demanded and received a vast pool of cheap and exploitable labor. This was following the pre-war prejudice against the Irish who flocked to America as a result of the potato famine of the 1840's. This was engendered by the fear of enhanced competition for available employment, but was also colored by religious considerations. The Jews, in their relationship to Christianity, had been subjected to intermittent persecution since the Middle Ages, not only in their faith but in the economic restrictions imposed upon them. As a result, this forced them into banking and money lending, which fanned the flames still further. This resentment was carried to the New World.

It was no doubt the fear of Jewish economic power that caused them to be singled out by some as a sinister force. From the time of the mid-19th Century, Jews faced restrictions in housing locations, memberships in certain social clubs and fraternal orders, along with admission to professional schools and colleges, which usually placed them, if at all, on a limited quota system. This widespread prejudice caused the majority of businesses and corporations to either deny or severely restrict the employment of Jews, especially if their position might include a high visibility. This ethnic and religious prejudice was widespread until the 1960's incidental to a more enlightened view of the matter following the upheavals of the Civil Rights Movement. While ethnic prejudice and anti-Semitism has been less widespread and generally unpopular politically in the United States, there has unfortunately been a resurgence in certain European countries following the collapse of Communism and signs of a rising fascism in some areas. In any case, ethnic prejudice within the domestic motorcycle industry during the first half of the 20th Century was well within the general state of thinking of the majority of businesses and industries.

By the mid-1930's the domestic motorcycle market had assumed a more or less predictable pattern. The country was now served by about a thousand dealerships for each make, the majority of whom operated from very modest premises. In spite of the efforts of both factories to encourage their respective dealers to present a respectable image to the public, many continued to operate out of premises that were less than presentable. On the other hand, most of the dealers in the larger cities had by this time updated their operations and the larger number of these operated from buildings that were on a par with contemporary automobile agencies.

Harley-Davidson dealers continued to feature their overhead valve EL and UL big twins as their top-of-the-line sales leaders. Milwaukee products also had the edge in law enforcement sales, abetted by the political efforts of the dealers to see that local municipal governments incorporated Harley-Davidson specifications into their procurement ordinances. They were often aided in this by the efforts of the factory travelers, who presented model specimens written by the factory legal department. While both factories stressed the touring aspects of motorcycling, this was given special emphasis by Milwaukee, who featured pictures of couples mounted on big twin machines fitted with touring equipment.

Indian dominated a specialized class of law enforcement machines with their four cylinder models which were the favorite mount of suburban or municipal patrolmen. Many of the country's larger cities, such as Seattle, Portland, San Diego, Phoenix, Houston, New Orleans, Kansas City, Atlanta, Wilmington, Newark, New York and Boston to name a few, all maintained substantial numbers. While these smooth running machines were well suited to this work, they were less than satisfactory when used for highway patrol duties involving high speed pursuits. They were vulnerable to mechanical troubles not encountered with either Chief models or VLP Harley-Davidsons. Verne Guthrie once estimated, from a private survey, that the nation's highways were patrolled by 70% Harley-Davidsons in Contrast to 30% Indian Chiefs.

The state of California, which operated the nation's largest number of patrol motorcycles, purchased mostly VLP and ELP Harley-Davidsons, with an occasional order of Chiefs. The Wigwam's status suffered in 1938, when Officer Ezra Eberhardt was instantly killed when his Chief somersaulted as the result of a broken front axle while he was pursuing a speeder on East Baseline Highway near San Bernardino.

In the summer of 1938, a race meet held on a half-mile trotting track adjacent to the village of Sturgis, South Dakota (also featuring a Gypsy Tour attended by club members from adjoining areas) received only passing attention. Organized by the local Indian dealer, Clarence J. Hoel, limited sponsorship from local merchants was solicited and through much publicity arranged by Hoel a creditable attendance was realized, compared with the sparse population of this northern plains area. Largely through Hoel's efforts, the event grew to the point that, for the next half century, excluding the war years, the Sturgis rally came to rival even Daytona as a motorcycling conclave. By the 1950's it had become a nationally recognized event.

The national organization of the AMA initially consisted of areas that were encompassed by states. It was soon noted that such was characterized by weak organization in less populated areas, as had been noted in the former FAM days. E.C. Smith, with the concurrence of the Competition Committee, redistricted the country in the mid-1930's into 38 divisions, starting with District 1 in the northeast and numbering them across to the Pacific coast, ending with District 38 in San Diego.

The more sparsely populated areas were incorporated into larger districts, with the more populated areas having much smaller geographical boundaries. In each sub-division, a District Referee was appointed by Smith; the appointments being rubber stamped by the Committee in nearly every case. Smith was careful to select only those individuals who were in agreement with current AMA policies and rule mandates and who were also personally loyal to himself. In the areas of larger population, Assistant Referees were also installed to assure adequate servicing of competition events, together with "commissioners" to aid in the administration of AMA affairs, if such were warranted.

This system gave Smith definitive administrative control of all AMA sanctioned events and helped to police the conduct of the membership, most especially in the perennial problem of combatting unsanctioned "outlaw" events and the censuring of AMA card holders who competed in them.

With their built-in loyalty to Smith, the District Referees were a decisive factor in enforcing the competition rules and their decisions in

The February 1935 issue of "The Harley-Davidson Enthusiast" was devoted exclusively to police motorcycles.
Don Emde Collection

The October issue celebrated Joe Petrali's National Championship victories at the Syracuse, New York mile and Hornell. New York hill-climbs.
Don Emde Collection

contested interpretations were invariably backed by Smith, should individual complaints be called to his attention.

While this rather autocratic control of AMA affairs undoubtedly was the prime factor in maintaining the necessary authority to keep all AMA affairs on an even keel, there was inevitably a substantial number of both members and competition riders who took issue with Smith and the competition Committee over their arbitrary control. The most frequent complaint was that no unaffiliated members, club personnel or competition riders had any voice in AMA policy making and that the membership of the Competition Committee was either factory personnel or trade representatives who, in some cases, were neither riders nor motorcycle owners.

A particularly controversial matter was that of the small purses sanctioned for competition events, entrants citing the costs of the upkeep of machines and travel expenses incidental to participation. The $500 purse allocated for Daytona was the highest of any AMA sanctioned event. The $300 purses for such nationals as Langhorne, Laconia, the Jack Pine and other major fixtures like the Pacific Coast Championships inaugurated in 1937, were the rule.

Smith's stock answer to critics was that with

the tight money situation throughout the country, larger purses would discourage promoters from providing risk capital to sponsor the events and that the even smaller purses of local club-sponsored events were necessary in encouraging these as well. In addition, Walter Davidson was adamantly opposed to the offering of more substantial awards, often stating that "young men shouldn't expect to get rich from entering motorcycle sporting events."

To combat rider complaints, Indian's top management continued the policy instituted by Frank Weschler of awarding small extra cash bonuses to successful competitors representing the Wigwam. As Harley-Davidson did not, the matter was still a bone of contention in the "name brand" controversy, although Milwaukee did on occasion supply spare parts and fund dealer's shop time for the benefit of their more successful enthusiasts.

The $10 per event fee advanced to District Referees for their services also came under fire and subsequently Smith would contribute five cents per mile for travel expenses if substantial distances were involved. In all cases, the Referees were paid by the promoters and Smith would usually add an additional billing for mileage in the award of sanctions.

There were also several AMA members who thought that the traditional $1 per annum membership dues should be raised to $2, mainly to fund a national advertising campaign to give more extensive publicity to the more prominent sporting events as well as the sport in general. Smith was adamantly opposed to this, stating that much of the AMA membership was recruited from Gypsy Tour participants who might oppose paying more than $1 for the privilege of attending just one outing a year and that adding to the AMA roster was essential to the strength of the organization.

With the general lack of publicity for some of the larger fixture AMA sanctioned events, the factories subsequently offered to fund a limited amount of advertising in local media outlets provided the dealerships adjacent bore a part of the cost on a pro-rated basis. As could be expected, some of the smaller dealerships in areas of low volume sales who never advertised themselves, objected to this practice as an unneeded expense.

While a number of AMA members and some dealers wrote letters to Smith and the Competition Committee airing their views (which in practice appeared to have been generally ignored because Smith did not believe in answering his critics) many of these complaints were sent to "The Motorcyclist." Arthur Welch, still an advocate of journalistic freedom, was of the opinion that some

THE COMPETITION ERA 1935-1941

recognition of the views of the AMA rank and file deserved an airing. He later told the author that he presented Smith with several dozen of these communications during one of his frequent visits to the west coast, with the suggestion that even a minority representation on the Competition Committee of rider members and competition participants would do much to create a minimal image of a democratic organization. Smith demurred, stating that any airings of discontent with the AMA's management or changes in Committee personnel would be a divisive factor in denigrating the AMA's image.

Arthur Constantine and Hap Alzina, who at one time or another were both members of the committee, later told the author that Smith only wanted members of the trade on the Committee because he considered it prudent to keep the inner workings and the deliberations of the Committee from public review.

Being denied any response to their complaints to the Committee and a public forum in "The Motorcyclist," many club members aired their opinions in their local chapter bulletins, many of which were exchanged between adjacent clubs. While only a very few copies of these bulletins survive, it appears that even at that time there was a strong undercurrent of opinion that the AMA management was highly undemocratic. Then too, Smith's often capricious and arbitrary decisions on the interpretation of AMA rules and by-laws added fuel to the fire.

The strained relationship between the AMA and Canadian riders and club men deteriorated still further during 1939, just before most civilian motorcycling terminated due to participation in Canada's war efforts. Walter Davidson, at long last, gave up his attempt to control the distribution of Milwaukee products in the north-of-the-border free market. Instead, with the cooperation of E.C. Smith, enthusiasts were importuned to join the AMA oriented clubs that were ostensibly organized for the benefit of the owners of American machines but in reality catered to Harley-Davidson owners. In his annual report rendered to the Competition Committee in 1940, Smith claimed that no less that 21 such clubs existed throughout the Ontario area, although Canadian motorcycle historians later stated that 11 had been the top number.

For competitive reasons and in an antagonistic gesture, these clubs scheduled their competition events, held under AMA Class C rules, as well as club outings and tours, on the same days that the Canadian clubs, featuring British machines and FICM oriented rules, held theirs.

Further antagonism was generated by the fact that a minority of Indian owners who attended the AMA sponsored meets subsequently complained that the Harley-Davidson oriented officials and referees treated them to such unfair ruling as to make their participation futile. One Indian owner from Hamilton, Ralph Donovan, wrote several letters to the AMA Competition Committee stating that Walter Davidson, Jr. and Hank Syvertsen, who frequently officiated at such meets, usually disqualified the occasional Indian owner who either won or placed in these events.

Aside from these tactics, which were clearly aimed to divide Harley-Davidson owners from the Canadian riders of other makes, the situation relative to the Wasaga Beach time trials was another matter of controversy. There was no AMA classification for 61 cubic inch overhead valve machines burning blended fuels in high compression (over 7.5:1) engines in the unlimited sprint class. Yet, such machines, including overhead valve Indian factory specials, were regularly entered by American contestants. The Harley-Davidson EL's especially built by Joe Petrali and Hank Syvertsen were the usual winners.

In the absence of any available British models to compete in this class, some Canadian riders were of the opinion that it was unsporting of the Americans to enter their own factory specials in an over-the-border venue when they were not sanctioned in their own country. The EL's reigned supreme until 1940, when Collin Fairly entered a winning Vincent HRD, one of 83 high performance big twins built in England just before the war.

The onset of the war in Europe and the immediate support by the Canadian government for England at once ended organized motor sport in Canada. The Wasaga Beach speed trials in the fall of 1939 was a competition event officially supported by the organized clubs.

A small number of Canadian competition riders, not immediately enlisted in the armed forces, turned their attention to south-of-the-border events under the reciprocity agreement with the AMA which was still in force with the somewhat reluctant approval of the Competition Committee. The machine of choice for these entrants was the Norton International, which, since 1932, had been the dominant marque in international competition. J.M. McGill, the Canadian importer for Norton, managed to secure a shipment of about 40 machines from the factory. Most of these were the overhead valve 500 cc Model 18's, which were Norton's over-the-counter offering, but included were about six Internationals. This was the last factory export of civilian machines before all its efforts were devoted to supplying vast

THE COMPETITION ERA 1935-1941

The starting lineup of a Targo Flio type race at Ascot Speedway. Such events were started in reverse of the usual direction of either conventional track or TT races.
Carroll Photo Service

numbers of 16H side valve models to the British War Department.

In noting the growing demand for Internationals, always a low production item due to their high retail price, McGill also rounded up about a dozen more, these being used samples purchased from such large London agencies as Pride and Clark, Neasdons and Marble Arch.

On the strength of Norton's now enviable competition record, McGill solicited a number of non-franchised motorcycle shops in the States as agents, offering mostly the new Model 18's. Sam Pierce, a one time Harley-Davidson and Indian dealer who held an almost fanatic affection for Indians, agreed to accept McGill's offer and ordered half-a-dozen machines. He told the author later that he regretted the decision, as the overhead valve roadsters had never been accorded the developmental attention by Norton's Chief Designer, Joe Craig, the rider-tuner who refined the previous work of Walter Moore and Arthur Carroll in perfecting the cammers. Craig had an agreement with the factory involving a bonus payment for competition wins and quite naturally spent all of his time and effort on this racing model, to the neglect of the production machines.

In the meantime, competition events were being carried on at an accelerated pace. E.C. Smith tirelessly traveled the country, promoting the activi-

ties of the established clubs and aiding in the formation of new ones. He was also ever watchful for non-sanctioned events, disciplining those riders caught participating, as well as attempting to recruit additional officials and referees, who always seemed to be in short supply. As a further stimulus to AMA membership, he importuned the manufacturers and suppliers of accessory items to mandate the membership of their representatives as a condition of admission to regional dealers' meetings. Yearly awards were presented to clubs on the basis of their receipt of favorable newspaper publicity as well as their participation in civic affairs. Recognition pins were also presented to individual riders on the basis of mileage ridden, which required verification from the dealer of the make involved.

With an eye to enhancing public recognition of AMA activities, Smith organized the Charity Newsies Benefit for the organization in Columbus in 1939. This was made up of a number of successful business and professional men in the area who had sold newspapers or who had serviced newspaper delivery routes in their youth and who had as their initial goal to provide for needy children in the Franklin County area. As an initial fund raiser, the group had planned to sponsor an air show featuring stunt flyers and parachute drops at the adjacent Ohio State Fairgrounds. Smith prevailed upon the group to sponsor a motorcycle race instead, on the grounds that such would draw a larger paying gate than an air show that could be viewed from outside the track area. The initial event attracted a crowd of 10,000 and for several years thereafter, discounting the war years, it became an annual event.

The extensive 1939 competition season, which included Langhorne, Laconia, Keene, New Hampshire, the Springfield Mile and the Pacific Coast Championships, was kicked off in March with the Daytona 200 for its third year. The heavily favored Ed Kretz blasted his way into an early lead and lapped the large field of over 100 riders but was sidelined, as was often the case, when his over-stressed engine blew up. Ben Campanale, riding a factory prepared WLDR Harley-Davidson kept a steady pace, saving his engine until close to the finish and took first place for his second straight win.

With an ever growing number of competition events, Smith decided to ease the administrative burdens of his staff at Columbus by establishing a branch office on the West Coast. Chester Billings, still Editor of "The Motorcyclist" and an AMA commissioner, was named to head this operation, with a salary of $50 per month for what was described as a part-time position. Arthur Welch was given an extra $25 per month over and above the production costs of the magazine for the use of office space. Billings spent most of his time overseeing the sanctioning and administration of West Coast events: 65% of the nation's motorcycling activity was still centered in this area. Welch later told the author that at this time he was less concerned with the financial position of the magazine, as circulation had grown and the demand for his other unrelated publications had also increased; this was due to improved business conditions brought about by the economic pressures of the war in Europe.

Later that year, Smith reported to the Competition Committee that the AMA now had 23,416 paid members, with 766 chartered clubs and that no less than 1,326 sanctions had been granted during the 1939 season. With the larger share of these being in the West, Billings kept the tabulations coordinated through telephone communication with Cora Reardon in Columbus.

The financial condition of the Indian Company was substantially improved in the fall of 1939, through an order placed by the French government for 5,000 military Chiefs and sidecars. At an agreed unit price of $600, this amounted to a $3,000,000 order.

Indian had already planned to introduce a spring frame for the Chief for the 1940 season and this was incorporated in the military order. The Chiefs were fitted with low compression commercial type motors, along with carburetor air cleaners, rear carriers, heavy duty stands, panniers and other military equipment including wide valanced mudguards. While during the last two decades the French had seen a proliferation of motorcycle manufacturers, the leaders being Gnome-et-Rhone, Terrot and Monet-Guyon, the typical Gallic individualism had seen an extensive growth in small capacity models. With the current emphasis on motorized motorcycle and moped type machines in Europe, none of the major factories had the facilities to turn out heavyweight military models.

Although the French government paid for the order mostly in cash, a part of the transaction involved Indian accepting 1,000 Peugeot mopeds as partial payment. Indian's management at once arranged to sell these at wholesale to several large department stores in New York and Boston.

As a historic footnote to the sale, the Chiefs were shipped in two increments to La Havre. The second shipment carried in the 10,000 ton freighter "Hanseatic Star" was lost, as the ship was torpedoed off Land's End by one of the German Navy's growing fleet of submarines. So some 2,500 Chief sidecar units now lie on the bottom of the Atlantic.

Indian had been hard pressed to fill the order due to the deficient state of their tooling. A number of retired employees were called back to help with the production. With round-the-clock shifts and the emergency acquisition of some used machinery, the order was ultimately filled just short of the agreed time.

The immediate effect of the war in Europe was a dramatic rise in both agricultural as well as industrial production. This factor at once brought about a partial relief from the long running Depression which, in spite of the pump priming from a myriad of expensive government social programs, was still unrelieved.

While the prevailing sentiment throughout the country was on the side of the Allies, there were many who were opposed to entering the war as a combatant; the mixed feelings over the realities of the Treaty of Versailles being still fresh in the minds of veteran politicians.

There were some minority groups who favored the German cause, such as the fascist leaning Ku Klux Klan, the Silver Shirts led by William Dudley Pelley and the German Nationalist group called the German-American Bund led by Fritz Kuhn. Included in the group were those advocating white supremacy as well as anti-Semitism. Another group which was more strictly isonalistic rather than eth-

The Drive side of the engine of a 1934 Harley-Davidson VLD.
Steve Iorio

A rider's eye view of a 1934 Harley-Davidson VLD.
Steve Iorio

nic in nature was the American First organization, a prominent spokesman being Charles A. Lindberg.

Political opposition in Congress was spearheaded by Senator Burton K. Wheeler of Montana, who harked back to the founding father's admonition to beware of foreign entanglements. President Franklin D. Roosevelt, however, who was well aware of the dangers of a German victory, was able to gather sufficient political backing to put a preparedness program in place, which also included a Lend-lease program to supply the Allied Forces with war material as well as foodstuffs.

The nation's transportation industry was, of course, a vital part of these programs, which naturally included the motorcycle industry. The War Department now called for prototype development of military machines. Both factories had already laid plans for this eventuality, with prototypes already on hand that were permutations of their in-place utility models.

Harley-Davidson offered their long standing WL models with a low compression commercial type engine fitted with a carburetor air cleaner, a skid plate under the transmission and rear chain, together with carriers, ammunition cases and other military gear.

Indian offered a somewhat smaller model with a 30.50 engine and similar equipment, the result being an admixture of Sport Scout and 30.50 components. The same machine with a 45 cubic inch engine was subsequently produced.

The author was fortunate, in the summer of 1939, to again interview A.B. Coffman. Coffman was in charge of a farm machinery exhibit at the World Trade Fair being held on Treasure Island.

The Island is a man made structure in the San Francisco Bay just north of Yerba Buena Island. While long separated from the motorcycle industry, Coffman had, in the interim, been in close touch with its on-going affairs. He somewhat ruefully noted that in his attempts to provide a strong leadership for the FAM he had been accused by some of being unduly dictatorial but E.C. Smith had been more successful with the management of the AMA through the employment of similar but even more aggressive tactics. He still mourned the destruction of his extensive collections of early day motorcycling memorabilia.

Another fortuitous interview that fall was with E. Paul and Francis I. duPont, which came about in a more or less oblique manner. The author's late father, Victor E. (1880-1966), a prominent California agriculturalist, was then a client of Francis I.'s stock brokerage firm. When an invitation was received to attend an open house for the opening of enlarged quarters in San Francisco's financial district on Montgomery Street, it was also noted that other members of the duPont family would be present.

E. Paul turned out to be a suave and sophisticated individual with the easy self-confidence of wealth and social position but was at the same time out-going and friendly in manner. He briefly reviewed Indian's past financial and managerial problems of the early post World War I era, together with the devastating effect of the Depression on the motorcycle market. He commented on the unfortunate aspect of the "New Jersey Jew" affair and stated that he had always attempted to maintain good relations with the Davidsons but at times, as he put it, they were "difficult." He also alluded to the well-known fact that Indian's survival during the early 1930's was due mainly to its integration with his more profitable group of companies and suggested that this fact might well be the basis of some resentment in Milwaukee.

The somewhat limited, yet growing, interest in foreign motorcycles in Southern California prompted a Triumph enthusiast, Al Fergoda, to open an Ariel and Triumph agency in San Francisco. He was, of course, encouraged by William E. Johnson, who supplied him with machines and parts stock along with repair tools but otherwise had no financial interest in the operation. Fergoda reported that during the summer of 1939 he sold 26 machines, including three Ariel Square Fours. He added that the distinctive burbling exhaust note of the Triumph Twins and Ariel fours was a sales inducement!

The growing popularity of low powered scoot-ers introduced by Cushman prompted a number of other smaller concerns to enter this market. These latter, unlike Cushman, used proprietary engines, mostly from Briggs and Stratton, although some were obtained from small firms like Lauson, Clinton and Onan. The former make was most popular, as Perry E. Mack, whom we have discussed before, devised a simple kick start mechanism that extended outside the engine compartment.

Many motorcycle dealers were now handling scooters, obviously a useful entry level two-wheeler for both the younger as well as the utility rider. The market for the former was extensive, as most states during that time were issuing driving licenses to youths when they reached the age of fourteen.

William E. Johnson and Albert G. Crocker also tentatively entered the scooter market with their own versions but dropped out after producing some prototypes and a few machines for the market. Various scooters were sold by Harley-Davidson dealers, even though they came from sources outside the factory: the dealers being adamant concerning their value as a two-wheeled sales leader. Sears and Roebuck, the pioneer general merchandise mail-order concern, also introduced some 1 1/2 and 2 horsepower models obtained from outside suppliers and sold under the name of "Allstate" at the bargain prices of $69.50 and $89.50.

Scooters generally gave good service provided the owners paid attention to servicing the engines periodically and their 20 to 25 mph cruising speeds were adequate for coping with the traffic conditions of the time. As a basically safe machine, with their low speeds and open frame design, the riders nevertheless had to be watchful against fouling the small wheels in ruts or railway crossings, as a fall could be the inevitable result.

In 1939, the contest for the "Most Popular Rider" was again sponsored by E.C. Smith, who urged all AMA members to send in their penny post card ballots. According to the 1938 winner, Ed Kretz, he again topped the field but was told by Smith that it would be awarded to another competition rider, preferably this time a Harley-Davidson enthusiast, to even things up. The award was then given to Arthur "Babe" Tancrede, a popular Milwaukee enthusiast from Connecticut who was active in the Eastern AMA Circuit and who had won the Keene, New Hampshire Classic in 1934 and 1935, gained second place at Savannah in 1936 and was also a perennial Daytona entrant.

Joe Tomas, the Newark, New Jersey Harley-Davidson competition rider who had changed his allegiance to BMW under New York City dealer Emil Recke, continued to campaign in the late

THE COMPETITION ERA 1935-1941

1930's. Due to the growing prejudice against German products, Tomas' entry was subjected to frequent exclusion or disqualification by AMA referees. The favored excuse was that his 500 cc super-sports Rennsport opposed twin was a racing model, although Tomas and Recke could always produce documentary evidence that it was a bona fide production machine. At any rate, it was decided to enter the machine in the National Springfield Mile event in 1938. His entry for the 25-Mile National was promptly disallowed but Recke threatened legal action against the AMA Competition Committee and his entry was accepted for the 8-Mile event. After a poor start, where he was impeded by the large field of starters, Tomas forged into the lead in the 7th mile for a spectacular win in a record time of 6 minutes, 27 seconds. He also set an all time lap record of 92 mph.

It was that same year the BMW factory rider Georg Meier won the Isle of Man TT on a Rennsport fitted with a supercharger. He took an early lead and was never headed, attaining a new record for the event at just under 90 mph. Momentarily eclipsing the long domination of the TT by Norton Internationals, his win brought about a banning of superchargers.

In 1940, the famous Jack Pine Run, inaugurated by Harley-Davidson dealer Oscar Lentz in 1926, saw its 14th running. Milwaukee's perennial triumph on this very difficult backwoods course was upheld by Theodore Kency who finished first. A place winner was Robert Dickinson, on a much modified Norton International, the first time a foreign machine was among the top placers.

By this time most of the Harley-Davidson factory prepared machines were fitted with aluminum cylinder heads and magneto ignitions and were fully competitive with the Special Sport Scouts. The formidable WLDR's as they were now catalogued, had a stiff challenge from Tom Sifton's specials; the noted Sam Arena beating a strong field of Milwaukee entrants in 1938. Babe Tancrede, on one of the latter, placed second in the Oakland 200 in 1939.

By this time foreign machines were much in evidence, with Canadian Bryan Sparks being a perennial entrant at Daytona with his 500cc Vincent HRD. The Langhorne 100 Miler was won in 1939 by his brother, Robert, on a 500cc Norton International: the first time a foreign machine garnered top honors on this very fast track with a speed of 82.28 mph.

Joe Tomas suffered from the now usual discrimination again in 1939 when, at Langhorne, he made the fastest recorded lap time; the prize for

this being a gold watch. At the last moment, the officials disqualified his BMW entry on the grounds that "...the timing apparatus had malfunctioned." After again being disqualified for his second try at Daytona in 1940, Tomas bowed to the inbuilt prejudice against German machinery and changed his allegiance to Norton.

Top Daytona honors again went to Milwaukee in 1940, when Arthur "Babe" Tancrede, on a specially built WRLD, forged past a large field of entries, including an again-sidelined Ed Kretz.

The Pacific Coast Championship races had their culmination as usual in the fall at the Oakland 200. After the elimination trials, 25 of the country's top riders, on a mix of 10 Harley-Davidsons and 15 Indians and foreign makes, lined up on this very fast course. Jack Cottrell, a promising newcomer on a WLDR Harley-Davidson set a blistering pace and came in the winner at 82.28 mph, in a 2 hour and 25 minute grueling run. Teammate Armando Magri was second, with Bud Lowrie and Don Rodman on Indians taking third and fourth places.

In spite of an impressive string of victories, partly because of potent machinery and partly because of Milwaukee's sponsorship of large fields of entries, Harley-Davidson's management, in 1940, decided that updated racing models were in order. While their much modified "W" series road machines had made a good showing, Indian was a frequent winner with their racing Scouts, which had lately undergone significant modifications.

The "Y" type Bonneville engines, with their enhanced breathing and racing type magnetos, saw a few improved models produced for factory riders with slightly enlarged crankcases to eliminate the occasional problem of oil surge at full throttle with the need for enhanced crankcase ventilation. Known as "Big Base" Scouts, their power had been increased by a private tuner, Arthur Hafer, who had modified some of the new as well as previous models with a cam gear that provided a "two cam" effect that gave higher engine revolutions. some having a top speed on the straights of 120 mph.

The WR's specifications now included larger intake and exhaust ports, with the valves moved closer to the cylinder bores and were of enlarged diameter. The cam gear of the stock WL's was modified to cut down the reciprocating weight. The machines were available either as a flat tracker without brakes that weighed about 300 pounds, or as a TT model with brakes and rudimentary mudguards.

For the 1940 sales season, both factories offered large section 5" tires on 16" rims as an option on their larger models. Up to this point, 4.50 section tires on 18" rims had been standard on "E" series

THE COMPETITION ERA 1935-1941

John Cameron with his stripped down 61 cu. in. Crocker.
John Cameron

Harley-Davidsons and Indian Chiefs and Fours for several past seasons, but it was suggested that the larger sectioned tires would give a softer ride.

Some riders, especially sporting types, thought the 5" tires gave less precise handling. In some cases, they retained the 4.50 type for the front wheel, but with the 5" type on the back. Numbers of machines ordered for highway patrol work ordered this specification.

In addition, Indian added the plunger spring rear suspension as standard on Chiefs and Fours that had been initially fitted to the French Army order on 1939. The range of travel was somewhat limited but the springing did much to alleviate the shock of severe bumps in the road, but at the penalty of an added 80 pounds of weight. Some riders complained, however, that the new soft tail combined with the traditional quarter elliptic front suspension gave imprecise handling at high speed.

Another Indian innovation for 1940 was the fitting of deep valances on the mudguards of the Chief and Four, the former open type still an option on the Sport Scout. Some riders claimed this fitting made handling difficult in high side winds, although many praised the protection from mud and water in rainy conditions.

Another innovation common to both makes was the elimination of the traditional pin striping on the fuel tanks and mudguard margins, the name plates now being metal badges, replacing the former roll-on transfers.

A forward-looking adjunct to organized motorcycling was created in the spring of 1940, with the launching of the Motor Maids of America,

an association of female motorcycle riders. It was founded by Vera Griffith, a Harley-Davidson enthusiast, who envisioned it as either an auxiliary to the established chartered clubs, or as an autonomous group, whichever category might suit local conditions. Griffith presented the idea by preparing and mailing, at her own expense, form letters to the chartered clubs outlining her proposition during the summer and fall of 1939. After receiving sufficient encouragement from the female membership, she next approached E.C. Smith and the Competition Committee, soliciting their approval and cooperation. The Committee gave their immediate blessing to the proposed organization and offered to charter either the Motor Maids as an in-place club auxiliary or as an autonomous group, whichever circumstance was most locally expedient.

While the Motor Maids were never a large organization, its membership spread throughout the country. Clad in their smart military style powder blue uniforms, they added a touch of class to club outings as well as their appearance at competition events. The sight of these well turned out riders, often with heavyweight machines, emphasized that the sport was not an all-male avocation.

In its initial organization the Motor Maids were centered in the midwest and most of the members favored Harley-Davidsons, often WL models due to their lighter weight and easy starting characteristics. Several chose Indians, some Sport Scouts, but more often than not, the 30.50 models that had the advantage of lower weight.

Skip Fordyce's attractive wife, Ruth, who was also active in her husband's very prominent Riverside Bombers Motorcycle Club, took and interest in recruiting western riders and several chapters were subsequently formed in the California area. Dorothy "Dot" Robinson, herself an active enduro rider, was also active in promoting Motor Maid activities and recruitment and in later years, served as a perennial national president.

During the winter of 1939 and 1940, E.C. Smith, together with a few members of the Competition Committee who lived adjacent to Columbus, met on several occasions to expand and update the AMA Rule Book. The original copies outlining the Class C concept had been published in January 1934. It was revised and updated again in 1936, and it was now considered necessary to publish a further update and to expand the work to clarify the various categories of the Classes of competition entrants. The status of Novice, Amateur and Expert had already been created. A beginning rider could advance from the Novice to

THE COMPETITION ERA 1935-1941

Ed Kretz, (#38), and Chuck Basney, (#6), at the starting line for the Bakersfield half miler in 1941.
Ed Kretz

Amateur Class provided a total of 25 point credits had been attained, even if accrued during the same competition season. An Amateur could advance to Expert after scoring 40 competition points. The overall scoring was based on the awarding of three, two or one points for qualifying for first, second or third place win in any sanctioned event.

While these rules had technically been in place for the past three seasons, the point system had not heretofore been specifically enumerated, and had been subject to rather broad interpretation by the various District Referees and contest judges. E.C. Smith himself was often under fire for his sometimes capricious interpretations of the rules, especially in the case of contested placings and lap scoring inconsistencies, and negotiated wins were usually settled somewhat arbitrarily.

Smith was always on the lookout for participants in "outlaw" events by AMA competition cardholders, who, if apprehended, could receive a year's suspension. He was also concerned with the prohibited entrance of more than one machine by a

contestant in any given event, as well as the surreptitious practice of changing engines, which sometimes occurred in the pits when judges were otherwise occupied. While such tactics were actually conducted to a limited degree, by this time they had become a type of game or carefully planned prank on the part of some individuals.

During 1939 and 1940, a number of prominent AMA members and dealers representing both makes suggested to E.C. Smith and some members of the Competition Committee that the AMA management should sponsor a compilation of the history of both organized motorcycling as well as that of the industry. According to later statements by Hap Alzina, Dudley Perkins and Ted Hodgdon, many of the veteran members of the industry considered that the rather vapid content of the motorcycling trade press between the wars, due to the management of the news by both the manufacturers as well as the AMA hierarchy, had caused a growing sentiment of disenchantment and a lack of confidence in the reporting of domestic motorcycling affairs.

THE COMPETITION ERA 1935-1941

It was suggested in some quarters that Verne Guthrie should be commissioned to compile such a history. As a pioneer rider since 1903, and an active member of the industry until 1925, Guthrie's general knowledge of the industry's doings, his broad acquaintanceship with past and present people in it, and his vast collection of motorcycling memorabilia qualified him to perform this task.

When this proposal was brought before Smith and the Committee during a meeting in the spring of 1940, both he and the assembled members turned the matter down after a brief discussion. In his private report to the proposers, which included Arthur Welch, who as ever was preoccupied with journalistic integrity, Smith outlined his reasoning. It was his contention that during the rather short 35 year history of organized motorcycling in the United States, the failure of the FAM, the controversies of the Coffman era, the near schism within the AMA over the proposed organization of the FWM, together with the near failure of the industry at the onset of the Depression, did not constitute a distinguished record of achievement.

Smith further stated that while, since the mid-1930's, the AMA had assumed a generally satisfactory state of stability, ongoing controversies, including "contested" events, "negotiated" wins, dissatisfactions with the offered prize money, and Smith's own personal critics who were airing their opinions, that a frank expose of the general state of motorcycling's affairs would do more harm than good. What he did not say, but which was generally known, was that he held a personal dislike for Guthrie, who, like Welch, was a disciple of objective journalism. His contemporary, candid reporting on the state of the automobile industry had its scathing moments.

Smith concluded that the reporting of motorcycling history should be in the hands of factory publicity writers, and that continued "management" of industry news would best serve to perpetuate the proper image to the general public. He also noted that Guthrie had left Harley-Davidson's employ in a disagreement over factory practices, and that his subsequent critiques of certain of the industry's policies rendered him unfit to assume the role of an industry historian. From these statements we can assume that Smith's concept of motorcycle history was that it should be interpreted as a propaganda medium rather than any considerations of factual objectivity.

In discussing his personal role in the affair in an interview with the author in 1946, Guthrie said that for some years he had been considering producing a definitive history of domestic motorcycle history, tentatively entitled "American Motorcycling: 1900-1940." To this end he had written a preliminary outline of the presentation, and had circulated this privately among a number of the industry's pioneers. It was the securing of their approval of his material that had prompted the suggested compilation of an officially sponsored AMA publication. He later presented the author with a copy of this outline, with the rather prophetic opinion that a professionally researched and objective presentation of domestic motorcycle history was still decades away![*5]

Another comment on the matter was later made to the author by James Wright. He stated that in some ways he tended to agree with Smith regarding the inadvisability of an expose of domestic motorcycling's affairs, but in his opinion the totally saccharine approach in the final analysis tended to make the industry look rather foolish in its assumption that riders and AMA members in general were totally unsophisticated.

Wright further ventured the opinion that Smith's reticence in regard to officially recording the internal affairs of the Competition Committee might well be due to his reluctance in having his private connection with the Davidsons, regarding his performance of public relations campaigns on their behalf, revealed in an official history of the AMA. While his activities in this matter were known to members of the Committee and to some of the top management people within the industry, it was not known by the general AMA membership.

Still another controversy regarding news management and slanted reporting in "The Motorcyclist" erupted after the following incident. In the fall of 1940, following Robert Spark's victory at Langhorne on a Norton International, Editor Billings, in laying out the next issue of the magazine, left a page open for the inclusion of an article describing the event, but did not produce it because he was called out of town on other business. As the deadline for printing approached, Welch wrote the article himself based on information received from two spectators who had attended the race. Up to this point, all race meet articles written by Billings featured only the action relating to the riders of American machines. If any foreign machines won or placed their mention was only noted in a box score at the end of the article.

In his report, however, Welch included a description of Spark's spectacular performance in the main body of the article. When the issue appeared, Smith at once challenged Billings concerning his deviation from the established policy. When Billings informed him of its source, Smith

THE COMPETITION ERA 1935-1941

A typical scene of the starting lineup on the old beach course at the Daytona 200.
William Tuthill

launched a blistering attack against Welch via telephone, suggesting that he was not properly supporting the best interests of American motorcycling. Welch replied that he had received numerous complaints from AMA members who favored foreign machines regarding discrimination against them in the magazine's sports reporting. He further stated that he was against the slanting of news as irresponsible journalism, and that with the growing enthusiasm for foreign machines, this policy was alienating an important segment of AMA membership. Smith was adamant, however, and reminded Welch of his obligation to follow established AMA policy in view of their financial support of the magazine. The dispute remained unresolved, however, and the relationship between the two was strained still further.

In February the United States Congress appointed President Roosevelt's Lend-Lease program to aid the embattled Allied powers in the "Arsenal of the Democracies" program to furnish them with war material. The initial action was to turn over to Great Britain 50 overaged destroyers left over from World War I to aid them in combatting the growing U-boat menace. The second was to award export permits to various U.S. industrial firms to provide other military aid items. Under this program, both domestic motorcycle manufacturers received large orders. Harley-Davidson contracted with the Canadian War Department for 10,000 WLA's. Following the shipment of the initial order the Canadians requested a modification of the specifications to include interchangeable wheels. The factory responded by fitting big twin forks whose

brake assembly accommodated this, and some models were also fitted with a hand activated clutch and foot activated gearshift. These models were subsequently designated as WLC's.

Next, both factories were offered contracts by the British War Department following the destruction of the town of Coventry by the Luftwaffe in 1940, which also destroyed the factory of prime supplier, Triumph.

In the subsequent expansion of the Lend-Lease program, large numbers of 30.50 Indians were shipped to Russia via the hazardous Arctic route to the port of Murmansk, and before the program was cancelled some 15,000 units were supplied to the Russian Army.

In addition, Harley-Davidson and Indian both supplied limited numbers of big twins as military machines; the UA and Chief models being fitted with low compression engines and wide section unvalanced mudguards along with the usual military equipment. Most of these were supplied as sidecar units, as neither the WLA's or the 30.50's had sufficient power for this use.

The Cushman Motor Company enlarged its plant at Lincoln, Nebraska to supply War Department orders for scooters, with models over 5 horsepower being optionally fitted with light sidecars. These were widely used as in-plant transportation. Cushman also undertook prototype experiments with low powered, four wheeled in-plant trucks, which were also employed as in-field transport for wholesale nursery operations and commercial truck gardeners. They also developed low powered, three-wheeled enclosed package trucks which were ultimately used for suburban mail delivery by the Postal Department.

The sobering thought of U.S. participation in the European conflict was brought home when Congress, at President Roosevelt's insistence, passed the Selective Service Act in June 1940, which was to be in force for the next 12 months. By the first of the following year over 10 million young men between the ages of 21 and 31 had been registered.

The only new model to be announced for the 1941 sales season was the 74 cubic inch Harley-Davidson FL. This was an overhead valve machine as a 74 cubic inch variant of the E and EL models, with an increased bore and stroke to enhance the cylinder displacement. It was considered as an alternative to the EL to provide increased power for both double riding as well as sidecar use. While it quite naturally provided more power, many enthusiasts preferred the E and EL models as their more nearly square bore and stroke made for a smoother running engine. The new F series went on to provide Milwaukee with another top-of-the-line overhead valve model, which, starting with the E series was in production for no less than 48 years!

With the sudden inflationary effect of the war in Europe, in its demands for increased industrial materials and foodstuffs, prices for goods in all categories rose accordingly. This was especially true for products using metal components, which, of course, included the motorcycle industry. The retail price of an Indian 30.50 was fixed at $275, the lowest priced machine on the domestic market. The usual price-and-policy fixing meeting between James Wright and W. Stanley Bouton of Indian and Arthur Davidson was held in Chicago that fall. The price of the 45 cubic inch WL and Sport Scouts were fixed at $375, the 74 cubic inch UL and Chief at $425, the 80 cu. in ULH was $20 more. The newly introduced 74 cubic inch FL, with no Springfield counterpart, was $525, and the Indian Four, in its own class, was now set at $965 - its car type engine being costly to manufacture.

The two decades-long practice of price fixing within the motorcycle industry was, of course, illegal under the Sherman Antitrust and Clayton Acts passed by Congress under President Theodore Roosevelt's administration earlier in the Century, but, through the between-the-wars period it was ignored more often than not by contiguous businesses and manufacturers. During the corruption of the Harding Administration, Attorney General Harry M. Daughterty was too busy covering his own tracks to prosecute anybody. Harding's successor, Calvin Coolidge, the dour Yankee who

avowed that "the business of the United States is business," firmly held to a hands-off policy involving corporate interpretation of its own needs. During the Depression, any firm or related firms who stayed afloat and provided employment could feel safe from any harassment. And, so it was that for two decades it was considered impolitic to examine corporate America too closely, in spite of laws to the contrary.

The 1941 competition season was kicked off as usual by the Daytona 200 held traditionally in March. It featured a stronger than usual entry of the top riders from both factories, riding the highly specialized WR's and WLDR's and racing Scouts, which by this time totally ignored the Class C concept and which, in reality, represented the now defunct Class A designation.

In the face of the domestic factories' determination to counter foreign competition, Canadian Billy Mathews was determined to compete with his Norton International. For several seasons he had been backed by Norton's North American distributor, J.M. McGill. McGill had generously supported Mathews with spare parts and the use of his shop facilities and mechanics; most of the parts being either supplied to him gratis or with generous discounts from the factory. In this instance, McGill refused to back him, stating the growing hostility of AMA competition officials who hoped to see the reciprocity agreement with the Canadian clubmen cancelled.

Mathews was adamant, however, and made plans to trailer his machine from Canada at his own expense. In later years, he told the author that he did not expect the Competition Committee to honor his entry for the usual trumped up technicalities, but it was his opinion that Milwaukee had put so much faith in their new WR's that they considered the usually formidable Nortons less of a threat.

Mathews' chances of success were enhanced by having one of the new spring frame models. In 1937, the factory entrants at the Isle of Man were so fitted and the next year they were offered on the market as a machine option. Mathews subsequently obtained a 1939 spring model that McGill had located in Raymond Way's London dealership. With the usual rough conditions of the beach course and the tarred back stretch, a solid frame competitor had his rear wheel off the ground for much of the time! At any rate, Mathews removed the highly tuned engine from his 1937 machine and installed it in the slightly used 1939 model.

The 1941 Daytona opened with Ed Kretz doing his usual sacrifice lead laps while he headed the field and, following his sidelining, the lead was

THE COMPETITION ERA 1935-1941

Young actress Shirley Temple made the cover of the December, 1935 issue of "The Motorcyclist." *Don Emde Collection*

taken by such ace riders as Ted Edwards and Jimmy Kelley on Sport Scouts and Armando Magri, Babe Tancrede and Junius "June" McCall on Harley-Davidsons. Mathews followed somewhat behind, saving his engine. Kelley took the lead from the 25th to the 58th lap, when he experienced engine failure. Mathews, who held second place at this point, forged ahead and kept the lead until the finish. Tancrede was second, McCall was third and Ben Campanale came up from behind to take fourth.

Mathews, of course, had long ago mastered the technique of exploiting the best of the Norton's capabilities. With its tall gearing it could be kept "on the cam" for its top engine revolutions, making frequent use of the gears to do so. These tactics, combined with the engine's now almost infallible reliability, and the advantage of the rear springing, spelled a certain finish among the top contenders in any case.

In reality, the International Norton was a detuned racer when taken off the shelf, needing only removal of the lighting and the installation of high compression pistons to enter competition. Any rider fancying one had to put up with a somewhat noisy machine that leaked oil copiously from the cam box, and had to cope with the tall gearing in traffic conditions. But, on the open road, the Norton could out cruise the competition on a long haul.

Mathews stated that for Canadian competition he had a top speed of 112 mph with an 8.5:1 piston and burning 90 octane "high test" aviation fuel. For AMA competition, a 7.5:1 piston and standard ethyl fuel would give him 100 mph, or slightly less. But with Norton's legendary road holding and steering, plus the handiness of the foot shift gear box, very high average speeds were possible.

In spite of the Norton's well known prowess, very few were actually sold on the North American continent. Selling for 90 Pounds in standard form ($450), one had to add the 10% tariff charge and a $65 shipping fee; the spring frame was $45 extra. This was quite a penalty to pay in a depression era when a 650 pound EL Harley-Davidson cost around $400, and in a time when money was indeed hard to come by. As a high priced machine,

the Norton cost vastly more than similar competitive makes on the home market; and production was necessarily small, being reported anywhere from 35 to 50 machines in any one year.

Mathews' seemingly easy victory had a salutary effect on the Competition Committee. One of the first considerations was the thought that it was a thinly disguised racing model, but, on the other hand, the WR's and Racing Scouts were nothing other than specialized machinery that were too intractable to ride on the street. In any case, bending the Class C rules to rule Nortons out of AMA competition could be a very controversial proposition.

Stephen duPont, a recent engineering graduate and presently a member of Indian's engineering staff and also a newly appointed member of the Committee, had already suggested lowering the mandated overhead valve engine compression ratio to 6.50:1. As noted, he had been put out by certain successes gained in the northeast in AMA club events by Canadian Norton riders. At any rate, he brought up the compression ratio matter again, and his suggestion was at once seconded by Walter Davidson.

In a subsequent discussion of the matter with the author, James Wright stated that he himself, as well as President duPont, did not approve of this proposal. The mandating of a 6.5:1 compression ratio ruling would at once make it impossible for foreign overhead valve machines to perform sufficiently well to make their entrance into competitive events worthwhile, and in effect, such a ruling would be publicly construed as an admission of inferiority of American machines to foreign makes of lesser cubic displacement.

Wright pointed out to the Committee that with the growing popularity of foreign motorcycles their owners would, in the foreseeable future, form their own competition organization. He pointed out that the rather tenuous position of the AMA as related to their relatively limited number of adherents could be seriously weakened if a rival organization were to dilute AMA's sphere of influence.

Stephen duPont at once defended his position, stating the American industry, having barely survived both the declining public interest in motorcycling as well as the devastating effect of the Depression, had every right to protect its own interests.

In the end, duPont and the Harley-Davidson majority marshalled sufficient votes to inaugurate the proposed new ruling, but ultimately decided to table the matter pending subsequent developments.

In spite of the general public apathy toward motorcycling and the marginal position of the

THE COMPETITION ERA 1935-1941

industry, its sporting aspect had attained a substantial spectator interest. The big national fixture contests had, since the mid-1930's, attracted substantial paying gates, which even extended to lesser events of a more local nature. It was noted with some chagrin by veteran members of the industry that the average spectator, while enjoying the sporting aspect of motorcycling, did not equate himself with either riding or purchasing a model for his own participation.

E.C. Smith, who had the statistical aspects of the sporting activities in hand since the Class C inauguration after 1933, announced that it was his estimate that more than 7,500,000 spectators had patronized competition events during the previous seven seasons. Cora Reardon, who had herself made up a summary of the estimated spectator attendance figures, later told the author that the figure should be nearer six million. In any case, these figures supported the long contention of many of the pioneers in the industry that the average man in the street viewed the various aspects of motorcycle sport as a hazardous gladiatorial contest that held a certain fascination for the risks involved for the competitors.

The matter of personal sexual freedom and the public discussions and disclosures in the matter as seen in the social revolution of the 1960's had, in actuality, been an adjunct in the human condition since time immemorial. Athletic and sporting contests, especially where elements of personal danger were involved, had long been known to provide erotic stimulation for members of both sexes. The high-born and aristocratic ladies of ancient Rome were known to have arranged trysts with gladiators following their bloody victories in the Coliseum. Latter day prize fighters, more often than not, found themselves the object of much feminine attention. The emergence of motor sports after the turn of the century in Europe and America added a new dimension to sports stimulated erotica.

In the motorcycling sphere such activity was no less intense, as was noticeably apparent at such big national races as Langhorne, Laconia, Springfield, and especially at Daytona. Veteran competitors in later years have spoken fondly (if privately) of the ready opportunity to meet nubile and not-so-nubile feminine fans adjacent to the race course, in the pits and loading areas during and after the contests, and especially at the bars and watering places and hotels in the area.

Participants noted an unusual amount of sexual variation, such as fetishists who demanded that their heroes perform with their racing leathers on! Others sometimes joining in the sport might be certain of the dealers or factory officials who rallied to the occasion with liaisons with other than their marital partners, who themselves, might be reveling in their own diversions. Such celebrations might well have been given certain impetus due to the long economic and social deprivations of the Depression, where opportunities for sexual adventures were perforce few and far between. While the term "groupie" had yet to be coined, it was later applied to those who favored public sporting and entertainment figures for special attention.

Another sexist feature of motorcycle sports was the ongoing practice of engaging some mildly prominent local beauty queen or aspiring actress to present the trophies and awards to the victors. At the big Nationals, where more often than not, certain celebrity enthusiasts were usually present, prominent motion picture and stage actresses often performed these honors. At less important local or regional contests, sometimes a waggish official would engage a local individual of dubious antecedents to do the honors, adding a touch of mischievous garishness to the event.

In spite of the heightening intensity of the war in Europe and the overriding specter of a draft to man the armed forces, the AMA Competition Committee responded to the calls for sanctions for the organizers of all of the big National fixtures. In actuality, most of the prominent star competitors were presently outside the Selective Service quota, being either over 31 years of age or married with families, as such categories were not yet subjected to conscription. In any case, Congress renewed the Selective Service Act in July, and mass participation was still in force under the law.

The prospect of being drafted quite naturally reduced motorcycle sales, but the factories were proceeding with accelerated production due to both the demand for military machines as well as enhanced orders from law enforcement bodies.

The active 1941 competition season had its climax at the annual fall running of the Pacific Coast Championships at Oakland. Always known as a very fast and hazardous course, the race was marred by what was perhaps the most tragic accident of the Class C decade.

Ed Kretz, who was involved in it, has left us his

The year 1935 saw the emerging presence of the British motorcycle industry in the United States. *Don Emde Collection*

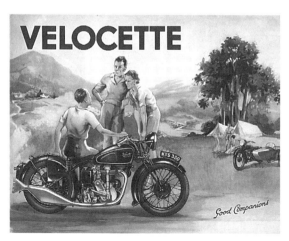

THE COMPETITION ERA 1935-1941

A posed photograph of Joe Petrali on the 61 cu. in. Special built by himself and Hank Syversten for an assault on the solo record at Daytona Beach in 1937.
The Harley-Davidson Motor Company

Petrali on his Harley-Davidson Peashooter in 1935. He went undefeated that season.
The Harley-Davidson Motor Company

personal recollection. He had lapped the field during the 38th circuit of the course, and was just behind and in the slipstream of Harley-Davidson riders Tommy Hayes and Ben Campanale. Just behind Kretz, in his slipstream, was Indian rider Jimmy Kelley and Harley-Davidson riders Sam Arena and June McCall. The closely packed riders were traveling at nearly 100 mph when Tommy Hayes fouled his front wheel in a rut and went down. Campanale hit the outer fence in trying to miss Hayes now lying on the track. Kretz grazed both Campanale's and Hayes' machines and proceeded in a 100 foot power slide that he managed to recover from. Kelley, still trying to regain control of his machine also hit the fence; Sam Arena went down between them, and June McCall spun out over the fence. Tragically, Hayes and McCall were instantly killed, and Campanale and Kelley were hospitalized for nearly a year. Arena was only slightly injured and Kretz was miraculously unscathed.

In reporting the accident, the news media, other than the trade press, were somewhat critical of motorcycle racing in general and the hazards it presented. In truth, the skilled riding of the professionals in the Expert Class had stood them in good stead in their previous years of survival in numerous similar close encounters.

Another tragic event that fall, unrelated to competition, was the death of Fred Ham. This colorful motorcycle officer, who, as a private Harley-Davidson rider, had established new Three Flag and 24-hour endurance records for Milwaukee, was pursuing a speeder on East Garvey Blvd. when struck by an automobile which drove out in front of him from a side street. This popular and well-liked individual, who was also noted for his athletic abilities, was mourned by a host of friends within the sport and industry.

During the late 1930's, which marked the high water mark of domestic motorcycle competition in the so-called Class A category, neither of the two surviving makes bested the other in the final analysis, competition results being of the seesaw variety. In general, Harley-Davidsons were more successful in the long distance events, with Indian predominating in the half-mile and milers. The handful of professional hill climb stars who were perennial competitors for many years sustained a give-and-take status in the National contests. The many imponderables of competition involved the skill of the rider, the condition of the course, and the ever unknown mechanical problems that could either make or prevent an ultimate victory.

The introduction of foreign machinery was a source of anguish to many of the adherents and competitors within the sport and certain leaders in the industry. But, at the same time, they provided increased spectator interest in what had become to some the monotony of the limitations of two-make competition.

While the side valve engine had been generally discarded in both Great Britain and Europe for other than utilitarian models, the American factory engineers, together with large numbers of private tuners and practical mechanics, had, through competition development, refined the side valve engine into a remarkably efficient and powerful entity. With sophisticated port breathing and valve sequence timing the 45 cubic inch side valver, with its inherently limited compression ratios and theoretically inefficient combustion chamber profiles, at the end of the decade could turn out 50 horsepower and propel a rudimentary solid framed racing machine at flat out speeds up to 120 mph. Such designs re-enforced the long standing Yankee concept of rugged, large displacement, lightly stressed engines that could provide dependability and longevity in heavyweight machines.

While the domestic industry provided a sport-ing showcase for motorcycling between the wars that reached a certain prominence in public interest by the end of the pre-war decade, the industry itself was actually in a state of decline from 1920 through 1940.

With the nation's population totalling 100 million in 1920, there were 3 million motor vehicles and nearly 200,000 motorcycles registered. By the time of the economic Depression in the 1930's there were 120 million people and nearly 20 million motor vehicles registered, but the two wheelers had declined to just under 100,000. By 1940 there were nearly 150 million people, nearly 40 million automobiles, and about 130,000 motorcycles, which included a few thousand scooters.

The decline in the numbers of motorcyclists in the face of an ever growing population and the increasing horde of automobiles was such that many motorists equated the motorcycle with law enforcement, with the sighting of the occasional traffic control officer. Only the weekend presence of a group of motorcyclists on a club run or limited numbers of touring groups participating in a Gypsy Tour served to remind the general public that motorcycling did exist.

The industrial might of the United States, which had grown steadily since the end of the Civil War, and the acceleration of production techniques had resulted in, among other products, the mass manufacture of automobiles which soon had their costs reduced to the point that nearly every family could afford one. This spelled the death knell of the family sidecar outfit, and the demise of the motorcycle as utilitarian transport. This trend rendered motorcycle ownership as a risky undertaking, especially as the question of noisy exhausts had never been resolved.

The spectator aspect of motorcycle sport and the inherent dangers emphasized in these public exhibitions, while offering vicarious excitement, served to alienate motorcycle ownership from the general public still further. Thus relegated to inferior transportation status, the majority of motorcycle owners were of the artisan-mechanic class, a group not noted for preoccupation with any fancied social status. This group was augmented by the thrill seeking undergraduate, the iconoclastic sportsman, the occasional feminine thrill seeker and the odd commuter.

With a total production of less than 25,000 units per year, motorcycle manufacture had become a strictly marginal affair, where the two ultimate survivors, in spite of an ongoing sub rosa collusion in price and policy matters, exhibited a public image of cutthroat competition. This had the unfortunate effect of stimulating violent confrontations between the adherents of each make which provided a roughneck image of two-wheeled ownership. With the majority of the dealerships being themselves marginal and understaffed operations housed in less than attractive quarters, it tended to put motorcycle sales and marketing at the low end of retail selling. The end result was that the manufacturers proceeded in an aura of grim determination, attempting to stay afloat through subterfuge and deception.

The position of the motorcycle industry in the United States was in direct contrast to that of Great Britain and Europe. With less developed manufacturing capabilities that precluded the mass production of automobiles, together with inordinately high fuel costs, the motorcycle was the best transportation compromise in these areas, creating what was to be historically considered, between the wars, as motorcycling's Golden Age.

The foreign trade press was less than kind in their comments on U.S. motorcycling, their journalists chiding our industry for a lack of technical progress and a failure to develop practical utility models and to augment our heavyweight big twins with middleweight types. Apparently unfamiliar with the U.S. market, they did not realize that with a very limited discretionary market, there was neither the incentive nor the funds available for extensive prototype development, nor to further explore the single cylinder market which had already been rejected by the American riders.

The ultimate development of organized motorcycling within the framework of the American Motorcycle Association served both the sport and industry well following the instituting of the Class C concept in 1934. As structured, with the financial and institutional support of the manufacturers and trade suppliers, there was sufficient strength to hold the organization together in difficult times. E.C. Smith, in spite of his often capricious and arbitrary administration of his executive duties, provided the necessary strong executive leadership that had heretofore been lacking during the earlier days of the AMA, a like situation being experienced previously in the failure of the FAM.

While many members (and others not within the organization) were highly critical of the undemocratic administration of its affairs, it was ultimately proved beyond any doubt that there were insufficient numbers of members and lack of financial strength within their ranks for a democratic administration to be effective.

In spite of the ongoing controversies regarding the conduct of competition activities, stern measures were necessary to maintain some semblance of order, and it was only Smith's tenacity that made this possible.

It must be emphasized that in any organized professional sport, as by necessity an adversarial proceeding, on-going controversy involving both the conduct of the events as well as the ultimate results are part and parcel of their makeup. This fact has resulted in dissatisfied factions that became strong enough to organize and maintain separate governing bodies within each sport. Today no less than three national organizations govern the automobile sport in this country, along with two each for professional football and basketball.

The governing and policing of such organizations to maintain the necessary rules is obviously a formidable undertaking. Yet, it is mandated by the need for keeping public support and confidence. The scandal involving professional baseball, the nation's first organized sport, occurred in 1919, when the members of the Chicago Black Box team were found to be fixing games in cooperation with certain gambling interests. In the face of much public loss of confidence, the owners of the leading national teams of the day met and selected a national overseer or "czar" with broad powers to observe the ball clubs' activities and to discipline both individual players as well as the clubs themselves for any flouting of either the established rules or legal or ethical infractions.

The man chosen was a retired federal appellate judge, one Kenesaw Mountain Landis, who for many years ruled professional baseball with an iron hand. While he frequently encountered much opposition to his usually arbitrary decision, he at least kept the sport generally free of corruption. E.C. Smith, also a baseball fan, much admired Landis, and was often heard to equate his own position in the motorcycle sporting sphere with that of the Judge.

While the strong sentiment on the part of the factories and many enthusiasts prevailing against the introduction of foreign motorcycles into the sporting scene (as well as the gamesmanship frequently noted on the part of the AMA officials in bending the rules against them) was, in most cases, patently unfair, it was not without reason. The memory of the Depression and the near failure of the industry had prompted such desperation that its leaders sought any means to protect their present hard-won situation. But in a relatively short time, changes in the motorcycling public's attitudes and altered marketing opportunities would greatly effect new directions in the domestic motorcycling market.

CHAPTER EIGHT

WORLD WAR II
1941-1945

WORLD WAR II 1941-1945

The war in Europe was somewhat remote in the thinking of many Americans during its early stages but, by the Summer of 1941, the possibility of United States involvement moved closer to reality. With the Continent of Europe and Norway in German hands, and England alone, beleaguered, but as yet unconquered, now fighting in Africa to save the Suez, coupled with the Japanese expansion in the Pacific theater, the Axis Powers were a real threat as possible world conquerors. The entrance of the United States into the conflict posed the question not so much as if, but when. The matter came to a head with the Japanese surprise attack on Pearl Harbor on December 7, 1941, and President Roosevelt, with the unanimous backing of Congress, declared war on Japan as well as Germany and Italy. With opposition to entering the war now all but muted, the country at once concentrated all its energies on the conflict.

Aside from an immediate mobilization of the Armed Forces, stringent controls on civilian activity became the order of the day. The Office of Price Administration instituted price controls on rents, foodstuffs, and other goods to prevent inflation. The production and sale of civilian commodities was strictly regulated in deference to the production of war material, and the sales of hard goods, such as motor vehicles and industrial equipment, building materials and the like, required official permission for purchase. Gasoline and petroleum products were rationed, as well as meat products, and a national 35 mph speed limit was imposed to conserve fuel and tires, as the supplies of crude rubber from Malaysia had been cut off by the Japanese.

The two major motorcycle factories at once stepped up production of their previously designed military models, each receiving open ended contracts from the War Department for as many machines as they could produce. The payment schedule, as for most war related products, was fixed at a cost plus 10% figure.

The Cushman Company stepped up production of scooters, the larger models usually fitted with forecars or sidecars, as well as in-plant vehicles, both being widely used now in the growing number of defense industries.

Certain motorcycles were made available under a priority system to essential users, most of these being either UL big twin Harley-Davidsons or 341 Indians, both usually as sidecar units; the Indian model having previously been supplied to the French government. Both makes were also made available in solo form for civilian law enforcement use. In addition, a limited number of low compression overhead valve "E" models were supplied to the Coast Guard for shore patrol, along with a number of Cushman scooters.

Indian's principal production involved the 30.50 models, initially designated as the 640. This model was subsequently joined by a 45 cubic inch machine with low compression Sport Scout engine. Most of these were kept in the United States, as they were preferred for their somewhat sprightlier performance over that of the heavyweight WLA's. There was some ambiguity over the designation of these Indian models. The original 640 designation later became the 640A as a 30.50, the 45 cubic inch model then being the 640B. Then the 640 became the 741A, and the 45 became the 741B. These somewhat confusing designations came about through a lack of coordination among the three technical writers engaged by the factory to produce the riders' instruction and overhaul and repair manuals for the Army. The writers were Ted Hodgdon, Matt Keevers, and later, Paul Brokaw. Purists to this day are still in contention as to what may be the correct designation of these models.

The social upheavals due to the demands of the war effort changed the course of most peacetime businesses, including that of the retail motorcycle dealers. Numbers of these dealers ceased operation in some of the rural areas and smaller towns and cities due to either service induction or the lack of customers. Many of the larger dealer-

WORLD WAR II 1941-1945

Seen here are the "Rough Riders" from Camp Carson, Colorado training on their Harley-Davidson military 45's.
The Enthusiast

ships in the more populous centers, together with some distributorships who possessed machine shop facilities, were able to secure contracts to fabricate small components for the large defense contractors. To ease the growing civilian manpower shortage, many overage workers remained in service, or came out of retirement.

As a paradox to the former indifference to the motorcycle as a utility ride-to-work vehicle, the shortage of automobiles and the growing price of used examples, coupled with the fuel rationing, now saw a demand for economical two-wheeled transport. Many dealers now ransacked their storage areas and lofts for machines once thought too obsolete to restore to running condition. Many defense plants now had numbers of forgotten models from

the 1920's, and even earlier, in their parking lots. Keeping these veterans on the road somewhat mitigated the loss of sales of new machines. With the lack of price controls covering used vehicles, the prices of late model used examples soared: a late model EL, UL, FL, or Indian Chief or Four could now bring from $700 to $800, or up to $1,000.

The initial defense effort was also an advantage to motorcycling, as many thousands of young draftees were being taught to ride at the many training centers throughout the country that were to provide vehicle operators for the Motor Transport Division, Signal Corps, Military Police, as well as other branches. With a shortage of enlisted personnel or non-commissioned officers that had previous experience as motorcyclists, Army procurement officials hired numbers of former competition riders, as well as dealers, former salesmen, and others so qualified to act as civilian instructors. Thus, many young men, and some women, who were formerly remote from the sport now found themselves with a new interest that might well be taken up in the future.

By this time motorcycles had become an integral part of military operations. The lessons learned

207

A 1941 74 cu. in. FLP Harley-Davidson police model. Pursuit light mounted on the handlebar, the siren being placed on the drive side of the machine on a pivot which can be moved to engage it against the rear tire. *Harley-Davidson Motor Co.*

by the U.S. Army during the Mexican Punitive Campaign as well as in World War I were not lost in the planning by the General Staff. British and European military planners were also cognizant of the usefulness of two-wheeled vehicles from the latter conflict. A more recent lesson was one learned in observing Hitler's Wiermacht in their blitzkrieg tactics in overrunning Europe. Many thousands of utility type 250 and 350 cc DKW made machines were employed as solo mounts for scouting purposes. In addition, heavyweight BMW and Zundapp shaft driven machines with horizontally opposed cylinders and fitted with sidecars were utilized by advance units. Most of these were fitted with sidecar wheeldrive shafts that were activated by transfer gears incorporated into the motorcycle's rear axles. These outfits were able to negotiate off-road terrain, but their drivers required special training to make the best of the capabilities. The German Army made use of all types of machines in their conquest of the of the Eastern front, the Low Countries, Norway, and in the North African Campaign in Tripoli and Libya. It was reported that they had nearly 200,000 units of all types on hand at the beginning of the war.

Great Britain employed large numbers of motorcycles in military service, including large numbers of late model 350 and 500 cc civilian type machines impressed from their private owners for Home Guard and military dispatch use in England. All the principal manufacturers, such as BSA, Associated Motorcycles making Matchless and AJS machines, Enfield, Norton, Triumph, including

lesser numbers of Velocettes, all of whom made military models, were used. Norton made small numbers of sidecar drive models based on their 640 cc sidevalve utility "Big Four" model. In all, the British industry supplied nearly 500,000 machines for the war effort, which included some special lightweight 125 cc models from James and Royal Enfield that could be dropped with paratroop units. Production was rationalized by the fact that most of the differing makes utilized Joseph Lucas electrics, Amal carburetors, Bowden handlebar controls and cables, and Burman and Albion type gear boxes.

In the fall of 1941, the U.S. War Department, noting the German successes with heavyweight machines, ordered both Indian and Harley-Davidson to produce similar prototypes for possible mass production. Each was authorized to manufacture 1,000 samples for testing and evaluation.

Harley-Davidson elected to produce a frank copy of the BMW R75, as employed by the Germans. This machine proved to be generally satisfactory for military use, but tests showed the lubrication system required further refinement. Milwaukee also experimented with sidecar drive versions, along with several other variants of the WLA and WLC models, as well as a light four-wheel scout car powered by a detuned "E" type V-twin. None of these underwent serious development, the sidecar drive model being considered too complex to be economically manufactured. John Nowak, Milwaukee's veteran Service Manager, was in charge of this experimental work, and personally tested the prototypes under field conditions.

WORLD WAR II 1941-1945

The leading link fork springing mechanism fitted to most Harley-Davidson models between 1907 and 1949.
Steve Iorio

A mechanics eye view of a 1947 74 cu. in. FLH Harley-Davidson's engine. First introduced as the 61 cu. in. "E" series in 1936, an enlarged version accompanied it in 1941. The knucklehead ohv engine was the basis of Milwaukee's big twin production for the next forty-eight years.

Indian's answer to this commission was to offer a 45 cubic inch V-twin; the engine set across the frame, with a four-speed, foot-operated gear box and shaft drive. An original design, which was largely the brain child of E. Paul duPont, it was conceived as a solo rather than as a sidecar unit. Another innovation, other than the shaft drive, was the fitting of a single leg link type fork which differed markedly from Indian's traditional trailing

link fork supported by a quarter electric leaf spring. The new design provided an increased rate of travel and was suspended by two hydraulically dampened shock absorbers.

The machine, described as the Model 841, was generally satisfactory, except that the driving pinions in the rear axle were subject to failure under severe conditions of use. The engine, however, performed smoothly in its 90-degree cylinder configuration, and as detuned and in a 500 lb. machine gave a top speed of about 68 mph. As a tribute to its basic design, the Italian firm of Moto-Guzzi offered a similar layout as a civilian machine two decades later.

Both John Novak of Harley-Davidson and John Taylor of Indian told the author in later years that the seven million dollar cost of the experimental work could be translated into the fact that 2,000 prototypes cost the American taxpayers $35,000 each!

While the War Department had offered open ended contracts to the two principal factories initially for as many machines as they could produce, both experienced difficulties in fulfilling their orders. For many years, each had been operating at reduced levels in antiquated 19th Century jack-shaft and belt drive factories that precluded the laying out of modern continuous flow assembly lines. The favored method of wheeling the units about on dollies to the various departments that fitted specific components led to much inefficiency and confusion. The recruiting of the work force required who might be familiar with these procedures was also a problem, and many overaged employees, or some already retired but called back to duty, were the backbone of the system. The wage and salary scale initially in place was also a problem in both factories, as the Depression-type wages and salaries formerly common in existing industry had not been raised substantially in newly created defense operations.

A case in point related to one young Linton J. Kuchler, whom we will be meeting again, who had been hired at Milwaukee just before the war as a production assistant at a salary of $100 per month. With the ever-increasing cost of living, which inevitably occurred due to the inflationary pressures of the war effort in spite of price controls, Kuchler found that his salary did not meet the needs of his young family. As the company refused to increase salaries at this point, he resigned to secure more lucrative employment.

The situation at Indian was somewhat different. President duPont, at the onset of the war contracts, at once announced a 20% increase in both the salary and hourly wage scales. His reasoning was that as long as Indian's contracts were based on a cost plus basis, there was no reason in subject-

The late William Hoecker's rare 1942 Harley-Davidson WLA War Department Model. The disc wheels were intended for use in desert sands.
George Hays

ing the workers to less than living pay scale.

While the two major motorcycle manufacturers were designated to produce what was the majority of War Department models, smaller firms also offered other designs. One such machine was designed by Powell Crosley, Jr. A multi-talented individual, Crosley had been a one-time disc jockey at a radio station in Cincinnati, Ohio. With initial capital raised through some shrewd investments, he was able to secure a majority ownership of the Cincinnati Reds, a professional baseball team based in that city. He subsequently, in 1939, entered the automotive field with a rather stark mini-car powered with either single or twin cylinder air-cooled industrial type Wisconsin engines. These vehicles could also be purchased in knock down kit form for home assembly, and represented the ultimate in low cost suburban transportation.

Just prior to the U.S. entrance into the war, Crosley offered the War Department his version of a military motorcycle for evaluation. It was powered by a fan-cooled horizontally opposed twin cylinder engine, being shaft driven through a four speed foot operated gear box, and fitted with car-type disc wheels. An unusual feature was the disposition of the fuel tank, which was shaped to an arc and carried over the rear wheel, reminiscent of Carl Oscar Hedstrom's early "camelback" Indians.

While the machine showed possibilities as an all terrain vehicle, War Department officials were not in

accord over its unorthodox configuration. In noting Crosley's somewhat limited production facilities, his proposal was not given serious consideration.[1]

The Simplex Manufacturing Company of New Orleans offered their Servicycle which had been marketed locally for several years. In its simplicity it was a somewhat crude but practical vehicle, and was now updated by the fitting of a kick-start mechanism. In addition to the basic solo model, it was also offered with both a lightweight sidecar and a forecar, the body being mounted between two front wheels. Limited numbers of these models were used in various defense plants, along with their in-plant trucks.

The Cushman Company, due to its substantial facilities, was able to produce large numbers of scooters fitted with engines of various powers, with sidecar and forecar options. Due to product demand, the company was able to secure a priority to requisition building materials to construct additional facilities to extend their assembly lines.

When the Army subsequently instituted the training of paratroops (made up of volunteers) to create an elite corps to be dropped behind enemy lines, it was decided to emulate the British system and provide some units with ultralight motorcycles. These had been provided with protective containers to allow them to be parachuted along with the troops. Limited numbers of small Cushmans were so fitted and used in training exercises, but none were

WORLD WAR II 1941-1945

The October, 1943 issue of "The Enthusiast" featured actress Barbara Stanwyck with her husband Robert Taylor. He spent the war years in the Navy which kept him away from his lovely wife and Harley-Davidson.
The Enthusiast

dispatched overseas to be used in actual combat.

The dislocations of the war at once had a profound effect on civilian motorcycling activities. With the extension of the conscription to include married men with limited dependents, and the acceptance of physically qualified men up to 41 years of age as volunteers, the ranks of active motorcyclists were obviously affected.

Most of the AMA chartered clubs suspended their activities, as those members not in service were often employed in defense related industries that now mandated six or seven day work weeks that often enforced much additional overtime as well.

On January 10, 1942, E.C. Smith issued an official statement that all competition events scheduled previous to the attack on Pearl Harbor were now cancelled. Ostensibly announced as a statement that such would be an unpatriotic diversion, any actual events were made impossible because of fuel rationing. At the same time, he also stated that any service personnel who were AMA members at the time of joining up would be carried on the roles for the duration of the conflict.

On February 15th, Smith issued another statement, in conjunction with a letter forwarded to the War Department, suggesting the recruitment of civilian motorcycle owners at home for traffic control, dispatch carrying, or to act as repair units for communication facilities in case of a military attack on the Continental United States. With the widespread numbers of trained motorcyclists now present in the various military installations across the country, Smith's suggestion was never acted upon, although he was tendered the official thanks of the War Department for his patriotism.

In the meantime, the two factories were in the process of gearing up for their War Department contracts. It was no small task to convert their antiquated facilities to large scale production, which now amounted to at least three times the output of their recent Depression volume. One problem was the state of their tooling, which had not been upgraded since the 1920's, replacements for which were in generally short supply. Indian was in particular difficulties, as its tooling was mostly in worn out condition and its best machinery had been sold off during the Bolles' administration, as noted. After much effort, President duPont was able to locate replacements for some of the more critical items. The storage of finished units was less of a problem in Springfield than it was in Milwaukee, as in later years production had taken place in only a small portion of the factory. In Milwaukee's case, additional storage space was leased adjacent to Juneau Avenue.

William E. Knudsen, President of General Motors, was now on leave to oversee the logistics of war production with the temporary rank of Lt. General. In his survey of domestic motorcycle production he noted the generally outdated condition of the industry's facilities, especially in Springfield, but commented that employee morale in both cases was high. In the end, both factories were awarded the coveted Army "E" for excellence in production performance.

Members of the Harley and Davidson families, company employees, and many dealers and enthusiasts were saddened at the news of the death of long time President Walter Davidson on February 7, 1942, in his sixty-sixth year. He had been suffering ill health from the effects of a chronic liver complaint, which was said to have been aggravated by the overwork entailed in the Herculean task of reorganizing the company's war-time production schedule. His survivors included his wife, Emma, sons, Walter, Jr., Gordon, and Robert, his brother, Arthur, and sisters, Janet and Elisabeth Davidson Marx.

A somewhat controversial figure within the industry, Davidson was possessed of a complex personality. Capable of exuding persuasive charm, he could also be vitriolic, profane, and overbearing. As a result he was admired by some and hated and feared by others. One of his preoccupations was maintaining the secrecy of the internal affairs of the company. Another was his paranoiac aversion to competition in the marketplace in any form, and it was often said that rather than meeting it in the usual manner he could only seek to destroy it. While his uncompromising and sometimes dictatorial policies often antagonized dealers and customers alike, his single-purpose dedication to the interests of the company he headed for 35 years was unquestioned. Whatever his personal faults, his unswerving insistence on quality of product and his heroic efforts to keep the company solvent during difficult times were a tribute to his executive abilities. While he never quite overcame his working class attitudes, he acquired a certain polish and sophistication as time went on, said to have been due to the influence of his wife, Emma, who was a woman of culture and refinement.

The value of his estate was reported as being close to three million dollars, consisting of his block of company shares, along with investments in banks, insurance companies, and public utilities. It was thought that he diversified his holdings as a hedge against the vagaries of the motorcycle business, using his company dividends as a means of investing in multiple holdings, most of which, at this point, had grown with the inevitable inflation

This technical manual was issued by the United States War department in 1942. It covered both the Harley-Davidson and Indian Military models.
Don Emde Collection

due to the stimulation of the war effort.

Throughout the industry it was considered that Arthur Davidson, as one of the original founders, would assume the presidency of the company. But such was not the case. For some time Arthur had not been in the best of health. Then, there was the unfortunate fact of his ongoing battle with alcoholism. According to his associates, he would sometimes absent himself for periods of time, returning in a shaken but repentant attitude, to carry on his sporadic duties as General Sales Manager.

After some consideration, the majority shareholders, including William S. Harley, the surviving Davidson heirs, and representatives of the Woods family, elected 37-year old William Herbert Davidson, son of the late William A., as president. It was subsequently suggested that this decision was somewhat influenced by the fact that the late William A. and his heirs at this time owned the largest number of company shares within the Davidson group. At any rate, and with the ongoing commitment to war production, there was no discernible change in company operations or overall policy.

With the suspension of all AMA sponsored activities and the termination of organized club affairs, E.C. Smith dismantled the operations at the Columbus headquarters. Cora Reardon resigned to assume a more lucrative position as a bookkeeper in a local defense facility, and the rest of the staff went their separate ways. Smith undertook limited duties in his home, mailing out an occasional newsletter to the officers of the now defunct clubs, with the suggestion that copies should be made and sent to members in the armed forces wherever possible. The limited clerical help that was required was provided by a part-time secretary. There was sufficient balance in the AMA treasury to carry these limited activities and to pay Smith's salary, as now there was no need for travel expenses.

The scope and content of "The Motorcycle" languished in the spring of 1942, following the publication of the last of the reports on the competition events of the past season. With advertising revenue dwindling due to the preoccupation of both the manufacturers as well as accessory suppliers with the war effort, the page content was drastically reduced. Johnson Motors, while concentrating on small machine fabrications for the aircraft industry, continued its advertising, as small shipments of Speed Twins in civilian finish were received from Triumph's recently acquired manufacturing facility in Meridan. The British government allowed this in order to earn the hard dollars so desperately needed to help finance their war effort.

Albert G. Crocker was able to secure a lucrative defense contract for the production of small aircraft components in his extensive premises on Venice Boulevard in Los Angeles. He also was able to clandestinely supply a small number of V-twin machines to a few favored customers from his remaining stock of previously finished parts.

By this time, both major motorcycle factories were well underway with their war contracts, along with a few machines with civilian finish for priority customers. Harley-Davidson produced limited numbers of 74 cubic inch UL models for law enforcement buyers, some with sidecars. Indian produced small numbers of their military Chiefs for the same market. Indian Four production was continued through March 1942 to fill a backlog of law enforcement orders, and about 450 units were turned out between January and March. Because of the rise in costs due to wartime inflation, the last models were priced at $1,095 - the same cost of a two-door eight cylinder Buick sedan!

During the fall of 1943, the Harley-Davidson Motor Company sustained another loss with the death of William S. Harley on September 18. He had been in poor health for several years, reportedly due to a chronic lung congestion. On the day of his death he played a round of golf at a local country club and, upon entering the clubhouse bar, collapsed from what was described as a massive heart attack.

As the principal designer of the original Harley-Davidson motorcycles with the collaboration of Arthur Davidson, he had, in common with most of the other pioneer experimenters, based his work on the previous designers of De Dion and Bouton. He had painstakingly developed his early engines until they were more rugged and dependable than many of those of other contemporary designers. During the earliest years of the company organization, he had earned an engineering degree from the University of Wisconsin, graduating in 1907, when the company formally entered the motorcycle market.

While his early engine was dependable, its mild performance limited the machine to utilitarian uses. When the company decided to meet the competition with a V-twin model in 1909, certain technical problems hampered its development. Seemingly lacking that innovative flair that was the attribute of certain contemporary designers, Harley wisely sought to recruit outside talent, which resulted in the hiring of William Ottaway who had already made a name for himself with Thor in creating high performance engines. Ottaway then provided the impetus for Milwaukee's subsequent competition successes just before World War I.

Described by contemporaries as scholarly as

WORLD WAR II 1941-1945

Harley-Davidson's offering for a military model was a modification of its long running WL 45 cu. in. series, fitted with non-valanced high clearance mudguards, a steel skid plate under the engine, gear box, and rear chain run, a low compression commercial type motor, heavy duty air filtration equipment, and saddle bags and sheet metal boxes for ammunition. Of necessarily mild performance, it proved to be a rugged and dependable machine. About 89,000 were produced, along with spare components that could be assembled into about 30,000 more. Dispersed world wide, rebuilt examples are still to be seen in daily use in various parts of the world.

Harley-Davidson Motor Company

In the Fall of 1941 the U.S. War Department requested that both Harley-Davidson and Indian produce prototypes of specialized Military motorcycles. Milwaukee's answer was a frank copy of the German R75 BMW, already in use in the German army. designated as the XA (Experimental Army) about one thousand units were produced. Prototype work was directed by John Nowak, long time H-D Service Manager. The machine was generally satisfactory, except that if the model had gone into serious production, the lubrication system would have been modified.

Harley-Davidson Motor Company

well as kindly in nature, Harley combined the somewhat opposed personal characteristics of engineering talent with interests in painting, drawing, and nature study; exhibiting a poetic and introspective outlook.

Harley's eldest son, William J., followed in his father's footsteps with studies in engineering, and acted as his assistant in the design department. After serving this apprenticeship, he was appointed to his father's post at his death. A younger son, John, also served with the company as an assistant in the parts department, but never attained management status.

Following William Harley's death, William Ottaway resigned from the company. Both Joe Petrali and Alfred Rich Child, who had kept in close touch with the state of affairs in Milwaukee, later ventured the opinion that Ottaway was well aware that changes in company policy were bound to occur. With the passing of three of the founders, the financial control of the company was now in the hands of the non-motorcycling heirs and the estates of the other deceased members, who would now, of course, dictate policy. Following his joining the company in 1913, Ottaway had enjoyed a cordial relationship with the founders, and it is possible that he felt at somewhat of a loss now that the former camaraderie had come to an end.

As far as is known, Ottaway was never a member of the close family circle, however, and in examining the fragmentary lists of shareholders available to the author, Ottaway's name does not appear. According to both Child and Petrali, Ottaway was awarded a yearly cash bonus in addition to his regular salary. While President Walter Davidson was known to frequently promise these to certain employees, Ottaway, and occasionally Hank Syvertson, were the only staff members who actually ever received them.[2]

Little is known regarding Ottaway's personal life, as he was essentially a very private and introspective person who rarely confided in others. Another pioneer motorcyclist, Herbert Ottaway, of Wichita, Kansas, who bore the same surname but was unsure of any relationship, later told the author that a number of Ottaways lived in England in a rural area of Kent. One branch of the family immigrated to Canada early in the 19th Century, where William was born in 1877. Studying engineering and mechanics as a youth, he subsequently moved to the States, where he held a number of positions in industry before joining Thor in 1909. Following his retirement, he is reported to have returned to Canada, where he passed away in 1952.

Ottaway's intuitions concerning eventual changes in the policies of the Harley-Davidson

(Above) A rider's eye view of the classic Harley-Davidson instrument cluster as fitted to a 1941 FL Model.
Steve Iorio

A rider's eye view of the experimental XA Harley-Davidson built for the U.S. War Department.
Harley-Davidson Motor Company

joining the company in 1929, he had had a significant role in the revival of Indian under duPont ownership. Possessed of a genial and persuasive personality, he had a host of friends within the industry and had contributed much to the cause of motorcycling; both with Indian, as well as his tireless efforts as the long-time President of the M&ATA and the AMA. Always a dynamic individual, he had become somewhat restless with the lack of normal sales activities as the result of the war. In assessing the current state of the industrial field, he decided that the machine tool sales field offered the most favorable outlet for his talents and, accordingly, accepted a position as Sales Manager with the Van Norman Machine Company. This company specialized in the manufacture of machine tooling used in gasoline engine rebuilding. He later acted in a similar capacity with the Hansen Screw Machine Company. His replacement at Indian was Harry A. Patton, who formerly managed an Indian branch office at 129 E. 129th Street in New York City.

Due to the dormant condition of the AMA during this period, the Executive Committee did not nominate Wright's replacement until 1944, when, at a meeting held on January 20th at the Lexington Hotel in Chicago, it was decided that with the long tenure of office held by an Indian representative, the presidency should now pass to a Harley-Davidson executive, and Arthur Davidson, presently Vice President of the Milwaukee company, was installed to succeed Wright.

In the meantime, Army procurement authorities had conducted a series of field tests on Harley-Davidson's XA and Indian's 841 experimental models at Fort Benning, Georgia, which was the official proving ground for prototype War Department vehicles. It was noted that while both machines proved generally satisfactory subject to minor modifications, there were now sufficient military models on hand and still subject to ongoing contracts. Tooling up for additional concentration of a campaign in the Pacific Theater against Japan, motorcycles, as compared to the four-wheeled Jeep, were unsuited for operation in jungle terrain.

During this period, the fortunes of the Western Journal Publishing Company continued to decline. With the restrictions of the War Production Board, civilian construction activities practically ceased, obviating the need for the advertising of building materials, architectural services, or contractor soliciting. Arthur Welch reduced his staff to one clerical assistant, and edited and composed "The Motorcyclist" almost singlehandledly. As noted, he was hard pressed to find material, resorting to review articles of the more spectacular sporting

Motor Company later proved true, as will be seen, and would have most probably not met with his approval.

Another significant change within the industry was the resignation of James Wright from the Indian Company. As its long-time Sales Manager since

events of the past, and even featuring fiction dealing with motorcycle themes. While the subscription roster naturally decreased, numbers of families of motorcyclists in the armed forces continued to send the magazine to their men through the special postal facilities maintained by the War Department. It was subsequently noted that motorcyclists in service often formed congenial groups within their units to review past experiences and explore plans for future activities once hostilities ended.

At the same time, E.C. Smith stopped using the facilities of the Western Journal Publishing Company and had his bi-monthly newsletters to the officers of the dormant clubs printed in Columbus, as well as the occasional flyers sent to the general membership. Welch later told the author that he thought that Smith welcomed the opportunity to distance himself from the activities of "The Motorcyclist". It was his opinion that with the resignation of Editor Billings, Smith thought that he had lost a valuable ally with the absence of his "Commissioner". One important source of revenue remained, however, with the ongoing sales of the "Uncle Frank" service guides.

In 1942, a somewhat surprising event in North American motorcycle publishing was the production by J.B. Nicholson, of Saskatoon, Canada, of the very comprehensive work, "Motorcycle Mechanics and Speed Tuning". Initially offered in paperback form, a subsequent somewhat enlarged edition was printed the following year in hardcover form. It covered comprehensive material on Harley-Davidson and Indian repair and servicing along with extensive data on the leading makes of British machines, both civilian as well as War Department models. In addition, it covered technical data on Burman and Albion gear boxes and clutches, Amal and Solex carburetors, Lucas, Miller and BTH ignition systems, with additional information on Villiers products. Also covered was data on speed tuning for competition machines. With the commercial publishing firms' general lack of interest in motorcycling subjects, the Nicholsons had the work published privately. It was noted that this work was the first comprehensive coverage of general motorcycle mechanics since Victor Page's "Motorcycles" in 1915!

In his further recollections, Welch stated that another controversy with Smith occurred in the fall of 1942, incidental to the publication of the Nicholson book. The authors contracted with Welch for a small advertisement to appear in the January 1943 issue of "The Motorcyclist" When this appeared, Smith telephoned Welch from Columbus with a blistering attack, stating that he

Don Emde Collection

was doing the American industry a disservice by promoting information that might encourage the purchase of foreign machines.

Welch countered that the tenets of ethical journalism mandated that the pages of a trade journal should be open to advertising all legitimate enterprises, and that the recent pre-war interest in British machines warranted the public dissemination of technical information regarding them. Smith then stated that he was shortly to visit the West Coast, in spite of the present difficulties of private travel, and that a personal meeting was now in order to attempt to iron out their difficulties concerning the status of the magazine in relation to AMA policies.

In a two day meeting held in Welch's office in early February, Smith stated that unless Welch was willing to offer more wholehearted cooperation in the promotion of the best interests of the industry and the AMA it would be better if the agreement with the magazine be terminated. Welch replied that he could appreciate Smith's attitude on certain aspects of news management. He cited the numerous complaints he had received regarding the arbitrary management of AMA affairs, and suggested that more flexibility on the part of Smith and the Competition Committee in allowing more rider participation in establishing policy might do much to eliminate controversy. But at the same time, he agreed that if the two could not come to some agreement concerning overall policy, it might be best to terminate their agreement.

In spite of a somewhat rancorous discussion, Welch reported that the two attempted to part on a somewhat friendly note. Smith stated that in spite of certain disagreements, the AMA's association with "The Motorcyclist" had proved valuable to both organized motorcycling as well as the industry during a critical period. Welch countered with the thought that the economic arrangement with the AMA had been a prime factor in keeping the publication afloat. Upon his return to Columbus, Smith drafted a formal letter to Welch on February 23rd, officially terminating the agreement between them.

Another significant event in the spring of 1943 was the resignation of G. Briggs Weaver from the Indian Company. He had been associated in engineering activities with E. Paul duPont ever since 1916, when duPont engaged in the manufacture of small marine engines, and later was involved with the design and production of the duPont automobiles between 1919 and 1931. While there was but limited innovative engineering in Indian's product line after 1930, Weaver was credited with the mild updating of Charles B. Franklin's basic designs in

the matter of styling. While Weaver's official title was that of Chief Engineer, much of the minor improvement in Indians along the way was accomplished through the collaboration of duPont with the company's long-time production force which included Erie Armstrong, James Hill, Allan Carter, and John Taylor.

Weaver's most important work was in connection with the revision of the Ace-type four cylinder engine during 1936 and 1937, and the subsequent designing of the new version in 1938. Given as his reason for leaving was his acceptance of a position with the Torque Engineering Company of Plainville, Connecticut, in connection with the development of a new product line of lightweight motorcycles. Also resigning from Indian and slated to also become associated with the Torque concern was an engineering draftsman, Clarence Washburn, and an assistant in Indian's advertising department, Harold Maredon.

Torque Engineering had been founded in 1940 by Ernest and John Stokvis, who had been formerly associated with the Holland based import-export firm of Stokvis and Sonen, which had been founded in 1944 by the Stokvis' great grandfather. From modest beginnings, the firm had grown to the point where it had branch offices all over the world. Among other diverse products Stokvis and Sonen had, for many years, acted as the European agent for Indian as well as Royal Enfield and DKW motorcycles. When the war broke out in Europe the firm prudently moved its liquid assets to banks in Switzerland, England and the United States, and its management and operating personnel left Holland ahead of the German invasion of the Low Countries.

The original firm also dealt in iron and steel, machine tools imported from the United States, sanitary equipment, Austin and BMW automobiles,

Velosolex mopeds, bicycles, and radio and television equipment.

The Stokvis brothers had long been in contact with the U.S. motorcycle industry through their agreement with Indian, and reasoned that the limited U.S. market could be expanded if lightweight European machines could be introduced.

Their initial operation in the States was wholesaling machine tooling, then a critical item for the burgeoning defense industries. After the course of the war presaged an Allied victory, they were prompted to plan for a post-war motorcycle program.

In 1944, Floyd Clymer (whose Indian franchise had been cancelled by the factory) and many others like him, were subsisting on the occasional sale of a used machine. Through the years, as an avid collector of automotive and transportation memorabilia, he had acquired a vast array of old catalogs and sales literature, along with copies of the early trade publications. The thought occurred to him that public interest in this nostalgia could be capitalized upon by the publication of reproductions of this material. The result was a small paperback volume that included mostly advertising material dealing with cars, but also included was a section on early motorcycles. Clymer included a brief text written by himself concerning his early day competition career, a somewhat amateurish effort reflecting his lack of formal education.

At any rate, the publication was an overnight success, and attracted favorable reviews, the most comprehensive being a write-up in "Time" magazine. Clymer subsequently published a series of these books, dealing with additional car and motorcycle material, steam cars, and a later edition dealing with both domestic and foreign motorcycles.

In the spring of 1944, Army procurement authorities cancelled the open-ended contracts for motorcycles, stating that sufficient quantities were on hand to supply the military both at home and in Europe. With thousands of models on hand at home, quantities of these were declared surplus, and offered for sale to individuals in lots of a dozen or more machines at various motor transport depots across the country. The initial offerings included 15,000 WLA's and 7,500 741's in both 30.50 and 45 cubic inch versions.

A number of dealers eagerly participated in these purchases, as there was now an accelerated demand for machines. A number of individuals seized the opportunity to enter the motorcycle retail market, including Ed Kretz, Harrison Reno, Frank Cooper and Joe Walker. Walker had left Johnson Motors when that company dropped Indian to concentrate on Triumph. Walker bought a sizable quan-

WORLD WAR II 1941-1945

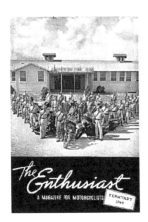

Don Emde Collection

tity of WLA's, and entered into a partnership with an established Harley-Davidson dealer, Jack Wagar, in Santa Ana, California.

The machines involved were mostly low mileage or even brand new models, and in competitive bidding could be had for anywhere from $75 to $150 each. The Office of Price Administration set a retail price of $550 on WLA's and $450 on 741's. Shortly afterwards the rejected shaft drive XA's and 841's were released, with a mandated retail selling price of $550. In addition, quantities of spare components were also offered for bids.

In the war production, Harley-Davidson produced a total of 89,000 WLA's and WLC's, together with sufficient additional components for about 30,000 more. In addition, about 3,500 big twin machines were produced for purchase by essential user which required official priority for acquisition.

Indian produced about 42,000 45 and 30.50 cubic inch 741's, along with the components of spare parts were to have an important role in the post-war motorcycling scene. In addition, thousands of surplus machines and parts were sold to individuals in England as well as on the Continent of Europe. Indian's total war production did not include the prior order for the French Army, as noted, with about 3,500 units sold to civilians for essential uses.

The following year about 15,000 more surplus machines, together with additional components were again offered to domestic bidders. The actual numbers and eventual destinations of domestically produced machines is somewhat obscured by conflicting reports issued through various government agencies. It is known that about 10,000 WLA's and lesser numbers of WLC's were sent to Canada, with some of the latter being transhipped to England. In addition, about 10,000 WLA's and WLC's were later dispatched to England, along with 7,500 30.50 741's. An additional 9,000 of the 741's were also sent to Russia via Murmansk. In 1943, an additional 5,000 741's and large stocks of parts went to Australia. As could be expected, an indeterminate number of machines were lost in transit through U-boat sinkings, especially on the run to Murmansk.

American and British service personnel were surprised by the capture of a number of Indian sidecar units at the defeat of the Field Marshall Rommel's Afrika Korps in North Africa. These were units taken from the defeated French Army after the fall of France and the institution of the Vichy Government.

The American military models generally provided very dependable service in the war effort.

Fitted with low compression engines and weighted down with military equipment, their performance was necessarily mild, but adequate for the work at hand. Some were of the opinion that the excessive weight of the equipment somewhat impaired their handling qualities. In any case, most dispatch riders, military police and motor transport personnel preferred the Yank machines over the British models because of the better rider comfort they provided, although their low ground clearance made them unsuited for off-road use. Many riders with prior experience were amused at the content of the operating instructions contained in a tag affixed to the tank top which warned the operator not to exceed 65 mph. In truth, neither model could actually be urged to within 10 miles of that figure! The 45 cubic inch Indian 741's were somewhat faster, but few of these were sent overseas, most being kept for use in the stateside installations.

As a historic aside, the author engaged in extensive world travel following his professional retirement in 1980. A surprisingly large number of well-worn ex-War Department models of both makes were noted as surviving throughout Europe as well as in North Africa, the Middle East, and even in India and Malaysia. These appear to have been kept on the road through the large stocks of spare parts that were also left behind. As an example, 30 tons of these spare parts lately came to light in Athens, being mostly for WLA's. Large numbers of both Indian machines and parts exist in Australia and New Zealand.

E.C. Smith and the Competition Committee had moved to increase the membership of that body from 16 to 22 in early 1941. It was their contention that with the increase in both club and sporting activities the governing body of the AMA should now be able to give broader attention to matters critical to the organization. It was anticipated that motorcycling activities in general would be increased during 1942. Such, of course, was not the case due to the intervention of the war. E.C. Smith had formally announced the cession of all competition activities in January 1941, but the following month he sent letters to the members of the Committee stating that all present appointments would remain in place for the duration of the conflict. He also emphasized that new and pressing problems would be facing both the industry and sport at the eventual end of hostilities, and that the members should be giving some thought to what course to pursue in the future.

In September 1944, Smith called a meeting of the Committee to be held in Chicago, the purpose of which was to include post-war planning of the

Don Emde Collection

AMA's future policies. In spite of the wartime restrictions on travel, 14 members were able to attend, which Smith declared sufficient for a quorum.

The main focus of the meeting, according to independent reports made later by Dudley Perkins and Ray E. Garner, was to discuss what was now considered by knowledgeable leaders within the industry as the post-war inevitability of foreign competition on the domestic market. It was well known that William E. Johnson had already announced that he was planning an extensive post-war expansion of his Ariel and Triumph dealership. Alfred Rich Child had also made public his intention to re-enter the industry through the importation of foreign machines. Such were sobering thoughts in the face of the realization that the domestic industry had not been able to successfully promote the development of middleweight machines presently covered by the British, and for which a substantial demand had already been noted.

This point of discussion at once brought up the problem of organizing competition to protect the domestic industry, as the proliferation of foreign makes could well dominate the field by sheer force of numbers.

Stephen duPont, with the support of Walter Davidson, had previously suggested, as has been noted, that the allowable compression ratio for Class C competition in all categories be lowered 6.5 to 1. It was then that Ray Garner brought up the point that if foreign imports should be introduced in substantial numbers, their distributors might then form their own competition organization outside the AMA which could seriously affect the strength of the AMA. In recognizing this point, Arthur Davidson stated that such a fact should be considered, but if government intervention in the matter of foreign imports in the form of imposing a restrictive tariff along with import quotas could be secured, the domestic industry could be further protected. After some discussion, the Committee

decided to table the matter of a 6.5:1 compression ratio until such time as the foreign import situation became more clear. It was also noted that with the anticipated controversy that was bound to ensue if such were instituted, it would be better not to mandate such a change at this point in time.

In spite of the usual secrecy that surrounded the internal affairs of the Competition Committee, word had already leaked out regarding the 6.5:1 proposal within the industry. Alfred Rich Child recalled that he learned something of the matter through his long friendship with Arthur Davidson. William Johnson also recalled that Ray Garner, who was not whole-heartedly in accord with the proposal, had broached the matter with several West Coast Indian dealers, including himself as well as Frank Cooper.

At any rate, the upshot of the matter was that Child alerted several prospective foreign machine dealers on the East Coast concerning the matter and, in a subsequent meeting in Los Angeles with Johnson, brought up the matter of forming a British Motorcycle Dealers Association to protect present as well as potential importers of these makes. It was at this juncture that he informed Johnson that he was in the process of communicating with James Leek, Managing Director of Birmingham Small Arms (BSA) concerning the establishment of his own organization in New York to import their motorcycle products.

Johnson concurred, and fired off a series of letters to satellite Ariel and Triumph dealers on the West Coast concerning the need for a formal organization of dealers representing British machines to protect their interests. While a formal organization was not at once instituted, veteran dealers later recalled that they considered the fall of 1944 the time at which the organization came into being in spirit, if not in actuality.

While winding down the contracts for military motorcycles in late spring of 1944, both factories engaged in the fabrication of products unrelated to the war effort. Due to the generally worn condition of their tooling, both factories specialized in small items using mostly fabrication facilities supplied by the prime contractors. In most cases these were parts for the hydraulic systems in aircraft consisting of valve assemblies, pump bodies, tubing layouts and the like.

Indian secured an open-ended contract with the Lawrence Aeronautical Corporation whose factory was situated just across the street. It was managed by one Rowland Burnstan, a talented graduate engineer who held the degree of Doctor of Philosophy in his field. Incidental to securing this

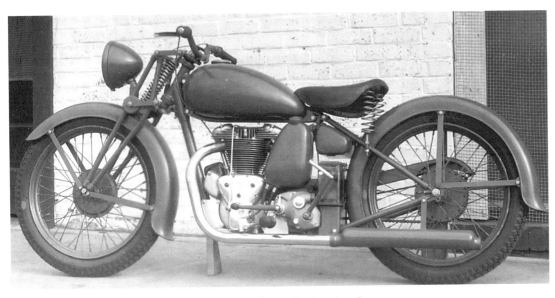

John Stokvis.

The fully assembled 250cc prototype built by the Torque Engineering Company.
Stokvis Collection

The 250cc engine prior to assembly.
Stokvis Collection

Edward Stokvis tries out his new creation in 1941.
Stokvis Collection

Edward Stokvis.
Shelburne Studios

These rare family-owned photographs document the Torque Engineering project to build a 250cc single cylinder prototype motorcycle in 1941. *Stokvis Collection*

contract, Indian's management purchased a book-keeping system from International Business Machines (IBM) which was intended to reduce the ranks of the current clerical help. When the war contracts were terminated it was discovered, to the management's consternation, that the system was defective in its scope, coupled with the fact that the billing sequences for thousands of small parts supplied to Lawrence could not be traced. According to Alexis I. duPont, there was a total of about $411,000 worth of products for which the company could not receive government compensation due to both the inefficiency of the system as well as mistakes made by those administering it. This disaster was a severe setback to the company, as this sum represented most of the war-time profits that were to have been utilized for post-war replacement of tooling and prototype development of new models.

Following the victory in Europe, War Department officials appointed a number of representatives of various industries to proceed to Europe to ascertain if it would be feasible to attempt to return all or part of the vast stock of military materials to the States. Among these were Stephan duPont, along with another member of Indian's Board of Directors. While these two were abroad during January of 1945, Dr. Burnstan took it upon himself to secure a bare majority of Indian's voting stock: the duPonts at this point holding but a slim majority that was now superseded.

The first public announcement on the matter appeared in the March 15th issue of the Wall Street Journal. On March 30th it was noted that Dr. Burnstan had been appointed as Indian's Vice President in charge of production, with Lawrence Aeronautical's legal counsel, Walter A. Boweres, now being an elected member of Indian's Board of Directors. It was also noted in the same issue that Lawrence had taken an option for the purchase of the Indian Motorcycle Company. While no other details were given, it was clearly apparent that Burnstan and his associates in Lawrence's top management had, in effect, taken over the company.

The details of this matter were not divulged until many years later when Alexis I. duPont told the author that it had transpired that during the latter years of the war Burnstan had engineered the acquisition of nearly 49% of Indian stock not held by the duPonts. It was in the absence of Stephan duPont that the Burnstan group was able to outvote the duPont contingent. Through this action, Lawrence Aeronautical was now in a position to make Indian a subsidiary.

Burnstan, however, did not at once move to take up the purchase option for Indian. Indian's

financial as well as physical condition, deteriorated premises and worn out tooling, together with the presence of an aged work force weary from the accelerated war effort, were scarcely an attractive acquisition. If Indian were to survive, it would take a massive infusion of capital and a thorough reorganization of its management. The crowning blow was perhaps the IBM fiasco which had stripped the company of its liquid capital.

At this juncture, Floyd Odlum, a prominent industrialist controlling a diverse group of manufacturing companies as well as General Dynamics and RKO Motion Pictures, enters the story. His prime interest was centered in his Atlas Corporation, a holding company controlling a number of manufacturing concerns. An individual who enjoyed a varied gamut of activity, he was also married to Jacqueline Cochrane, the famed aviatrix of the 1930's. With his ongoing interest in the various facets of domestic industry, he had long been aware of the redundant position of the motorcycle industry: its low production as well as its limited range of model types. In being well aware of the role of motorcycling overseas, he reasoned that new domestic markets could be opened up if advanced types of lightweight machines could be introduced. In learning of the plans of the Torque Engineering Company, he envisioned a breakthrough in motorcycle sales increase.

At any rate, Odlum was acquainted with one Ralph B. Rogers, a rising young New England industrial entrepreneur who had lately been successful in forming the Diesel Engine Sales Company to market an advanced type of lightweight diesel engine recently perfected by a onetime backyard tinkerer, Clessie L. Cummings. Rogers also controlled a group of companies that manufactured sheetmetal fabrications, lawn mowing machinery, and railway cars.

The story goes that Odlum and Rogers met at a social function in New York City early in the spring of 1945, at which time Odlum advanced the idea where Rogers would purchase the ailing Indian Company and merge it with Torque for a broader range of machines in anticipation of an accelerated market. With Indian's present condition and the nebulous position of Torque at that time, with only a skeleton engineering staff headed by G. Briggs Weaver, it made for a rather indeterminate situation. At any rate, Rogers stated that he would consider it.

In the meantime, as the war in the Pacific was winding down, Frank Cooper joined William E. Johnson and Alfred Rich Child in making plans to import British machines. In July he journeyed to

WORLD WAR II 1941-1945

Don Emde Collection

England to meet with Norton's Managing Director Gilbert Smith, as he had been previously impressed with their competition prestige. Smith informed him, however, that at this point, with the problems in converting their war-time production they had not settled on a post-war program, and were therefore not in an immediate position to make any firm commitments on overseas marketing. Cooper next contacted another prominent motorcycle manufacturer, Associated Motorcycle, Ltd.

Associated Motorcycle, Ltd. consisted of a merger, during the Depression year of 1931, between Harry and Charles Collier, pioneer manufacturers of Matchless Machines and another pioneer firm, AJS, headed by Joe Stevens and his four sons. With high quality products and an aggressive marketing program, the firm, through shrewd management and careful attention to its financing, had not only weathered the Depression but had, in 1938, acquired the manufacturing rights to the Sunbeam motorcycles. This latter firm, prominent in the classic era, had lately been concentrating on automobiles and other unrelated products to the neglect of motorcycle production.

Cooper, being impressed with AMC products, then executed a preliminary agreement with septuagenarian Charlie Collier, still active in the business, for the North American import rights.

In the meantime, G. Briggs Weaver had completed the design work for his proposed Continental-type lightweight motorcycles. The result was a two model range of both single and vertical twin cylinder machines whose engines, of modular designs, offered rationalized production using identical frames and interchangeable components. The Stokvis brothers, who were not conversant with the technicalities of motorcycle production, questioned only Weaver's choice of 13 and 26 cubic inch displacement, and in the fall of 1945 authorized the assembling of prototype machines.

It was during this period that Alfred Rich Child concluded his agreement with BSA for the U.S. import rights for their machines. He had made at least three prior journeys to England incidental to these negotiations, one being made before the Allied assault on D-Day. He was somehow able to book passage on a freighter bound for Liverpool. On the return trip, his ship was torpedoed, but he fortunately escaped injury during the attack and made the hundred mile trip to the New Jersey coast through rough seas in a motor lifeboat.

Not to be outdone, Edward Turner came to Los Angeles immediately following the Japanese surrender to finalize the agreement with William Johnson for the post-war Ariel and Triumph import program.

It is an interesting vignette of history that Johnson had not been the original Ariel importer in California. One William Gibson had arranged for the importation of Ariel, BSA and Calthorpe machines in the spring of 1935, operating out of minimal premises on West Pico Boulevard in Los Angeles. With very limited financing and the inability to arrange conditional sales contracts with potential customers, the business floundered after only a handful of machines were sold. Johnson was able to purchase Gibson's interest for $1,500 in 1937. Johnson's initial Ariel and Triumph dealership was incorporated into his Indian dealership in Pasadena, but was shortly moved to the West Pico Boulevard location. After the war ended, he was able to secure a permit to construct a luxurious 25,000 square foot building to house showroom, repair and service, and warehouse facilities on Colorado Boulevard in Pasadena, which became his permanent headquarters.

As news of the construction of what was to be the largest and most luxurious motorcycle facility in the country spread, numbers of other dealers made it a point to visit the site.

Following the Japanese surrender, E.C. Smith called a meeting of the in-place Competition Committee in Chicago in late September. With a full complement of members on hand, a comprehensive discussion of post-war AMA activities was now undertaken. Smith, in a lengthy address to the members, stressed the fact that both the revitalization of the clubs as well as a comprehensive competition program were necessary to promote the recovery as well as the expansion of the domestic motorcycle market. He noted that the latter was especially important to showcase the industry, in view of the fact that motorcycling in the U.S. involved sporting and recreational interest as its primary focus: utility and transportation application having long ago been pre-empted by the automobile. He emphasized that with the general news media viewing motorcycling with either apathy or hostility, the spectator aspect of competition was a vital factor in attracting general public interest.

In noting the agreements already in place involving the importation of British machines, Smith noted that while motorcycling in general should be given encouragement, steps should be taken to insure that the interests of domestic manufacturers be protected. To this end, he suggested that the reciprocity agreement with Canadian competition riders be terminated, noting their predilection for FICM rules, and that AMA activities north of the border should be limited to encouraging the participation of those clubs, mostly in the Ontario

221

region, whose members favored American machines and who conducted competition events according to the established Class C rules. He further noted that the free marketing conditions long present in Canada were not generally acceptable to the exporters of American machines, and that it would be to the best interests of both parties that the Canadians now be left to their own devices.

It was at this point that Arthur Davidson suggested that with the difference of opinion between the manufacturers of domestic machines and the importers regarding competition rules, it might be best to separate the two by lowering the present compression ratio mandate from 7.5:1 to 6.5:1. In this he was at once supported by Stephan duPont, who had suggested this change before the war.

Some members of the Committee, including Erle Armstrong and Eugene Shilingford, disagreed, stating that the 6.5:1 ruling would be divisive in eliminating foreign competition entirely, as highly tuned overhead valve engines could not be made to run properly at this setting. They suggested that the elimination of foreign machines would tend to establish two-make competition and lead to not only monotonous contests, but would be a tacit admission that the imports were considered superior. In addition, the 6.5:1 ruling might well lead to the formation of a separate foreign competition organization that would be divisive and detrimental to ongoing spectator support.

When the matter came to a vote, however, the Milwaukee majority, with duPont's support, voted in the 6.5:1 ruling. Smith at once suggested that a public announcement of both this as well as the decision regarding the elimination of the Canadians should be withheld until the inauguration of the 1946 competition season the following spring. He also mentioned that the 6.5:1 ruling might well be publicly justified as mandating a safety measure in order to reduce the danger to the riders by reducing the ever-increasing speeds attained during both track and TT contests.

It might be emphasized that from the time of the inception of the M&ATA control of organized domestic motorcycle competition in 1920, and through the 1924 inception of the AMA, the membership of the Competition Committee was made up of approximately equal representation of Excelsior, Harley-Davidson and Indian personnel.

After 1932, when the Excelsior representation was phased out, the membership was indicated as equally staffed by the two survivors. While this was supposed to indicate an equality between them, in practice a tie vote was broken by Smith who, having constitutionally mandated voting power, invariably sided with the Milwaukee contingent. With the growingly indeterminate position of Indian, the post-war control of the Competition Committee was solidly in the hands of the Harley-Davidson majority.

As a final order of business, the current members of the M&ATA were assessed a total of $3,500 to fund the now nearly depleted treasury, which had not been replenished during the wartime inactivity of the AMA.

On November 30, 1945, it was announced in the Wall Street Journal that Ralph B. Rogers had acquired majority control of the Indian Motorcycle Company. Included was a statement by Rogers that he planned to undertake a revitalization of the company with an augmentation of the present product line, although no further details were forthcoming.

The actual details of Rogers' acquisition of Indian are somewhat clouded due to conflicting statements later made to the author by both Rogers and Floyd Odlum. Odlum stated that he had not only been the prime mover in Rogers' consummation of the deal, but that he had arranged for the financing for the purchase of the stock. Rogers later admitted Odlum's participation in the matter, but stated that he had secured his own financing through his ongoing connections with the Chemical and Marine Midland Bank in New York City. The matter is further clouded by the later claims of certain veteran Indian employees that Rogers never actually purchased a controlling number of shares but rather forged a coalition to control the company through organizing certain of Indian's minority stockholders.

With the end of hostilities in August with the surrender of the Japanese, the war-time wage, price and rent controls remained in force through the government's attempts to control the inevitable post-war inflation; although gasoline and fuel rationing and the 35 mph speed limit on highways was rescinded, as was meat rationing.

While the AMA Competition Committee had as yet no organized plans for any sanctioned competition activities, a few short track races were held in Central California that fall, which were promoted by Harley-Davidson dealer Frank J. Murray of Sacramento. The venues included Hughes Stadium at that city's community college, the oval at Fresno State Teacher's College, and the refurbished half-mile course at Lodi.

With ten years of economic depression followed by four years of participation in global conflict, the United States was now facing the challenges of a new era of economic, political and social adjustment.

CHAPTER NINE

THE POST WAR DECADE
1945-1955

THE POST WAR DECADE 1945-1955

Ralph Burton Rogers.
Gittings - Neiman Marcus

William Herbert
Davidson, 1905-1993. He
was President of the
Harley-Davidson Motor
Company from 1942 until
1973.
*Harley-Davidson Motor
Company*

While the wartime hostilities ended in August 1945, it took nearly a year for the country to assume a somewhat normal economy. The logistics of twelve million service personnel to be demobilized and the retrieval of a portion of their far-flung military equipment was a monumental undertaking. The production of the usual civilian goods was by necessity on hold, as most of the country's manufacturers had been heavily involved in the war effort. Those who had anticipated updated and newly formulated products after the war's end were doomed to disappointment, as when production of civilian goods haltingly began, they were merely slightly warmed over pre-war editions.

In anticipation of an inflammatory situation due to the soaring demand for civilian products, Congress authorized the continuation of the war time price controls on a wide range of goods and products, including rents and a ceiling on wages. This caused many economic dislocations, as supply and demand in the marketplace saw increased inflationary pressures. It was so acute that many manufacturers held back on inaugurating increased production on the premise that there was no point in the latter if the profit aspect was being suppressed.

This mandate caused problems in the labor market, as the inevitable rise in the cost of living at once created inequities when compared to the policy of many manufacturers of reinstating a pre-war wage scale. The Harley-Davidson Motor Company attempted to follow this trend, and Lin Kuchler, who returned briefly to his former position after being separated from the service, resigned when he noted that his pre-war salary was totally unrealistic. In any case, a wave of labor unrest and a series of strikes throughout the country's industries complicated the hope for rapid post-war economic recovery still further. Added to this was the uncertainty of the requisite market in various raw materials, both in availability as well as delivery capabilities.

The whole series of problems was overshadowed by uncontrollable inflationary pressures.

Harley-Davidson, in the fall of 1945, announced a product line for the forthcoming sales season identical to their pre-war program. This consisted of the UL and ULH side valve models, together with the overhead valve EL and FL series, along with the WL and the limited production ServiCar based upon it. With only a few internal mechanical updates, the resumption of the former line was no doubt a wise move in view of the current problems, especially as production was well rationalized. The factory had received some inquiries from both dealers and enthusiasts regarding the possible introduction of a civilian XA model. The response was that as it was largely a hand fabricated machine there had been only minimal tooling set up for the project, and in any case, the XA was too much at variance with the in-place product line to warrant its continuance.

While Indian's post war program had yet to be announced, the long running Chief was continued as a civilian model, again with rear springing and the full valanced mudguards. The only visible change was the fitting of the hydraulically suspended single leg link fork formerly fitted to the military 841 as designed by E. Paul duPont. Three variants in specification were offered, with options in the range of equipment. There were a number of requests, mostly from law enforcement bodies, for a resumption of Four production, but the response was that post war production costs were such that its retail pricing would be prohibitive under present conditions.

There is no record of any sub rosa meetings between the top management at Milwaukee and Springfield after the war, but Indian Production Foreman Erle Armstrong later reported that he conferred with his opposite number, Hank Syvertsen, concerning pricing matters, and that both factories subsequently set the figures for the top-of-the-line Chief and FL models at $775 for 1946.

Conditional sales contracts for the purchase

of motorcycles lagged behind that of automobiles for many years, as the auto factories set up their own finance companies. In the late 1930's the Davidsons established such a facility for their motorcycle sales, named the Kilbourne Finance Company, which was managed initially by Joseph C. Kilbert. With its main office in Milwaukee, the consummation of individual contracts was somewhat cumbersome, and the approval of the applicant for installment credit was largely left to the discretion of the dealer, who had to guarantee the loan in any case. But at the same time, the establishment of a loan service was of significant benefit to the industry, as the more usual finance companies would have nothing to do with motorcycles. The Kilbourne Finance Company serviced their contracts mainly in the midwest after World War II, due to the fact that the Bank of America in the western states now offered motorcycle financing. This forward looking institution, founded by A.P. Giannini as the Bank of Italy in 1906, was oriented toward the needs of small business. After the war, A.P. Giannini, Jr., who succeeded his father as president, extended finance opportunities for all manner of goods, household and otherwise, which encompassed very modest purchases in many cases.

In relation to motorcycles, in most cases the purchaser was required to pay at least 25% of the cost as a down payment. The interest rates on the unpaid balance were usually around 15% per annum. In addition, the bank returned 2% to 3% of the value of the contract to the dealer as a bonus. In most cases the contracts were seldom written to extend over 24 months.

The interest rates for Kilbourne Finance loans were somewhat higher, as the company operated by borrowing its capital from commercial banks at 7% to 8%, making its profit by floating its contracts at 18% to 20% per annum.

The fortunes of the Western Journal Publishing Company also enjoyed an upturn at the close of the hostilities. With advertising contracts from various dealers, importers, and accessory manufacturers "The Motorcyclist" expanded from its former pamphlet format. Arthur Welch, reveling in the casting off of the aura of E.C. Smith's news management, commented editorially that the magazine was now independent of industry control and, henceforth, would be "Free, fearless and fair." To aid in his expansion, he engaged a young motorcycling journalist, William Smith, to act as Editor. The two began a broad personal coverage of motorcycling activities, and discerning readers at once noticed that the scope of the reporting of competition events covered a broad spectrum of the various makes of machines entered, with fair credits to winners and placers alike.

Welch recalled that his last contact with E.C. Smith was a long distance telephone call in which Smith was highly critical of his handling of a news item. It seemed that in the late fall a group of

Dick Milligan takes a fall from his Sport Scout on the rough course at the Blackwell Ranch.
Ed Kretz

THE POST WAR DECADE 1945-1955

Indian restorer Bob Stark with one of the last 80 cubic inch Blackhawk Chiefs.
George Hays

celebrity riders of the Hollywood Motorcycle Club had made a weekend run over the Ridge Route. On the return home, Randolph Scott (George Randolph Craine) had been forced off the road by an oncoming motorist and had sustained painful injuries requiring his hospitalization. After noting that Welch had mentioned the incident in the Club News section, Smith protested that printing any accounts of rider injury was prejudicial to the best interests of the sport and industry. Welch replied that an element of risk was inherent in motorcycling, and that the omission of such items, already reported in the general print media, lacked journalistic responsibility. Scott later informed the author that, while he made an uneventful recovery, he concluded that motorcycling was endangering his professional career and he never rode again.

In the meantime, E.C. Smith continued to issue his bi-monthly "AMA Report" now urging a reactivating of the disbanded clubs together with a suggested drive to reinstate former members and to recruit new ones. He also announced that an augmented Competition Committee, as well as his staff at Columbus, stood ready to aid in the scheduling of events for 1946.

A special meeting was announced in October 1946, consisting of long standing AMA officials and Competition Committee members, but which did not actually meet in Columbus until the following January. In attendance, in addition to E.C. Smith as Chairman, were Al West of Springfield, Massachusetts; Bruce Walters of Peoria, Illinois; Johnny Van of Battle Creek, Michigan; Reggie Pink of the Bronx, New York; William H. and

Walter Davidson, Jr., of Milwaukee, Wisconsin; Oscar Lenz of Lansing, Michigan; Jim Davis of Columbus, Ohio; Fritzie Baer of Springfield, Massachusetts; Dudley Perkins of San Francisco, California; Eugene Shillingford of Philadelphia, Pennsylvania; and Marion Diedricks of Seattle, Washington. Hap Alzina of Oakland, California, was absent due to illness, and Stephen duPont was still in Europe on the war material retrieval program. It was noted that Harley-Davidson factory personnel and dealers formed a strong majority, and that no active competition riders were present at the meeting.

The agenda included a vote to publish a new Competition Rule book, with emphasis on the enhanced enforcement of the categorization of the Novice, Amateur and Expert classes, which were reported as having been subjected to lax enforcement during the immediate pre-war season by appointed AMA officials and referees.

Also to be re-emphasized were the original 1933 Class C rulings regarding the prohibitions against modifications to the bore and stroke of 45 cubic inch side valve engines, alterations to the frame and forks, as well as other deviations from standard roadster specifications. (As a historic aside, critics of the AMA rulings subsequently pointed out that this new emphasis merely added fuel to the fires of controversy when the ongoing production of specially tuned Sport Scouts and WR specials was currently in place in the factories.)

The most sweeping and controversial ruling, however, was the first public announcement of the new Class C mandate for the lowered compression ratio of 6.5 to 1 that had been under consideration since just before the war. A storm of protest was forthcoming when the news was printed in "The Motorcyclist", not only from the importers and dealers of British machines, but from many owners of domestic machines as well. While the original announcement had been piously described as a safety measure to protect the riders in the face of the high speeds now present on both track and TT courses, it was obvious that the ruling was aimed at eliminating British machines from competition, as the overhead valve 500 cc models could not be made to run well at ratios under 7.5 to 1.

Arthur Welch, who had hoped to more or less soft pedal his differences with AMA policies in the interest of more objective reporting, was drawn into the fray by the hundreds of letters that poured into his office disputing the ruling. He offered his dissenting opinion editorially, along with the printing of representative sample letters from outraged owners.

THE POST WAR DECADE 1945-1955

A single cylinder 13 cubic inch 149 Torque Model in original condition.
George Hays

This ruling also had its repercussions in Canada, as the Competition Committee's prior decision to phase out AMA reciprocity with competitors north of the border had not yet been made public. The Canadians were already somewhat incensed by the immediate pre-war activities of certain AMA clubs in the Ontario area (who had gone their own way in sponsoring closed Class C competition events and their conflicting scheduling that had hurt attendance at other locally sponsored events) and were now alienated further.

C. Gerald Barker called a special meeting of the British Empire Motorcycle Club in Toronto, also inviting the officers of as many adjacent Provincial clubs that he could muster, to discuss this new turn of events. The general reaction from those present was that the AMA had taken this arbitrary stand to force the Canadians to either limit their competition activities to American machines or else remain outside the realm of Class C activities altogether. Adding fuel to the fire was the now-noted stand of the Harley-Davidson clubs in restricting their competition activities to Milwaukee made products only. It was also noted that specially built overhead valve 61 cubic inch EL's, which were outside of any Class C categories, were still being entered in Canadian club sponsored unlimited events, such as the speed trials at Wasaga Beach.

Barker, who was well known in motorcycling circles south of the border, contacted both E.C. Smith as well as other prominent American motorcyclists regarding the matter. While his initial correspondence was ignored by Smith, he received a substantial amount of support from disapproving AMA members. Barker subsequently told the author that he thought it was grossly unfair of Smith to have acted against the Canadians in an oblique manner, rather than simply terminating the pre-war agreement by a direct communication.

The reaction from the prospective British importers was immediate. Both Alfred Rich Child and William E. Johnson fired off letters of protest, each stating that the AMA and Smith could have at least invited British representatives for a prior discussion of the ruling before arbitrarily implementing it. Johnson contacted as many British dealers as possible in order to formalize the organization of a British Motorcycle Dealers Association, being assisted by Triumph dealers Al Fergoda of San Jose and Joe Sarkees in Sacramento. During their survey, both later reported that many Indian and some Harley-Davidson dealers were sympathetic to their position in agreeing with the unfairness of the ruling. At the same time, both Child and Johnson suggested to Smith that, in view of the current hostility to foreign imports, dealers and owners of such should organize their own separate competition organization. As a point of beginning, they further suggested that piston displacement should be the only criteria for various classes of competition.

In the meantime, Ralph B. Rogers concluded an agreement with Ernest and John Stokvis for the purchase of the manufacturing rights, some tooling, and the prototype machines from the Torque Manufacturing Company and announced, on March 1, 1946, that he was integrating Torque products into the Indian line. John Stokvis later told the author that, in spite of their differences with Briggs Weaver regarding the basic design of the Torque prototypes, he and his brother had initially been willing to proceed with their manufacture. Other factors had intervened, however, as additional funds were needed at this time to shore up the Stokvis' operations in Europe following their wartime dislocation. Rogers had offered $120,000 for the Torque operation, but this, in the end, amounted to a transfer of Indian Motorcycle shares in that amount, with a promised buy-back at double the initial purchase price within three years. As events later transpired, as well be seen, Indian Motorcycle stock became virtually worthless.

As Briggs Weaver had departed to work in other engineering fields, one time Indian engineer Clarence Washburn was re-employed by Rogers. What was not known at that time was that Rogers ordered Washburn to streamline the Torque designs for the ultimate in low production cost. This reduction in quality was to have a drastic effect on Indian's forthcoming fortunes.

In the meantime, the importers of British machines were now engaged in organizing their corporate activities.

227

The Cushman Motor Works, who were the country's largest producer of scooters that became popular in the late 1930's, adapted their standard model for commercial urban delivery use as well as an industrial application as in-plant carriers. Large numbers of these outfits were employed in the wartime defense establishments.

Alfred Rich Child leased a suite of luxurious offices on Madison Avenue in New York City, together with an adjacent showroom to exhibit sample BSA's. At the same time, he secured warehouse facilities in nearby Nutley, New Jersey, which also included a parts and service department. Long a widower, Child had recently remarried, and his attractive young wife, Helen, managed the Madison Avenue establishment while Child set about visiting both established as well as potential motorcycle dealers, presenting an extensive advertising program. Child was quick to point out that dealers in British motorcycles had the advantage of an unrestricted market and that they had the choice of carrying product lines from a diverse group of manufacturers.

As could be expected, the British motorcycle manufacturer had numerous difficulties in inaugurating their post war manufacturing programs. With worn out tooling and replacements in short supply, the critical shortage of both raw materials as well as bought-out items, and suppliers in the same difficulties, all acted to curtail predictable production schedules.

While the BSA factory had announced an initial three model range of post war machines (the 250 cc C11 and 350 cc B31 singles, together with an in-line shaft-driven 500 cc twin with the Sunbeam name attached) the factory could only initially supply a batch of War Department type M20 side valve 500 cc singles in civilian finish.

William E. Johnson's Ariel and Triumph organization was well organized early in 1946, with Edward Turner in attendance to aid in converting the operation from a dealership into a distributorship. The actual management of the operation was in the hands of Wilbur Ceder, who, for some years, had acted as both secretary and comptroller for some of Johnson's other corporate enterprises. Eugene W. "Pete" Colman (the well known competition rider and formerly a mechanic in Earl Ferrand's Glendale Indian agency, along with the noted Indian tuner Ray "Pop" Schunk) was installed as Service Manager. Colman, who had a broad background in general engineering, also fulfilled other roles in the company such as overseeing sales, recruiting dealers, and managing a competition program.

Johnson and Turner had, through the years, become warm personal friends. The Johnsons were prominent socially, Mrs. Johnson being related to the Salsbury family of industrialists who manufactured centrifugal drive systems and who were to subsequently launch the Salsbury scooter. The Johnsons occupied a palatial mansion in La Canada's exclusive Flintridge district where they entertained many members of Hollywood's motion picture industry. Turner enjoyed this opulent atmosphere, and arranged to spend about six months of the year in Los Angeles, where he maintained a suite at the Ambassador Hotel.

Frank Cooper was soon integrating his Associated Motorcycle imports with his Los Angeles Indian Agency. The Matchless-AJS post war line at first consisted of 350 and 500 cc models that shared the same cycle parts. While bearing contrasting silver and gold name badges and striping, the only actual difference between the two "makes" was the position of the Magdyno; it being placed in front of the cylinder in the AJS and behind it on the Matchless! Both makes featured the hydraulically dampened plunger forks that they had pioneered on their War Department machines, AMC having previously developed these based on the German BMW type. Most of the earliest post war British imports featured the old style girder forks with the single barrel coil spring, plunger forks not becoming universal until the later 1947 season.

Jack Frodsham negotiated a North American distributorship with Veloce, Ltd. for the continued sales of Velocette machines, concentrating on their 350 cc MAC and 500 cc MSS models. The 350 cc overhead cam KSS was also featured, but due to high production costs appeared only in limited numbers. Frodsham shortly sold his interests to Louis Branch, a Los Angeles motorcycle accessory dealer, and retired to a coastal village in Mexico's Baja California.

THE POST WAR DECADE 1945-1955

The January, 1947 edition of "American Motorcycling" was the premier issue of the AMA's new "official publication".
Don Emde Collection

J.M. McGill, the Ontario, Canada, Norton North American distributor, announced that manufacturer's post war program, and made a direct mail solicitation for a dealership that was still in the hands of Sam Pierce in San Gabriel, California. The only initial roadster model imported was the Model 18, a 500 cc single with a push rod engine, also available as the ES-2 with plunger rear springing.

In the lightweight category, the 125 cc James (a civilian adaptation of the paratroop model fitted with the familiar 125 cc Villiers two-stroke engine-gear unit) was imported by the Hambro Trading Company of New York but was supplied through their warehouse facilities in New Orleans.

Another 125 cc model was the Excelsior (British) fitted with the same power plant and was subsequently distributed through Ariel and Triumph dealers.

Some time after relinquishing the Torque models to Ralph B. Rogers, the Stokvis brothers re-entered the industry by forming the Whitehall Distributing Company based in Washington, D.C., for importing Royal Enfield motorcycles. These consisted of the 350 cc Model G and the 500 cc Model J, which shared the same cycle parts, and the 125 cc R.E., a 'civilianized' paratroop model based originally on the pre-war DKW patents. A vertical twin was later added to the line to compete with Triumph. After the Brockhouse Group took over the Enfield importation, the Stokvis brothers bought out Roy Hostetter, who, for a time, handled the eastern states importation of Matchless and AJS.

The high performance 61 cubic inch overhead valve V-twin Vincent-HRD was handled on the east coast by Rod Coates, with Vincent L. Martin in charge of the west coast.

Hap Jones, San Francisco Indian dealer and now operator of a growing accessory business, announced his appointment as U.S. distributor of Douglas machines, a post war revival of a once famous line of horizontally opposed twins.

In addition, the New York City based Industrial Distributors announced their importation of two lightweights from Czechoslovakia, the Jawa and CZ.

Imported as well as domestic products were still mandated by law to have their selling prices fixed by the Office of Price Administration, having been set through the joint efforts of committees of marketing experts from the Department of Commerce in consultation with the various importers. In the case of imported motorcycles, the retail price was fixed at 100% over the landed cost

to the distributor. This meant that a 500 cc 5T Triumph and an Ariel Red Hunter in 1946 carried a selling price of $775, with a lesser $535 ceiling on a 350 cc Ariel, Triumph 3T, or Model G Royal Enfield. All lightweight machines in the 125 cc category had their prices fixed at $375. Within a couple of years the latter were reduced about $40. In 1947, the prices of the 500 cc and 350 cc machines were raised about $60..

In theory, this gave the distributors and retailers each a 25% markup. But the distributor had to pay an 8% import tariff on the landed cost plus the shipping cost, which reduced their margin to about 18%. The markup on spare parts and accessories was more generous, the retail pricing reflecting an allowed 100% markup for both.

When the first small shipments of British machines began arriving in the late spring and summer of 1946, most casual observers who were unfamiliar with foreign models thought that they were probably new post war designs, but such was not the case. As in the case of domestically produced goods, and most especially in the vehicular field, the manufacturers were hard put to reproduce even their immediate pre-war designs, what with the logistics of changing over from war products, material shortages, plus attendant labor problems, et cetera.

The British imports were actually in design identical to those produced in the mid-1930's. Due to the innate conservatism of both motorcycle buyers in rejecting radical innovation, together with the traditional caution of the British manufacturers, the slow updating of the motorcycles reflected this philosophy. Saddle type fuel tanks had gradually replaced the squared-off between-the-rails type in the late 1920's and early 1930's. Foot shifted transmissions came into being in the mid-1930's, with such machines being produced as War Department models and carried forward for the post war programs. The only real post war innovation was the almost universal fitting of plunger forks, although the lightweights still carried the familiar parallel ruler girders. The overhead valve engines were another matter, however, and while being foreign to American riders, most British roadster models had been so fitted ever since the mid-1920's, mostly mandated by the results of class racing under ACU and FICM rulings.

Taking advantage of his newly acquired journalistic freedom and the termination of E.C. Smith's and the Competition Committee's news management, Arthur Welch introduced two new features in "The Motorcyclist" that were conducted by Editor Bill Smith. One was a section entitled

Scenes at the 1947 Riverside TT races. (Top photo) Ed Kretz (#38) and Floyd Emde (#7). (Bottom photo) A group of riders enter a tight turn.
Armando Magri

"The Battle of the Motors," where readers could write in commenting on their reactions to both domestic and imported machines. The other was a series of objective road tests of various machines conducted by Smith; an area that had been strictly off limits for American trade publications for the past two decades.

The number of dealers for both domestic makers had declined markedly with the onset of the war, there currently being about five or six hundred each, down from the thousand each pre-war. There was, of course, a new statistic in the now-growing number of new dealers handling British makes. Some were new to the game, others were domestic defectors who were reveling in the long standing British system of free market franchising and the lack of factory interference in the conduct of their operation. The main problem facing both groups was the lack of new machines, as the manufacturers on both sides of the pond were facing production problems with the lack of both raw materials and bought-out components from outside suppliers. Under such conditions, it was now definitely a seller's market. Late model used machines in good condition were not subject to OPA pricing schedules, and more often than not, had identical price tags to new models.

Many dealers were able to fill a part of the demand with war surplus models, and some dealers refurbished these in civilian finish which could then bring premium prices.

The serious shortage of new automobiles was an important stimulus to two-wheel vehicle sales which was mainly noted in the new demand for moderately priced scooters. The Cushman Company, with the advantage of their War Department mandated factory enlargement, at once stepped up production; their only problem being the shortage of the air-cooled industrial engines. Briggs and Stratton, who supplied many of the castings for both the Cushman in-house models as well as their own complete units, was reported as having bought a sizable block of Cushman shares. This firm also manufactured low cost models for both Sears-Roebuck and Montgomery Ward mail order houses who marketed them in their catalogs under other names.

Other firms entering the scooter market included Salsbury, who also supplied their patented centrifugal clutches in various sizes and models for application in other industrial products. Others included Powell, which featured engines utilizing Ford automotive parts; the Doodlebug, which used both Wisconsin and Lauson engines, and a number of smaller firms who catered to local markets

Don Emde Collection

throughout the country. A later make with some sporting proclivities was the Mustang, designed by R.M. Forster and manufactured in Glendale, California. Featured was a well made, high performance, side valve engine which was fitted with Albion or Burman gear boxes imported from England. A noted feature was its 16" wheels, which made it somewhat of a hybrid motorcycle. It was offered in a three model range with varying specifications and with either disc or wire wheels.

Another machine which was more in the ultra-light motorcycle category was the Servicycle, John Paul Treen's 1935 introduction manufactured by the Simplex Company in New Orleans. This was launched nationally with a media advertising campaign. Treen offered 80, 115 and 150 cc variants with optional lightweight side-cars, still adhering to the single speed belt drive arrangement, controlled by a centrifugal clutch.

A revival of the 1920's Shaw motor-bicycle attachment principle was seen in the newly re-introduced Whizzer, which for $59.50 would supply a small single cylinder four-stroke engine, fuel tank, belt pulleys, and other parts needed to convert a heavyweight roadster bicycle to power. A similar unit, but with a horizontally opposed twin cylinder motor, was also offered by Marmon. The sudden popularity of these units prompted Schwinn to offer a special bicycle with heavy duty wheels and a cartridge sprung fork, along with a cranked front down tube to accommodate them. These models made power conversions more practical as ordinary bicycles showed both rapid wear as well as early structural failures from the higher speeds attained, not to mention the pounding received on rough roads. The popularity of both these units, as well as scooters, was enhanced by the fact that many of the states had lately relaxed their vehicle licensing laws to allow 14 year old riders to legally operate on the roads.

One make of machine not revived after the war was the now famous Crocker. Establishing as it did an enviable reputation for high performance among experienced sporting riders with a pre-war production of just 65 units,[*1] its maker in Venice, California, was importuned to resume its production. Crocker refused on the grounds that while he was enthusiastic about the machine's future, the fact that he had lost about $2,500 on each unit produced due to the high expenditure for tooling was now a mitigating factor. While Crocker had prospered handsomely with his war time production of defense components, his immediate family members were adamantly opposed to the dispersal of any more capital for motorcycle production.

THE POST WAR DECADE 1945-1955

E.C. Smith scheduled a meeting of the M&ATA in February at the Lexington Hotel in Chicago for an initial discussion of post-war policies by the leaders of the industry. He informed the members that he had already outlined to the Competition Committee his plans for enhanced club activities, including a revitalization of those inactive, a continuing Activities Awards program, expanded plans for re-establishing the Gypsy Tours in connection with important sporting events, and a general expansion of the AMA staff at Columbus to better expedite an anticipated post-war competition program.

To aid in this he announced that he had just hired Jules Horky as his assistant to be in charge of keeping the records of competition activities and to aid in the enforcement of the Class C rulings, as well as scheduling sanctioned events and other details, at a salary of $3,000 per year.

Horky, a life long motorcyclist, had also been a professional mechanic, and just before the war had taken over the retail sales outlet located in the basement of the Indian factory that had been formerly operated by Fritzie Baer. During the war, he acted as a civilian instructor in teaching motorcycle operation at various military installations.

Smith reported that well over half of the 635 pre-war AMA registered clubs were viable, mostly those who operated from their own premises. He also noted that well over 15,000 former members had renewed their registrations and could be considered ready to resume normal activities. He stated that he was still vigorously campaigning for a revitalization of the inactive clubs and that mailings had been sent to the last known addresses of former members who had not yet renewed.

Dudley Perkins and Ray E. Garner later told the author that they both had second thoughts concerning their initial support of the lowering of the compression ruling, and during the proceedings had voiced their opinions, although such was not recorded in the minutes of the meeting.

It was their contention that while they supported a protectionist attitude toward the domestic industry, they were apprehensive about the possible formation of a separate competition organization for imported machines. They further pointed out that rumors were emanating from Springfield that the Sport Scout was not immediately planned for post-war production, and if this were true, one make participation by Milwaukee could not inspire much public interest in continued Class C competition.

In the meantime, reader opinion in the matter, continually being voiced in the pages of "The Motorcyclist", supported the idea that a return to the former 7.5-1 ruling was threatening the whole future of any extensive planning for expanded post-war competition.

Heeding this, and advice from others (including many Harley-Davidson enthusiasts as well as dealers) Smith called an early meeting of the Competition Committee to again review the matter. Subsequent to another meeting in Chicago in March, where a majority vote not supported by the Davidsons overturned the previous ruling, Smith announced on March 31 that the old rule had been reinstated.

While there was a general feeling of relief among enthusiasts, club members, and dealers at this news, it was hoped that the bitterness within the sport and industry would die down. There was much ill feeling among the importers and new converts to British machinery who quite logically contended that the Competition Committee, long controlled by the domestic industry, had attempted to suppress a revitalization of the long dormant American market. As matters now stood, however, the battle lines between the two were being drawn.

While the Competition Committee, led by Smith and Horky, had planned a resumption of an extensive post-war competition program, conditions existing from the dislocations of the war prevented much activity in this direction until the summer of 1946. It was too late to plan for the annual Daytona classic, but plans were made to schedule the pre-war big fixture contests such as the Jack Pine, Langhorne and Laconia. A few dirt track races had been held in the fall of 1945, as noted, in California. There was also an early revival of Class A racing in 1946. These were promoted by Frank J. Murray at the Hughes Stadium in Sacramento and also in Fresno, and several meets were promoted by Floyd Clymer in the Los Angeles area. Many of the pre-war stars participated. An outstanding winner who was ultimately made to enter in strong handicap starts was Wilbur "Lammy" Lamereaux.

Jules Horky reported that E.C. Smith and Harley-Davidson renewed their previous pre-war agreement for the former to perform certain public relations duties on behalf of that company, the financial details not revealed.

In April, Smith circulated a confidential memoranda to the members of both the M&ATA and the Competition Committee advocating the inauguration of a magazine which was to be the official AMA publication. He mentioned that the former AMA affiliation with "The Motorcyclist" had fulfilled the needs for the AMA and the industry as a media outlet during difficult pre-war times, but that the present editorial policies of that magazine were no longer compatible with the best interests of the AMA. It transpired that Smith had already approached several members of both bodies regarding the matter, and had received a favorable response, along with the suggestion that for more comprehensive coverage of national motorcycling affairs the publication had best be produced in the Midwest.

Smith took charge of the matter and subsequently collected $1,200 on a pro rata basis from the M&ATA membership to advance the initial expenses. In the meantime, he continued to send out the AMA newsletter on a bi-monthly basis to both the chartered clubs and registered members.

With the now growing activities in the Southern California area, a new AMA referee was appointed for District 37, Royal Carroll. With Carroll's cooperation, Floyd Clymer and Paul A. Bigsby expanded the promotion of Class A racing to include night meetings at various tracks such as

Lincoln Park, Ascot and the Santa Monica Stadium.

As the competition season got under way in Southern California, still the most active area of the country's motorcycling sporting activity, many of the riders who had been dissatisfied with both the often dictatorial policies of the AMA Competition Committee as well as the tactics of certain of the race promoters, found an outlet for their expression in the formation of the Competition Riders and Owners Association. It was founded by Bruce Pearson, a pre-war Indian and Ariel rider, who initially acted as its president. Pearson announced that the purpose of the organization was to improve the status of the riders as well as to enhance their safety requirements and to present a better image of motorcycle competition to the public. In the matter of the purses, it was requested that these should amount to a total minimum of $250 to cover winners and placers, or 30% of the gate receipts, if there was insufficient revenue to meet the former figure. In better paying major events, if the $250 figure was met it was to be augmented by an additional 35% of the gate. In addition, the promoter was to contribute $25 from his share to the riders' insurance fund. In addition to that, $100 was to be awarded any rider who sustained an injury.

Other stipulations required that only mechanics remain in the pits during the races: all other individuals being banned. In addition, all mechanics and track officials were to wear clean white coveralls. Qualified marshalls in sufficient numbers were to keep all spectators off the track surfaces, and a physician and an ambulance should be in attendance for the duration of any contest. The condition of the track itself would be subject to an inspection by a committee of riders, with special

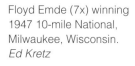

Floyd Emde (7x) winning 1947 10-mile National, Milwaukee, Wisconsin.
Ed Kretz

Langhorne, 1947. Eugene Shillingford (r.) presents the trophies. (From left) Billy Miller, Chet Dygraaf, Ed Kretz, and Mrs. Kretz. *Norman P. Speirs*

attention to the elimination of dangerous ruts and the suppression of excessive dust, this latter to be controlled by either water sprinkling or by the use of chemicals.

Pearson told the author that a matter of contention between the riders and promoters was the quality of the purses, the rates of which had not been raised since the inauguration of Class C competition in 1933. He blamed both E.C. Smith and the late Walter Davidson for this situation, claiming they purposely kept the purses low to attract more promoters into the game, much to the rider's detriment.

During the late fall of 1946 and early spring of 1947, the starts of several race meets in the Los Angeles and San Diego areas were delayed by the riders when they were not sure that the promoters involved were willing to accede to their demands.

Pearson also stated that a list of the riders' demands had been forwarded to Smith in Columbus in August, and that in reply Smith offered to appoint a committee from the membership of the M&ATA and the Competition Committee to consider their demands. Pearson at once fired back an answer stating that the matter required immediate action rather than going through the cumbersome process of assembling a committee whose deliberations could well be lengthy. Smith's reply was to threaten to suspend both Pearson and his most enthusiastic supporters if they persisted in disrupting the competition schedule. In the meantime, the groundswell of support from both the clubs as well as from many AMA cardholders from the general membership was such that Smith backed down and acceded to

the riders' demands.

By the summer of 1946 there was a substantial demand for new motorcycles which was greater than either the two domestic factories or the newly instituted importers could supply. The domestic manufacturers were still contending with their outmoded 19th Century facilities, and were further hampered by the shortage of raw materials and accessory items. The picture was further clouded by the still existent OPA authority which, in theory, was kept in place to control inflation, but which, in reality, exerted a strangling effect in the market place due to the pressures of readjustment which had raised prices and production costs all along the way. Rather than operating at a loss or with minimal profits, many manufacturers of various products held back production in the hope that the OPA could be forced into termination. As a side effect, the inevitable black market condition permeated critical industries.

In spite of unfilled orders from their dealers both Harley-Davidson and Indian exported substantial numbers of machines to Central and South America to fulfill military contracts, much to the retailer's consternation.

While the importers of British machines through their advertising had in effect heralded a new era in American motorcycling, the actual shipment of machines was curtailed by adverse economic conditions in Great Britain. In an intense effort to provide as much volume of exports as possible to fill the need for hard currency to help pay for the staggering cost of the war, raw materials and bought-out components were in short supply. At this point, due to the export drive, British citizens found the purchase of new vehicles almost impossible. The picture was further complicated by their government's levying a 25% purchase tax on most durable goods. Furthermore, the sale of motor fuel was severely restricted, and during some periods strict rationing forbade its use for pleasure driving. When available it took the form of a low 72 octane product called "pool", which offered inferior performance at best.

While the U.S. importers enjoyed sporadic shipments of machines, accompanying spare parts were in short supply, and many dealers were forced to cannibalize new machines in stock to keep previous buyers on the road.

As the motorcycle market slowly expanded during the fall and winter of 1946 and 1947, it became apparent that through their individualistic designs, there was a strong divergence of application between the domestic and imported machines. The long evolving domestic heavyweight V-twins were best suited to the stringent demands of law enforcement and commercial use as well as that of long distance touring at high average speeds. In addition, as long wheelbase models they were better suited for both double riding and carrying the necessary luggage. The light and middleweight imports were best suited for solo use and, of necessarily smaller piston displacement and lighter construction, could not maintain the high average speeds for long periods in extended highway travel. The demands of vast distances of the North American continent generally mandated the choice of imported 500 cc machines, and it was this category of displacement that came to dominate the U.S. import market. The initial vertical twin Triumphs were especially suited to the American market, as their higher power development over the singles of the same displacement gave them the edge in top speed. This started the fashion in vertical twin configuration, and BSA shortly brought out their A7 twin, followed by the Ariel Huntmaster and the Norton Dominator, and, at a later date, the Enfield.

No British firms resurrected any of their pre-war V-twin designs, which had been produced mainly to compete with the Americans on the export market, the more important manufacturers being AJS, Matchless and BSA. The only two heavyweight British models to be imported post-war were the newly designed 61 cubic inch overhead valve Vincent-HRD and the 61 cubic inch Ariel Square Four. The former, capable of fantastic performance and offered in three variants of top end performance, was a somewhat temperamental machine best in the hands of a mechanically oriented owner. The Square Four, a smooth running machine possessed of vivid acceleration and superlative power, was handicapped by being susceptible to overheating in the West and Southwest areas: the locale of the major motorcycle markets. Both of these high priced mounts failed to threaten the markets for those traditionalists who favored heavyweight domestic V-twins.

In any case, it was the middleweight imports that attracted immediate public attention. Not only was there a market stimulus from the recent exposure of former GI's to two wheels as noted, but also the alternative from the former monotony of a two-make market offering a limited range of models.

The middleweight concept was also an attraction to former mildly interested potential buyers who were intimidated by the bulk and weight of the domestic offerings, and it was at once noted that a more conservative type of customer was being attracted to the game.

While American conditions of space and travel focused the market on the 500 cc twins and singles, there was also the mandate of this displacement for potential sporting participation under the long-standing AMA ruling.

(As an aside, with the current shortage of new automobiles due to the difficulties mentioned, the scooter market for utility riders was booming, with 50,000 units sold by the end of 1947.)

While a sellers' market was well in place due to the pent-up demand for domestic models, a sobering disadvantage was the loss of most of the former export markets which had long been a prime factor in the domestic industry's survival. The still-devastated economies of Japan and Europe due to the dislocations of the war precluded their buying power, and a struggling Great Britain raised their tariffs on the import of foreign vehicles to 50% in an effort to protect their home markets. As the battle lines between the domestic manufacturers and the importers became more finally drawn, this latter fact became an important matter of contention.

While the enthusiasm for the British machines and the early development of their market was apparent, not all was lovely in the garden. Many of the newly franchised dealers, while motorcycle enthusiasts, lacked business and managerial experience, or were under- capitalized to the extent that they could not outlast an initial growth period, and a substantial number failed.

Another problem was in parts and service. The former was mentioned earlier, and the latter was sometimes handicapped by a lack of skilled mechanics. Motorcycle trade schools were not in existence in those days due to the limited pre-war market and the distributors attempted to fill the gap by offering short crash courses in the rudiments of repair and service.

The middleweight British machines, quite naturally, did not feature the rugged construction of the American machines, mainly because the service demands of England and Europe, with smaller areas of travel and generally good roads, were subjected to less stress. Many British models showed structural and lubrication failures when subjected to prolonged high speed running, especially in the unfamiliar summer climate conditions of the West and Southwest. Then too, American riders, accustomed to the rugged gear boxes and heavy duty clutches of the domestic machines, frequently subjected the light pattern drive trains of the imports to unintentional abuse.

The Lucas electrical system fitted to most British machines was another point in question, as

(left to right) Erwin G. "Cannonball" Baker, Noel McIntyre and Ed Kretz share a happy moment with race winner Floyd Emde and his wife Florence following the 1948 Daytona races.
Ed Kretz

was the sensitive adjustments required to keep the Amal carburetor in proper tune. The tendency to flooding, especially when the engine was hot, often made restarting difficult for those unfamiliar with the procedures involved.

Enthusiastic buyers of British machines had one single advantage, however, in that there was a vast amount of published information dealing with both the generalities of ownership as well as the specifics of operation and maintenance. Where the Americans had "Uncle Frank", and later the Nicholson books, the British offered the manuals published by Iliffe and Temple Press, as well as the extensive service manuals that came with the machines, along with the specialist books on specific makes such as Pitman and Haycraft.

A wholesale book dealer in England, Vivian Grey in Sussex, obtained mailing lists of American owners of British machines from licensing agencies and sent over thousands of flyers listing dozens of books available. Floyd Clymer, flushed with the success of his series of historic motor books, inaugurated an import business in British motorcycle publications. Sometime later, however, he ran afoul of the international copyright laws when it was discovered that he was printing pirated copies, including the Nicholson books, without paying royalty benefits to the original publisher. Both Iliffe and Temple Press at once terminated

their prior agreements with him, and a shipment of material from both publishers was seized by police at the docks through a court order.

On the journalistic side, a group of budding authors entered the field with occasional articles adversely comparing the American control systems with those of the British. Noting that the latter offered easier control with their hand-clutch-foot-shifting arrangement, they were critical of Yankee arrangements. This latter was a fallacious suggestion, as the high torque resistance of the heavy pattern clutches responded more easily to the leg power than to the hand power of the rider.

While the British were eager to fulfill their agreements with the American importers, they were less cooperative in making any design changes to better serve the American market. They tended to encourage the emphasis on 250 and 350 cc models; whereas the 500 cc sizes were best suited to the long distance travel that was part and parcel of American operation.

The majority of exporters were not enthusiastic about the adaptation of their products for competition, their native emphasis being more on transport and touring. Alfred Rich Child often stated that the BSA development of the A7, and later 650 cc A10 vertical twins and eventually the high performance 500 cc Gold Star models, was due to his table pounding sessions with Managing

The Post War Decade 1945-1955

Floyd Emde, the winner of the 1948 Daytona 200 with his racing Scout. He was sponsored by San Diego Indian dealer Guy Urquhart, and his machine was tuned by Noel McIntyre who was the Shop Foreman.
Don Emde

Director James Leek during his frequent visits to the factory.

Edward Turner was never whole-heartedly enthusiastic about racing but, due to American pressure, brought out the Trophy model whose aluminum engine was derived from a war-time portable electric generator set. This machine was subsequently fitted with a kick starter and a rudimentary lighting set to comply with AMA's Class C rulings. Turner was ever ready to point out that the indeterminate financial position of Norton was due to their vast expenditures allocated to the development of their competition models.

Frank Cooper recalled his good fortune with Associated Motorcycles beefing up their engines for American conditions noting the life long interest of Charlie Collier, who had been a competition enthusiast since the turn of the century. The AJS and Matchless machines were improved early on with the updating of cam profiles, larger valves and the fitting of heavy duty lower bearings.

The other British single which was more suited for competition was the Ariel Red Hunter, which had more specialized design features than the standard touring models. Early post-war successes on the dirt as well as TT's by Shorty Thompkins and Bruce Pearson were proof of this point. But the more massive internal construction of the Harley WR's and Indian Scouts was often

the telling factor against the more nimble imports, especially in long distance events. The International Norton, however, by its inherent design features, was always in a class by itself.

While the 1946 competition season did not include the Daytona 200 and few of the big pre-war national fixture contests, the Illinois Springfield Mile was scheduled in September. This well established event by tradition gave the winner the coveted Number One Plate in what was a "sudden death" affair that decided the National Championship taking precedence over all other big fixture contests.

This 1946 event was significant in that the Harley-Davidson and Indian majorities on the AMA Competition Committee now threw down the gauntlet to the foreign machines in seeking to showcase domestic domination of motorcycle sport.

A looming confrontation was provided by the announced entrance of one of the country's top riders, Chester "Chet" Dygraaf, a usual Indian rider now campaigning with an International Norton. The Competition Committee had taken exception in allowing this model for Class C events due to its impressive pre-war performance and, in fact, it had already been barred from dirt tracks by the AMA referees in some districts on the ruling that examples had been modified from standard for such contests. It had, however, been allowed in numbers

237

The Post War Decade 1945-1955

Some of the country's most outstanding competition riders gather at the 1948 Daytona 200 for the crowning of AMA's Most Popular Rider contest. Ed Kretz was again accorded the honors, having been the winner in 1938. From left, Dick Klamfoth, Bobby Hill, Leo Anthony, Billy Huber, Ed Kretz, Joe Weatherly, Jimmy Chann, Bill Tuman, Chet Dykgraaf, Bill Miller.
William Bagnall

of TT races, as it was in fact a legally cataloged model since 1932. Billy Mathews had been allowed to enter the 1941 Daytona on the grounds that it was classed as a TT, together with the fact that Harley-Davidson had put great faith in the abilities of their newly introduced WR, which was actually an out and out racing machine not suited for street use. Mathews' spectacular win at that time was now a factor to consider.

With the information of Norton's admission into past events now out, the Committee was on the horns of a dilemma regarding the Springfield classic. After some deliberation, the Committee decided that both Harley-Davidson and Indian would boycott the event and not enter any factory teams in the race, and dealers who had planned to sponsor riders were ordered to cancel their entries. While the boycott was actually honored, both Harley and Indian riders, who already had their own racing machinery, opted to enter anyway as privateers. Dygraff was an easy winner. The experienced Indian riders who already had their own well tuned machinery, such as Art Hafer, Johnny Spiegelhoff, Ted Edwards, Freddy Bellibeau and the Castonguay brothers, took the next places. As the experienced Harley riders generally heeded the boycott, the few less experienced Milwaukee contingent who entered were all at the back of the pack.

According to a later account of the matter by Jules Horky, the North American distributor, J.M. McGill, somehow learned of the Competition Committee's unofficial edict and at once telegraphed his U.S. regional distributors, including Sam Pierce in San Gabriel, about the matter.

Pierce, in high dudgeon, attempted to contact E.C. Smith by telephone. Failing to get an answer, he boarded a DC-3 airliner for Ohio to face Smith in person. But wishing to avoid any legal action against the AMA or the Committee on the part of either Norton distributors or a coalition of foreign dealers, the wily Smith sidestepped the issue by informing the irate Pierce that the barring of International Nortons from either dirt track or TT events had come about through the decisions of the local AMA district referees and that the Competition Committee had, in reality, taken no official action against Norton entries. Pierce, still not mollified, returned home and spent a whole day telephoning all the U.S. Norton dealers and those of other foreign makes as well. Pierce later gave the author his account of the matter, which substantiated Horky's initial report.

The California based British Motorcycle Dealers Association (BMDA) held an emergency meeting at the Johnson Motors headquarters the following month; all U.S. British distributors and dealers being given prior notice. The members present at the meeting voted unanimously to expand the BMDA into a formally organized national association to present a united front against Smith and the Committee. BSA distributor Alfred Rich Child offered to help in recruiting British dealers east of the Mississippi. He fired off a strong letter to Smith, stating that the growing presence of imported machines on the domestic market was now a fait accompli, but that the market as a whole was not yet strong enough to support a separation of the two factions in organized competition. He added that if the present infight-

THE POST WAR DECADE 1945-1955

In an effort to improve the public's view of motorcycling, the factories were quick to feature celebrities in their in-house publications. Here, football star of the 1940's Johnny Lujack poses for "The Indian Magazine".
Don Emde Collection

San Diego's Floyd Emde was shown on the cover of the March, 1948 issue of "Motorcyclist" in a rather unenviable position. He was featured again the next month when he won the Daytona 200.
Don Emde Collection

ing continued to the point of attracting more public attention, the adherents of both domestic and foreign makes would suffer. Child later reported that Smith at once contacted him by telephone and stated that both he and the Committee now hoped for some sort of a compromise.

In the meantime, a committee of California BMDA members, consisting of Johnson, Frank Serveti of San Jose, Joe Sarkees of Sacramento, and Sam Pierce of San Gabriel, inaugurated a letter writing campaign contacting all the dealers of foreign machines throughout the U.S. and by the following January, nearly all of them had joined the organization.

In spite of the conciliatory statement from Smith, Norton enthusiasts did not win a single victory. District referees continued to ban Internationals from dirt track events, although they were admitted to TT's and to their now tenured position at Daytona. Sales of these machines remained quite limited in the States, no doubt due in large measure to their high selling price of $1,095.

The author subsequently purchased a 1947 International as a matter of personal interest concerning the ongoing controversy. With its superb race-bred steering and handling and its high power development even in road-going tune with attendant 90 mph cruising speed and vivid acceleration, to the experienced rider it appeared to offer the zenith in British engineering. The price paid, however, was its somewhat intractability in traffic due to its tall gearing and its chronic habit of leaking copious quantities of oil from the cam box and the exposed valve springs.

The Model 18 push-rod Nortons never fared too well on the U.S. market, although the spring framed ES-2 version (which shared the 18's good handling and was pleasant to ride) did. The power development was inferior to that of the Ariel Red Hunter, Velocette and Triumph of like displacement, and the extremely heavy steel push rods required replacement with light alloy members to reduce noise and excessive wear on the tappet followers. As Norton's Joe Craig's contract with the factory did not extend to the push rod models, their development never paralleled that of the cammers. Norton sales of these models languished within a couple of seasons, but were revived somewhat in 1950 with a vertical twin model designed by Bert Hopwood.

In the immediate post-war period a trend in motorcycling took place that was disturbing to the management of the domestic factories, the AMA, the M&ATA hierarchy, as well as many thoughtful

motorcyclists. This was the emergence of an increasing group of enthusiasts who favored stripped and modified mostly domestic big twins, usually with noisy exhausts. They favored bizarre or often downright disreputable dress, and when congregating in groups they often exhibited rowdy and sometimes antisocial behavior, which, on occasion, bordered on the obscene. Whatever their individual preferences, their general ambiance branded them as "outlaws".

Initially, both the factories as well as the dealers were put off by the image these outlaws presented to the general public, especially as the recent pre-war era had seen too often in the public mind the idea that motorcycling was a "roughneck" sport. At any rate, these post-war groups almost at once organized themselves into fraternal type clubs. The most prominent of these were the Hell's Angels, organized in Oakland, California, under the leadership of Ralph M. "Sonny" Barger.[*2] Others included the Hessians, the Mongols, the Chosen Few, Satan's Sinners, and, at a later date in the Southwest, the Bandidos.

Most of the registered AMA clubs were antagonized by these groups when they were uninvited attendees at club runs, Gypsy Tour events, and competition meets where they sometimes engaged in disruptive behavior.

In the meantime, certain sociologists and psychologists speculated as to the root causes of this antisocial defection. Some claimed that it was a manifestation of the natural disillusionment of ex-service personnel following the war, and that the motorcycle as a vehicle for iconoclasts became their media of expression of personal freedom. This became an extension of social rebellion, relating to the living of a life of total freedom.

Others claimed that it was a reaction of free thinkers against the somewhat rigid concepts of the factories who had long advocated certain modes of dress and the "dresser" type of machines, as well as the mandate of uniform attire presently the style of the organized clubs.

The "bikers", as they now preferred to be called, however, were not subject to universal condemnation by certain segments of the public who may or may not have had a connection with motorcycling. Some socially oriented liberals praised them as unfettered individualists who had the courage to indulge in free expression, citing the personal satisfaction to be gained in Bohemianism. Others likened them to the rugged trappers and mountain men who opened up the early western U.S. before the California gold rush. Others admired them as Samurai types, or a courageous

Win Young, with friend, entered in a 1948 race at Lincoln Park.
Win Young

"warrior class" who epitomized the bravery of the total macho image. Many feminine admirers of the total male, whether themselves riders or not, reveled in their participation in the movement with a chosen mate or mates. At any rate, a new and suddenly growing counterculture was now in evidence and as a group were, in the coming decades, to exert a significant influence in the course of domestic motorcycling.

In the meantime, the Motor Maids of America had been reorganized for post-war activity and Vera Griffith, with the help of Dorothy "Dot" Robinson and Ruth Fordyce, scheduled a national convention that was held in Sonoma, California. It was reported that more than 500 members were now enrolled on a national basis.

January 1947 saw the resurrection of the pre-war Big Bear Run, a Southern California cross-country event sponsored by the Three Point Motorcycle Club of Hollywood, with the assis-

tance of several other participating groups. Starting at the edge of the desert at Saugus, it featured 126 miles of an incredibly rough course of a terrain of sand, rocks and brush over the San Gabriel foothills and terminated up at Big Bear Lake at 7,000 feet. Only a few of the 225 riders who entered were able to finish, the ultimate hero being Dick Page on a stripped 74 cubic inch FL Harley-Davidson. Second place went to Ray Tanner on another stripped big twin Harley which was modified for enhanced ground clearance, and third place went to Stanley Irons on a Matchless.

This type of event had been originally suggested by Frank Cooper, the AJS-Matchless distributor, who had been lately promoting English type trial events and Hare and Hound races, as well as more demanding types of cross country Enduros. It was Cooper's contention that with the now-growing popularity of British middleweight machines, their appeal could be heightened in staging events well suited to their weight and ground clearance. He envisioned such events as an outlet for sporting riders who did not favor either the expenses involved or the risk of formally organized AMA dirt track or TT competition.

In fact, Cooper had, during the past season, made personal contacts with the leading organized clubs in the Southern California area in company with Ernie May, to promote the organization of such events, which of course was a stimulus for the sale of British machines. He soon gained the support of Skip Fordyce, an active member of the Riverside Bombers, who also organized an ongoing schedule of such events. Eventually, during the spring, summer and fall seasons, such events were held nearly every weekend at some venue. Cooper subsequently formed what he called the Sports Committee, a loosely organized group of club officers as well as dealers to encourage the sport and to schedule meets. This type of event soon spread to other parts of the country.

The first post-war meeting and trade show of both the AMA and M&ATA was held in Chicago in January 1947. It was restricted to the exhibits of American made machines and accessories only, together with products of the allied trades such as Diamond and Duckworth chains, Mesinger saddles, Delco and Geneto electrics, Edison-Splitdorf ignition parts, Firestone and Goodyear rubber products, and accessories offered for American machines.

Arthur Welch attended the meeting, which was duly reported in "The Motorcyclist". A climatic event, related to the ongoing controversy between Welch and E.C. Smith over current AMA policy matters, was a confrontation between Welch and Arthur Davidson, the subject being the articles on

THE POST WAR DECADE 1945-1955

the matter which, since the end of the war, had been appearing in the magazine. Davidson made it clear to Welch that Smith was himself representing the edicts of the entire Competition Committee, and that personal attacks on Smith were unfair. He further suggested that dissident members of the AMA should be encouraged to consult with local area members of the Committee over policy matters which they did not agree with. Welch countered with the thought that such AMA members had complained that when they had done just that their feelings had been ignored, and that the Committee constituted an unresponsive dictatorship. Without a consequent meeting of the minds, the parting of the two was on an acrimonious note.

Smith had announced in his November and December AMA newsletters that an official AMA magazine was to be launched early in 1947, and the initial issue of what was called "American Motorcycling" was mailed to all AMA members in February. Its Editor, hired by Smith, was a non-motorcycling journalist, E.W. Henn, and it was published in Chicago. Its advisory staff was made up of representatives of the two domestic factories. A technical staff consisted of two Harley-Davidson dealers, H.E. Jameson, and Reggie Pink, who had recently terminated his contracts with the British factories and was now allied with Milwaukee. The Indian factory member was Earl Robbins, with young competition rider and photographer T. Jacques duPont included.

As anticipated, the overall theme of the publication stressed the dominant role of the AMA in motorcycling activities with the prime interest centered on the American factories and their products. The photographic content rarely showed more than a glimpse of foreign machines. The reports of competition events featured mainly those where domestic machines were the winners. The coverage of the growingly popular off-road events was almost non-existent as the heavyweight American models with their bulk and low ground clearance were not suited to these contests. In the earlier issues at least, only domestic products and accompanying accessories were admitted to the advertising pages, although this ban was soon relaxed when the need for additional advertising revenue became apparent. The overriding theme of the magazine was to showcase the domestic motorcycling scene and to picture the affairs of the AMA and actions of the Competition Committee as the ultimate of serene perfection.

The first post-war Daytona Classic was inaugurated on February 23, 1947. As usual, the main event was the 200 Miler, with an innovative 100

Miler for contestants of current AMA Amateur status to be run after the main event. As pre-race ceremonies, Billy Huber, a popular Harley-Davidson rider, was awarded the 1946 Rider of the Year trophy.

The race was started by the veteran Jim Davis, after Reggie Pink, Indian representative Earl Robbins, and Milwaukee engineer Hank Syvertsen had checked the entrants' motor for correct displacement and compression ratios.

With an incredibly large field of 172 entrants, no less than 160 lined up for the start of the 200. The riders were lined up in rows of 14, with ten second intervals between their starts. The ten second interval was added to each row's final finishing time, a hoped-for innovation for less chaotic results; a rather haphazard system, as final evaluation proved.

The very tough course offered its usual challenge to even the most seasoned riders, but the indefatigable Ed Kretz, in his usual charging style, blasted into an initial lead and led the pack until sidelined with a blown engine in his racing Scout. The rate of attrition was especially severe, with only 76 riders still in contention by the 36th lap. The usual retirements were spills, blown engines, sand in the carburetors, failed brakes, broken control cables, flat tires, and in some cases, the total exhaustion of the rider.

By the 185th mile, only 40 machines remained in the running. Johnny Spiegelhoff of Milwaukee, the one time Harley star who was a pre-war defector to Indian, was a consistent but conservative front runner to the end, saving his engine for the final laps. This was the same pre-war "big base" machine that had just won him a victory at Langhorne, PA. The timers had little difficulty in checking his progress, as he remained close to the lead throughout the race. This happily avoided the usual disputes seen in many of the Nationals, with split prize money and negotiated wins. Other riders in either place or field positions were less than happy, however, and there were many challenges to the decisions of the lap scorers. Spiegelhoff's time was 2 hours, 35 minutes, 33 seconds for an average of 77.14 mph. This was somewhat slower than Billy Mathews' 78.08 mph ride in the 1941 contest. Second place went to Ted Edwards of Atlanta, also Indian mounted, who came in 90 seconds behind the winner. Third place went to Al Quattrocchi of Providence, Rhode Island, on a Harley WR, who would have been a formidable contender had he not fallen and lost valuable time in remounting.

The 100 mile Amateur Race held the next day

was a ragged affair, with only 11 riders finishing the 32 laps. The winner was Jack Horn of Rosemead, California, on an Indian Scout with an average speed of 73.4 mph. Bill Huguley of Miami, Florida, also Scout mounted, was second; with Al Wilcox of Trenton, New Jersey, third, on a Harley WR.

The 200 was marred by two fatalities. Porter Clack, Harley mounted, went down and was run over by three following riders in the 12th lap. Another death of an unnamed rider occurred in the 34th lap.

An unheralded sixth place finisher in the 100 Miler was Scout mounted T. Jacques duPont, a son of E. Paul. He was a perennial entrant at Daytona for several seasons, and in later years entered several Isle of Man TT's on a Matchless.

Other activities included a Saturday night dance at the Pavilion on the Daytona pier. Featured was a Popular Lady Contest which was won by Bernice Miles of Peoria, Illinois, who was crowned National Motorcycle Queen.

Much of the visiting motorcyclists' activities were centered on continual parading through the streets of downtown Daytona, interfering with normal traffic, with numerous traffic tickets being issued for speeding and open exhaust pipes. A number were also arrested for drunk driving and rowdy behavior, all of which elicited editorial attention from the local news.

E.C. Smith's writeup in the "American Motorcyclist", as expected, was a sugar-coated tribute to the event, lauding both the entrants and the officials involved, with no mention of the fatalities or the controversial conduct of some of the visitors. It was also pointed out that this was the first time the report of a big National was featured in a national magazine, this being in Colliers, entitled "Handle Bar Derby."

In the meantime, personnel changes were under way at "The Motorcyclist". Editor Bill Smith had departed in November 1946, for more lucrative endeavors, and a present contributor, Harry Steele, was installed in his place.

After a few issues, Steele resigned, expressing the intention of starting a new trade magazine. He was followed by Paul Brokaw, a one time aviator, mechanic, journalist, and practical engineer who, before the war, had been both a Harley-Davidson and Indian dealer in quick succession: an action which did not endear him to either faction. As a forthright and outspoken individual, he had become a figure of controversy when he advocated the free marketing of machines, along with the parallel retailing of foreign machines in categories not presently covered by the domestic factories. In his new position he was assisted by his wife, Neda, who was a professional journalist and who subsequently wrote many of the reports that appeared in the magazine.

Brokaw's earliest effort was his report on the recent Daytona 200, a first-hand account of the proceedings as he spent over a week in the Florida city.

In his article in "The Motorcyclist" he complimented the extensive promotional work performed by William France, who was also a stock car impresario, who managed the event with the help of Frank Harvey and Jim Roberts, but tempered with candid observations.

He noted that no grandstands were provided, the landward side of the course being simply blocked off by a wire fence which was patrolled by walking marshals. The paid access gates were at the turns, where about 24,000 spectators were charged $3.00 admission. Several thousand additional non-paying onlookers lined the poorly surfaced asphalt road that made up the backstretch. Only primitive sanitary facilities were provided, these being temporary wooden privies set up over open pits.

Effective crowd control was lacking, spectators being able to cross the course at will: a hazard both to themselves and the contestants. There was also uncontrolled public access to the pit areas, which interfered with the rider's stops for quick adjustments and refueling.

A most serious deficiency was the lack of emergency medical facilities, there being only one physician, two assistants, and one ambulance engaged to care for injured riders. This could and did cause a time lapse of at least 30 minutes before a downed rider could be cared for.

There was also a shortage of course marshals, and numerous near- accidents were noted when warning flags were not displayed for the benefit of downed riders. On several occasions the ambulance was seen weaving its way to its destination, with oncoming riders treating the vehicle as part of the race!

Brokaw also noted what he considered a lack of adequate prize money. Only 28 winners and placers received minimal awards. In addition, dozens of machines were destroyed, and there were numerous painful, if relatively minor, injuries. It was his conclusion that the conduct of the whole affair was a brutal exploitation of the contestants.

Some European journalists later expressed amazement at the overall haphazard conduct of the affair, and the general cowboy atmosphere that pervaded it.

THE POST WAR DECADE 1945-1955

Ed Kretz's post WWII Triumph competition team, following his assuming a Triumph dealership in 1949. (From l.) Ed Kretz, Fred Ford, Eddie Jr., Charles White, and Jack Horn.
Arnold Halstead

Some subsequent articles in the general press called attention to the fact that the large crowds now attracted to motor sporting and athletic events were due to the pentup demand for public entertainment that had been thwarted by a decade of economic depression together with the later restrictions of the war years.

As a stimulating spectator spectacular, the usual bevy of groupies noted as attending the immediate pre-war motorcycle contests were seen in greater numbers at the Big Nationals, especially Daytona. Some of the contestants subsequently reported that the possibilities of erotic entertainment were now almost unlimited. Added to this were tales of participation by certain unnamed members of the industry itself.

The AMA Competition Committee held a meeting for the purpose of organizing the balance of the season's events. Those factory and dealer personnel attending included Jim Davis, Marion Diedricks, Dudley Perkins, Stewart Champlin, Bruce Walters, William J. Harley, Walter C. Davidson, Jr., Oscar Lenz, E.C. Shillingford, Reggie Pink, Earle Robbins, A.J. West, Erle Armstrong, Fritzie Baer, with Ted Edwards who was admitted as a token rider representative. They met in closed session to select dates and venues for

coming National Championship events in the 200, 100, 50, 25, 15, 10 and 5 mile contests. As usual, E.C. Smith chaired the meeting.

Following this two day gathering, the city and county officials of Daytona area hosted a banquet for the Committee at the Sheraton Plaza Hotel. Mindful of the outside money brought into the Dade County area, the various officials lauded the entertainment value of the races, and complimented the management of the affair. E.C. Smith, in a self congratulatory speech, praised the public support of the now growing interest in motorcycle sport, and described the AMA as "a rider controlled organization and a true representation of American Democracy"!!!

The second most prominent sporting event that spring was the initial running of the first Greenhorn Enduro. Sixty-three contestants were flagged off at 6:00 a.m. on May 1, at Johnson Motors headquarters in Pasadena, at one minute intervals. The route varied from pavement to backwoods dirt roads, sand, brush country, and assorted roughery. An average speed of 24 mph had to be maintained for the 250 mile route, the riders being observed at various checkpoints. Mandatory equipment included speedometers, stop watches, maps and route cards. By Saturday night, those riders fortunate enough to survive the initial part of the course arrived at the peak of the 6,000 foot Greenhorn Mountain east of Bakersfield. The following morning the pack was flagged off for the return trip. An unlikely winner was Max Bubeck on a stripped Indian Four. His performance was no doubt aided by the fitting of Vard hydraulic forks and rubber mounted Flanders handlebars. Cliff Onan was second on a stripped Harley FLH. Most of the entrants, however, favored British machines, due to their lighter weight and greater ground clearance.

The event was sponsored by various dealers and cooperating AMA clubs, with Frank Cooper heading the organizers. The Greenhorn was the forerunner of a number of similar events that were becoming fixtures on the cross-country contest scene.

The summer of 1947 saw the launching of another motorcycle magazine by sixty-one year old R.W. "Pop" Cassell. Born in England, he had enjoyed a varied career, starting with menial employment, becoming involved in pioneer motorcycling, and ultimately engaging in sales promotion of industrial products, coming to the States just before World War II. He had been employed as an engineer in a defense plant, and after the War was an industrial journalist. Noting the presence of only one motorcycle magazine, he had planned the inauguration of his own in the fall of 1946, apparently unaware of E.C. Smith's planned founding of an official AMA publication.

Cassell later told the author that he had planned the magazine as a Chicago-based effort to give broader coverage to midwestern and eastern affairs, though admitting the importance of the Los Angeles based "Motorcyclist" in the area of the country's greatest motorcycling activity. At any rate, he had intended to orient its theme to the reporting of dealer activities and new news items and personnel doings within the industry, along with sports coverage. Incidental to the launching and first printing of what he named "Buzz-zz Motor Cycle News", Cassell arranged a conference with E.C. Smith in Columbus in the hopes of soliciting his cooperation in obtaining future announcements of upcoming AMA events.

Cassell recalled that he met with a decidedly cool reception from Smith, who apparently sensed him as a less-than-welcome competitor. At any rate, Smith informed Cassell that the AMA would not deviate from the long-standing policy of managing the news of the sport and industry. No derogatory editorialization or criticism of AMA or Competition Committee policies would be permitted, and all technical material regarding the domestic manufacturers' products must be subject to prior review by

the factory in question before being printed. Cassell at once took issue with these statements, declaring that freedom of the press was a prime constitutional right and cited the strong position of the British trade press in acting as a watchdog for the motorcycle industry in the United Kingdom. Smith countered that the near redundant condition of the American industry between the Wars required protection of its public image, and that the factories, with the help of the AMA, were on record as doing just that. Smith further remarked that unless Cassell was willing to cooperate in the management of trade news, access to AMA programs and reporting would only be available for his use after it had appeared previously as a public announcement in the official AMA publications.

With this somewhat acrimonious debate, Cassell then saw that his only role as a journalist would be that of both monitor and critic of both the AMA and the motorcycle industry.

Following the end of hostilities, the U.S. government awarded the British with favored trade agreements to encourage their U.S. exports in order to give them hard currency with which to purchase sorely needed domestically produced foodstuffs and other necessities for their post-war recovery. This policy aroused no little resentment within the U.S. industrial community, as the British already had raised formidable tariff barriers against American imports to further aid their own economic recovery and encourage their own industry.

A further handicap to domestic industry was the inauguration of the Marshall Plan. This policy, enacted by Congress, included both monetary loans and priority preference of certain raw materials to European countries to speed their post-war recovery and to fill an economic vacuum in the hopes that such could forestall the spread of Communism. This policy at once imposed production difficulties upon all manufacturers, including the domestic motorcycle industry.

At any rate, a side effect of the tariff concessions was the post-war importation of British automobiles, which somewhat eased the shortage of domestic cars, whose makers were still in the process of converting to civilian production after being totally preoccupied with war production.

British cars were something of a novelty, as only a few luxury models, mostly Rolls-Royce, had been imported between the wars. To capitalize on the burgeoning U.S. prosperity, importers sought to encourage a hobbyists' market by specializing in sports type vehicles, such as the MG Midget, the Jowett Javelin, M-Type Jaguars, and subsequently the Austin Sprites and Healeys. The

THE POST WAR DECADE 1945-1955

Ed Kretz riding his trusty Indian Scout at a field meet.
Ed Kretz

American drivers could now indulge in high performance cars that had taught suspension, superior cornering, and distinctive styling that offered fun driving in vehicles that could actually be steered rather than aimed!

Domestic automotive journalism had languished during the Depression, but now that motoring had entered the recreational stage and driving could in some aspects be classed as a fun activity, a host of new publications dealing with automotive matters became available.

Some of these were now offered by a young automotive technician and journalist, Robert B. Petersen, who successfully launched "Motor Trend" and "Hot Rod" to cater to the new hobby of altering domestic models, and "Kustom Kar", a further extension of the latter. Some magazines, such as "Popular Mechanics" featured road tests and the personal critiques of Tom McCahill, a former race driver, whose cowboy type of reporting and exaggerated journalistic hyperbole entertained domestic car buffs.

It was at this point that Bob Steele launched his announced entry into the motorcycle journalistic field with a magazine called "Cycle". His intended format was to emphasize the technical aspects of the subject, with articles on both mechanics as well as road tests. Being lightly financed, he ran into difficulties after a few issues, and the upshot of the matter was that Petersen decided to buy Steele's rights and add "Cycle" to his list of automotive publications. He followed both Steele's and the British format as to content, tending to minimize competition

reporting and to ignore the now acrimonious controversy concerning AMA policy. Petersen edited the first few issues himself, and then turned the job over to one Bob Greene, an experienced rider, mechanic, and journalist.

The summer of 1947 saw the ultimate official separation of the AMA with the Canadians. As noted, the Competition Committee had already decided to sever their north-of-the-border connection at the end of the War, but E.C. Smith had given no official notice of the fact other than to ignore the written request of Canadian riders for U.S. AMA competition cards under the pre-war agreement. In the meantime, representatives of most of the formally organized Canadian clubs had met on several occasions during the winter of 1946-1947, to officially organize the Canadian Motorcycle Association. Prime movers in this were C. Gerald Barker and Ted Buck, both members of the British Motorcycle Club in Toronto, and who, for more than a decade, had been tireless advocates of a national Canadian organization.

In May 1947, Barker contacted Smith regarding the latter's withholding competition cards from Canadian riders in the abrogation of the pre-war reciprocity agreement which, to his understanding, was still in place. Before replying, Smith held an emergency meeting with some of the members of the Committee, and then informed Barker that the Committee was of the opinion that competition reciprocity between the two countries should be terminated.

Barker at once objected, stating that with the

THE POST WAR DECADE 1945-1955

Kretz takes a fall at the 1948 Laconia Races. His machine is somewhere to the left of the camera. *Wally Huntington*

post-war resurgence of motorcycling interest, such would not be in the best interests of all concerned. He then suggested that a meeting between himself, Smith and representatives of both meet and attempt to arrive at some sort of a compromise.

Smith agreed that a formal meeting should be called to settle the matter, and in June, Barker, Buck and two members of Ontario clubs met in Chicago at the Blackstone Hotel with Smith, Jules Horky, Arthur and Walter Davidson, and two other members of the Competition Committee.

Barker presented his case, first noting that all were aware of the differences of opinion regarding the AMA Class C concept and the preference of Canadian riders for the ACU and FICM systems. He then suggested that a two-stage set of rules be inaugurated so that the adherents of both sides could compete in separate categories under their respective rulings. He also revealed that the two more prominent members of the British Motorcycle Dealers Association, Alfred Rich Child and William E. Johnson, had been in contact with him over the problem of the bitter fratricidal warfare currently being suffered between the advocates of domestic and foreign imports. He stated that both had ventured the suggestion that such a compromise might be the answer to what was becoming an unhealthy division within the industry.

Arthur Davidson at once objected to this proposal, stating that even with growing numbers of foreign imports, the AMA was not strong enough to survive a fragmentation of its membership. He

further stated that the American manufacturers who had supported organized motorcycling through the lean years would not be amenable to relinquishing their control over domestic motorcycling affairs to what was considered foreign interlopers. He also emphasized that he did not favor Canadian Harley-Davidson owners participating in club activities where a majority of the members favored foreign machines.

His remarks were seconded by Walter Davidson, Jr., who stated that many members of the American industry considered it unpatriotic to favor foreign machines. In a rare gesture of extending the olive branch to Springfield, he hoped that Indian owners would see fit to give unqualified support to Milwaukee in the matter of retaining domestic supremacy in regulating the industry.

Barker and Buck countered with the statement that in the face of the superior marketing trends favoring British machines the AMA's stand on letting the American industry dominate motorcycling affairs was undemocratic, and that the Class C rulings tended to stifle technical development, whereas the ACU and FICM mandates had been responsible for the between-the-wars progress in the production of high performance engines.

Some of the Indian representatives on the Committee suggested that perhaps some further study of a possible compromise might well be in order, but when the matter came to a vote the Harley-Davidson majority, supported by Smith, made the decision to cancel the former reciprocity agreement with the Canadians.

In relating the details of this meeting to the author in later years, both Barker and Horky stated that they had each hoped that some sort of compromise could be worked out, if only to ease the current bitter feelings that existed both in the States as well as across the border.

A later report on the meeting appearing in "American Motorcycling" was limited to a terse statement that Canadian competition riders could no longer compete in American events, and the minutes of the meeting were never included in the AMA archives.

To further add fuel to the fire, Milwaukee' factory travelers were instructed to urge the more prominent Harley-Davidson dealers in Canada to sponsor clubs intended for the exclusive membership of their customers, in effect creating an AMA presence in Canada of one brand of machines. Most of these clubs continued the pre-war practice of scheduling events such as rallies, tours, field meets and sporting gatherings on the same dates of CMA events. The resultant ill feeling between the

THE POST WAR DECADE 1945-1955

Lincoln Park Speedway, 1948. This was Pete Colman's last year of professional Class A competition. Colman, Number 1, is challenged by Byrd McKinney.
Lincoln Park Speedway Association

two groups lasted for decades afterwards, and the whole affair represented a less than pleasant episode in motorcycling history on the North American Continent.

A more positive act of the Competition Committee at a meeting in July was to finalize negotiations with an insurance company to extend health and accident insurance to AMA competition riders participating in AMA sanctioned events. It offered single day or weekend policies with a $1,000 award for death or dismemberment; $3,000 for injuries requiring hospitalization; $100 for minor injuries; the entrants being charged $1 for registration. The principal premium payment was charged to the promoters, their compliance a condition of being granted an official AMA sanction. A side effect of this program was that it tended to discourage rider participation in "outlaw" events, but, in any case, the program was greeted with wholehearted rider approval.

The perceptibly growing numbers of the so-called "outlaw" motorcyclists attending AMA sanctioned events as well as the Gypsy Tours were ultimately subjected to public scrutiny on July 4, 1947, at Hollister, California, a small agricultural community in the Salinas Valley south of San Francisco. An AMA sanctioned race meet at a newly opened half mile track also included a Gypsy Tour and rally, which was attended by several thousand riders from the central California area.

A large group of these free-swinging riders in

attendance antagonized the club members by their rowdy behavior, and a number of fights between the two factions broke out. The "outlaws" proceeded to terrorize the town, riding their machines on the sidewalks, frightening the townspeople, and even riding into the bars and other ground level buildings. When the rioting overcame the abilities of local police, law enforcement personnel from other areas, including highway patrol officers, were called in to assist. It took nearly twenty-four hours to quell the disturbance, with numerous participants being arrested for drunkenness, disturbing the peace, indecent exposure; many for relieving themselves on the sidewalks and against buildings.

The national press and radio news media had a field day in reporting the incident, the most prominent exposure being extensive coverage in Life Magazine, with the now-classic photo of an inebriated rider of a stripped Harley-Davidson hoisting a bottle of beer. In spite of the lurid descriptions of the episode being played up by the news media, many of those present later stated that the intensity of the affair did, in no sense, live up to the sensational reports that were released to the public.

Of course the affair was a source of consternation to the entire industry, including both the distributors and dealers handling British machines. Harley-Davidson's and Indian's top management were particularly incensed, as the "outlaw" element favored their machines and the

THE POST WAR DECADE 1945-1955

One of Indian's star riders, Johnny Speigelhoff, being congratulated for his 1949 win at Langhorne.
Bob Stevens

perpetuate the roughneck image of motorcycling in the public mind, in spite of the fact that increased sales of British machines were attracting a more restrained group of enthusiasts. That summer, veteran domestic factory personnel, dealers and enthusiasts were saddened by the death of Verne Guthrie from a massive heart attack. Guthrie had been a participant in both the automobile and motorcycle industries since their earliest days. While he had severed his connection with the latter in the mid-1920's, he had always kept in touch with its ongoing affairs during his later role as both a transportation historian and freelance journalist. As a gregarious and charismatic individual, he had a host of friends within both industries, and many oldtimers had referred to him as "Milwaukee's Frank Weschler". With Guthrie's encyclopedia knowledge of the past events of the industry, the author has ever been grateful to his memory for both his cooperation in efforts to record domestic motorcycle history, as well as his friendship.[*3]

whole episode ran counter to their ongoing campaign, begun in the 1930's, to upgrade the public image of motorcycling.

E.C. Smith wrote an editorial in "American Motorcycling" stressing the fact that only a very small percentage of motorcyclists were involved in such activities, and suggesting that the media had tarred the entire sport and industry with the same brush.

Paul Brokaw pursued a smaller course in "The Motorcyclist", sending copies to the leading newspapers of the country who had printed sensationalized accounts of the matter, in an attempt to persuade them to take a more moderate view of the matter. In siding with Smith, Brokaw, in his gesture of support to the industry, was in a somewhat incongruous position. He had lately been printing a column, "We Lead With Our Chin", critical of the AMA's dictatorial management and calling for more rider participation.

At any rate, the Hollister incident served to

It was during these immediate post-war years that the author was fortunate in having two lengthy interviews with James Wright, who visited the West Coast during the summers of 1946 and 1947, in connection with trade fairs relating to industrial products and machine tooling. Wright elaborated on his earlier experiences within the industry, as well as his sensitive contacts with Harley-Davidson's top management in the ongoing secret meetings involving price and policy fixing.

While during the immediate post-war years Harley-Davidson's top management continued to mandate that their dealers stock merchandise obtained only through factory sources, paradoxically they were allowed to sell Cushman scooters. The speculation regarding this phenomenon was that in some way Walter Davidson, Jr.'s marriage into the Briggs family, who then owned a sizable block of Cushman shares, had something to do with the matter. However, in the spring of 1947, the factory ordered their franchised dealers to

248

Down the beach at Daytona.
Don Emde Collection

cease selling Cushmans. The order went so far as to demand a notarized statement from each dealer attesting to the cancellation of their sales agreements with Cushman as a condition of renewing their franchises with Harley-Davidson.

The story went that some Cushman executives who had visited the Juneau Avenue factory had been heard to compare it unfavorably with the former's new and enlarged facility at Lincoln, Nebraska, which, of course, antagonized the Davidsons. Whatever the truth of the matter, there was, as will be seen, a subsequent reason for Milwaukee to terminate their dealerships as an outlet for Cushman products.

Substantial numbers of domestic motorcycle enthusiasts with superficial knowledge of the post-war production problems facing the factories were now questioning the lack of updated models from both Milwaukee and Springfield. There was emphasis on the need for middleweight models to compete with the British imports, particularly from those who subscribed to brand name loyalty.

Both Indian dealers and enthusiasts were particularly concerned with the indeterminate situation at Springfield, with the sudden changes in Company ownership, which was heightened by the sporadic production of Chiefs, there being more orders than could be filled. Ralph B. Rogers at length responded by announcing that a new line of machines was in the planning stage that would cover the light and middleweight market, although technical details and production dates were still lacking. But to supply Indian dealers with the much-needed increase in the numbers of machines available for sale, Rogers also announced that he had formed a new subsidiary, the Indian Sales Company, which would shortly supply some leading makes of British machines that would be available to all franchised Indian dealers.

This news was received with mixed emotions by the dealers and enthusiasts. Not a few of these who were loyal to Indian products had already agreed with the sentiments in Milwaukee, as well as Harley dealers and enthusiasts, that the domestic market should be protected from foreign competition. Sentiments of patriotism were augmented by the thought that with the privations and difficulties of the domestic factories in surviving the Depression, they now deserved a controlling interest in the prospering post-war market. In addition, there was much opinion within the industry that Roger's move was one of desperation to overcome whatever difficulties he was having in finalizing the production of a new line of machines.

Harley-Davidson's stand in the matter of post-war designs was best illustrated from reports of a conversation between Arthur Davidson and Maldwyn Jones, who is recalled as a pioneer motorcyclist and one-time competition rider with Flying Merkel, Harley-Davidson, and later Excelsior. He was then an engineer with Wheeler-Schebler and had many years of intimate contacts within the domestic industry.

Jones subsequently told the author that Davidson had informed him that numbers of Milwaukee's dealers had suggested that an updated overhead valve version of the discontinued Model C 30.50 cubic inch single could well be the answer to offering competition to the middleweight British imports. The factory's answer to this was that post-war production difficulties and the critical situation in the acquisition of raw materials precluded the inauguration of any new models that could not be rationalized with the present big twin production. Then there was the emerging problem of introducing a new model and the facing of the inevitable teething difficulties involved in offering competition to the British machines that had already seen several decades of evolvement. Davidson also referred to the fact that the non-motorcycling shareholders of the Company were now in the majority, and that their prime interest was in collecting their usual dividends as opposed to the expenditure of internally generated profits on future product development.

This policy was opposed in the immediate post-war years by President William H. Davidson, who, in 1946, had hopefully hired a small group of professionally educated engineers and draftsmen for the express purpose of creating new designs to update the Company's product line. This group was headed by one John R. Bond, a graduate automotive engineer, whom we shall meet again. They were encouraged to design some modern prototypes, some of which showed promise. But when it came to assembling prototypes, the majority of shareholders refused to sanction the requisite funds. It was noted concurrently that they were also critical of what they considered the inordinately high salary scales allotted to the professionals, which amounted to $300 per month, and the following year, according to later reports by Bond, they were all discharged. The limited updating of the Company's pre-war product line then reverted to the veteran empirical mechanics who worked under William J. Harley, who reportedly acquiesced to the conservative policies of the shareholders.

Arthur Davidson subsequently defended these ongoing regressive policies in noting the consternation on the part of many Indian dealers and

THE POST WAR DECADE 1945-1955

Max Bubeck with the 80" "Chout" built by Frank Chase and Bubeck, with cams engineered by "Pop" Schunk. As a "laker" it made a solo run with Bubeck aboard at 135.58 mph. It featured a much modified Chief engine in a 101 Scout frame and Vard forks.
Max Bubeck

enthusiasts regarding President Rogers' announced intention of a revised product line and the threatened suspension of future Chief production. To the dealers it sounded a warning that the domestic factories should not jeopardize their market for the traditional types of machines by venturing into uncharted waters.

This point may have been well taken, as many Indian dealers were indeed apprehensive concerning the future of the production of the long-standing classic models, not to mention that of many enthusiasts. In fact, when it was learned that the Sport Scout was not to be included in the post-war

line, a group of dealers and private owners, headed by the indomitable Sam Pierce, actually journeyed to Springfield and angrily invaded a Board of Directors meeting to protest this decision. Following a stormy session in which Rogers defended his position of catering to what he hoped was an expanded motorcycle market, he hired a group of security guards to keep unauthorized visitors off the factory premises.

Following this episode, and in the face of a number of dealers dropping their franchises, substantial numbers of which changed their allegiance to Milwaukee, Rogers not only reaffirmed the decision to continue Chief production, but also embarked on a personal crusade to bolster the confidence of Indian's remaining dealerships. In an attempt to raise their morale, he traveled the country with a program of seminars presented at a series of previously scheduled meetings in which he presented updated sales and marketing techniques, a subject in which he was well versed. It was to Rogers' credit that he recognized the need for innovations in retail motorcycle marketing, which included the cleaning up and refurbishing of dealers' premises, a problem which had long plagued the domestic industry. However important the increase in professionalism was clearly needed to complement the now-enhanced public interest in motorcycling, not all the dealers contacted were in accord with this campaign. Many veterans disputed the necessity of the added expense of expansion, and some of the more rough-hewn among them could not relate to the suave and sophisticated Rogers, who represented a philosophy with which they were unfamiliar.

At any rate, Rogers' ongoing personal contacts with his dealership now reinforced his decision to at least continue Chief production, noting that the American market by tradition had always supported the big twin as the top-of-the-line sales leaders.

On the competition side, Harley-Davidson's prestige on the West Coast circuit was enhanced by Sam Arena's performance on Tom Sifton's reworked WR motors, winning most of the local races. Arena's triumphs were confined to the West, however, as he did not choose to undertake the extensive travel necessary to compete in the big Nationals.

The Jack Pine fixture revived in 1946, the surprise winner being Claude Goulding riding a 350 cc B31 BSA. This event was usually thought of as a Harley-Davidson showcase, but in any event was a very severe test of both rider and machine.

Through the intense lobbying of both dealers and top competition riders, Ralph Rogers some-

THE POST WAR DECADE 1945-1955

Ernie Roccio takes the lead at the Box Springs TT course in 1949. This venue in the mountain foothills was an unusually tough course.
John Cameron

what reluctantly agreed to authorize the assembly of fifty "big base" racing Scouts, now designated as the Model 648. This number of manufactured machines complied with the long standing AMA ruling in order for a model to be eligible for competition. In common with the long established pre-war practice of flouting the basic Class C concept, the 648's were no more standard roadster models than were the WR's. This emphasis on special racing machines still saw a revived criticism from the ranks of pre-war competition riders who were still more or less adhering to the original Class C rules, and who felt that they were being hopelessly outclassed by the factories who were still demanding their brand name loyalty. At any rate, the new batch of Indians were assembled under the direction of James Hill, the Wigwam's noted racing specialist.

In the fall of 1947, Harley-Davidson's management held a special national meeting of their dealership in Milwaukee, where in effect they threw down the gauntlet to the foreign competitors. Billed as an affirmation of loyalty to the Milwaukee brand and a celebration of the need for patriotic support of American industry, the affair turned out to be less of a love feast than was described by E.C. Smith in a report published in "American Motorcycling" or in the Company distributed "Enthusiast".

Prominently displayed were the top-of-the-line EL and FL big twins, carried forward with revised valve gear as the "panhead" enclosure, along with the introduction of an updated lubrication system that included hydraulically activated valves, following contemporary automotive practice. The

venerable 45 cubic inch WL model was carried forward, as was the Model G Servi-car based upon it. To further rationalize production, the side valve UL and ULH models were not cataloged, although they were still available to special order.

In addition, an extensive line of accessories was prominently displayed, and it was also emphasized that all franchised dealers were expected to offer only such ancillary products that were supplied by the factory. It was also suggested that dealers who stocked merchandise from other sources would have their franchises reviewed in the usual yearly factory assessment for possible cancellation.

A surprise announcement was that the Harley Davidson factory had recently acquired a new manufacturing facility on Capitol Drive west of Juneau Avenue for the assembly of engines and transmissions. As a large single story building, it was well adapted to modern flow-line assembly, which would obviously offer enhanced efficiency over that not possible at the original plant. The assembled dealers were transported en masse to view the new facility.

Another surprise was the unveiling of a new model at the traditional banquet, a 125 cc lightweight two-stroke that was designated as the "125". The machine was a frank copy of the DKW that had been designed by Dr. Ing H. Schnurle and initially introduced in Germany before the war. Its engine was an advanced design that featured a flat topped piston and sophisticated flow metrics made possible by a patented system of porting. The power development was such that the machine showed much better performance than contempo-

rary designs, such as the long running models produced in England powered by Villiers.

The patent rights, among other industrial entities owned in Germany, had been appropriated by the Allied War Commission as part of the reparation penalties invoked following Germany's unconditional surrender, and as such, were now declared in the public domain. Other countries which built DKW copies of the 125 were Russia, which designated it as the Moska, and in England where it subsequently appeared as the BSA Bantam and the Royal Enfield R.E. It was later produced in Japan as the Yamaha YA-I.

Milwaukee's appropriation of this design was a shrewd method of penetrating the booming lightweight market without incurring the expense of extensive prototype development, which in any case, would not have been sanctioned by Harley-Davidson's ultra conservative Board of Directors.

This now explained why the factory had ordered their dealers to cancel their long running agreements with Cushman for retailing their scooters, which now cleared the way for the new model to hopefully supplant the latter at the low cost end of the market.

The 125 was an exact copy of the original, down to the rubber band front suspension, the only innovation being the fitting of larger sectioned 3.25" tires and the reversing of the foot gearshift and brake controls to conform to American practice.

While the appearance of the new model was greeted by some dealers as a needed step to broaden Milwaukee's market penetration, there were a few who considered that its OPA sanctioned $375 price tag was more than double that of the lower echelon Cushman's it was to replace. Other dealers, while approving of penetration of the lightweight market, at once noted that the factory was still ignoring the middleweight market now covered by the British imports that was capturing the most active segment of the market.

In a rather tense question and answer session following speeches dealing with the matter by Sales Manager Arthur Davidson and his assistant, Walter Davidson, Jr., a somewhat surprising response to the above question was forthcoming. In his opening address, Walter, Jr. following his usual recitation of the Company's past historic role in the industry, made Milwaukee's marketing position clear. It was stated that after manufacturing motorcycles for over forty years, the factory knew what types of machines were best suited to the American rider, that the main product line followed this schedule, and it was now up to the dealers to sell them! Following this statement, it was reported

that a substantial number of those present walked out of the meeting.

A rather anachronistic occurrence at the close of the conference was the presentation by E.C. Smith of a handsome trophy to Vice President Arthur Davidson. Its purpose, stated Smith, was to honor the recipient as one of the Company founders, together with his many contributions to the industry and his many years of loyal support of the AMA, which Smith somewhat optimistically described as currently having over 50,000 members. The presentation was viewed by some as being contentious, as Smith's financial connection with the Company over the years in his role in promoting their sales was well known.

In subsequent interviews with the author regarding the context of this meeting, a number of prominent dealers were of the opinion that the Company was short-sighted in ignoring the middleweight market, even in the face of current production difficulties connected with the shortage of materials. While many were not at all in sympathy with Indian's Ralph Rogers' recent introduction of British machines into the Wigwam's network, they had hoped for the possibility of an updated single from Milwaukee to compete in this market.

Harley-Davidson's emphasis on heavyweight models was not at all illogical, however, as they had been currently able to sell all the EL's and FL's that they could produce, and many dealers were now carrying a backlog of orders from enthusiasts. In addition, Indian's stepped-up production of Chiefs was being well received by its dealerships, as the traditional market for big twins was still strong, both from the wartime hiatus in the market the growing enthusiasm for club activities, as well as the new popularity of touring.

In the meantime, Indian's production of Chiefs had been advanced to 6,500 units in 1947, with a three model line based upon it designated as the Sportsman, Clubman and Roadmaster variants, according to equipment and detail finish. In addition, and for the anticipated middleweight Torque model production, Rogers announced the recent purchase of the Hendeeville plant built under the direction of Oscar Hedstrom in 1913. In 1920, this plant had been sold to other interests, and had been acquired in 1920 by American Rolls-Royce for the production of an Americanized version of this British classic. During the war it was subsequently utilized by defense contractors and when the Depression had terminated the luxury car market in 1931, it was taken over by the Hauk Wheel Company.

The cavernous and now run down State Street

THE POST WAR DECADE 1945-1955

Two familiar sights at motorcycle races in the late-1940's were the Motor Maids of America and young Teddy Edwards riding the little home made mini-bike built by his dad, Ted Edwards.
Don Emde Collection

plan was sold. When the news came out a large number of Indian enthusiasts were on hand when the storage area was cleaned out and many old racing machines, as well as some weird and wonderful prototype models, were saved for posterity.

On the competition side, Milwaukee stepped up production of their WR models, and urged their dealers to reactivate available pre-war WLDR machines for the benefit of novice riders to enter competition. The strategy was to enable Milwaukee iron to fill as much of the card as possible at race meets in order to help "blanket off" the growing number of British machines.

Jimmy Hill managed to assemble fifty big base Scouts in time for the 1948 competition season, but there were many disappointed enthusiasts as the demand far exceeded the supply. Some Indian contestants were arousing the ire of both their Milwaukee as well as British counterparts with the revival of the "H-D strokers". The lower bearing assemblies of the stock WL 45's were somewhat more rugged than those usually fitted to the standard Sport Scouts. Ingenious mechanics were again substituting these WL units, making a rather potent engine with a longer stroke, raising the displacement to 52 cubic inches, a flagrant violation of Class C rules. The Competition Committee now issued a special warning to referees and scrutineers to be on the watch for this practice.

Milwaukee's Racing Department was now in contention with ace tuner Tom Sifton. Working in his well equipped shop in San Jose, California, Sifton's much modified WR engines were making a name for themselves on the Western circuits, with a new talented rider, the diminutive Larry Hedrick. The factory was accusing Sifton of making a name for himself at their expense, with his self promotion of "Sifton Engines". A point of argumentation was that Sifton refused to share his tuning secrets with the factory. One of Sifton's favorite stories was that one of his engines was somehow removed from his van adjacent to the pits at a race meet, and found its way in a suitcase to the Harley-Davidson factory. Incidental to this "love-hate" relationship with Milwaukee's top management, Sifton, at various times, was either welcomed or snubbed, depending on the current state of competition. It was noted that on occasion Harley-Davidson enthusiasts and factory personnel actually rooted for Sifton's competitors in race meets, whether from Springfield or even Great Britain!!

The 1948 Daytona 200 held in March saw Johnny Butterfield, a popular midwest Harley rider awarded the Most Popular Rider trophy, the balloting for which had been announced the previous

July. The race was won by Floyd Emde, a one-time both Harley and Indian dealer, on a "big base" Scout and sponsored by San Diego Indian dealer Guy Urquhardt. The machine was tuned by shop foreman Noel McIntyre, a legendary west coast tuner. Emde kept well in the lead throughout the race, closely pursued by Canadian Billy Mathews on a Norton International. The race was actually decided in a pit stop, where Mathews' crew inadvertently spilled gasoline all over the machine, losing two minutes in the process. Emde's thirty-six second stop put him well in the lead, with Mathews ultimately a few seconds behind to come in second.

With the prohibition of honoring Canadian entrants competition licenses formerly in place, Mathews, who had shortly returned from England and a season of speedway racing before Daytona, circumvented the ruling by entering into a fictitious corporate partnership with Jerry Man who had a Norton dealership in Buffalo, New York. The Competition Committee, who at the time of Mathews' entrance were in doubt as to just how he had obtained an AMA competition card, decided to let the matter stand, noting his outstanding performance, along with the fact that amateur Don Evans had also won the concurrent 100 Miler on a similar machine.

It was subsequently learned that several Canadian riders had been following the same practice with the help of American collaborators, as well as obtaining AMA competition cards by registering under false names and fictitious addresses.

While Smith's report of the Daytona races in "American Motorcycling" was, as usual, highly laudatory, Paul Brokaw's comments in "The Motorcyclist" and R.W. Cassell's in "Motorcycle News" were more candid. Both commented on promoter Bill France's moving of the course somewhat south of its original site to better connect with the local access roads as an improvement. They took issue with the ongoing lack of proper sanitary facilities, the ineffectual crowd control, and above all, the confusion and controversies over the results due to deficiencies in the scoring system.

In a rebuttal to these comments in a subsequent issue of "American Motorcycling", Smith published the names of the current Competition Committee, citing their reputations as long supporters of the best interests of the AMA, with the disclaimer that in spite of certain adverse comments in other trade press publications concerning the Committee being controlled by the factories, such was not the case. Many of those concerned at once branded this statement as patently absurd, as the roster contained the names of the usual majority

The Post War Decade 1945-1955

Top two in 1949 Daytona 200. Billy Mathews (#98) finished 2nd to Dick Klamfoth, both on Manx Nortons. Tex Luse, also Norton-mounted, made it a 1-2-3 sweep for Nortons that year. Winner's speed: 86.42 mph.
Bill Bagnall

of factory employees and dealers.

In spite of the lack of wins in the two post-war Daytonas, Milwaukee enjoyed a triumph at Springfield, Illinois, that fall with veteran rider Jimmy Chann taking the number one plate as the year's National Champion. It was alleged that Chann's machine was powered by the wayward Sifton engine.

In the fall of 1948, more fuel was added to the fires of international rivalry when Gilbert Smith, Managing Director of Norton Motors, issued a blanket challenge to any American machine to compete in a European Style road race at a venue of the American's choosing. E.C. Smith at first ignored the challenge but, at length, answered a third cablegram by stating that American Class C "stockers", as he put it, were not about to enter a contest in competition with foreign factory prepared "specials". Gilbert Smith then replied that the present highly tuned factory WR's and big base Scouts could scarcely be classed as road going machines, which was obvious. Other communications in the matter were ignored by both Smith and the Competition Committee.

When news of the matter became known, some Yankee tuners declared that both the WR and racing Scouts were as fast as the Nortons, citing some recent speed trials held on the dry lakes in California.

On the journalistic side, Petersen Publication's "Cycle" magazine continued to grow through the general high quality of its reporting of selected competition events, along with Editor Bob Greene's emphasis on technical reports of new models of machines, by necessity mostly British, and his commendable objectivity. As far as the

ongoing controversy concerning AMA affairs, Greene assumed a somewhat neutral approach, although he was seen to admonish the industry that it should move with the times and heed the nature of consumer opinion.

The editorial strength of "The Motorcyclist" as produced by Arthur Welch's Western Journal Publishing Company was enhanced with the association of the latter's son-in-law, Charles D. Baskerville, who had married Welch's daughter Lenore just before the war. After his war-time service in the Merchant Marine, Baskerville, for a time, had been employed in the sales department of a dairy products concern, Adohr Farms, Incorporated. Welch, who was now approaching seventy years of age, rightly felt the need for a relief of some of the responsibilities of producing a diverse group of publications, which Baskerville was able to assume. Paul Brokaw continued as Editor, still campaigning for a more democratically oriented AMA.

R.W. Cassell's "Motorcycle News", through objective reporting, continued to gain strength, especially in the midwest, and followed a similar but somewhat less adamant policy toward the AMA.

All three magazines enjoyed substantial advertising support from the British importers as well as the trade accessory suppliers for these as well as domestic makes. Harley-Davidson and Indian at this point sustained advertising contracts with the AMA sponsored "American Motorcycling" in apparent support of its ongoing policy of closely managing the news of both the industry and the AMA Competition Committee, and thus made a pointed effort to ignore the other publications that subscribed to journalistic objectivity.

THE POST WAR DECADE 1945-1955

A youthful Dick Klamfoth on his Manx Norton wins the 1949 Daytona 200. The 1941 winner, Canadian Billy Mathews, similarly mounted, was a close second.
Dick Klamfoth

A new publication which related to the transportation industry but didn't deal with motorcycling was to later exert a profound influence on the quality of the latter's productions. This was the founding of an automotive magazine, "Road and Track", by John R. Bond.

Bond, following his discharge from Harley-Davidson in late 1947 by William Davidson following the latter's failure to convince his majority shareholders of the need for forward product development, had engaged in both freelance engineering consultation as well as technical writing, in which he excelled. In noting the somewhat uneven quality of the contemporary automotive publications, he had for some time contemplated the launching of a magazine that could provide the technical information that heretofore had not been seen in that media. With limited capital at his disposal, he was able to gain the sponsorship of a large printing company in Glendale, California, Griffin and Patterson. The management of this firm had become both convinced of Bond's abilities as a

technical analyst as well as the need for a really professionally oriented publication. The project was then launched on a small scale, Bond's office being initially housed in a mobile home located at the rear of the main printing plant.

In the meantime, and possibly in the face of the ongoing attitudes of the current motorcycling publications, the Competition Committee reinstated the somewhat dormant $1,000 claiming rule regarding racing motorcycles. This in effect mandated that anyone could purchase the machine of any AMA competition rider following a contest for that sum. This rule was intended to indicate that as Class C competitors, the machines were in fact converted road going models. It also gave a somewhat oblique notice to the foreign competitors that any disguised and costly high tech machinery could be acquired for the same price as regular production machines.

The pre-war interest in solo speed trials on the dry lake beds in Southern California was revived in the late 1940's, some of which were observed by AMA officials, but more often than not, were conducted without official sanction or observation. The Indianapolis Indian dealer and distributor, Rollie Free, was also selling Vincent big twins under Ralph Rogers' newly instituted importation of British machines through his agreement with John Brockhouse. In what was categorized as both a courageous and foolhardy event, Free stripped to swimming trunks and tennis shoes, and lying prone over the fuel tank of a Vincent supersports Lightning model, racked up a new record for a two-way run over a three mile course of 149.6 mph, on the Bonneville Salt Flats in Utah, establishing a new high for the 61 cubic inch class.

John Chase, with the help of ace tuner "Pop" Schunk, prepared a 1929 Indian 101 Scout fitted with a much modified Chief engine and Vard type hydraulic forks for a competing attempt with a domestic machine. Selecting the 135 lb. enduro rider Max Bubeck as the rider, a two-way run of 134 mph was recorded. While the record was eluded, the event qualified Chase's machine as the world's fastest Indian.

The big Western National, the 100 Mile 1948 Championship TT race, was held near Riverside, California on July 5, which also featured a well supported AMA sponsored Gypsy Tour. Held over a very rough course, it was won by an unbeatable Ed Kretz, with placers being Harrison Reno, 1947 winner Ray Tanner, and Armando Magri. Both Kretz and Reno wore the skin off the palms of their hands, attesting to the severity of the course and the effects of the summer heat. The event was spon-

THE POST WAR DECADE 1945-1955

Alan Ladd was another celebrity who hitched up with Indian in the 1940's. *Don Emde Collection*

sored by the active Riverside Bombers Motorcycle Club, being directed by Harley-Davidson dealer Skip Fordyce with the assistance of Frank Cooper and Ernie Mann.

The event was marred by the antisocial activities of a number of outlaw riders who came in conflict with certain of the Tour and Club riders in a disturbance similar to that of the previous year at Hollister. The general news media once again had a field day at motorcycling's expense, although law enforcement officials and other observers later reported that the severity of the altercation had been greatly exaggerated. A report of the matter was not published in "American Motorcycling", but the editors of both "The Motorcyclist" and "The Motorcycle News" named the implications of rowdyism and sporting events as detrimental to the movement as a whole, and were further critical of noisy exhaust systems which were still a point in question with many non-motorcyclists.

The pre-war interest in hill climbing was not revived, the factories no longer officially supporting it. The former National races at Michigan, New York and California were now receiving limited participation by such private entrants as Windy Lindstrom and Sam Arena on Harleys, and Howard Mitzel with his stable of Indians. The last two riders were perennial supporters for the next two decades.

There was little, if any, participation by British enthusiasts in hill climbing, as the high revving 500 cc overhead valve singles did not possess the torque characteristics of the larger capacity Yank twins, and, in any case, to lengthen the wheelbase of the singles would have required the fabrication of special frames.

In the fall of 1948, Ralph Rogers announced the launching of his Torque models with extensive advertising in the trade journals. His approach was to encourage the possible family market, with advertising picturing adults riding the twin 440 cc 249 models and teenagers mounted on the 220 cc single 149 models. In addition, a number of Hollywood actors and sports figures were paid to endorse the sport in general, and a noted sports newscaster, Howard Stern, was retained to write a series of articles extolling the joys of the sport. Rogers had envisioned the extension of the movement to include a new class of "gentlemen" motorcyclists.

In addition to the media publicity, Rogers continued to criss-cross the country to convince his dealership to update their sales campaigns.

By this time, those Indian dealers who still remained with the ship were concentrating on the sales of the Chief, of which 11,500 units had been produced for 1948. Most dealers were not happy

with the announcement that this model's production was to be suspended for 1949 in favor of the Torque machines.[4] In order to participate in the expanding middleweight market serviced by the British imports, a substantial number of the dealers were selling AJS, Matchless, Norton, Royal Enfield and Vincent machines obtained through the Indian Sales Company activated through the arrangement with Brockhouse, although few, if any, dealers were stocking the complete line.

The Torque models included both standard and deluxe types: the standard with solid frames, the deluxe with rear springing, with slight variations in detail finish. While the machines were attractive in their overall appearance and symmetry of design, knowledgeable motorcyclists were quick to note some skimping of details, such as the lack of chain tensioners for the rear axles. On the other hand, the engine and gear cases were well executed castings formed by the newly developed injection system as opposed to the old style sand molding.

The general unsuitability of the Torque's overall design almost at once came to light. The small sized Edison magneto would inevitably burn out under prolonged high speed running and lower bearing failures in many cases would accompany this, due to its undersized dimensions. The light pattern clutch and gearbox would not hold up under the usual hard usage meted out to it by riders who were used to the traditional big twin designs.

The acid test of the twin models was to come at the Laconia races, where a factory team of twelve riders was entered. All of these retired during the early laps with blown engines. In addition, dealers from all over the country were returning wrecked engines to the factory to hopefully have the usual warranties validated. The dealers were, of course, furious at having an inferior product foisted upon them, and Indian enthusiasts were, of course, abysmally disappointed, especially as the new models were obviously unsuited to any sort of competition.

The original designer, G. Briggs Weaver, came under fire for his part in the matter, but claimed that Rogers had ordered his successor, Clarence Washburn, to cut further corners in the final production sequences to reduce costs. It was noted, however, that Weaver's forte was, in reality, more in the designing of small marine engines and automotive products, and that his later tenure at Indian had been in the realm of styling rather than any re-engineering of the basic designs of Charles B. Franklin.

The affair was also an embarrassment to several publicity writers, including Ted Hodgdon, who

Don Hawley with his 500 cc Triumph Trophy Model at Ascot Speedway in 1952. The trophy girl is unidentified. *Campbell Photos*

potent performer, but lacked the staying power to be competitive in the endless demands of track racing. Max Bubeck campaigned briefly on a Warrior, winning the Cactus Derby, but the model attracted little attention due to the bad publicity surrounding the original models.

What actually sounded the death knell for even the most serious potential efforts to have improved the Torque models was the devaluation of the pound by the British government in the early fall of 1949. Due to Great Britain's economic troubles following the war, the pound had dropped from its pre-war $4.84 value to a little over $3.00. In order to preserve a precarious trade balance, the pound was then allowed to float, resulting in a $2.80 valuation. The effect, of course, was to decrease the retail pricing of British motorcycles, and the Torque machines displayed in dealer's establishments alongside the British machines floored under the Indian Sales Agreement were not only well proved models but were priced at least 15% cheaper. For Rogers, the game was up.

Noting the precarious state of Indian's finances, John Brockhouse sent his factory manager, one Frederick B. Stote, a 300 pound giant of a man, to Springfield to monitor both Rogers' activities and to watch over the interests of the Indian Sales Company.

In the interim, Floyd Odlum, mindful of the $700,000 stake the Atlas Corporation had risked in Rogers' reorganization venture, took over the domestic manufacturing side of the company and inaugurated the resumption of Chief production for the 1950 sales season. Slightly updated as the Blackhawk, its cylinders were stroked out to 80 cubic inches, and a four speed gear box and plunger forks based on the Vard patents were added. The assembly was moved to the small premises on Worthington Street, where George M. Hendee had manufactured his bicycles before the turn of the century and where Carl Oscar Hedstrom had created the first Indian motor-bicycles! This operation was carried on under the management of an Atlas subsidiary, the Titeflex Company.

Rogers, of course, came under severe criticism for his brief years with Indian from both dealers and enthusiasts alike, who could not envision the motorcycle world without their treasured models. The basic problem appeared to be that Rogers was a sales promoter, with a previously well proven track record, but he did not possess the technical knowledge to assess the possibilities of a new design. Furthermore, as a non-motorcyclist, he approached the matter from a marketing aspect rather than taking the proffered advice of the old

had been induced to concoct glowing technical descriptions of the machines as advanced publicity.

Rogers at once instituted a crash program in an attempt to rectify matters, and the veteran Arthur A. Constantine was called in as a consultant. A minor re-engineering of the 440 cc Torque twin was the boring out of its cylinder to bring its displacement up to 500 cc, and the fitting of an improved magneto. Constantine later told the author that he was skeptical of the new model, now billed as the Warrior, due to its overall lightness of design. As it was, the machine was now a rather

Ernie Roccio on his Ariel
Red Hunter with tuner
Jerry Fairchild.
John Cameron

hands at the factory who were well acquainted with the demands of Indian enthusiasts. Rogers was correct in assessing the redundant state of the pre-war domestic motorcycle market, and he was also sincere in his attempts to bring Twentieth Century sales engineering to a dealership that had subscribed to haphazard methods of retail selling. As it was, according to his own later statements to the author, he lost nearly $7,000,000 in his three year campaign with his Torque models, and the ultimate production of about 19,000 units. Many of the units survive as restored machines, and appear to perform well, but require careful riding at modest speeds. Rogers went on to build another fortune in Dallas, Texas, with a holding company, Texas Industries, which enjoyed the profits from a number of diverse holdings.

In the end, what proved to be one of the greatest disasters in domestic motorcycle history was a sad lesson that was to be repeated again in other venues: namely that non-motorcycling sales engineers rather than experienced enthusiasts have no record of successful management of motorcycle

manufacturing.

As a historic aside, the author's later interviews with E. Paul duPont's surviving sons and production managers, Erle Armstrong and Allan Carter, about the Indian debacle brought out an interesting footnote to the matter. During the latter years of the war after the production of War Department models had wound down, the Indian Company, in common with many manufacturers, secured contracts for diverse products required for the war effort. In agreement with the Lawrence Aeronautic Company whose factory was located on the opposite side of State Street, Indian manufactured pump and hydraulic valve assemblies supplied to aircraft manufacturers. Coincidentally an IBM bookkeeping system was installed to monitor both the supply and costing of the Lawrence agreement. Former Indian employees do not agree as to the details of just why the system was not effective. It was suggested that either the system was at fault, or whether the clerical employees were not instructed in its operation. At any rate, Indian at the war's end was left with over $400,000 worth of porduct supplied to Lawrence that could not be accounted for and could not be billed to the account. This serious loss precluded the planned development of a post-war updating of Indian's line of models.

Following this fiasco, veteran staff members offered a practical means of overcoming the lack of forward development capital. This was to present a three model post-war range based on the Sport Scout. It was to consist of the in-place pre-war side valve model, still an odds-on favorite, together with an overhead valve 45 cubic inch version, and an identical model bored and stroked to 61 cubic inches. Prototype costs would have been minimal, as the overhead valve design was already a proven mechanism as previously developed in past racing models. All that would have been needed was a full enclosure and a position oiling system. E. Paul duPont had agreed, but he lost control of the Company at that juncture through the raid by the Burnstan group. When the same project was suggested to Rogers, it was reported that he saw the wisdom of the idea, but that he demurred on the grounds that he had tied up all the available company funds in the ongoing Torque project. At any rate, the contemplation of such a move might well have saved the Company. Such is the fascination of conjecture!

In the meantime, a significant updating of Milwaukee big twins occurred in their 1949 sales program in the production of a hydraulically dampened plunger type fork in the EL and FL models.

THE POST WAR DECADE 1945-1955

Based on the Vard patents, the new models, now billed as the Hydro-Glide as so fitted, gave a very smooth ride in combination with their 5 inch section tires and the traditional spring seat post. The new suspension was an improvement over the traditionally fitted girders in that it was predictably accurate at high speeds, obviating the frightening speed wobbles that the latter sometimes suffered. A design fault noted in some of the earlier Hydro-Glides was that the assembly allowed excessive bottom deflection on rough surfaces. The risk was, as the author noted in his 1950 purchase of an FL, that in a tight turn on a rough road the lower edge of the crash guard was subject to hitting the ground, making a spill possible. The factory at once offered a kit, supplied through the dealers, that corrected the fault through an improved metering of the movement of the hydraulic fluid.

Harley-Davidson's adoption of the 125 DKW was a fortuitous move, as the performance was much better than the competitive British Villiers engined lightweights, and offered the intrinsic attraction of being an American made model. As the result of this and a vigorous advertising campaign, more than 10,000 units were sold during the first year. Some dealers, however, disputed the prohibition against their continued selling of Cushman scooters, as the simpler models were priced well under the $375 fixed priced entry level product. At the same moment, a substantial number of dealers were continuing to importune the factory to develop a middleweight model to compete with the ever growing British competition.

The venerable WL, while still in limited production, retained a certain appeal to a small number of utility as well as feminine riders due to its easy starting capabilities, as well as attracting some sales south-of-the-border as a military model. But as a weighty and underpowered machine, as a roadster type, it had long ago lost its appeal as a sporting entity, and was mainly considered the precursor of the Model G Servi-car.

By this time the scooter market as well as that for the lightweight machines continued to be firm. With the lifting of government price controls and the abolition of the Office of Price Administration, automobile production was now accelerated to fill the pent-up public demand for new cars, but with the inevitable steep increase in price due to the post-war inflation. This made the low cost two wheelers an attractive proposition for newsboys and student buyers as well as those seeking ride-to-work machines and those living near adjacent employment. The sophisticated Salsbury machines with their handy centrifugal gearing were at the top

of the line, followed by Cushman, who was now developing more advanced models, together with the Mustang, which was more nearly a motorcycle in type and actually offered sporting possibilities.

Meanwhile, at the pre-race activities at the 1949 Daytona 200, the redoubtable Ed Kretz was accorded top spot in the "Most Popular Rider" postcard voting that had been previously announced to be in place during 1948. In duplicating his 1938 selection, in the post-war years this veteran rider had continually impressed the crowds with his impressive charging style and lion-like courage, even though more often than not he retired before the finish with a blown engine. With his handsome, virile appearance and swashbuckling manner, he was a favorite with the feminine enthusiasts, and a general crowd-pleaser with his natural flair for showmanship.

Billy Mathews was one of the pre-race favorites to win in 1949, following his impressive showing the previous year, but the initial phase of the race saw Californian Jack Horn blasting into the lead on a Triumph, Horn was never headed until the 35th lap when he retired with a blown engine. Mathews then forged on to duel with another up and coming rider from the midwest, the youthful Dick Klamfoth from Groveport, Ohio, another Norton International rider who had lately been making a name for himself in the cornbelt circuits with the aid of ace tuner Clarence Czysz. In a wheel-to-wheel duel, Klamfoth took the checkered flag with a 10 second lead over Mathews, followed by another Norton rider, Tex Luce, from Burbank, California.

The Norton entourage was aided in the preparation of their machines by the presence of Francis Beart, the legendary Norton tuner, who has been sent over to Daytona by Norton's Managing Director, Gilbert Smith. Beart was assisted by Indian's James Hill, also of legendary abilities. Beart, a private preparer of Norton racing machinery, conducted his own operation in England, but was on good terms with the factory and shared many of his modifications with Norton engineers. The Americans initially considered him overzealous in his lengthy attention to detail, but his efforts were applauded in the end for the faultless running of the machines over the grueling beach course.

The pre-race activities were marred by a dispute between the AMA and G. Briggs Weaver and his friend, Jerry Fairchild, over the entry of an Italian super sports machine, a 500 cc horizontal overhead cam single cylinder Dondolino model that Fairchild had obtained from the Moto Guzzi factory in Milan. He had obtained the data relating to its cataloged production status from factory representative Fabio Calcaprina, and its entry had been accepted by the Competition Committee with Ernie Roccio as the rider. Just prior to the race, the Committee changed its original ruling and barred the machine from the event. As the sponsors had had the machine shipped from Italy at considerable expense, they at once lodged a protest that was ignored by the Committee. Their next move was to engage a newspaper reporter to aid in publicizing the injustice of the matter, and the reporter telephoned the AMA office in Columbus and stated that newspaper articles accusing the Committee of unsportsman-like conduct would be aired, along with the filing of legal action. The Committee backed down and allowed the Guzzi to enter. Roccio made a spectacular showing in the early laps of the race only to retire in the 70th lap with a broken valve. It was later thought that this had occurred through misinterpretation of a translation of the Italian instruction book that outlined the clearances.

In the meantime, distributors and dealers of British machines were expanding their activities to capitalize on their now increasing markets. Edward Turner, who was by this time spending over half the year in the States, urged William Johnson to open a branch in the eastern U.S. to better serve Ariel and Triumph expansion in that area. Johnson had already expanded his Pasadena operation with the recruitment of additional dealers, and was actively supporting competition riders with a racing department under the direction of the veteran Pete Colman. Turner was informed that due to his diverse corporate activities, Johnson did not wish to expand his operation to include an eastern outlet, so Turner, utilizing both his own as well as factory funding, established a branch near Baltimore with Dennis McCormick, a factory manager brought over from England, to head the operation.

Alfred Rich Child also expanded his activities by inducing Hap Alzina in Oakland to head a western distributorship. Alzina was already disenchanted with Indian's recent marketing fiasco with the ill-fated Torque venture and, after over twenty-five years of Wigwam loyalty, transferred his allegiance to BSA, much to the discomfiture of many still-loyal Indian dealers. In consummating the deal, Alzina furnished Child with a letter of credit in the amount of $250,000 to insure his initial ordering of a large group of machines, along with a supply of spare parts and shop tooling. In addition, he was to pay Child 5% of the landed cost of each unit shipped from the factory for a period of three years, these being shipped directly to San Francisco.

Child was also able to persuade BSA

April, 1950 marked the entrance of Robert E. Petersen into the motorcycle sport with his new publication "Cycle." It would go on to become one of motorcycling's premier titles during the decades to follow.
Don Emde Collection

Managing Director James Leek to resurrect BSA's pre-war 500 cc super sports Gold Star Model, which had appeared briefly before the war. Its performance was enhanced by an alloy engine, enlarged valves, high lift cams, and a big carburetor. Child was able to import the first six machines for the following season, and cannily supplied previously printed catalogs to the AMA Competition Committee in order to qualify the Gold Stars for Class C competition even though the required fifty machines had not actually been produced at that time. The Gold Stars were said to be faster than the currently popular A7 vertical twin.

Frank Cooper's growing AJS-Matchless operation was expanded by the establishment of additional parts depots in Illinois, Pennsylvania and Georgia. The initial line was augmented by AMC's acquisition of the Francis-Barnett lightweight line of 125 and 197 cc Villiers powered machines. He was able to induce the still active Charlie Collier to bring out stripped versions of these lightweights as entry level machines for aspiring off-road and enduro riders, as he was still actively promoting these now increasingly popular events.

In addition, those Indian dealers who still supported the Indian Sales operation were supplying the makes from this source as mentioned, along with a very limited number of Blackhawk Chiefs which were in small production in the Titeflex operation in Springfield.

The domestic machines were selling well also, as the Harley-Davidson EL and FL and Indian Chief big twins were still the backbone of AMA club activities and for the touring enthusiasts who preferred the comfort of the heavyweight models for long distance passenger carrying travel.

While domestic motorcycling was by this time enjoying enhanced popularity, it must be emphasized that the now increased market was still relatively small as compared with the overall population of the country and the ever increasing number of automobile registrations. The actual sales of motorcycles during the fifties decade averaged between 55,000 and 60,000 per year: a figure that relegated motorcycling and its related activities to the status of a minor industry. The then current members of the industry had no means of visualizing the twenty-fold increase in sales volume that would take place two decades later!

The status of the AMA during the 1948-1949 period, as reported by Jules Horky, saw a total of 41,356 paid up members, with 1,652 affiliated clubs. The income totaled $68,000, 90% of which was derived from membership fees and payments for sanctions. The largest expenditure was for

A group of Indian competition riders gathered at the Hendeeville factory in the late 1940's. Included (from left) Bobby Hill, Bill Tuman, Ralph B. Rogers (then Indian President), Harry Foster, Ed Kretz, Leo Games, Lee Potter, and Oscar Skinner.
Indian Sales Company

salaries, being $4,800 for Smith, $3,600 for Horky, together with five clerical employees who received a total of $13,780. The details of Smith's financial involvement with Harley-Davidson's Publicity Department were not disclosed.

During the 1948 calendar year, a total of $28,351 was paid to injured riders, the first year of operation for the Motorcycle Riders Benevolent Fund. In 1949 this had increased to $34,697.

Indian enthusiasts, dealers and other members of the motorcycle industry were saddened in the fall of 1949 to learn of the passing of James Wright, long-time Indian Sales Manager and President of the AMA from 1928 through 1943. He had taken the train in Washington, D.C. for an overnight journey to New York City and, upon arrival, was found dead in his berth from an apparent massive heart attack. He had exerted a profound influence on the course of events within the sport and industry, especially with his ongoing association with Walter and Arthur Davidson and others from Milwaukee in the establishment of AMA policies during their clandestine meetings through the years. With his honesty and sincerity of purpose, together with his tactful and sympathetic demeanor, he had enjoyed a

wide circle of acquaintanceships. The author was also indebted to him for his cooperation in recalling and helping to preserve the many important facets of domestic motorcycle history.

With the growing popularity of British imports, William Johnson, with the cooperation of a number of western dealers, sought to strengthen the British Motorcycle Dealers Association. Led by Johnson, several of them installed themselves as a functioning Board of Directors and, to enhance eastern representation, the newly appointed east coast manager, Dennis McCormick, was elected National President.

In order to strengthen the market, the subject of instituting a national publicity director by the AMA for the purpose of obtaining more coverage of motorcycling affairs in the national media was suggested to E.C. Smith, who had previously vetoed the idea. He again offered a negative opinion, stating that the AMA lacked the funds to implement such a project. Johnson and McCormick then suggested that the annual AMA membership dues be increased to $2.00 to cover the costs. Smith then stated that a large portion of the AMA memberships were obtained through the

261

Jack Horn (31) leading Ernie Roccio as they broadside out of the north turn of the Fresno, California, track. Both are riding Indian Sport Scouts.
John Cameron

on-the-spot registrations for participation in the now popular Gypsy Tours, and that he did not wish to diminish rider interest in this program.

Many within the industry subsequently were of the opinion that Smith's refusal to consider the solicitation of added national publicity was because of the fact that the imports were now out-selling the domestic machines, such a program would put Harley-Davidson at a distinct disadvantage. Then there was the matter of Triumph's introduction of a new 650 cc model, called the Thunderbird, that had been designed with increased cylinder displacement specifically to fulfill the needs of the American market.

In addition, production had been increased for the competition model, the 500 cc Trophy, which was fitted with a kickstarter and rudimentary lighting sets to conform to Class C rules. Both these new models had been subjected to rigorous testing, with attendant publicity; the Thunderbird prototypes having been run for a 24 hour 100 mph average on the concrete oval at Montlhery, France, by a team of factory riders.

The manifestation of some of the Harley-Davidson dealers' dissatisfaction over the factory's barring the sale of Cushman scooters by their franchises came to a head late in 1949. A dealer in Minnesota, who claimed he had been driven to bankruptcy through the loss of entry level

machines, together with some other dealers in the midwestern area, filed a class action suit against the factory under the Clayton Act through the Department of Commerce, charging illegal restraint of trade. The complaint was channeled through the Chicago office of Federal District Attorney Beecher Asbury, who had previously gained national prominence through his connection with the local crime fighting force known as the "Untouchables," led by Elliot Ness. A deputy, Emmett Caulfield, was appointed as a presiding commissioner, and a hearing in the matter was scheduled. As the plaintiffs clearly had legal grounds for their action, the complaint was settled in their favor. In an apparent move to conclude the matter as quickly as possible, the factory attorneys entered a plea of nolo contendre (no contest). The Commissioner levied a token fine against the factory, with an injunction that the dealers' sale of goods not supplied by the factory was not to be prohibited.

In spite of this defeat, factory travelers were at once instructed to warn the dealers that their voluntary compliance with the Cushman ban would count heavily in their favor when the yearly review of their franchise contracts took place. A few dealers braved factory disapproval, however, and continued to stock the scooters. The only trade magazine which reported the incident was Cassell's "Motorcycle News", which printed a detailed account of the proceedings.

As far as scooter popularity went, the trade magazines were featuring a section dealing with both activities connected with it as well as light-weight motorcycles. Various feature articles appeared advocating these machines for short distance touring and mild off-road excursions. The overriding theme was the entry level aspect of preparing an owner for the acquisition of larger capacity machines. Cushman dealers were encouraged to sponsor local clubs of scooter owners.

In the fall of 1949, Arthur Welch more or less phased out his management of the Western Journal Publishing Company in favor of his son-in-law, Charles Baskerville, whose name now appeared on the masthead as Editor and Publisher. Paul Brokaw, who had conducted a vigorous editorial campaign in the avocation of a more democratically controlled AMA, suddenly resigned in a dispute with Welch over salary considerations. It was somewhat previous to this time that the photographic content of "The Motorcyclist" was enhanced by the contributions of young William A. Bagnall. Bagnall, who was born in Taft, California, and subsequently moved to Huntington Park, had grown up with a consuming interest in photography and had later studied the subject at a local photographic trade school. After becoming interested in motorcycling, he purchased a Norton in 1947, and attended competition events where he perfected an ability to take action photographs. He submitted an ongoing number of these to "The Motorcyclist", which were usually selected for publication. Along with being required to furnish descriptions of his subjects, he was soon furnishing detailed reports as formal presentations which earned him by-lines in the magazine. He was subsequently hired by Welch on a 90-day trail basis as a full-time editorial assistant. For some unknown reason, Welch fired him on the last day, but he was rehired two years later by Baskerville and became a full-time member of the staff.

Pioneer members of the industry, and veteran dealers and enthusiasts, paused to honor the memory of W.G. Spacke, Who died in the fall of 1949. The early day motor-bicycle designer and manufacturer played a prominent part in the industry during the heyday of domestic motorcycling. Between 1910 and 1915, he produced motorcycles that bore his own name and which were also marketed by others under the names of DeLuxe, Sears-Roebuck and Eagle. He also supplied engines to the Dayton concern. During the 1914-1915 cycle-car boom he supplied numbers of engines to various experimenters, most of whom were limited to

building prototypes that never went into series production. His main products were high quality 61 cubic inch V-twins that were of advanced design. During World War I his company secured a contract from the U.S. government to build a number of French Gnome-et-Rhone rotary aircraft engines under a licensing agreement with the French originators. These powered the Thomas Morse Scout pursuit airplanes that were developed too late to take part in the war, but were in service with the U.S. Army from 1920 through 1923. Spacke later joined the Revere Automobile Company of Logansport, Indiana, as both an engineer and investor, but lost heavily when the company went bankrupt in 1926. A fortuitous inheritance enabled him to re-establish himself, and he managed a number of commercial real estate investments in Chicago until his death.

The AMA Competition Committee met in the fall of 1949 for its usual pre-season conference to establish the rules for the coming year. After some discussion it was voted to increase the allowable compression ratio for 500 cc overhead valve motors from the time honored 7.5:1 ratio to 8.0:1. According to later reports of the meeting by Dudley Perkins and Hap Alzina, this was done to silence the well publicized ongoing complaints of the British importers, dealers and enthusiasts that the factory controlled AMA was unfairly penalizing foreign competition.

The main reason, however, was that after four seasons of Class C competition it was noted that while the imports might at times have an advantage in TT contests with foot change gear boxes and rear springing, their performance in dirt track racing was something else again. The results of these contests had shown that the American machines with their broad range, high-torque characteristics and side-valve engines, along with the ban on gear changing, gave them a noticeable advantage. As most of the big Nationals were involved with dirt tracking, the AMA Committee felt that giving the imports a slight advantage on power would not jeopardize domestic supremacy. Then, too, as not revealed at this point in time, Milwaukee was already planning to update their competition planning with a new side valve engine in the traditional Class C mode.

This decision, which was at the moment a closely guarded secret, involved a somewhat controversial discussion between Harley-Davidson's top management and their non-motorcycling shareholders regarding what the former considered was a long overdue development of forward products. This took the form of both an updated racing engine, the shareholders having already been resigned to the necessity of supporting competition for the sake of marketing prestige, and the introduction of a middleweight roadster to accede to the ongoing pressure from the dealerships to compete head-to-head with the imports. This decision, as will be seen, resulted in the KR and KRTT competition machines to replace the now outclassed WR, and a new model, the K series 45 cubic inch roadster. Prototype work on these projects was started under the direction of Chief Engineer William J. Harley early in 1950.

In the meantime, Frederick B. Stote, who had been directing the affairs of the Indian Sales Company since the resignation of Ralph B. Rogers the preceding fall, was named as its President. The Tite-Flex operation involving the production of Chiefs was now moving forward under the direction of Henry Vernon, with James Badger as Sales Manager. A few Warrior models were later produced, but their overall performance and quality of construction did not measure up to the competition and, in any case, Indian's long suffering dealers were deserting the company in increasing numbers.

As a historical footnote to the ill-fated Torque episode, Edward Turner was once shown the shop drawings for the machines before they went into final production, and declared that the design was inherently faulty in many respects. Arthur Constantine, who had been called into consultation for the ultimate development of the Warrior, later told the author that nothing short of a completely redesigned machine would have corrected its difficulties. In addition, Rogers had completely disregarded the advice of Indian's veteran production force in their preliminary condemnation of the efficacy of the whole project.

The usual pre-race ceremony for the presentation of the Rider of the Year Award at Daytona was cancelled for 1950. Since Dick Klamfoth's spectacular victory the preceding year, along with his impressive string of wins on the midwest circuit, there was a groundswell of support for his 1950 nomination. According to Rollie Free and Clyde Benton, a substantial number of postcard ballots were sent to the AMA headquarters during the preceding fall. E.C. Smith and the Competition Committee had other ideas, however, and in a flyer sent to the AMA chartered clubs, it was announced that "insufficient" votes had been received to warrant the presentation of an award. The private declaration was that the award had been originally conceived to honor the riders of domestic machinery. This announcement was received with mixed emotions by the club members, even though most

of them were made up of a mixed group of Harley and Indian riders. As matters stood, there were at that time relatively few owners of British machines supporting the AMA chartered clubs, due to the rivalry and frequent downright hostility present between domestic and imported machine owners. Further divisiveness was noted in that a number of clubs had been organized, mostly in the west, that were made up of British machine owners who made no effort to affiliate with the AMA. At any rate, no further efforts were ever made to reinstate the Most Popular Rider Award.

A rather small crowd of less than 8,000 spectators attended the 1950 Daytona classic, said to be due to the inadequate grandstand accommodations. At any rate, the Norton contingent was out in full force following the encouraging wins enjoyed the previous year including Dick Klamfoth, Billy Mathews, Bill Tuman and Ernie Roccio.

Ed Kretz, who had now switched his allegiance to Triumph, took his usual early lead. But at his pit stop for refueling, a helper held the clutch released with the machine in gear, and the resulting burnout sidelined Kretz after a few subsequent laps.

With the now legendary Norton dependability and the aid of Francis Beart, who was again on hand with factory subsidy, it was a win for Mathews, who narrowly beat second-place Klamfoth, with Tommy McDermott on a BSA Gold Star, third. Bill Tuman, on another Norton, was fourth, with teammate Ernie Roccio, seventh. Harley rider and pre-war winner, Ben Campanale, came in fifth. The best showing made by Indian was done by Jimmy Kelley, who came in 17th; few of the Redskins being entered because of a lack of machines and the absence of factory support.

A Moto-Guzzi Gambalunga model entered by John Cameron was refused participation, again on the grounds of being a racing machine, although it was registered as a legally produced catalog model with over fifty examples previously sold. Cameron at once lodged a protest, which was ignored by the AMA Committee. While the model was less potent than Jerry Fairchild's Dondolina, apparently the officials were apprehensive about the potential capabilities of the Italian machines.

This year was significant in that it showed graphically the decline of Indian as a potent force in AMA competition. The emphasis of the Brockhouse-owned Indian Sales Company was now focused on the marketing of British machines, along with the promotion of the Norton in competition. The Tite-Flex operation was concentrated on Chief production, with no provisions made or funds available for further development of the big

THE POST WAR DECADE 1945-1955

Competition riders who participated in the 15-mile National held in Milwaukee in 1951 visit Harley-Davidson's Capitol Drive plant. From left, back row: Bill Miller, Ed Kretz Jr., Everett Brashear, Tommy Byars, Alex Swing, Don McHugh, Julian Wooleyhan. Middle row: Billy Huber, Jimmy Phillips, Paul Albrecht, George Cooper, Buddy Baker, Kenny Eggers, Clarence Wilerson. Front row: Boog Schroerlucke, Joe Leonard, Roy Andres, Harry Van Doorn, Leo Anthony, Ed Kretz.
Clair Wilson

base Scouts. Bobby Hill, Bill Tuman and ace tuner Art Hafer, as privateers, were still working with the Scouts, however, and in Indian's twilight years achieved some remarkable results. Ball bearings were inserted in both ends of the main shafts, as well as in the big ends of the connecting rods. Another tuner, Dick Gross, reworked Scout engines fitting a four lobe cam mechanism, with four cam lobes instead of two. Many of these parts were reworked from Harley-Davidson components, especially the lower bearing assemblies, as they were considered to be more rugged than the originals! Some now claimed that these "four cammers" were capable of 125 mph on the straight.

The author had continued his extensive research into both past motorcycle history as well as the contemporary progress of the industry. He had also purchased a succession of British motorcycles, including Ariel, Triumph, Royal Enfield, Francis Barnett, and Norton, as well as an FL Harley-Davidson for testing and evaluation. This program was financed through the proceeds of a modest inheritance from the estate of Evelyn Gunn Van Wormer, who passed away in 1941, and the cash flow from professional activities. With the fortuitous presence of the still surviving pioneers of the early days of the industry, the idea of now assembling a formal history of the sport and industry covering the first half century of its existence appeared to be in order.

This proposal was inspired by the publication

from the Iliffe Press in England, publishers of the pioneer trade magazine, "The Motorcycle," of a history of the sport and industry's initial half century entitled "Motor Cycle Cavalcade". It was written by a pioneer motorcyclist who was also an Anglican clergyman, Basil Henry Davies, who for some years had written commentary columns for Iliffe under the pen name of "Ixion". Davies, who was then 70 years of age, rightly concluded that such a history should be undertaken while substantial numbers of pioneers still survived to allow for an accurate summation of past events from the personal observations of these participants.

Davies' effort, which like most British products on transportation subjects, was a dignified and scholarly as well as fairly comprehensive coverage of the British industry since 1900. The reading of this work inspired the author to consider a similar effort dealing with the domestic subject. A further encouragement was that there was already on hand comprehensive source material that had been gathered by Thomas Callahan Butler, L.D. Richards, Ted Hodgdon, and others, who were already more than willing to cooperate in such a venture. Up until this time there had been no efforts to produce a professionally researched and objectively oriented work on the subject.[*5]

Some representative pioneers of the industry who were still active, were as encouraging as the formerly mentioned individuals who had already organized some background material. Dealers such

265

THE POST WAR DECADE 1945-1955

Enduro rider Joe Gee made the cover of the October, 1951 issue of "Buzzzz. The Motorcycle News" after winning the prestigious Jack Pine Enduro.
Don Emde Collection

as Ray Garner, Hap Alzina, Dudley Perkins, Claude Salmon and William Ruhle were in sympathy with such a project, for they individually were not in agreement with the official AMA concept of managing the news of both the sport and industry and the cloaking of quasi historical reports as sales promotion efforts.

Both Hap Alzina and Dudley Perkins reminded the author that such a proposed history suggested by the late Vern Guthrie had already been voted down by E.C. Smith and the Competition Committee in 1940. Then it was also a well known fact throughout the industry that the Harley-Davidson Motor Company had officially condemned the author's efforts in 1938. It was their opinion that the AMA hierarchy would offer no official cooperation in such a project.

Nothing daunted, the author put together an outline of his proposal and submitted it to no less than six of the country's then leading publishers.

In due time the replies received were all rejections. A composite of the statements of the editors was that the domestic industry was but a minor activity within the transportation scene, that motorcycling affairs in general had not merited widespread public approval, and that the average motorcycle owner who might have a possible interest in such a subject was not generally considered to be interested in literary efforts! While this wholesale lack of interest on the part of the publishers was a disappointment, the author could also deduce that the generally amateur quality of motorcycling literature produced to date in the trade publications could scarcely have inspired first line publishers to consider seriously the proposals for a formal work by a motorcycling journalist.

In the meantime, the so-called Big Three of the British importers were enjoying an expanded scope of activity. The Triumph organization by this time had nearly 800 dealers throughout the country, and were selling between 6-8,000 units a year. The runner up, BSA, was selling about 5-6,000 units per year through about 600 dealers. The third runner up, AJS and Matchless, had sold somewhere over 4,000 units each year, the make being favored for off road competition.

Aside from the now universal fitting of plunger type hydraulically dampened forks and a bit of cosmetic face lifting, the British products were still basically as produced in the mid-1930's. Some updating occurred in the early and mid-1950's, however, with the optional fitting of various types of rear springing. Triumph introduced a spring hub, a revival of a design proposal suggested during the pioneer days, but this proved to be

somewhat less than practical as after some mileage, normal wear allowed for lateral movement of the wheel which upset the handling. Ariel offered an optional plunger type device that allowed limited travel in an arc at the rear axle, but its extreme flexion under severe conditions caused premature chain wear.

The most effective rear springing was an option on the AMC models intended for off road use. Charlie Collier had attempted to negotiate for a system devised by the McCandless brothers, but the deal fell through when the designers were said to have demanded what was described as too high a price for a royalty. A simpler system, based somewhat on the pre-World War I Hedstrom system once fitted to Indians and suggested by Frank Cooper, was ultimately fitted to certain AJS-Matchless models.

The offerings of the Indian Sales Company sustained less popularity. The Vincent HRD attracted a limited following due to its complexity and its high selling price. The Royal Enfield machines, while soundly built, did not offer the performance of the Big Three models. John Brockhouse, in an attempt to capitalize on the Indian name, brought out a 250 cc side valve three speed lightweight single, made in his factory at Southport. With its mild performance from a cylinder displacement that never enjoyed notable popularity in the U.S., it was ignored by stateside buyers, many considering the appellation "Indian Brave" an insult to Springfield tradition. Very few were ever sold domestically, and the machine ultimately enjoyed some mild popularity in Spain and Portugal as a utility mount.

Another British production from Brockhouse, a folding scooter powered with a 98 cc Villers engine-gear unit and first built as the "Welbike" for paratroop units, was offered in the States as the "Indian Papoose". Being of very limited performance capabilities, it was little more than a novelty, and was soon withdrawn.

While the 500 cc British vertical twins and singles made a radical change in the domestic competition scene, only two models were actually well suited to the demands of high performance in stock form. These were the push rod Ariel Red Hunter that came with a massive lower end and advanced porting and, of course, the immortal Norton International with its overhead camshaft.

The principal American importers were constantly urging the British factories to beef up their engines to make them more dependable in the traditional rough and tumble AMA competition. After much urging, Edward Turner authorized the development of the Trophy model, which subsequently

THE POST WAR DECADE 1945-1955

Larry Everhold (l.) and Chuck Basney at Ascot Speedway in 1954. The trophy girl is unidentified.
Chuck Basney

A 1954 photograph of Eddie Kretz with an unidentified trophy girl at the old Ascot Speedway.
Knighten Photos

enjoyed a substantial following in England. After much urging, and "table pounding", as he often described it, Alfred Rich Child induced BSA to reactivate their pre-war Gold Star single. They also ultimately brought out a high performance version of their vertical twin with twin carburetors.

Frank Cooper recalled that AJS was the most cooperative of all the British manufacturers in this regard, relating it to the competitive spirit of Charlie Collier. The original mild performing AJS-Matchless models were given stronger lower ends, larger valves, and enhanced breathing capabilities, and, as noted, made notable records of off-road competition.

Most of the pioneer British importers agreed that the manufacturers were essentially conservative in their outlook, and tended to be satisfied with an ongoing design if such attracted sufficient sales response to make a profit. They tended to subscribe to the premise that any upward improvement should, in the marketplace, recoup advanced tooling costs within their initial year of sales. In any case, most of the victorious British models, other than the International and Red Hunter, required extensive preparation for competition events, and even then many of the models lacked the stamina to run the whole course.

With the impetus of the funding from the Marshall Plan, Germany, by the early 1950's, was well on its way to re-establishing its industrial capabilities. The large BMW concern (Bayerische Motor Werken) was now in full swing in automobile production, and they also reactivated their pre-war motorcycle production with their horizontally opposed 500 and 600 cc overhead valve "R" series twins. Their obvious quality and high performance had brought them a certain following when imported before the war by Emil Recke, as noted, but they were handicapped in public acceptance due to the overtones of the Hitler government. An accessory concern in New Jersey, Butler and Smith, executed an agreement with the factory in 1951, and shipments were inaugurated in 1952. Butler and Smith then entered into an agreement for their west coast sales through Earl Flanders who, after the war, had set up an accessory manufacturing concern in Pasadena.

A venture to import Italian machines from similarly reviving manufacturers in that country was that of Cosmopolitan Motors, headquarters in Washington, D.C., and formed by a partnership between Ernest Wise and his son Lawrence and Joseph Berliner. The principal makes initially imported were a post-war Moto Guzzi V-twin based on E. Paul duPont's 841 shaft drive military Indian,

A group of motorcyclists gathered for the start of a Sunday run at Ed Kretz's Monterey Park dealership. The size of this establishment is typical of many of the country's post WWII dealers premises.
Edward Bates

along with various Ducati models fitted with desmodromic valve gear. The partnership was later dissolved, with the Wise's taking over the Parilla motorcycles and Vespa and Lambretta scooters.

On the competition side in 1950, Milwaukee, while losing out at Daytona, saw prominent wins on the west coast with Tom Sifton's re-engineered WR's ridden by Larry Hedrick. The factory was not happy, however, over the emphasis on the "Sifton" engines, rather than on the factory's own productions. Hedrick swept the board with winning all the Three Mile Nationals as well as the 15-Miler at Milwaukee. Additional prominence was attained by another young newcomer, Joe Leonard, also a protege of Sifton.

Other factory sponsored riders did well on the Eastern circuit, with Billy Huber in a spectacular win at the Langhorne 100-Miler, and Bill Miller's win at Laconia. In mid-season, Hedrick's win at the Springfield Mile gave him the honor of mounting the Number One plate.

A spectacular ride in the Jack Pine Enduro was that of one Jerry McGovern, who piloted a Harley-Davidson 125 over the rough 500 mile course, an emphasis that a lightweight machine with adequate power was gaining a place in colonial type terrain. His machine was fitted with a swinging arm rear springing devise, a fact suppressed in factory reports!!

An added interest in newcomers to competition was the debut of 18- year old Ed Kretz, Junior, who joined his famous father that season in their dual campaigning on Triumphs. Eddie, as he was

known, won some initial west coast races, including a five-mile National.

Veteran Indian dealers, enthusiasts, and other members of the industry joined the duPont family in mourning the passing of E. Paul from a sudden massive heart attack in September 1950. He was 63 years old. The important roles in Indian affairs played by E. Paul, along with his brother, Francis L., had up until that time not been widely recognized, due most likely to E. Paul's self-effacing stance in the industry's affairs. The duPonts had become substantial shareholders in Indian during the 1923 reorganization and its transition from the Hendee Manufacturing Company to the Indian Motorcycle Company. It was their acquisition of the majority control of the company late in 1929 that no doubt saved Indian from oblivion at the hands of the Bolles-Levine group. Then, during the difficult Depression years, the duPonts' dedication to the cause of Indian and their employment of the assets of their more lucrative industrial holdings kept motorcycle production intact.

The Indian Company had been fortunate during its post-Hedstrom days in having the leadership of two able executives: Frank J. Weschler and E. Paul duPont. Weschler was in command of company operation after 1916, and was single-handedly responsible for the 1923 recovery and its prosperity up until his forced resignation in 1927. Both Weschler and duPont were effective managers as well as being possessed of sensitive and charismatic personalities, and these attributes, along with their inherent sense of diplomacy, created a good ongoing relationship with both dealers as well as customers. Then, too, both men were able to maintain good will and cooperation within the factory operation itself; the camaraderie existing among the production force at Springfield being legendary. It was this overall era of good feeling that no doubt helped to earn Indian the long traditional appellation of being "America's best loved motorcycle."

In later years, duPont's surviving sons told the author that their father's light-hearted bantering manner and self-depreciating and modest approach to management sometimes laid the way for others within the Indian management to assume more credit for Indian's successes than they otherwise deserved. It was also probably the reason why E. Paul's profound technical knowledge of both automotive and motorcycle engineering were not generally acknowledged in his own lifetime.

The domestic motorcycle industry sustained another great loss in December with the tragic death of Arthur Davidson, then 70 years of age, and his wife in an automobile accident. The couple was returning to their home in a suburb of Milwaukee and, while making a left turn into the entrance of their driveway, they were struck head-on by another driver traveling at high speed and who was later found to have been intoxicated. The other driver was subsequently cited for manslaughter.

A driving force within the Harley-Davidson Motor Company, Arthur was, in company with the late William S. Harley, the originator of the initial machines. The early models, their engines based upon the early designs of De Dion and Bouton, were characterized by somewhat more rugged construction than many of their contemporaries and, after several seasons of prototype development, were formally introduced to the market in 1907, when the other two Davidson brothers joined in the founding of the company.

Convinced of the soundness of their product, it was Arthur who initially assumed the role of Sales Manager and, in the years before World War I, tirelessly traveled the country soliciting dealerships from the bicycle shops that were the early retail outlets for the newly introduced motor-bicycles.

Described by contemporaries as perhaps the most personable of the Davidson brothers, Arthur, with his genial personality, made a host of friends throughout the years with both dealers and enthusiasts. Being more diplomatic than his somewhat bombastic brother, Walter, he was able to often smooth the waters coincidental to the often stormy relationships that were a part of the sometimes arbitrary and restrictive policies in the company's

marketing and distribution methods that affected both the dealers as well as enthusiasts.

With an early cognizance of the importance of organized motorcycling to promote the interests of both the sport and industry, he was a consistent supporter of the FAM, the M&ATA, and later assumed an important role in the ultimate creation of the AMA, and took an ongoing part in its continuing activities. Since the resignation of James Wright he had, for the past seven years, served as President of these two organizations.

In the meantime, the staff at the Juneau Avenue factory were busily engaged in the development of both a new roadster as well as a racing model, and employees later told the author that the intensity of these activities had not been felt since the development of the EL and UL models during 1935 and 1936.

The 1951 competition season opened as usual with the Daytona Classic. Flushed with the victories of the past two seasons, the Norton team, well supported by both the Indian Sales Company and the factory in England, again saw the subsidized presence of Francis Beart to oversee machine preparation. The strong team of Norton riders included Dick Klamfoth, Bobby Hill, Bill Tuman, and an up-and-coming newcomer, Dick Curtner.

Klamfoth and Hill forged into an early lead, and were never headed after the twenty-fourth lap. Klamfoth was a narrow winner over Hill, with Tex Luce and Don Bishop on Triumphs taking third and fourth places. The best a Milwaukee rider, Eddie Conley, could do was eighth, with Earl Givens on an Indian Scout trailing in seventeenth place. A surprise entrant was long time Indian rider Rody Rodenberg on a BMW, who had problems with sand in his carburetors and came in twentieth. Only forty-four Harleys were entered, down from nearly double that number in the first post-war races. While the factory sponsored several riders, private entrants were said to have been discouraged from signing up in the face of the formidable Norton campaign.

A significant occurrence on the motorcycle marketing scene was a dealer's revolt against the restrictive retailing mandates of Harley-Davidson's top management regarding the stocking of competitive makes. The matter was brought to a head by Arthur "Skip" Fordyce, veteran motorcycle rider, former stunt show manager, and long time dealer in Riverside, California. Fordyce had long been a sponsor of the very active Riverside Bombers Motorcycle Club, which, since before the war had been giving broad support to a heavy competition schedule in the Riverside, San

THE POST WAR DECADE 1945-1955

One of Southern California's popular off-road racers was Bud Ekins, seen here in a 1950's scrambles event on a Triumph. Ekins was also well known in European off-road events.
Bill Bagnall

Bernardino, and desert regions. In addition, Fordyce's wife, Ruth, had long been active in the west coast affairs of the Motor Maids of America, and had recruited numbers of new enthusiasts in California and the Southwest.

At any rate, in March, Fordyce announced that in addition to his continuing Milwaukee franchise, he had now signed with Johnson Motors to handle Ariel and Triumph. He subsequently told the author that while his sales of Harley big twins and 125's had been heavy, the lack of a middleweight model to compete with the growing popularity of British machines was such that he believed Milwaukee was putting its dealers at a disadvantage by not allowing them to stock a full line of machines that covered the whole spectrum of the market, irregardless of the source. The response from the factory was immediate, with the dispatch of a telegram threatening an immediate revocation of his franchise unless he took steps to cancel his agreement with Johnson Motors. He was also treated to a hostile visit from the regional factory traveler, A.S. Goodwin. At the outset, Fordyce said that he intended to follow through with Triumph. His main defense in the matter, other than the logic of expanding his product line, was that he had legal grounds against Milwaukee regarding franchise revocation under the Sherman/Clayton Antitrust Act involving the restraint of trade, which had been on the books since the administration of President Theodore Roosevelt, who had advocated their inception.

Fordyce later stated that during the altercation with the factory he was receiving dozens of letters and telegrams from Harley-Davidson dealers all over the country, both encouraging his action as

well as expressing the intention of following suit.

With the widespread opposition to the factory's long standing restrictive marketing practices, the threat of government action and the precedent of the 1949 past official injunction against the ban on the sale of Cushman scooters, Harley-Davidson's management bowed to the inevitable and no franchises were revoked. However, while some dealers did at once take on other makes of machines in the middleweight category, the majority were still loyal to the factory. As big twin enthusiasts with a firm market from like-minded enthusiasts, they continued to restrict their sales programs to Milwaukee manufactured machines. Those who chose to follow the factory precedent were rewarded with preference in the matter of the supply of the more popular models and color finishes.

At a special meeting of the AMA Competition Committee and members of the M&ATA, George D. Gilbert, President of the Baldwin-Duckworth Chain Company of Springfield, Massachusetts, was nominated and unanimously elected to the presidency of those bodies to fill the vacancy left by the death of Arthur Davidson.

As an innovative addition to the usual AMA sporting fixtures of the big National track and TT contests as well as the increasingly popular desert races and enduros, a group of enthusiasts sought to organize yet another special interest event. The venue selected was Catalina Island, an arid mountain top 26 miles off the California coast west of the Los Angeles basin. To be billed as the Catalina Grand Prix, it was actually in the form of a TT contest, but was also an attempt to inaugurate out-and-out road racing.

The prime movers behind the proposal were Howard Angel; "Swede" Belin, Frank Cooper, Earl Flanders, Frank Kennedy, Harry Pelton, Aub LeBard and Del Kuhn, all of whom were exponents of off-road competition. The thought behind the proposal was that it could provide a counterpart to the classic Isle of Man contests, as well as offering a road course event that had long been advocated by foreign motorcycle enthusiasts.

The organizing committee had entered into prolonged negotiations with the local government of the mile square incorporated village of Avalon, as well as with the Santa Catalina Island Company that owned the rest of the island outside the town. This part was then controlled by the heirs of the Wrigley family, who managed the agricultural activities conducted there as well as the operation of the small airport located on the north end of the island.

The island authorities ultimately gave permission for the staging of the races, with certain restrictions on the area of the course and details of its operation. A committee, headed by veteran enduro racer Aub LeBard, laid out a ten mile circular course that covered roads on the central part of the island, as well as a segment that included a portion of the streets of downtown Avalon. In order to control the speed and as a protection to spectators, haybales were placed at strategic spots to act as chicanes.

One of the restrictions was that only the motorcycles of the competitors were to be allowed on the island, this access being controlled by the race committee who engaged a barge to transport the machines from a marshaling point in San Pedro.

No cash purses were offered, the only prizes being the trophies, and the entry fee of $25 per machine covered both the chartering of the barge and tugboat, with enough left over to pay the balance of the expenses.

As expected, the well publicized event, which was held on the first weekend of May, attracted a large crowd of spectators, including the author. The Island Company arranged for extra sailings of the 300 foot, 1,200 ton, 1,500 passenger steamer that regularly served the island, and it was estimated that more than 10,000 spectators were on hand.

Incidental to the transportation arrangements, a group of outlaw motorcyclists attempted to circumvent the restrictions against non-competitive machines by building a large wooden platform that was supported by several dozen large truck tire inner tubes for flotation. Before the raft was completed however, it broke away from its mooring in the Los Angeles harbor and, before it could be retrieved, it was sunk by the Coast Guard as a menace to navigation.

The very rough course included sea level to mountain terrain, and included varied surfaces from the paved streets of Avalon to graveled roads in the interior, and rough mountain trails that required skillful riding.

The two-day event included a six lap 50 mile race for lightweight machines up to 150 cc which included scooters, along with a class for machines under 250 cc, these being run on Saturday. The Sunday event was for machines over 250 cc and up to heavyweight 74 cubic inch classes.

Forty-five riders entered the Saturday event, which was won by Nick Nicholson on a 250 cc C11 BSA. Tommy Bizzari, on a Mustang, was second, with Charlie Cripps on a just imported 250 cc Jawa, third.

The Hundred Mile Sunday event saw a line-up of 132 riders who were flagged off in Avalon in groups of five at six second intervals. The indefatigable Walt Fulton, on a Triumph Trophy, starting near the end of the pack, blasted to the lead in the fifty-first mile. Ed Kretz, also Triumph mounted, was among the leaders from the start, but near the end was sidelined with a blown engine.

The placers included Chuck Minert, BSA, a close second, with Del Kuhn, AJS, third, and Nick Nicholson, BSA, fourth.

The overall organization of the event was complimented by the riders, and was a thrilling spectacle for the spectators, and a financial success for the various concessionaires on the island who offered the usual tourist trap merchandise.

The race committee was somewhat taken aback that the AMA Competition Committee refused to sanction the event on the grounds that the contest was a road race and not a bona fide TT, which was declared outside the current rules. Critics at once held that this decision was based on the fact that the solid frame WR racers and Sport Scouts, along with the domestic big twins were not suited to this type of terrain, due to their low power-to-weight ration, and that the Committee did not wish to sanction events that showcased foreign machinery.

In fact, E.C. Smith issued a preliminary warning that those AMA competition cardholders who participated in what was termed an "outlaw" event faced a year's suspension. In spite of this warning, Jules Horky later told the author that Smith retreated from his original position when it was found that the majority of the competition cardholders in District 37 and a substantial number from District 38 (San Diego County) had participated in the island races. Thus, disciplinary action against the entrants would, in effect, have terminated all AMA competition activities in Southern California for a whole season! As it was, Smith ignored the island races the following year, but granted an official sanction for the meet in 1953.

A critical factor in the post-war domestic motorcycle market was the matter of import tariff. It must be noted that the United States government had, since the earliest days of the industry, been notably lenient regarding charges levied against foreign vehicles. As the world's largest manufacturer of motor vehicles, with a healthy home market and the principal supplier of vehicles to foreign countries, domestic manufacturers had little to fear from foreign competition. What few automobiles were imported consisted mostly of a small number of expensive luxury models.

An initial tariff act, inaugurated in 1910, had imposed an initial surcharge of 10% against the landed cost of all classes of foreign vehicles, along with the same levy on spare parts. This law was

Through the sand at Daytona.
Don Emde Collection

reviewed in 1930, the same levy against imported vehicles was retained, but increased the charges on spare parts to 25%. The matter was again reviewed in 1947, by the Senate Select Committee on Tariffs, who decided that a minimal rate should be charged for the benefit of the recovering Allies who were recipients of foreign aid through the Marshall Plan. There were also the pressures from the farm lobby who cited the need of hard currency by the imports of foreign goods so that they could then pay for much needed foodstuffs.

During the winter of 1950 and 1951, Harley-Davidson's top management viewed with some alarm the domestic motorcycle market which showed their own static sales position in contrast with the growing increase in sales of imported machines. Coupled with this, they had, since 1946, been contending with a restive dealership that was demanding that they develop new middleweight models to provide a segment of the market which they had heretofore ignored.

While the company had already undertaken at long last the development of two new models as mentioned, they had hoped to keep this a secret until actual production facilities were in place. It was also announced that a newly updated line of two stroke DKW-based models was undergoing development,and would be marketed toward the end of the year. With a revitalized product offering, Harley-Davidson was ready to reverse its past two decades of declining fortunes.

The factory travelers, in the spring of 1951, were authorized to inform the dealers that new models were in the works without divulging any of the details of the designs.

With plans at the factory now being implemented, management came up with what they considered an expedient action to protect and enhance the market for their new middleweight product. This simply was to persuade the U.S. Tariff Commission to raise the levy on foreign machines. Accordingly, in the spring of 1951, Harley-Davidson, through their legal counsel, served a petition to the Commission for relief against the import of foreign motorcycles. In their pleading, the company cited a static volume of sales, with declining profits through continuing inflation eroding the dollar, together with the fact that they faced the added penalty of competing with low cost foreign labor. As a further consideration and as a projected penalty against the imports, it was suggested that the tariff be increased to 40%, and that the allowable number of foreign machines imported would be placed on a quota system which was based on the small number of such machines that

had been imported before 1941.

The news of the filing of this petition at once caused great consternation among the importers, who interpreted the proposal as simply a means of putting them out of business. They noted that the imposition of a 40% tariff would at once put the retail price of a middleweight 500 cc machine well over that of an EL or FL Harley and an Indian Chief, and that the proposed quota system would very nearly shut off the supply of machines entirely.

The British Motorcycle Dealers Association, which up to this point had not been overly active, at once galvanized into action. President Dennis McCormick called an emergency meeting of the Board of Directors, which included the heads of the three most prominent importers, along with some prominent dealers and distributors. The immediate problem was to raise funds for an adequate legal counsel. Following a three day meeting at the eastern Triumph headquarters in Baltimore, sufficient funds were pledged to engage the prominent Washington, D.C. law firm of Coulter, Collier, McGinnis and Klein, who specialized in tariff law, and who met with BMDA officers to prepare a rebuttal.

The proposed hearing was to be conducted by a group of legal officers from the office of the Tariff Commission, who then met privately to study the submitted briefs and to set the agenda for the formal consideration. The officers were Oscar B. Ryder, Chairman, members Lynn R. Edminster, Edgar B. Brossard, E. Dana Durand, John P. Gregg, George N. McGill, and Secretary Donald N. Brent.

Harley-Davidson had submitted their application on May 21, 1951, and the Commission met on June 9, in the Senate Office Building to undertake a preliminary investigation of the matter, following the receipt of the BMDA's rebuttal on June 7. On July 19, the Commission extended the scope of their investigation to the importation of spare parts. The public hearing had been originally set for August 1, but due to the large amount of material submitted by both sides, it was postponed until September 1.

The protagonists ultimately faced each other in a large hearing room in the Senate Office Building, facing the discomfort of the summer heat, which in those days had to be suffered without the benefit of air conditioning. Each side brought a number of representative machines for exhibits, and it was noted that with some difficulty a full dress Harley FLH was loaded into the elevator for the trip to the second floor.

In their opening statements, it was noted that the Milwaukee contingent was somewhat at a dis-

THE POST WAR DECADE 1945-1955

Photographed at Catalina in the 1950's: (l.) Dave Ekins, Ralph Adams, and John McLaughlin.
Bates Photographers

advantage, as they had brought their own legal counsel from Wisconsin who were not as well versed in tariff law as were those retained by the BMDA and based in Washington, D.C. At any rate, Harley-Davidson now contended that they had, since the war, sustained a serious loss of business and consequent profits through competition from foreign imports and had been forced to lower their retail prices in an attempt to retain their position in the market. It was also noted that they were faced with problems of ever increasing overhead through post-war inflation, citing the fact that the average hourly wage of production foremen and workers had grown from 84 cents in 1941 to $1.65 in 1951. They concluded that the 8% tariff against the imports, being based on the landed cost per unit, represented an actual surcharge against only one-half of the retail price of the machines, as the distributors' and dealers' markups were outside the tariff levy. Also noted was the alleged unfairness of the tariff barriers erected overseas against American products, and that Harley-Davidson exports were now practically non-existent.

The counsel for the importers, in his opening statement, at once noted that his clients' main offerings were middleweight machines, calling attention to the examples on view as contrasted to the American heavyweights, and that the former offered alternatives rather than direct competition to domestic products. It was also emphasized that, in the opinion of the importers, Harley-Davidson was attempting to seek the imposition of punitive tariff laws to defeat the importers without they

themselves entering the competitive market.

When called to testify, BMDA's President McCormick stressed the fact that the proposed 40% surcharge and the imposition of the suggested quota system would, in effect, put the importers out of business.

He also stressed the fact that nearly 2,000 dealers presently retailing imports represented substantial employment of several thousand people, the termination of which would cause a great economic loss to both business and the tax increments that helped to support essential public services.

During a following recess in the proceedings, some of the members of the import industry warned McCormick that his enthusiastic portrayal of the monetary volume involved might well jeopardize their case.

At any rate, when McCormick again took the stand, he offered the opinion that the hard dollars earned by Great Britain through their exports made it possible for them to purchase American produced foodstuffs and other domestic goods.

The most significant testimony on behalf of the importers was offered by Alfred Rich Child, one time Harley-Davidson factory traveler, and later the proprietor of Milwaukee's Japanese export facility, presently the head of BSA import operations in the United States. Reading from a prepared statement, Child reviewed the long-established marketing practices of the domestic motorcycle industry. He described the highly restrictive franchise conditions of the manufacturers, notably Harley-Davidson and with somewhat lesser intensity, Indian, wherein neither would allow their dealers to handle the products of any other manufacturer, whether machines or accessories. He also mentioned how the major manufacturers, surviving into the 1920's, had entered into sub rosa agreements to both control the industry and fix retail prices in defiance of the Sherman/Clayton Antitrust Laws, and that in so doing they froze out the lesser volume manufacturers and otherwise imposed restraints on the trade.

He further stated that both factories had neglected to develop lightweight models that could have extended the scope of the motorcycle market, but instead had followed a retrograde policy of attempting to force a limited range of heavyweight models on the marketplace with a view to rationalizing their own production at the expense of public interest. He described the Harley-Davidson Motor Company as the domestic industry's strongest survivor and an entrenched monopoly that was now attempting to force on the American market a type of machine that had a limited appeal, and were tak-

THE POST WAR DECADE 1945-1955

The 55 cubic inch K series introduced by Harley-Davidson in 1952 superseded the long running 45 cubic inch W series, which was also accompanied by the KR competition models. In keeping with tradition, these were powered by side valve engines.
George Hays

ing a dog-in-the-manger policy of attempting to terminate a segment of American free enterprise by cutting off its source of product.

While Child's forthright stand in the protection of the imported motorcycle business was no surprise to the others of like association, his long connection with Harley-Davidson and his personal friendship with the founders were also well known, and many of his cohorts were surprised at the vehemence of his allegations. At any rate, the effect of his statements on the assembled Harley-Davidson contingent was devastating, according to later statements of some of those present, and it took several minutes before they gained their composure.

In addition to the testimony offered by the opposing sides, a number of witnesses representing the dealerships were heard; the Milwaukee adherents describing their loss of business, and the foreign dealers expressing the financial losses possible through the shutting off of their supply of machines.

The lengthy hearings, which are a matter of public record and which are preserved in transcripts of the proceedings, lasted nearly three

weeks. The upshot of the matter was that a solid majority of the commissioners decided in favor of the importers, with the recommendation to the Senate Committee that the present tariff structure regulating the imports be allowed to stand.

Alfred Rich Child later told the author that he regretted the effect that his public revelations about the past internal workings of the industry had on the Davidsons, but the possible loss of several million dollars that was at stake in his BSA operation was a risk that he could not afford to take. As an aftermath, his former long-standing friendship with those in Milwaukee was terminated, and it was only during the last few years of his life that he was able to re-establish a somewhat restrained friendship with the founder's survivors.

A further analysis in later years of the Commission's decision, from individual members, elicited the fact that the evidence of Harley-Davidson's attempts to control the market without themselves offering a product line that served the importer's market was a deciding factor.

The results of the hearings were given nation-

THE POST WAR DECADE 1945-1955

On board the S.S. Catalina bound for the 1952 Catalina Grand Prix are (l. to r.) Pete Colman, William E. Johnson, Fay Johnson, Jeanie Colman, Walt Fulton, and Maureen Fulton.
William Bagnall

wide publicity through a report from the Associated Press, and were printed in the country's leading newspapers. Full reports of the matter subsequently appeared in both "The Motorcyclist" and "Motorcycle News". Predictably, the matter was ignored by "American Motorcycling", although two of the staff members attended the hearings.

The management of "The Motorcyclist" was now in the hands of Charles Baskerville, who was listed as both Editor and Publisher and who was also in charge of the Western Journal Publishing Company's other industrial publications with the final retirement of Arthur Welch. Much of the motorcycling content, articles of general interest, reports of competition events and accompanying photographs, were contributed by Associate Editor William Bagnall, who traveled on occasion to cover the various events. Most of the local coverage was handled by Baskerville.

The Petersen Publishing Company sold the publication rights of "Cycle" to Floyd Clymer in 1951. It was reported that with the increased growth of "Motor Trend' and other of the firm's

automotive magazines, it was decided to direct the staff's efforts in this field to the exclusion of motorcycling. Clymer's other publishing activities had undergone a decline following his being denied source material from England after he had been caught pirating copyrighted material without royalty payment. Bob Greene, "Cycle's" long time editor, was slated to carry on in Clymer's employ. In his usual expense cutting tactics, Clymer reduced the staff and loaded extra duties on the survivors without raising salaries. Greene then departed, along with the rest of the staff, and Clymer undertook to edit the magazine himself. The technical coverage which had been "Cycle's" tour de force at once deteriorated, and due to Clymer's lack of journalistic experience and his poor command of English, the magazine took an amateurish tone.

The agreed selling price of the magazine was reported as being $1,000 with $500 down and the balance within six months. Clymer attempted to either evade or at least postpone the final payment, and only the threat of foreclosure against the publication rights at long last saw him paying the

Frank Cooper (l.) with Associated Motor Cycle's Sales Manager Jock West during a visit to the London factory. *Associated Motorcycles Ltd.*

agreed installment. The extremely low price of the sale was later said to have been due to Petersen's bookkeeping strategy to lower his current income tax liability.

Clymer's first move was now to suggest that a domestic syndicate be formed to purchase the manufacturing rights of Indian motorcycles from the Brockhouse Group, citing the prostitution of the Indian name by affixing it to the ill-fated Brave model. What Clymer did not know was that the manufacturing rights of the classic Indians was presently in the hands of the Atlas Corporation that was currently manufacturing the Blackhawk Chief and, of course, Brockhouse ignored his letters and telegrams requesting a conference on the matter.

Another of Clymer's activities promoted through the magazine was that of a projected revival of the pre-World War I National Championship races once sponsored by the AMA at Dodge City, Kansas. He eventually was able to sponsor two 100 Milers during 1951 and 1952, neither of which was well supported. The three mile oval was plagued with problems such as excessive dust, the location was too far from the population center with insufficient spectator accommodations, and it was subject to the excessive summer heat of the Kansas prairie. After the popular Milwaukee

star Billy Huber died from heat prostration following the 1952 race, the event was discontinued. Clymer had a personal interest in Dodge City — as a twenty-year old rider he had won a National Championship race there in 1915.

On the competition side, 1951 saw the ever decreasing number of Indian Scouts entered in the big Nationals, and by mid-season, no Redskins had won any of these titles. The list of entrants now was made up of a majority of British machines to contend with Harley-Davidson. The Harley wins, especially on the western circuits, were garnered by Sifton- prepared motors. Bob Schantz, reporting in "Cycle" magazine, wrote a series of articles featuring Sifton's activities and his star rider, Larry Hedrick; a fact that did not endear the publication to Milwaukee. At the same time, Sifton was looking forward to the rumored appearance of updated racing machinery by Harley-Davidson, as the few reworked "double cam" specials based on the big based Scouts now had the edge over Sifton's machines. As it was, Milwaukee did not win at either Daytona or Laconia, although Billy Huber had racked up a signal victory at Langhorne, the event being run in two successive days due to rain.

Veteran motorcycle enthusiasts, dealers and pioneer survivors of the early days of the industry paused to honor the memory of Perry E. Mack, who passed away at the age of 71 in the fall of 1951. As a pioneer experimenter with motor bicycles, he designed the Waverly, Jefferson and, subsequently his own make, the PEM. He also designed the 61 cubic inch overhead valve V-twin in 1910 that powered the last Pope machines, as well as building a similar model adapted for cyclecars, sharing this short lived market with the Spacke productions.

Following the collapse of the domestic industry, he fulfilled a number of consultation assignments in the automotive industry and, in 1925, joined the Briggs and Stratton organization where, for many years, he was their chief designer.

In the fall of 1951, Harley-Davidson announced its 1952 marketing program at a general dealer's meeting in Milwaukee. Current production was rationalized by dropping the long running 61 cubic inch EL model in favor of continuing the top-of-the-line 74, much to the chagrin of many EL enthusiasts who liked the smoother running characteristics of the short stroked 61. The venerable WL 45 cubic inch side valve was dropped as a solo machine, but was carried forward as the basis for the long running Model G Servicar. The now popular 125 was updated with a plunger fork in place of the rubber band supported girder, now listed as the "Hummer". This model was outdistancing the outdated British Villers engined lightweights due to its superior DKW based design, and was averaging around 10,000 sales per year.

The introduction of two entirely new models, the K roadster and the KR racing variants to replace the now outdated WR, was described by veteran factory employees as being the most extensive design effort since the phasing out of the A, AA, B, BB, and C singles and the introduction of the overhead valve E and side valve U and ULH models in 1936.

While the KR model, as will be seen, was to usher in a new era in Milwaukee's competition successes, the road-going K model at once became the center of controversy. Its overall design configuration was attractive in that it carried rear springing as a compliment to its plunger fork as a concession to modernity, but its 45 cubic inch side valve engine owed more to the classic 1920's era. Offered as a middleweight machine to hopefully compete with British machines in a long neglected segment of Harley-Davidson's market, it appeared that the Company was attempting to combine the traditional side valve with updated chassis design. While the engine retained the classic long stroke cylinder dimension of 2-7/8" x 3-13/16" bore and stroke that harked back to the earlier R, D, and W

45 inches, it was a new configuration of in-unit construction with the primary drive train and foot shifted, four speed gear box.

The accompanying KR racing engine was offered as both a rigid framed dirt tracker and a rear spring KRTT road race TT model. While the KR engine was also an in-unit design, it differed markedly from the roadster model in having larger valves for enhanced breathing, special porting with advanced flow metrics, and could turn out an incredible 45 plus horsepower on a compression ratio of 5-1/2 to 1. With some further development, as will be seen, it began a new era of Milwaukee competition supremacy.

While the introduction of the new K series and its immediate acceptance by both dealers and riders was heavily played up in a subsequent issue of "The Enthusiast", many Milwaukee fans were skeptical concerning its in-unit design which mandated total disassembly of the unit to adjust both the clutch and gearbox internals. While the engine was said to develop 40 hp in bench tests, its power as transmitted to the rear wheel turned out to be substantially less, and mated with a 480 lb. machine the actual top speed and acceleration capabilities did not live up to the claims of being a high performance machine. Being somewhat short on power, it was not suited to the double riding capabilities demanded by the tourists, nor was it adaptable to the fitting of a sidecar.

The author was loaned a demonstration machine by Santa Ana dealer Joe Walker for testing and evaluation. A good handling machine with a comfortable ride and easily controlled with its hand controlled clutch and foot shifted, four speed gear box with well chosen rations, its main drawback was its apparent lack of power, especially in the hills, and its limited capabilities of acceleration.

It was during this period that solo speed trials were popular with tuning enthusiasts, some of which were conducted at Rosamond Dry Lakes, the more serious contenders traveling to the dry salt lake course at Bonneville, Utah. Dick Dale piloted a specially tuned fuel burning Harley WR to a new Class C 45 cubic inch record of 123.5 mph, topping the 115 mph 1938 run by Fred Ludlow on a Sport Scout.

Class A records with no restrictions on compression ratios or types of blended fuels were considerably higher. Eugene Thiessen managed a new 47 cubic inch record of 143.6 mph with a BSA Golden Flash. Lloyd Bulmer, with a 21 cubic inch KSS Velocette, managed an incredible 105.6 mph. Bud Hare established a new record with a 30.50 Triumph of 126.7 mph.

"Moto" magazine was a popular 1950's magazine published on the west coast.
Don Emde Collection

Johnson Motors sponsored record runs with a team of Ariel Square Fours. Blackie Bullock attained 132.9 mph, with Sam Parriott a close second with 1 mph less, both tuned to Class C specifications by Cal Makela.

These and other records were run under the supervision of the Southern California Timing Association under the management of Earl Flanders, who oversaw the use of electronic timing equipment.

The 1952 Daytona was another triumphant year for Norton as well as for BSA and Triumph. Dick Klamfoth took on an early lead with his Manx Norton, and easily toured to victory closely followed by Cliff Farwell, similarly mounted. Jimmy Phillips on a Triumph was third; Bobby Michael, Norton, was fourth; Al Gunter, BSA, fifth. Sixth and seventh places went to Norton riders Bobby Hill and Tex Luce. One time Norton star Billy Mathews elected to ride a BSA and was a hard luck twentieth.

Francis Beart was again on hand to fine tune the Norton members, with the assistance of Jimmy Hill. Beart later stated that he had to coach the American riders how to get the most out of the Nortons by using the gears to keep the engines revving "on the cam", a technique not before required on the domestic models that, by tradition, employed their higher torque characteristic of their larger displacement engines.

Milwaukee was not prominent in this year's contest: its best showing was fifteenth place by privateer Herb Groves. It was now agreed that the WR was at long last outclassed, the time being ripe for its replacement.

In spite of the adverse legal decision against Milwaukee regarding both their now banned restrictive trade policies and failure to erect a punitive tariff wall against the imports, there was little concerted action on the part of Harley-Davidson dealers to take on foreign franchises. Most of the dealers had their own built-in core of big twin enthusiasts who subscribed to brand name loyalty; many considering it unpatriotic to not support American industry. Many former Indian dealers were of the same opinion, also enjoying the same customer support and substantial numbers of them did not support the Indian Sales Company's campaign to introduce foreign imports. Many of those who did switch to British machines took on either BSA or Ariel-Triumph franchises, which was sometimes interpreted as a protest against the innovative policies now emanating from Springfield.

Many Harley dealers ultimately stated that the main advantage of the adverse decision against Milwaukee was the relaxation of the often overbearing attitude of the factory travelers who formerly had made it a point of their visitations to closely inspect the dealer's stocks of accessory merchandise for non-compliance in the stocking of unauthorized goods from outside sources. Many stated that some of the more bellicose travelers now assumed a genial attitude!

It was during this period that the German motorcycle industry, dormant since the end of the war except for BMW, was now undergoing a period of revival. Due to a current shortage of fuel, the West German government had encouraged motorcycle manufacture by offering state subsidized, low interest loans, much of the funding for which was derived from the credits provided by the Marshall Plan. From this encouragement such firms as Zundapp, NSU, Maico, Horex, TWN (German Triumph), and others were now entering the market with not only small utility models, but with larger capacity machines as well.

In spite of the attempts of most of the German firms to penetrate the now substantial U.S. market, most were not successful. Aside from the now well entrenched BMW, which was gaining a cult-status foothold as a touring machine, there were few serious importers who could raise sufficient venture capital to set up competitive operations in the face of the now established British markets dominated by Ariel-Triumph, BSA and AMC. While there were some limited attempts to introduce revived pre-war makes of German machines, the lack of capital for sales promotion and the inability to induce dealers of established lines to expand their operations to include them was prohibitive.

Two of these makes, Maico and Zundapp, enjoyed some success at a later date when off-road enduros metamorphosised into the sport of motocross, when high performance two strokes proved to be well suited for this use. Another exception was the introduction of the high performance, four stroke overhead valve 125 cc NSU which gained a few adherents in lightweight racing classes such as at Catalina.

As a historic aside, government policies of encouraging fuel saving vehicles in Germany saw a brief revival of the cycle car. This included the Messerschmidt and the BMW-Isetta, the latter developed in conjunction with an Italian moped manufacturer, and others in conjunction with Fiat. These included the Goggomobile, Bianchina, along with miniature four-wheelers from NSU and Maico. Parallel attempts to introduce these models into the United States failed, as the underpowered bollides were not suited to the now growing pres-

THE POST WAR DECADE 1945-1955

Photographed at a Southern California field meet: (from left) Al Titus, Billie Adams, Del Kuhn on a Matchless, and Frank Cooper handling the fuel hose.
Frank Cooper

ence of freeways.

With subsidized loans the German motorcycle and cyclecar manufacturers produced an excess of vehicles that glutted the domestic market. When fuel became more plentiful in the mid-1950's, the prospering Germans now preferred higher powered conventional vehicles, and the former market collapsed overnight.

By the spring of 1952, fair numbers of Harley-Davidson's Model K had reached the dealers, and a limited market for what was termed an entry level Milwaukee product was attained. Certain problems with the clutch and gear box appeared, and the dealers complained that the unit construction design precluded easy access to these parts, with complete dismantling of the unit mandated to do repair work.

With the machine's mild performance, some dealers interviewed, concerning their opinions of

the model, privately speculated on the possible state of the U.S. motorcycle market had the proposed recent tariff adjustment been adopted: it would have made the Model K the only middleweight machine available to American riders!

The annual TT races at Peoria, Illinois, had long been the post-war venue of Harley-Davidson victories, but 1952 turned out to be a Triumph year with the top spots won by Jimmy Phillips, Ed Kretz, Jr., and Walt Fulton.

The KR racing models were not fully developed for successful competition during 1952, as noted, but in 1953, ushered in a new era for Milwaukee when an up-and-coming young rider, Paul Goldsmith, came in first at Daytona on a KR for a record of 94.5 mph average. This was the KR's initial success in a big National although the previous summer Everett Brashear had piloted an example to its first victory in the Five Mile National at Sturgis, South Dakota.

The KR, in concept, was hopelessly obsolete as far as contemporary international motorcycle design was concerned: being a low compression side valve engine with inefficient combustion chamber profiles, in all aspects adhering to the time honored AMA Class C concept. But with large valves, high volume breathing capabilities, and internally polished porting, it showed an impressive power output after extensive experiments on the part of Hank Syvertsen and his staff in the Racing Department. It was found that private tuners who attempted to improve on its original internals generally ended up with a reduced power output.

As noted, the KR was offered both as a rigid framed track machine and a swinging arm model for TT and road racing. In addition, an off-road model designed as the KRM was placed in limited production, its modification included a skid plate under the crankcase. It was hoped that the KRM could offer an effective challenge to the British machines' domination of the enduro and desert type contests. The Matchless-AJS off-road racing star, Bud Ekins, was offered factory support to campaign with a KRM, but as the machine outweighed his present mount by over sixty pounds, he declined the offer. Del Kuhn, another AMC rider, was importuned to campaign with a KRM, but was unable to duplicate his previous performances on British models.

The general motorcycle market was somewhat depressed in the early 1950's incidental to the Korean War, which saw the resumption of the Selective Service Act and the resurrection of the draft of young men between the ages of 18 and 31 years of age. The uncertainties of being called into service saw many potential draftees putting aside plans to purchase new machines. Particularly hard hit were many small volume dealers in the more rural areas. One such was Lin Kuchler, who had just taken up a Harley-Davidson franchise in a suburb of Ann Arbor, Michigan. Due to the falling off of business, Kuchler dropped the agreement late in 1952.

On the journalistic side, Floyd Clymer, who, as editor of "Cycle" had altered the original format of the magazine into a rather folksy publication filled with his personal reminiscences and with much emphasis on historical motorcycling, saw a marked decline in its circulation. He then advanced a staff writer, Bob Schanz, to the post of Editor, in the hope of changing its direction. With the usual Clymer policy of paying minimal salaries, Schanz soon departed for Cleveland, Ohio, to become associated with a competition products firm. His place was taken by Donald J. Brown, a young competition rider, who had just joined the staff following his employment as a sales trainee for the Blake, Moffitt, and Towne Company, a prominent manufacturer of paper products. He was the son of the late Ray W. Brown, a once prominent aeronautical test pilot and a one-time associate and friend of the noted Jimmy Doolittle, also a contemporary and later famous as leading the carrier based bomber attack on Tokyo. Brown at once sought to bring the magazine's standards up to a more professional level.

Arthur E. Welch, now well into his 70's, had retired from active management of the Western Journal Publishing Company and Editor of "The Motorcyclist" in favor of son-in-law Charles D. Baskerville. In 1953, staff writer and photographer William A. Bagnall was advanced to the post of Editor. Bagnall enhanced the scope of the magazine in both content and photographic material. While his editorial policies regarding the AMA and industry were more conciliatory than that of his predecessors, he campaigned consistently for a more democratically controlled AMA and for their affiliation with the FICM to end isolation from international competition.

"Pop" Cassels continued as Editor of "The Motorcycle News", its format being objective in its reporting of both news of the internal affairs of the industry and the AMA, still campaigning for more rider participation in the AMA's management. The publication ceased to exist in the late 1950's with Cassels' death, his heirs finding no one to take up its publishing rights.

"American Motorcycling", the official AMA publication, continued to serve the AMA membership, but lost much of the credibility of its reporting due to its format slant to Harley-Davidson affairs

Paul Goldsmith gave Harley-Davidson its first Daytona 200 win in over twenty years when he won in 1953. It was the first Daytona race for the new four speed KR model motorcycle.
Don Emde Collection

and interests to the exclusion of those of the industry in general.

In its annual fall meeting, the AMA Competition Committee zeroed in on the position of the Norton International in domestic competition, noting its four seasons of dominance at the Daytona 200 and its now growing number of entrants in TT events. Late in 1951, Norton's racing designer, Joe Craig, had adopted what was known as the "featherbed" frame, which continued to offer the International's legendary steering and handling but now gave more travel with its swinging arm rear suspension. This unit replaced the long standard "garden gate" frame with plunger rear suspension that had been adopted in 1947, and which was also fitted to the ES-2 pushrod engined roadster.

In accepting the International's 1952 Daytona entries, the Committee barred the featherbed frame as non-standard, so all the numerous Norton entrants were fitted with garden gate frames and, in fact, most of the International's limited production for 1951 as garden gate models had gone to both the U.S. and Canada.

For 1953, Norton introduced the updated International as the "Manx" model, which was now fitted with dual rather than single overhead camshafts and was built as a short stroke model with nearly "square" piston dimensions.

The Committee at once took exception to this model, especially as it had an altered engine design and the fact that it required "run-and-bump" starting, illegal under Class C rules, as it had no kickstarter.

Norton enthusiasts at once protested that the model was no less specialized than the recently introduced KR's, and that the Manx was sufficiently tractable to be ridden on the road which the KR was not. In addition, J.M. McGill was importuned to enlist factory support for the fitting of kickstarters. The situation was further complicated by the fact that the Bracebridge Factory had lately suffered financial problems, together with the fact that Managing Director Gilbert Smith was of the opinion that Norton had proved its point as a superior performer in the American venue, and that there was now no point in engaging in a hopeless battle with the AMA Competition Committee which, in any case, had the power to inaugurate further restrictions to simply bar Norton machines from U.S. competition without any reasonable recourse from their rulings.

Edward Turner, in commenting to the author in the matter of competition, reiterated his theory that the expending of the factory's cash reserves in extensive racing development was highly imprudent. He referred to the fate of such once prominent makes as the original Sunbeam concern, Rudge-Whitworth, and Chater-Lea, who went to the wall in the 1930's in a blaze of racing successes. As it was, the AMC concern ultimately took Norton under its wing as a subordinate company and terminated Joe Craig's contract for further extensive development of competition machines. In any case, with the ongoing emergence of highly sophisticated multicylinder designs from the Italians, such as the Mondial and MV-Augusta, the days of single cylinder racing machinery were numbered. While Manx Nortons continued to be a factor in international competition for a few more seasons, its declining successes were due more to their superb handling and dependability in making a finish.

Indian product in its classic form was ultimately ended in 1953. According to Production Foreman Walt Brown and Sales Manager Harry Savage, between 3,600 and 3,800 units had been assembled by Titeflex during the preceding four seasons. Built to dealer's orders, only a few of the latter were still loyal to the make, and with the low number of retail outlets, the small production became unprofitable. Floyd Odlum told the author that he regretted the end of the classic Blackhawks, but that the Atlas Corporation's Board of Directors saw no other choice than to terminate the operation.

The last models had been somewhat updated with a hand operated clutch, a four speed foot-shifted gearbox, along with the Amal type carburetors. While thousands of Indian enthusiasts were saddened by the demise of a once proud line of machines, the complications of the failure of the various changes in company management had created a series of insoluble situations. The Indian Sales Company, still a separate entity from the Titeflex operation, and under the control of the Brockhouse Group and managed by Frederick Stote, attempted to capitalize on the Indian name. The product line of Royal Enfield was made over with Indian red paint finish and the Indian logos, which as will be seen, was not well accepted by Indian purists.

Velocette machines had not, up to this point, been prominent in competition, as their small production of classic models due to the factory's emphasis on utility machines saw only limited numbers allocated to export. The California distributor, Lou Branch, received sufficient machines to supply only a small number of dealers. They made their mark in the Catalina Grand Prix in the 1953 contests, however, with enthusiast John McLaughlin making two spectacular wins in two classes. In the Saturday 250 cc race, he took a first

place with an MOV model, and another on Sunday in the unlimited race with a 350 cc MAC. The two machines were supplied by Branch. McLaughlin credited his win to his pre-race practicing on various mountain trails on the mainland.

With initial technical problems now solved, Harley's KR models came into their own in 1953. Joe Leonard won four Nationals, including the California Mile, Bay Meadows, a roadrace in Pennsylvania, Sturgis, and the Peoria TT. Everett Brashear won two half-mile events, and Paul Goldsmith complimented his Daytona victory by winning at Langhorne.

Indian star Bobby Hill was favored to repeat his two past season's winning of the Springfield Mile for the National Championship in 1953. During a hard fought race on the very fast track, he gained an early lead, but had to drop out in the eighth lap with a broken valve. Bill Tuman, also Scout mounted, then engaged in a give-and-take duel with the leaders, and by the twentieth lap, was in a wheel-to-wheel contention with BSA mounted Al Gunter. In a fierce contest close to the inner rail, Tuman was the ultimate victor by a wheel length. Joe Leonard and Don Hawley on KR's were strong early contenders, but were passed by the leaders midway in the contest.

By the mid 1950's, BSA was becoming a strong contender in competition. The super sports single cylinder Gold Star model was starting to fulfill the role formerly held by Norton now that the new Manx model had been barred from AMA contests. In addition, the 500 cc twin carburetor Star Twins were coming to the fore. These models had been developed by the factory at the insistence of Alfred Rich Child, with the cooperation of Managing Director James Leek, as a challenge to Triumph's prominence in U.S. competition.

In the fall of 1953, Child and Hap Alzina had engaged the services of Tom Sifton to tune a group of Star Twins for the 1954 competition season. Sifton had just sold his San Jose Harley-Davidson dealership to former shop foreman and pre-war racing star, Sam Arena, and was now engaged in speed tuning on a full-time basis.

The commission paid off at the 1954 Daytona, when BSA swept the board with the first five places; the riders being Bobby Hill, Dick Klamfoth, Tommy McDermott, Al Gunter and Kenny Eggers. Triumphs took sixth and seventh places, ridden by Alvin Shaffer and Mike Dottley. Harley-Davidson KR's trailed in tenth and eleventh places, ridden by Don Hutchinson and Leon Applegate.

The highly tuned British machines, with their fast turning engines, had the advantage on the turns

THE POST WAR DECADE 1945-1955

A team of Enduro riders sponsored by Frank Cooper. (From l.) Aub LeBard, Del Kuhn, and Ernie May. Cooper's famous stretch limousine in the background.
Gilbert Travis

through their lightweight and enhanced acceleration.

The Race Committee and Bill France paid special attention to safety considerations, in noting the two deaths and two serious injuries of the preceding year. Cliff Farwell had hit a spectator crossing the track, and both had succumbed to their injuries in the hospital. In the same race, Jimmy Chann and yet another spectator were seriously injured in the same manner.

There was much speculation regarding the future of the beach course, as encroaching subdivisions with now limited spectator access and complaints from adjacent residents concerning noise becoming a critical factor.

An innovative event for the 1954 season was the April 4th running of the first Willow Springs Road Race, a course located 80 miles north of Los Angeles in the Mojave Desert. The two and one-half mile irregular course had been built in 1950 by a group of sport car enthusiasts to promote continental type racing, and had been used for informal speed trials by small groups of motorcyclists shortly thereafter.

The 125 mile event was inaugurated through the efforts of a number of British dealers in the area

who were members of the BMDA. A request for an AMA sanction had been sent to E.C. Smith during the preceding January, which was ignored. On March 20, William E. Johnson telephoned Smith regarding the matter and was told that the Competition Committee did not favor road race type contests, citing considerations of "safety for the riders." Johnson replied that plans for the event were well in hand, and that a large contingent of prominent contestants was already signed up. Smith at once brought up the matter of suspensions attendant to participation in an "outlaw" event. Johnson countered with the threat that the non-compliance of the AMA would be publicly advertised as a discrimination against the owners of British machinery and, in the end, Smith capitulated and issued a sanction, but levied a punitive $150 sanction fee in retaliation.

The event was a showcase for BSA and Triumph. Kenny Egger, who headed the field from the start, was a strong contender. Ed Kretz, Triumph, was also a strong contender, but gave way to Jimmy Phillips, also Triumph mounted, when he had a fall in the twentieth lap. He managed to remount, but was well behind Phillips when the

282

THE POST WAR DECADE 1945-1955

Off road legend Bud Ekins showed good form on the cover of the March, 1953 cover of "Motorcyclist".
Don Emde Collection

Everett Brashear was a big star in the 1950's winning numerous dirt track events.
Don Emde Collection

latter shed a chain. The only consistent Harley entry was Don Tindall, who stayed in the running but did not place. Kenny Egger was the victor, with Ed Kretz second, another Triumph rider, Johnny Gibson was third, and Al Gunter and Gene Thiessen, both BSA mounted, fifth and sixth.

Stung by the outstanding BSA wins at Daytona, Milwaukee's top management swallowed its pride and negotiated with Tom Sifton to engineer a KR engine for its up-and-coming rider, Joe Leonard. Sifton was subsequently retained by Harley-Davidson as a consultant for a $3,000 yearly retainer. Sifton ultimately hammered out an agreement with Walter Davidson, Jr., and set to work. He altered the KR's porting, revised the cam profiles and substituted a set of double valve springs previously developed by Triumph tuner Tim Witham, which helped to reduce valve float at high throttle openings. He also developed rotating valve lifters to reduce temperatures at the seats, a frequent cause of distortion and engine failure.

The end result was that the Sifton engine had a considerable edge on power over the standard KR's with factory tuning. Leonard went on to win no less than eight Nationals, including the Laconia 100 and the Springfield Mile, to gain the coveted Number One National Championship plate.

Following the Indian victories at Springfield during the past three seasons, the Competition Committee decided to change the rules governing this long running event. Instead of a "sudden death" winner-take-all event, the contestants' standing was dependent on points accrued from wins at other Nationals. This effectively precluded the chances of a lucky win on the part of private participants, and favored factory riders whose sponsors fielded active teams of multiple riders in preceding competition. There was, as was to be expected, much criticism of this decision from numbers of competition riders as well as enthusiasts in general. "Pop" Cassells had at one time editorialized in "The Motorcycle News" that the new ruling would have the effect of further narrowing competition in this fixture event, as well as discouraging public interest on the part of spectators. In spite of these sentiments, there was no appeal from the Competition Committee's decision.

In the face of lukewarm public interest in the Model K roadster, the model was updated by Milwaukee engineers by boring out the cylinders to increase the displacement to 55 cubic inch. In addition, the drive train was altered to hopefully overcome previous weaknesses in the design and to improve access for servicing. Cataloged as the KH for 1954, the improved model attracted some new-

comers as an entry level Harley-Davidson for its comfortable ride and ease of control with its foot shift gear box and hand controlled clutch. While the increase in displacement improved the machine's hill climbing abilities, its overall performance was not noticeably enhanced.

With the expansion of the sales of imports after 1950, many dealers sought to obtain law enforcement contracts from their local municipalities. Of course, such markets were by tradition bastions of domestic name brand loyalty. It was noted that up to this point about 70% of the market was dominated by Harley-Davidson, the minority of 30% going to Indian. Then the penetration of this market was further complicated by the inclusion of the technical specifications of a favored brand into the purchasing ordinances; a policy first inaugurated in the 1930's by Harley-Davidson.

A few municipalities, especially in the Los Angeles basin, had been importuned to purchase a limited number of foreign machines for police use, the dealers gaining a slight foothold on the issue of fairness to local business concerns. In such cases, Harley-Davidson at once took the initiative to terminate such purchases. Under the leadership of factory travelers, local as well as adjacent dealers were at once recruited to protest the foreign invasion, citing the patriotic consideration of the necessity to allocate taxpayer's funds for the support of American industry. Such proceedings saw considerable pressure being brought to bear on city councilmen, purchasing agents, and other concerned officials.

Ed Kretz recalled selling an Ariel Square Four to the city of Monterey Park in the early 1950's for suburban police patrol. Led by a factory traveler, such pressure was exerted on the local city council members by adjacent Harley-Davidson dealers that ultimately the machine was condemned out of service after a few months, in spite of the fact that it gave satisfactory service.

A notable event in 1954 was the founding of the Antique Motorcycle Club of America. For several years following the war, a small group of enthusiasts in the northeastern states had been meeting informally at times to display old machines and to trade for spare parts. It was then decided to create a formal organization, the details of which were effected by a father and son duo of industrialists, Henry Wing, Senior and Junior, Ted Hodgdon and Emmett Moore. These founders were joined by a small group of enthusiasts who personally funded the inauguration of a quarterly magazine, along with a public solicitation of other enthusiasts with like interest. The initial emphasis was on the collection of machines manufactured

THE POST WAR DECADE 1945-1955

Frank Cooper's motorcycle shop in Los Angeles in the early 1950's. His franchises included Matchless, AJS, Norton, Francis Barnett, Puch, and Powell Scooters.
Frank Cooper

before 1915 but, as the movement gradually expanded, the interest expanded to between-the-wars models.

The organization of the Antique Motorcycle Club was patterned somewhat on the Vintage Motor Cycle Club of Great Britain, which had been founded in 1946, under the leadership of C.E. Allen.

A valuable function of both these groups was the preservation of the general history of the industry as well as that of individual machines, so much information from knowledgeable individuals found a clearing media that otherwise would have had no other outlet.

The market for scooters remained fairly active, and for lightweight motorcycles was enhanced by the fitting of larger 198 cc Villiers engine-gear units to such makes as James and Francis Barnett, both of which were now a part of the AMC group. The Harley-Davidson Hummer was improved by boring out its cylinder to 165 cc. Competitive with the British models, its good performance was attracting about 10,000 buyers each year.

Not to be outdone, the Cushman Company had

brought out their Eagle model with a high performance 250 cc engine of their own manufacture that gave a top speed of 60 mph. While it still carried the small wheels, it was fitted with a motorcycle type fuel tank and appeared as somewhat a caricature of the Harley-Davidson big twins. It later assumed a cult-like stature among some enthusiasts.

A notable advance in scooter engineering and design was provided by the Vespa, manufactured by Piaggi Engineering SA of Genoa. Imported by Ernest Wise's Cosmopolitan Motors, it set a new performance standard for the 125 cc class with a top speed of 60 mph. Advanced design features included a high revving engine in-unit with the drive train to the rear wheel, stub axles to facilitate tire changing, and gear change controls incorporated in a twist grip.

Vespa was soon to enjoy worldwide sales from an enlarged factory and an "Ape" model three wheeler was developed as both a passenger carrying vehicle as well as miniature delivery truck and van models for third world countries. Sears Roebuck later negotiated an agreement with the

284

factory to market the Vespa through their mail order outlets as the "Allstate".

By the mid-1950's the biker cult had increased to the point that a substantial industry had grown up to date to the market for custom accessories and given an engine and gear box it was possible to construct a complete machine from the ground up. These universally followed the "chopper" style, and while a small number were based on the Indian Chief, most were now Milwaukee replicas.

With public attention now focused on the biker movement, it was inevitable that Hollywood would feature the more sensational aspects of it. This finally occurred when the director of controversial films, Stanley Kramer, assembled a company to produce a movie in the summer of 1953 for 1954 release. Entitled "The Wild One", the plot was loosely based on the Hollister incident. The principal star and anti-hero was Marlon Brando, supported by Lee Marvin, Mary Murphy, Brian Keith, and a crew of authentic bikers as extras. The machines appearing were a nondescript mix of both domestic and foreign models, the name plates were obscured in the interests of anonymity, but the hero, somewhat improbably, rode a pristine Triumph. While there was much violence portrayed as the outlaws took over the town and the outraged citizens planned to assault the leader, there was much philosophizing on the part of Brando and others regarding the free living aspects of the biker mode.

Many "straight" motorcyclists, especially organized AMA club members, were outraged at the film, and groups of them picketed the entrances to some of the theaters that exhibited it. But as a media for portraying both off-beat and violent drama, "The Wild One" presaged the ongoing production of biker films that have continually appeared through the years featuring many of Hollywood's prominent actors.

Another literary effort featuring a motorcycling subject appeared at this time written by "Cycle" Editor Don Brown in collaboration with a staff member, Evan Aiken. Entitled "How To Ride and Win", it contained much practical advice for aspiring competition stars based on Brown's own experiences as a successful enduro rider. Being faced with the usual rejection from major publishers concerning its publication, the authors formed a private company, National Sports Publications, to produce it. The initial 5,000 copies were printed at $3.00 per copy, most of the sales being handled directly by Brown. An additional 5,000 copies were printed in 1955.

The domestic competition picture changed markedly during the 1954 and 1955 seasons.

Don Emde Collection

Norton's supremacy was now in a decline following the official barring of the Manx model. While Norton imports were handled by the Indian Sales Company, their current emphasis was now on selling the Royal Enfield line carrying the Indian trademarks, to the exclusion of Norton's lately introduced vertical twin which had showed promise due to its advanced technical features. The recently updated BSA Gold Star single was now starting to take the place of the Norton International, as its performance was comparable and it was a less costly machine and easier to repair and maintain. Of the 18 big Nationals conducted in 1954, 13 were won by Harley-Davidson and the balance by BSA.

The fiftieth anniversary of the development of the first Harley-Davidson machine suitable for public sale occurred in 1953. Accordingly, in 1954, the Company selected its top-of-the-line FLH as its Anniversary Model. In addition, it had published a paperback book purporting to be a history of the company. Ostensibly written by members of the publicity department, it bore no author's title and, as a typically oriented in-house publication, its content was more of a sales effort than an actual account of the true facts of company history. There was also little emphasis on the company's role in AMA affairs. It was distributed mostly through dealer outlets, and its main value to historians was a chronological outline of the company's past extensive number of models.

In the Spring of 1954, George D. Gilbert, President of the Baldwin Chain Company, resigned as President of the M&ATA and the AMA. He was replaced by Carl Swenson, President of the Milsco Company of Milwaukee. With the dominant position of E.C. Smith, who, as Secretary-Manager, chaired the Competition Committee that implemented M&ATA and AMA policy, the office of AMA President had become largely a ceremonial position.

By the mid-1950's, the increase in the number of AMA chartered clubs had slowed markedly, now standing at about 1,600. The growth of AMA membership was also static as a result. A contributing factor according to statements by Jules Horky, was the reduced number of Gypsy Tours due to the problems engendered by the growing number of outlaw types who were forming a fringe element at such gatherings. By 1954, AMA membership was reported as being 48,764.

Club growth was somewhat inhibited by the reluctance of many new owners of foreign machines to join up, these often being discouraged by the covert and sometimes open disapproval of

THE POST WAR DECADE 1945-1955

Tex Luse, 1958 winner
of the Riverside 100 with
Patty Michael.
Bill Campbell

some veteran members owning American made machines who resented the overseas invasion of what they considered an American institution. A number of groups of owners of imported machines formed their own clubs that were organized without benefit of an AMA charter, these being mostly in the West and Southwest.

By this time Canadian motorcycle activities were, of course, isolated by the growing strength of the well organized CMA. According to C. Gerald Barker, the various affiliated clubs were almost exclusively populated by owners of British machines, although Indian owners were welcome. There was little restriction as to the technical details of competition machines other than piston displacement as mandated by FICM rules. Competitors entering side valve Indian machines were given a wide latitude as to specification, no doubt due to the neutral position of the factory during the recent battles with Milwaukee.

A handful of AMA affiliated clubs, made up

exclusively of Harley-Davidson owners and mostly sponsored by dealers, carried on in the Ontario area. These remained isolated from CMA affairs, and conducted their own social and competition events under AMA Class C rules.

The character of the domestic motorcycle market quite naturally changed markedly from its pre-war status during the first post-war decade. The introduction of the foreign imports with the now wide range of machines available at once attracted new and expanded markets within classes of enthusiasts whose interests had formerly been entirely neglected. By 1950, the sales of machines of all types had approached nearly three times that of 1940, the retail market being served by nearly 3,000 franchised dealers. By 1955, this latter group was augmented by about 1,000 non-franchised outlets offering not only repair and service facilities but a growing market of after market accessories for those with an interest in customized machines. The sales of foreign imports accounted for about 3/4 of the new machine market which, by 1955, ran between 55,000 and 60,000 units; a marked increase over the 20,000 odd retail sales volume of 1940.

The sales leader of the post-war era was Triumph, whose aggressive marketing program and the continuing expansion of its dealer network now had distribution points located on both coasts. The BSA operation was a close second, with a similar aggressive policy and distribution. The AMC operation was third, its sales interest was oriented toward special models for the post-war interest in off road and enduro type riding, along with an aggressive promotion of competition events within this category.

The marketing activities of the Indian Sales Company ran a distant fourth, with emphasis on the Enfield Indians, at the expense of the better performing Norton vertical twin which did not receive the attention it deserved. The high performance Vincent V-twins were no longer available: Phillip Vincent announcing in the spring of 1955 that the high cost of its manufacture, which included the single cylinder version known as the Comet, rendered the operation unprofitable. Production at the small factory at Stevenage had run about 100 units per month during the decade of manufacture, the bulk of the 12,000 units produced during that period going to the U.S.

The position of the German made imports has already been discussed, the well established BMW being the principal survivor, and enjoyed a modest but well supported market from touring enthusiasts.

The export market for domestic machines, which had never regained its pre-war status due to

THE POST WAR DECADE 1945-1955

the economic dislocations of the war and the reaction to foreign tariff barriers, saw a modest revival when Alfred Rich Child's son, Richard, returned to Japan. He had secured the import rights for BMW automobiles in that country in 1952, and through negotiations with Milwaukee, re-established the importation of Harley-Davidsons in 1954. The Japanese manufactured Rikuos, whose operation had been seized by the government in 1937, had been revived after the war by a couple of manufacturing concerns, but the genuine Milwaukee models had always commanded an ongoing market. In spite of the high tariff penalty against them, the big twins appealed to a limited group of well-to-do fans.

The ambiance of most dealerships, whether specializing in either domestic or foreign products, had assumed a club-like atmosphere: the Saturday gatherings at the motorcycle shops offering a kaffee-klatch type of socializing. With the sharp division of preference for either middleweight imports or heavy big twin domestic machines, each faction more or less withdrew to their own sphere of interest. The factory continued to urge all Harley-Davidson dealers to either inaugurate or strengthen their support of local AMA chartered clubs, and sought to promote dealer cohesiveness through a strengthening of their regional dealers' associations.

On the sporting side, the ongoing development of Milwaukee's KR models were proving to be formidable contenders in competition, and from the mid-1950's on, Harley-Davidson assumed a dominant position in the big Nationals. While the engineering background of the KR was based on obsolete side valve concepts, as a rugged design

with highly developed breathing and porting, it reinforced the now traditional AMA emphasis on this type of power plant. Further advantages were Milwaukee's ability to recruit top flight riders, who competed in sufficient numbers to give the advantage of substantial support through large entries. Then, too, the Milwaukee dominated Competition Committee made sure that sufficient National races were scheduled to provide the types of track racing events that were the best venue for KR participation. The usual 5, 10, 15, 20, 50 and 100 Mile Nationals were often augmented with 3, 6, or 7 Mile events to round out the season, in addition to the traditional Springfield and Daytona races. These track events balanced out the Big Bear Runs, Cactus Derbys, Catalina Grand Prix, and other enduro type events that showcased the foreign machines, but were not well suited to Milwaukee participation.

The year 1955 saw the increased effectiveness of the KR's. Leonard Andres, the San Diego Harley-Davidson dealer, purchased the highly developed Joe Leonard KR from Tom Sifton for his son, Brad, an up-and-coming Amateur rider. Brad came in first at Daytona at a record speed of 94.5 mph. He next racked up victories at both Laconia and the last running of the Dodge City Event, as this was now an unpopular venue; the original 100 mile distance having been shortened to 75 in deference to the severity of the summer heat and its dangers to the riders. Between Andres, Joe Leonard, and Everett Brashear, 15 of the 17 big Nationals went to Milwaukee. Tom Sifton now commented that his highly developed and much altered KR's were at long last faster than the special Sport Scout "cammers" that had been designed by Bill Tuman and Art Hafer, the top speeds of the KR's on the straights being nearly 130 mph.

Public support of motorcycle competition on the part of spectator attendance was increasing, and numbers of knowledgeable leaders of the industry were concerned that the motorcycle market was not growing in proportion. Some were of the opinion that the same situation existed that had been noted in the earlier days of the domestic industry; that the gladiatorial aspects of motorcycle competition entertained spectators who could not equate ownership, of what was generally considered an inherently dangerous vehicles to themselves.

While post-war sales had markedly increased, as noted, neither the newly introduced middleweight imports nor the historically evolved domestic heavyweight big twins, as far as their technical features were concerned, offered the buyer other than limited compromises. The British machines were based on pre-war designs that were at least two decades old and, in the interim, had only been subjected to minor face lifting. The traditional Lucas electrical systems were prone to a variety of ailments, and there were ever present problems with clutches and drive trains. In addition, most makes could be counted on to leak a steady stream of lubricating oil. The engine and gear cases were not designed to be oil tight! Their dependability after high mileages for any sort of long distance travel was often open to question.

The German made BMW, as a post-war creation, was infinitely more refined with dependable Bosch electrics and shaft drive which eliminated the continual problem of chain adjustment, not to mention rear springing as standard. But its necessarily high price and limited availability limited its market, and its low ground clearance and the difficulty of altering its gear ratios eliminated it as a sporting contender.

At any rate, the immediate post-war motorcycle market had its greatest appeal to the young and athletic, this being served by the imports. A hard core of veteran older enthusiasts, many of whom supported club life and touring, continued to support tradition by buying the domestic product. But in any case, the overall market was still limited, its numbers remaining small in proportion to the now vastly increased number of automobiles and the explosive increase in the nation's population.

In the organizational sphere, American motorcycling was continually embroiled in conflict between the enthusiasts for imported and domestic machines. The now seemingly insolvable differences between the two factions was no doubt heightened by the fact that in both basic design and application the domestic and foreign machines represented entirely opposed considerations. While the British manufacturers ultimately came to realize that more substantially built models were necessary to compete successfully on the American market, their inbred conservatism prevented them from making radical changes in their basic designs.

In the matter of competition, British importers and enthusiasts had, from the beginning, emphasized what they considered the unfairness of the AMA rules regarding piston displacement and compression ratios that penalized the performance of their machines.

On the other hand, if the Competition Committee had relaxed the rules to enable the imports to compete under the non-restrictive ACU-FICM rules in the early post-war period, the technical development of the imports as compared to domestic models would have placed the domestics at a serious disadvantage.

Then the issue of fairness raised the question of the position of the domestic manufacturers. Having survived the near demise of the industry after World War I, as well as the devastating effects of the Depression, it would have been an inequitable situation to have allowed the post-war importers to overwhelm the market with the middleweight designs that the domestic manufacturers never had the prior assets to develop.

In view of these conditions, it is little wonder that the adherents of both factions had, up to this point, not been able to arrive at a cordial meeting of the minds.

The ongoing bitter controversy regarding the autocratic position of the AMA and its Competition Committee still remained unresolved, but, at the same time, any dilution of its central authority would have resulted in a breakdown of the competition organization that the industry needed for its survival.

It must be emphasized that while Harley-Davidson, as the long time dominant force within the M&ATA and the AMA, was the leader in the fight against the intrusion of the imports, Milwaukee had substantial support from other than just their own dealers and enthusiasts. A substantial number of former Indian dealers and owners, as well as a few veteran Super-X and Henderson enthusiasts, were firmly on their side. These people were sympathetic to the position of the domestic industry on the grounds of both patriotism as well as in support of its past struggles to survive.

CHAPTER TEN

A TIME OF CHANGE
1955-1965

A Time of Change 1955-1965

The beginning of the second decade of the revitalized post-war domestic motorcycle saw many of the leaders within it speculating upon the reasons for its static condition. It was noted that the average yearly retail sales had leveled off at between 50,000 and 60,000 units. In comparison, automobile sales were soaring, and the nation was undergoing a population explosion. Some marketing analysts were of the opinion that the low birth rate experienced during the pre-war Depression years had now resulted in fewer young motorcycle buyers. Others thought that the lack of new innovative designs from both the British as well as the domestic factories was responsible for a leveling off of public interest now that the novelty of the availability of imported models had worn off. Others cited the effects of the Korean War in discouraging potential draftees from purchasing machines.

Another factor affecting the domestic manufacturers was the almost total loss of their once-important export market, where formerly often 45 to 55% of the yearly output went overseas and had been a critical item in keeping the ailing industry afloat. Henry Vernon, who headed the Titeflex operation that had produced the Blackhawk Chiefs, stated that had a viable export market been in existence, their manufacture could have survived the decimation of Indian's domestic dealership. Harley-Davidson's 1955 production had dwindled to about 9,500 units, relying now almost wholly on domestic sales and with only a handful of machines exported to Japan and South America. High foreign tariffs were of course the answer, and in an attempt to aid in overseas offshore recovery and to halt the spread of Communism, the U.S. government still implemented the Marshall Plan. In addition, the low tariff on foreign imports brought a return of the hard currency that allowed the purchase of domestically produced foodstuffs.

On the sporting side it was now apparent that Harley-Davidson KR models were in the ascendancy. With the refinement of its design favoring the Class C concept, and the factory's control of the AMA Competition Committee that insured the predominance of dirt track events that were the essence of KR supremacy, the British were now at a distinct disadvantage.

In commenting on this situation, noted tuner Ray "Pop" Schunk later told the author that while the British factories had somewhat reluctantly slightly beefed up their engine designs to better contend with the rigors of American competition, such were not sufficient to stand up to the more rugged KRs. It was his opinion that if the British engines had been made 10% more rugged, their chances of overall victories would have been enhanced 100%!

This new trend was not lost on British enthusiasts, and a group of California dealers, led by Joe Sarkess of Sacramento and Al Fergoda of San Jose, proposed a remedy. It was their contention that the Competition Committee had unfairly rigged both the technical rulings regarding 500 cc overhead valve motors as well as the venues of competition. As a compromise it was suggested that the allowable compression ratios for such engines be raised from 8:1 to 9:1. To give effect to this intent, it was now proposed to file legal action against the AMA and the Competition Committee to enforce a change in the rulings.

With the concurrence of some other Triumph as well as BSA dealers, members of the BMDA, Sarkees engaged the services of a local attorney, Walter B. Henretty, to inaugurate such an action on the allegation that the AMA was engaging in a restraint of trade. Henretty, who was a personal acquaintance of the author, subsequently privately stated that he saw little merit in the BMDA's contention, as the AMA was a private organization not connected with industry. On this promise, the provisions of the Clayton and Sherman Antitrust Acts could not be applied.

Rather than going to the effort of preparing a formal pleading, Henretty sent a letter to the Competition Committee, stating the BMDA's com-

A Time of Change 1955-1965

plaints and suggesting a compromise to forestall the
formal filing of charges. Harley-Davidson's legal
counsel privately agreed with Henretty's opinion in
the matter, and so stated in a subsequent conference
with the Competition Committee. While the
Committee was sure of their ground, they decided
that the publicity created would highlight an ongoing warfare between the domestic factories and the
importers and would have further adverse effects on
the industry. Now, confident in the advantageous
position enjoyed by the KR, the Committee voted to
raise the allowable compression ratio of 500 cc
overhead valve machines to 9:1.

As matters now stood, the KR's operating ratios
in the hands of different tuners ranged from 5-1/2 to
6:1; it's optimum spread for the most effective
power development. While the raising of the overhead valve motor ratios to 9:1 allowed them to
attain more power through increased engine revolutions, the consequent stresses induced reduced reliability so, in the end, the import's advantage in the
matter was indeterminate.

During 1955, Alfred Rich Child reassessed his
position with BSA. While he had created a substantial market for their motorcycles through both his
own East Coast market and the association in the
West with Hap Alzina, he was now uncertain about
the future of the U.S. situation in regard to the situation with BSA's top management.

The Birmingham Small Arms organization
came into being in the early years of the 19th
Century to supply the British forces who, during the
Victorian era, were engaged in consolidating Great
Britain's far flung colonial empire. As the company
prospered during the succeeding territorial expansion, other diverse manufacturing activities were
added and, after the turn of the century, comprised
at least 20 subsidiaries including automobiles, and
in 1910 motorcycles were added. This industrial
empire was presided over by Sir Bernard Docker as
Chairman of BSA's central Board of Directors, who
followed a policy of encouraging the autonomy of
each of the subordinate companies as long as they
continued to be profitable. After 1950, the free
wheeling Docker's management was challenged by
a new group of substantial shareholders. Child, who
had enjoyed a working relationship with the motorcycle division's director, James Leek, had ultimately
encouraged the development of machines adapted to
the American market. With a threatened change in
overall BSA policy, Child was apprehensive regarding his own position in the company. By this time
Child had amassed a considerable fortune and, near-
ing 65 years of age, decided to call it a day. As his
import business was highly profitable, he
approached BSA's top management with the suggestion that the company assume direct management of the U.S. operation and purchase his

A TIME OF CHANGE 1955-1965

interests. After some negotiations, the agreement was finalized, with Child receiving $1,250,000. Child at once moved to Las Vegas, as the state of Nevada, then as now, levied neither income or inheritance taxes due to the overriding income from the taxes on legalized gambling.

After BSA took over the American operation, Ted Hodgdon was appointed to the post of General Manager, which, as will be seen, was to have an indeterminate effect on the company's fortune in the States.

Hap Alzina's western operation was unaffected, as Child's operation was limited to the territory east of the Mississippi, and in any case, Alzina had already negotiated a renewed five year duration contract with BSA in 1954. He continued to receive machines and spare parts shipped directly to Oakland by steamship.

In the meantime, transportation events in Japan, virtually unknown in the western world at the time, were taking place which were to cause revolutionary changes in both the world's automotive and motorcycling industries.

The story has been told many times concerning the post-war activities of one Soichiro Honda, who was born in Osaka in 1906, and whose spectacular career personifies one of the world's most astounding success stories. An indifferent student, Honda dropped out of school to become a mechanic.

During the late 1920's he developed a penchant for American cars and motorcycles, owning several examples of cars as well as a later Sport Scout and a VL Harley-Davidson. An interest in race car building came next, and he ultimately obtained a patent for his design of lightweight aluminum automobile wheels. Noting the shortage of spare parts for American products, he formed a small company, Tokai Seika, to manufacture pistons and piston rings. Experiencing a lack of both theoretical and technical knowledge in mechanical engineering, he enrolled in a part time engineering course.

Following the War, and noting the lack of motorized transportation facilities, not only in Japan but throughout the Pacific Rim due to the destruction from military action, he proposed his own solution in a most unique manner. The great bulk of personal transportation in the Orient had been long provided by the bicycle, but Honda reasoned that such could provide a stop-gap until more developed transportation could be made available.

Japanese military aircraft were fitted with small electric generator units as auxiliary power, these mostly being powered by small 50 or 100 cc, air-cooled, single cylinder, two stroke, gasoline engines built in large numbers by Mikuni and Tohatsu. Large numbers of these units were available as surplus, and Honda adapted the engines as "clip on" units for roadster bicycles. With the

A Time of Change 1955-1965

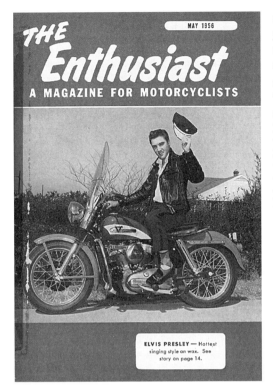

Harley-Davidson scored big when it lined up Elvis Presley for the cover of "The Enthusiast" in 1956. *Don Emde Collection*

shortage of motorized transportation in Japan, his venture was an immediate success: Honda's small firm at once sold all it could put together. As the supply of surplus motors diminished, Honda formed the Honda Motor Company in Hammamatsu, and proceeded to design motors that possessed better longevity than the surplus units had sustained under continuous use. He was able to secure a substantial loan from the Mitsubishi Bank, having proved his commercial venture as a viable reality, and came to the U.S. to purchase suitable machine tooling. Now with adequate financing he was able to purchase a large order from the Houdaille Company. On his return to Japan, and with the help of his brother Benjiro, he inaugurated a three model range of machines. These were the "A" Model, a motorized bicycle; the "B" Model, a tricycle; and a "C" Model, a miniaturized motorcycle with the fuel tank in the conventional position above the motor. In the need for expansion of the company, Takeo Fujisawa joined the firm as business manager in the fall of 1949. In the same year, a larger 100 cc Model "D" was introduced with all chain drive and a two speed gearbox. A larger 150 cc "E" Model, called the "Dream" came in 1951.

Expansion of the market was halted in 1953 by the economic depression in Japan after the Korean War and Honda then concentrated on the lower priced "clip on" models in the interim. With better times near the end of 1955, a new and more luxurious model, the 250 cc overhead camshaft "Dream", appeared for that sales year. At this point, Honda was Japan's leading motorcycle manufacturer, its product line emphasizing four stroke engines.

As was to be expected, other Japanese firms entered the motorcycle market following Honda's initial successes. Yamaha, a leading manufacturer of musical instruments as well as a broad range of sporting goods and leisure time products, entered the industry with a two model line of 50 and 80 cc miniature motorcycles with two stroke engines. Suzuki, a large conglomerate with a special interest in manufacturing textile processing and weaving machinery, also entered the industry with 50 cc

"step through" type two stroke, along with a similarly powered miniature motorcycle, and a low geared trail bike version for off road use. These were also two stroke powered.

Other smaller firms entering the field were Tohatsu, who made the basic small engines during the war effort, and Bridgestone, a large tire manufacturer who also made other industrial products. Other minor participants were Lilac and Marusho, the latter making rather inferior copies of the German BMW.

The market for any sort of vehicles in the Pacific Rim and Malaysian areas was, of course, a fertile field of endeavor, as their transportation units were mostly a few well worn automobiles and trucks that had survived the war, augmented by limited numbers of surplus military vehicles left over from the conflict. By 1955, Honda was the largest motorcycle manufacturer in the world, with a huge factory complex with multiple assembly lines turning out 500,000 units per year. The rest of the industry expanded rapidly to add 300,000 units yearly to this total. With a now expanding export effort, Japanese machines were penetrating the Australian and New Zealand markets, as well as Africa, and by the late 1950's were extending their markets to Europe and the Middle East.

As a paradox, this expansion took place as the German made machines declined due to the causes mentioned, though NSU, with their advanced overhead camshaft models, survived, as did Maico, who also made light two stroke powered automobiles and the Maicoletta scooter.

It was during this period that the Italian motorcycle industry underwent a recovery with an emphasis on mopeds, autocycles, and miniature motorcycles. The miniature motorcycles were caricatures of Grand Prix type machines, a manifestation of the Latin propensity for high speed travel. Due to the shortage of automobiles and their consequent high prices, the industry concentrated on lightweights through such firms as Garelli, Minerella, Aermacchi, with Moto Guzzi being the most prominent. Two of Moto-Guzzi's larger models were well-proven pre-war types: the 250 cc Astore and the 500 Falcone. The 500 Falcone was a civilianized version of the Italian Army machines. These were of the "Gambalunga" or "long leg" type, with horizontally disposed single cylinder configuration. These proved to be rugged and almost indestructible models, and were imported in limited quantities by Lou Branch, the pioneer Velocette distributor in Los Angeles. Smaller numbers of high performance Benellis and MV machines were also imported. Intermittent produc-

Milwaukee's record breaking streamliner fitted with an Aermacchi 250cc racing engine which attained a speed of 158.6 mph at Bonneville for a new class record.
Harley-Davidson Motor Company

Racers such as Brad Andres and Joe Leonard kept Harley-Davidson in the spotlight in the 1950's.
Don Emde Collection

tion was a weakness of the Italian factories, as was the unavailability of spare parts. A source of problems was the often weird and wonderful vagaries of Italian electrical systems, as well as their small and rather hard saddles. Branch's rather limited financial structuring together with the Italian's somewhat unorthodox design features limited sales to those iconoclastic buyers who fancied something distinctive and out of the ordinary.

During the mid-1950's E.C. Smith broached the subject of his desire to consider retirement, after an almost thirty years tenure as the AMA Secretary Manager, to the Competition Committee and the officers of the M&ATA. After some discussion of the matter, President William H. Davidson suggested the name of Lin Kuchler to be considered as his replacement. Kuchler later recalled that his long association with both the Davidsons and his subsequent employment at the factory was originally due to his being a Milwaukee native and having grown up and been schoolboys with the younger Davidsons, Allan, Gordon, and Robert. His pre-war factory employment and his later brief post-war connection has been noted, along with his

brief tenure as a franchised dealer in Ann Arbor.

Between his very brief post-war association and the Ann Arbor connection, Kuchler had found other employment. But, after giving up the latter, he had conducted a limited operation as a non-franchised service facility to maintain his former customer's machines as well as servicing two adjacent police departments who were long time Harley-Davidson buyers.

At any rate, President Davidson's recommendation of Kuchler was based on both their long standing friendship and the fact that through his official connections with the company he enjoyed a wide acquaintanceship with Harley-Davidson dealers, especially throughout the Midwest where loyalty to Milwaukee was the strongest.

After some negotiations, Kuchler accepted the appointment which was confirmed by both the M&ATA and the Competition Committee, and which was based on Kuchler's willingness to serve in the capacity of Smith's assistant until 1958, in order to effect an orderly transfer of the office. The starting salary was agreed upon as $3,000 per year, plus attendant travel expenses when required.

A Time of Change 1955-1965

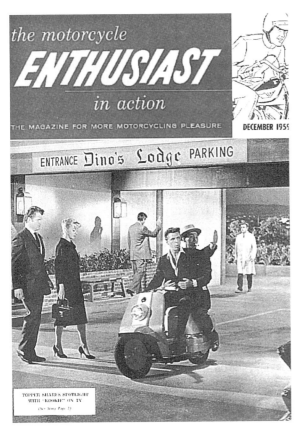

the motorcycle
ENTHUSIAST
in action
THE MAGAZINE FOR MORE MOTORCYCLING PLEASURE   DECEMBER 1959

ENTRANCE Dino's Lodge PARKING

TOPPER SHARES SPOTLIGHT
WITH "KOOKIE" ON TV
(See Story Page 2)

Another top celebrity riding Harleys in the 1950's was Ed "Kookie" Burns. His choice of machinery was the Topper scooter. *Don Emde Collection*

Kuchler recalled that while Smith was initially cordial to his appointment, he was less than cooperative after Kuchler settled in at Columbus, and appeared reticent about acquainting him with the intimate details of the AMA operation. The staff at that time consisted of Smith, Jules Horky as his assistant in charge of sanctioning of events and record keeping, Marie Jenkins, who had succeeded Cora Reardon as office manager and who was also Smith's secretary, and four female clerk-typists. Mrs. Jenkins turned out to be somewhat hostile toward Kuchler, and he was denied access to certain of Smith's private files as well as the office safe that contained material relative to the Committee's financial matters. At any rate, Kuchler's initial duties were to take over the issuance of some of the sanctioning details of adjacent AMA clubs and outside promoter's proposals for the same. Kuchler also noted that the Davidsons did not extend to him the same arrangement that Smith enjoyed as a paid public relations agent to the Harley-Davidson factory, which, for many years, had been a private association not connected with either the M&ATA or the AMA. At the same time, Kuchler only functioned initially on a part-time basis, as he was traveling two or three days a week to Ann Arbor to close out his shop activities there.

When Smith first announced his intention to retire, there was some speculation within the AMA whether or not Horky, who had been a full-time AMA employee for the past decade, might assume Smith's position. However, Horky later informed the author that he preferred what he called the inside work of record keeping and sanctioning supervision rather than outside travel away from Columbus, and that he did not relish contending with the complex political considerations that were ever a part and parcel of AMA operation.

On the journalistic side, there were now only three motorcycle trade publications after the demise of "Bzzz. The Motorcycle News". They were "Cycle", "The Motorcyclist" and "American Motorcycling". The first two were oriented to general news of the trade, reports of competition activities and technical articles and road tests. The last one, of course, was dedicated toward self-serving news of AMA activities and promotion of the interests of the domestic factory products and accessories.

The staff at "Cycle" was headed by Editor Don Brown, with the assistance of Evan Aikin and Bob Schanz, together with Hank Elfrink land Eric Arctander as contributing journalists. These were all independent thinkers, and in general were often in a somewhat underground contention with Floyd Clymer, who at the same time was somewhat deferential to their superior talents as professional writers and their in-depth knowledge of the trade and industry. In addition, Brown was an active competition rider, his main interest being in enduro type off-road events. He had become quite active in this area after 1951, when he competed on Matchless and AJS machines. In 1953, he rode with Harley-Davidson sponsorship, an experimental 45 cubic inch overhead valve prototype racing machine at the Catalina Grand Prix, which proved unsuitable due to its excessive weight penalty as an enduro entrant. In 1956, he placed third at the Island on a specially prepared MAC Velocette supplied by Lou Branch in the 350 cc class.

At any rate, and faced with a growing apprehension concerning Clymer's sometimes disapproving attitude, Brown elected to resign his position and move on to other interests within the sport and industry. He next acted as a sales representative for after market products, calling on various dealers, as well as promoting the sale of the second edition printing of his book, "How to Ride and Win."

Another notable activity was his inauguration of a half-hour radio program, sponsored by Johnson Motors and dealing with motorcycling, which aired over local Los Angeles station KHJ. This was the first time that such a broadcast was ever featured in the U.S. dealing specifically with the industry, and for a time it enjoyed a good response, being aired on prime time in the 7:30 p.m. time slot.

It was during the 1956 Catalina races that William Johnson offered him the position of General Sales Manager for Johnson's Ariel-Triumph distributorship.

On the competition side, Harley-Davidson was now in a dominant position in AMA contests, with

Celebrants crowd a Daytona saloon incidental to the 200 Classic.
Jimmy Roberts

another increase in horsepower due to both factory development and the efforts of Tom Sifton. With pre-race time trials now instituted at Daytona to determine starting positions, Brad Andres on a KR topped the field for the 1956 event at 126.3 mph. Second was Joe Leonard with 124.1 mph. The first place for British machines was taken by Dick Doresteyn on a Triumph at 121.6 mph.

The race was won by Johnny Gibson on a KR, at 94 mph, after fellow Milwaukee riders Paul Goldsmith, Brad Andres and Joe Leonard were all sidelined with blown engines. A strong BSA challenge was mounted by Dick Klamfoth, George Everett, Tommy McDermott and Eugene Theissen, who took second to fifth places. These were followed by another pack of KR riders who took sixth to tenth places. Bobby Hill, now KR mounted, was twelfth, and Indian had its Daytona swan song with Claude Mook who came in eighteenth.

Harley-Davidson riders swept the 1956 season by winning all of the National Championships, proving that the 9:1 compression ratio concession for 500 cc overhead valve machines did not offer a formidable threat to Milwaukee.

With the newly instituted point system, Joe Leonard kept his Number One plate, which gave the advantage to consistent high point winners throughout the ongoing season.

It was now apparent to the more casual observers of AMA competition, and somewhat grudgingly admitted by the distributors, dealers and tuners of British machines that, apart from the technical development of KR Harley-Davidsons, Milwaukee's domination was in no small way due to their organization and single minded dedication to Class C competition. With a well organized racing department and the production of a substantial number of machines, together with the control of the venues of competitive events, Milwaukee's campaigning was most effective. In addition, they were able to recruit top flight riders by offering attendant financial inducements.

On the other hand, the British manufacturers could not be persuaded to alter their basic engine designs for improved performance and dependability. The factories offered little in the way of subsidy for competition activities, such being left to either the distributors, dealers or private entrants. In the absence of such support, the actual numbers of British competition machines was far less than those fielded by Harley-Davidson, which in itself was a distinct advantage.

In addition, Harley-Davidson's shareholders were in accord with the need for substantial sup-

A TIME OF CHANGE 1955-1965

port of competition as a marketing adjunct and the funding required to serve it. These factors gave credence to the old adage that victories in the field of motor sport invariably accrued to those who could spend the most money.

With the adequate production of new automobiles to serve the contemporary market, together with the consequently moderate prices asked for used cars, the market for scooters now leveled off. There was always a hard core of those seeking the ultimate economies in basic transportation, however, along with the ongoing numbers of youthful riders who sought entry level sport and utility. In the face of substantial production from larger manufacturers, such as Cushman and Salsbury, many of the smaller firms, catering to local markets dropped out of the picture. There was also a substantial demand for the more sophisticated high performance Vespa and Lambretta models.

One mitigating factor was the effect of the increase in the building of the nation's network of freeways and expressways. Many states now prohibited the low powered scooters from them on the reasonable conclusion that such vehicles were at risk when mixed with high speed traffic. Then too, a number of states rescinded the fourteen year age minimum of licensing scooter riders on the grounds of an increased number of accidents. The Whizzer organization at once terminated the marketing of their bicycle clip-on units, and the operation was moved to Holland, where much of that country's

transportation was centered on bicycles.

Harley-Davidson had entered the scooter market with a model called the Topper. It was powered by the well proven DKW engine-gearbox unit fitted with a centrifugal drive based on Salsbury patents. In addition to a standard model, a detuned version with a small carburetor and restricted breathing was offered to conform to certain licensing restrictions on power development in some states. Its retail price of $600 was not competitive with most of the rest of the market, but as a well built and rugged machine it was generally trouble free and gave good service. Its prototype costs were moderate, involving mostly the fabrication of a simple chassis; the engine unit being already in production for the Hummer motorcycles.

With the disappointing response to the KH 55 cubic inch side valve model, Harley-Davidson was now considering updating the machine. Potential customers for middleweight motorcycles apparently were not attracted to an obsolete side valve engine mated to a contemporary chassis, especially as its overall performance was unimpressive. As it was, the overall design was generally considered as a 20th Century anachronism. Early in 1956, some prototype experiments were undertaken with an overhead valve 55 incher with high camshaft valve action. Provisionally designated as the KL, the project was dropped in the face of design problems, and it was then decided to proceed with a more conventional overhead valve engine fitted with push rods. The valve gear design was based on what had been fitted to the 500 cc CAC racing model as developed by Joe Petrali in 1931. Joe had based this design on one already developed by J.A. Prestwich in England, in relation to its valve operation, and the new model, catalogued as the Sportster, was launched for the 1957 sales season. With its enhanced performance, it was hoped it would fulfill the need for both an entry level big twin and get the interest of the sporting rider. But its long stroke engine combined with the inherent rocking couple of the narrow angle V-twin engine produced excessive vibration at its upper range revolutions. Unsuited to long distance travel, it now became considered a cafe cruising type, and for decades has been a controversial model.

Milwaukee's ongoing successes continued into the 1957 season, with Joe Leonard heading the field with a win at Daytona, together with four of the eight big Nationals, and wins at the Laconia 100 and the Twenty-Miler at Springfield.

Making his debut that season was Carroll Resweber, who was distinguishing himself on half-mile and one-mile tracks and ranked fourth in point

A TIME OF CHANGE 1955-1965

Gil Stratton, television sportscaster, one time motion picture actor, and Triumph enthusiast on his Tiger Supersports model with Don Brown as a passenger. The photograph was taken incidental to Stratton's hosting Brown's KHJ weekly radio broadcast sponsored by Johnson Motors.
Ralph Poole

Triumph Service Manager Cal Makela (l) and Don Brown with a 1956 Ariel Red Hunter scrambler model.
Don Brown

A Time of Change 1955-1965

Carroll Resweber wore the #1 number plate for Harley-Davidson for four straight years in the late 1950's and early 1960's. *Don Emde Collection*

"Cycle" magazine had a wide variety of coverage in the 50's and 60's. *Don Emde Collection*

standing. BSA riders managed to win two National races, with Al Gunter coming close to Joe Leonard in points, winning second spot.

At the season's end, the veteran Hank Syvertsen, who had been associated with Milwaukee's racing activities since 1920, and who had assumed command of competition activities in 1945, elected to retire. He was succeeded by Richard "Dick" O'Brien, a talented self-taught engineer in the manner of Tom Sifton, who had a distinguished record in building automobile racing engines.

Harley-Davidson previously had updated its FL models with the offering of an optional hand controlled clutch and foot operated gear changing mechanism in response to public demand. The design was based on a pre-war after-market fitting that had been first offered as an accessory in 1938. In 1957, a plunger type rear springing was added as a standard fitting, with an eye to bringing the model in line with current practice. The arrangement was actually somewhat less than effective as the top attachment of the unit was set rather far forward on the frame just behind the seat brackets. This was done to reduce what would have been a rather wide silhouette when either the universal saddle bags or police equipment were positioned on either side of the rear wheel. While sufficient resiliency was attained to counteract the more severe road shocks, many enthusiasts claimed that, as a strictly highway machine, such was not necessary due to the action of the sprung seat post and the 5" sectioned tires that already offered a very comfortable ride. In any case, the new arrangement added an additional 80 pounds to an already heavy machine. The new models were catalogued as the "Duo-Glide."

Erwin G. "Cannonball" Baker, long a professional rider, was perhaps the only motorcyclist who had enjoyed national recognition for his well publicized transcontinental record runs on both motorcycles as well as automobiles. With his interest in colorful exploits, it had often been suggested by members of the industry that he write his autobiography. Baker was often in agreement, but privately hesitated because of his lack of literary abilities due to the neglected formal education from his youth. The author had already become well acquainted with Baker through ongoing contacts in relation to attendance at Trailblazer gatherings; Baker offering much valuable historical material on the earlier days of the motorcycle industry.

The matter of recording Baker's life and times came into focus in 1957, after several meetings with the author, Baker now suggested that he could ghostwrite his memoirs. The main problem was to locate a publisher, mindful of the reticence with which leading literary concerns were known to view motorcycling. The most promising compromise appeared to be Floyd Clymer, then the most prolific purveyor of motorcycling books, although both Baker and the author were skeptical of his business methods, which, in the past, had shown that he was averse to allowing any of his contributing authors to share in profits from sales.

At any rate, Baker and the author made an appointment with Clymer, who immediately expressed an interest in producing Baker's memoirs. When Baker brought up the matter of negotiating a formal contract covering financial details, Clymer at once demurred, stating that "only a handshake was necessary". In noting what appeared to be Clymer's typical strategy, Baker stood up, motioned to the author to follow him, and angrily left the office. Any possible future opportunities to formally record Baker's exploits came to an end with Baker's failing health due to the onset of crippling arthritis, which he attributed to the rigors of his years of record breaking, and his passing in the summer of 1960, at his home in Indianapolis at the age of seventy-eight.

Hap Alzina's BSA operation prospered in the nineteen western states under his capable management that featured an aggressive recruitment of new dealers with an accompanying sales campaign, together with a substantial support of competition activities. But sales of BSA products leveled off in the eastern states, which was attributed to Ted Hodgdon's tight-fisted management. After assuming control, he closed the Madison Avenue office in New York City, moving the executive offices to Nutley, New Jersey. He then moved the operation from the spacious warehouse facilities established by Alfred Rich Child to less suitable, but less costly, quarters in a former Kaiser-Frazer automobile dealer's premises in Nutley.

When Hodgdon was installed as General Manager by the factory-owned operation, he was instructed to set up both a profit sharing arrangement and pension as well as health care agreement with a group of new employees. This Hodgdon agreed to do, but actually did not. In addition, he instituted a wage and salary scale for the employees which was substantially substandard. In his initial agreement with BSA, Hodgdon was allowed a generous financial yearly bonus arrangement based on overall sales in addition to a regular salary. After establishing substandard wages and salaries and denying any other benefits, the accrual of

A TIME OF CHANGE 1955-1965

funds from gross sales was increased by this practice, to Hodgdon's advantage. George S. Alexander, who initially was employed as a bookkeeper, and Emmett Moore, who later became Sales Manager, later reported that Hodgdon paid himself over a million dollars in bonuses during the ten year period that he managed the operation. It was noted, however, that the efficiency of the branch suffered through the high turnover of employees caused by Hodgdon's penurious tactics.

In the meantime, the Japanese motorcycle industry was undergoing a rapid expansion, due to the demand for utility transportation throughout the Pacific Rim area. Honda, Suzuki and Yamaha set up marketing and service outlets through the Pacific Island chain, as well as in the Philippines, Borneo, Malaysia, the Adaman Islands, Australia, New Zealand, Taiwan, Sri Lanka, India, Madagascar, and into South Africa.

Taiwan, as an emerging industrial nation, negotiated with the major factories for the assembly rights for certain models under license in that country. There was some resistance to Japanese products in Australia and New Zealand due to the overtones of prejudice left over from the war.

The Japanese firms were producing larger capacity models by 1960, most of the initial offer-

ings having been in the 50, 80, and 100 cc categories. Their superiority in both quality and performance over the traditionally manufactured British makes was at once apparent and, due to the position of the yen, could be marketed at substantially lower prices. Then, too, with their advanced designs, the small capacity Japanese machines could outperform the comparable British models which were still mostly powered by the venerable 9D and 10D Villiers 125 cc engine-gear units whose basic designs were little changed from the early 1930's. These makes included James, Francis Barnett, Tandon, Ambassador and a few others which, in any case, were produced in such small numbers that they were simply overwhelmed by the extensive Japanese production.

Members of the Harley and Davidson families, factory employees, dealers, and enthusiasts were saddened, in the summer of 1957, by the death of young Gordon Davidson after a brief illness. It was reported that he had suffered from an acute inflammation of the kidneys, which associates alleged was complicated by his addiction to alcohol. Like others of the Davidson's younger generation, he had grown up within the activities of the factory and had recently been a member of the production staff.

A Time of Change 1955-1965

Don Emde Collection

Yamaha was the next
Japanese manufacturer
to hit it big in the U.S.
Don Emde Collection

In June of 1958, E.C. Smith formally retired from his position as AMA Secretary-Manager in which he had served for thirty years. This had run concurrently with his nearly forty-five year connection with various branches of the sport and industry, notably as an early day race promoter. The occasion was marked by a banquet held in Columbus, attended by members of both the M&ATA and AMA Competition Committee, as well as dealers and many AMA members-at-large. Smith received many accolades for his long years of service, including a number of citations and trophies from various members of the motorcycle industry. Long a controversial figure, his management of the AMA had been accompanied by almost continual turmoil. While he conducted his office in a dictatorial and often arbitrary manner, his dedication to promoting the best interests of both the sport and industry was never questioned. In noting this turbulent history, many knowledgeable leaders within the industry were in agreement that an organization composed of regulating both the affairs of the industry as well as its sporting aspects was inevitably subject to ongoing controversy. In contemplating the unfortunate past histories of both the FAM and the M&ATA, which preceded the formal founding of the AMA, it was strongly indicated that only a forthright and aggressive leadership could have held the present organization together.

While the initial and ongoing support of the factories, both administrative and financial, and their consequent role in commercial dictatorship was much cause for criticism, at the same time the AMA could never have survived under a less structured organization. With Harley-Davidson's ultimate dominant role in the AMA as the domestic industry's sole survivor, it inevitably became the target of much criticism, whether justified or not.

At any rate, and perhaps to avoid further controversial reviews of past AMA policies, Smith took with him many of the official records, original copies of the minutes of the meetings of the Competition Committee's more controversial decisions, along with the records of his financial involvement with Harley-Davidson as a public relationship advocate. It was subsequently alleged, but never proven, that most of these records ultimately passed into the possession of the Davidson family.

Upon taking over Smith's office, Kuchler recalled that he at once faced a dual organization totally controlled by a private club made up of Harley-Davidson factory employees and dealers, together with their component suppliers, which formed an entrenched clique in the "good ol' boy" tradition.

At the same time, the M&ATA and AMA were suffering from a depleted treasury, as most of the operating income had lately been received from sanctioning fees for competition events. This weakness was in part caused by the minimal dollar-per-year membership dues and the low subscription cost of the magazine; both of which Smith had purposely kept low in the theory that it increased membership. Membership-at-large had recently been static, due to the phasing out of most of the Gypsy Tour programs due to the growing problem of conflicts taking place between AMA members and certain of the outlaw groups who caused disturbances when the two factions came together.

In an initial effort to increase income, Kuchler was able to convince the Competition Committee to raise the subscription fee of "American Motorcycling" to $3.00 per year. In its initial reports of the change in the AMA's top management and a discussion of Kuchler's past career activities, it was stated that he had formerly been associated with "a prominent Milwaukee manufacturer" — an effort to publicly play down Harley-Davidson's dominant position in the AMA.

A more immediate problem was the AMA's status with the Internal Revenue Service, in relation to their income tax situation. Kuchler, who had some background knowledge of bookkeeping and accounting, early on noted to his dismay that in its 1928 incorporation the AMA had been organized as a non-profit entity. But since the inception of the Class C concept in 1933, the income from sanctions had not been reported. Up to this point the IRS had not challenged the AMA's non-profit status and Kuchler rightly feared that if such action were instituted, the consequent demand for back taxes and accrued penalties could result in the AMA being put out of business. He contacted the IRS headquarters in Chicago regarding the matter, explaining the problem. The agency was cooperative in the matter, especially as Kuchler had personally initiated a review of AMA status, and worked out a yearly payment schedule that staved off any potentially embarrassing legal action.

Another ongoing problem was the overall poor public image suffered by motorcycling, now focusing on the conflicts with the outlaw element that was receiving media attention, and backstopped by the continuing fratricidal warfare between the competing domestic makes which had begun in the 1930's, and was now intensified by the post-war introduction of imported machines. Kuchler proposed that the Competition Committee authorize a professionally conducted public relations campaign to correct this unfavorable impression, not-

A TIME OF CHANGE 1955-1965

Rider awards being presented at an Edward Turner sponsored event in 1963. Don Brown and Turner on the right.
Ralph Poole

ing that neither Smith nor the Committee had seen fit to make substantial effort in this direction.

Certain members of the Committee countered that the AMA had officially encouraged support of the March of Dimes campaign first inaugurated by the President before the war and continuing in the 1950's. It also noted that the AMA had given official support to the National Safety Council, as well as Red Cross fund drives, the Charity Newsies program, and that many local AMA chartered clubs had given public support to various charities. It was noted that the hiring of professional public relations firms had been suggested before, but the high costs of such a program was too prohibitive.

Kuchler then called attention to the very minimal $1.00 per year membership fee for individuals, and at long last, in 1959, convinced the Committee to raise the dues to $2.00.

Following this enhancement of the M&ATA's and AMA's financial situation, Kuchler was able to convince the Committee to engage a professional public relations firm to enhance motorcycling's image. The advertising firm of Klaus Van Peterson-Dunlap, which had such facilities based in Chicago and New York, was awarded a contract

to fulfill this assignment. They were able to forward reports of various major competition events to some of the larger newspapers for insertion, along with articles concerning certain charitable drives that the organized AMA clubs were participating in, together with other material favorable to motorcycling. Not forgotten was the AMA's support of the National Safety Council's effort to reduce the number of traffic accidents.

On the competition side, 1958 saw the growing prominence of Carroll Resweber as one of Milwaukee's star riders who was destined to leave his mark as one of motorcycling's all time greats. In the point system, he was able to win out over Joe Leonard by one digit in a 36 to 35 accounting. Leonard garnered his second Daytona 200 and Springfield wins, but lost out at mid-season because of an injury.

In the overall picture, British machines were able to take one-half of the victories in the big Nationals. Of ten such events, Harley-Davidson won five, with BSA winning four and Triumph one. This was the first post-war year when Milwaukee failed to win a majority of these events.

Tom Sifton, in his making peace with

Eddie Mulder shocked the motorcycle world when he won the prestigious Big Bear Run at the age of 16 in 1960.
Don Emde Collection

Milwaukee, had been appointed a member of the Competition Committee, and had shared his tuning secrets to aid in Harley-Davidson's growing supremacy. He later told the author that at long last he had become disenchanted with the continual quarreling over the side valve/overhead valve controversy, which his new membership on the Committee had brought more sharply into focus.

In a personal revolt against the Committee and Harley-Davidson dominance in its affairs, Sifton decided to turn his attention to BSA products, no doubt to prove his versatility in motorcycle engineering. He next reworked a Gold Star for Everett Brashear, a now disenchanted Milwaukee rider, for a big National that was held at the fast track in San Jose, California. During the qualifying time trials that preceded the race, Brashear broke Joe Leonard's record in a 43.49 mile run, breaking the past year's by a fraction of a second. During the 25 mile race, Brashear narrowly beat Carroll Resweber, now a formidable competitor. Sammy Tanner, also mounted on a Sifton-tuned Gold Star, came in second. Sifton noted that both the KR's and the Gold Stars showed identical power, each kicking out 58 h.p. at somewhat variable engine revolutions. Again referring to the long standing contention over engine types, Sifton offered the theory that Milwaukee long ago should have brought out a 500 cc overhead valve engine to offer more fair competition to the British, rather than continuing to support tradition with obsolete designs of side valve engines.

In the meantime, both BSA and Triumph organizations continued their aggressive sales campaigns. Hap Alzina conducted a vigorous dealer recruitment program directed by Sales Manager W.C. "Bill" Meyer, as did Triumph's Don Brown, backed by the efforts of Service Manager Pete Colman, who managed an augmented parts and service organization. In a ploy to increase dealer representation, Brown offered a dealership to any individual who would purchase just one machine with a basic supply of spare parts. They would be able to purchase a new machine at 10% over dealer's cost, with the option to purchase spare parts at a figure allowing him a 50% markup. This, together with the mandated purchase of an electrically lighted official plastic-faced neon Triumph sign, would enable the initial start-up of a factory approved dealership.

The operations of the west coast Triumph organization was sometimes rendered indeterminate by the health problems of both William E. Johnson and Wilbur Ceder. Both were confirmed alcoholics and Ceder also suffered from crippling arthritis; his drinking problem said to have been induced by his constantly being in severe pain. At any rate, the pair's late afternoon drinking bouts had become legendary in their intensity.

In the meantime, William E. Kennedy, President of the Rex Chain Belt Company, had been elected president of the M&ATA-AMA, and had pledged his support to Lin Kuchler in attempting to update and enlarge the scope of influence of the organization for the improved interests of the motorcycle sport and industry.

As predicted by some of the minority of dissidents on the Competition Committee, the membership roles did fall off with the raising of the dues to the 1950 number of about 50,000. But, encouraged by the dedicated efforts of a new Secretary-Manager, the total number of AMA cardholders increased gradually to over 72,000, more than doubling the income to an annual $144,000. This enabled Kuchler to improve his own as well as the staff's salary level to more realistic figures, and to replace the long antiquated office equipment and furnishings at the Columbus AMA headquarters.

As an additional source of income, the sanctioning fees were raised to nearly double the old rates, and those competition riders cited or suspended for infractions of the rules were subjected to fines of either $25 or $50, depending on the severity of the case.

With additional funds for travel at his disposal, Kuchler embarked on a national visitation program

A panel discussion aired in a San Francisco television broadcast concerning compulsory helmet laws for California motorcyclists. Pictured are (from l.) Hells Angels founder and perennial President Ralph M. "Sonny" Barger, California State Assemblyman John Foran, Joe Hope, and sportscaster Joe Dolan.
Joe Hope

to enhance both general AMA membership as well as to recruit more Dealer Classification members. It was his initial intention to bring more owners and dealers of British machines into the fold. Numbers of these dealers subsequently told the author that Kuchler had taken on a difficult job of fence-mending. Most of the owners of British machines, as well as their dealers, had become disenchanted with the M&ATA and the AMA following the bitter warfare instituted by Harley-Davidson against them after the war. Many only bought membership cards in order to receive competition licenses as sporting contestants. Small numbers had become inactive members simply to participate in the odd Gypsy Tour, and most of the dealers not only boycotted the Dealer Classification but often sponsored clubs that took part in their own sphere of interest and avoided securing AMA charters.

Undaunted, Kuchler inaugurated his campaign to recruit those connected with foreign

imports into the AMA, and spent most of his traveling time in the west where traditionally 65% or more of the nation's motorcycling activities took place. While some of this group remained unimpressed, substantial numbers of dealers and members became sold on the idea that a revitalized AMA had their best interests at heart and, to look out for these and to combat the ever present threat of hostile anti-motorcycle legislation at both the local as well as the national level, the AMA was the only game in town!

In the face of a mostly successful recruitment campaign, Kuchler came in for some strong criticism from Walter Davidson, Jr., who stated that Kuchler was spending too much with the foreign element and not enough time with Harley-Davidson dealers and owners who, by tradition, were the actual backbone of the whole AMA concept. Kuchler countered with the statement that Harley-Davidson sales were presently far below that of the imports, and with the growing strength

A TIME OF CHANGE 1955-1965

Enduro star and motion picture stunt rider Bud Ekins in a posed publicity shot.
Universal Pictures

of that segment of the industry the AMA could no longer be considered a private club run for the benefit of Milwaukee and their ancillary suppliers.

Further fuel was added to the fire when the California Triumph Dealers Association, a rather loosely organized group, sent a letter to the Competition Committee, stating that while they were in accord with supporting a revitalized AMA that could include an interest on their behalf, they were not in agreement with the Committee's long standing policy of maintaining competition venues advantageous to Harley-Davidson.

AJS and Matchless dealer Eddie Arnold, with the approval of Frank Cooper, also sent in a letter critical of the Committee's reluctance to award sanctions to certain enduro, desert runs, road races and Grand Prix type events, such as Catalina, that were best suited to imported machines.

In the fall of 1958, when Frank Cooper paid his annual visit to the AMC factory, he was informed that his long standing import agreement was being reviewed. Then, without warning, the following year his agreement was cancelled, the factory taking over the U.S. import business without offering to pay him for the operation he had

built to impressive proportions since inaugurating it in 1945. Cooper, however, still owned his parts depots and continued to service his former sales outlets for several seasons thereafter. The AMC factory sent over a manager and a team of employees to manage the importation of machines. But a combination of lack of experience in two areas—in dealing on the American market and in general management—saw their operation failing a little over a year later.

Cooper had devised a re-design of AJS and Matchless engines to improve the oiling system to enhance their performance in high speed running, and most especially to stand up to the rigors of enduro riding. These models continued to offer strong competition in the hands of private owners for several reasons.

The top management of the parent BSA group underwent reorganization during 1958 and 1959, under the leadership of Sir Bernard Docker, who was subsequently ousted from his position as Board Chairman of the group's diverse manufacturing activities and was replaced by Eric Turner (no relation to Edward). The BSA group then took over the management of Triumph, although the

305

A TIME OF CHANGE 1955-1965

operation was kept separate from BSA's motorcycle division, and Edward Turner was retained as its Managing Director. It was noted that under his past connection Triumph had maintained a much higher profit ratio than did the BSA operation, and it was suggested that for this reason BSA wished to acquire it. Triumph market penetration had recently been enhanced by the introduction of a new model, the lightweight 150 cc Cub, which could be slightly modified for a rather sprightly performance. The eastern Triumph operation in Baltimore was now merged with Johnson Motors, still managed by Denis McCormick. The western operation, covering the nineteen western states, was now conducted more as a distributorship to serve the growing roster of dealers, and the Service Department, headed by Pete Colman with Andy Anderson as his assistant, was greatly expanded.

With the failure of the factory managed AJS-Matchless U.S. distributorship, the AMC management executed an agreement with the still viable

Indian Sales Company to take over this distributorship of their products. Indian terminated their agreement with Royal Enfield, ending the marketing of their models painted Indian red and bearing their trademarks. This venture had never been overly successful, due to the resistance of bona fide Indian enthusiasts and the fact that the Enfields were, by their basic design, not outstanding as sporting vehicles. In 1958, Reddich had introduced their newly designed 700 cc vertical twin into the U.S. as an "Indian Chief", fitted with five inch sectioned tires, widened mudguards and footboards in the American style. Interest in this model was negligible, however, and when anticipated law enforcement contracts did not materialize, the model was offered for only two seasons.

Frank Cooper subsequently negotiated an agreement with Enfield to assume their U.S. importation, and also included the marketing of the Maico line, one of the few German firms, other than BMW, that survived the marketing fiasco of the late 1950's that occurred in Germany.

As a historic aside, the Japanese were a surprise entry in the 1959 Isle of Man TT with a newly developed overhead cam 125 cc vertical twin racing machine. At vast expense, the Honda organization sent over a team of five riders with five machines, a comprehensive supply of spare parts, along with complete machine shop facilities. The 175 pound machines developed 18 hp at 14,000 rpm and, while they did not garner a win, the sophistication of their design and their obvious technical innovation were at once noted as a formidable challenge to the still complacent British motorcycle establishment.

As a further indication of their intention to create a place for themselves in the world's motorcycle market, Honda sent over another team in 1960 with a slightly larger variant in the 250 cc class, the engine design now being a cross-the-frame four cylinder overhead cam model, in essence being two of the former 125 cc cammers featuring four valves per cylinder.

In the meantime, Lin Kuchler continued his efforts to update the standing of the M&ATA-AMA organization and to bring it more in line with the expanding needs of the domestic motorcycle industry. With the enhanced financial structuring, the Columbus headquarters were moved to more spacious facilities at 5030 N. High Street. Additional business machines and mailing equipment were installed, and the staff was augmented to a total of seventeen.

The new public relations program was paying off, with ongoing news releases to the general media. The Highway Samaritans program was inaugurated whereby motorcyclists were publicly recognized for offering assistance to stranded motorists as well as other motorcyclists in difficulties encountered on the nation's roads. This was integrated into a new slogan: "Put Your Best Wheel Forward". A leading journal of general athletic activities, "Sporting Illustrated", now featured national coverage of major motorcycling sports events, such as Laconia, Langhorne and Daytona. Champion riders, such as Roger Reiman, were interviewed on NBC-TV, and Kuchler himself was able to participate in a number of TV interviews encompassing various motorcycling activities. In addition, the AMA was officially supporting, with club cooperation, the ongoing Red Cross Blood Bank enhancement.

In the meantime, there had been much discussion within the Competition Committee regarding the future of the Daytona 200 in relation to its beach location. Encroaching business develop-

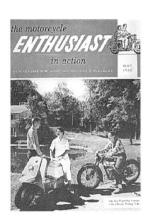

It can never be said that Harley-Davidson Motor Company didn't try to address the growing interest in lightweight motorcycles and motorscooters.
Don Emde Collection

ments and access considerations could shortly force the abandonment of the present venue, and with that threat, promoter William France and his association considered the construction of a more formally presented raceway with a circular track and adequate grandstanding and crowd containment facilities that had never been possible with the old beach course. The main problem was, of course, finances, aside from the cooperation of the adjacent cities in providing the proper zoning. France was ultimately able, after some months of negotiations with various unnamed individuals, to raise the necessary funds.

A long simmering problem within American organized motorcycling was the post-war refusal of the M&ATA-AMA to accept the membership of those formally affiliated with the import of foreign machines. With the initial hostility of members of the domestic industry, most of the early importers, distributors and dealers returned the compliment by being both highly critical of the AMA's monopolistic policies and were initially not inclined to affiliate with it.

As the imports came to assume a dominant role in the industry, it was, as noted in the late 1950's, that the market for Harley-Davidson machines commanded only 25% of total domestic sales that were served by a like percentage of the total number of dealerships that came to serve the domestic market.

Some of the leaders of the import industry were taking note of this fact and, due to the incongruity of having control of 75% of the industry, they did not even have token representation in the sole national organization that controlled all aspects of motorcycle sport as well as general public policy. Alfred Rich Child, William E. Johnson, Frank Cooper and others within the import group had been considering inaugurating an organized movement to gain official M&ATA membership. In the meantime, a number of these individuals had written letters to E.C. Smith during his tenure as AMA Secretary-Manager concerning the matter. At first these were simply ignored at Columbus and when, on occasion, queried about the matter, Smith's stock answer had been that, "The AMA functions to support the interests of the American motorcycle industry."

To combat this attitude, an unorganized campaign slowly got under way on the part of some of the import group, which found its voice by importuning numbers of the official AMA referees in some of the 37 official AMA districts across the country concerning the matter, with the result that the Competition Committee became well aware of the growing groundswell of opinion.

It was during the 1950's period that the American motorcycling public was generally unaware of the rapidly growing might of the Japanese motorcycle industry. But, at the same time, a rather surprising manifestation of this was graphically illustrated at the 1958 Catalina Grand Prix, when a high performance 250 cc Yamaha two stroke was entered in the Lightweight Race program. This had come about through the efforts of two U.S. born Japanese motorcycle enthusiasts, Jimmy Jingu and Matt Matsuoka, who had already been exploring the proposition of the future of the importation of Japanese machines and who had been in correspondence with the leading Japanese factories.

Their action had motivated Yamaha to initiate a showcasing of their products by sending over two racing machines specifically for competing at Catalina. An arrangement was made with Pierre Marty, of Marty's Foreign Motors of Inglewood, to receive and set up the machines. One, piloted by Japanese racing star Fumio Ito, finished the race in the top 15 entries, though Ito had little time for practice and was unfamiliar with the course. The high pitched yowl of the Yamaha was a spectacular feature of the contest.

The Catalina Grand Prix had become a popular event, with an ever growing list of entries each year. In 1957 a spectacular win in the unlimited class was by the well known enduro star Bud Ekins. Catalina's last year was 1958, due to a number of adverse factors that were actually influenced by the intensive interest in the event, both from the large number of entrants and the expanded spectator interest. During the last two years of the event the big island steamer made no less than four daily roundtrips to accommodate the visitors. At this point, the business interests in Avalon protested both the congestion caused by the large crowds and the fact that the crowds were not interested in purchasing the requisite volume of tourist goods. The restaurant operators complained that they did not have the facilities to accommodate the demands for service, and that a number of unpleasant incidents occurred when they ran out of food. Then, too, many of the residents who were retirees complained of the excessive noise and overall congestion in the small town. The Island Company and the Avalon Merchants Association ultimately gave notice to the promoters that henceforth the island venue could no longer accommodate the event. As a grand prix event it was regrettable that the island could no longer be utilized, as such it was the only event of its kind ever staged by organized American motorcycle sport.

In the late 1950's the Ariel Motorcycle Company revised its general policy regarding the design of its product line. While offered initially in the U.S. along with Triumph, its emphasis on single cylinder models was somewhat downgraded in comparison with Triumph's vertical twins which offered better performance. The sporting Red Hunter, although a potent performer in the hands of skilled tuners, had a certain appeal but again, in this sphere, was overshadowed by Triumph. The unique Square Four had a cult-like appeal to iconoclastic enthusiasts but, as a rather high priced machine, it enjoyed a limited market and as such was always in small production. The Huntmaster vertical twin, introduced in 1950 in competition with Triumph, never attained Triumph's popularity and as a sound design it never really received the attention that it might otherwise have deserved.

In 1958, Ariel phased out its long standing classic line in favor of a lightweight twin, called the Leader, which did not have a marketing appeal in the U.S. This model, together with some later scooters, subsequently enjoyed a limited market in England as the intense competition from the Orient was already a factor.

The appearance of the Yamaha marque at the Catalina Grand Prix was a graphic example of the emergence of Japanese motorcycles on the international market. Frank Cooper, who was in the process of losing his import franchise of AJS and Matchless, decided to explore the possibilities of negotiating an agreement with this Oriental firm. An inquiry to Yamaha International resulted in a visit by Age Kiraguchi, who was the head of the export organization, which resulted in the consummation of an agreement for Cooper to handle Yamaha machines in the U.S. Cooper recalled that while the contract gave him the rights to sell Yamaha products, it did not obligate the company to supply him with their machines other than at their option.

The initial models he received at the Port of Los Angeles were the YD-1 250 cc two stroke parallel twins, which were a frank copy of the recently produced German Adler which was currently being phased out with the Japanese securing the patent rights. While the styling of the YD-1's and their dull brown paint finish were not overly attractive, the machines were outstanding performers and their high revving engines made them nearly as fast as the more usual four stroke 500's. Cooper's Sales Manager, Don Watkins, at once inaugurated an extensive sales campaign, concentrating on the western states where the majority of the nation's dealers were located. Within a short time he had

A Time of Change 1955-1965

Triumph Publicity
Directory Ivor Davies and
Chairman of Triumph
Engineering Department
Frank Docker (from l.)
confer with Pete Colman
following the testing of a
revised frame design for
the Thunderbird at the
Motor Industry's test facil-
ity in England, 1964.
*Triumph Engineering
Company*

signed up over 200 retail outlets. Most of these dealers were agents for British machines, although a handful of Harley-Davidson dealers joined in on the premise that the 250 cc Yamaha's were not competitive with Milwaukee's big twins.

Yamaha's top management, in order to facilitate a sales blitz, initially made a very generous offer to Cooper in that they financed the flooring of the machines, with payment from the dealer due only after their delivery to a customer. As it was, Cooper reported that over 1,000 YD-1's were sold before the end of the first year.

In order to update the YD-1, Yamaha introduced an updated model, the YD-2, which was designed for increased performance with more compression and altered port timing. This proved to be a near fatal mistake, however, as the YD-2 at once evidenced certain serious faults. The fast revving 10,000 rpm engine was subject to piston ring breakages, burned pistons and gear box failures due to the clutch being attached at the crankshaft, its high speed operation causing difficulties in meshing the gears, with subsequent loss of dependability.

Cooper at once called the factory's attention to the problems of these early models, but when a delegation of Japanese engineers visited his newly occupied facility on the corner of Broadway and Slauson Avenue, they declared that the problems

were caused by customer misuse rather than through any basic fault in the design! In the meantime, and with a shop floor covered with blown engines returned by the dealers for validation of the guarantee, Cooper and his staff were faced with the problem of attempting to correct the troubles themselves.

As an inevitable result, Yamaha's initial image suffered and a substantial number of dealers canceled their franchises. This at once opened the way for Honda's traveling sales force, who were conducting their initial efforts to introduce their line of four stroke 50 and 80 cc step-through lightweights to the American market.

In the meantime, factory engineers were in the process of correcting the YD-2's faults and, at the same time, were hurrying the production of 50 and 80 cc two stroke models to counter those now being introduced by Honda. It will be noted that it was Yamaha, not Honda, contrary to popular opinion, who first made a serious attempt to penetrate the U.S. market and, in fact, the initial national advertising attendant to the importation of Japanese machines was noted in the fall of 1959, in an announcement in "Cycle" magazine.

At this point, in a visitation to Cooper's headquarters by a delegation from the factory, Yamaha formerly notified him that his import agreement was

A Time of Change 1955-1965

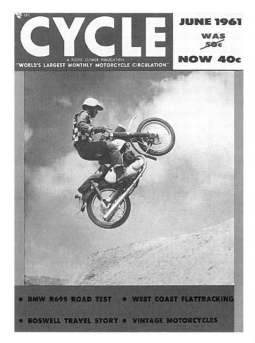

By the early 1960's, Japanese machines were hitting the covers of the major publications. *Don Emde Collection*

terminated. The reason given was the factory did not have sufficient production to supply Cooper in the face of their forthcoming assault on the European market. Cooper at once noted that Yamaha was already making plans to take over the sales to the U.S. market through their own organization.

In referring to his original contract, Cooper noted that while he had been initially awarded the U.S. import rights, the factory did not legally commit itself to any obligation to supply machines on Cooper's demand. As matters now stood, Cooper suffered a severe financial loss in his brief association with Yamaha.

In the meantime, the leaders of the British motorcycle industry were painfully aware of the Japanese assault on the world's markets, and belatedly began considering ways and means to protect what had once been their dominant role as the prime supplier of the world's two wheelers. In the summer of 1960, Edward Turner decided it was high time to make a personal survey of the Japanese industry to more clearly assess its relationship to the future of the British position. Accordingly, he made arrangements with the three leading factories, Honda, Yamaha, and Suzuki, for a visitation and was given a very courteous reception.

Turner's conclusions were that Japanese production totaled over 500,000 units per year, in comparison to about 140,000 units at home, with facilities that were far and away more elaborate and efficient than had ever been noted within either the British or American experience. He at once noted that his observations exploded the pre-war myth that Japanese goods were cheap imitations of western products. The manufacturing facilities, tooling, forward product research and marketing and distribution practices were of very high standards, and as such, the Japanese were in a position to dominate the world's market.

In a somewhat naive conclusion, he noted that at this time Japanese production was concentrated on machines of under 300 cc, and the British concentration was on the larger types of machines this still left the home industry with the alternatives of supplying this market.

At the Honda factory, Benjira Honda assured Turner that the Japanese at this point were not attempting to take over the existing motorcycle market, but rather to create a new interest in two wheeled vehicles among the entry level class of buyer. In any case, however, it was illogical of Turner to assume that once the Japanese had gained a foothold for their lightweight products they would not move forward to expand their product line to heavyweight machines.

Turner noted that the Japanese were in a very favorable economic position with a wage scale that was less than half that seen in both England and Europe, and that production workers were housed in company owned apartments and were charged minimal rents, with food available at cost in company managed outlets. Furthermore, massive financing was available at low interest rates guaranteed through the government sponsorship, as well as no excise tax levies on goods produced for export. In addition, income tax levies on individuals was minimal as, by the terms of their revised constitution instituted by the U.S. Occupation government administrated by General MacArthur, the country was spared the expense of maintaining a large defense establishment.

The consequent low retail prices of Japanese motorcycles was reflected in these favorable conditions, such as $250 for a step through 50 cc Cub or miniature motorcycle, or $595 for a 250 cc high performance two stroke. Another advantage that enhanced Japanese production was the position and attitudes of their labor force. By tradition, management took a paternalistic policy toward employees in providing low-cost housing and subsidized food supply and, in periods of diminished market demands, sacrificed profit taking to avoid laying off production workers. The bonus for the companies in the light of such attitudes promoted employee loyalty and fostered a spirit of family participation.

This situation was in direct contrast to employee/management relations in the western world. Labor relations in the U.S., by tradition, had been proceeding for well over 100 years in ongoing strife not conducive to either productivity or the enhancement of quality control. The situation in Great Britain had lately been even more critical. The focus on the differences within the country's stratified class system had only recently been somewhat resolved; it was only after 1910 that the average working class Englishman had acquired the right to vote, a privilege formerly enjoyed only by the titled aristocracy and the landed gentry. Labor had at long last gained political power between the wars, and had made sweeping demands for socialistic advantages. The post-war labor government had become even more militant

A Time of Change 1955-1965

Pete Colman tests a 1957 Triumph thunderbird on the Motor Industry's test facility in England, with Triumph Sales Manager Ivor Davies in attendance. *Triumph Motor Company*

and, in the demand for improved working conditions, the adversarial climate resulted in greatly reduced productivity that at once put British industry in a disadvantageous position. Under such conditions, the Oriental manufacturers now had overwhelming industrial powers, giving them a commanding position in the world's markets.

At this point, the top management of the Harley-Davidson Company were assessing their position in the marketplace. With the export of American made vehicles curtailed by protective tariff barriers erected by foreign countries seeking to encourage their own industry, the market for their machines was now largely restricted to domestic sales. While Milwaukee had long enjoyed the loyal support of big twin enthusiasts, the now expanded sales of imports to entry level buyers included only a limited group of the latter. These factors, for the last several seasons, created a more

or less static demand for American made machines, which now averaged about 12,000 units per year.

At the same time, the market for domestically produced machines had been limited from the legacy of the between-the-wars declining market, and both Harley-Davidson's and Indian's production facilities were limited to an archaic institutionalized situation. Since 1920, the management at Milwaukee had never visualized their production as a high volume operation and had prudently geared production to market demand through dealer's orders. At the same time and with a conservative outlook, the introduction of either new or a diverse range of models had never been in management policies to encourage them to expand production. To do so would have entailed the hiring of a professional engineering staff and the acquisition of enhanced outside risk capital with a radical change in their operations which, in any case, would not have been allowed by the company's non-motorcycling shareholders whose prime interest was the funding of their own personal estates.

The obvious solution to expand the product line without drastically altering in-place production scheduling and the financial expansion involved would entail the incorporation of models acquired from outside suppliers. Such a decision was made in an agreement with an Italian manufacturer, Aeronautica Macchi, located in Varese. This pioneer company, which had its origins following World War I, was once connected with elements of the French concern that manufactured Nieuport aircraft components. The latter reorganized concern, subsequently known as Aermacchi, manufactured aircraft engines for the well known Macchi fighter planes of World War I. Reorganized after this war as a diverse manufacturing group, it entered the motorcycle industry using the Aermacchi name. While it produced a line of utility machines, its management concentrated on racing, and made a name for itself on the Continent with overhead camshaft 250 and 350 cc single cylinder models.

In following the Norton path of spending vast sums on developing competition machinery, the motorcycle division ran into financial difficulties which enabled Harley-Davidson to purchase half interest in the company in 1960 for what was variously reported as either $247,000 or $261,000. It was later reported that this bargain price was not contested by Milwaukee's tight-fisted shareholders who, at this point, were well aware that the company badly needed expanded marketing capabilities to enhance their marketing position.

The initial 250 cc Aermacchis were introduced into the U.S. market for the 1961 sales season,

Catalina Island, 1958.
Dave Ekins (#128) on an
NSU, Ralph Adams (#58)
on a Francis Barnett and
John McLaughlin (#18) on
a Velocette.
Frank Cooper

being cataloged as the 61-C "Sprint" model. A long time member of Milwaukee's engineering staff, Wilbur Petri, was sent to the factory at Varese to oversee the modifications of the Sprints to conform to American specifications such as control systems, widened mudguards, enlarged fuel tanks, and attempts to sort out problems with the often mysterious Italian electrical systems.

The introduction of the Sprint was not too well accepted by the Harley-Davidson dealerships. Being traditionally oriented toward the big V- twins, they were not especially cordial to the idea of promoting light or middleweight machines. Then, too, there was the matter of the financial responsibility of stocking a separate line of spare parts. As it was, the 250 cc machine was never popular in the U.S., except perhaps for some limited interest from a relatively small group of utility riders.

In the meantime, and while the Japanese motorcycle manufacturers were gathering their forces to inaugurate a penetration of the U.S. market, a new aspect of motorcycle sport had manifested itself in Europe and England and was now becoming popular in the States. The long popular English style trials which featured slow riding over rough colonial terrain had now been extended to what was known as "scrambles". The courses for this, while adapted for undulating country, were intended for high speed running and required a more high powered version of the usual stripped trials machine.

The initial interest in scrambles was said to have had an early inception by Edison Dye, the recently appointed western distributor for the Swedish Husqvarna motorcycles. They were one of the pioneer manufacturers in the Scandinavian area

A Time of Change 1955-1965

and also one of the first to build specialist scrambler machines. The Sports Committee, led by Frank Cooper, at once paid special attention to the matter in the way of promoting scrambler events. Cooper recalled that he personally supervised the establishment of about 30 such courses in Southern California's rural areas where parking was available and where the location was such that complaints concerning the noise factor were not a problem. The use of road graders and bulldozers was employed to construct the courses, and spectator interest was enhanced by making the course of the closed variety within a somewhat limited area. The most popular course initially was the one pioneered by Dye, adjacent to the City of Carlsbad, just north of San Diego.

All of the major British factories were now including limited numbers of 350 and 500 cc machines adapted to scrambling, such as BSA, Triumph, and Velocette. The last four stroke models produced by the now financially ailing AMC group were scrambler types, in addition to limited numbers of 125 and 200 cc Francis-Barnett two strokes in similar models.

While the initial interest was in the adaptation of four stroke models, high performance two strokes were coming to the fore, due to their high power to weight ratio and the 350 cc models were able to successfully challenge the 500 cc four strokes. The 350 cc models were featured by the Swedish built Husqvarna and the German made Maico.

The Spanish motorcycle industry was now making a place on the international market. Spain's transportation industry had made a slow recovery following the close of their savage civil war that ended in the Fall of 1939. Little progress had been made during World War II due to the diversion of world markets to war production. Spain had initial problems in resurrecting their agricultural capabilities which had been devastated by the war. It was noted that fully one half of that country's population had died as the result of their civil war through battle casualties, starvation, malnutrition and disease. By the early 1950's some progress had been made in re-establishing heavier industries, and initial motorcycle manufacture had been based on the importation, or manufacture under license, of small capacity engine-gear units of Fichtel and Sachs or Zundapp manufacture. One of these firms, headed by Alberto Montesa, was now producing sporting models in association with designer Francisco Bulto. Small numbers of these sporting models appeared in the U.S. after 1960. Bulto broke away from Montesa as the result of a

Hillclimbing has remained a popular form of motorcycling over the years.
Don Emde Collection

policy dispute and founded his own organization that marketed both utility types as well as high performance two strokes under the trade name of Bultaco. His sporting models subsequently gained popularity in the U.S. with both scrambler types as well as a high performance 200 cc super sports roadster called the Metralla, with a high revving engine capable of 100 mph.

A later Spanish entrant on the sporting scene was the Ossa with their own versions of the scrambler and trials machines. Both the Montesa and the Ossa took second place to the Bultaco in overall performance capabilities and, with the minority position in the market enjoyed by Spanish products coupled with their relatively small production and competition from the massive Japanese production and large dealer network, only the Bultaco enjoyed a significant market.

In the meantime, the syndicate of investors organized by William France had obtained the financing of the new Daytona racetrack which was opened in time for the 1961 classic, ending the use of the old beach course. The new two-mile oval track provided not only acceptable accommodations for the spectators but enhanced the financial returns through providing strict crowd control. France had a previous opportunity to perfect the management of the course, as he had promoted a few Stock Car races there the previous fall. The AMA Competition Committee had reservations regarding safety considerations of the 33 degree banking on the turns. After some discussion, it was decided that the motorcycles would be raced on the two-mile paved road course situated on the infield, avoiding the use of the banked turns, and the speeds were reduced somewhat by having six turns on the road course to negotiate.

Roger Reiman, on a Harley-Davidson, set the fastest qualifying time of 72.3 mph for the pole position. The race began with Reiman contending with Carroll Resweber, also Harley-Davidson mounted, and Don Burnett on a Triumph. During the initial dueling, Resweber was sidelined with engine trouble and Reiman forged ahead to win just in front of Burnett, second, and George Roeder, also on a Harley-Davidson, coming in third. Warren Sherwood, BSA, was fourth. Reiman's winning average was 69.2 mph, much slower than the latter times on the beach course due to the greater number of turns.

The 1959 through 1961 period saw the continuing dominance of Milwaukee riders, due to the development of the KR's, the choice of venues that favored the make, and Harley-Davidson's recruitment of top flight riders. It was this point in time that saw the rise of the great Carroll Resweber, who won the Number One plate every year since 1959. His best year was 1961, when he won no less than five National Championships. His versatility was proven in his performances on short tracks, half mile, mile and TT contests. On the other hand, his luck seemed to desert him at the Daytona classics.

The most outstanding British motorcycle model during this period was the BSA Gold Star. It's top rider was Dick Mann who took the Peoria TT. Second ranking was Triumph, which offered strong contention with two factory teams. Milwaukee, with the fielding of large numbers of riders, in the end, won about three-quarters of the top spots during this period.

Aside from Resweber, Brad Andres was a strong Milwaukee contender who, in 1959 and 1960, garnered his second and third wins at Daytona. This last took place at the final running of the classic on the old beach course. It was in this year that Harley-Davidson captured 17 of the 20 first places; the other contenders being one BMW and two BSA's.

During a meeting of the AMA Competition Committee in the fall of 1961, the three firms importing and distributing British machines were finally granted representation on that governing body. These were BSA, Incorporated, the Triumph Corporation, and the Indian Sales Company that had recently taken over the distributorship of AJS and Matchless. This came about through the long continuous campaigning of British distributors for a place on the Committee and the efforts of Lin Kuchler who, since the beginning of his term as AMA Secretary-Manager, had urged the expansion of industry participation in AMA affairs. Critics of the AMA at once noted such an action was long overdue, seeing that the imports now enjoyed a four-to-one ratio of sales over the domestic product. In spite of this, Milwaukee had, during most of the post-war era, fielded the largest number of racing machines and, in the expansion of the membership of the Committee, Harley-Davidson's factory and supplier members still held an overwhelming majority of voting power.

With the growing popularity of scrambles and the increased number of closed courses under construction, the big point-to-point off-road races, such as Big Bear, the various hare-and-hound contest and Cactus Derbys, faded from the scene. One of the difficulties had become the increasing number of contestants which made for logistical and organizational problems. Then the Big Bear classic had come into ill repute when, in 1961, it was discovered that many of the contestants were faking

their route cards and checkpoint tallies to enhance their scores. Then there came into being small (but vociferous) groups of environmentalists who were questioning the possible damage caused by the large number of motorcyclists passing over areas of still natural terrain, whether in the mountains or the deserts.

A notable literary event in 1961 was the publishing of a motorcycle history book by the Bookman Transport Press in London and written by James Sheldon, a long time observer of the British motorcycling scene. Entitled "Veteran and Vintage Motorcycles", it reviewed the British industry from 1900 to 1930. Somewhat following the format of "Motor Cycle Cavalcade", previously written by Basil Henry Davies, it offered more details of the life and times of nearly all of the British motorcycles and the people involved in the industry, although the work covered only the first three decades of the 20th Century. The book was well received in England and enjoyed modest sales in the U.S. from British enthusiasts.

In the meantime, the Yamaha organization was engaging in the dual activities of rectifying the design deficiencies on the ill-fated YD series, perfecting new small capacity utility type models, and continuing to support their extensive world wide competition program. It will be recalled that Yamaha was the first Japanese manufacturer to take part in international competition, although Honda was not far behind. As noted, Yamaha had sponsored two entries in the last Catalina Grand Prix in 1958, and subsequently, fielded teams throughout Europe, South Africa and in various South American countries. European motorcycle historian and one time competition rider, Dr. Ing Helmut Krackowizer recalled that by 1959 the company had over 50 factory machines in the hands of professional riders in various parts of the world and, in addition, had opportuned some of them to act as salesmen!

Following the termination of their agreement with Frank Cooper, who was their initial importer, Yamaha's top management sent over a team of middle management executives to reorganize their U.S. marketing program. Establishing an office and warehouse headquarters on West Pico Boulevard in Los Angeles, they engaged one Bert Smith, a former Wyoming outdoorsman and hunting enthusiast, as General Sales Manager. A short time later, however, the post was offered to the Texas born Nisei, Jimmy Jingu. Jingu had first been connected with the Yamaha operation following the war when he had set up an import business to distribute their extensive line of pianos and other musical instruments.

A Time of Change 1955-1965

Motorcycles lent themselves well to pin-up photography, as evidenced in this 1952 photo of Maxine Raney and a Triumph Thunderbird. Widely circulated photo appeared on cover of four different motorcycling magazines from all corners of the Earth.
Bill Bagnall

His experience with Japanese affairs in the U.S. had also been broadened by his acting as a consultant to the Japanese Embassy in Los Angeles regarding the promotion of U.S. trade and import matters; this was after the Embassy was established early in 1948. Jingu's immediate problem was to attempt to mend fences with Yamaha's dealerships and to assure them that the technical faults of the earlier models were being rectified and that a new line of entry level lightweight machines would round out the product line.

As Yamaha's activities expanded, their headquarters were moved to larger quarters in the Los Angeles industrial suburb of Montebello. A new Service Manager was installed, Leo Lake, who possessed an interesting background. His parents had been Protestant missionaries posted to Japan after World War I, where Lake was born in 1921. He grew up speaking Japanese as well as English. At an early age, he showed an interest in mechanics and when the family was expelled in 1935,

when the militaristic government took over, he found employment as both an automobile as well as a motorcycle mechanic in the Los Angeles area. He subsequently mastered the technical details of Yamaha's initial line of two stroke machines, and offered the factory the benefit of his advice on the preferences of entry level American riders.

In the meantime, Honda, still Japan's largest motorcycle manufacturer, was preparing to expand its activities to the American market. General Manager Takeo Fujiwasa appointed Kihachio Kawashima as Sales Manager for the newly formed American Honda Corporation. Kawashima arrived in Los Angeles in the fall of 1959, to make a preliminary marketing survey. In his travels about the country he astounded some of the competitive dealers in stating that Honda planned to sell 12,000 units a month in the U.S. Heretofore, an importer who sold a like number in a year's time was considered to be making a good showing!

Kawashima recruited a sales force of about 25 American enthusiasts who, during the summer of 1960, had a sales blitz the magnitude of which had never before been seen in the annals of the American motorcycle industry. Introductory sales promotional meetings were scheduled in hotels, motel complexes, civic center facilities, and in any locale where a crowd could be induced to attend. Many of the established dealers handling previously imported foreign machines with their preconceived antipathies to the Japanese image refused to participate. In the end, however, some capitulated in adding Hondas to their established lines and, in addition, dealerships were placed in sporting goods stores, hobby shops, hardware outlets, in agricultural implement dealers in rural areas, and anywhere they could get a foot in the door.

This program was helped by the fact that machines, initially of the 50 cc step-through "Cub" models and miniature motorcycles, were placed in dealer's hands on consignment, which meant the factory did not expect payment until the machines sold. Due to some confusion as to the exact locations where the machines had been placed and the lack of a comprehensive centrally located bookkeeping system, the payment for substantial numbers of machines was overlooked. This problem was complicated by the diverse character of the sales outlets. These could be anything like Robert "Evel" Knievel's small town sales outlet in rural Washington to Norm Reeves of Fullerton, California, who early on established multiple dealerships. As a result, the initial sales campaign saw gross sales of over $500,000 for the dealers but a net loss of $54,000 for the company.

The sales campaign was further stimulated by the low retail cost of the machines, due to Honda's efficiencies in high volume production, their very low wage outlay, and the current position of the yen in relation to the dollar. A Cub motorcycle as the entry level models carried a price tag of about $260. The subsequent two cylinder overhead cam 125 cc super sports Benley model retailed for about $550. The later Hawk, which followed the now popular Street Scrambler design, a 305 cc overhead cam twin whose engine could rev to 9,500 rpm and outrun the current 500 cc 5T Triumph twin, went out the door at $795. At such prices, spur-of-the-moment purchasers were encouraged to ride a model home after presenting a credit card!

Aside from the modest selling prices, the initial Honda models were attractive from the standpoint of being oil tight and electrically started, an innovation in the industry, as well as their almost unfailing freedom from mechanical failure.

The initial marketing of Honda products in the U.S. was bound up in the early career of one Jack McCormack. A wartime Marine officer, he was a swashbuckling and ebullient individual who had become a convert to motorcycling at the end of the war. His enthusiasm was such that he voluntarily attached himself to Triumph's racing organization and Pete Colman recalled that he had, more often than not, acted as an errand helper for his pit crew during race meets in Southern California. McCormack's background was that of a younger member of an affluent family who owned a prosperous button manufacturing organization that had extensive markets within the local garment industry as well as upholstery industries in the Los Angeles basin. In his motorcycling enthusiasm, McCormack usually rode his Triumph wearing a three piece business suit while making his rounds as a company salesman, with his sample case strapped to the carrier.

McCormack's family took a rather dim view of his motorcycling activities, which ultimately did not stop him from quitting the family business to become a salesman at Johnson Motors. He held this position for several months, when intense pressure from his family caused him to resign. Following some further dissension from his family, he again expressed his intention to return to his old position. At this juncture, Johnson Motors General Manager, Pete Colman, suggested that he might do well to apply to the newly formed American Honda Corporation as they were seeking a new sales manager and, as the result of this, he joined that company in the spring of 1963.

Filled with enthusiasm, he crisscrossed the country with another blitz sales program. The slogan, "You meet the nicest people on a Honda", was broadcast and there is some difference of opinion as to whether this was originated by McCormack or by the prestigious Gray Advertising Company of New York who had been retained to provide a national promotional campaign.

The stressing of the utilitarian advantages of the lightweight machines was bearing fruit as thousands of entry level former non-riders bought machines, many of whom, such as the well known, politically conservative author, TV personality and magazine publisher William F. Buckley, became Cub riders. As a result of this growing interest, a group of New York executives actually formed the Madison Avenue Motorcycle Club.

Close on the heels of the Yamaha and Honda incursion into the U.S. market, the Suzuki organization had instituted its own sales campaign. Michio Suzuki, an early day company executive, had directed his son, Shunzo, to set up an American operation, concluded in the spring of 1963, by establishing headquarters in Santa Fe Springs, a suburb of Los Angeles. A 50 cc step-through model, similar to the Honda Cub, called the "Mikick", along with a miniature motorcycle, the M12, of similar capacity, and a 125 cc Colleta type Two, were the initial offerings. Suzuki had, by this time, perfected an oil injection system that metered the lubricant into the fuel that obviated the rider's manual mixing of the two, always considered a disadvantage of two stroke operation. This technical innovation put Suzuki directly in competition with Yamaha, who also featured a similar system, which, in turn, made both competitive with Honda, who, at this point was exclusively committed to the four stroke engine principle.

Suzuki's entry into the U.S. market coincided with a contemporary expansion of their production facilities which was enabling them to increase their sales campaign into all of the Pacific Rim countries, Malaysia, Taiwan, and the Pacific Islands.

During the initial phase of the Oriental penetration of the American market, the three principal firms were in strong competition with each other. But, at the same time, their coincidental marketing surveys had led them to the cumulative conclusion that a free, rather than a restrictive, marketing concept was beneficial to all. It had already been noted that the long in-place restrictive marketing practices imposed by the American factories had, in the end, the effect of inhibiting the market as a whole. The fact that a prospective dealer had the option of handling either one or all of the Japanese makes

A TIME OF CHANGE 1955-1965

Harley-Davidson was tough to beat on the National circuit in the early 1960's.
Don Emde Collection

Floyd Clymer published a weekly motorcycle magazine for a few years called "Motor Cycling News".
Don Emde Collection

was a further inducement to accept a franchise.

In the matter of Japanese manufacturers' sales organizations set up in the U.S., the initial steps were undertaken by English speaking executives from Japan. The strategy was to then recruit both American middle management and sales personnel to staff the headquarters and necessary branches. This was considered a sound policy in order to somewhat neutralize the still latent prejudice in the U.S. against Japan, left over from the bitter feelings caused by the war, and left the Japanese administration in a low profile position.

Japanese firms were generally able to recruit effective American management and sales personnel by offering fair salaries and certain fringe benefits that might include a modest yearly financial bonuses that depended on increased corporate expansion. In spite of this, the opinions expressed to the author by numbers of these American personnel interviewed, indicated that all was not lovely in the Japanese garden. The Japanese were careful never to elevate any American to top management positions or to give them authority in ultimate policy decisions. This became especially frustrating on some occasions to sales personnel experienced in the domestic motorcycle market when sometimes quaint Oriental ideas on procedure ran counter to prior policies that had been proven traditionally acceptable. In addition, performance bonuses were never offered as options to purchase company stock, the manufacturers seemed to be most definitely opposed to allowing any occidentals to gain any foothold as shareholders.

Another problem that interfered with the bonus situation was that when the company profits increased, which they characteristically did in an impressive way, additional Japanese employees from Japan, as well as friends and relatives of the top U.S. Japanese management suddenly appeared in the U.S. Ostensibly arriving as visitors, they were quickly placed on the payroll, their duties in most cases being both nebulous and insignificant. The bottom line of this policy was to define the role of the American employees as expendable entities and with a rather narrow role in the corporate structure. This policy was, as will be seen, to have future repercussions within the management structure of the Japanese-American motorcycle market.

In the meantime, certain changes were taking place in the administration of Triumph, both in the U.S. as well as in Great Britain. It will be recalled that the BSA Group took over ownership of Triumph in 1959, although the latter firm retained its autonomous status under the management of Edward Turner and was actually competing with

BSA products. While Edward Turner was still Triumph's manager, he no longer had a financial interest in the company as he had sold his shares to BSA in the 1959 merger for approximately $4,000,000. Eric Turner (no relation) had succeeded Sir Bernard Docker as BSA Board Chairman and subsequently, laid plans to further BSA's control over Triumph by projecting a purchase of the Johnson interest in Los Angeles. To work out the details of this proposal, the matter was placed in the hands of a middle management BSA employee, Harry Sturgeon, who later would replace Edward Turner as Manager of Triumph.

In the meantime, William Johnson's health had been deteriorating from the effects of a number of ailments that were complicated by his addiction to alcohol. While he was seen less and less in connection with Triumph activities it had not affected the company's operation. Wilbur Ceder had always acted as the overseer of Triumph's day-to-day operations. When the original Triumph operation was organized in the late 1930's, Ceder was already the general manager as well as the comptroller for Johnson's corporate activities. When the corporation was altered to include the Triumph operation, the details were handled by Johnson's corporate attorneys, the Los Angeles law firm of Lantz, Leibowitz and O'Connell. In this reorganization Ceder was awarded an interest in the Triumph operation that consisted of 10% of its shares, presumably as an inducement for his taking on the added responsibilities of Triumph's operation.

After the war, when Johnson's health problems became more acute, a codicil was added to his contract with Ceder wherein the latter was provided additional control of another 50% of company stock, in the event of Johnson's demise, although this voting control did not include actual ownership. Legal work for the firm was subsequently handled by Clarence Flemming, a recent law school graduate who was also Johnson's nephew. Coincidental to these later events the BSA group in England was negotiating the purchase of the U.S. Triumph operation with Harry Sturgeon in charge. This had not been made public yet when Johnson ultimately passed away in the summer of 1962. By the terms of Johnson's will, this left Ceder in control of the company's management, although the surviving Johnson heirs, led by Flemming, were trying to contest his authority by virtue of the fact that he did not actually own the shares he had the power to represent.

In the midst of this infighting, Harry Sturgeon, acting under the authority of the BSA group, approached the members of the Johnson family regarding the purchase of their majority shareholdings. It was later reported that he moved quickly in the matter before the internal troubles could affect the company's operation. The upshot of the matter was that the Johnson family sold their interests to BSA for a reported $2,700,000. Sturgeon, in the interests of executive continuity, reaffirmed Ceder's position as company president, although there was some internal opinion that his crippling arthritis might impair his managerial abilities.

It was during 1960 and 1961 that Joseph Parkhurst gave serious thought to the publication of a new motorcycle magazine. Since an early age he had expressed an interest in motorcycling and his education was in liberal arts with an interest in photography and journalism. In 1956 he had been a staff member of John R. Bond's new prestigious "Road and Track" magazine. In 1960 he took a year's sabbatical leave, enjoying a photographic expedition to Europe. It was during this time that he began considering the launching of a motorcycling magazine based on the high standards and format of the successful Bond effort. Upon his return from Europe he joined the staff of the Pelzer publication, "Karting", which was then catering to the rather brief popularity of these miniature four wheelers, and shortly afterwards he became its editor.

In noting the quality of the current publications, "The Motorcyclist" and "Cycle", Parkhurst saw that they tended to be mostly industry newsletters devoid of comprehensive technical data covering current new models. In this their technical features and performance figures tended to reflect the reports of their manufacturers rather than being subjected to independent objective evaluation. Of the two, "The Motorcyclist" tended to be more informative, but its scope was hampered by Editor Bagnall's rather limited financing. Clymer's "Cycle" reflected its publisher's archaic and folksy outlook on the industry, and his low salary scale for his employees precluded the presence of any sort of journalistic talent.

In the end, Parkhurst launched "Cycle World" in January 1963, while still editing "Karting", on a $500 per month salary. Its publisher, Jack Pelzer, financed the publication of the initial issue. The founding of the magazine was most definitely on a shoestring basis, Parkhurst having raised the modest sum of $11,000 as an initial effort by mortgaging his modest home in Costa Mesa, California, and using his garage as an office. Pelzer withdrew his support after the first issue but, as a last ditch effort, Parkhurst was able to work out an agreement with one Lew Kaufman, who was currently publishing a series of what would today be called

soft core pornographic magazines. Parkhurst later recalled to the author that Kaufman's credit terms were such that he could not afford to be overly choosy, and the initial issues rolled off the presses.

During "Cycle World's" initial days, Parkhurst was encouraged by the late Henry Manney, a motoring journalist and antique automobile enthusiast, who took over some of the reporting assignments and book reports on current motorcycling publications. The initial four member staff included Carol Sims, Patsy Platt and Gordon Jennings, a professional engineer as well as a competent technical writer who was also a competition rider. This group was later augmented by the addition of Ivan J. Wagar, a former Canadian 350 cc road racing champion who was also well grounded in motorcycle engineering.

At once Parkhurst went forward with his original intention to provide technical descriptions of currently marketed motorcycles as well as offering comprehensive analysis of their performance through road testing by both himself and other staff members. Rather than accepting any of the manufacturer's or distributor's performance figures, each model was timed in a suitable venue with a battery of accurate stop watches which were soon being augmented by a high-tech Krondek electronic timing system.

This policy at once antagonized the representatives of the more prominent manufacturers, especially the management of the Eastern Triumph branch and Ted Hodgdon's New Jersey BSA facility, as the timed results were always less impressive than those published from "official" sources. A hostile Floyd Clymer organized an advertising boycott with the support of the above, along with Harley-Davidson, on the premise that the "industry didn't need another magazine". It was also agreed that advertising contracts awarded to another publication would add to overall costing problems.

When Parkhurst subsequently solicited Milwaukee's top management for advertising he was informed that it would not be forthcoming unless the Company was extended the right of prior review and censorship of any articles appearing in the magazine dealing with their products. In noting this attempt to reinforce the industry's old line policy of news management, Parkhurst wrote off any hopes of Milwaukee's cooperation.

In the earliest days of "Cycle World's" existence there were many emerging makes of machines for a buyer to choose from. The explosive growth of the Japanese manufacturer's production and the consequent increased worldwide interest in motorcycling saw several European

A Time of Change 1955-1965

Scene at the old Riverside TT course. This was a rough venue plagued with problems with dust.
William Bagnall

manufacturers expand their activities in an attempt to gain a better footing in what was now a growing market. The more or less dormant German market now saw firms like DKW and Zundapp offering new designs of 250 and 350 cc scrambler types machines in addition to their 50 cc moped lines. The British industry, while their export market was suffering from the effects of the Japanese expansion offered scrambler versions of the 350 and 500 cc four strokes, and the Villiers concern brought out 250 and 350 cc two stroke engine-gear units which were fitted by the small Greeves Company that was attempting to penetrate the growing popularity of street-scrambler trends.

The German Maico concern brought out an expanded line of similar models of 350 cc and 500 cc two strokes which were now imported by Frank Cooper. In order to facilitate easier starting, Cooper fitted compression release valves in the cylinder heads and was soon taking about half of Maico's production of these models. Maico's fortunes were improved with the acceptance of a military version

of their scramblers for off-road use by the armed forces of the North Atlantic Treaty Organization (NATO). The production of the Swedish Husqvarna models was also increased, most of them coming to the U.S. through Edison Dye in San Diego.

A motorcycle marketing anomaly in the U.S. was the offering of Austrian manufactured machines by the pioneer mail order merchandiser, Sears Roebuck. In 1963 they executed an agreement with Steyr-Daimler-Puch for the importation of their 250 and 350 cc models. These were powered by the twin piston or "split single" engines first developed and patented by Dr. Ing Joseph Erlich before World War II, which improved the efficiency of the intake and exhaust cycles over the basic single cylinder models invented by Sir Dugald Clerk in the late 1880's.

Sears had always adhered to the policy of marketing basic utility type machinery, such as smaller types of marine outboard engines, the simpler models of motor scooters and, even after World

319

War II, the compact automobile, the "Henry J", offered by Henry J. Kaiser. All of these products were offered under their trade name of "Allstate".

The Puch machines were the utility types, being substantially built without any pretense of sporting performance. Within the trade they were often referred to as "non-motorcyclist's motorcycles". Initially priced at $467 and $545, they were a definite transportation bargain, and proved to be generally reliable and trouble free. Distributed through Sears' retail outlets or shipped via mail order to the customer in assembled condition, a surprising number of 13,000 units were sold during their five years of sales life. Most of them were sold in the eastern and midwestern states to non-sporting riders, and many were still in use two decades later. Their eventual disappearance from the market was due to Sears' inability to set up an effective service program. This was in the days before they developed their later effective automobile service program. Many buyers were put off the road through the difficulty of obtaining needed spare parts.

In the meantime, Floyd Clymer was carrying on his campaign to discredit Parkhurst, but without much success. Parkhurst was enlarging the scope of "Cycle World" by conducting more road tests, accurately recorded with special equipment, and utilizing the newly opened road race course at a rural area near Riverside, California. In addition, and to add prestige to his efforts, he was engaging well known racing stars such as Al Gunter, Ron Grant, Don Vesco, Skip Van Leeuwen, Gene Romero and others, in addition to himself and Assistant Editor Ivan J. Wagar.

It was alleged that much of Clymer's animosity was caused to Parkhurst's adding Carol Sims to his staff after she had left the staff of "Cycle", following Clymer's refusal to increase her salary. Then, too, Parkhurst had lately negotiated an agreement with Iliffe and Temple Press in England to market some of their publications in the U.S. after they terminated their agreements with Clymer. This was after they had found out he had pirated editions printed without honoring their international copyrights. Shortly afterwards, Pete Colman and Don Brown of the Western Triumph operation refused to continue the eastern branches', BSA's, and Harley-Davidson's advertising boycott against Parkhurst and made their own agreement with him.

In the meantime, Jack McCormack (the former salesman for Johnson Motors who had left the company in 1962 to join Honda's North American operation in a similar capacity) was shortly to become involved in yet another business deal. It was noted that both Honda and Yamaha had greatly expanded their operations and, McCormack, as a sales executive for the former company, had traveled extensively through the U.S. to promote new dealerships. While he had been producing results, the Japanese management questioned the overuse of his expense account on lavish entertainment of potential clients and his own travel expenses. Getting wind of his superior's disenchantment, McCormack decided the prudent course of action to insure his own future was to find himself alternative employment before the axe fell. Accordingly, and while still technically in Honda's employ, he traveled to Japan for this purpose.

It was at this point that Suzuki, while having gained a foothold in the U.S. market far behind both the leader, Honda, and the number two competitor, Yamaha, was seeking ways to improve its marketing position. To make a long story short, McCormack was already aware of this situation and was able to negotiate a contract with Suzuki to manage their U.S. marketing program. The agreement involved the formation of a new company, headed by McCormack, which took over the sale of Suzuki products in the U.S. in consideration of a 25% markup, before taxes, on landed merchandise. On his return to the States, he concluded some sales agreements on Honda's behalf, during which time their top management caught up with him and terminated his association with the company.

In the meantime, Frank Cooper, who had given up on his attempts to breathe life into the wavering Royal Enfield sales efforts in the U.S., now concentrated his attention on expanding the Maico line, whose rugged and well engineering machines were exhibiting their growing acceptance in the scrambler and off road sphere.

The domestic scooter manufacturers had formed a somewhat informal association before the war under the leadership of Servi-cycle's John Paul Treen. This was mainly concerned with establishing certain safety standards involving handling and braking, but this languished with the withdrawal of Treen from the market in 1960. The sale of scooters was threatened two or three seasons later by competition from the sale of Japanese lightweight motorcycles, along with the further threat from various state governments who were in the process of abolishing the rather liberal licensing ordinances that allowed 14 year olds limited operation of small capacity machines. In addition, most low powered scooters were now being barred from high speed freeways and expressways for safety reasons.

Bud Ekins won the Big Bear Run in 1963.
Don Emde Collection

A TIME OF CHANGE 1955-1965

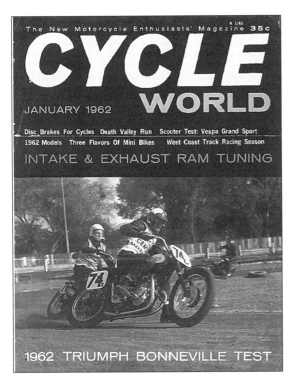

In 1962, Joe Parkhurst's "Cycle World" hit the market. It continues today as one of the sport's leading publications.
Don Emde Collection

In an attempt to counteract this trend, the scooter manufacturers reactivated their organization and hired Robert J. Rawlings, a Chicago based accessory salesman, to perfect their association and to act as a lobbyist to counteract restrictions against scooters. Rawlings' efforts were somewhat hampered by both the lack of adequate funding and the fact that they worked on a part-time basis only. The leading manufacturers, such as Cushman, Salsbury, Mustang and Harley-Davidson (who was still producing the Topper model) together with some smaller concerns, sent representatives to a general meeting in Chicago.

The upshot of the matter was that the manufacturers increased their funding and hired William T. Berry, a resident of Colorado, to act as a full time lobbyist for what was now to be known as the American Motor Scooter Association. The Berry family, as pioneer residents of Colorado, were well known in the transportation circles. For some years the senior Berrys had operated a Dodge-Plymouth agency in Canon City. Young Berry subsequently became the Sales Manager and, as an ebullient and gregarious individual, was later the President of the Colorado Motor Car Dealers Association. Berry was well acquainted with the scooter industry from his contacts with the distributor for Cushman products in that state, which also included the marketing of Cushman's suburban mail cars and in plant industrial trucks. Berry at once launched proposals for a scooter manufacturer's advertising campaign, and individual dealers were urged to sponsor clubs in their local areas to promote sociability between owners, and to organize tours and field meets of a mild nature to hopefully broaden the scope of scooter interest.

Berry was less successful in persuading state legislatures to rescind restrictive operational ordinances involving the general use of scooters on main highways and expressways, but his extensive nationwide travel schedule calling on dealers helped to strengthen the Association both numeri-

cally as well as financially. In 1964, Berry suggested to the Board of Directors and Lin Kuchler, AMA Secretary-Manager, that the Association should officially amalgamate its activities with the M&ATA. His proposal was that, as two wheeled vehicles, the use of scooters and motorcycles offered the public a related appeal, and the scooter as such was a natural entry level step to the later purchase of larger machines.

Kuchler at once was in favor of such a merger, and commented on the fact that Berry's extensive excursions into the country's political sphere for the benefit of the two wheeled industry showed that new doors could be opened in the realm of public acceptance. Both the AMA Board of Directors and the Competition Committee saw the advantages of the merger in the needed strengthening of the influence of the AMA generally, and voted to inaugurate the finalization of such a reorganization.

What was not publicized at the time was Kuchler's private intention to leave the AMA in favor of becoming the Competition Manager for the National Association of Stock Car Racing (NASCAR) at the invitation of its President, William France. Kuchler later recalled to the author that a number of controversial events within the AMA organization during the recent past had a definite influence on his ultimate decision.

After ignoring the growing interest in off road events the Competition Committee finally approved a set of rules to govern what was now being termed Moto Cross (MX) to take effect in the 1962 season. These rules were similar to those previously adopted in foreign countries. The point system outlined for Moto-Cross scoring awarded 400 points to the winner down through 1 point for the 20th place finisher. Season totals then indicated the standings of the riders. By this time most of the leading British manufacturers were offering four stroke machines suitably modified for MX, but lighter weight, high performance two strokes were gaining popularity. Harley-Davidson presently had no models suitable for MX, but later, during the opening MX season, offered a modified 250 cc version of the Aermacchi Sprint model suitably lightened and built with a high ground clearance. In order to enhance the so far limited appeal of the road model, the cylinder was bored out to 350 cc for the following sales season, along with the announcement that the imported Aermacchi line was shortly to include a comprehensive line of two stroke machines.

A notable event in American motorcycle history was the filming of the National Championship races at Louden, New Hampshire, through the efforts of Lin Kuchler in obtaining the cooperation of the Columbia Broadcasting Company. Over 50,000 feet of film were shot which was then edited into a one-hour program to be subsequently televised as a CBS Sports Spectacular.

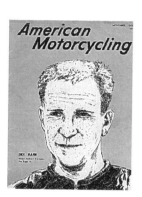

Dick Mann made news in 1963 when, as a privateer, he won the AMA Grand National Championship.
Don Emde Collection

In the early 1960's there was a growing sentiment among a number of competition riders, the majority of whom favored imported machinery, for the establishment of a set of regulations by the AMA Competition Committee to govern European Grand Prix type off road racing. At the same time, there was some pressure from within the ranks of the AMA membership as well as from William Bagnall, Editor of "The Motorcyclist", who was subsequently joined by Joe Parkhurst of "Cycle World", for AMA affiliation with the international FIM. Lin Kuchler brought up the matter with the Competition Committee, who voted an investigation into the possibilities of such affiliation but took no further action.

In the meantime, a group of competition riders, led by Edison Dye, the San Diego based Husqvarna importer, in company with Wes Cooley, formed the United States Motorcycle Club. The purpose of this was to form an association to promote enhanced moto-cross and European type road racing, not favored by the AMA Competition Committee up to this point. This group also favored affiliation with the FIM, also an action not favored by the AMA Competition Committee, which would materially strengthen the USMC. To this end, Dye opened up correspondence with the FIM headquarters to Geneva to consider the matter. In 1962, following a personal visit to Switzerland, the FIM governing committee accepted the USMC's petition for affiliation. This opened the way for American riders, as members of the USMC, to compete in International events held in Europe.

The AMA hierarchy at once took a dim view of the activities of the USMC, considering this a divisive factor in motorcycle sport as well as a challenge to their long domination of domestic motorcycling affairs. Their initial reaction was to suspend the competition licenses of AMA cardholders who supported the USMC and entered events sponsored by them.

The eastern activities of the USMC were given much publicity by Bernard Kahn, sportswriter for the Daytona Evening News, who noted that the fledgling organization was now challenging the arbitrary rule of the AMA. Active support to Grand Prix type racing at the newly opened Daytona Speedway was offered by William France, who, with William Tuthill, was the founder of NASCAR. Tuthill was active in promoting early

USMC affairs, along with Tom Galan of New Jersey, who was the USMC's eastern organizer.

In 1963, it was noted in the trade press that the American Motor Scooter Association had consolidated Chicago and Provo, Utah, into one headquarters in William T. Berry's home city of Denver, Colorado.

During the winter of 1963-64, the three Japanese importers, Honda, Yamaha and Suzuki, sponsored a series of meetings attended by their representatives in view of organizing a movement to gain membership in the AMA-M&ATA. With their rapidly growing market they considered they now had a right to a voice in organized American motorcycling affairs. The upshot of this activity was the later formation of the Southern California Motorcycle Safety Council, so named because the warehouse facilities and corporate offices of these makes were all based in the Los Angeles area.

During the spring and summer three letters were dispatched to the AMA headquarters concerning SCMSC Class B affiliation, all of which were ignored. Walter Davidson, Jr., on numerous occasions now publicly stated that his company would never permit the Oriental interlopers to join the AMA whose prime function was to promote the interests of the American manufacturers. This was taken as a rather contentious attitude, noting that with the rapid increase in the sale of Japanese products, Milwaukee's actual share of the market was now far and away a minority position. In any case, the sale of Oriental machines was seeing a credible increase, augmented by growing numbers of German, Polish, Austrian and Czechoslovakian imports, who were also active in the marketplace. Motorcycling in general was enjoying the aspects of a major boom.

The American public was, by this time, well aware of the growing industrial power of Japan, especially as Honda, along with Suzuki, had announced plans to manufacture a line of automobiles and trucks and Toyota and Nissan, as non-motorcycle manufacturers, were also preparing to penetrate the U.S. market.

At this point, few members of the American public were aware that the growing general industrialization of Japan was due to American influence. General Douglas MacArthur, as head of the Japanese occupation forces at the close of the war, at once noted the necessity for reviving Japan's industry for economic recovery after the war's devastation. Back in 1947, MacArthur had engaged the services of W. Edwards Deming, a renowned American expert on industrial organization, to come to Japan and inaugurate such a program. Deming, a

A TIME OF CHANGE 1955-1965

professional engineer, had rendered practical application for a number of advanced theories on production planning, quality control, material acquisition, time and motion efficiency, cost control, and other techniques for achieving enhanced production. He spent several months in Japan, accompanied by a team of assistants, lecturing Japanese production engineers (through interpreters) on methods of building improved industrial systems. It was their employment of the Deming theories that enabled Japan to quickly create their fabulously successful industrial rebirth.

Strange to relate, American manufacturers, while somewhat familiar with Deming's recommendations, were slow in updating their post-war production programs or in replacing obsolete plant facilities. It was only in the late 1970's, when Japanese import goods were posing a serious threat to American industrial markets, that Deming's proposals received widespread attention at home.

In the meantime, and accompanying the now rapidly growing interest in motorcycling on the part of the general public and the expansion of its market, a new segment of the domestic market was assuming substantial proportions. This was the recent steady growth in the manufacture of motorcycle acces-

sories that was the outgrowth of the custom chopper or cruiser type of modified machines favored by the biker devotees. While some Indian Chiefs and limited numbers of British machines were altered, the make of choice was Harley-Davidson FL and F models. Early on the factory had frowned on the biker movement for the public image it presented, the lack of accessory purchases associated with the factory promoted "dresser" type scorned by the bikers, and cottage industries came into being to market the style of parts favored by custom builders. These were to grow into such leading firms as Jammers, Gary Bang, and Custom Chrome, which offered a comprehensive range of products. In addition, dozens of smaller operations offered such specialized items as custom style frames, forks, engine and transmission cases, stroker type cylinder barrels and other parts. By this time it was possible to build up a counterfeit Harley-Davidson from these parts.

While many of the accessories were domestic manufacture, by this time there were other sources of supply provided by a myriad of manufacturing firms in Japan, Korea and Taiwan, the latter two countries now following the example set by Japan with extensive and ever expanding industrialization. In addition, most of these concerns also supplied custom type parts to fit both domestic and foreign manufactured automobiles.

A TIME OF CHANGE 1955-1965

The aftermarket motorcycle market was now expanding to cater to the rapidly growing biker movement, iconoclastic and counterculture sentiments being stimulated by the general interest in various manifestations of social protest. This coincided with the so-called Haight Ashbury syndrome that spawned the flower child movement, together with the protest against the Vietnam War.

Some social behaviorists were arguing the point as to whether the bikers were primarily motorcyclists, or whether the motorcycle, as an iconoclastic vehicle, was the logical extension of the free swinging biker lifestyle.

During the late 1950's, Charles "Chuck" Clayton, an experienced journalist with a special interest in automotive and motorcycling subjects, founded a publication with a newspaper format which he called "Cycle Sport", initially published bimonthly in Long Beach, California. This was intended to fill the void left by the demise of "Bzzzz Motorcycle News", with an emphasis on sports reporting. Clayton was able to provide a broader coverage of such events than "The Motorcyclist" as well as the AMA publication "American Motorcycling". In comparison with the latter, "Cycle Sport" offered expanded coverage of

events featuring the participation of foreign machines, which had never been emphasized by "American Motorcycling" whose quite natural principal coverage dealt with sporting events involving only American machines.

"Cycle Sport" was circulated initially through display sales in motorcycle shops. As sales increased, Clayton expanded his coverage toward marketing promotion aimed at retail selling as well as articles of general rider interest, and inaugurated a sales campaign to increase advertising content from both commercial firms and want ads from private owners. With additional financing he bought out a rival journal. He changed the name to "Cycle News" and it appeared weekly.

In editorial comments, he advocated a more democratic AMA as well as affiliation with the FIM to allow U.S. participation in international events. In his expanded coverage of sporting events, he engaged a group of traveling reporters to provide on-the-spot coverage of the major seasonal fixtures. Among these reporters was a young former graduate student with a Master's Degree in English from the University of Oklahoma, Ed Youngblood, whom we shall meet again. The publication was subsequently expanded to include an

Eastern edition, although the main office continued in Long Beach.

Within a couple of years after its founding, Joe Parkhurst's "Cycle World" had become the leading general motorcycle publication. With well written and comprehensive technical articles covering contemporary design progress, a broad coverage of sporting events, together with Parkhurst's policy of road testing any new or updated model on two wheels, reader interest in the rapidly expanding motorcycle market was well covered.

This, along with Parkhurst's realistic road tests of current machines, did not endear "Cycle World" to Milwaukee. Word subsequently circulated within the trade that the magazine was anti-Harley-Davidson. Parkhurst, in answer, published an editorial stating that this was not true, and that the magazine's policy was to treat each make of machine objectively, although he did not retreat from his policy of advocating a restructured AMA.

The proposed Southern California Motorcycle Safety Council, as organized by the Oriental importers, had made little if any progress in their campaign to secure membership in the M&ATA, as their formal correspondence to the AMA headquarters had been ignored.

While a series of meetings of representatives of both groups was going on, the Board of Directors of the parent BSA organization in England authorized Harry Sturgeon to negotiate with Hap Alzina, BSA's western distributor, for the outright purchase of his operation. While Japanese machine sales were making serious inroads on the American market, as well as creating a new class of buyers, BSA's and Triumph's were also selling well, and the factory sought to take over the whole operation to enhance their profit picture.

At the same time, BSA's directors had privately arrived at the decision to replace Ted Hodgdon in the New Jersey branch. While sales had been steady, it was noted that his tight-fisted control of the operation as a private fiefdom mainly was oriented toward his own sales commissions. A rapid turnover of employees due to his low wage scale and lack of benefits, his reluctance to maintain an adequate supply of spare parts, and his often non-cooperative attitude toward the interests of the dealers indicated that BSA's interests were not being well served.

In the meantime, Wilbur Ceder had delegated Vice President Pete Colman, who acted as Western Triumph's General Manager, to negotiate with Hap Alzina for BSA's purchase of that distributorship. Following a series of personal conferences, Alzina agreed to relinquish his holdings for $975,000. As

(Top and bottom) 1964 was a very good year for Kewanee, Illinois' Roger Reiman. In addition to winning the Daytona 200 that year, he won the AMA Grand National Championship and also set speed records at Bonneville.
Don Emde Collection

the details of his operation came to light, it was noted that his old friend and competitor, Dudley Perkins, also had a substantial financial interest in the operation. He had been invited by Alzina to participate in his initial 1949 assumption of BSA's western distributorship. In later years Perkins told the author that while his interest in the BSA operation was wholly legitimate, the matter was kept a carefully guarded secret so as not to complicate his sometimes tenuous relationship with the Harley-Davidson factory.

Following the consummation of Alzina's sales, he financed the purchase of "The Motorcyclist" magazine by William and Sherlee Bagnall, whose names subsequently appeared as the publishers on the masthead. The former owner, Charles D. Baskerville, who had inherited the operation from his father-in-law Arthur E. Welch, now pursued other interests.

After a series of meetings between William T. Berry, the manager of the Scooter Manufacturers Association, and AMA Secretary-Manager Lin Kuchler, the latter presented the matter of combining this with the M&ATA to the M&ATA Board of Directors. Kuchler, who had materially strengthened the latter organization by bringing both the distributors and owners into the fold, reasoned that scooter owners, as entry level riders, could well graduate to motorcycles with the advocacy of AMA membership, not to mention the financial advantage of augmenting Class A membership. The Board at once saw the wisdom of Kuchler's suggestion and the scooter organization was voted into the AMA-M&ATA with Berry being incorporated into the staff. The name of the M&ATA was now officially designated as the Motorcycle, Scooter, and Allied Trades Association.

The ranks of scooter manufacturers were somewhat reduced when Harley-Davidson dropped the Topper model in favor of entering the golf cart manufacturing field, and were now testing both gasoline and electrical powered prototypes. The Salisbury concern also discontinued their once popular scooter models in favor of concentrating on the sales to industry of their patented centrifugal drive clutches. In any case, Berry was hopeful that M&ATA affiliation would somehow strengthen the marketing position of the surviving scooter manufacturers, as the sales of lightweight Japanese motorcycles had already eroded the domestic scooter market. The high tech, high performance Italian scooters remained popular, however, being represented by Piaggi's Vespa and Innocenti's Lambretta. The former was the most popular, however, being imported through Ernest Wise's

A Time of Change 1955-1965

Cosmopolitan Motors as well as being handled by Sears-Roebuck under the name of Allstate in a separate import agreement.

A personal change within the industry was noted at this time with the resignation of Don Brown as General Sales Manager for the western division of Triumph. While he had done a creditible job of expanding both Triumph's dealer network and retail sales, long standing personal differences between himself and Wilbur Ceder were given as the reason. Shortly after that Brown was offered a like position by Jack McCormack in the American Suzuki Corporation. The energetic McCormack had, within a short time, increased Suzuki's market share from 5% to 15% with an aggressive marketing program, aided by the parent Japanese factory's introduction of an expanded range of models. New dealerships as well as in-place operations were now expanding Suzuki sales.

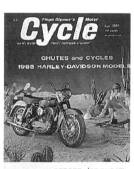

Don Emde Collection

For 1965, Harley-Davidson brought the top-of-the-line FL models into the modern mode by adding electric starting, although the kickstart mechanism was retained. The attachment was engineered by the Homelite Corporation, manufacturers of both portable and stationary generating sets. Due to the heavy current draw needed to rotate the large piston, the whole electrical system was converted to twelve volts. The Homelite system was hastily installed to replace the initial system engineering by Outboard Motors Corporation, which for some implausible reason was found to be vulnerable to problems of shorting out in wet weather, although the mechanism was derived from similar fittings recently produced for large outboard marine engines. Electric starting was hailed as an encouragement to feminine riders who favored heavyweight machines, although Harley-Davidson's were traditionally easy starters without it if the proper drill was carried out. As it was, the system added another 80 pounds to an already weighty vehicle, although the twelve volt system was an improvement for the current demands of police work. The 1965 big twins were now cataloged as the Electra-Glide.

Harley-Davidson production, not including the Aermacchi models, averaged between 10,000 and 15,000 units between 1960 and 1965. There was, of course, a built-in market of loyal Milwaukee enthusiasts who would consider no other make, and the big twins and surviving Indian Chiefs were almost the standard choice of the AMA chartered clubs that still prospered. With their ability to carry two riders along with a substantial amount of luggage over long distances in reasonable comfort, they were the machine of

choice for such activity. Their only challenger was the BMW which, although a high priced machine imported in small numbers, was already assuming a cult-like status of its own.

The sales of Milwaukee's Italian imports turned out to be disappointing. Much of the resistance to their sales came from the dealers themselves, who were not oriented toward small capacity machines and did not relish the investment in a comprehensive spare parts inventory to serve them. Numbers of owners who purchased Sprint models might well find themselves off the road for a time for the lack of some component that more often than not had to be back ordered. After 1965, Aermacchi brought out a line of small two strokes, a type not favored by veteran dealers and, in any case, these lagged behind the growing horde of Japanese imports in technical development and in overall dependability.

During the mid-1960's there were persistent rumors that Harley-Davidson's top management had put forth confidential proposals to such midwestern firms as Caterpillar, John Deere, DeLaval, and other firms, concerning their purchasing of the Company. Insiders alleged that the shareholders' constant demands for high returns on their stock, which had precluded updating the firm's product line, were eroding the operating capital. By this time, President Davidson was well aware that in order to modernize the Company's product line and its long antiquated manufacturing facilities would require a radical restructuring of its financial structure, together with the hiring of a professional engineering force; innovations which would not be sanctioned by the conservative shareholders. Then, too, the Company had no existing family members who were either willing or competent to take over the responsibilities of management. It was later learned that the outside firms who were approached regarding the purchase of the Company were not encouraged with the prospect of having to invest large sums for plant modernization or engaging in extensive prototype development to update the now venerable line of Milwaukee products.

There were also unsubstantiated rumors that small increments of Harley-Davidson stock had been acquired from some of the original shareholders by Cuban capitalists who had escaped from that beleaguered country just ahead of Castro's revolution in 1959. Whatever the details of the matter, this situation of Harley-Davidson shares was to have a critical effect on the Company's future.

Milwaukee continued to figure prominently in AMA competition. Brad Andres won the 1960

A Time of Change 1955-1965

Daytona for a third time, with the first 14 places going to Harley-Davidson riders. The focus was starting to shift to Grand Prix type competition with the increasing activities of the United States Motorcycle Racing Club, which was staging FICM type events.

Preston Petty and Bob Rickard formed a Honda Racing team on CB 92 Model 125 cc Honda Benleys, and ran in the first lightweight contest held on an airport north of Daytona. Harley-Davidsons were still well in the picture, however, with Carroll Resweber winning his third Grand National title in Ionia, Michigan, in the same year. Stu Morley won the 1960 Pacific Coast Championship on a Gold Star at Sacramento. Al Gunter, BSA mounted, won the Eight Mile National at Ascot.

The USMC inaugurated FIM type Grand Prix racing at the Daytona Speedway in February 1961. Riders from six countries competed in 100 and 200 kilometer distances.The race was billed as "The Grand Prix of the United States", and was the forerunner of subsequent similar events at the same venue. USMC founders Bill Tuthill and Tom Galen, in Florida, had received a FIM sanction, and a group of overseas entrants in the 100 kilo event included Moto Kitano from Japan on a Honda four cylinder special who won over second place Englishman Mike Hailwood on an Italian Mondial, with Guatemalan Luis Giron on a German NSU coming in a close third.

The 200 kilo event was again won by Kitano on a Honda 250, entered in the 500 cc class. Hailwood and Tony Godfrey dueled on Manx Nortons, along with Buddy Parriot similarly mounted. Hailwood was sidelined with engine trouble, and Godfrey won at 90.62 mph. By this time, increasing numbers of European machines were being brought to the States, such as the Parilla by Cosmopolitan Motors, the Ducati by Berliner Corporation, and the Moto Guzzi and Rumi by the Berliner organization. All of these swelled the ranks of USMC organized events which were to form a prominent role in Grand Prix type competition in the U.S. during the balance of the decade.

An account of the various USMC competition events during this period would fill a large volume, a report of which is more or less beyond the scope of this history. The USMC was a separate organization from that of the AMA and was somewhat in competition with it.

The AMA hierarchy was, of course, strongly opposed to FIM sanctioned contests, which were rapidly winning public spectator interest because of both the novelty of this type of racing as well as the fact that a diverse class of machines from 50 cc upwards were now featured.

Some contemporary journalists, who were in favor of AMA traditions and the restrictive rulings in place through the efforts of Milwaukee, tended to downgrade the importance of the USMC. It was also noted that the AMA Competition Committee initially attempted to class USMC programs as "outlaw" events, but with many new riders not bothering to affiliate with the AMA in preference to USMC competition, AMA suspension threats were virtually meaningless.

The AMA, however, continued to put its emphasis on the dirt track National circuits. Don Burnett won the Daytona 200 on a Triumph, breaking Milwaukee's seven season series of wins; as Carroll Resweber and Joe Leonard, in an early lead, sustained blown engines. The popular Ascot races featured a number of seesaw contests between BSA, Triumph and Harley-Davidson riders.

In the 1962 season, Milwaukee's Carroll Resweber, Bart Markel and BSA's star Dick Mann were running wheel-to-wheel for the Number One plate. During the Lincoln, Illinois Half Miler, Resweber lost his chance to take his fifth straight title in a severe accident on a dust shrouded track. Jack Gholson was killed and three other riders were injured. The most seriously hurt was Resweber who was sent into retirement seriously crippled. Bart Markel went on to win the Lincoln contest and later the Sacramento Half Mile and won the Number One plate.

Another Harley-Davidson rider, Tony Murguia, won the 120 Miler at Indianapolis, adding another National victory to Milwaukee's crown.

The 1963 Daytona 200 was a race plagued with mechanical failures. Only 18 out of 65 entrants crossed the finish line. Ralph White, riding a conservative race, piloted his Harley-Davidson through the race for another Milwaukee victory. BSA's star rider, Dick Mann, was a favored winner but the AMA Competition Committee disqualified his Matchless G50 on the grounds that it had a nonstandard frame. Through some intense politicking, the machine was qualified two years later.

The Competition Committee inaugurated the sanctioning of the AMA Speed Trials at Lake Bonneville, with regulations intended to insure the safety of the contestants by enforcing certain technical details on the machine's construction. Long time AMA referee Earl Flanders was designated as the chief inspector, and presided over the Speed Trials for 17 years.

A spectacular entrant in the 1960's was New Zealand's Burt Munro who, in his late 60's and early 70's, was a perennial visitor with his much modified

A Time of Change 1955-1965

1920 Indian standard Scout with a streamlined fairing. His peak performance was ultimately a 190 mph record in the 61 cubic inch class.

In 1964, the Daytona course was lengthened to 3.8 miles by utilizing a major portion of the outer oval. It was now considered to be both safer and faster due to the elimination of some of the sharp turns. This race featured a duel between front runner Roger Reiman and George Roeder, on Harley-Davidsons, and Triumph mounted Gary Nixon. After a hard fought contest Roeder was the winner at 94.8 mph. The 1963 winner, Ralph White, Harley-Davidson mounted, was fourth, and Dick Klamfoth, out of retirement riding a Matchless G50, was fifth. This was the first year that streamlined fairings were permitted. The conservative AMA Competition Committee had resisted their sanctioning for several past seasons.

Events outside of the usual AMA sanctioned contests (but mentioned due to their historic significance to the domestic motorcycle industry) included the participation of Bud and David Ekins, Cliff Coleman, actor Steve McQueen, and John Steen in the 1964 International Six Days Trials held in Germany. These riders were eligible due to their membership in the USMC. The team missed a Team Prize due to accidents sustained by both Ekins and McQueen, but Dave Ekins and Cliff Coleman were awarded Gold Medals, with John Steen getting a Silver. Bud Ekins was distinguished to have been the USMC entrant during the 1962, 1966, and 1967 events, winning Gold Medals. He also won a Silver in 1961.

The 1965 Daytona was a Milwaukee victory with Roger Reiman and Mert Lawwill taking first and second places. Triumph riders George Montgomery and Gary Nixon came in third and fourth. Due to wet conditions, because of sudden heavy rains, the speed of the winner was down to 90.04 mph.

A portent of things to come was the news from Japan that the Kawasaki conglomerate was intending to enter the world motorcycle market. This giant concern consisted of a diverse group of activities such as shipbuilding, heavy equipment manufacture, railway cars and equipment that included complete suburban transport systems with cars, track and switching facilities. It also was involved in aircraft manufacture and, during the war, had turned out vast numbers of engines for the Japanese armed forces. It was now noted that Kawasaki was experimenting with prototypes of small capacity two stroke motorcycles, as well as a four cycle twin that was a frank copy of the current BSA A10 that was noted for being very well finished and which did not

leak oil! That fall, a team of economic analysts from Kawasaki toured the U.S. in order to survey the American market.

With the virtual boycotting of the USMC news and competition reports on the part of AMA's "American Motorcycling", Charles Clayton was expanding the news coverage of "Cycle News" to accommodate this, and added additional staff for this purpose.

William Bagnall also expanded his journalistic scope by founding a magazine called "Motorcycle Dealer News", in partnership with Larry Hester. Hester was an advertising salesman for Petersen Publications as well as being an enthusiastic motorcyclist with a special interest in off-road events. The initial issue was launched in June of 1965, as a 24 page pamphlet, but soon grew to respectable proportions with added scope and enhanced advertising sales. The magazine was intended as a controlled circulation production distributed to dealers and members of the trade exclusively, and specialized in featuring marketing reports, sales data, news of new product lines, and items of more or less confidential variety not intended to air before the general public. The partnership of Bagnall and Hester existed until 1971, when Bagnall sold out to Hester.

Members of the industry, dealers, and numerous enthusiasts have cumulatively told the author that the decade of the 1960's was more or less a second Golden Age for domestic motorcycling. There was, by this time, almost an infinite variety of machines of all capacities and sizes and types on the market from Europe, Great Britain, Scandinavia and the Orient. Competition in the market place was still extensive, as the Orientals had yet to completely fill the spectrum of choice, and retail prices were quite reasonable. Licensing and insurance requirements were not repressive and organized environmental groups had not raised a formidable outcry against the use of public lands and uninhabited areas for off-road events. Federal and State legislation mandating compulsory helmet laws and other ordinances aimed at restricting motorcycling activities had yet to appear.

In this happy era of unfettered freedom of choice and scope of activity, public interest in motorcycling grew by leaps and bounds with nearly a million machines registered nationwide. Historically, this period in domestic motorcycle history could well be compared to the salad days in the U.S. between 1910 and 1915, when the motorcycle technically came of age and was the choice of both sporting and utility riders due to its low first cost and wide availability.

Chapter Eleven

The Later Years

During the fall of 1965, the Kawasaki survey team completed their analysis of the American motorcycle market. Finding favorable prospects of its penetration, the group, headed by S. Kenogshima, leased a large warehouse with office facilities in Avenal, New Jersey, an industrial suburb of Newark. Their initial model introduction was to be a line of small capacity, two stroke machines in the street scrambler style popular at the time.

Emmett Moore, who had become disenchanted with his $10,000 per year salary from Ted Hodgdon as BSA's General Manager, at once accepted a similar post with Kawasaki at double the salary. With a large stock of product now on hand, Kawasaki opened their sales campaign early in 1966.

In the meantime, Don Brown had been considering an offer from M. Eguchi of Yamaha to accept a position as Vice President in charge of marketing, but made the decision to join Jack McCormack's Suzuki operation in a similar position with a profit sharing agreement along with a regular salary. McCormack's operations had taken off encouragingly, but certain policies inaugurated by the parent company had recently eroded his profit pictures. As the operation expanded, an increasing group of Suzuki personnel had been sent over uninvited which featherbedded the payroll.

McCormack, in reviewing this situation, claimed a breach of the original contractual agreement and filed legal action against Suzuki, retaining the law firm of Flemming and Anderson to represent him, with a junior partner, Richard Darby, managing the case. Suzuki retained the most prestigious law firm in Los Angeles, Gibson, Dunn and Crutcher. The focus of the affair centered around an arbitration agreement written into the original contract, and the attorneys spent five weeks in negotiation. The judge ultimately ruled in favor of McCormack, but Suzuki at once filed notice of an appeal. But at this point, both parties

had tired of the protracted struggle and Suzuki at length came forward with an offer of settlement.

The action provided that Jack McCormack terminate his arrangement with Suzuki's U.S. distribution, such being a part of the settlement. Suzuki at once put their own management organization in place headed by Japanese executives. Brown remained for a short time as head of marketing before resigning to seek other employment.

A factory authorized history published in 1980, of the entire Suzuki operation, from the manufacture of textile proceeding machinery through the manufacture of both motorcycles and later light automobiles and commercial vehicles written by British transportation historian Jeff Clew, did not mention either the incident or the fact that McCormack was ever connected with the company.

In the spring of 1966, Lin Kuchler decided to act on his long standing plan to resign his AMA position and join William France's NASCAR organization. His official position would be Competition Manager. While Kuchler's initial appointment had been criticized in some quarters due to his former close association with the Davidsons, he had at once acted as his own person in the inauguration of certain innovative policies. He mended fences with many of the foreign machines dealers as well as their enthusiasts, many of whom heretofore had not favored AMA affiliation due to Harley-Davidson's monopolistic policies. His ability to bring many of these groups into the AMA did much to enhance its scope of activity. This improved financial picture was aided by raising membership dues, which enabled an updating of office facilities and the raising of salaries of the clerical force, as well as his own to $15,000 per year.

In tendering his resignation, Kuchler later recalled that up to that point he was of the opinion that he had progressed about as far as possible with the ultra conservative Competition Committee who, for the most part, were too old to ride motorcycles, resisted change, and based their thinking on the practices of the past. He also recalled the end-

Joe Parkhurst, who founded Cycle World Magazine in 1962. On the cover page to this chapter Parkhurst is seen at speed somewhere in Baja California, his favorite off-road venue.
Parkhurst Publications

less political situations that were a part and parcel of AMA activities, together with the fact that the growing influence of the U.S.M.C. was complicating the AMA's relationships with their own membership. Then there was the growing pressure for a complete reorganization of the AMA to include the representation of the Oriental factories, which was already meeting with strong resistance from Milwaukee. An important facet of Kuchler's legacy was the enhanced efficiencies of the AMA's bookkeeping and financial control systems along with a complete and intact set of records compiled during his tenure of office. Kuchler later recalled that a great inducement to join NASCAR was France's offer of continuing his $15,000 salary.

The Competition Committee took some time in selecting Kuchler's successor, and finally decided to elevate William T. Berry to the post, with the title of Executive Secretary. Berry had spent his first year in promoting the cause of the scooter industry, as well as learning the procedures laid down by Kuchler. Berry had hoped to assume Kuchler's salary scale, but the Davidson contingent, who were ever an advocate of modest wages, held out for a final offer of $13,500.

Not everyone in the AMA hierarchy was happy with Berry's appointment. Many felt that he was not a motorcyclist in that sense of the word, and that his past experience with scooters was overshadowed by his broader previous role in the sale of Cushman mail cars and industrial trucks. As it was, he was not personally oriented toward fitting in with the "good ol' boy" group that made up the Competition Committee, and to effectively manage the affairs of both the AMA and the M&ATA he indeed faced a rather formidable task.

A change in the motorcycle trade publication picture occurred in 1966 when Floyd Clymer sold "Cycle" magazine to the New York based Ziff-Davis publication group, who had previously entered the transportation field with "Car and Driver". Clymer, who had contended with numerous personal problems within his staff, no doubt induced by his traditional low salary scale, was reported to have been happy to step down in favor of the $200,000 purchase price offered by Ziff-Davis director David I. Davis. The latter at once reorganized "Cycle's" staff and enticed rider-journalist Gordon Jennings away from "Cycle World" to serve as editor. The technical content and scope of reporting as well as a greatly improved literary style at once became apparent. This was carried forward by a subsequent editor, Phil Schilling, who later wrote a non-controversial and artistically conceived anthological overview of the motorcycling

scene, "Motorcycling World", which was published as a limited edition by Random House.

The biking world was the subject of a full length motion picture, "Hells Angels on Wheels" in 1967, featuring Jack Nicholson and Adam Rourke in starring roles, with appearances by founder Ralph M. 'Sonny' Barger and numerous members of the Angels' California chapters. In noting the often violent and antisocial depictions, some esoteric biker publications and newsletters complained that the devotees were subjected to unfair treatment and that the biker mode encompassed a broad spectrum of personality types that did not subscribe to violent or criminal activities. By this time, the biking movement sought to legitimatize itself by local sponsorships of charity drives, blood bank contributions, "Toys for Tots" features at Christmas and widely supported runs and gatherings for the financial benefit for the relief of muscular dystrophy.

Following the ground previously broken by Lin Kuchler, motorcycling events were now being seen in television features, as well as motorcycles being used as an adjunct to plot sequences in feature productions. Bud Ekins was the early supplier of motorcycles and attendant stunt riders, and had strong connections in the entertainment industry as well as being a mentor for actor Steven McQueen in his participation in motorcycle sports events.

As the motion picture industry expanded its scope to produce feature pictures for television, producers entered the subliminal advertising field for enhanced revenue. For a fee, shots featuring a variety of commercial products appeared as backgrounds, such as billboard advertising, various store fronts, items of food products, etc. The use of various makes of vehicles was a prominent feature, and auto makers whose products were an invariable adjunct to plot lines were frequently shown.

One such feature with a motorcycling theme, "Along Came Bronson", appeared as a two-season television series starring Michael Parks and Bonny Bedelia. The theme was that of a knight errant rider, and the personal situations encountered on California's coastal highways. Bud Ekins cooperated with cinematographer Raymond Flin in the construction of camera bearing machines with seats over the front wheels to facilitate action camera shots. Both Flin and Ekins had originally planned to feature Triumph machines but then, according to both Flin and Triumph manager Pete Colman, the producers demanded $40,000 as an advertising fee. Colman refused to comply and the matter was resolved when Harley-Davidson agreed to participate if the cast rode Sportsters. Ekins then supplied two identical machines, with Milwaukee contribut-

A much modified
Harley-Davidson
ServiCar altered to make
a chopper styled rick-
shaw.
Joe Teresi

ing to production costs.

Colman, however, cognizant of celebrity advertising value, presented several Thunderbird models to various Hollywood riders. Motion picture and nightclub artist Ann-Margaret (Ollsen), shrewdly managed by her actor-husband, Roger Smith, were Triumph enthusiasts, and in two of her Las Vegas spectacular stage shows and one TV spectacular, the dance scene was enhanced by a montage of Triumphs as static displays.

In the meantime, while the BSA-Triumph combination continued as the principal makes of British representation in the U.S., the rest of the British industry was in sharp decline. Enfield closed down their operation at Redditch, and subsequently sold the manufacturing rights and tooling to a firm in Madras, India, which continued the manufacture of 250, 350, and later 500 cc 'Bullet' models. For reasons of economy and to accommodate the low octane gasoline produced in that country, these models were non-sporting types and were intended for utility transportation only. The once

popular Panther line produced in Yorkshire also closed down, ending Ed York's limited operations as a distributor in a suburb of Sacramento, California. Most of the Villiers engine lightweights went out of production in the mid-1960's due to competition from the low cost, high performance Japanese machines; a Suzuki distributorship having been established in Great Britain as early as 1963, with other makes soon following suit.

The supply of 350 and 500 cc Velocettes available in the U.S. was greatly reduced after 1967, as Veloce, Ltd. concentrated on lightweight machines in an attempt to compete with the Orientals, as well as experimenting with scooters, types which did not find favor in the U.S. market. Veloce ultimately ceased production at the end of 1970. BSA attempted to market 75 cc four stroke lightweights called the 'Beagle', which failed technically. Many enthusiasts were disappointed at the phasing out of the Gold Star, which had replaced the Norton International which disappeared with the reorganization of that company into Norton-Villiers.

THE LATER YEARS

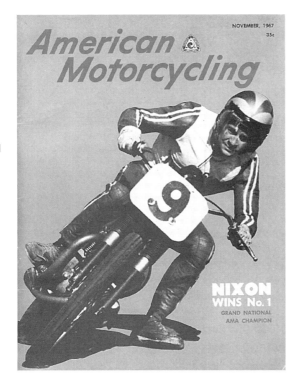

In spite of Oriental competition, the BSA-Triumph group continued to produce machines principally intended for the U.S. market. Triumph's top-of-the-line 650 cc Thunderbird, 500 cc Trophy, and 200 cc Cub models were carried forward. BSA emphasized their 650 cc Lightning and Rocket twins, the 500 cc A7, and were experimenting with a 750 cc, three cylinder model with vertically positioned cylinders. This was badge engineered as the Triumph Trident and the BSA Triple and introduced in 1968.

In the western U.S. BSA-Triumph continued its active participation in competition under the management of Pete Colman. This also included the remaining supply of Gold Star models which were set up in dirt track, motocross, and some Grand Prix types. A newcomer in 1965 was the 441 Victor model, a four stroke machine originally conceived as a 250 cc model to compete with the growing number of foreign high performance two strokes that in 360 cc form were invading the 500 cc motocross class. BSA's factory team had been making a good showing in some European events and Colman promoted this machine actively on the West Coast with Dick Mann on the central California circuits, the noted 'Feets' Minert campaigning in the south. The Victor enjoyed some mild popularity as a street model, although it had a reputation as a hard starter.

Colman came into the overall management of both Triumph and BSA operations in the western states with the sudden death of Wilbur Ceder from a massive heart attack in the fall of 1966.

In spite of the growing activities of the U.S.M.C. and the various types of events sponsored by them, which were outside the scope of the long traditional AMA Class C events, the ultra-conservative Competition Committee continued to ignore this interest both from within and without the sport. Suggestions to include the fitting of streamlined wind fairings and clip-on type handle bars in AMA approved racing events were passed over. In noting this trend Lin Kuchler, just before his resignation as AMA Secretary, had personally authorized their fitting on behalf of a small AMA chartered club in Southern California, called the Motorcycle Road Racing Association, at the urging of Pete Colman.

In the meantime, the BSA factory continued with its plans to reorganize its eastern branch at Nutley, New Jersey. The ailing Managing Director, Harry Sturgeon, was replaced by Lionel Jofeh who came over from Birmingham to take over the reorganization. In addition, another factory person who entered the picture was Eric Turner, who was the Board Chairman of BSA-Triumph. At this point, Ted Hodgdon, who had been aware for some time that his days at Nutley were numbered, in a series of press releases to the trade, announced his impending retirement from the motorcycle industry. His former sales manager, Emmett Moore, later told the author that Hodgdon did not wish to endure the stigma that he was actually being fired. Jofeh, at this point, was on the West Coast interviewing potential managers to head the Nutley Operation for BSA. Jofeh ultimately made an offer to Don Brown and, after some negotiating, Brown moved to Nutley to assume management of the branch. The operation at this point was nearly at a standstill, with a badly depleted parts inventory, rundown premises, and a dispirited staff of employees. To add to the difficulties, the branch was being picketed by the Teamsters Union as being unfair to organized labor.

Ted Hodgdon retired to his former home in Springfield, and next assumed the role of an elder statesman in the growing interest in old machines with his activities within the Antique Motorcycle Club of America. He was ultimately to write a book entitled "The Golden Age of the Fours", published by the Bagnall Publishing Company, which centered on its author's life-long interest in this type of machine.

Following his separation from Suzuki, Jack McCormack conceived a new venture within the motorcycle industry. It was planned to import a complete line of motorcycles from Europe from 50

Kawasaki flies at Bonneville

First time out at the salt and Kawasaki sets 14 new A.M.A. speed records...the most records ever established in one year by any motorcycle manufacturer.

Here's the score!

Kawasaki Bonneville records

Disp.	Class	Rider	Speed
100cc	PS-A	Thomas Kuntze	73.251
	CC	Harry Sullivan	76.909
175cc	PSA	Bob Vaughan	86.023
	CA	Bob Vaughan	89.361
	APSC	Bob Vaughan	83.567
	AC	Bob Vaughan	90.870
	CC	Bob Vaughan	87.007
250cc	APSC	Thomas Kuntze	96.771
	AC	Thomas Kuntze	101.425
	AA	Thomas Kuntze	106.912
	PSA	Darrel Krause	118.421
	CA	Darrel Krause	111.633
	APSA	Darrel Krause	122.396
650cc	APSC	Roger Hall	102.769

Subject to final A.M.A. certification

Now Kawasaki has proven the quality performance of aircraft manufacturing precision applied to motorcycles ...proven that Kawasaki builds motorcycles for people who know what it's all about. Now, are you the Kawasaki kind?

See your dealer today! Get a Kawasaki winner. And get a winning factory written warranty. An unbeatable 12,000 mile/12 month assurance of dependability.

650 W2SS COMMANDER   350 A7 AVENGER   250 A1SS SAMURAI

Kawasaki Motorcycles

Kawasaki was the last of the four major Japanese manufacturers to make a push in the United States. *Don Emde Collection*

The July 1967 issue of The Enthusiast featured rising star Cal Rayborn. He would go on to become one of America's best-ever road racers. *Don Emde Collection*

cc upward to compete with the Oriental imports. Utilizing some of the funds from his financial settlement with Suzuki, he entered into an agreement with Richard Darby, his attorney in the Suzuki litigation, in which Darby was to organize a projected $3,000,000 fund to implement the operation. Meanwhile, McCormack entered into an agreement in Italy with the Laverda concern, whose top-of-the-line 650 cc parallel twin was a very potent performer. Naming the machine "The American Eagle", an ambitious advertising campaign was launched in the trade press, and a limited number of dealers took on franchises. About 180 machines were imported during 1967 and 1968, but the addition of other machines stalled due to Darby's inability to raise sufficient risk capital to fund the venture. As funds dwindled, the importation of Laverdas ground to a halt. McCormack has been compared to the automotive industry's William Crapo Durant's ventures, being adept at organization but inept in management. The Laverda machines gained some notoriety when employed by the daredevil stunt rider Robert 'Evel' Knievel in his early exploits.

Following the sale of "Cycle" magazine, Floyd Clymer took it upon himself to reactivate the Trailblazers organization, which had languished since the death of its original founder A.F. Van Order. Clymer obtained the records and mailing list from Van Order's widow and, with the aid of Earl Flanders and William Bagnall, scheduled a meeting in the spring of 1967, which was held in the Rodger Young Memorial Auditorium in Los Angeles. The revival of these yearly meetings met with much enthusiasm.

William Berry assumed the leadership of the AMA-MS&ATA with the new title of Executive Director. To replace himself as the former head of the Governmental Relations Committee, he hired Paul McCrillis, a former account executive with a Pennsylvania based investment firm. He also engaged Garry Payne as his executive assistant.

Berry next moved the Government Relations section and the AMA head offices to larger quarters at 5655 No. High Street in Columbus. A West Coast information office for the MS&ATA was already in place in Los Angeles. These changes saw the virtual separation of AMA and MS&ATA operations, with McCrillis ultimately overseeing the functions of the MS&ATA. The AMA was now operating with its director not immediately connected with the motorcycle trade organization.

While there were a number of officers who were active members of both the AMA and the MS&ATA, and most Class B (members of the trade) belonged to both, the separation of the two entities was now apparent.

Early in 1967, at the urging of Walter Davidson, Jr., Berry reviewed the present structuring of the AMA in an article in "American Motorcycling". He also voiced strong criticism of those within the AMA as well as the trade press for their ongoing complaints concerning Milwaukee's long-standing dominant role in AMA affairs. He suggested truthfully that, without the financial support offered by the trade through the years, the AMA would have ceased to exist shortly after its initial founding.

The scope and content of "American Motorcycl-ing" had become greatly diminished due to the increasing prominence of the U.S.M.C., whose competition events were quite naturally not reported through AMA channels, the magazine featuring only articles and reports on AMA sanctioned events. The bulk of sports reports was now fully covered in "Cycle News" as well as the usual trade journals, and the AMA publication was shortly to be reduced to a mere pamphlet form.

Floyd Clymer's next move, after selling his magazine, was intended to be an innovation in motorcycle marketing with his introduction to the U.S. of the Munch Mammutt (Mammoth). Friedel Munch was a German motorcycle dealer and practical engineer who had been employed in German automobile factories as well as in the now defunct Horax motorcycle concern. With a keen interest in high performance machinery, he had conceived a design based on the 1100 cc engine gear unit developed by NSU for their Prinz model automobile. Set across the frame, the high performance overhead cam design was carried in a heavyweight featherbed type chassis. In prototype experiments, the torque of the engine was such that it could collapse the standard wire spoked rear wheel, and Munch devised a heavy duty alloy type wheel with solid type spokes cast integrally with the rim.

The Mammoth was essentially a very low pro-

THE LATER YEARS

California Highway Patrol Officers check a group of biker's machines as to the legality of equipment.
Steve Nelson

duction hand-built vehicle, being run off in small batches whenever Munch could find someone to finance his efforts. Clymer negotiated an import agreement with Munch early in 1967, with an initial shipment of reportedly 6 machines. Clymer suggested that these should be sent over on a consignment basis, but the wily Munch collected about $3,200 for each unit as his manufacturer's price before shipment.

The Mammoth was a genuinely powerful, high performance machine, capable of an honest 120 mph top speed, but its handling characteristics were noted as being something else again. Presaging as it did a future popularity of the superbike, the formidable appearing Mammoth and its then-high retail price tag of $4,000, made its appearance somewhat ahead of its time. The total production of the model is open to question, but sources in Germany have reported that somewhat less than 150 units were ever built. In each case, the detail specifications varied widely, and engine capacities varied from 1,000 to 1,300 cc. It is thought that less than twenty five were ever sold in the U.S.

Clymer subsequently contracted with an Italian accessory firm to hand build an updated prototype of the Indian Sport Scout with plunger forks and a spring frame. Its engine was a 42-degree V twin whose lines and layout were a copy of the original. Prototype tests revealed that the 45 cu. in. side valve engine was handicapped by its heavy frame, much as seen in the early Harley-Davidson K models. Clymer had appropriated the Indian trademarks and registered it under his own name in a hoped-for Indian revival. But, as matters stood, the Scout, as it was called, never went into production.

Clymer's next flirtation with Italian engineers was to purchase Velocette 500 cc MSS type engines and gear boxes from Veloce, Ltd. An attractive machine based on conventional practice, examples were marketed briefly in the U.S. with the Indian logos on the tank sides. Its principal buyers were Velocette enthusiasts who were mourning the shortage of Veloce's traditional larger displacement models. Many removed the Indian decals and replaced them with those of Velocette. With Veloce's emphasis on lightweight machines and scooters, the supply of power plants ran out and, what with Veloce soon to go into liquidation, assembly in Italy ceased. It is thought that about 150 units in all were produced and sold, mostly in the United States.

In the meantime, President William H. Davidson was in negotiation with two different conglomerates for the outright purchase of the

The 750cc four cylinder Honda virtually started the Superbike category of motorcycles.
Don Emde Collection

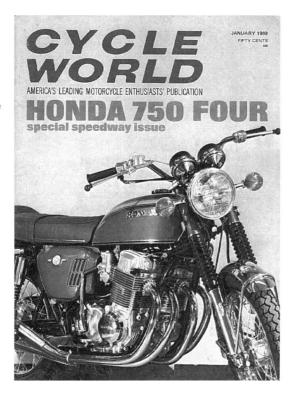

CYCLE WORLD

AMERICA'S LEADING MOTORCYCLE ENTHUSIASTS' PUBLICATION

JANUARY 1969
FIFTY CENTS

HONDA 750 FOUR
special speedway issue

Harley-Davidson Motor Company. With the lack of cooperation from the non-motorcycling shareholders in the matter of updating the company's line of machines and the upgrading of production facilities, coupled with the shareholders' desires to liquidate their stock to further fund their personal estates, it appeared no other choice was possible.

As noted, Davidson had been unsuccessful in interesting a number of heavy manufacturing concerns in the midwest in buying the company; mainly because they viewed the necessary reorganization of the Milwaukee operation excessively formidable. But Davidson had a champion in Rodney C. Gott, the Board Chairman of the American Foundry Company, which had been founded before the turn of the century. Its diversified holdings had included the manufacture of railroad cars and equipment, heavy industrial products, a boat and yacht building yard, and the manufacture of marine engines. In the post-war years, the company had changed its emphasis to leisure time products such as bowling equipment and alleys, pool and billiard tables, and various sporting goods products, along with a boatyard that built plastic sailboats. Gott, who had been a Harley-Davidson enthusiast in his youth, was convinced that the manufacture of motorcycles would be a helpful adjunct to the company's present sporting emphasis.

In the course of the negotiations, Gott experienced some opposition from his Board of Directors

who were familiar with the situation in Milwaukee and could relate to the doubts expressed by Caterpillar, DeLaval, John Deere and others who had had serious objections to the purchase of Harley-Davidson. One Board member, Ray Albert Tritten, was particularly vocal in this regard but, in the end, Gott was able to rally a majority of the members to his cause.

The other conglomerate in the picture was Bangor-Punta, which owned a diverse group of companies such as a feeder line railroad in Maine, the Waukesha Motor Company, firms manufacturing industrial machinery and, at one time, sugar processing mills in Cuba. With the aggressive management of President David Wallace and Cuban born Board Chairman Nicolas G. Salgo, an ongoing series of acquisitions and diversements of various holdings had increased the corporate worth up to $167 million, according to Standard & Poor's Corporation index. A significant fact at this time was Bangor-Punta's holding of over 28,000 shares of Harley-Davidson stock, which had been sold by dissident shareholders who wished to cash out.[*1]

President Davidson was against dealing with Bangor-Punta on the grounds that Harley-Davidson might well become another pawn in their corporate dealings, rather than a long term operation that would preserve the company. The coming battle between the American Foundry Company and Bangor-Punta for Harley-Davidson's acquisition would, as will be seen, become perhaps the most critical period in the history of the Milwaukee operation.

In spite of the upheavals within the industry, BSA, Harley-Davidson, and Triumph continued active support of competition. Buddy Elmore won at Daytona in 1966, at a new record speed of 96.38 mph on an updated T100R Triumph. Cal Rayborn, Harley-Davidson, had been favored to win as his qualifying speed had been the fastest on the oval at 138 mph. The new Triumphs matched the Harley-Davidson entrants on the track, however, but the Milwaukee riders, George Roeder and Gary Hall, came in second and third respectively.

Rayborn, on a KR sponsored by San Diego's Leonard Andres, won his first National at Carlsbad, California. Gary Nixon, riding for Triumph, gained the second spot in National standings in 1966, with fellow rider Eddie Mulder coming in fourth.

An outstanding Harley-Davidson rider was Bart Markel, three time Grand National champion. In 11 years of competition, he won 28 victories. These included 18 half milers, 6 TT's, a Two-Mile

THE LATER YEARS

A typical Biker Bar.
Steve Nelson

national, and several short track events. His career included the third largest number of victories in AMA history.

The innovative Gordon Jennings, in collaboration with ace tuner Jerry Branch, built up a KR special with a lightened Sprint frame and 18 in. wheels which resulted in a diminutive machine that was 35 lbs. lighter than the standard KR. The engine was destroked to increase its rev count and fitted with a special Fairbanks Morse magneto. Requiring factory sponsorship for his intended Daytona entry, Jenning's request was not favored in Milwaukee, which did not prefer to officially sponsor machines built by outsiders. They finally capitulated after Jennings threatened to air the matter in "Cycle" magazine where he was the current editor. The machine provided an impressive number of initial laps, but was found to have insufficient braking power. Jennings suffered further ill luck when an object thrown up from the track broke his goggles. He was ultimately sidelined with a broken wrist pin.

In 1967 Milwaukee experimented with a modified 'lowboy' type frame. One of the first competitors to employ one of these was California rider Lance Weil. Fitting a factory tuned Sportster engine, he went to England to compete in road racing events. His entry caused a sensation among British racing enthusiasts, as it was the first time in over 40 years that an American V twin had been entered in competition, recalling the nostalgic memories of the Brooklands era when American twins had enjoyed some popularity. Weil was initially successful in some 1,000 cc class races at Brands Hatch, Mallory Park and Oulton Park. His machine was originally fitted with fairings, but the race promoters insisted that he remove the lower sections so the spectators could see the engine! Weil's successes were cut short due to the lack of on-hand spare parts for maintenance.

The amalgamated BSA-Triumph organization on east and west coasts underwent accelerated sales and competition programs under the respective leaderships of Don Brown and Pete Colman. Colman hired Joseph Hope, who had enjoyed extensive sales and marketing experience in the retail field as an Industrial Sales Manager for the 19 western states. Brown temporarily engaged Albert Close, a west coast mechanic, to reorganize the long ailing parts and service department at Nutley. Difficulties were experienced when shipment of 4,000 twins from the factory were found to have rust deposits inside the cylinders and had to be returned for overhaul. The factory charged this work to the branch's account, which caused critical financial difficulties. Brown ordered the refurbishing of the premises at Nutley and, subsequently, purchased an adjacent industrial site for the projected construction of enlarged quarters.

By 1967 the domestic motorcycle industry was in the midst of what was described as explosive growth, with over 600,000 units sold during that year's sales season. Due to an unusually aggressive sales campaign, along with the establishment of dealerships in such non-traditional outlets as hardware stores, sporting goods outlets, agricultural equipment concerns, and even automobile dealerships, Honda now commanded 50% of the total market. Suzuki and Yamaha were also expanding their activities, now joined by Kawasaki, which had added a 650 cc vertical twin similar to the in-place BSA models, a well designed machine which, unlike its competitor, did not leak oil! By the end of the year it was estimated, through several independent surveys, that the Japanese enjoyed 83% of the retail sales. The other 17% was filled with machines from Germany, Italy, Sweden and Milwaukee.

At that point, the industry was publicly represented by the MS&ATA yet none of the Japanese firms were members. It was reported that a couple of years before Honda's top management had applied for membership, which had been refused,

Ace motorcycle mechanic and engineer Johnny Eagles with the 1936 Norton International he restored for the author. As the vintage and classic motorcycle hobby developed more interest in the 70's and 80's, restorers like Eagles with expertise in the old classics were in demand.
George Hays.

although the author, up to this point, has not been able to verify the details of this. In any case, Harley-Davidson's management had publicly expressed much bitterness regarding the Japanese invasion, reviving the hostility engendered by the war and stressing the patriotic necessity for public support of the domestic industry. The situation had come to the point that many public gatherings featuring Harley-Davidson club members and owners, such as picnics or charity runs, had as an entertainment feature the invitation to attack a still viable Japanese machine with sledge hammers provided by the organizers!

The lack of official recognition by the MS&ATA and the highly visible prejudicial attitude as noted above was taken as a deep insult by the Japanese and, in the serious emotion of the Oriental concept of 'losing face' any further efforts to become integrated into the domestic industry on their part was now unthinkable.

The lack of a truly representative trade organization on behalf of the motorcycle industry was at once causing grave problems. Hostile legislators, insurance companies and other groups that held prejudice against motorcycling in general and the marketing of related products were having a field day. This sort of activity was noted as a continuation of the problem attendant to the marketing of two-wheeled vehicles, which had been noted as far back as the introduction of the high wheeled bicycle after the Civil War! There were also comments from both inside as well as outside the industry that incriminated certain antisocial behavior from the biker movement and added fuel to the fires of prej-

udice. In any case, the lack of trade representation on the part of over 80% of the industry created an impasse that had placed it in a hopeless position in regard to either promoting its own interest or in combating outside hostile forces.

Leaders within the industry had been well aware for some time of the lack of an organized effort on the part of manufacturers, especially in the face of its rapid growth, but it was Hope and Colman who made the initial efforts to rectify the problem. In their discussions of the matter, both agreed that inasmuch as the Japanese would never consent to join the MS&ATA, the problem would never be solved as long as the MS&ATA was the only option for industry unity. This led to the idea that another association should be formed, and that all the Japanese manufacturers be invited to join. They also reasoned that if over 80% of all industry membership were to be represented, a proposal could be made to the minority group comprising the MS&ATA suggesting both a merger and the formation of a totally new organization.

Early in 1968, Hope met with Matt Matsuoka, PR Director of Honda, and his like number Jimmy Jingu of Yamaha, in Jingu's office, and perfected an organization of what was to be initially called the Southern California Motorcycle Safety Council. This name was suggested because by this time all the Japanese's manufacturers had headquarters in California; Kawasaki having just acquired substantial marketing and warehouse facilities there as well. In the end, both Suzuki and Kawasaki agreed to the proposal, which of course, included the BSA-Triumph operations as well. Hope recalled that at no time during the initial discussions were any officers or members of the MS&ATA made aware of the planning.

The SCMSC immediately went into action. Members made themselves available to the media and service clubs as speakers, cooperated with other safety organizations, produced a 35mm film that was made available to schools outlining motorcycle safety, and offered cooperation with the National Education Association, all aimed at promoting both motorcycle safety as well as the industry itself. It was intended that this barrage of publicity would effectively counter the activity of those organizations and individuals who were hostile to motorcycling and legislators who might be considering introducing adverse legislation. The aggressive activities of the SCMSC were at once successful, and the trade press was soon giving wide coverage to the drive to promote motorcycle activities as well as safety.

As the scope of the educational drive expanded, the name of California was dropped, the organization now being known as the Motorcycle Safety Council. Early in the proceedings, and with the aid of John Marin, Editor of Sports Illustrated, a dinner meeting was arranged at the Los Angeles Athletic Club, of which Marin was a member. To this dinner were invited corporate officers of every major manufacturer and distributor within the industry. Hope addressed the assembly with carefully prepared remarks, outlining the weaknesses of the industry's present position and the need for a new organization that could offer both protection as well as advocacy for the best interests of motorcycling. Hope recalled that his remarks were well received, as most members of the industry were by this time well aware of their situation. A committee was formed to implement organization, and Hope was elected president.

In the meantime, AMA President William Kennedy decided to resign due to the pressure of his ongoing business commitments, which presented the problem of nominating his successor. It was tacitly agreed that perhaps someone not directly connected with the industry could be chosen to succeed him, and the choice ultimately centered on William Bagnall. As editor of "The Motorcyclist" and as a journalist he was in a somewhat neutral position in regard to the industry. It is well known that he favored reorganization of the AMA that was tempered by his conciliatory attitude, as well as his past track record in being able to get along with the Davidsons. Bagnall recalled that an offer of nomination was made to him by Jimmy Jingu during a golf game, and the upshot of the matter was that he was elected President of the AMA in the fall of 1968.

In the gradual separation of the activities of the AMA and the MS&ATA, Paul McCrillis' position of management of the MS&ATA's affairs was phased out in favor of formally electing Ivan J. Wagar, Associate Editor of "Cycle World", as President of the MS&ATA.

It was during this period that the complex negotiations between Harley-Davidson's top management, the American Foundry Company, and Bangor-Punta were resolved when matters were finalized to sell the company to AMF. The complex maneuvering between the three has already been covered, including legal action filed by Bangor-Punta against Harley-Davidson over a technicality involving their ignoring an offer to exchange Harley-Davidson's shares to Bangor-Punta ownership. The consummation of the matter took place following a series of shareholders' meetings presided over by President William H. Davidson during which he stressed the importance of accept-

ing AMF's offer. According to later statements by Lin Kuchler, Alfred Rich Child and Joe Petrali, the pivotal decision in favor of AMF was made by Walter Davidson, Jr., who at that point owned a large block of company stock. At any rate, the transaction involved a little over $21,000,000. The majority of the shareholders were greatly relieved to be separated from the motorcycle business and to be able to fund their own estates with a substantial profit. AMF officially took over Harley-Davidson in January 1969.

Also in 1969, Floyd Clymer negotiated yet another agreement with a foreign motorcycle manufacturer with an announcement in the trade press that he was to import a substantial number of 50 cc engine-gear units from the Italian firm of Minnareli. Clymer's intended strategy was to offer these to domestic manufacturers as an opportunity to build mopeds and lightweight motorcycles in order to cash in on the rapidly expanding market and to compete with the Japanese. Clymer stated that huge shipments of these units were shortly to begin, but actually he only ordered 50 units in order to test the market. When few, if any, orders were forthcoming, he had a couple of dozen miniature motorcycles with 16 inch wheels made in Italy, and offered them as entry level machines for juvenile riders at premium prices. He affixed Indian transfers on the tank sides, to the obvious amusement of members of the industry. It was later reported that only a few of these were ever sold.

A new set of problems was presented to American industry in the general sense by the rise in what was termed 'consumerism', with buyers of manufactured goods of all kinds being advised to take a renewed interest in the overall quality and ultimate customer satisfaction of the product. The principal exponent of this trend was one Ralph Nader, whose most notable campaign was against the automobile industry, focusing attention on the real or fancied unsafe design of General Motors' air-cooled Chevrolet model that had been recently introduced as the Corvair. Following a series of tests it was claimed that the model, which had a rear mounted engine, possessed unsafe handling characteristics which were discussed in his book, "Unsafe at Any Speed". This, amid speculative questioning of the quality and usefulness of certain other diverse products led to the enactment of 'Lemon Laws' designed to protect the customer, which brought forth other legislation at both the state and federal levels dealing with product liability.

This state of affairs was complicated by certain Supreme Court decisions outlawing the prohi-

After the Honda 750 came the same 4-cylinder concept in smaller sizes.
Don Emde Collection

Dignitaries at Daytona - This 1968 photo shows, from left: Bill Appleby, Renold Chain Distributor for U.S.; Bill Tuthill, well-known motor sports journalist and head of Daytona's Museum of Speed; Shirlee Alzina Bagnall, wife of then-AMA President Bill Bagnall, and daughter of the next gentleman in the photo, Hap Alzina, western states BSA Distributor; and Jim Davis, famed early day motorcycle racer.
Bill Bagnall

bitions in force by professional groups against commercial advertising. The legal profession at once took advantage of this, and lawyers began to solicit clients by advocating lawsuits on the part of consumers against producers and retailers for real and imagined damage claims. The courts became clogged with filed actions. The motorcycle industry also came in for its share of such actions. Often where accidents occurred the litigants claimed faulty machines were the cause. Veteran Yamaha Service Manager Leo Lake stated that he was spending much time in court as an expert witness in defense of his company's products; the other manufacturers contending with the same problems.

In the meantime, William Berry was launching a program to expand the scope of the AMA, and most particularly to expand the Governmental Relations Committee, initially proposed by Lin Kuchler, in order to counteract the hostile legislation being suggested in some states against motorcycling which had come into being with the sudden increase in motorcycle sales and public interest in the sport. With the gradual separation of the activities of the MS&ATA and the AMA itself, which was now more oriented toward the interests of individual members, there was a growing movement toward granting more authority to the members at

large in implementing overall policy. This centered on the expansion of the Competition Committee to include a rider's majority, long a bone of contention within the AMA. This growing trend was vigorously advocated by Pete Colman and other veteran referees who noted that the expanded sales of machines now represented a much greater group of manufacturers than Harley-Davidson, BSA and Triumph, along with Milwaukee's ancillary suppliers who had too long controlled the Competition Committee.

In the April 1967 issue of "American Motorcycling", Berry indicated that the fundamental structuring of the AMA should undergo some radical changes. It was also announced that discussions were now in progress among certain AMA officers that a study should be made into this matter. Their recommendations, announced in the December issue, stated that the traditional Competition Committee be replaced with a Competition Congress consisting, at least in part, of elected representatives. Class B commercial AMA members were balloted by mail to solicit their opinions. As a result, the new Competition Congress was voted into the bylaws. Its structuring was to consist of two representatives from each of the manufacturers or distributors of two-wheeled vehi-

THE LATER YEARS

A "chariot race" in progress at a field meet sponsored by Easyriders. *Paisano Publications*

cles; one AMA member-at-large from each of the country's 36 districts elected by the chartered AMA clubs, with each club having one vote; 6 professional licensed competition riders, 2 from each region to be elected by other professional riders from within each region; and 2 AMA staff members, one being the Executive Director who would act as Chairman of the Congress.

The first AMA Competition Congress met in October, 1968, to formulate rules for the 1969 season. The first proposal was to increase the displacement limit on approved overhead valve machines (non-Harley-Davidsons) to 650 cc. Walter Davidson at once moved that the motion be amended to increase the displacement to 750 cc. This would allow Milwaukee to alter their KR's without drastically changing their basic design. The motion was passed, and Davidson then made a motion to delay the enactment of the new formula until the 1970 season, obviously to buy time for the redesign of the KR. His proposal was voted down, the result being that for the 1969 season Harley-Davidsons were competing with foreign overhead valve machines of 750 cc displacement.

It was, of course, during this period that the Motorcycle Industry Council was undergoing its formation as instituted by Pete Colman, Joe Hope, Matt Matsuoka and Jimmy Jingu, which was to take over and supplement the MS&ATA. While the AMA itself and the MIC were now to exist as separate entities, their common interests and ongoing cooperation were required for the best interests of the industry.

The complexities of the formation and ultimate organization of the Council are best summarized by its founders and, as a separate subject, are elaborated upon in the Appendix.

With the separation of the activities of individual AMA members and the control of competition activities from the domination of the factories, the latter within the Council now undertook to oversee technical matters and to work for the benefit of the economic side of the motorcycle industry. The manufacturers had, in effect, formally loosened their control over the AMA to the extent that the enthusiast membership were now in control of their own destinies. This decision ushered in a new era for the AMA, and opened up a new and exciting, as well as controversial period in the history of organized motorcycling.

William T. Berry is perhaps best remembered for his role in the reorganization of the AMA in the development of the Competition Congress. He also presided over an expansion of competition activities and an aggressive move into matters of both legislation and politics. In order to facilitate the anticipated expansion, Berry augmented the staff and installed an updated IBM data processing system to assist in record keeping.

A feature of the now expanding competition activity was seen in the sanctioning of a $6,000 purse National Short Track Championship that was held in the newly completed Houston Astrodome. For several seasons these races became a prominent fixture in the Southwest. In addition, a new system for implementing and expanding the selection of district and regional referees was put in place, along with improved methods of managing and officiating such races. A new rule book was put in place dealing with the expanding interest in motocross, now a rapidly growing sport that was attracting enhanced spectator interest. Berry also made an initial trip to Switzerland to negotiate for the affiliation of the AMA with the FIM, the world

A group of members of the Southern California Chapter of the Antique Motorcycle Club of America take off for a Sunday ride, circa 1969. Johnny Eagles, 101 Indian Scout in background, Ernest Skelton, BMW R 50 at left, and the author on a 1938 Indian four.
George Hays

sanctioning organization.

While Berry had taken an aggressive role in the AMA reorganization, all was not well within the ranks of top management. There had been frequent personality clashes, and Berry was cited in some quarters as being undiplomatic in the handling of controversial matters. One such matter was that of his role in Don Brown's promotion of a solo record setting attempt with BSA's newly introduced 750 cc, three cylinder "Rocket 3". Brown had negotiated an agreement with Berry that the latter would privately sanction such an attempt involving the renting of the Daytona Speedway. In this the results would be kept confidential if the attempt failed; these would be made public only if new records were established. To head the event, Brown had hired the Canadian star Yvon Duhamel. New records, racked up as official, in the 5 through 200 mile distances were established; being 131.72 for 5 miles, 127.62 for 100 miles and 127.61 for a 1-hour run. Dick Mann, Gordon Jennings and Ray Hempstead then took turns setting a new 4-hour record of 117.97 mph which included stops for both fuel and rider changes.

The Rocket 3 had a stock engine, and the only modifications were racing tires and clip-on handlebars. Brown's strategy was to advertise the prowess of the newly introduced model, which was now being challenged by the 1969 introduction of the four cylinder CB 750 cc Honda. While the

records were certified by Berry, his sub rosa action in allowing the running of the affair immediately aroused a storm of protest from Milwaukee and their adherents as being partial to BSA's interests, with Berry bearing the brunt of the criticism. In the end, BSA did not benefit unduly, as the model retailed at $1,795, and the CB 750, which would out perform it, was initially priced at $1,295. In addition, the CB 750 had electric starting and did not leak oil. In noting the advantage, Honda at once raised the CB's price to $1,495!

Berry was also in contention with the AMA Directors in his lately voiced dissatisfaction with his $13,500 yearly salary, claiming that the time and effort now required in overseeing the expanded AMA activities was worth more. In the end, Berry was asked to resign in May, 1970. The Executive Committee noted that a study was now being undertaken to more clearly define the duties and responsibilities of the Executive Director. Berry's duties were at once taken over by his deputy, Garry Payne, with AMA President William Bagnall acting as an advisor.

During this time, the magazine "American Motorcycling" was discontinued as it had deteriorated into more of a pamphlet, and carried on in reduced format as "The AMA News". The Executive Committee also rescinded an earlier vote to raise the annual dues to $5.00, returning to the former $2.00 fee and leaving optional the subscrip-

THE LATER YEARS

In 1970, the BSA factory fielded a full team in the TRANS-AMA motocross series, sweeping the first three places. Of note in this photo is Jeff Smith (far left) the former World Motocross Champion who is now head of the American Historic Racing Motorcycle Association. Next to Smith are the American riders on the BSA effort Charles "Feets" Minert (#30) and David Aldana (#3).

tion to "The AMA News" for an additional $3.00 per year. In the meantime, Garry Payne resigned, after being rejected to succeed Berry.

Berry's tenure of office lasted little less than 4 years. In retrospect, the scope of his accomplishments overshadowed his personality conflicts within the AMA hierarchy, such as his contributions in the AMA reorganization and its consequent expansion. At his leaving, his efforts as well as the ongoing growth of the motorcycle industry saw the AMA membership exceeding 100,000. Not to be forgotten was his installation of the IBM data processing system which facilitated the need for an effective tabulation of the vastly expanded competition records. He was reported to have returned to his native Colorado.

In January 1970, Floyd Clymer, who was previously reported to have enjoyed good health, was found dead at his desk, the victim of a massive heart attack. He had been prominent in the motorcycling world ever since he won the National

Championship in 1915 at Dodge City, as a 20-year old amateur rider. Although he spent a lifetime within the industry, many of his business dealings had larcenous overtones, and those who had occasions to have dealings with him more than often viewed the associations with distrust. The subsequent Trailblazers banquet featured recognition of his past participation in the sport and industry. Veteran members formerly acquainted with him were invited to comment publicly on his life and times, but the few that did so were circumspect in their comments in deference to his widow, who was present as an honored guest.

In the negotiation of the purchase agreement with Harley-Davidson, AMF's Board Chairman Rodney C. Gott persuaded President William H. Davidson to remain with the operation on salary as head of the Motorcycle Division of AMF, with Walter Davidson, Jr., employed as General Sales Manager. Gott was of the opinion that such a move would indicate to loyal Harley-Davidson

343

The 1969 solo speed record event to publicize the newly introduced BSA Rocket 3 model that was conducted at the Daytona Speedway. (from l.) AMA Executive Director William T. Berry, rider Dick Mann, Official AMA Timer Paul Shattuck, and Don Brown. Berry's sanctioning and participation in the event caused a controversy within the AMA hierarchy that eventually caused his forced removal from office. *Daytona International Speedway*

enthusiasts that there was continuity between the past and present.

The explosive boom in general motorcycle sales saw Gott ordering Harley-Davidson to increase the unit production of their domestic model of motorcycles and golf carts, as well as production at Varese, Italy, of the Aermacchi machines. This order, however, caused problems in the beginning. Back in Milwaukee, the Capital Drive plant was well suited to the manufacture of engines and transmissions, but the antiquated Juneau Avenue plant was not laid out for series assembly of chassis parts. The current top management and production foremen were not conversant with streamlined continuous flow assembly, and there were problems in inventory control. Added to this, there were dislocations due to a restive labor force who at once demanded wage increases. The dealers were soon unhappy over the receipt of poorly assembled machines which required much

adjusting or rebuilding at the expense of much shop time before they could be delivered.

During 1969, AMF engineers partially updated the long-obsolete FL models by installing a solid state breakerless ignition system. This was to conform the engine design to the Environmental Protection Agency's (EPA) mandate that gasoline engines with breaker point ignitions were 'dirty engines' from the standpoint of air pollution. With a pancake type alternator fitted in the crankcase on the drive side of the crank, the gear train to the former generator was eliminated, making for a much quieter engine. The following two seasons saw the fitting of hydraulically activated disc brakes, and improvement in the heavy machine's stopping power that was long overdue.

A surprise model introduced for 1970 was the "SuperGlide", an FL variant based on custom chopper lines with a Sportster fork, 21 in. front wheel and a bobbed rear mudguard. AMF's sales

The year 1977 saw three of the best motorcycle racers ever doing battle: Kenny Roberts, Gary Scott and Jay Springsteen.
Don Emde Collection

department reasoned that with the phenomenal growth of the biker movement, and the burgeoning aftermarket industry based on Harley-Davidson designs, but now far surpassing it in dollar volume, it was time for the company to put aside its prejudice against stripped machines. Widely noted in the trade press, it was described in "Cycle World" as an 'institutionalized chopper'!

During the buyout negotiations with AMF and Bangor-Punta, Harley-Davidson's publicity department engaged the services of Maurice Hendry, an Australian automotive journalist, to write yet another 'history' of the company. The text emphasized the role of the founders through the years, eulogizing their accomplishments. Also included was a description of Harley-Davidson's complex range of past models. As a typical in-house publication, few pertinent facts concerning the internal affairs of the company were included. When Hendry included a few personal observations, such were deleted, the text showing the effects of official censorship. Published as a paperback by Ballantine Books, a limited edition was sold through dealer outlets.

In the meantime, the once-great BSA conglomerate and its Triumph subsidiary were suffering from growing financial troubles due to Japanese world-wide competition, along with ineffectual management, although both makes continued to find a substantial market in the U.S. Pete Colman at once urged Triumph's top management

and their chief designer, Bert Hopwood, to update the 650 cc engines to 750 cc to conform to the displacement now sanctioned by the AMA to keep the marque competitive in the sporting venue. With typical British conservatism, Hopwood declined, stating that, "It's never been done." At this point, he had been working on a design project for BSA that featured the modular concept in engine design to rationalize production in using like components for engines of 250 to 1,000 cc's. After several futile trips to England, Colman ordered some new cylinder barrels cast domestically, converting some 204 examples of 650 cc Thunderbirds to 750 cc, the number insuring that the 200 model rule demanded by the AMA was adhered to. The conversions were assembled in Triumph's Duarte, California warehouse. A short time later, Triumph's top management ordered Hopwood to update the Thunderbirds to 750 cc.

In the reorganization of BSA North American operation, Don Brown was able to correct most of its problems, but overall sales were moderate due to the massive competition from the Japanese and their increase in dealerships. The once-giant BSA conglomerate in England was struggling with their financial problems brought about by the global competition from Japan and their own failure to modernize their production methods.

The motorcycle division was overburdened with engineers, most of whom were non-motorcyclists, along with middle management advertising specialists and marketing experts who were in the same category. The publicity department was constantly calling public attention to prototype motorcycles and scooters of supposedly advanced designs, none of which were in actual production. It was said that top management was attempting to reassure the shareholders that forward planning was instituted to turn the company around.

One big problem that British industry as a whole faced was their archaic banking and finance systems. Industrial loans were extended on an 'overdraft' system, wherein a company was given a certain line of credit upon which they could draw for operations. This allowed the loan managers to keep a close watch on these operations, often questioning the management's methods when, in many cases, they were unfamiliar with the businesses they were attempting to advise, a system which more often than now was in a state of chaos.

Another problem was the laws governing the rights of the shareholders. Investors purchasing shares were entitled to instant dividends on their shares, differing from the U.S. practice which allowed a corporation some breathing time for

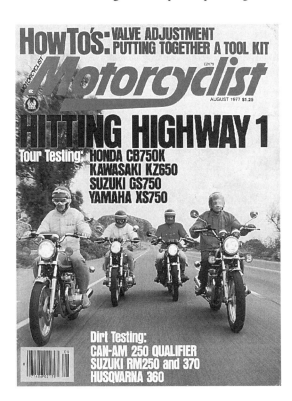

By the mid-70's, consumer magazines had comparison tests in full swing.
Don Emde Collection

THE LATER YEARS

Ted Evans, President of the California Motorcycle Dealers Association accepting a plaque from Pete Colman on the occasion of their joining the Motorcycle Industry Council in 1971.
Pete Colman

plant improvement and product development before dividends were declared, at the option of management.

Then, too, the British Labor government, sympathetic with labor unions, laid down strict rules protecting the workers, and it was difficult to discharge personnel or streamline an operation that more often than not was inefficiently overstaffed.

With British labor being generally an adversary of management, the latter's attempts to create plant efficiencies were usually resisted and, in many cases, labor retaliated by sabotaging the products. Many managers in the U.S. involved in motorcycle importing, such as Joe Hope, Frank Cooper, and Pete Colman, told the author of numerous instances where machines were deliberately shipped over with missing or maladjusted components.

BSA's top management in England sought to bolster their sagging U.S. market by reorganizing its operation that was managed by Brown as a corporate Vice President, who also presided as National Sales Manager, but was not involved with Triumph. Pete Colman was Triumph's Vice President in charge of engineering and service as well as managing competition.

In 1970, BSA's Board of Directors ordered Lionel Jofeh to bring in an outside advertising agency, which saw the appointment of one Peter Thornton, president of Sales Communications,

Inc., a subsidiary of Inter-Public Advertising Company of Detroit, which was said to have had contracts with the Ford Motor Company. It was indicated to the staff that Thornton's retention was to analyze the branch's sales and advertising programs, but it soon became apparent that he was shortly to take over its management.

In a series of staff meetings, Thornton informed Brown and his associates they had not been effective in sales and marketing, even though BSA's marketing position had improved since the new management had taken over. At a subsequent "must attend" meeting at the Pierre Hotel in New York City, Jofeh introduced Thornton as the new President of the American BSA and Triumph organization, and announced that he had just been elected to BSA's Board of Directors in England. It was also announced that the BSA-Triumph operations were to be merged. Colman was retained in his west coast position and Brown was still Vice President in charge of BSA's national sales, although he was not involved with the Triumph operation.

Eric Turner now ordered Brown to sell the previously purchased industrial site at Nutley, New Jersey. This was effected for a profit of $48,000. A new location was set up at Verona. Brown then decided to resign and return to California where he took a year's sabbatical to enjoy flying time in his Commanche 260 airplane. He received a year's salary as severance pay and BSA also assisted in the sale of his Verona home. He later undertook sales and marketing analysis for the motorcycle industry as a consultant, for both the Japanese firms as well as Husqvarna.

Joe Hope had joined the BSA sales force in Verona, New Jersey, but returned to California to accept an employment offer from Dennis Poore to head U.S. sales for Norton-Villiers-Triumph, a new operation. Poore was an English capitalist who had made a fortune in gambling casino operations in London, following their legalization after World War II. Poore also organized another industrial complex, Manganese-Bronze Corporation, and in a raid on what was left of the BSA empire, transferred its remaining assets to MB.

Poore planned to revitalize Norton, which was combined with Villiers, the latter firm now specializing in industrial engines. A talented engineer, John Favel, designed the 650 cc vertical twin cylinder Norton Commando, which was subsequently marketed in the U.S. in an 850 cc version as well. Labor troubles and component supply problems ended this venture after a couple of years, although the Commando became somewhat

346

American Motorcycle Association Executive Director Russell E. March (l.) conferring with a group of riders at the 1971 International

of a cult object among some U.S. enthusiasts.

The remains of the Triumph operation were salvaged in the organization of a cooperative setup by a former management executive, Bryan Jones, who obtained permission from the British Board of Trade to operate under employee ownership. With limited funding, inadequate quarters, and badly worn tooling, Triumph production proceeded at a trickle until 1983. The last few models were somewhat updated, with electric starting, five speed transmissions, and spoked alloy wheels.

In the meantime, AMF's Board Chairman Rodney C. Gott, board member Ray Albert Tritten, and some of AMF's advertising staff met with William H. Davidson and members of the Motorcycle Division in an attempt to assess Harley-Davidson's troubled position. However, Gott's conferees were not conversant with the details of motorcycle production and Harley-Davidson's management was not familiar with updated manufacturing or component supply methods and, in addition, were handicapped by operating in outmoded premises. Matters were also complicated by the retirement of most of Harley-Davidson's experienced production personnel,

many of whom had measured their term of service in decades.

At the suggestion of AMF's marketing department, Harley-Davidson reviewed the status of their dealerships. Many of the ones who still operated from rundown or substandard premises (in the opinion of AMF) were ordered to either update these or move or their franchises were terminated. A number of veteran dealers whose dealerships had existed for decades, and who in some cases were approaching senility, and whose activities had declined to the occasional sale of a machine, were arbitrarily terminated. While Harley-Davidson's management claimed that servicing these veterans was not an economical proposition, many enthusiasts considered this action rather heartless in view of their long-term loyalty to Milwaukee.

In reviewing Harley-Davidson's advertising and sales program, Walter Davidson, Jr.'s long standing position as General Sales Manager came under scrutiny. He had been appointed to this position in 1950, following the death of his Uncle Arthur, who had managed the company's sales program since the 1907 incorporation. Walter, Jr. had fulfilled the office in a somewhat inconsistent fash-

347

THE LATER YEARS

The BSA factory sponsored racing team at Daytona in 1971. (from l.) Don Emde, Mike Hailwood, Dick Mann (that year's winner), David Aldana, and Jim Rice.
Dave Friedman photo/courtesy of Infosport

ion, due to his addiction to alcohol. During the 1960's, he had undergone a drying out process and in the buyout negotiations he had assumed a more aggressive position in company affairs, according to Alfred Rich Child and Lin Kuchler. His traditionally bombastic and often emotional speeches at dealers' meetings and within the AMA, delivered in a florid manner, along with his standard references to the supposed machinations of Jewish bankers, had become an embarrassment to some of the lately affiliated AMF personnel. It was ultimately suggested to him that he should tone down his rhetoric, especially as anti-Semitism publicly expressed was not considered in good taste. Walter at once took exception to this criticism, and abruptly resigned, stating that, "He wouldn't be told what to do". Although now officially separated from the company, he continued to publicly support Harley-Davidson's interests and was a consistent attendant at race meets and competition events until his death in the late 1970's.

Following the resignation of William Berry, AMA's Board of Directors made an assessment of his term of office in relation to what direction their policies should now take. Berry's enhancement of the AMA's scope of activity, his augmentation of

the office facilities, and the overall growth of the membership were weighed against his sometimes abrasive manner and lack of diplomacy in dealing with staff members. His most controversial action had been entering into a secret agreement with Don Brown in BSA's record breaking attempt at Daytona. Acquiescing to withhold an announcement of the results should these fail to make new records was particularly criticized by the Milwaukee contingent and their supporters as being a tacit attempt to favor a foreign make of machine. In regard to the affair, some Board members who supported Berry called attention to the fact that former Secretary-Manager E.C. Smith had been, for many years, on Harley-Davidson's payroll as a public relations agent outside of his duties with the AMA.

After some deliberation, the Board of Directors of the AMA selected one of their own members, Russell E. March, to succeed William T. Berry as Executive Director. There was some negotiation over his salary, as March held out for a $25,000 yearly stipend, stating that part of Berry's problems with his position stemmed from the fact that he felt he was underpaid for the time and effort involved. After some discussion his request

348

THE LATER YEARS

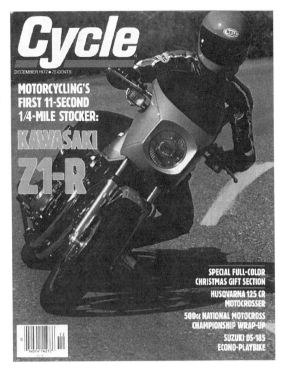

Kawasaki upped the performance ante in 1977 with the introduction of its Z1-R model. It would run 110 miles per hour in the quarter mile.
Don Emde Collection

was granted.

March was born in 1937 in Pottstown, Pennsylvania, where he grew up and attended local schools. He subsequently enrolled in law school but dropped out to join Standard Oil of Ohio in a management training program. Two years later he joined American Honda as a regional, and later, a national sales manager. His next position was with the American Safety Company, manufacturer of seat belts and other equipment for automobiles and trucks. He was appointed to the position of sales manager and later head of the Buco Helmet Company, a subsidiary of ASC.

In his position with Buco he became a Class B member of the AMA and was elected to its Board of Directors in 1968. He was elected to the position of Executive Director in March 1970, at a board meeting held in Phoenix, Arizona. He was strongly backed by board member Jess Thomas who was also on the staff of "Cycle" magazine. This particular meeting was a marathon, five-hour affair, with intensive discussion of how the future of AMA policies should be conducted. In the end, March's appointment was confirmed by a four-to-two vote, with Thomas and the Japanese members providing the majority votes. The Harley-Davidson member opposed, together with William Bagnall who usually sided with Milwaukee.

March recalled that as Executive Director he had initially three goals under consideration. These were: raise the yearly membership dues, which for the past decade had been at a rather unrealistic

$2.00, in order to increase capital for the general fund and to allow for the re-establishment of the defunct "American Motorcycling"; officially affiliate the AMA with the FIM; and to acquire a suitable building of sufficient size to accommodate the anticipated expansion of AMA activities. This latter project came to fruition in the fall of 1971, with the negotiation of an optioned lease on a large industrial type building in the Columbus, Ohio suburb of Westerville. It had adequate floor area to accommodate executive offices, meeting rooms and space for the projected printing plant to allow in-house production of the magazine.

The projected dues increase was initially opposed by the Harley-Davidson members, but was supported by the Japanese contingent as well as the two members representing "Cycle" and "The Motorcyclist", who were of the opinion that the AMA should have its own medium for reporting its activities. After an examination of the financial projections, the dues were set at $7.00.

The FIM affiliation was also opposed by the Harley-Davidson board members but supported by the majority, and ways and means were next explored for the petitioning of the international body for AMA membership. March recalled that a political problem existed because the U.S.M.C. was already a part of it and had been affiliated with the FIM since 1961. The U.S.M.C. was largely controlled by Edison Dye of San Diego, who had been managing the extensive motocross program, and administration activities had been placed in the hands of Wes Cooley. This was undertaken on a part-time basis, the office expenses being paid through the on-going sale of membership cards and competition licenses along with the awarding of sanctions to the promoters of competition events. Cooley and Dye were in control of all U.S. FIM sanctioned activities, as the only rule was that the various classes of machines were indicated by piston displacement only.

In the meantime, March hired Ed Youngblood who had for some time been a staff reporter for Charles Clayton's "Cycle News" as the editor of the projected revitalized AMA magazine. In anticipation of some searching investigation of the status of the AMA attendant to its affiliation petition, March directed Youngblood, who was assisted by Jess Thomas, to write a presentation booklet outlining past AMA activities. This material was printed by the "Cycle" staff at their own expense. Youngblood also prepared a slide show presentation.

March journeyed to Europe that fall to confer with FIM President Nicolas Rodil and the Board of Governors. While the meetings of the FIM were

The Later Years

Team BSA and Team Triumph dominated the 1971 Daytona event, placing 1st, 2nd, and 3rd in the 200 mile road race. Dick Mann (BSA) repeated his previous year's victory by winning in record time. Dick was followed to the checkered flag by AMA Grand National Champion Gene Romero (Triumph) and Don Emde (BSA). The team effort was organized by E.W. "Pete" Colman, Vice President of Engineering and Director of Racing for the BSA/Triumph Group in America.
Dave Friedman photo/courtesy of Infosport

usually held at Geneva, this time they were convened at the French coastal resort of Cannes. Rodil and the Governors made a searching examination of the U.S. motorcycling scene and promised to announce their decision at the next regular meeting.

At any rate, March returned to Switzerland, this time accompanied by AMA President William Bagnall. In the vote admitting the U.S. into FIM participation, Sweden, Australia and Belgium indicated that they supported the present Dye-Cooley arrangement. The British representative, Fred Dixon, sided with the U.S. position, and was able to inaugurate a compromise where the AMA would be allowed to sponsor a couple of FIM events each year. They were now formally affiliated with the international body. The AMA then made application for a sanctioned International Six Days Trial, long an international fixture, to be held in the U.S. in 1973. After some deliberation, the Board of Governors granted this request.

It was during this period of reorienting certain

of the AMA's activities toward international competition that John Harley, along with some of the AMA Board members who were loyal to Milwaukee, publicly expressed their opposition to both FIM affiliation and the holding of its sanctioned competition events in the U.S. They claimed that the identity of U.S. motorcycling affairs was being undermined by foreign competition.

During 1971 public interest in motocross saw expanded coverage of this activity. Mike Goodwin, a former rock music concert promoter, secured sanctioning for a series of these events in the Los Angeles Coliseum. Bruce Cox, part owner of the industry news magazine, "Motorcycle Weekly", obtained sanctioning for a series of motocross contests at Carlsbad, including the first FIM motocross Grand Prix to ever be held in the U.S. He was able to stage another series in the Los Angeles Coliseum.

Plans were now set in motion for the AMA sponsorship of an International Six Days Trial, the

THE LATER YEARS

Don Emde, winner of the 1972 Daytona 200 at speed on his 350cc Yamaha TR3, the smallest engine size and first two stroke to ever win that event.
Dave Friedman photo/courtesy of Infosport

first to be held in the U.S., which had been scheduled for the fall of 1973. It was initially planned to hold the affair at Fort Hood, Texas, a disused Army base, but public controversy and adverse agitation incidental to the war in Vietnam suggested that the contest might be compromised by holding it on a military reservation. It was subsequently decided to transfer the venue to the Berkshires, a mountainous area on the east coast. An initial expense fund of $50,000 was suggested as the AMA's contribution, which was ultimately collected from the motorcycle distributors, although Harley-Davidson, who was against the international affiliation from the start, refused to contribute or participate in any way.

In the meantime, March made an extensive journey across the country to meet with members and officials concerning their thoughts on general policy matters, reminding them that the AMA was now essentially a rider's organization, free from its former manufacturers domination, and soliciting their support and participation. He subsequently amplified his program by inaugurating a dues increase to $7.00 per year in order to pay for an anticipated expansion program of AMA activities. An important item was March's proposal for a comprehensive accident insurance plan, which was

to be instituted under the management of insurance agent Greg Mosher. Underwritten by the Continental Casualty Company of Chicago, the program offered the amateur competitor as well as the road rider $1,000 in death or dismemberment insurance and $10,000 medical coverage in case of accident. The program was announced in 1971. At the same time, a full-time AMA sponsored legislative program was announced along with a safety program featuring televised announcements urging motorists to "Watch out for motorcycles". Another innovation was a noise suppression program, with the emphasis on the public relations ploy of countering anti-motorcycling sentiment.

The Traveling Ambassador program was instituted, with Ben Harrel criss-crossing the country on a full dress Harley-Davidson touring machine, meeting with clubs and recruiting new members. This was later augmented by dispatching five staff members in commercial sedan type delivery cars, meeting with clubs and others, explaining the updated AMA rider programs and soliciting new memberships as well as hearing complaints.

An important result of the decision of the newly formed Competition Congress to increase the allowed displacement of competition machines in National competition was the Auto-Cycle Union

351

AMA Executive Secretary Annette Kern, newly elected AMA Executive Director Ed Youngbood, and retiring acting Executive Director Lin Kuchler at an awards banquet honoring the latter for his services. He was also presented with the prestigious Dudley Perkins Award for meritorious service to the AMA and the domestic motorcycle industry.

of Great Britain establishing a new rule for international road racing, Formula 750. This was noted as an example of America's new influence as a member of the FIM, as 750 cc powered competition machines had been the basis of U.S. competition.

Another program was the proposal for a national mini-cycle organization aimed at encouraging under 16-year olds to participate in elementary motorcycling under controlled safety conditions. Later in 1971, Bob Jalbert was appointed to explore ways and means of implementing this program.

The FIM now expressed interest in encouraging a revival of speedway racing, and dispatched the former Polish racing star Wladyslaw Pietrzak to the States as an observer of the American system of management and its point scoring system.

The publicity surrounding the institution of the insurance program was a potent force in attracting new members, and the 100,000 figure noted at the end of Berry's tenure of office was now said to exceed 140,000. This was of course accelerated with the explosive growth of the motorcycle industry, fed by the ever increasing choices of innovative models from the Japanese, along with the increased production from Spain and Italy.

Another project was the Political Frontiers program. Headed by Bill Lowe, one of the most prominent political organizers in the country, seminars were held in conjunction with various AMA clubs throughout the country to show motorcyclists how they could have recourse to political maneuvering to advance their interests on the legislative front.

A landmark in AMA history was the licensing of a female motorcycle racing participant, Kerry Kleid, in 1971, along with authorizing lady mechanics who were qualified for licensing as technicians to work in the pits.

Another significant occurrence in 1972 was that the Grand National Champion, Mark Brelsford, earned over $100,000 attaining the crown, a tribute to the newly formed AMA Racing Publicity Department which had been campaigning in the best interests of the riders. This was a far cry from the days when contestants were awarded prize money only barely sufficient to pay their transportation to the race meets.

In a concentrated effort to combat public preoccupation with the noise problems the AMA made sound meters available to chartered clubs that could be employed at race meets to chart decibel

Motorcycle Weekly was started in 1968 and was a serious competitor to Cycle News for about ten years.
Don Emde Collection

frequencies where critics often exaggerated the sound emanations from competition venues.

In line with the expansion of AMA membership, two additional regional offices were established in Atlanta and Los Angeles.

Active participation in national politics by the AMA was first seen in the 1972 national elections when a National Committee for the Re-election of the President was put in place which backed the winner, Richard M. Nixon. The reason behind this move was Nixon's prior announcement for plans to regulate the use of public lands, much of which, at least in the West, was lately being used more extensively by off-road motorcyclists. Russell March, in foreseeing a possible problem, had instigated what was called 'Operation Alert', the first excursion of the AMA into the national political arena. Chartered clubs and dealers were treated to a barrage of posters, together with releases to the print media in an 'Alert' campaign, urging the President to be fair to motorcyclists In the proposed land use guidelines. In addition, AMA staff members circulated petitions at race meets and club gatherings urging motorcyclists to write to the President as advocates for granting them the same rights to public land access as the general public enjoyed.

With widespread response from motorcyclists in supporting this drive, the President, on August 17, acknowledged the fact in a letter to AMA headquarters recognizing motorcycling as "one of our Nation's fastest growing outdoor activities as a recreational outlet."

On September 12, representatives of both the AMA and the Motorcycle Industry Council joined together to deliver a petition advocating the rights of motorcyclists with over 250,000 signatures to the White House in a sidecar motorcycle. The two organizations then joined forces to conduct a series of meetings with land use managers and key political figures concerned with the BLM. The upshot of the matter was that the BLM decision was to permit motorcyclists access to more than 5 million acres of public land, with certain restrictions on some areas where ecological damage to plant and animal life might be experienced. While the matter was settled for the time being, the use of motorcycles on certain public land areas would become a factor to be reckoned with some decades later.

In February 1973, a highly significant change in the bylaws of the AMA was made when the advocacy of March for more democratic governing was implemented in permitting the election of two Class A members to serve on the Executive Committee. In 1974, this edict was revised to include no less than 3 Class A members, one from each region to be elected by other Class A members, to positions on the Board of Trustees.

While March's ongoing proposals for the expansion of AMA activities and services to members had generated much general approval, it was now becoming evident that programs were outdistancing the financing to support them. The initial response to the rider's accident insurance plan had been substantial, and the coverage for death and dismemberment had been raised recently to $5,000. At once it became apparent that the Continental plan had been under funded in the face of the number of claims submitted. As an emergency measure, and in hopes of staving off financial disaster from the effects of other extended programs, the Executive Board hurriedly raised the annual membership dues from $7.00 to $12.00, in January of 1973.

In an attempt to further cushion the insurance program, an alternative proposal was to have the rider pay the first $1,000.00 as a deductible, with the promoting club picking up the liability from $100 to $900, and the membership benefit policy to cover the range from $1,000 to $10,000. The changing of the plan to $1,000 deductible for the rider at once set up a storm of protest, and numerous of the insured simply dropped their policies. As matters stood, another proposal was advanced and generally agreed to for the insurance to be made available through the promoting club, this being in force at their option. In the end, Continental Casualty sustained severe financial losses and, as by prior agreement with the AMA, it was now liable to make up the shortfall.

While the tremendous strides made in AMA progress generally mitigated some of the criticism from the membership, March's part in the affair did much to dampen his popularity.

It was another recent event, however, that triggered March's undoing. A short time earlier, Greg Mosher had organized a corporation to offer both advertising and general business services to corporate bodies and had invited March to join in the venture. March agreed and purchased 20% of its shares for $5,000. Mosher then secured a contract with the AMA for certain advertising programs. March's participation did not come to light until it was noted that he had been handed a check for $750 as his share of a quarter's profits. As the Executive Committee had already launched an investigation into the background of the insurance problem as well as the AMA's now overextended financial situation, it took exception to March's connection with Mosher and, citing this as a serious conflict of interest, asked for March's resigna-

THE LATER YEARS

The XCLR 1000cc Cafe Racer was a radical departure in Harley-Davidson engineering in 1976, which featured continental type styling. Technical problems with engine vibration in relation to the light frame structure and buyer resistance to a radical departure from Milwaukee's traditional design sequence caused the model to be discontinued after about 3,000 units were assembled. *Benton & Bowles, LTD.*

tion in August of 1973.

Upon leaving the AMA, March participated in various business ventures, and later founded Marich Management Corporation, which is based in San Juan Capistrano in Southern California. The company deals with seismic testing equipment, with financial and insurance plans to complement it.

In later years, March subsequently told the author that his participation in the affair was not illegal. He was then of the opinion that if he had informed the Executive Committee ahead of time of Mosher's proposal, they would not have taken the action against him. But, at the same time, he had exercised poor judgment in getting involved in the affair in the first place.

The dynamic approach to expanding the scope of the AMA was typical of March's optimistic and positive executive style and, most particularly spectacular, was his involvement in the AMA in the international scene. He was frequently complimented by many members for bringing the AMA into the 1970's coincidental to the dramatic growth of the motorcycle industry, and his making it both a responsive and responsible membership organization. It was further noted that he was quick to capitalize on William Berry's initial efforts to affiliate the AMA with the FIM, as well as to implement the expansion of activities necessary to serve the growth in membership. In commenting on the 7 year history of the AMA that encompassed both

Berry's and March's stewardship, it was a time of the greatest growth and innovative change that the AMA had enjoyed during the 50 years previously.

The Executive Board next appointed Ed Youngblood as Acting Executive Director and, at the same time, implemented emergency controls over finances and authorized a thorough audit of AMA funds. A study was also undertaken to ascertain just why things had gotten out of control. It was noted that the simple financial operation set up years before by E.C. Smith was like that of working out of a cash register, with no further sophistication in place when March took over. Now facing a serious debt situation at the close of 1973, it was voted to thoroughly update the accounting procedures and to name Bob Thompson of Morgantown, West Virginia, as comptroller and watchdog over the dispersal of funds. The conclusion was that the AMA had fallen victim to too much expansion in too short a time.

Early in 1974, the executive powers were placed in the hands of Youngblood, Thompson and Bill Boyce who was to manage competition affairs. The three would share equal responsibility and authority, answerable to the Board of Trustees.

In passing, the Executive Committee noted that with the rapid expansion of the motorcycle industry it was now attracting increased attention from certain state as well as federal legislative bodies in regard to a possible increase in regulatory ordinances, and that Operation Alert as conceived by March, had been the first step in illustrating how an organized effort by the AMA at self protection had come none too soon.

Other changes within the AMA executive structuring had been the appointment of Robert Rasor as editor of "American Motorcycling" to allow Ed Youngblood to devote more time to the monitoring of legislative proposals at both the state and national levels, as well as his present role in sharing the executive duties.

William Bagnall, who had been re-elected to the office of AMA President, resigned in order to devote more time to his private activities. He later noted that the office had recently become more of a ceremonial position. In his place the Executive Board elected J.R. Kelly, of KK Cycle Supply, to replace him.

Due to the fact that the AMA was now heavily in debt, certain members of the operational staff were discharged and plans for an expanded campaign for promoting observed trials were dropped.

With the growing interest in motocross, Frank Cooper, who had had a leading role in its initial promotion, re-entered the industry with a new make of motorcycle, appropriately named the Cooper. It was based on an Italian design, the Islo, which was a 175 cc two stroke. The original machine was a utility type of modest performance, but was altered by Cooper's engineer, Bryan Fabre, into becoming a high performance 250 cc. Based somewhat on the already successful German Maico, the frames were also redesigned to conform to their pattern. Cooper contracted with a manufacturing plant in Saltillo, Mexico, 250 miles south of Laredo. Following prototype testing, the engine was provided with stronger crankcases and a bored out 400 cc version was added.

Cooper marketed the machines in the U.S. through a number of motorcycle dealers with whom he had a wide acquaintanceship. During 1971 and 1972, he produced 1,200 units. Most of the components were manufactured in the Saltillo plant, in conforming to Mexican law. He later sold the manufacturing rights to a motorcycle accessory firm in the States, who failed to maintain proper parts and service commitments and operation ground to a halt.

In 1971, motorcycle historian James Sheldon revised and updated his book, "Veteran and Vintage Motor Cycles", for the benefit of British enthusiasts. Inspired by Sheldon, and in response to the evergreen interest in Indian motorcycles and at the urging of some enthusiasts, the author negotiated a contract with

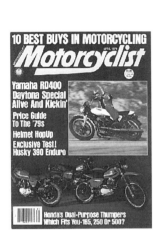

Motorcyclist Magazine is the longest running American motorcycle publication. It's roots go back to Pacific Motorcyclist prior to World War I.
Don Emde Collection

Haynes Publications of Sparkford, Somerset, England, for the writing of Indian history. The project was promoted by Jeff Clew, himself a motorcycle historian and also then the Editorial Director of Haynes and a prior acquaintance of the author through mutual membership in the Vintage Motor Cycle Club of Great Britain. This comprehensive history was supported by the author's vast collection of source material, aided by the contributions of a substantial number of former Indian factory personnel still surviving.

While the reorganization of the AMA and the launching of the MIC was heralded in the trade press as featuring both the cooperation and the acceptance by Harley-Davidson, such was not the case, however, with many members of Milwaukee's top management expressing disapproval of what was called their diminished influence in the domestic industry. Walter Davidson was especially bitter, and made no secret of his aversion to the inclusion of Japanese manufacturers' influence in domestic motorcycling affairs. When the manufacturers were called upon to contribute financially to sporting activities involving the FIM, Harley-Davidson generally refused to participate.

With all the problems attendant to the unprecedented expansion of the industry, it was most certainly fortuitous that both the AMA and the MS&ATA had been reorganized and expanded to cope with the many problems now facing them.

In the meantime, motorcycle sales generally were assuming unprecedented expansion. With machines from Spain, Czechoslovakia, Italy and other countries, in addition to the imports from Japan, together with accelerated production from Milwaukee, a buyer now had well over 200 types of diverse models from 50cc to 1200cc capacity to choose from. To serve this expanded market, the representation of nearly 7,000 franchised dealers was now in place, with perhaps two times that number of independent repair shops and retailers of general after-market and retrofit merchandise, which also included an expanded market in wearing apparel.

The now impressive motorcycle market had brought both the sport and industry into expanded public focus. This at once had accelerated public attention to the more controversial aspects of motorcycling. These included the matter of excessive exhaust noise and pollution, awareness of an increased accident rate with attendant insurance problems and the concerns of a growing number of environmentalists about the massive invasion of off-road riders on public lands. The burgeoning

Honda's Gold Wing re-shaped the world of motorcycle touring.
Don Emde Collection

growth of the biker movement and both the appearance and deportment of bikers and some of the fraternal type organizations also attracted public attention. This was emphasized by Hollywood in their exploitation films dealing with biking that usually portrayed violent behavior.

The biker movement by this time was almost wholly centralized on Harley-Davidson products. With the factory's rejection of the biker movement per se, the after-market suppliers and attendant non-franchised shops were outstripping the dollar volume of the parent company by a huge margin. In deference to the biker movement, such magazines as "Big Bike" and "Street Chopper" had already appeared as an adjunct to this market, the most significant one that came into being in 1971 was "Easyriders", launched by one Joe Teresi in association with Lou Kimzey.

Teresi, of Italian parentage, was born in Minneapolis in 1941. As a young schoolboy, he had developed an early interest in two wheelers, starting with a Hiawatha Doodle Bug, and proceeding through Cushman Eagles and on to a full dress Indian Chief. With a native ability in mechanics and an innovative turn of mind, Teresi was constantly experimenting with ways and means of enhancing a machine's performance in his home workshop. After noting the enhanced tuning possibilities of overhead valve engines over sv types, he turned his attention to EL and FL Harley-Davidsons. His basic strategy was to lighten the

cycle parts of the machine along with seeking ways and means to increase the engine power. He was soon entering his machines in drag strip contests in the Minneapolis area where they gave a good account of themselves.

Attracted to the mild and all-weather riding climate of California, Teresi came west in 1959. He found employment in phonograph record manufacturing, but continued building and experimenting with modified machines in his home workshop.

While remaining in the record business, Teresi continued to build his customized Harley-Davidsons in his home shop, these being distinguished by artistic paint finish and extensive chromium plating, unlike many contemporary examples which were not well detailed. His productions were featured in articles, complete with photographs, in trade magazines, initially in "Modern Cycle", and later in "Cycle Guide", both of which had lately entered the field due to the increasing interest in motorcycling. A later entrant in the custom cycle journalistic field was "Big Bike", produced by Daisey Hy Torque.

"Big Bike" magazine was published by Bill Golden, and featured articles and photographs of a wide range of custom choppers, but he had a policy of showing pictures of individuals. Many felt this inhibited its scope of general interest. At any rate, Teresi subsequently made the acquaintance of a professional journalist and publisher, Lou Kimzey, who had initially published color catalogs for the Jammer accessories concern. It was during this time, in the late 1960's, that Teresi originated the extended narrow type of springer fork, which at once inaugurated a new styling trend in chopper fabrication.

In the meantime, both Teresi and Kimzey agreed that the featuring of human interest material in addition to technical data focusing on the biker lifestyle could have a broader appeal to these enthusiasts. In the fall of 1970, the two incorporated what was to be called 'Paisano Publications, Inc.' The word "Paisano" being the English translation of the Italian word for "friends". The first issue of the magazine was distributed in May 1971, under the name "Easyriders". Its broad appeal soon caught on with biker enthusiasts, and it soon dominated the field with increasing circulation.[2]

Another change in motorcycle trade publishing was Joe Parkhurst selling his interest in "Cycle World" in 1972 to CBS Publications for $1,700,000. As part of the agreement, he stayed on for a time as its managing publisher, and in addition, he continued his preoccupation with off-road riding and ultimately published a guide book to aid

THE LATER YEARS

Charles E. Larson (seated) Vice President of the AMA Board of Trustees as well as Vice President of the American Kawasaki organization confers with Lin Kuchler concerning AMA administrative affairs.
Lin Kuchler Collection

in the exploration of the Baja California peninsula.

The competition situation quite naturally underwent drastic changes following the reorganization of the AMA and the institution of a democratic Competition Congress. But in the late 1960's, Milwaukee, still competing under the old AMA Class C rules, dominated the competition with their still potent KR's and through their control of the racing venues. Cal Rayborn, on an updated KR, won the 110 Mile Indianapolis road race in a hard fought duel with Gary Nixon on a Triumph. George Roeder enjoyed an excellent season, winning a number of contests which included the Sacramento Mile. In spite of strong opposition from Milwaukee, Gary Nixon finished the season with 505 points to Roeder's 451 to win the Number One plate for 1967.

For 1968, Dick O'Brien re-designed the KR into its 'LowBoy' form, with 7 riders, entering them as a team for Daytona. These riders included Dan Haaby, Mert Lawwill, Walt Fulton, Fred Nix, Bart Markel, Cal Rayborn, and Roger Reiman. All qualified in the top 10 qualifying trials and Rayborn won the race, his pre-race time trials showing a remarkable 149 mph.

The 1969 Daytona was run under the new Competition Congress ruling that allowed 350 cc two strokes to enter in the 750 cc class. As the Harley-Davidson contingent was experiencing tuning problems with their Tillotsen carburetors and reverse cone exhaust megaphones, a two stroke victory was predicted. The 350 cc Yamahas racked up the fastest qualifying speeds, with Yvon Duhamel topping the list with 150.5 mph. These high revving machines were advantageously fitted with five speed gear boxes, another innovation under the new rules. Duhamel, Rod Gould and Ron Pierce of Yamaha gained an early lead, with Cal Rayborn on a KR running fourth. Prolonged fuel stops and minor mechanical troubles ultimately slowed the leaders, however, and Rayborn managed to take the lead in the last laps to win. This was the last year for a Milwaukee win at Daytona. This was the first year that a Suzuki team put in an appearance, with Al Baumann and Ron Grant riding 500 cc two strokes, the former retiring with a fractured expansion chamber.

The first two stroke exponent to win an AMA Grand National race was Art Baumann, again on a 500 cc Suzuki, coming in first with a wide margin at the Sears Point Raceway near Vallejo. Teammate Ron Grant made a good showing until sidelined with a blown engine. Ron Pierce, on a 350 Yamaha, was second, and Roger Reiman and Mert Lawwill on KR's were third and fourth.

Mert Lawwill won the Number One Plate for 1969, in a surprise win over formerly strong BSA and Triumph riders who experienced a disappointing run of mechanical troubles.

Dick Mann, who had never enjoyed a win at Daytona in 15 years of participation, finally attained a victory in 1970, riding a racing version of Honda's CB Four. Honda had prepared 4 machines for the contest for Irish riders Ralph Bryans Tommy Robb, and British Honda dealer Bill Smith. BSA, Triumph and Suzuki fielded several entries, but all were sidelined with engine troubles except Gene Romero on a Triumph, who came in second. Mann's winning time was 104.7 mph.

The newly designed Harley-Davidson 750's were not in the running, as their four-man team was retired with engine trouble. A gallant rider who finished in sixth place was Walt Fulton, riding his own KR. The XR's, with their iron engines, had their share of teething troubles for the first two seasons but were improved with the fitting of alloy engines, later in some cases sporting twin carburetors.

The side valve KR's were now hopelessly outclassed but had served Milwaukee well for nearly

THE LATER YEARS

Executive Director Ed Youngblood presents Lin Kuchler with a Honda Electric Generator as a gift from himself and the AMA staff upon the latter's retirement.
Lin Kuchler Collection

two decades, as noted in the record books. Dick O'Brien and his mechanics had done a masterful job in wringing the performance that they did from an engine that was little different in principle from the Powerplus designed by Indian's Charles Gustafson in 1915, itself being based on the French Peugeot originally conceived in 1905.

With the AMA reorganization, the sporting picture now featured a wide variety of both makes and models, with technical progress now the hallmark with the elimination of the long outmoded Class C concept. The renewed interest in competition ushered in a decade whose racing programs increased to the point that it would require a large volume to chronicle.

The AMA-FIM affiliation sparked an accelerated interest in international competition, as well as increased emphasis on motocross, which in itself stimulated the interest of the more casual rider in off-road activities.

The year of 1973 saw the high water mark in American motorcycling, with nearly 1,750,000 units of all classes sold. While this was an encouraging sign for the industry, the AMA itself was now facing administrative problems in attempting to serve the interests of competition, club activities and the needs of the individual rider. This was complicated by the fact that it was facing a $2,000,000 deficit from the over-expansion that had taken place during the March era. The situation was also complicated in that the Executive Board had yet to select an Executive Secretary-Manager; the board itself being in a state of indecision as to just what course to pursue to put its house in order.

Also in 1973, Rodney T. Gott and the Board of Directors of AMF decided to move Harley-Davidson's assembly operation to a large single-storey factory building owned by them in the industrial city of York, Pennsylvania. The site had been built for the manufacture of defense products during the war but was now vacant. The Capital Drive plant in Milwaukee, as a modern structure, was well suited for the continuing manufacture of engines and transmissions and it was hoped that the York facility would help to solve the many problems attendant to final assembly that existed in the outmoded Juneau Avenue facility. Then there was the matter of the restive labor force in Milwaukee and the growing strength of union power. A new industry would be welcome in Pennsylvania, which was already starting to lose its traditional smokestack industry and it was possible to utilize available labor that was not only more docile but could be hired at a basic wage of $6.00 an hour.

The news of the intended move raised a storm of protest in Milwaukee, as more than 750 jobs were at stake and staying on with the company would entail the financial commitment of both moving as well as taking a cut in pay. In spite of the local objections, AMF put the plan in motion and by summer machine assembly was undertaken in York; engines and transmissions being shipped by truck over the 700 mile distance to Pennsylvania.

That same year, American Honda announced the purchase of a large factory site near Marysville, Ohio, for the assembly of large capacity motorcycles as well as Civic automobiles. Kawasaki made a similar move with the purchase of a large factory site adjacent to Lincoln, Nebraska, both indicating that they were permanently entrenched in the American market.

In the fall of 1974, Honda announced the introduction of a new model expressly intended for the tourist market, which was called the Gold Wing, with a horizontally opposed, liquid cooled, 61 cu. in. four cylinder engine with shaft drive. Expressly designed for low maintenance and longevity, its smoothness and low noise level placed it well within the category of a two wheeled luxury automobile. Prototypes had been subjected to rigorous testing by a factory team over a 2 year period in California's Death Valley where the searing heat of summer imposed stringent operating conditions. This model, offered in both standard as well as increased luxury specifications in Interstate and Aspencade versions, at once attracted a new market of tour enthusiasts who appreciated its dependability which almost at once became legendary. Old timers noted that the "gentleman rider", as envisioned by Ralph B. Rogers three decades previously, had at long last become a reality. Two rider organizations at once came into being, one sponsored by the factory, the other by a private group. To highlight their ambiance in the world of motorcycling, representatives of the private group staffed booths at trade shows dressed in tuxedos and occasionally in white ties and tails! To compete in this new market, the other three Japanese manufacturers soon brought out similar models, with BMW also offering their traditional Boxer models with full touring equipment.

Japanese motorcycle production for the world's markets had, by this time, reached an all time high, offering a bewildering array of models in all categories. In a visit to these factories, the author was impressed with the advanced technology of their manufacturing procedures, which rivaled in sophistication and rigid quality control those of the manufacturers of such high quality automobiles as BMW and Mercedes-Benz in Germany and Volvo in Sweden, which had been visited previously.

The Japanese, under the new AMA competition rules, were now taking a leading role in American competition. With newly developed machines, Honda had petitioned the Competition Congress to void the long standing $1,000 claiming rule which had once been intended to rule out expensive factory specials. In the end, claiming was not eliminated but the rate was raised to $2,500. While this could not cover the actual value of the factory exotica, anyone validating a claim would face the resistance of the factory in the matter of providing spare parts and maintenance.

A notable event in 1974 was the negotiation of an agreement between the Competition Congress and the R.J. Reynolds Tobacco Company for the latter's commercial sponsorship of AMA sanctioned motorcycle racing. The immediate effect of inaugurating what was now to be called the Camel Pro Series, so named for Reynolds' top-of-the-line cigarette brand, was the strengthening of the sport and underlining the importance of American motorcycle racing to organizations outside the industry itself.

The leading tobacco product manufacturers, such as Reynolds and Liggett and Meyers (Lucky Strike) had, for some years, allocated multi-million dollar budgets to advertising campaigns. They often sponsored certain sports programs then being aired on television. This was in the days before the Federal Communications Commission banned tobacco product advertising from the airways.

The Reynolds campaign regarding motor racing had its inception in 1970, when it began sponsoring NASCAR events, under a contract with their head, William France. Reynolds' marketing director, Ralph Seagrave, had reasoned that more advertising exposure was possible when company names and logos were continually visible during the contest when affixed to the bodies of the race cars than was possible in having just spot commercials aired between events. In noting the agreement, NASCAR's Contest Chairman Lin Kuchler suggested to Seagrave an extension of this program to motorcycle racing for added advertising exposure, seeing that machines now entered in Grand Prix type events were fitted with fairings that could carry highly visible advertising material. Following the inauguration of the Camel Pro Series, Reynolds added the name "Winston", another of their product designations, to certain Grand Prix events as well.

With the explosive volume of motorcycle sales, the industry was faced with the problems attendant to the public focus on consumerism and the consequent matter of product liability. Sparked in no small degree by the machinations of certain members of the Trial Lawyers Association, certain individuals sustaining accidents ventured the charges that in some manner some parts of the machine, such as suspension units, brake assemblies, or controls, might have been defective. Yamaha Service Manager Leo Lake's comments have been mentioned previously, and it was now noted by others in like positions that they were now spending more time in court defending their products. After-market accessory manufacturers were not exempt from liability claims as well, particular-

Alan R. Isley, President of the Motorcycle Industry Council.
MIC

THE LATER YEARS

The Evolution look of a new breed of Harley-Davidsons. This FXRT model designed by Erik Buell featured detachable carrier bags and a wind fairing that enhanced touring facilities but could be quickly detached for the custom cruiser look. This model was also modified for law enforcement use, and fitted with a special wind fairing could then attain the 100 mph speed required by most purchasers.
Harley-Davidson Motor Company

ly in disputes over the possibility of leaking fuel and oil tanks having a bearing on the course of the accident. With the attention to quality control paid by the Japanese and other foreign manufacturers, most of these were able to win their cases.

Harley-Davidson was in a less fortunate position, however, due to their ongoing problems with production and the intermittent effectiveness of their quality control. For some time the company had experienced problems with misalignment of the swinging arm assemblies on the FL models. There had been reports of these machines suffering from speed wobbles, particularly when employed by law enforcement bodies and incidental to high speed pursuit episodes. It was reported that the company settled several lawsuits out of court before the fault was corrected by altering the position of the frame gussets. Many of the legal actions against the various motorcycle manufacturers, even though they were considered without merit by the defendants, were settled out of court with proffered minimal damages in order to save the ever increasing costs of formal litigation, as well as the time involved on the part of key employees.

Another problem, this within the industry, was

that of warranty reimbursement. This initially involved customers' claims, in some cases obvious, of mechanical failures due to some part of the machine's components being of defective manufacture. As the retailer, the dealers were of course initially contacted by the owners for remedy of the claimed defect. It was then up to the dealer to ascertain if a real defect existed, or whether the problem was due to the owner's misuse, abuse or neglect. In most cases, the dealer's best interests in the matter was to placate the customer but, at the same time, in case of a proven component defect, looked to the manufacturer or the distributor to not only replace the part in question but to recompense the dealer for the shop time involved. In most cases, the manufacturer or distributor would slant their decision toward both the interests of the customer and dealer.

The relationship of the motorcycle industry to the law enforcement market continued as an ongoing problem, as previously described. Harley-Davidson had of course dominated this market after 1960, when the last of the Indians had reached the end of their days. The Japanese manufacturers, as by tacit agreement, had refrained from

The Later Years

In the mid-1980's Petersen Publishing launched Dirt Rider Magazine and switched the editorial format of Motorcyclist strictly to street bikes.
Don Emde Collection

entering this field. With their domination of the general market, coupled with Milwaukee's obvious production problems, they thoughtfully considered that public ill will might well be generated if Harley-Davidson's last bastion of strength were to be overwhelmed. This policy was given special attention by Honda, still far and away the U.S. sales leader with nearly 50% of the market. They had, for some years, built special police models, now based on the CB 750 four, which they did not import into the States. They also built a three-wheel traffic and parking control model, similar to the Harley-Davidson Servicar, but this was never imported either, even after the Servicar was dropped from the line in 1973, due to its high production cost. As a labor intensive item the Servicar could no longer compete with the sale of the export type sedans employed in law enforcement that were now $1,000, or more, less than the $3,500 Servicar. Then, there was the added situation of the still lingering animosity left over from the war toward the Japanese in general, of which the Japanese were still well aware.

While the venerable FL Harley-Davidson police models were adequate for suburban patrol duty, they were no longer suited to highway patrol work where high speeds in pursuit conditions were often required. The gear ratios on their four speed transmissions were such that the engines would over-rev on high speed running. The uneven firing sequence of the V-twin engines then set up a vibration syndrome that was destructive to both the engine as well as the whole machine. The need for five speeds was often discussed among enthusiasts, but the factory never responded, although aftermarket manufacturers subsequently offered conversion equipment to provide it.

In the end, states in the far west ultimately ordered the 850 cc Moto Guzzi Police model for highway patrol duties, along with similar numbers of Suzukis and CB 750 Honda fours. Kawasaki later seriously entered the law enforcement field with their 1,000 cc KZP model especially equipped for this work, including all radio and electronic equipment. Capable of at least 120 mph, the model found favor in many parts of the country and many municipalities ordered examples for suburban duty. Most departments, however, kept a few overaged Harley-Davidson FL models on charge to lead parades and other politically oriented public affairs for their visibility factor where the featuring of Japanese models might have been impolitic.

Charles Clayton's "Cycle News" had lately been expanded to include both eastern and western issues, and as a weekly publication could give comprehensive coverage to the increasing number of seasonal sporting events, enhanced by the phenomenal growth of motocross. Clayton, like Joe Parkhurst with "Cycle World", had early on adopted an independent editorial policy, and offered frank comments on new models of machines as they were introduced. This did not please many of the manufacturers, but did much to attract a large number of enthusiasts due to his broad coverage of both the sport and industry. Also featured were frank comments on the role of the AMA, with Clayton's advocacy of the democratic AMA, coincidental to the expansion of the United States Motorcycle Club which had broken away from the AMA's rigid Class C rulings. Clayton ventured the obvious opinion that high tech development of racing machinery would be of benefit to the updating of motorcycle design, and that an early revision of the rules was in order.

The year 1974 marked the 50th Anniversary of the official founding of the AMA, and in the fall of 1973, Clayton ordered some of his staff members to prepare an extra edition of the magazine to contain a brief history of this along with material on the previous constituent organizations. Issued in the spring of 1974 as a supplement entitled "The AMA, the First Fifty Years", the 30 page offering which included much advertising, gave a general overview of the subject and marked the first time that a rather frank discussion of the many controversial issues was included. In deference to the current financial problems of the AMA, the matter was not discussed, nor were details of the recent AMA reorganization, the founding of the MIC, or the ongoing role of the U.S.M.C. in inaugurating a new era in motorcycle sport. Due to space limitations, the presentation was necessarily condensed, but provided an effective overview of the AMA. The supplement was well received and about 200,000 copies were printed.

Following this, Clayton received an acrimonious telephone call from Walter Davidson, Jr., who chastised him for publishing the article, stating that certain of his revelations were prejudicial to the best interests of the AMA in general and to Harley-Davidson in particular. He added that the Company would not have contributed accompanying photographs if it had been alerted ahead of time as to Clayton's handling of the subject, and that the usual request for prior review and possible censorship in such cases should have been imposed.

Clayton, who himself was well grounded in the historical facts of both the industry as well as its constituent organizations, was well aware of the long standing traditions involving news manage-

A factory produced model derived from the custom-chopper era - Milwaukee's Evolution engined Low Rider.
Harley-Davidson Motor Company

ment. In noting the past experiences of the author in the same matter, in a later discussion, he agreed that any journalist who proposed to air a frank expose of the industry was subject to condemnation by certain segments within the industry.[*3]

In the mid-1970's, Carl T. Wicks, an electronics salesman and also the owner of a funeral escort service as well as a life long Harley-Davidson enthusiast, founded the Harley-Davidson Owners Association. In noting the current difficulties of the Company, and the concern of the many enthusiasts for its future, his thought was to offer both encouragement and expressions of on-going support for its management. Being based in Los Angeles, Wicks initially organized a couple of chapters in that area as well as in San Diego. Later groups were organized in Texas and Arizona, and one later in Michigan.

Wicks' strategy was to encourage dealers to sponsor chapters and provide meeting venues on their premises which, of course, was of mutual benefit. In due course a magazine, "The Gear Box", was published, edited by E.L. Stillman, a veteran Harley-Davidson mechanic and the owner of a non-franchised shop in Monterey Park, California. Wicks earlier had contacted the Harley-Davidson Public Relations Manager, Robert Klein, concerning the Company's possible official recognition of the H.D.O.A. Klein congratulated Wicks on his loyalty to the cause but stated that it was a long standing Company policy not to officially

affiliate with any outside groups unless the Company itself had full control of the operation.

"The Gear Box", which was published irregularly, soon featured articles by E.L. Stillman concerning various of the Harley-Davidson model's more glaring deficiencies and methods of counteracting them, all of which did not please the management at Milwaukee. At a later date, the author was awarded an honorary membership, and was appointed as the official H.D.O.A. Historian, with the stipulation that an occasional article dealing with some aspect of Harley-Davidson's past or present activities be submitted for publication.

The H.D.O.A. offered a varied social program of weekend outings, group rides, and participation in such events with proceeds allocated to charities such as Red Cross Blood Bank renewal, Muscular Dystrophy, toys for needy children at Christmas, and similar activities. All Harley-Davidson riders were welcomed into membership with the stipulation that members of in-place fraternal groups not wear their "colors" at H.D.O.A. functions. With the aid of dealer participation, the Association for a time was a prominent fixture on the motorcycling scene.

In 1975, Rodney C. Gott resigned as AMF's Board Chairman due to ill health. During his tenure of office he had been instrumental in the acquisition of Harley-Davidson but, due to various problems, production efficiencies were not implemented and forward product development never

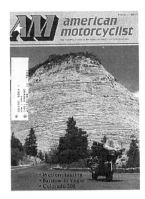

In the 1980's, American Motorcyclist covered touring as well as racing events to give its members plenty of things to do. *Don Emde Collection*

The 1980's also saw the Japanese manufacturers moving aggressively into the accessory business. *Don Emde Collection*

got off the ground. Gott's one successfully completed project was establishing a museum to display the collection of the Company's past products, which was named in his honor.

Gott's hand-picked successor, Ray Albert Tritten, became Board Chairman, and at once turned his attention to the ailing subsidiary. Tritten had been against the Harley-Davidson acquisition from the start, citing the run-down condition of the company and the attitude of its non-motorcycling shareholders in milking the company of its capital with the lack of foresight in forward product development. He noted that presently product defect was running at 50%, the continuing loss of public confidence, low dealer morale with substantial defections, and the company's inability to inaugurate efficient production.

In a copyrighted article in "Nations Business", Tritten outlined AMF's present position in the leisure time field, along with the comment that Harley-Davidson was and had been an albatross around AMF's neck and that the company should either face drastic improvements or else be dropped entirely.

After some lengthy discussions, AMF's Board of Directors authorized Tritten to attempt to salvage the operation. In the meantime, he had been investigating modern production and quality control procedures, based on the Deming principles, as well as canvassing the field of available production executives with formal backgrounds in engineering. This was in contrast to the traditional practice in Milwaukee of the injudicious cost cutting practice of delegating critical engineering and design work to empirical mechanics. Following both investigations and interviews with potential executives to reorganize the motorcycle division, L. Vaughn Beals, Jr. was offered the position on a salary and bonus basis. A graduate of the Massachusetts Institute of Technology, with a degree in mechanical engineering, Beals had enjoyed a successful track record in the design and manufacture of logging machinery in the Northwest. Upon making a thorough analysis of Harley-Davidson's unfortunate history, he assured both Tritten and the AMF Board that he fully understood what course of action to pursue to turn the operation around. Dealers and enthusiasts were greatly heartened at this news, and at the same time both Tritten and Beals were well aware of the hardcore name brand loyalty possessed by both dealers and enthusiasts, as evidenced by the continuing forbearance displayed by the majority of them in their consideration of the company's recent problems.

In the meantime, the AMA's top management was attempting to contend with reorganizational problems along with the overhanging cloud of a financial deficit. At the same time, the membership roll had increased, and the expanding activities of a now democratic organization were demanding attention. In an editorial statement commenting on the AMA's current situation, Ed Youngblood wrote:

"In the first place, the whole structure was due for review anyway. The past year has proven that. So, that's one basic problem. The AMA, with all the right ideas and good intentions in the world, just didn't develop the machinery, over something like 47 years, to be a 150,000 member, high powered organization with a clientele as broad as the scope of motorcycling is today. The conditions, and thus the impetus for change really didn't exist until the Russ March era. Then, there is the matter of the 'tunnel vision' that befell everybody, including the AMA, during the early 1970's, the major manufacturers and all the leading bike publications. We all became performance oriented with the development of the off-road motorcycle. We all thought everybody wanted to be a racer or at least look like a racer. The average street rider, the whole realm of road rider activity and, for that matter, the motorcycle club as a social group, were all virtually ignored. The big emphasis on road race insurance, which got us into a lot of trouble to begin with, stemmed from this attitude.

Now we're encouraged to see the pendulum beginning to swing back. The AMA, with its new structuring, is prepared to respond to a much broader concept of motorcycling than before. Examples of the pendulum swing are increased sales of road bikes, new emphasis on motorcycle safety and a real explosion of observed trials."

Youngblood went on to comment on the fact that blaming Bill Berry and Russ March for all of the AMA's current problems was unfair, as much progress had been made in the expansion of AMA activity, particularly the Operation Alert program to monitor potential hostile anti-motorcycling legislation at both the national and state levels. The development of machinery to continue this action now had become one of Youngblood's high priorities.

According to later statements by Lin Kuchler and other AMA veterans, the administrative problems of the AMA were complicated by some skepticism concerning its new leadership, in view of the problems of the Berry and March tenures of office. Then, the presence of an interim temporary management of a tripartite nature made pressing executive decisions difficult. Following the Berry and March years, the Executive Committee was hesitant to make an early decision concerning the selection of a new Executive Manager, all of which tended to inhibit decisive leadership.

It had been hoped that a substantial bank loan could be obtained to aid in easing the handling of the financial deficit but, in view of the past problems, local Columbus banks could not be persuaded to step into the picture.

Some Board members, led by John Harley and seconded by prominent dealers and formerly prominent members of the industry such as Dudley Perkins, Hap Jones, Rich Budelier and others, contacted Lin Kuchler regarding the possibility that he might return to manage AMA affairs, noting the success of his term of office following the retirement of E.C. Smith. It was noted that the interim leadership had not experienced extensive organizational management, together with the fact that they were not well known personally to the membership at large. At this point, Kuchler declined as he was happily involved in his position with NASCAR.

The Antique Motorcycle is a publication for members of the Antique Motorcycle Club of America. It primary focus is on the restoration and collecting of old American-made motorcycles.
Don Emde Collection

Another problem facing organized motorcycling was the specter of legislation mandating the wearing of crash helmets by motorcyclists. The matter had been under consideration in some quarters since the early 1960's. Lin Kuchler and a committee of veteran AMA members had encouraged potential manufacturers to have their prototype designs submitted for testing to insure that the fiberglass shells and internal padding were made to withstand substantial impact. Many touring enthusiasts had already accepted the helmet but, at the same time, a number of manufacturers had been driven into bankruptcy as the result of adverse decisions in damage suits brought on by motorcyclists injured in crashes and claiming defective design if helmets were impacted.

The bikers, with their basic philosophies of unfettered freedom of choice, were at once against mandatory helmet laws. Such organized fraternal groups like the Hells Angels, Hessians, Chosen Few, Mongols, Outlaws, Sons of Silence, Bandidos, etc., at once concentrated their efforts in mass gatherings at either legislator's headquarters or at government offices where helmet proponents were available. The AMA went on record as advocating the voluntary wearing of helmets as a matter of individual choice but did not support mandatory laws requiring them. While the MIC and the AMA were in general agreement in most policy matters regarding safety and legislative surveillance, the MIC went on record as supporting helmet laws.. Harley-Davidson withdrew from MIC membership in 1975, the allegation being that they did so in support of their enthusiasts who were universally against such laws. The helmet matter was to intensify in later years.

In the fall of 1977, E.C. Smith passed away of natural causes in his 88th year. Following his retirement as Secretary-Manager of the AMA in 1958, he had busied himself with private projects, but kept in close contact with motorcycling affairs. Mellowed with age, he had put aside his somewhat acerbic attitude and made an effort to keep in contact with his former acquaintances in the sport and industry. He favored the author with several interviews, recounting some of the generalities of past events. However, he could never be lured into a discussion of the more controversial aspects of his tenure of office. Long a figure of controversy, his dedication to the support of motorcycling was unquestioned, and he was a guiding force during the industry's more difficult days. In recognition of his past and to aid him in his personal maintenance during inflationary times, the MIC awarded him a pension supplement of $300 per month. His widow was accorded the same courtesy until her death at the age of 92.

The German firm of Fichtel & Sachs was a pioneer manufacturer of heavy industrial machinery, specializing in the production of ball bearings in Schweinfort. Leveled during the war by intensive Allied bombing, it was rebuilt afterwards with aid through the Marshall Plan and extended its product line to suspension units for Volkswagen cars and Mack trucks. It also made wheel hubs and other small parts for Schwinn bicycles. Early postwar expansion saw the mass manufacture of small two stroke engines, with various designs to power chain saws, leaf blowers, lawn mowers, and more importantly, small capacity engines and drive units for ultralight motorcycles and mopeds.

Coincidental to the rise of the burgeoning Japanese world wide motorcycle market, Fichtel & Sachs' top management decided to enter the field to challenge the Orientals in the European market. Several firms bought large quantities of power plants for the assembling of mopeds, which by this time were popular with a broad spectrum of utility riders. In noting the unprecedented boom in motorcycle sales in the U.S., it was decided to enter this market with entry level mopeds of 50 cc capacity which, in the States at that time, could be sold exempted from formal license registration provided their top speeds were under 30 mph.

Accordingly, a marketing team was dispatched to the U.S., setting up headquarters in Cleveland, Ohio, which was considered advantageous as being in the heartland of the country. Advertisements soliciting domestic management personnel were

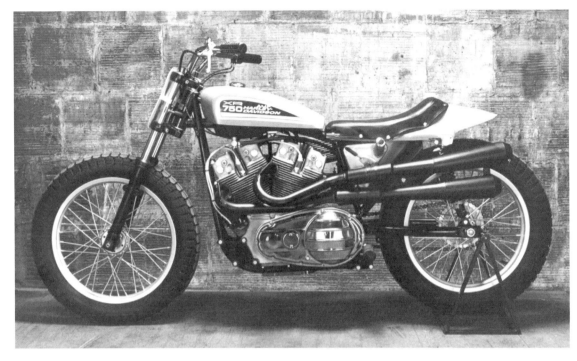

A 1980 edition of the Harley-Davidson XR750.

placed in the Wall Street Journal as well as in some of the newspapers in the larger cities. A number of past and present members of the domestic industry submitted resumes, including Pete Colman who was no longer connected with Triumph. Colman was selected to head the U.S. operation, with the stipulation that he move from his long time residence in Southern California to Cleveland, which, after some discussion, he refused to do, commuting by air to the Ohio headquarters. Colman was able to convince Fichtel & Sachs' management that basing the warehouse and some office facilities in California was advisable due to its prominence in the motorcycle market.

The machines dispatched to the States were mopeds, fitted with pedals for starting up, the chassis parts being supplied by the German Hercules firm, and marketed under this as the trade name.

Colman inaugurated a nationwide marketing network, hoping to establish retail outlets in bicycle shops. This was not entirely successful, as many of these were not allowed to sell gasoline engined products due to zoning restrictions. Colman recalled that he was not entirely satisfied with the product, as the seats were quite small and uncomfortable and the single geared units were somewhat short on power development as compared with the multigeared transmissions of comparable Japanese units. Colman was able to place substantial orders in a variety of outlets, however, such as hardware and sporting goods stores, and certain retail outlets in rural areas. It is estimated

that within about a year-and-a-half some 250,000 units were sold. The moped concept, in the end, did not catch on too well with American buyers, as all weather riding for utility use was not universally possible, and the machines were underpowered to contend with the ever increasing speeds of urban and suburban commuter traffic.

Formidable competition in the rather limited ultralight U.S. market was noted in multigeared like models from Honda and Yamaha, especially Honda's Express model built in vast numbers in a plant recently established in Holland, which was in effect a miniature motorcycle and showed much better performance. After a couple of disappointing sales seasons, Fichtel & Sachs called it a day and, in the ensuing years, disused Hercules machines could be seen moldering away in many garages and garden sheds in residential areas. The company subsequently attempted to enter the booming motocross market with new designs of 125 and 250 cc engine gear units, but these turned out to be inferior to the products of the more established manufacturers in the field.

By the late 1970's the smaller capacity Japanese machines almost completely dominated the market, although small production foreign firms such as BMW and Ducati served their own enthusiasts. The Spanish imports, Bultaco, Montesa, and later Ossa, had enjoyed popularity as high performance models of high quality, and their motocross machines had given a good account of themselves. But their production ceased following the death of Spain's long time dictator,

Generalissimo Francisco Franco in 1975. During the consequent political and economic upheaval, certain Communist activists within the labor force had invaded the factories, stopped production, locked out the management personnel and made impossible demands for both increased wages and managerial authority. Being such small operations with limited financial strength and unable to meet the militant's demands, all three companies were forced into bankruptcy.

Harley-Davidson's Aermacchi line of imports had never fared well on the American market, being indifferently supported by the dealerships, for reasons already noted, together with the fact that many enthusiasts condemned them out of hand in their resentment of foreign machines labelled as Harleys. It was also noted that their line of two strokes, more recently introduced, were technically inferior to the Japanese models of similar capacity, as the latter were marketed at prices substantially below that of the Aermacchis. Milwaukee now elected to retaliate and, in the Spring of 1978, filed legal action through the U.S. International Trade Commission charging that the Japanese, and most particularly Yamaha whose machines formed the bulk of competition, were guilty of 'dumping' - i.e., selling the machines at lower retail prices in the U.S. than in Japan.

Following Yamaha's North American operation receipt of the notice from the ITC, all of the Japanese firms banded together to defend the action, sensing that if one of them could be penalized, further charges against the others might well be forthcoming. In a series of conferences with their attorneys, the Japanese coalition secured the services of Joe Parkhurst as their principal witness. While he was no longer officially connected with the industry, he had, since the founding of "Cycle World" in 1962, been a strong advocate of free access of all importers to the American market.

The hearings were conducted in a large auditorium in the ITC building in Washington, D.C. The proceedings were similar to the 1951 tariff hearings conducted under the auspices of the Senate Select Committee of Tariffs.

After Harley-Davidson's attorneys had presented their pleadings, Parkhurst was called to testify on behalf of the Orientals as their principal witness. In his testimony, Parkhurst stated that the Aermacchi machines were inferior both in quality and performance to the Japanese models, introducing copies of road tests conducted previously by staff members from both "Cycle" and "Cycle World". On this basis he claimed that the Aermacchis were not competitive in the market-

place and that the financial damages sought by Milwaukee were a subterfuge to make up for deficiencies in the product.

In the matter of retail pricing, Parkhurst admitted that the Japanese had undercut Milwaukee, but that the position of the yen in relation to the dollar had created this condition.

During the course of the hearing, evidence came to light that in some ways the Japanese were in fact guilty of dumping, but some burden of proof could be borne against Harley-Davidson for attempting to protect an inferior product.

Following a grueling two-day session, the testimony was concluded, and the ITC Commissioners retired to arrive at a verdict. While Parkhurst's testimony dominated the defense's case, also to be considered was the testimony of several Harley-Davidson dealers who stated that Milwaukee had importuned them into handling an inferior product. It was stated by some that this was partly in retaliation against the Company's often arbitrary refusal to honor their claims for warranty reimbursement. In the end, the Commission's judgment was that while the Japanese were technically guilty of dumping, Harley-Davidson had been in a non-competitive posture in offering an inferior product, and levied no fine or penalties against the Japanese.*4

Parkhurst later told the author that he felt it was his duty to protect the best interests of the industry as a whole in his advocacy of a free and competitive market, and that, as a result, he had incurred the lasting enmity of Milwaukee's top management.

The Trailblazers Club's annual meetings following the death of Floyd Clymer were suspended. Harry Pelton, a one time Indian and later Harley-Davidson dealer, had been named to succeed him. Pelton did not follow through in organizing subsequent meetings due to health problems, and the organization languished. It was revived in the later 1970's through the efforts of Earl Flanders and William Bagnall. They co-chaired the annual meetings until 1984, at which time Flanders passed away. Bagnall then assumed the leadership by carrying on as President, much to the approval of the membership who through the years had given strong support to the organization.

In spite of the near financial collapse of the AMA, together with a severe reduction of activities, the paid up membership continued to increase. This was attributed to the fact that in the new democratization rider input and participation did much to put aside the former fratricidal warfare that had gone on when all authority came from Milwaukee. Then, too, with the end of the rigid

Don Emde Collection

Class C rulings, all classes of machines could now be considered for competition within their designated displacement category.

In an effort to more strictly control the handling of AMA funds, Treasurer John Harley took over an enhanced control of finances, reviewing receipts and payables on a weekly basis and establishing a central accounting system under a comptroller from outside the AMA Board. He also arranged for an outside auditor. He attempted to negotiate a line of bank credit to aid in funding operations in the face of the deficit, but was unable to obtain a sufficiently large enough amount to overcome all of the problems.

At this point Harley had little to do in the Juneau Avenue factory, as he had never attained management status. It was reported that his main duties had been the collection of scrap metal for recycling incidental to component manufacture, and the breaking up of rejected prototype machines. In his role as AMA treasurer, he was fortunate in having the backing of certain of the factory's clerical staff in performing the bookkeeping, together with the time available to oversee it.

The AMA administration at this time came under some criticism for having a preponderance of industry members in control, and subsequently two seats were added on the Board to admit members-at-large. In ensuing years more of these members came into Board membership.

In the mid 1970's the scope of the "American Motorcyclist" was expanded to include the interests of the non-competitive riders in dealing with touring, club activities, and stories about the exploits of individuals, and otherwise in the direction of upgrading motorcycling's image in relation to the general public. At the same time, attention was given to the accurate and comprehensive coverage of sporting events. In fact, since reactivated in 1970, this reporting resulted in the magazine being an accurate summation of the results of such contests as a point of reference to those interested in past statistics. This upgrading had been originally undertaken following the suggestion of some representatives of British interests on the Board that the magazine should be sold to outside interests because of alleged undue emphasis on Harley-Davidson affairs. At any rate, the enhanced format did much to provide a wider interest to members-at-large.

The name "American Motorcycle Association" had long ago been copyrighted as a trade name and, in 1975, another version was registered as the "American Motorcyclist Association" to designate the now more universal appeal to riders of all makes of machines and their diverse persuasions.

The vote to incorporate the sponsorship of the R.J. Reynolds Tobacco Company was contested by a Board member representing a Japanese firm on the grounds that their advertising would tend to overshadow the brand name of the entrant, but this was overridden by the majority who saw the advantage of enhanced financial participation from outside sources. It was noted by some that the long standing domination by Milwaukee of competition activity could just as easily be usurped by the Japanese, in case they could gain sufficient power on the Boards! A significant action at this time was the Board's establishing regulations to enforce decibel limitations on exhaust noise on both roadster as well as competition machines to counteract a long standing source of public criticism of motorcycling in general.

With the now wide open access to foreign machinery in the competition sphere, the matter of exotic and high tech factory machines conceived through vast expenditure of money now proposed a threat to a more desired participation within the sport. The matter of the traditional claiming rule, as noted, again came under consideration in an emergency meeting of the Board called during the Daytona 200. Terry T. Tiernan, heading American Yamaha, proposed a temporary suspension of the rule in regard to what was considered a costly 'rule charter', the TZ 750 specials entered by that company.

This at once brought forth accusations of a promotion of special interests. While Tiernan, for some reason, was able to preside over the meeting, the "temporarily suspended" rule was never reinstated in road racing and was later diluted in dirt track racing. As it was, Honda had won the 1970 Daytona with a specially built version of the CB 750 BSA had its Daytona swan song in 1971 by a win with its Triple cylinder Rocket 3 ; and Don Emde rode to victory on a 350 Yamaha in 1972, to begin a 13 year domination by that make of this classic event. With the multiplicity of classes of machines now contained with the AMA racing venue, the tradition 'Grand National' concept in American racing came to an end.

A more positive and definitive action with clear cut objectives was the strengthening of the government relations programs, largely overseen by Ed Youngblood, to deal with the evergreen threat of anti-motorcycle legislation at both the state and national levels. The state problem was monitored by volunteer groups about the country who kept abreast of legislative actions.

In 1977 the author's work on Indian, "The Iron

THE LATER YEARS

The ultimate in Harley-Davidson touring luxury: The FLT Tour Glide with side panniers, scoot boot, and a full handlebar fairing with radio, tape deck, and provision for installation of a citizen's band two way radio.
Harley-Davidson Motor Company

Redskin" was published by Haynes Publications in England, and marked the first time that a professionally researched history, backed by past and contemporary members of the domestic industry, had ever appeared. With the scope of the in-depth research and the intense cooperation from those in authority, the work was generally accepted as a definitive treatment of the subject. As the long defunct company was neither an economic force nor a political threat to the industry, an enthusiastic review was forthcoming in "American Motorcyclist". The author was subsequently offered a contract by Haynes to produce a similar work on Harley-Davidson. The editorial staff was of the opinion that such a production by an author unconnected with either the company or the industry, who already had a vast file of source material on hand, could offer a more definitive and authoritative overview of the subject in contrast to the usual in-house presentations which were thinly veiled sales promotions.

Another problem in the competition sphere involving the AMA Board was that of speedway racing, which had its rules interconnected with the FIM. Harry Oxley, a west coast promoter, filed legal action against the AMA, claiming that in this relationship the AMA-FIM were, by their control, engaging in monopolistic practices which were a restraint of trade. In a settlement of the matter following prolonged negotiations, Oxley was granted the promotion of the first individual Speedway World Championship Races, subject to certain rulings. Other sanctions were eventually awarded, taking place mostly on the west coast.

Other legal battles were experienced over the overall control of Supercross sanctions brought on by the personal practices of former rock show musical promoter Mike Goodwin, who had

attempted personal control of this now popular sport.

The AMA was still operating without a formally appointed Executive Director, with various Board members chairing the meetings dealing with diverse problems attendant to the AMA's overall authority. By this time Ed Youngblood was overseeing the bulk of the administrative problems, and it was suggested by some that he should now be elevated to that office. Treasurer John Harley was now Harley-Davidson's chief spokesman on the Board, as Walter Davidson, Jr. had departed his company in 1971, and William H. Davidson had retired as the AMF's Motorcycle Division head in 1973.

At any rate, a new problem was facing the Board. In addition to on-going financial problems attendant even with an expanding membership, a pro-racing advocate on the Board, Douglas Mochette, was overstepping budget restrictions in the administration of competition programs. The matter was complicated by ambiguous rules governing such matters which had never been clarified by William T. Berry during his term as Director.

At this point, John Harley, for a brief time, was serving as AMA Board Chairman, and it was his suggestion that Lin Kuchler be importuned to return to the AMA as Director, noting his past track record in reorganizing Association affairs during the critical period following the retirement of E.C. Smith. In recalling the matter, Kuchler told the author that he viewed this offer, which was sanctioned by majority vote of the Board, with mixed emotions. He was happy with his association with NASCAR in overseeing their competition programs, together with the fact that he was now approaching retirement age. Both his interest in the cause of motorcycling and his long time loyalty to the AMA in the end overcame his doubts and he offered to rejoin the Association as Director under certain conditions. These were that he would assume the office for a specified period of 3 years under a legal contract. This specified that if he could not turn the AMA around and hopefully solve its financial problems within 2 years, his contract could be terminated at his option. But, if he could see his way clear to attain the desired results, he would remain as Director for 3 years, terminating his position at that time. In any case, his contract called for a yearly salary of $35,000. After some discussion, his offer was accepted under the conditions outlined.

In further reviewing the matter, Kuchler recalled that while the Board had expanded heroic efforts to maintain the status of the AMA, there remained the lack of a strong central authority.

Critics of AMA policy matters felt many in the membership considered this lack undermined confidence in the organization. The tripartite management and government through this and temporary chairmen in his mind were not going to offer definitive leadership.

Kuchler's ascension to power was at once an advantage due to his already in-place personal prestige among AMA members, dealers and other long standing contacts he had established as a result of his participation within the industry and his service to it. He at once took charge of all AMA operations beginning October 1, 1978. From past experience he was able to establish a firm control of finances, including the runaway competition problem. He was also able to terminate the hiring of outside auditors and accounting firms. While the in-place staff was not reduced, personnel were given notice that any resignations would not have replacements. Cost of living wage increases were terminated for the time being as well. Aside from the tightening up of the whole operation, the yearly membership dues were increased by $2.00 and the sanctioning fees were raised in moderate amounts.

Ed Youngblood continued with the strengthening of the government relations program and, in recognition of his past performance in overall management, Kuchler designated him as his chief deputy along the way, with the private intention of recommending him as his eventual successor as Executive Director.

One of Kuchler's strengths was his wide acquaintanceship with the nation's motorcycle dealer network. These were contacted to solicit their ongoing support by aiding in conducting membership drives on behalf of the AMA; new riders being especially targeted when they purchased machines.

Meanwhile, L. Vaughn Beals and his newly recruited force of production people were in the process of straightening out the multitudinous tangle of Harley-Davidson's manufacturing problems. Beals then announced his plans for replacing the company's decades old and long obsolete designs. At this point, Board Chairman Tritten was advocating to AMF's Directors that the corporation should divest itself of the motorcycle division. AMF's production staff were not familiar with motorcycle manufacture and attempts at communication between them and the Harley-Davidson operation had been nothing short of chaotic. At the same time, AMF was divesting itself of its leisure time products in favor of entering the public utility service field dealing in petroleum and gas products. Ways and means of selling Harley-Davidson to a group of investors headed by Beals was now

under consideration.

Motorcycle sales had peaked in 1973, and experts were noting that the market was reaching a saturation point. It was also noted that after nearly 2 decades of massive production of machines in Japan and intensive world wide marketing, the same condition was occurring overseas. In spite of this, the Japanese factories were still in heavy production, mainly to follow their accepted practice of keeping their work force on the job. In Oriental parlance it was most advisable to maintain employment, even if profits had to be sacrificed to do so.

The continued massive shipments of machines to the States resulted in a growing backlog of warehoused units. The author visited a number of football field sized warehouses, mostly in the Southern California area, that were crammed to the ceilings with crated machines of all models.

The author's second one-make history, "Harley-Davidson: The Milwaukee Marvel", was published late in 1981. The work was based on a comprehensive backlog of prior source material, with contributions from an enthusiastic group of past and present factory employees, past and present dealers, sporting riders and veteran enthusiasts. It had been agreed that a realistic summation of the Milwaukee operation, the sole survivor of the domestic industry, was long overdue. Cooperation from Milwaukee was not forthcoming, the 1938 edict condemning the author's exploration into the domestic motorcycle scene was allegedly still in force. The work was generally well received and subsequently serially reprinted and updated, as well as produced in Japan in a Japanese language edition.[*5]

Another work that appeared shortly afterward compiled by a young emerging historian, Jerry Hatfield, entitled "American Racing Motorcycles", was published. Its author's contract with Haynes Publications was backed by this author. Hatfield, with the specialized interest in the technical details of antique machinery, traced the development of early racing types going back to the pioneer era. A somewhat esoteric work perhaps, as most of the makes described were long defunct,. it was nevertheless a valuable work that preserved historic data that otherwise would have been lost.

It was during this period that numerous publishers, mostly in Great Britain, brought forth a whole series of motorcycle books, dealing mostly in one-make subjects written by marque enthusiasts. While the British industry was dead, the enthusiasm by individuals was not. These works helped to bring on the birth of a myriad of cottage industries that made components and undertook

The high performance Sportbikes of the 1980's grabbed the headlines in virtually every issue.
Don Emde Collection

rebuilding to keep the cherished veterans on the road. These books were at once marketed in the U.S., and were well received by the still substantial numbers of British enthusiasts.

By 1981, the heroic measure undertaken at Westerville by Lin Kuchler and his staff paid off with the AMA's financial situation coming to an even keel. With Kuchler's backing, Ed Youngblood was named Executive Director, the job title being soon changed to that of President which was stated as being more indicative of overall authority. Shored up by a line of credit negotiated by Kuchler at a local bank, and carefully proceeding with cautious fiscal restraint, the AMA was now to enter a new era of enterprise.

Early in 1981 it was announced in the Wall Street Journal that a small group of investors headed by L. Vaughn Beals, Jr., was purchasing the assets of the Harley-Davidson Motor Company for $80,000,000. Described as a heavily leveraged buyout, the financing was provided by Citicorp of New York, with AMF backing a portion of this as guarantor. In noting the rundown conditions of the company before the AMF takeover, and the subsequent unsolved problems sustained during the 11 years of AMF ownership, there was now considerable skepticism within the financial community concerning the company's possible survival. Plus factors, however, were Beals' proven abilities as an administrator and progress already made in production procedures, together with the presence of a substantial number of hard core enthusiasts and the loyalty of surviving dealership. Beals at once announced that updated manufacturing and production procedures and an updating of Harley-Davidson's long obsolete designs were to be undertaken.

In the meantime, the ancillary after-market, retrofit parts and accessory suppliers and others geared to the Harley-Davidson presence, were prospering in what was presently a multi-billion dollar a year business. Mostly oriented toward the biker syndrome, such firms as Custom Chrome, Jammers, Gary Bang, Paughco, Drag Specialties, Motorcycle Nostalgia and others, offered a comprehensive line of products. Other smaller specialized concerns in the engineering field offered retrofit engine crankcases, gear box shells, custom sized cylinders and other items, the magnitude of which easily enabled a mechanically minded rider to build an individually customized machine from the ground up.

The overall motorcycle market had retreated somewhat from its 1973 peak, but sales of machines and accessories were holding firm.

American Motorcyclist, the AMA's in-house publication grew larger in the 80's along with the association's membership. *Don Emde Collection*

Motorcycle economists, however, were noting what could be an ominous change — the weakening of the dollar and the rising value of the yen on the international monetary scene could have an untoward effect. The market for Japanese machines was seen as being sustained from the vast backlog of warehoused units on hand, which had been shipped anywhere from 2 to 4 seasons past and which were being retailed as current models for whatever season they were offered.

At this point, the various dealers were holding blitz sales campaigns, especially in the larger trading centers featuring knockdown prices. It was noted that medium to large displacement machines that could, in ordinary trading, retail at something over $4,000 were selling for anywhere between $2,500 to $2,900. While such trading could move the product, it tended to create an artificially low set of values in the public mind.

Many veteran dealers who had progressed from domestic franchises through British and lately Japanese products were now becoming concerned that the frantic competition created a situation where there was insufficient mark-up in cut-price structuring, threatening business survival.

An analysis of the market during this period showed 609,000 units sold in 1965, raising to 1,000,000 in 1970, 1,520,000 in 1973, with a gradual downturn thereafter. At any rate, sales held fairly firm through 1984.

Government standards implemented through the Department of Transportation now governed noise and exhaust emission restrictions. This latter mandate saw the necessity of phasing out two stroke models for road use, being now classed as 'dirty' engines, and offering them at off-road markets in the small displacement category only. The last big year was 1984, with 1,305,000 units sold, including ATV's, and a high dollar volume of $2,383,000,000. This peak was caused by the inevitable rise in retail prices due to the yen/dollar ratio changing, the leftover warehoused units being cleared out.

The observable decline in new motorcycle sales are attributed to the smaller number of young people who were born during the post-war baby boom period, together with rising prices.

The Japanese manufacturers, in the face of inflationary trends in their own country, were forced to make certain adjustments. Production of small capacity machines was cut back to concentrate on larger types which brought in higher returns, as in a labor intensive product, concentrating on the smaller types was less profitable. Then, there was a significant market effect with the

THE LATER YEARS

A group of Pre-Sixteen riders gather at a 1982 rally at St. George, Utah. Organizer Bud Ekins is on the right.
Bud Ekins

decrease in the 25 to 35 year old baby boomers, together with the lessened sales to the 18 to 25 year olds whose more usual choices were the smaller capacity machines. A sidelight to these conditions was the edict of the Japanese government that curtailed the domestic manufacture of large capacity machines. Honda's Gold Wing and Nighthawk models, assembled in Ohio, were now exported to Japan for the home market, as were certain larger Kawasaki models assembled in Nebraska. Some of the larger volume dealers with bloated inventories were now dealing with traders and exported some of these excess machines back to Japan! The whole pricing structure was rapidly changing as the recent $1.00 to 242 yen ratio was now $1.00 to 123 yen.

The sharp rise in retail prices in the mid-1980's was at once noted as a deterrent to sales, but other factors also intervened. In the prospering U.S. the choices of recreational outlets had lately increased. The availability of family billiard parlors, increased facilities for tennis and racquetball, accelerated building of both public and private swimming pools, the popularity of physical fitness programs in burgeoning health spas as well as private participation, the development of more winter sports venues, all had the effect of offering wider choices of recreational outlets which overshad-

owed motorcycling.

The development of a new product in motor sport, the All Terrain Vehicle (ATV), had lately come into the marketplace as an adjunct to the motorcycle. Pioneered by Honda, the other Oriental manufacturers soon joined in producing them. The ATV's widened the already popular sport of off-road motorcycling, due to the increased lateral stability over the two wheelers. The earlier models were three wheelers in varying engine capacities, fitted with very large sectioned low pressure tires which obviated the need for sprung suspension. Initially fitted with solid chain activated rear axles without deferential action, as such they presented handling difficulties that could cause control problems unless the operators had special training in their operation. As motorcycle derived, they were of course added to dealer's offerings, but many were additionally marketed through franchises such as hardware stores and sporting goods stores not originally in the two wheel trade.

The ATV's were soon applied commercially to land and range management duties, conservation control and the herding of food animals. In some cases, they were used in agriculture for light hauling with small trailers, light duty plowing and culti-

371

THE LATER YEARS

vating and residential landscape maintenance.

The ATV's also added complications to the controversies with the growing concern of environmentalists over natural habitat destruction. The three wheelers ultimately came under fire because of the large number of accidents experienced by under age and/or unskilled riders. Under pressure from private and governmental safety groups, the models were discontinued. Their place was taken by four wheeled types; i.e., quadricycles, but still with motorcycle saddles and handlebar controls.

Some purists declined to classify ATV's as motorcycles, but retailed largely by established dealers, they were categorized as such and were statistically included by the MIC in sales, marketing and economic reports.

The AMA's sports programs accelerated during the early 1980's, due to the increased public interest in motorcycling, both by individuals in the game and strong spectator interest. This interest was stimulated by the opening up of new competition classes in varying cylinder displacements. The administration of competition was aided by allowing various areas of the country rather broad authority to set their own rules, thereby keeping the

inevitable controversies over certain details from becoming a national source of friction. This was an improvement over former days when all decisions on the rules were handed down through Milwaukee.

The leading spectator sport during this period was motocross, with various promoters staging stadium events in different parts of the country and often program airing was sold to local television outlets, a few larger events being seen nationally.

AMA membership had now grown to well over 150,000, stimulated by both the overall growth of the market and the democratic climate present under the reorganized management. Youngblood recalled the financial caution which characterized AMA policies at this time, in view of the hard lessons learned from the injudicious implementation of expanded activity and the need for tightly controlled top management to prevent it.

It has often been noted that the AMA, as the sole entity that formed motorcycling's formal organization, has never enjoyed the personal and financial support from motorcyclists in general it deserved. With well over 7,000,000 machines registered nationally, paid up AMA participation even today is just over 200,000. In the past, when the AMA's emphasis was on the overseeing of competition and club activities, the average rider, as an individual outside these spheres, might have been justified with disinterest. But with the later challenges to the industry and sport from hostile interests, any enthusiast now has a stake in support of AMA advocacy. As it is, the cause of every 100 motorcyclists is backed by about 4 AMA members.

The Harley-Davidson Motor Company under private ownership was now undergoing extensive reorganization. The production force at York was cut to the bone and technically advanced production methods were implemented. With computerized control of component inventory, the "materials as needed" from outside suppliers reduced overhead. Efficiencies frankly copied from Japanese manufacturers, as outlined by W. Edwards Deming in the U.S. decades before, were put to use. Production experts with previous experience and trained engineers for forward product development were being put in place.

The years between 1981 and 1984 were critical for the company, with it's diminished market share, 4% of the total, and a somewhat dispirited dealership who were now expected to see a cut in machine and parts markup as a part of the overall belt-tightening process. Company management, with justifiable optimism, was counting on the long standing brand name loyalty of Harley-Davidson owners to share their anticipation of updated designs that would carry on tradition.

The general motorcycle market was now seeing the change of product emphasis, as noted. The importation of small capacity machines was sharply cut back, with enhanced attention to middle land upper-range displacement machines with advanced sophistication in design that gave the ultimate in performance. The so-called "Ninja" type of multi-cylinder power plants, with high compression multi-valve design, were now showing top speeds of 140 to 150 mph, with acceleration to match that could be "0 to 60 mph" in 3 seconds!

While the technical writers for the consumer magazines reported with relish the details of these rocket like creations, the actual operation of these by exuberant young riders caused no little adverse comment from the general motoring public, and the appalling number of fatal accidents was shortly to have repercussions from within the insurance industry.

In order to cover a broad spectrum of a hoped for increased market, the Japanese entered the V-twin field to capitalize on the American's traditional preoccupation with that type. Yamaha brought out their 500 and 750 cc Virago models; Suzuki's counterpart being the markedly similar Intruders. Both were sophisticated designs with counterweighted crankshafts to help neutralize the V-twin offbeat firing order and had shaft drive as well.

Honda offered their V-twin Magna, a 1500 cc model with enormous power. They also offered what was called an entry level custom cruiser based on the chopper theme, called "The Rebel", a small machine with a somewhat extended fork and a bobbed rear mudguard. The buyer had a choice of two forwardly inclined vertical twin engines in either 250 or 400 cc displacement. Numbers of Harley-Davidson dealers sought out used examples for the benefit of female riders seeking to enter the sport due to their lightweight and low riding position.

Source material for a description of Japanese imports included Jeff Clew's history of Suzuki, and in 1989, Honda published a 316 page book describing all of their models marketed since 1959. Both were handy references for those enthusiasts investigating histories of these makes.

The ongoing relationships between the various factories and their dealerships has been a traditional source of discussion within the industry. As has been noted, such more than not had their stormy periods. The desires and theories of factory top management and/or their marketing personnel were often at variance with those of their dealers who lived on the actual firing line of retail merchandising.

Many dealers of Japanese products have stated that penetrating the almost impenetrable wall surrounding top management was very nearly impossible. As noted, the Japanese made a practice of hiring Caucasian managers to head their U.S. operations, the Orientals themselves keeping a very low profile. But American top managers would inevitably find that a glass ceiling walled them off from invading the echelons of top management. Americans were never appointed to Board of Director status in Japan, nor were they provided with options of stock purchase, which could then allow economic penetration. Due to the traditional Oriental practice of decision-making by internal consensus, such were often very slow in implementation. This as no doubt due to the prime consideration of providing "face saving" within their own groups. Decisions involving renewing dealer franchises or the transferring of ownerships took inordinately long to resolve, often causing financial hardship to those involved. The same problem existed when product orientation required altering to suit conditions on the American market. Most

Updated Sportster
Models fitted with the
newly designed Evolution
type engines were
offered in 1986, with
optional displacements
of 883 and 1100 cc's.
The latter models were
subsequently bored out
to 1200 cc. The models
were later improved with
five speed gear boxes
and belt drive replacing
the rear chain.
*Harley-Davidson Motor
Company*

dealers ultimately gained the overall impression that, while the Japanese were anxious to do business in the States, they preserved their Oriental clannishness. The few Nisei or U.S. born Japanese employed within the industry have stated that, as American citizens by birth, they were regarded in the same category as native Caucasians, and received no special favors.

On the competition side, interest remained high for motocross and the Camel Pro Series under R.J. Reynolds' sponsorship attracted spectator attention at such venues as Loudon, New Hampshire, Daytona, and Riverside, Laguna Seca and Sears Point, California. There was some controversy over the admission of high tech factory specials whose performance was enhanced by the vast amount of money spent on their development. Such machines could well discourage privateers whose financial resources mandated the use of the more standard types of sports models.

THE LATER YEARS

Following the reorganization of AMA management and the solving of recent financial problems through the heroic efforts of Lin Kuchler, incoming President Youngblood and dedicated staff members, the Association now faced the multitude of problems facing the industry in the coming decade. The AMA was governed by the Board of Trustees, which oversaw the general business matters and administration, and the Competition Congress, made up of representatives elected from the charter clubs, to oversee competition activities. In addition, the AMA's top management had established a set of rules called the Administrative Code which governed both parliamentary procedures as well as defining and regulating their competition activities.

The balance of the decade was given over to the expansion of AMA activities to cover all aspects of motorcycling interests to serve a broader spectrum of member interest and enhance its general appeal. An important facet of activity was to enhance and protect the public image of motorcycling.

An ongoing problem was the projection of media advertising that usually, in the subliminal sense, downgraded the motorcyclist. One such example was the subsequent airing of a 15 second TV commercial where an ill-kempt individual in ragged clothing, with a motorcycle in the background, was employed by the James Rivers Company to advertise Brawny paper towels. This, and several other similar presentations, inferred that motorcycling was either dangerous or populated with less than attractive individuals who were portrayed as being socially unacceptable. The AMA issued strong protests along the way which, in most cases, caused their immediate withdrawal.

As a result of a 1986 industry conference held in Palm Springs, California, the MIC subsequently launched a major public relations campaign, known as "Discover Today's Motorcycling" (DTM) included personal communications with media representatives who were known to show hostility to motorcycling, along with literature on projected safety programs and other positive information.

The program with an initial budget of $400,000 provided by the four major Japanese companies would prove to be a very effective tool in improving the public impressions about the sport and continues today. The AMA continued an aggressive campaign to reassure all members that brand name preference was a thing of the past, and that all makes of machines, no matter what origin, were considered worthy of general interest. Also stressed was the democratic make-up of the AMA, with solicitations of members to take part in any facet of activity that was their special interest. The expanding scope of the AMA included observed trials, motocross, supercross, dirt track, Grand Prix and Superbike type road racing in all displacement classes, together with emphasis on various aspects of touring and camping. In order to aid in membership recruitment, a large number of active, high mileage road riders, about 80 in number, were appointed to circulate in their respective areas of the country to promote new riders or unaffiliated veterans to join up. These "Rep Riders", as they were called, provided effective public relations through personal contacts. In addition, all dealers in new machines were again reminded to promote AMA memberships to buyers of new machines.

The promotion of club life was also stressed, members and prospective members being reminded that the orientation of the various chartered clubs could range from those interested in socializing and mild road runs all the way to those preferring the sponsorship of competitions, or serious personal participation in them, and that club life could offer something for everybody.

Both individual and club participation in AMA affairs on a volunteer basis was encouraged by offering a series of awards each year to those offering meritorious service. There were a series of awards for clubs; i.e., "Top Club" awards, for various activities such as public service participation, charity drives, special events promotions, and the like. The most prestigious individual presentation was the Dudley Perkins Award, instigated in the 1970's by that pioneer rider and dealer, for the AMA member who performed outstanding service for the good of motorcycling.

The annual dues were raised to $20 in 1984, and an increase in paid up membership to 130,000, along with an increase in sanctioning fees, helped to fund the ongoing expansion of all facets of AMA activities.

The format of the "American Motorcyclist" was changed to include expanded news coverage. An innovation was the complete reports of meetings of both the Board of Trustees as well as those of the Competition Congress to keep the membership informed of administrative matters. Also included were news items involving new models of machines, new products, accessories, and the like, although critically oriented road tests of machines were avoided as being potentially stimulating of divisive opinion. A critical section was the ongoing reports on impending or proposed legislation at both the national and state levels involving the regulation of motorcycling, alerting members to make their views known to their representatives regarding hostile legislation.

THE LATER YEARS

The ultimate in aftermarket production. The Super Vee motorcycle designed by Richard Crawford, the engine being a V-twin based on the well known Chevrolet V-eight engine using many standard General Motors parts for economical upkeep. The concept was the brainchild of Steve Iorio, founder of the Motorcycle Nostolia concern, and fitted to a special frame e along with other replicated after market parts supplied by the latter firm. What with 94 cu. in. displacement and high torque capabilities, the machine is a potent performer.
Steve Iorio

Harley-Davidson's top-of-the-line Heritage Softtail model, a frank replica of a 1950's FL which carries out the Milwaukee theme of motorcycle nostalgia. The author acquired one of these models for testing and evaluation, and noted that in out-of-the-crate stock form, its performance was almost identical to its ancestors.
Harley-Davidson Motor Company

Another worthwhile service rendered by the magazine was that of forecasting the television programming of various sporting events, such as championship motocross and Camel Pro events, for both the interest and entertainment of enthusiasts as well as encouraging the promoters and boosting viewer ratings.

In the initial reorganization of Harley-Davidson under its new ownership, President L. Vaughn Beals, Jr., again considered the matter of an attempt to protect the company's position through tariff relief. It was now an admitted fact throughout the industry that warehouse stocks of Japanese machines were at an all time high, that competition among the dealerships was such that unrealistic price structures were in place, and that substantial numbers of dealers were contemplating closing out their operations.

A petition for tariff protection against unfair foreign competition was filed on behalf of the company by Harley-Davidson's legal counsel early in 1981, with the International Trade Commission. The company's hardship position was stated, along with the proposal that a tariff against all imports over 700 cc be imposed, such to be levied against them after an initial 6,000 units had been imported. Exempted were importers such as Ducati and BMW whose yearly average sales had lately been under 4,000 units.

The proposed tariff rates were to run for 5 years, admittedly to allow for Milwaukee to make itself competitive in the marketplace. This would include a 45% surcharge the first year, 35% the second, 25% the third, and 5% for the fourth and fifth year.

Harley-Davidson's third effort at obtaining tariff relief was much better organized than previously, with competent legal counsel who presented a well prepared case. The problem of adverse testimony by dissident dealers was overcome by calling a group of carefully rehearsed individuals who were in sympathy with company policy, and who testified as to the damage inflicted on their business by 'Japanese cut-throat competition'.

A witness for the government was Gordon Jennings, who played the role of devil's advocate. In his testimony, he brought up the matter that since AMF had taken over the company in 1969, four successive CEO's of the Motorcycle Division, William H. and John Davidson, John O'Brien and Gus Davis, had failed to effectively manage the company, and that during the ensuing decade product defects had been running from 50% to 80%.

Beals admitted that many problems had existed, but at the same time outlined remedies that were already being implemented to update production methods and enhance quality control. A group of professional engineers, headed by John Favel lately of Norton-Villers, were currently working on updated engines and gear units, and that Erik Buell, another talented engineer, was revamping the overall design of their top-of-the-line big twins.

At any rate, the three ITC Commissioners retired to examine the evidence and ultimately approved the proposed tariff relief which was signed into law.

The Japanese presented a defense, but the four defendants did not consolidate their efforts, and in any case, could not negate the evidence that their overproduction brought about dumping of products. Some top Japanese executives expressed bitterness at the outcome, and it was suggested that President Ronald Reagan was somehow implicated in the affair as a means of inaugurating retaliation against Oriental imports, using Harley-Davidson's position as the opening wedge to bring this about.

The reorganization and updating of the AMA and its emergence as a truly effective voice for the advocacy of motorcyclists' rights came none too soon. During the late 1970's and early 1980's forces representing anti-motorcycling legislation, compulsory helmet law adherents, environmentalists, the accident insurance industry, campaigners for limited motorcycle access, and certain members of the legal profession, were setting about to weave a restrictive climate against motorcycle ownership.

One initial move to legally bar motorcycle use of certain public access facilities occurred during Lin Kuchler's initial term as Executive Director. Following the near completion of the nation's first expressways (the New Jersey Turnpike and the Pennsylvania Turnpike), certain legislatures in both states were importuned by anti-motorcyclists to forbid them access to both facilities. Kuchler recalled that he was able to personally head off these restrictions with the aid of some aggressive AMA members in these districts.

The City of Brockton, Massachusetts, passed ordinances barring motorcycles from access to roads through both their city parks and certain thoroughfares adjacent to them. It took five years of litigation and several court appeals for the AMA's legal counsel to have these overturned, which was ultimately effected through an appeal to the Massachusetts Supreme Court.

The government relations program instituted through the efforts of Ed Youngblood was further strengthened, after the AMA reorganization, through the appointment of Robert Rasor, AMA Vice President, to administer the program on a full time basis.

The advocacy of compulsory helmet laws became a familiar subject during the1980's, following much discussion during the previous decade. The matter came to a head in California with the activities of an anti-motorcycling legislator, Assemblyman Richard E. Floyd of Gardena. His stand was that serious head injuries sustained by motorcyclists in accidents could cost the state anywhere from $65 to $100 million a year in medical care, on the premise that most motorcyclists were indigents unable to acquire adequate accident insurance. His bill passed through the legislature several times, but was vetoed by conservative Governor Deukmajian after the AMA intervened along with other interested organizations such as the fraternal clubs, the MMA and ABATE. California was looked upon as a state where the passage of helmet laws was critical, as the registration of over 750,000 machines made it the leader in motorcycle use.

An embittered Floyd, following the rejection of his bill, made the remark that all non-helmeted riders should have their machines impounded to get them off the roads.

Floyd's helmet law was ultimately passed in 1990, and signed into law by Governor Pete Wilson, who had previously supported a federal highway bill when he was U.S. Senator that had advocated such. It was later alleged that Floyd had utilized accident statistics that included motorists in general in addition to motorcyclists to shore up his arguments.

During this same period the MIC, under the leadership of President Alan Isley, made possible rider safety programs by providing teams of instructors to implement courses in road craft for beginning as well as experienced riders. The worthiness of this program has brought good results when statistics dealing with motorcycle accidents are examined. While much of the cost of setting up these programs is borne by pro rata contributions from MIC members, once in place they are usually self-sustaining by adding a minimal amount to the annual motorcycle registration fees charged by each state.

Many of the legislative restrictions against motorcyclists and motorcycling had their inception during President Jimmy Carter's administration when he appointed Joan Claybrook to head the National Highway Traffic Safety Administration (NHTSA). Claybrook, a non-motorcyclist, appears to have received some bad advice from so-called experts who advocated a front wheel driven, rear wheel steered machine. Advocated as a safe design, experienced engineers declared it unridable! Also advocated were seat belts intended to prevent the rider from falling off the machine! Another innovation was the suggested inclusion of an air bag carried in the steering head. Then, if the front wheel fouled in a rut or struck a small object, the rider would at once be enveloped in the bag!

For the 1985 sales season, Harley-Davidson introduced a new series of FL and FX type big twins powered by an updated V-twin engine. Similar in appearance to the former iron engines and displacing 80 cu. in., the Evolution series, as they were named, were a definite improvement, with alloy cylinders and generally updated by precision manufacturing techniques. A new model in custom cruiser style was the FXRT Sport Twin developed by Erik Buell. A variant fitted with a special wind tunnel tested fairing that enabled 100 mph speeds to qualify for law enforcement specifications was introduced as a Police Model, enabling Milwaukee to again compete for this market. All the big twins now had a newly designed five speed gear box, a long overdue improvement which enabled a more effective utilization of the engine's power band, and did much to neutralize the inherent vibration of the V-twin firing sequence. It was also announced that a newly updated line of Sportster models was undergoing development, and would be marketed toward the end of the year. With a revitalized product offering, Harley-Davidson was ready to reverse its past two decades of declining fortunes.

In addition to the formidable array of hostile legislative proposals now facing domestic motorcycling, the insurance companies, in many cases, were entering the picture. In an effort to reduce their liability claims, several companies that had been serving the motorcycle market now announced a drastic upward revision of their premium rates. The Insurance Institute for Highway Safety (IIHS) issued a set of statistics purporting to show a recent increase in motorcycle accident rates, and many owners now reported that their policies were either cancelled or subjected to drastic increases in premium rates. Some buyers of new motorcycles over 600 cc displacement have stated that the quotes for premiums for an initial year nearly equalled the cost of the machine!

Another and perhaps more sinister piece of anti-motorcycling expression was in connection with a new crime control bill introduced into the U.S. Senate. It was designed to broaden the statutory powers of law enforcement bodies in dealing with organized crime, and referred to what was called Recognized Racketeering Influenced Corporate Operation (RICCO). Senator Dennis De Concini, D., Arizona, who was a member of the committee, added a rider to the proposed bill dealing with motorcyclists. His reference was to a method of controlling "motorcycle gangs" on the allegation that some of them were known to be manufacturing and distributing illegal amphetamine drugs. In analyzing this section, Robert Rasor and the AMA legal counsel interpreted it as allowing law enforcement officers to interdict, question and possibly incarcerate for further examination any group of motorcyclists traversing public highways. Through concerted action, the AMA was able to convince De Concini of the unconstitutionality of this part of the statute and have it removed from the bill.

Observers, in noting the widespread proposals to inaugurate anti-motorcycling legislation as an attempt by some legislators to capitalize on public sentiment, in some quarters feel this is a ploy to recruit new voters to their causes. It was also noted that as motorcyclists and motorcycle owners as a class were in a minority position in contrast to motorists in general, as such they might not have the voting power to counteract discriminatory statutes. This same minority situation was also employed by legislatures in attempts to override the interests of motorcyclists in side-tracking funding set aside for both rider education as well as the upkeep of off-road trails and recreational areas already available for such use. In mounting strong opposition to such proposals, both the AMA and the MIC have been, in many cases, instrumental in heading off such proposals which, along with the actions of some insurance organizations, appear to have been part of what are considered conspiracies to simply legislate and regulate the motorcycle industry out of business.

The strength of the AMA's legislative watchdog program is largely due to the extensive publicity aired each month in "American Motorcyclist" concerning current legislative actions related to motorcycling. Telephone numbers of legislators involved in such matters at both the federal and state levels are also published for response by the general membership, and anti-motorcyclists within government bodies can today usually expect vigorous responses to their activities. In commenting editorially about membership participation in AMA affairs, President Youngblood has said that the growing strength of the AMA at all levels is due to the actions of individuals and members as well as from chartered clubs.

After the mid-1980's, Harley-Davidson experienced an encouraging upturn in sales following the gradual introduction of Evolution engined models in both big twin and Sportster types. The latter was offered in two models: an 883 cc version as an entry level machine priced initially at $3,995, as well as a bored-out 1200cc version. A marketing program offered an 883 buyer the option of full credit on its purchase price for the acquisition of a

Classic Bike Magazine, a British publication was launched in the late-1980's to address the growing world-wide interest in vintage and classic motorcycles. It was largely distributed in the U.S.

Don Emde Collection

big twin if consummated within a year's time.

While the resurgence of Harley-Davidson was encouraging to both dealers and enthusiasts, the 1982 through 1984 period had been the most critical in company history. Management had been concerned with both the updating of product as well as the difficulties of carrying its heavy debt service. Chairman Beals had been critical of the dealers' abilities to hold the retail market during the transition period, and the dealers, numbers of whom defected, resented the factory's reduction of their markups, especially during a period when they were forced to give heavy discounts to customers to encourage sluggish sales.

Milwaukee's dealerships had long been represented through factory sponsored organization known as the Harley-Davidson Dealers Advisory Council. This had traditionally been staffed by hand-picked dealers known for their cooperation with factory policies. A group of dissident dealers, dissatisfied with some of these policies and the lowered markup situation, organized an independent dealer's group, which was known as the Harley-Davidson Dealers Alliance, to act as a collective bargaining agency. Founded by a group of midwestern dealers, the Alliance, in its initial organizing, was headed by Westminster, California dealer James Wismer. At one point, nearly half of the dealerships, numbering about 300, paid $100 yearly dues to support the HDDA, and included many prominent long-time dealers across the country. The factory officials refused to recognize this insurgent group, but representatives met unofficially with HDDA members and some of the difficulties with factory policies were worked out through compromises.

The Harley-Davidson Owners Association was active until the mid-1980's, still headed by President Carl T. Wicks, but with increasing managerial participation by E.L. Stillman, editor of the club journal, "The Gear Box". Both Wicks and Stillman had importuned Milwaukee to recognize the HDOA officially, but had been informed by Milwaukee's publicity director that it was against company policy to affiliate with any ancillary group that they themselves did not control. The company also disapproved of "The Gear Box", as Wicks would never accede to the company demands for the right of prior review and possibly censorship of materials.

Milwaukee subsequently organized their own auxiliary club which they called the Harley Owners Group (HOG) under factory management. Notices were sent to all Harley-Davidson owners regarding it, and they were urged to join subject to a $35

THE LATER YEARS

Erik Buell's Bimoto type racing model, the RS 1200, fitted with a Harley-Davidson Sportster engine-gear unit.
Buell Engineering Co.

yearly membership fee. Factory travelers now informed the dealers who had been HDOA sponsors to transfer their support to the HOG. The object behind this club was to offer a social outlet for the benefit of Harley-Davidson owners and to consolidate name brand loyalty, such as it had promoted during the former days of the early AMA. With substantial yearly dues and factory sponsorship, the HOG quickly attracted members. The privately funded HDOA did not attempt to compete with the HOG, and officially disbanded in the fall of 1986.

In addition to the ongoing struggle against compulsory helmet laws that began in earnest during the early 1980's, the battles against hostile legislation from the government bodies and the machinations of the insurance companies, the AMA became increasingly concerned with the anti-motorcycling activities of certain environmentalists. Many of the off-road recreational areas already in existence throughout the country were under critical review by some groups. The ploy was that motorcycle operation was destructive to the environment through exhaust emission pollution and hazardous to wild life. The politically powerful Sierra Club, with is then 500,000 membership, was particularly active in the west, and turned most of its attention to the vast desert areas of California, Nevada and Arizona,much of which was government owned and under the control of the Bureau of Land Management (BLM). They advocated severe restrictions against the use of both dune buggies (highly tuned Volkswagen conversions) and three

and four wheeled ATV's as well as motorcycles. The Sierra Club was particularly concerned with the well-being of the desert tortoises, as well as rodents, birds, and insect life. Agitation had started well before World War II during the heydey of the motorcycle desert races, and the legal battles over the running of the classic Barstow to Las Vegas races each year had become fixtured events. The AMA Congress had repeatedly pointed out that this event was run over the dirt tracks already in place that serviced the high tension electric power lines that radiated from the Pit River and Lake Mead facilities.

While both sides fielded their own expert opinion makers, the Sierra Club had along the way weakened their own position by approving desert access to certain mining, prospecting and ranching interests who paid substantial sums of money into the Club's war chest.

The matter more-or-less came to a head in the late 1980's when California Senator Alan Cranston proposed his California Desert Protection Act. This, in essence, followed Sierra Club mandates and would effectively restrict all access to about 7 million acres of Southern California desert territory. Led by the AMA, there was substantial resistance to Cranston's bill from numerous other groups, including mining and cattle organizations. This battle would wage on, eventually losing in the years to come.

A noticeable feature of motorcycling involvement, both domestically as well as overseas, was the preoccupation of many enthusiasts with the nostalgic aspects of the sport. The growth of international interest in machines of the past as well as the details of motorcycling's history was noted, as indicated by the growing strength of antique motorcycle organizations in all parts of the western world. The interest in Grand Prix type racing in the U.S. appeared to be waning, but preoccupation with machines of the past was evidenced by the growing prominence of the American Historic Racing Motorcycle Association, which was promoting events around the country featuring antique racing machinery. To this end, the AMA took steps to organize the American Motorcycle Heritage Foundation, to feature the establishment of a museum at the AMA headquarters in Westerville with rotating exhibits of historic machines and the collection of historic data and memorabilia dealing with domestic motorcycling history. President Youngblood considered that an inclusive collection of such material would focus general interest in the broad spectrum of domestic history.

The nostalgic aspect of motorcycle interest is often centered on the yearnings of a young person for a motorcycle that is financially out of reach, or its access barred by parental disapproval. When a later day arrives when these objections are no longer valid, thoughts may well turn to the model that was the object of youthful desires.

The nostalgic factor is well illustrated in the recent resurgence of the Harley-Davidson Company. In upgrading its product in both technology and quality, its overall designs follow a traditional format adhering to a hallowed past. In a brief flirtation with proposed high tech models, intended to compete with the Japanese and engineering in prototype form by Porsche in Germany, the Company's marketing executives found that their traditional customers would not be interested in this type of design.

The sales of new motorcycles declined markedly in the 1980's since the peak year of 1973, due to socio-economic factors already discussed. Inflationary forces precluded Japanese production of low cost entry level models, but to adjust to current markets they reduced their number of models and put more emphasis on middle range machines.

On the plus side, the Italian manufacturers have reorganized their production methods and there was an amalgamation of some formerly ailing companies. On the domestic front, Harley-Davidson closed out the 1980's focused on a strategy to feed the lifestyle needs of riders who associated 'Harley-Davidson' with 'American'. In future years, the trademarks of the Harley-Davidson Motor Company would attain a value never dreamed of by the company founders.

In spite of downward marketing trends, the AMA has, during the past two decades, enjoyed a moderate but steady growth in membership. This appears to be due to two principal factors: the democratization and reorganization in 1970, when the domination of the interest of one domestic manufacturer and the strengthening and expansion programs of 1981, when a broadened spectrum of activities came to appeal to motorcyclists of every persuasion and the owners of all brands of machines.

An important rallying point for motorcyclists' support of the AMA has been concentrated assaults by legislative, corporate and environmental interests that, left unchallenged, could well spell the death knell of the sport and industry. A well planned and extensive public airing of these activities, along with a vigorous campaign to combat these forces, has highlighted the fact that the AMA is the major defender of the rights of motorcycle ownership. While the battle against compulsory helmet laws nationwide has yet to be concluded, much hostile legislation and many discriminatory laws against motorcyclists has been beaten back. As a fairness issue, the AMA deserves more general support from motorcycle owners at large, all of whom benefit from AMA activities. The role of the MIC must also be recognized for its general support from motorcycle owners at large, all of whom benefit from AMA activities. The role of the MIC must also be recognized for its general support of the industry. Acting on behalf of manufacturers, distributors and accessory suppliers, it offers sales and marketing aids and economic analysis along with implementing rider safety education programs. It has been stated that while the AMA and the MIC are on opposite sides of the street, they are both headed in the same direction.

Epilogue

The casual observer and the entry level motorcyclist often express amazement upon encountering some of the basic facts of the history of the domestic industry and its constituent organizations. When compared with that of some other American industries, the history of its motorcycling activities seems almost unbelievable as a collection of bizarre occurrences, illogical situations, inexplicable political ramifications, and often unorthodox and frequently outrageous behavior on the part of some members of the industry. The answer to these questions may well be explained by the controversial nature inherent in the motorcycle itself.

Let us look back...

Any vehicle supported by two wheels set in tandem lacks lateral support, a fact that presupposes a certain danger to anyone who operates it. When technical progress saw the invention of drawn steel tubing and the tangently spoked wire wheel after the American Civil War, the consequent introduction of the high wheel bicycle saw it rightly condemned as a dangerous vehicle for the rider and a further hazard to traffic in general as its appearance frightened horses.

The introduction of the improved "Safety" bicycle saw public condemnation in some quarters for its high speed capabilities, its contribution to traffic congestion in urban areas, and the social liberties it afforded young people who could venture unchaperoned into the countryside.

The appearance of the primitive motor-bicycles compounded these objections. With the capabilities for high speeds then unheard of even in the early horseless carriages, the rattle of its exposed machinery and the noise of its poorly silenced exhaust, the obvious poor handling exhibited by some versions, coupled with the inefficiencies of its braking power, all combined to alienate a substantial segment of the public.

As improved models subsequently gained ground as a low cost utility vehicle amid the high cost of early automobiles, the sporting application of the motorcycle came to the fore. Racing bicycle promoters, who had had a field day with variations of the safety bicycle, now staged speed contests on the wooden velodromes for motorcycles, and soon enlarged versions called "motordromes" with subsequently even larger board tracks were built. Dozens of these temples of speed were built adjacent to nearly every large urban center in the country, a lucrative spectator sport that flourished between 1912 and 1925. While the board tracks enjoyed a popular appeal, the average spectator could scarcely visualize himself as the purchaser of one of the fire belching monsters, the dangers of which saw an appalling number of accidents that put motorcycle racing in the category of a bloody gladiatorial spectacle.

When the introduction of the cheap automobile supplanted the motorcycle or motorcycle-sidecar outfit as a utilitarian vehicle after World War II, the industry faced a near collapse almost overnight. With 85% of the manufacturers retired from the market, the few survivors were left with only the support of those who rode for the sport of the thing, and now catered to a narrow market that favored heavyweight machines capable of high speeds that required some athletic ability to start and control.

Faced with diminished public interest and supported in large part by the demands of the export market, the manufacturers more-or-less tacitly agreed on a news management program that mandated all reports of the industry be controlled by the factories. This was supported by a dwindling number of trade magazines that once served a flourishing pre-war industry. The general public was then further confused when a casual reader of a trade publication was exposed to articles describing the activities of a successful industry that was producing machines of superlative technical excellence in increasing quantities when, in fact,there were few such to be seen on the roads. In fact, the average motorist could travel for days on end without ever encountering one!

The devastating effects of the Depression wreaked havoc on the domestic motorcycle industry and, in a desperate attempt to survive, the two remaining factories found themselves in a fratricidal warfare that further diminished public approval of motorcycling. With the support of the factory supported AMA, the surviving sporting aspects of motorcycling were carried forward which, while shoring up the industry, further eroded public approval in carrying out the image that motorcycling was a roughneck and thoroughly declasse' undertaking.

During this period, there was much rider antagonism to the AMA which was, by economic necessity, under the firm control of the industry and subservient to their interests. While the natural American sentiments of adherence to democracy by individual enthusiasts persisted, the result was a decade of continual quarrelling over the issue.

Following World War II, the domestic industry was threatened by the importation of British middleweight models which captured what was not a new market, but one which the formerly depressed domestic suppliers never had the resources to develop. The AMA was only able to come of age when the massive importation of Oriental machines opened up the marketplace, provided better dealer expansion and independent free markets not previously possible.

Added to the aforementioned chaotic situations, the growth of the biker movement and the widespread public exposure to an iconoclastic free-swinging lifestyle could be and was an unsettling factor in the public image of motorcycling. In an age and time characterized by a newly acquired tolerance of diverse social behavior, the influence of Hollywood in a series of motion picture productions featuring excessive violence has had its effect on public opinion.

The effect of long standing industry control of motorcycling activity, its dominance of constituent organization and news management, has discouraged independent examination of both the sport and industry in its historical aspect. Only in recent years has there been substantial public opinion in favor of a formally presented overview of the subject. But there are still those within the industry that believe the past is best forgotten. Then, any professional journalist who undertakes such a project becomes a part of the controversy itself.*6

The motorcycle industry and its organizations have been presented with many challenges in the late 20th Century, many of which are still unresolved. Some time down the road it will then be the task of 21st Century historians to interpret their resolutions.

CHAPTER NOTES

CHAPTER I

1. In the mid 1880's, Lucius D. Copeland and Sylvester Roper, working independently in the Philadelphia area, fitted ultra light steam power plants to the upper frame rails of high wheeled bicycles. The machines were predictably unstable, but could be made to run, although the necessarily small size of the boilers gave them a cruising range of only a few hundred yards.

2. A clause added later to the constitution specified that only manufacturers representatives could have voting power. This explains why in later years E.C. Smith would never allow public scrutiny of a copy of the document. Blacks were never excluded from either the FAM, the M&ATA, or the AMA, but it was not until the 1990's that they were specifically invited to join the AMA.

CHAPTER II

1. In common with many immigrant arrivals to this country, Brinker had "Americanized" the family surname. Originally it was Steinove in Russia, Brinkerhoff in Holland, and eventually it became Brinker in the United States.

2. Jerome Charles Bonaparte, brother of the Emperor Napoleon, came to the U.S. in 1803, settled in Baltimore, and married Elizabeth Patterson, daughter of a wealthy and socially prominent merchant, incidental to also being the King of Westphalia. The couple had a son, Jerome Napoleon (1805-1870), who father Charles Jerome (1851-1921) who attended Harvard University and attained a law degree in 1873. As a prominent attorney in Baltimore, he entered politics, and was successively Attorney General and Secretary of the Navy in the administration of President Theodore Roosevelt between 1903 and 1909. His involvement in the Thornley affair, due to his prominence, received much attention in the newspapers of that day.

CHAPTER III

1. The initial design of the Excelsior lightweight was British in origin, and was first produced in 1912 by Triumph. Ignatz Schwinn bought the patent rights and briefly manufactured the model under license.

2. The two stroke engine was a frank copy of the British Union design.

CHAPTER IV

1. President Walter Davidson's reservations about hiring Child as a factory representative were his fear that Child's ethical concepts might have been corrupted by having been formerly employed by a Jewish merchant.

2. The FICM (Federation Internationale des Clubs Motorcyclists) was founded in Austria in 1904 by an amateur motorcyclist, Dr. Weiss von Tessbach. It was formed for the purpose of supplanting the somewhat poorly organized competition bodies then in place in Europe. Gaining strength through the years, FICM headquarters with a permanent staff were located in Geneva, Switzerland, and well before World War I were in control of Europe's motorcycle competition. It later assumed international scope, and after World War II its name was shortened to Federation Internationale Motorcliste (FIM).

3. After rejecting AMA affiliation with the FICM in 1924, the Competition Committee paradoxically later that year went on record as favoring such, but with nor further action being taken in the matter.

4. The lack of individual AMA member participation through lack of voting power was emphasized.

5. A.B. Coffman remained in office as an ex-officio Chairman until the late Fall of 1924 through action of the Competition Committee.

6. All of the correspondence relating to Hobart's negotiations with both the Auto-Cycle Union, William H. Wells, and the FICM staff at Geneva were later destroyed through orders of President Walter Davidson, and no reference to Hobart's activities are to be found in the incomplete archives of the AMA.

7. It was about this time that President Walter Davidson suggested that all news releases regarding the Domestic motorcycle industry be subjected to strict factory control.

8. The once great Arnold Schwin organization declared bankruptcy in 1992, citing their inability to compete with foreign competition.

CHAPTER V

1. The problem with recurrent failures in cylinder head gasket sealing and consequent blowing was eventually cured in 1936 with the fitting of nine stud cylinder head fastenings instead of the previous seven.

2. Sidecar production along with that of rear cars was carried on between the wars by Australian Immigrant Claude Goulding and lasted until the early 1950's. Much of this production was exported.

3. The Hanlon Brothers, David and Daniel, based in Minnesota, proposed a revival of the Super-X and Henderson marques with updated models in 1994.

4. E.C. Smith's suggestion marked the first formal inauguration of news management by the AMA, following President Walter Davidson's mid 1920's advocacy of such a policy.

5. While only a few dozen foreign machines were imported into the United States during this period, there was much apprehension among leaders in the

CHAPTER NOTES

industry that an import organization might be instituted.

6. As a matter of ongoing policy, no articles dealing with specific details of past AMA history ever appeared in AMA sponsored publications.

CHAPTER VI

1. An allweather highway spanning Canada from coast to coast was ultimately completed in 1948 under the sponsorship and financing from the central government in Ottawa.

2. The AMA Competition Committee was hard pressed to find a rule enabling the barring of the International Norton from domestic competition. In production since 1932 and marketed as a road going machine, sufficient numbers had been marketed to qualify it as a cataloged model. In actuality, however, the model was a slightly detuned racing machine, needing but minimal modifications to put it in competition trim.

3. The AMA Competition Committee secretly sanctioned the utilization of Wasaga Beach in Canada for the testing of experimental U.S. made prototypes that were far removed from Class C designation.

4. While officially accepted for AMA competition, Norton Internationals were barred in some venues at the option of local AMA referees.

CHAPTER VII

1. The history of the Cushman organization by Ron Rae is available.

2. While Ignatz Schwinn refused to join with Harley-Davidson and Indian executives in their annual price-and-policy fixing meetings, he frequently conferred with them concerning the protection and/or registration of patents on components. The designation, "Excelsior" was terminated for the V-twin models in the Fall of 1925 in favor of the term "Super-X" in deference to the protests of the British company who had first registered the name as an internationally designated patent.

3. The specifications of various Cushman models are shown.

4. Editors of the AMA magazine rejected articles submitted by individuals dealing

with details of AMA history.

5. E.C. Smith usually destroyed such material.

CHAPTER VIII

1. Crosley ordered the four prototypes of the rejected military models destroyed. He subsequently developed a design for an ultralight automobile with a four cylinder 1000 cc engine.

2. The non payment of promised cash bonuses to certain Company employees by President Walter Davidson was long a matter of contention with the organization.

CHAPTER IX

1. While the number of the V-twin model Crockers was usually considered to be about 65 units, subsequent information indicates that there might have been a dozen or so more assembled.

2. Barger is alleged to have served approximately twelve years in prison on various conspiracy charges. In 1990, he was reported to have opened a motorcycle accessory shop in Oakland, California.

3. Vernon Guthrie subsequently supplied the author with much valuable historical material dealing with the first four decades of the twentieth century.

4. Approximately twenty five thousand 74 cu. in. Indian Chiefs were produced at Springfield between 1945 and 1949. This does not include the production of 80 cu. in. Blackhawk models between 1950 and 1953.

5. E.C. Smith and the Competition Committee had traditionally opposed any objective examination by outsiders of either the past state of the industry or any material surviving in the AMA archives.

CHAPTER X

1. Francisco Bulto was abducted by Mideastern terrorists in 1985, was directed to go to his bank and withdraw a large sum of money. To insure his compliance, they taped an explosive device to his body, with a warning that if he attempted to remove it, it would explode. Bulto disregarded their advice, and in attempting to remove it, he was blown apart.

CHAPTER XI

1. A detailed account of the transactions

involving AMF and Bangor Punta is to be bound in Chapter Ten of the Author's Harley-Davidson: The Milwaukee Marvel, and in "Well Made in America, by Peter C. Reid.

2. By 1990, Paisano's various publications circulation figures, including their foreign language magazine editions, exceeded that of the total output of the more conventional U.S. motorcycle trade journals.

3. In addition to refusing to entertain Vernon L. Guthrie's offer to produce a comprehensive history of AMA activities up to and including events up to 1940, similar offers by Thomas Callahan Buther in 1952 and Leslie D. Richards in 1957 were refused by E.C. Smith on the grounds that such public disclosures would be prejudicial to the best interests of the AMA.

4. Following their failure to induce the ITC to rule in favor of Harley-Davidson against the Japanese motorcycle importers, Milwaukee ceased the importation of Aerrmachi products. The latter Company was later taken over by the Cagiva concern, an Italian based conglomerate.

5. Reviews of The Milwaukee Marvel published in various motorcycle trade journals both at home and abroad dealing with the first edition early in 1982 accepted the authors conclusions as authoritative, based on both his prior research and the collaboration of contemporary witnesses. In a review appearing in "American Motorcycling" in April, the AMA's position was that the work was an embarrassment to the domestic motorcycle industry. This statement suggests that the AMA was still adhering to its long tradition of news management.

6. During the middle and late 1980's incidental to the production of this book, copies of preliminary manuscript material were forwarded to the AMA management. Following some rather vague responses and comments, the author was served by a formal notice from the AMA's legal counsel, the law firm of Bricker and Eckler of Columbus, Ohio, that the AMA refused to officially accept the author's overview of the domestic industry's and the AMA's history. This notice was served on the author on August 11, 1992.

APPENDIX

UNITED STATES MOTORCYCLE PRODUCTION
1920 TO 1940

	HARLEY-DAVIDSON MOTOR COMPANY	INDIAN MOTORCYCLE CO.	ARNOLD SCHWINN & CO. (HENDERSON, EXCELSIOR, SUPER X)
1920	18,180	19,608	4,678*
1921	10,202	13,862	4,067*
1922	12,759	6,344	3,657*
1923	18,430	7,409	2,753*
1924	13,996	6,991	1,956
1925	16,929	8,678	2,234
1926	23,354	11,654	3,058**
1927	19,911	10,834	2,319**
1928	22,350	6,352	2,006**
1929	21,142	1,356	2,768**
1930	17,422	6,897	3,089**
1931	10,503	7,665	457**
1932	6,841	5,751	
1933	3,703	1,657	* Includes small numbers of 61 and 74 cu. in. V twin Excelsiors and Hendersons.
1934	10,231	2,809	
1935	10,368	3,715	
1936	9,812	5,028	** Includes 45 and 61 cu. in. Super X's and Henderson (40 - 50% of Excelsior-Henderson production was exported)
1937	11,674	6,030	
1938	9,994	3,651	
1939	8,355	8,883	
1940	10,855	10,923	

	READING-STANDARD MOTOR COMPANY	IVER JOHNSON MOTOR COMPANY*	SCHICKEL MOTOR COMPANY**
1920	1,854	345	226
1921	996	167	301
1922	454	67	71
1923	—	34	43
1924	189	27	39

    * Assembled to special order
    ** Assembled to special order

	NERACAR MOTOR COMPANY	CLEVELAND MOTOR COMPANY	CROCKER MOTORCYCLE COMPANY
1920	3,609	5,607	
1921	3,441	4,960	61 to 90 cu. in. V-twin machines assembled in irregular series from 1936 through 1941. A total of 65* V-twin units were produced.
1922	3,058	5,109	
1923	2,178	3,560	
1924	2,678	4,012	
1925	1,780	2,693	
1926	—*	541*	About 35 30.50 cu. in. speedway machines assembled in same period.
1927		171*	
1928		467**	
1929		451**	

Production ceased in U.S., but continued in England until 1928.

    * T-head Fowler designed four.
    ** 45 and 61 cu. in. F-headed models.

APPENDIX

The Emblem Motor Company produced about 2,500 lightweight 32 cu. in. V-twins per year between 1920 and 1925, but all were exported to Europe.

The Ace Motorcycle Company, whose products were based on the original Henderson designs, was organized in 1919 and about 6,000 units were assembled between 1920 and 1923, when financial difficulties intervened. The factory was moved from Philadelphia to Blossburg, Pennsylvania, under a reorganization where very limited production occurred. Financial difficulties again caused manufacture to cease. The remains of the company were sold to Michigan Motors in Detroit, but few if any units were assembled. The manufacturing rights were acquired by the Indian Motorcycle Company in 1927, and about three hundred units were assembled from original tooling. In 1928, the engine-gear units were fitted to a modified 101 Scout chassis, the name being changed from Indian-Ace to Indian Four. This model, with updates in 1936 and again in 1938 was in limited series production until March of 1942, sales being mainly to fleet orders from law enforcement organizations. About 9,400 "Fours" were produced by Indian, including Ace models from 1927 until the last days of manufacture.

* Later estimates dispute this figure

The Evans Powercycle, based on a heavyweight bicycle, was in very limited production after 1921, with the manufacturing rights being sold to a German form in the mid-1920's. It was powered by a two cycle engine with belt drive.

The Servicycle, a belt driven lightweight with a two cycle engine was in limited local production and sold locally in New Orleans prep from 1936 onward, the make not being marketed nationally until after WWII.

The Whizzer, a four cycle power attachment for bicycles was in limited production after 1939, with accelerated national sales after WWII.

The Marmon, also an attachment for bicycles, featuring a horizontally opposed

two cycle engine with belt drive, was marketed briefly, but never attained the popularity of the Whizzer.

Between 1920 and 1940, domestic motorcycle production averaged somewhat under 25,000 units per year. Of this number from 30% to 55% of domestic production was exported to various foreign countries.

Between 1945 and 1960, domestic motorcycle sales averaged about 60,000 units per year. Following the introduction of Japanese imports, sales doubled and redoubled until the peak sales figure of 1,450,000 units was reached in 1973. Due to various social and economic forces, sales saw a steady decline thereafter.

The sidecar became popular for transportation of the young family after 1912 when the fitting of change speed gears to twin cylinder machines made them practical. Most manufacturers offering sidecar machines supplied the chassis equipment, but usually had the bodies fabricated by specialist manufacturers. The B.F. Rogers Company of Chicago was a prominent supplier.

The Goulding concern of Saginaw, Michigan was in limited production of sidecars until the 1950's. Their products between the wars were mostly exported, as their lightweight models were more suited to 37 and 45 cubic inch domestic models because of their light weight and their patented suspension systems provided a more comfortable ride than did the versions produced by the larger factories.

Goulding also built rear car attachments suited for American big twins, these being in very limited production and were mostly seen on the export markets.

The following list of American-made motorcycles includes only those which were actually in production for a time and offered for commercial sale. It was prepared with the advice of the late Erwin Tragatsch, who spent a lifetime in compiling a comprehensive list of the world's motorcycles. While over two hundred makes have been listed, many were one-off prototypes by individuals that never went into production.

A.C.E. - A.C.E. Motor Corporation, Philadelphia, Pennsylvania. 1919 - 1929

A four cylinder machine designed by William Henderson in 1918 after he resigned from the Excelsior Motor Company who bought the manufacturing rights to his popular Henderson machine in 1917. After Henderson's death in 1922 the firm passed to the ownership of Michigan Motors in Detroit, with some machines being built in Blossburg, Pa. The ACE was purchased by the Indian Motorcycle Company in 1927 and became the Indian Four.

A.M.C. - Allied Motor Corporation, Chicago, Illinois. 1912 - 1915

A heavyweight V-twin machine built in small numbers with a swinging arm front fork which carried a trussed coil spring in its center.

AMERICAN - American Motorcycle Company, Chicago, Illinois. 1911-1914

Produced both 34 cubic inch side valve singles and 61 cubic inch twins in small numbers. A prototype horizontally opposed twin never went into production.

ARMAC - Armac Motor Company, St. Paul, Minnesota. 1904 - 1907

A conventional clip-on type machine fitted with a 2 1/2 horsepower DeDion type engine and flat belt drive. The company claimed to have originated twist-type engine controls. About 150 machines were produced and sold locally.

AUTO-BI - Buffalo Automobile Company, Buffalo, New York. 1902 - 1911

Originally a clip-on type pedal cycle machine developed in the pioneer era, the Auto-Bi later featured rearward facing 2 horsepower engines designed by an automotive engineer, E.R. Thomas, who later headed the Thomas Automobile Company.

AUTOPED - The Autoped Company of America, New York City. 1915 - 1921

A very small scooter with a 150 cc four stroke motor driving a roller on the front

386

APPENDIX

wheel, the operator riding in a standing position, control being effected by a moveable steering column. It was made in small numbers under license in both Great Britain and Czechoslovakia. It was never commercially successful.

BADGER - Badger Motor Company, Racine, Wisconsin. 1914 - 1915

An unorthodox design lightweight machine with a small 165 cc four stroke motor carried in the rear wheel. Only about 200 machines were produced.

BAYLEY-FLYER - Bayley-Flyer Autocycle Company, Chicago, Illinois. 1913 - 1917

An unorthodox design originally built in Portland, Oregon. It was equipped with a horizontally mounted twin cylinder engine with shaft drive and a hand start mechanism. Fewer than 300 machines were ever produced.

CLEVELAND - Cleveland Motorcycle Company, Cleveland, OH. 1915 - 1929

This company, which also built Cleveland and Chandler automobiles built the 13 cubic inch two stroke utility type machine that sold well both at home and abroad, totally about 5,000 units per year until 1925. In 1926, a T-head light four cylinder was offered. This was followed by a 750 cc four and a 1000 cc four in 1928 and 1929. Only a few of the latter were sold.

COLUMBIA - POPE Manufacturing Company, Westfield, MA. 1900 - 1905

This machine was the original Pope, with small de Dion type engines fitted to Columbia pedal cycles. It was redesigned as the Pope in 1908.

CROCKER - Crocker Motor Company, Los Angeles, California. 1934 - 1941

Albert G. Crocker built 500 cc speedway machines in 1934-1935 and in 1936 brought out his high performance V-twin that was custom built to various displacements from 61 through 90 cubic inches.

CURTISS - Glenn Curtiss Manufacturing Company, Hammondsport, New York. 1903 - 1908

This aviation pioneer built high performance motorcycles along with aircraft engines during the belt drive era. After concentrating on aircraft, the motorcycle design

rights were sold to the nearby Marvel Manufacturing Co.

CUSHMAN - Cushman Motor Company, Lincoln, Nebraska. 1939 -

Pioneer maker of small industrial engines who produced small scooters powered with their small air cooled models and fitted with centrifical clutches. The line included small industrial trucks.

CYCLE-SCOOT - Cycle Scoot, Inc., Rockford, Illinois. 1953 - 1955

A small scooter fitted with both Cushman and Briggs and Stratton engines of the industrial type. Only about 500 units were produced.

CYCLONE - Joerns Motor Company, St. Paul, Minnesota. 1913 - 1920

This company also built the Theim motorcycle, 1903-1914. The Cyclone which was designed by Andrew Strand was an advanced type of ohc 61 cubic inch motor that had numerous racing successes in 1914-1915. Ongoing financial problems caused intermittent production and only a few hundred were ever built.

DAYTON - Huffman Manufacturing Company, Elkhart, Indiana. 1911 - 1917

Dayton also built sewing machines as well as this high quality 61 cubic inch V-twin machine fitted with proprietary Spacke engines with bevel driven magnetos. Dayton offered an unorthodox machine with a small engine fitted in the front wheel in 1920 which was not successful.

DELUXE - Excelsior Cycle Company, Chicago, Illinois. 1912 - 1915

Conventional but high quality 61 cubic inch V-twins fitted with Spacke engines made by the F.W. Spacke Machine Company who also supplied engines for Eagle, Dayton, Sears and other manufacturers as well as units for cycle cars.

EMBLEM - Emblem Manufacturing Company, Angola, New York. 1909 - 1925

High quality belt driven single and later V-twin machines designed by William C. Schrack. His 1916 76 cubic inch V-twin was first U.S. big displacement machine. This was discontinued in favor of a lightweight V-twin produced for the export market after 1919.

FREYER & MILLER - Freyer & Miller Manufacturing Co., Cleveland, Ohio. 1902 - 1909

This make featured a large single cylinder engine mounted behind the saddle tube. It was one of the first makes to fit magneto ignition. It enjoyed only limited sales in its own locality.

GREYHOUND - Greyhound Motor Company, Chicago, Illinois. 1905 - 1907

A rather obscure make of conventional belt driven clip assembled from proprietary cycle parts and fitted with 2-1/2 hp Thor engines.

HARLEY-DAVIDSON - Harley-Davidson Motor Co., Milwaukee, Wisconsin. 1903 -

Originated by William S. Harley and Arthur Davidson, Harley-Davidsons were in limited production until 1907 when the firm incorporated and included William and Walter Davidson. The Company grew by continued refinancing of its operation and ultimately became the largest U.S. manufacturer after 1921, forging ahead of the long time leader, Indian. The Company was sold to American Foundry Company in 1969 and again to a private group in 1981.

HENDERSON - Henderson Motor Company, Detroit, Michigan. 1910 - 1931

William Henderson devised the first practical four cylinder machine in 1909 in Rochester, New York and later found capital to inaugurate manufacture in Detroit. The Company was sold to Exelsior in 1917 and Henderson resigned in 1919 to produce the ACE of similar design. Arthur O. Lemon carried on as designer for a time and the last models were designed by Arthur A. Constantine, 1929 - 1931. Production was terminated that last year.

HILAMAN - A.L. Hilaman Company, Moorestown, New Jersey. 1906 - 1912

First featuring motor powered bicycle types, the Hilaman in 1909 offered twins of conventional design. With limited facilities, the Company enjoyed sales only in its home locality.

IMPERIAL - Imperial Manufacturing Company, Pittsburgh, Pennsylvania. 1903 - 1907.

A motorized pedal cycle with a forward-

387

ly inclined 400 cc four stroke engine. It was marketed in small numbers through the Company's own retail outlets in Philadelphia and New York City.

INDIAN - The Indian Motorcycle Company, Springfield, Massachusetts. 1901 - 1953

Founded on the designs of Carl Oscar Hedstrom in partnership with George M. Hendee, proprietor of a bicycle factory, Indian soon established a position of leadership through Hendee's shrewd management and ultimately enjoyed world wide sales. The partners lost control of the company in 1913 when it oversold its stock to enable extended expansion. Hedstrom resigned in 1913, with Hendee leaving in 1916. Although the Company was preeminent until 1920, its ownership by non-motorcycling stock speculators was nearly its undoing. Rescued by E. Paul du Pont in 1930, it operated under his vast corporate umbrella until 1945. Later ownership under Ralph B. Rogers saw the development of untried designs which proved to be unreliable. Indian was ultimately controlled by the British Crockhouse concern which suppressed the American style machines in favor of its own imports.

IVER JOHNSON - Iver Johnson Arms and Cycle Works, Fitchburg, Massachusetts. 1907 - 1925

This well known fire arms manufacturer first diversified into bicycles and later motorcycles with some very well made single cylinder machines and in 1912 produced heavyweight V-twins. Of strictly utilitarian type, they were noted for their high quality and longevity rather than performance. Their highly advanced two speed 61 cubic inch twin of 1915 was available to special order as late as 1925. It was a favorite of rural mail carriers.

JEFFERSON - Waverly Manufacturing Company, Jefferson, Wisconsin. 1911 - 1914

This make featured well designed ohv single and V-twin engines designed by Perry E. Mack who briefly produced a limited number of similar machines under the name of P.E.M. A few engines for cycle cars were produced during 1913. Mack later was chief designer for the Briggs and Stratton Company until 1949.

KENZLER-WAVERLY - Kenzler-Waverly Motor Company, Cambridge,

Wisconsin. 1910 - 1914

K-W machines were a variation of Perry E. Mack's Jeffersons produced under a licensing agreement with that company. They also featured ohv models.

MARSH - Marsh Motorcycle Manufacturing Company, Brockton, Massachusetts. 1900 - 1905

Probably the first U.S. motor bicycle manufacturer, they first featured French Aster engines copied from early de Dion & Bouton products. This company was closely allied with the adjacent Orient-Aster assembly plant with later designed Heinrick Metz machines, using Marsh cycle components.

MARVEL - Marvel Motorcycle Company, Hammondsport, New York. 1910 - 1913

This company bought out the manufacturing rights to the Curtiss machines after the latter decided to concentrate on aircraft products. It did not survive past the belt drive era.

MIAMI - Miami Cycle and Manufacturing Company, Middletown, Ohio. 1905 - 1923

This branch of the Miami organization that produced the Flying Merkel also built the Miami, an ultralight pedal cycle type powered by a small rearward facing engine. In 1920 a motor wheel was added to the line. This was later built in limited numbers by the Hendee Manufacturing Company (Indian). All production declined after 1920.

The Flying Merkel motorcycles were developed by a talented engineer, Joseph Merkel, shortly after 1900, and soon evolved into designs more sophisticated than the primitive belt drivers. Both single and twin engines of advanced design were developed, making much use of ball bearings. Eclipse type clutches as well as two speed sliding gears were featured after 1910. Miami's in place bicycle outlets were used to advantage to promote motorcycle sales, and the Flying Merkel soon shared popularity with the so-called "second string" motorcycle manufacturers, Excelsior and Pope, ranking below the industry sales leaders, Harley-Davidson and Indian. Merkel racing machines were also widely seen in both board and dirt track competition. Between 1910 and 1915, nearly 10,000 units were sold through a string dealer network each year. Production came to a halt in 1915, the European war precluding the

import of ball bearings and other components, a fact that saw 85% of the domestic manufacturers to cease production.

MICHAELSON - Michaelson Motor Company, Minneapolis, Minnesota. 1910 - 1915

High quality products from this small firm included 500 cc single and 1000 cc ohv V-twins, the latter having two speed gears. Production was never large enough to enable the company to build up a national market.

MILITAIRE - The Militaire Auto Company, Cleveland, Ohio. 1911 - 1920

One of the most unorthodox designs ever built in the United States. Early single cylinder models featured a car type frame, wooden spoked artillery type wheels and folding auxiliary idler wheels along with car type steering wheels. In 1916 a four cylinder air cooled engine was optional. Technical difficulties saw numerous suspensions in production. Several sponsoring firms lost heavily in building these models, the last being built in Springfield adjacent to the Indian factory. An attempt was made to market the fours in Europe where it was known as the "Militor." In all, fewer than 500 units of all types were produced.

MINNEAPOLIS - Minneapolis Motorcycle Co., Minneapolis, Minnesota. 1910 - 1916

Conventional machines with side valve single cylinder engines incorporating a two speed gear box in unit with the engine and all chain drive. Also featured were three wheeled delivery vans of the forecar type. All were high quality products but the company was never large enough to capture a national market, although a few dealers handled the make in the Midwest.

M & M - American Motor Co., Brokton, Massachusetts. 1904 - 1909

The M & M was a powered pedal cycle typed that was associated with the Metz engine unit that also powered some models made by E. R. Thomas, Holley, Royal and Marsh. Its designer was also at one time associated with Orient.

MONARCH - Ives Motorcycle Co., Oswego, New York. 1912 - 1915

This make featured 500 cc single and 1000 cc V-twin models. The single had prima-

APPENDIX

ry chain and final belt drive, the twin an all chain drive. Fewer than 500 units were built and sold locally before the company suffered financial problems although the make had a reputation for high quality products.

MUSTANG - Gladden Products, Glendale, California. 1956 - 1958

A rather curious machine, part scooter, part motorcycle, with 20" disc wheels. It featured a side valve 200 cc engine of own manufacture with British made Albion gear boxes. It was also produced in limited numbers as a side car or three wheeled commercial model.

NERACAR - Neracar Corporation, Syracuse, New York. 1920 - 1926

The brain child of Carl A. Neracher, co-designer of the two stroke Cleveland, the Neracar was a car-like two wheeler with a very low channel type frame and featured center pivot steering. Its wide mudguards gave good weather protection and the machine was inherently very stable, attracting novice riders. It was also built coincidentally in England by the Sheffield-Simplex Group who fitted small Blackburne engines in place of the 13 cubic inch two stroke fitted in he U.S. models which was much like that of the Cleveland. The machine was marketed outside the usual motorcycle channels, advertisements being placed in farm and general circulation publications such as the National Geographic. Its initial strong financial support was withdrawn in the U.S. when a mass market was not forthcoming. The Neracar suffered from its unorthodox appearance. It fared better in England where it was favored by rural mail carriers, visiting nurses, and other commercial users requiring low cost transportation.

NEW ERA - New Era Autocycle Company, Dayton, Ohio. 1913 - 1914

An unorthodox machine with an open frame and the rearward engine under a form fitting seat, the fuel tank being over the rear wheel. Featured were all chain drive and a two speed gear box with foot change mechanism. In spite of a national advertising campaign fewer than 200 units were sold.

ORIENT - Waltham Manufacturing Company, Waltham, Massachusetts. 1900 - 1910

Probably the earliest pioneer U.S. manufacturer, the first Orients featured French Aster engines copied from current de Dion Boutons. It later fitted engines designed by H. Metz, and appears to have been a part of the Marsh-Metz group of small assemblers who also featured the Holley and Thomas products. The Orient was prominent in early competition events and was sold in California and the West Coast. It passed from the scene when more substantial designs with chain drive and change speed gears became mandatory, the makers apparently not wanting to seek additional capitalization.

PIERCE - Pierce Motorcycle Company, Buffalo, New York. 1909 - 1913

Motorcycles of superlative quality originated by Percy Pierce, the son of George N. Pierce who originated the Great Arrow (later Pierce Arrow) luxury motor cars. A 500 cc belt drive single was initially made, followed by a T-head four cylinder design with two speed gears and shaft drive designed by L. E. Fowler. With the single priced at $250 and the four at $400, far above the contemporary competition, sales were limited and the company folded after about 3,500 units were produced.

PIRATE - Milwaukee Motorcycle Company, Milwaukee, Wisconsin. 1913 - 1915

The Pirate was an inferior copy of the contemporary high quality Harley-Davidson models, and featured both single and V-twin types with all chain single geared drives. In spite of extravagant claims for performance and design, the make happily disappeared after some 250 units proved to be inferior products.

POPE - Pope Manufacturing Company, Hartford, Connecticut. 1901 - 1916

The Pope was one of the earliest motorcycles, originally powered as a "clip-on" with various versions of the de Dion-Bouton engines. These were marketed through the company's vast bicycle retailing empire. After 1910 the company expanded its forward product activities to offer improved products with all chain drive ohv engines, two speed gear boxes and rear springing. both single and V-twin models were offered. The 1913 and 1915 models were noted for both comfort and performance. After the death of Col. Pope in 1910, the company underwent managerial problems and production was suspended in the Fall of 1915. It was reinstituted in a small factory in Westfield, Mass. in 1916, activated by the assembly of the spare parts inventory of the preceding year. Production in 1917 was not

carried forward and the make disappeared from the market.

READING STANDARD - Reading Standard Company, Reading, Pennsylvania. 1903 - 1924.

A pioneer in the industry, Reading Standard initially produced clip on belt drivers and progressed to optional chain drive and two speed gears. Charles Gustafson designed side valve power plants with mechanical inlet valves copied from the French Peugiot in 1905, which were superior in power output over the then more common atmospheric type. The company specialized in V twins after 1915, first with an overhung reduction gear on the engine shaft and later fitted three speed sliding gear types. During 1919 and 1920 a few ohc racing engines were built based on Cyclone patents. The marketing of too many models within a limited production range caused the company's downfall in 1922. It was purchased by Cleveland in that year and an abortive attempt at revival caused the company to suspend production in 1924. Gustafson resigned to join Indian in 1909 and later designed the Powerplus models, still based on the Peugot type.

ROYAL - Royal Motor Works, New York City, New York. 1902 - 1904

A short-lived make based on the original Hedstrom designs that enjoyed a brief vogue in the New York area.

SALSBURY - Salsbury Manufacturing Company, Los Angeles, California. 1939 - 1953

Introduced a primitive type scooter in 1939 utilizing small Briggs and Stratton and Lauson engines. In 1946 a new streamlined high performance model was offered with a 300 cc two stroke engine of own manufacture with a patented flexible drive and centrifical clutch. In 1953 the company was purchased by Wayne Equipment Company, manufacturers of heavy industrial products. The Salsbury drive is still fitted to various of their products.

SCHICKEL - Schickel Motor Company, Stamford, Connecticut. 1912 - 1925

Norbert Schickel specialized in large capacity single cylinder two stroke designs. Produced 500 and 650 cc models with both single gears with Eclipse clutches and later two speed countershaft gears. As a subsidiary of the Stamford Foundry Company specializing in aluminum castings, the frame and fuel tanks were made of this material. Of limited performance, but possessed of good pulling power, most of the unites were used as commercial sidecars. The make enjoyed a limited market locally and was available to special order until 1924.

SEARS - Sears Roebuck & Company, Chicago, Illinois. 1912 - 1916

The Spacke concern which also supplied power plants to other makers as well as marketing the de Luxe make, supplied this famous mail order company with a similar model with the Sears nameplate. The were high quality machines, but built down to a price they were fitted with a single drive gear and countershaft clutches.

SHAW - Shaw Manufacturing Company, Galesburg, Kansas. 1918 - 1922

A power kit consisting of a small four cycle engine and belts and pulleys for converting a bicycle into a motorcycle. The company also built a toy type racing car with all parts supplied for home assembly. These products were phased out in favor of powered garden tractors.

STEFFEY - The Steffey Motorcycle and Manufacturing Co., Philadelphia, Pennsylvania. 1902 - 1907

A pioneer manufacturer, the Steffey was a conventional clip on machine of its day that featured both air- and water-cooled single cylinder engines with atmospheric inlet valves. Early examples were based on the Columbia utility pedal cycle.

SUPER-X - See Excelsior

THEIM - Joerns-Theim Motor Co., St. Paul, Minnesota. 1903 - 1914

The Theim was a pioneer make which carried on with more advanced designs after 1910. These were both single cylinder and V-twin types of good quality in limited production. In 1912 they introduced a two speed rear hub. The make was dropped in 1915 to enable the introduction of the very advanced design of the OHC Cyclone, which was in production for only a few months.

THOR - Aurora Automatic Machinery Company, Aurora, Illinois. 1903 - 1916

This large diverse manufacturing and foundry company built proprietory engines based on Hedstrom designs, supplying both Indian and later themselves as well as other obscure motorcycle assemblers. They later developed their own line of single cylinder and V-twin machines of high quality and advanced design. William Ottaway developed their competition machines after 1909 and Thors were once a noted contender on both board and dirt tracks. Ottaway left the firm to join Harley-Davidson in 1913 and thereafter Thor's fortunes declined. Motorcycles were dropped in 1915 to enable the company to concentrate on their extensive home appliance and machine tool business.

TIGER - The Tiger Autobike Company, Chicago, Illinois. 1914 - 1916

The Tiger was a lightweight fitted with a 250 cc Fredrickson engine and a direct belt drive. It weighted 112-1/2 lbs and sold for $112.50. Small production never allowed for a national market and the few hundred made were sold locally.

TRIBUNE - A pioneer make of assembled machine of then conventional belt drive type that fitted first imported French aster and later Hedstrom types made by Thor.

WHIZZER - Whizzer International, Inc., Pontiac, Michigan. 1947 - 1954

An engine and belt drive assembly designed for converting roadster pedal cycles. The low speed side valve engine was well designed and of commendable longevity. Its one time popularity cause the Schwinn concern to offer a special bicycle with spring forks to accommodate it. With sales oriented toward young riders, a series of accidents caused various states to raise the age for vehicular operation from 14 to 16 or 18 which eventually killed its market. The outfits were later manufactured in Holland where bicycling was historically most popular.

YALE - Consolidated Manufacturing Company, Toledo, Ohio. 1902 - 1915

A pioneer in the industry, the Yale developed soundly designed single cylinder and later V-twin types after 1910. They then concentrated on their 1000 cc twin fitted with a two speed gear box that was from 1913 through 1915 a sales leader for $260.

THE CYCLECAR IN AMERICA

Transportation historians are in disagreement whether the cyclecar should be classified with motorcycles or automobiles. But as early motorcycle manufacturers accepted the cyclecar as a variant, the author follows this alternative.

As soon as the motor bicycle was technically practical, experimenters at once began to consider a four wheeled version as an economical alternative to the then high priced automobiles. The earliest known example in the U.S. was said to be the Orient Buckboard, prototypes of which were built by the Orient Bicycle factory in Waltham, Massachusetts. It was said to have consisted of a flexible platform body made of thin hardwood battens supported by four heavy duty bicycle wheels, a single cylinder air cooled de Dion type engine being mounted behind the seat that drove one rear wheel via a belt. There is not record that it ever achieved commercial success, and no examples are known to survive, although a few were built between 1905 and 1909.

Serious production of cyclecars occurred in Europe. M. George Bourbeau in Paris built a prototype of such vehicle in 1908. It consisted of a narrow ladder-like frame built of hardwood, with a motorcycle engine in front that activated belt drives to the rear wheels through a friction drive attached to a countershaft that carried the pulleys. With a narrow track of 36", the driver and passenger were carried in tandem seating, the former being in the rear. For simplicity, clutch action was effected by a movable rear axle that either tightened or loosened the belts, and the steering was by a central pivot through the front axle, much like a child's coaster wagon, movement being controlled by a wire and bobbin system attached to the steering column. Commercial production was inaugurated in 1910, with other concerns coming into the field in both Europe and Great Britain, most of whom copied Bourbeau's basic format. The cyclecar enjoyed some popularity in these areas before World War I due mainly to the presence of suitably surfaced roads.

The idea was not slow in being taken up in the U.S., stimulated by the then growing popularity of the motorcycle, and during the winter of 1912-1913 numerous experimenters were building prototypes. G. Marshall Naul, Bud Ekins, and F.J. Sedgewick, who later

APPENDIX

extensively researched the subject have estimated that at least three hundred different prototypes were built by either individuals or existing commercial firms.

A national organization was actually suggested in the Fall of 1913 by William B. Stout, an automotive and aeronautical engineer, and was formally organized in March, 1914, utilizing the motorcycle trade magazines as a means of correspondence and the exchange of information. The cyclecar was officially designated as a vehicle having an engine of less than 70 cubic inch and a gross weight of under 750 pounds. Suggested prices were fixed at $250 for a single passenger model, and not over $300 for two passenger types.

The cyclecar was a logical attempt to provide basic economical transportation comparable to that offered by the motorcycle but featuring lateral stability and hopefully some weather protection as well. It was intended to create a low cost alternative to the growing number of automobiles which at that point in time were far too expensive for the average working man's budget. Even the Model T Ford in 1910 being priced at $850.

As attractive as the cyclecar appeared in theory, any realities of being successful were stacked against it. Its ultralight construction mitigated against its durability, a few dozen miles of travel over roughish roads could cause a model to literally disintegrate. Then as a low powered vehicle it had difficulties in negotiating the unpaved rural roads of the period which in rainy weather required substantial power for travel, not to mention the mud clogging the belt drives which most had affected for economical manufacture. Most examples were fitted with either 36" or 42" wheel tracks, making the negotiation of the rutted country roads difficult which accommodated the 56-1/2" railroad gauge wagon tracks universally in use, that had been established during the Civil War.

Henry Ford, who was intending to put the world on wheels for the lowest possible costs was keeping a close watch on the Cyclecar boom. In 1912 his Model T touring car and roadster were priced at $590 and $570. By 1915, his increased production had lowered these figures to $460 and $440 respectively. While these prices were marginally above that of the average $375 cost of a cyclecar, the advantages of buying the former were so great the latter lost its potential market before its industry could get off the ground. Sales fell to the point that in February

of 1915, the Cycle Cars National Association announced in its monthly newsletter that it was disbanding. William B. Stout, who had been its principal organizer a d had served as its national Secretary later had a hand in designing the famous Ford Trimotor, the country's initial prime passenger and freight carrying airplane, and the Scarab automobile, an unconventional design that never caught on commercially.

The CCNA listed 162 firms that had announced a cyclecar production program during the Spring of 1914. The majority of these were located east of the Mississippi, the reason probably being that the roads of this area were more suited for motoring than the vast distances and the then undeveloped highways of the west. Most of these firms were already engaged in some sort of manufacture, many being related to the automotive industry. In addition there were probably around 150 other individuals who had expressed intention of entering the field. The picture is somewhat confusing when the large number of advertisements in both motorcycle and automotive trade magazines announcing new arrivals to the field. It was noted that many of these consisted of having built a prototype or two and then resorted to an advertised announcement in order to test the response to a projected marketing program. In most cases these operations were too lightly financed to weather an initial development period.

The basic weaknesses of the cyclecar at once became painfully apparent. Once Paul E. Hawkins, who had launched the Acme and Xenia makes from a small plant in Xenia, Ohio frankly stated in an article in "Motor Age" that after a few units had been sold the cyclecar market had dried up, this in December of 1914. Others in the game had stated privately that it was difficult to sell a prospect when a model sold six months previously had already disintegrated.

One problem facing the potential manufacturers was that of obtaining power plants. The larger manufacturers, such as Excelsior, Harley-Davidson, and Indian would not divert engines from their already committed production schedules. A proprietary manufacturer of engines, the Spacke concern, who not only built a machine under their own name, but also supplied De Luxe, Dayton, Sears-Roebuck and a few others could and did supply such to the cyclecar trade, as did Perry E. Mack. But trade discounts were not offered in

the purchase of limited numbers of units to individual builders.

The most successful model was the Imp, offered by the McIntyre Motor Company of Auburn, Indiana, who already made automotive components. The Imp, sometimes marketed as the McIntyre, was typical in having a Spacke engine, friction type clutch, and final belt drive, and like most was a narrow track design with tandem seating. About four hundred units were sold between the Fall of 1913 and the Spring of 1915 when the market finally collapsed.

Scripps Booth, of Detroit, also an automotive component manufacturer, built a similar model which sold in like numbers, and in 1915 was redesigned as a light automobile with a four cylinder water cooled engine, sliding gear transmission, and a differential rear axle. The firm was sold to General Motors in 1918, and portions of Scripps Booth design was incorporated in the newly introduced Chevrolet 490 model which offered competition to Ford's Model T.

A few of the larger volume cyclecar producers followed a similar course in changing over to light cars, but by 1920 most had been overwhelmed by the now massive Model T production which undercut them severely in retail price.

While a few cyclecar manufacturers survived in Great Britain and Europe after World War I, the American market was totally defunct by the Spring of 1915, the concept having proved woefully unsuited to both design criteria, the road system, and Henry Ford's competition.

THE A.M.A CONGRESS

It was October 28th, 1968, when the American Motorcycle Association took a giant step, moving from autocratic to reasonably democratic. On that day, an A.M.A. Congress representing all segments of the sport of motorcycling, replaced the old Competition Committee as the rule making body for A.M.A sportsman and professional events.

The Congress originally promulgated professional rules as well as sportsman, and professional racers were also elected to the Congress by their peers.

The requirements for promoting and marketing professional motorcycle racing events became too complex to be handled on a day-to-day basis by the Congress.

In 1974, Professional Racing was trans-

391

ferred from the Congress to A.M.A. headquarters, and was guided by the Director of Professional Racing. Each segment of Professional Racing is coordinated by a Manager who reports to the Director.

So that professional racing rules could remain fair and equitable, advisory committees comprised of riders, tuners, promoters, and others concerned with racing, work with A.M.A. staff members for the advancement of the sports.

BACK TO THE DINOSAUR DAYS

The scenario leading to creation of a more democratic A.M.A. Congress during the 1960's was filled with an abundance of political maneuvering, industry intrigue and frustration. The A.M.A. Board of Trustees was often divided on this subject, due to "fear of change", combined with empathy for the "old Competition Committee."

A few Competition Committee members, and a large number of professional racers were less than happy with some of the Class "C" competition rules. As a result of this unrest, Pete Colman envisioned the creation of a more democratic "Competition Congress" to replace the Competition Committee.

FOREFATHERS OF THE A.M.A. COMPETITION CONGRESS

History tells us that the forefathers of the A.M.A. Competition Congress were E.W. "Pete" Colman, Frank Heacox, Wilbur Cedar and Bill Kennedy.

Colman was Vice President/General Manager of BSA Motorcycles-Western and VP of the Western Triumph distributor Johnson Motors, Inc. In 1966, he was promoted to VP/GM of both companies, following the untimely death of Wilbur Ceder. Colman was a former world class speedway star and a 4-year member of the A.M.A. Competition Committee. His corporate responsibilities for the Triumph/BSA group included the creation of Team Triumph and Team BSA, which successfully campaigned for the Grand National Championship in 1970 and 1971. In 1970, he was elected President and Board Chairman of the fledgling Motorcycle Industry Council (MIC), and re-elected in 1971. He was also a founding member of the Motorcycle Safety Foundation (MSF).

Frank Heacox was Vice President/General Manager of Bell Toptex Helmets, with a long background as a motor-cycle enthusiast and Southern California enduro rider. In 1968 Heacox was elected VP of the A.M.A., and in early 1970 he served as interim President of the MIC.

Wilbur Ceder was President of Johnson Motors, Inc., and President of BSA Motorcycles-Western. He had been a senior executive of Johnson Motors since 1939.

William E. Kennedy represented Rex Chainbelt Company on the A.M.A. Board, and served as a three term President of the A.M.A. He was also elected President of the MS&ATA and was subsequently elected President of the Motorcycle Industry Council (MIC).

CREATION OF THE COMPETITION CONGRESS

Colman started his drive to create the Congress on a cold February night in Chicago - the night before the 1966 Annual Meeting of the A.M.A. Board of Trustees. Little did he realize that he was on the brink of a battle that would take nearly three years, and generate long lasting hostility towards Colman and other perpetrators of a Congress. On that night, Colman launched a "trial balloon" and tested his plans for a Congress during dinner with A.M.A. President Bill Kennedy.

Kennedy listened while Colman outlined the need for a new and democratic organization. Pete told Kennedy that he had discussed the plan with his boss, Wilbur Ceder, and had gained Ceder's full support. He also told Kennedy that plan for an A.M.A. Congress had been discussed several times with Frank Heacox, and included Heacox's input and support.

Colman then asked Kennedy if he should make a proposal for creation of an A.M.A. Congress to the A.M.A. Board of Trustees. Kennedy noted that Ceder, Heacox and Colman all represented Class "A" member companies of the A.M.A., and, as members of the Board of Trustees, such a proposal would certainly be in order.

At the A.M.A. Trustees meeting the next day, Colman was ready to present his proposed plan. Unfortunately, Chairman Lin Kuchler (Executive Director of the A.M.A.) failed to give Colman the floor to make his proposal, allegedly under orders from Milwaukee.

During a short recess of the Board, President Kennedy advised Colman and Ceder that word of the proposed Congress had leaked, and the opposition was so strong that Colman was not likely to have an opportunity to speak. Kennedy suggested that Colman ask to be excused early to catch his flight back to San Francisco. He believed that following Pete's departure, Wilbur Ceder could propose the formation of an A.M.A. Competition Congress.

According to the official minutes of that meeting, Ceder did make the proposal. It was quickly seconded by Walter Davidson, with an amendment to put the plan into a study committee - an old ploy often used in meetings to "bury a proposal." Pete's plan had been given a "death sentence" - or so the opposition thought.

President Kennedy named Bill Harley (a Harley-Davidson VP) as Chairman of the A.M.A. Congress Study Committee. He also appointed Colman and Heacox to the committee, and instructed them to present their findings at the next Board meeting scheduled for February 8, 1967. The plan to form a Congress now faced a one year delay - at best.

While preparing for the 1967 meeting, Colman and Heacox met several times to review and finalize plans for the Congress. They hoped that the Board would approve the plan, following discussion of the details.

Study Committee Chairman, Bill Harley, did not schedule a meeting with Colman and Heacox, and when asked at the 1967 Board meeting to give his report, he stated that the committee "did not have time to meet", so there was nothing to report.

Colman quickly asked for a recess so the study committee could meet. He explained that he and Heacox had developed a discussion paper. He believed the Study Committee could make an official report to the Board following a short recess. The chair granted Pete's request.

A news report of that historic meeting appeared in the April 1967 edition of American Motorcycling. It stated in part..."The Board of Trustees listened and later joined into a discussion of a study committee's proposed Motorcycle Congress...those who criticize the present system say it is not truly democratic in as much as members remain on the Competition Committee year after year" ...the study committee was appointed by Association President William Kennedy, many months before this annual meeting, "...the present members of the study group are: William Harley, Chairman; W.T. Berry, Jr.; E.W. (Pete) Colman; and new members: Robert B. Hicks

APPENDIX

and Frank Heacox. There have been others on the committee in the past... the committee will meet again on May 20."

"GREEN LIGHT GIVEN TO AMA STUDY COMMITTEE."

That bold headline appeared in the June 1967 edition of AM. The article stated in part, "American Motorcycle Association Executive Director, William T. Berry, Jr., announced the association's Executive Committee has given a go-ahead on further development of a Competition Congress idea after hearing a report from a five man study group on their recommendations to revise the present Competition Committee."

The Executive Committee scheduled the inaugural meeting of the new AMA Competition Congress for October 28-30, 1968, at Columbus, Ohio. Bill Bagnall was elected AMA President on February 12, 1968, and presided over the first annual meeting of the Congress.

Prior to formation of the Competition Congress, members of the Competition Committee were appointed by the Executive Director (or Executive Secretary) of the A.M.A. In 1966 and 1967, the membership also included two professional competition riders who were elected by their peers, and two staff members from the Columbus headquarters of the American Motorcycle Association.

The final meeting of the Competition Committee convened on October 30th, 1967. Members in attendance were: Leonard Andres, Al Arnold, W.T. Berry, Jr. (Executive Director of the A.M.A. and Chairman of the Competition Committee), Walt Brown, Rabun Chambles, John Ciccarelli, Rod Coastes, E.W. Pete Colman, Walter C. Davidson, William G. Davidson, Jim Davis, John Esler, Earl Flanders, Horace Fritz, Jules Horky (A.M.A.), Oscar C. Lenz, Dick Mann (competition rider), R.H. O'Brien, Dudley Perkins, Phil Peterson, Earl Robinson, Bruce Walters, Ewin Warmack, Earl Widman (competition rider) and Peter W. Zepka.

The Committee members each had long and outstanding backgrounds in various types of A.M.A. competition and attempted to pass competition rules in a democratic manner. Unfortunately, Japanese brands had no representation on the committee, and, the voting on Class "C" rules was often slanted to favor Harley-Davidson dirt-trackers.

Had it not been for Pete Colman's dream and his tenacity to follow through...the strong

cooperation of Bill Kennedy, Frank Heacox and Wilbur Ceder...the contributions from many AMA trustees...and the affirmative vote by the AMA Board; the 25th Annual Meeting of the AMA Congress might never have been held in 1993!

E.W. "Pete" Colman
Joseph Hope

CREATION OF THE MOTORCYCLE INDUSTRY COUNCIL, INC.

During the 1960's, the fate of the American motorcycle industry was guided by the Motorcycle & Allied Trades Association (M&ATA) and the American Motorcycle Association (AMA). The merger of the M&ATA with the Scooter Association did little to change the course, except the name was changed to Motorcycle, Scooter & Allied Trades Association (MS&ATA).

The MS&ATA and the AMA had the same membership roster, the same Board of Trustees and corporate officers. As the meetings of both organizations were conducted in the same room, it was often difficult to ascertain which meeting was in session.

Although the membership included British and European motorcycle manufacturers, the voting strength was in the hands of Harley-Davidson and Allied Trade members who were suppliers to Harley-Davidson.

Honda's application for membership had reputedly been "blackballed" by at least one member of the membership committee, and membership applications from other Japanese manufacturers were unofficially discouraged.

By 1967, the MS&ATA claimed to represent the industry, even though the members companies were selling less than 10% of the motorcycles. Some of the members, including those' from the BSA and Triumph felt that an organization representing 100% of the motorcycle brands and aftermarket companies was needed.

1968

In early 1968, a new motorcycle trade association was formed in Souther California by Joe Hope, Sales Manager for BSA Motorcycles-Western, Inc., Matt Matsuoka, American Honda Motors Corp., and Jimmy Jingu, Yamaha Motors Corp. The new association was originally named the Southern California Motorcycle Safety Council, but shortly thereafter was renamed the California Motorcycle Safety Council (CMSC).

Joe Hope acted as president of the

CMSC, and his participation in the CMSC was encouraged by his boss, E.W. "Pete" Colman (Vice President/General Manager of BSA Motorcycles-Western).

The membership grew with the addition of U.S. Suzuki, Kawasaki Motors Corp., and Johnson Motors, Inc., (Western Triumph distributors). John Marin, Sports Illustrated joined as an associate member. Monthly dues were $100, providing the CMSC with an annual budget of $7200.

1969

In February 1969, Hope and Matsuoka organized an industry dinner. The location was the Los Angeles Athletic Club, made possible by John Marin's LAAC membership. The LAAC was in the Union Bank Building at Wilshire and Western in Los Angeles, and the industry function was held in the top floor dining room.

84 industry leaders attended the CMSC dinner, (a no host affair) and for the first time in industry history, the leaders of Japanese, British, and European motorcycle companies in the USA dined together. There was no "head table", and a mixture of guests from the various manufacturers and American aftermarket companies were assigned seats at "round" tables.

The guest list read like "Who's Who in the Motorcycle Industry." It included the senior executives from Honda, Yamaha, Suzuki, Kawasaki, BSA and Triumph. Attending were H. Nakamura, VP and General Manager of American Honda; H. Kawashima, VP and General Manager of Yamaha Corporation; K. Iizuka, Executive Sales VP of U.S. Suzuki; George Hamawaki, Executive VP of American Kawasake; Don J. Brown, VP and General Manager BSA Incorporated; Earl Miller, VP and General Manager of the Triumph Corporation (Eastern Triumph); and E.W. "Pete" Colman, VP and General Manager of BSA Motorcycles-Western and Johnson Motors, Inc. (Western Triumph).

The dinner guests also included magazine publishers and other important suppliers of motorcycle industry goods and services.

CMSC President, Joe Hope was master of ceremonies and keynote speaker. Joe outlined the progress made by the CMSC since its inception. Hope's speech included this statement, "It is absolutely essential for any major industry to have a well-organized, cohesive group that is able to speak for that

APPENDIX

industry and to act constructively in cooperation with other segments of our society..."

Joe Hope and E.W. Pete Colman were quietly working behind the scenes to bring about a merger of the CMSC with its diverse membership, and the MS&ATA.

At board meetings of the MS&ATA during the 1968 and early 1969, President Bill Kennedy called on Colman to update the members on the activities of the CMSC.

Ivan Wager, Editor of Cycle World was elected President of the MS&ATA at the 1969 Annual Meeting. At a subsequent meeting held in Loudon, New Hampshire, the subject of a merger with the "California Association" was discussed with favorable results.

On October 9, 1969, the final meeting of the CMSC membership was held at the International Hotel in Marina Del Rey, California, and the plan for a possible merger was approved. Joe Hope was given the green light to discuss the CMSC's merger hopes with MS&ATA president, Ivan Wagar.

The merger of the CMSC and the MS&ATA took place at the International Hotel on November 20, 1969. Shades of David and Goliath! The tiny CMSC won a majority of the seats in the Executive Committee of the resulting organization. The name was changed to the "Motorcycle Industry Council" (MIC), and the assets of the old MS&ATA (including a large bank account and interest bearing investments) provided the new MIC with reasonable funding to accomplish its first year's goals.

The founding board of directors elected Joe Hope (Sales Manager for BSA Motorcycles-Western) President, Frank Heacox, (VP/GM of Bell Helmets) Vice President, Paul McCrillis, (former Executive Secretary of the MS&ATA) Secretary and John Harley, (Harley Davidson) Treasurer. These were interim appointments. It was agreed that new officers would be elected at the first annual meeting of the MIC to be held in Washington, DC in March of 1970. It was also agreed that the MIC headquarters be moved to Washington.

The BSA and Triumph distribution companies in America, headed by Pete Colman, Don Brown and Earl Miller were merged into a new corporation known as the Birmingham Small Arms Company Incorporated, with Peter Thornton as President.

Joe Hope was transferred to the group's corporate headquarters in Verona, New Jersey as PR Manager. Earl Miller became VP of

Operations and maintained his office at the Old Triumph Corporation in Baltimore.

Don J. Brown was appointed Sales VP for BSA, and moved from Nutley to Verona. E.W. Pete Colman was appointed Engineering VP and Director of Racing, and organized the BSA and Triumph Technical Center in Duarte, California (the former distribution facility for BSA-Western and Johnson Motors).

Hope was forced to resign as president of the MIC because Norton Villiers was not an MIC member. MIC VP Frank Heacox filled the vacancy as MIC president until the forthcoming Annual meeting. John Harley's election as Treasurer was to offer token representation to Milwaukee, even though Harley-Davidson did not approve of the changes in organizational direction.

1970

At the annual meeting in March, 1970, Heacox told the MIC Board of Directors that he was unable to continue as president. He then nominated E.W. "Pete" Colman as his replacement.

Colman won the election as President of the MIC and Chairman of the Board, by unanimous acclimation. Matt Matsuoka was elected Vice President, John Harley was elected Treasurer and Paul McCrillis was named Executive Director.

President Colman's administration faced many problems that needed immediate attention. Fortunately, Colman was able to spend the necessary time away from his Duarte office to move assets of the MS&ATA from Columbus, Ohio to Washington, DC and to organize the MIC Headquarters offices on Connecticut Avenue.

Paul McCrillis informed Colman that he didn't want to reside in Washington and could not continue as Executive Director. Colman and Dick Orth (Sales VP of US Suzuki) started a search for a replacement for McCrillis. They finally located a candidate in Los Angeles (a motorcycle riding politician who was also a Los Angeles City Councilman under Mayor Yorty). His name was Jim Potter. During interviews with Potter, Colman and Orth learned that Potter was well connected in Washington, DC and that he was L.A.'s representative at the Federal level. They recommended the employment of Potter as Executive Director, and Potter's appointment was subsequently confirmed by the MIC Directors.

The MIC also needed a Washington-

based attorney to look after legal affairs of the association and to act as parliamentarian at all board meetings. Colman and Potter located a young attorney named Stewart Ross, and Ross was retained as legal advisor, (a position still held by Ross when this history was written).

Another important member of the MIC staff was employed after interviews by Potter and Colman. His name is Mel Stahl. At this writing, Stahl is Vice President of the MIC, and heads the DC office as legislative Analyst.

The MIC needed to develop a working relationship with the National Highway Traffic Safety Administration, (the government organization charged with promulgation of standards affecting motorcycle safety). Stahl and Colman had their work cut out for them. They gained appointments with various members of the NHTSA, including Doug Toms, NHTSA Administrator and one of President Nixon's lower Cabinet members.

The industry worked hand-in-hand with the NHTSA. The MIC helped to educate employees of NHTSA about motorcycles. Nearly 200 attended class room studies about motorcycles (conducted by employees of the various motorcycle manufacturers). Following the classroom presentations, the NHTSA employees attended rider training classes conducted by the MIC at Bolling Field.

1971

On one occasion, Doug Toms and his son rode motorcycles in a special "Executive Class" at the National Championship Enduro in Talladega, Alabama - along with Frank Heacox, Pete Colman and other industry executives.

Pete Colman was re-elected as President and Chairman at the 1971 Annual Meeting of the MIC. Willie Tokishi (Honda) replaced Matsuoka as Vice President. Dick Orth continued to work hard for the MIC< and coordinated various PR campaigns, such as the successful "<SOUND = >GROUND", which was covered by public service radio announcements and billboards.

Another giant step by the Colman Administration was a decision by the directors to establish "association memberships" in the MIC for motorcycle dealers.

This membership drive was coordinated by Don Graves (Kawasaki). The first membership meeting was conducted in Houston, Texas, following the National Championships at the Astrodome. At this membership meeting, Graves, Colman and other MIC members convinced most of the dealers in attendance to sign up as Associate Members. As a result of this successful membership drive, it was agreed that if some "California prune-pickers (as called by Texans) could convince Texas dealers to join - they could sign-up Associate members in every State."

Colman recalls another interesting "happening" during the races at the Astrodome. Top executives from the BSA/Triumph Group had invited Mr. Honda and a group of top management from American Honda to view the races with them in Judge Hofheintz's suite, high above the action in the Astrodome.

Colman was introduced to Mr. Honda, and shortly thereafter, Colman was asked if he could bring Dick Mann up to the suite so Mr. Honda could personally congratulate Dick for winning the Daytona 200 miler on a 750 Honda. Pete sent a message back to Mr. Honda that this was a National Championship event, and that Mann was now riding a BSA. He said he couldn't take Mann away from the pits at this crucial time to meet Mr. Honda.

The messenger soon returned with another request from Mr. Honda: "Would Mr. Colman please escort Mr. Honda to the pits and introduce him to Dick Mann?"

Colman agreed that he would, so off went the entourage of Honda, BSA and Triumph executives - down the elevator and to the pits - with Pete Colman and Mr. Honda leading this strange group of people - dressed in business suits and ties - into the pits.

The racers, mechanics and officials were surprised to learn that Mr. Honda (in person) was bowing and shaking hands with Dick Mann.

1972

The membership program was so successful that nearly 3200 dealers became Associate Members of the MIC, and dealers were permitted to nominate their representatives as members of the MIC Board of Directors.

At that point in time, the Motorcycle Industry Council had fulfilled its by-laws - to represent the best interests of the motorcycle industry. This addition of dealer members provided the MIC with a grass-roots organization of employers, property owners and taxpayers in nearly every community - and in every State.

Dealers were encouraged to organize in every state, and many adopted "MIC" as a

part of their association name, (like the California Motorcycle Industry Council, with dealer Ted Evans as its President).

At the end of Colman's second term as MIC President, an industry banquet was held at the Washington Hilton, with Pete Colman as the Guest of Honor. Nearly 200 guests were in attendance, including Congressmen, Senators, and members of the NHTSA as well as MIC members.

The Master of Ceremonies was James Drury, TV's Virginian and Malcolm Forbes was the Keynote Speaker. Following Forbes' interesting talk about his motorcycle riding adventures, his motorcycle dealership (Sleger Forbes) and his short political life where he "lost the election as Governor of New Jersey by a landslide:, a final surprise awaited Colman.

Pete was called to the podium, where a large oil painting depicting his "life story to date" was unveiled and presented by Jim Potter in appreciation of Colman's work for the motorcycle industry.

At the 1972 Annual Meeting of the MIC, Tom Heininger, co-owner of the aftermarket company, Webco, was elected President.

1973

At the end of another successful year, the MIC was preparing for the 1973 Annual Meeting. Suddenly, rumors were circulating to the effect the John Harley was going to campaign for the post of MIC President. Although board members generally believed that it was time for a Harley-Davidson representative to be elected President, most disagreed that John Harley was the right person for the job, noting his problem with alcoholism.

Pete Colman thought that Bill Kennedy would be the best alternative to John Harley. Kennedy had already served as President of the AMA and the M&ATA. He was a close personal friend of John Harley, and should be acceptable to Harley-Davidson. Pete called Kennedy and after explaining the problem, asked Kennedy if he would accept the nomination for President, and compete with his friend John. Bill wanted time to think it over, and finally agreed to run. Colman assured him that he would work hard to gain the support of other directors.

The plan worked. Bill Kennedy was elected President and led the MIC through another year of progress.

During the fall of 1973, the Motorcycle Safety Foundation was spun-off from the

MIC, became a separate organization and moved its headquarters. The MSF directors approved the appointment of Dr. Charles Hartman as Executive Director, and the MSF increased the scope of the MSF under Hartman's direction.

Towards the end of 1973, Dennis Poore made a corporate raid on the Birmingham Small Arms Company Limited in England. The company had already ceased production of BSA Motorcycles, leaving Triumph as the last remaining motorcycle company in the group.

Poore's new British company operated under the name of Norton Villers Triumph (NVT). However, shortly after Poore's takeover, the employees at the Triumph Engineering Company Limited in Allesley, England, shut the factory doors and went on strike.

Colman arrived in England with 400 American dealers on two stretched DC8s. At a banquet on the first night in London, the dealers were disappointed to learn that they would not be able to visit the factory because of the strike.

1974

The remaining Triumph organization in U.S.A. (owned by Dennis Poore's NVT) was now combined with Norton, and were to distribute Triumph and Norton from the Duarte, California facility. The new corporate President was Dr. Felix Kalinski.

On February 1st, Kalinski returned to his office following a trip to London, only to learn that "his resignation had been accepted" by Dennis Poore. He told his Vice President, Pete Colman, what had happened, advising Colman to be prepared - because they swung the axe early in the morning.

As predicted, Colman was asked to "take early retirement", putting an end to Colman's 26 years plus one day of association with Triumph motorcycles.

At the 1974 Annual Meeting of the MIC, Honda's Matt Matsuoka was elected President.

Matsuoka's administration made two substantial changes in the operation of the motorcycle trade association. First, the directors voted to eliminate the Associate Membership provisions that permitted dealer members.

The dues collected from dealers was turned over to each dealers State Association.

During another board meeting, the directors voted to move the MIC headquarters to Southern California, and, to employ a long

APPENDIX

term corporate President to run the MIC, rather than elect one of the directors to serve as President for a one year.

In late November, application for the position of President were accepted from Alan Isley of Kawasaki and Pete Colman, now an independent industry consultant.

Both candidates campaigned hard for support from the MIC membership. Then, at the last minute, Everett Brashear, a former sales representative for Triumph, also became a candidate. It appeared to some industry members that Brashear's entry into the race was planned to take votes from Colman. When the votes were counted, Alan Isley was the MIC President, defeating Colman by one.

1975

In February 1975, Isley opened a new headquarters office for the MIC in Costa Mesa, California. Some of the old MIC staff moved to California, while Mel Stahl remained at the old location in Washington.

Isley quickly expanded the effectiveness of the MIC to meet the ever changing needs of the industry. In 1983, Isley was also named President of the Motorcycle Safety Foundation (MSF) and the Specialty Vehicle Institute of America (SCIA). These two associations also operated out of the Costa Mesa headquarters.

The ATV Safety Institute (ATVSI) was added to Isley's responsibilities in 1988, and the requirement for additional space brought about a move to a new and larger facility in Irvine, California.

MOTORCYCLE INDUSTRY COUNCIL, INC., ITS FUNCTION, AIMS, AND PURPOSES

Reprinted from the MIC Statistical Annual

Motorcycling continues to be a popular recreational activity and a source of transportation. An estimated 31 million people operated a motorcycle, scooter, or ATV in the past year, which is comparable to participation in other recreational activities such as camping (42 million), fishing (40 million), and golf (23 million). Motorcycles, scooters, and ATVs are also used by industry and government agencies in such varied applications as agriculture, law enforcement and land resource management.

There are currently about 7.3 million motorcycles, scooters, and ATVs operating in the U.S. Motorcycles and scooters represent over two thirds (69%) of the vehicle population while three and four-wheeled all-terrain vehicles (ATVs) make up the remaining one third (31%). The motorcycle industry generated about 7.0 billion dollars in consumer sales and services, state taxes, and licensing fees in 1990.

Approximately 462,000 motorcycles, scooters, and ATVs were sold new in 1990 at an estimated value of 1.8 billion dollars. Off-highway motorcycles and ATVs accounted for half (50%) of total retail sales while on-highway motorcycles and scooters made up the remaining 50%. Six major distributors accounted for roughly 99% of the annual motorcycle, scooter, and ATV retail sales.

In 1990 the motorcycle industry supported over 9,600 retail outlets selling either new vehicles or specializing in motorcycle related services, parts, and accessories. These outlets employed over 46,000 people at an estimated annual payroll of $756 million. In the last several years many motorcycle retailers have expanded their business to include other products such as snowmobiles, personal watercraft, or other power products.

In 1987 the MIC launched a long term public awareness campaign, "Discover Today's Motorcycling" to stimulate greater interest, involvement and understanding of motorcycling among the general public. The MIC also sponsors a public service program to encourage motorcycle rider responsibility in noise reduction and environmental protection.

The MIC actively works with state and Federal government agencies to encourage intelligent land planning and management. MIC endorses multiple use, which is equitable to all outdoorsmen, including those who ride the 3.8 million motorcycles and ATVs used for off-highway recreation. The MIC has joined the U.S. Forest Service in its "Tread Lightly" Campaign, an environmental awareness program aimed toward motorized recreationists.

Motorcycles in the 1990's are cleaner in terms of air pollutants than motorcycles in the past. National exhaust emission controls for new motorcycles began in 1978. Although motorcycles contributed less than 1 percent of the total hydrocarbon emissions nationwide before controls, the motorcycle industry supported the adoption of uniform national standards to regulate exhaust emissions.

The motorcycle industry's continuing commitment to reduce sound levels in our environment has been demonstrated by the production of quiet motorcycles and aftermarket exhaust systems. Many new models are as quiet as new automobiles. With the support of the industry, the U.S. Environmental Protection Agency set uniform national noise standards for new motorcycles and moped produced after 1981. MIC actively assists noise enforcement authorities in cost-efficient programs for motorcycle noise control.

FROM THE PRESIDENT OF THE MOTORCYCLE INDUSTRY COUNCIL

The MIC offices were established at 501 Connecticut Avenue S.W., Washington, D.C. when I came into the industry in 1971. I worked at Kawasaki Motors Corp. U.S.A. as Director of Marketing. Jim Potter was the full time Executive Director of MIC when I was appointed to the Board of Directors in 1973. My association involvement included being Kawasaki's appointed Board member of the AMA as well as the MIC, but there was no legal or official connection between the trade association (MIC) and the rider association (AMA).

MIC activities during 1973 through 1975 involved a wide range of issues important to the business members, These members included not only the major manufacturers, wholesale distributors, publications, insurance companies, and professional services. The issues were wide ranging, including land use, no-fault insurance, helmet use, emission control, noise reduction, public relations, equipment regulations, and safety.

A heavy emphasis was placed on soliciting retail dealers as Associate Members to MIC. Dealer dues were split between their home state dealer association and the MIC. A large part of the MIC staff was devoted to dealer membership solicitation, newsletter publication, and state level legislative issues by 1974.

By August of 1974 the annual budget had been depleted, causing a series of meetings that led to a restructuring of the MIC membership and a change in staffing. The large overhead of the retail dealer Associate Membership was a major drain on MIC member dues. MIC discontinued associate membership for retail dealers and reduced its paid professional staff by approximately 10 people.

The state dealer associations formed the National Motorcycle Dealer Association (NMSA). Under the leadership of Minnesota dealer Bob Illingsworth, the NMDA retained

APPENDIX

a Washington DC area firm to represent dealers nationally. Several MIC members, Honda, Yamaha, Kawasaki, and Suzuki assisted dealers with "Automatic Billing Request" dues collection. Dealers who wished to belong to their state association could have their dues added to their parts account automatically and forwarded to the state association. The MIC Board also set up a dealer Legislative Contingency Fund, $25,000 annually, to match dealer association funds and address issues of mutual concern.

MIC relocated the administrative offices to Southern California to be closer to a majority of its membership and the industry trade media. I was hired to succeed Jim Potter, tighter financial controls were implemented, and the activities of the reduced MIC staff were focused on matters of urgent concern to the members. Mel Stahl continued to head the government relations office in Washington, D.C. Harley Davidson chose to follow an independent government relations agenda and withdrew from MIC in mid 1975.

From 1975 to 1990 the MIC has followed a consistent course. The purpose of the MIC is to preserve and promote motorcycling by serving the interests of individual members, the industry, and the general public. This is accomplished through activities in government relations, statistics, off-highway vehicle planning, technical programs, aftermarket programs, and public awareness..

MOTORCYCLE SAFETY FOUNDATION, INC.

In the Fall of 1972, the MIC served as spawning ground for the Motorcycle Safety Foundation (MSF). Matt Matsuoka and Willie Tokishi from American Honda Motor Co. advanced the concept of a long term increased emphasis on motorcyclist safety. They envisioned a $1 million annual budget and offered to pay half of this amount if the remaining industry would fund the other half. Yamaha, Kawasaki, Suzuki, BSA-Triumph, and Harley Davidson agreed to the concept and became the founding members of a new separate association from MIC.

Originally called the Motorcycle Industry Council Safety and Education Foundation (MICSEF), the new organization was housed with the MIC staff briefly in late 1972 and early 1973. A national search for a chief executive officer resulted in the hiring of Dr. Charles Harman, ex-deputy administrator of the National Highway Traffic Safety Administration. The association name was shortened to the present Motorcycle Safety Foundation (MSF). Their offices were moved to Linthicum, Maryland in 1974, and to Chadds Ford, Pennsylvania in 1979. Dr. Hartman served as president of MSF from 1973 to 1983, during which time the association was successful in launching programs in safety research, rider training, law enforcement, licensing, and public awareness.

BSA-Triumph resigned from MSF membership in 1973, and Harley-Davidson resigned at the end of 1982. in late 1983, Dr. Hartman left the MSF to pursue other interests. The Board, now consisting of Honda, Yamaha, Kawasaki, Suzuki, and new member BMW of North America, took this opportunity to consider ways to improve communications and cost efficiency. In the interim, I was requested to serve as temporary MSF president under a contract between MSF and MIC. After approximately 1 year of bi-coastal management (MIC in Costa Mesa, California and MSF in Chadds Ford, Pennsylvania,) the Board decided to move MSF offices to California in October of 1984.

By sharing and coordinating some common functions of MIC, MSF, and the new Specialty Vehicle Institute of America (SVIA), economies were brought to all three associations. Shared office space, reception, telephone system, accounting, data processing, reproduction, shipping, and executive staff allowed more of the financial resources to be applied to association program services. Since 1983 this concept, separate associations sharing common resources, has proven successful in getting the most cost effective benefits for each associations members.

SPECIALTY VEHICLE INSTITUTE OF AMERICA

In the Fall of 1982, the MIC also served as the spawning ground for a new association dedicated to the safe and responsible riding of All Terrain Vehicles. Discussions among MIC members determined that the all terrain vehicles were different from motorcycles, and the issues surrounding their use were also different. The Specialty Vehicle Institute of America (SVIA) was conceived to be a broad trade association for non-motorcycle products, some of which were still not in production, or even on the drawing boards.

Incorporation of SVIA took place in February of 1983 with Honda, Yamaha, Kawasaki and Suzuki and the founding members. All terrain vehicles, being the first significant non-motorcycle product in distribution, were the subject of SVIA's initial activity. A contract was negotiated with MSF for ATV rider training curriculum and safety brochure development. David Sanderson, Executive Director of the New England Trail Riders Association, was contracted to mitigate trail disputes between ATV riders and snowmobile riders. The MIC was contracted to provide administrative, land use, government relations and statistical resources.

Activities of the SVIA were focused on the ATV rider safety issue in the period from 1984 through 1987. Full time professional staff was fired during that period to implement an increasing series of safety programs. In 1988 the U.S. ATV distributors agreed with the U.S. Consumer Product Safety Commission to provide free rider training to purchasers of ATVs and members of their immediate family, so long as they met age guidelines. A training division, call the ATV Safety Institute (ASI), was created within the SVIA to deliver this free training.

As of 1990, all three trade associations, the MIC, MSF, and SVIA, are sharing office space and some staff resources in Irvine, California. The Boards of Directors (called "Trustees" for MSF and SVIA) meet separately and fund their associations through individual budgets. The trade associations have unique missions to accomplish for their members, yet work is unduplicated through careful management and oversight. The relationships of MIC, MSF, and SVIA with the American Motorcyclist Association are cooperative and based on friendly communication. There are no financial ties, membership privileges, or Board relationships. The work of each association is coordinated when necessary buy staff interaction. Information is exchanged frequently, and issues are addressed for the good of the sport of motorcycling. I feel fortunate to have participated for nearly 20 years in a successful relationship with AMA based on personal confidence in our respective staffs, and a mutual respect for the mission of each association.

Alan R. Isley
President
Motorcycle Industry Council, Inc.
Motorcycle Safety Foundation, Inc.
Specialty Vehicle Institute of America, Inc.

BIBLIOGRAPHY

Publications and photographs publicly circulated by the Harley Davidson Motor Company

The Archives of the Hendee Manufacturing Company

The Archives of the Indian Motorcycle Company

Archival material from the American Motorcyclist Association

The United States National Museum, Department of Transportation

The United States Congressional Record

The Reports of the United States Select Committee on Tariffs

The Reports of the United States International Trade Commission

The United States Department of Justice, Bureau of Prisons

The Federal District Court, Denver, Colorado

The Superior Court of Cook County

The Superior Court of Monroe County

The Detroit Public Library

The Milwaukee Public Library

The Springfield, Massachusetts Public Library

The Los Angeles County Public Library

The Orange County Public Library

Bibliotica Nationale, Mexico City, Republic of Mexico

Motorcycles, 1915 Edition, Victor Page

Motor Cycle Cavalcade, Ixion, (Cannon B.H. Davies) Iliffe Press

Vintage Motorcycling, (Australia) Margaret A. Bull

Vintage Motor Cycles, James Sheldon, Batsford Press

The Golden Age of the Fours, Theodore A. Hodgdon, Bagnall Publishing Company

The Story of the TT, G.S. Davison Temple Press

Triumph, Ivor Davies, Haynes Publications

The World's Motorcycles, Erwin Tragatsch, Temple Press

American Racer, 1900-1940, 1940-1980, Stephen Wright, Megden Press

The Daytona 200, The History of America's Premier Motorcycle Race, Don Emde

Well Made in America, Peter C. Reid, McGraw-Hill

Motoraad, Dr. Ing. Helmut Krackowizer

Motorcycle Mechanics and Speed Tuning, Nicholson Brothers

The Iron Redskin (Indian history), Harry V. Sucher, Haynes Publications

Harley-Davidson: The Milwaukee Marvel, Harry V. Sucher, Haynes Publications

The World's Automobiles, G. N. Georgana

Standard and Poor's Corporation Index

Moody's Corporation Index

Barron's Weekly

Nation's Business

The Motor Cycle

Motorcycling

The Western Motorcyclist and Bicyclist

Motorcycling and Bicycling Illustrated

The Motorcyclist

American Motorcycling (AMA)

Cycle World

Cycle

Easyriders

Supercycle

Iron Horse

Custom Chopper

Street Chopper

Cycle News

Automotive Illustrated

Motor Age

Automobile and Motorcycle Trade Journal

The New York Times

The Los Angeles Times

The San Francisco Chronicle

The San Francisco Examiner

The Milwaukee Sentinel

The Milwaukee Journal

The Wall Street Journal

The Journal of the Antique Motorcycle Club of America

The Official Journal of the Vintage Motor Cycle Club of Great Britain

The Journal of the Classic and Antique Motorcycle Club

Dean Witter Reynolds

The First Boston Company

Robert W. Baird, Incorporated

The Atlas Corporation

The Titeflex Corporation

E.I. duPont De Nemours

Delco, Incorporated

Bangor Punta, Incorporated

The American Machine and Foundry Company

Who's Who in America

The Baldwin Chain Company

The Diamond Chain Company

Francis I. duPont & Company

Unpublished manuscripts and extensive source material dealing with the early days of the American motorcycle industry and its constituent organizations donated by Thomas Callahan Butler, Vernon L. Guthrie, Leslie D. Richards, and Theodore A. Hodgdon. Additional material was supplied by Charles Clayton.